Agrarian Change in India

Readings on the Economy, Polity and Society

This series of readers is meant to introduce university students and research scholars to important research that has been published in the *Economic and Political Weekly* in specific areas. The readers draw on the large number of research articles that has been published in *EPW* over the decades. Each set of readings is compiled by a senior academic who has also written an introductory essay for the volume. *EPW* is grateful to the authors of the articles included here for permission to reproduce them.

Recently Published Titles

Gender and Education, eds **Vimala Ramachandran and Kameshwari Jandhyala**

Sectarian Violence in India: Hindu-Muslim Conflict, 1966–2015,
eds **Sanjay Palshikar and Satish Deshpande**

A Handbook of Rural India, ed. **Surinder S. Jodhka**

Social Policy, ed. **Jean Drèze**

Water: Growing Understanding, Emerging Perspectives,
eds **Mihir Shah and P. S. Vijayshankar**

Agrarian Change in India

Edited by

Surinder S. Jodhka

AGRARIAN CHANGE IN INDIA: READINGS ON THE ECONOMY, POLITY AND SOCIETY

ORIENT BLACKSWAN PRIVATE LIMITED

Registered Office
3-6-752 Himayatnagar, Hyderabad 500 029, Telangana, India
e-mail: centraloffice@orientblackswan.com

Other Offices
Bengaluru, Chennai, Guwahati, Hyderabad, Kolkata,
Mumbai, New Delhi, Noida, Patna

First published by Orient Blackswan Pvt. Ltd. 2022

ISBN 978-93-5442-228-7

042813

Typeset by
Le Studio Graphique, Gurgaon 122 001
in Adobe Garamond Pro 10.5/12.5

Printed in India at
Kensington Printing & Packaging, Noida 201 301

Published by
Orient Blackswan Private Limited
3-6-752 Himayatnagar, Hyderabad 500 029, Telangana, India
e-mail: info@orientblackswan.com

Contents

Section III

The Green Revolution and Market Edifice

Section IV

Relational Structures and Transitions

Tables and Figures

Tables

Figures

Abbreviations

AICC	All-India Congress Committee
APMC	Agricultural Produce Marketing Committee
APCLC	Andhra Pradesh Civil Liberties Committee
APMRA	Agricultural Produce Market Regulation Act
ASI	Agricultural Sustainability Institute
AWB	Australian Wheat Board
BC	Backward Castes
BJP	Bharatiya Janata Party
BKU	Bharatiya Kisan Union
BSP	Bahujan Samaj Party
CCI	Cotton Corporation of India
CLASCO	Latin American Council of Social Sciences
CODESRIA	Council for the Development of Social Science Research in Africa
CPI	Communist Party of India
CPI-M	Communist Party of India (Marxist)
CSC	Civil Supplies Corporation
CWC	Congress Working Committee
DMK	Dravida Munnetra Kazhagam
DPP	Deficiency price payment
ECA	Essential Commodities Act
EPW	*Economic and Political Weekly*
ERS	Economic Research Service
FCI	Food Corporation of India
FDI	Foreign direct investment
FHP	Farm harvest price
FPO	Farm producers' organisations
GSDP	Gross state domestic product
HYVP	High-yielding Variety Programme
HYV	High-yielding varieties
IAAP	Intensive Agriculture Areas Programme
IADP	Intensive Agricultural Development Programme
IARI	Indian Agricultural Research Institute
IAS	Indian Administrative Services
IAY	Indira Awas Yojana

ICDS	Integrated Child Development Services
IDEAS	International Development Economics Associates
IFPRI	International Food Policy Research Institute
ILO	International Labour Organisation
IT	Information technology
ITI	Industrial Training Institute
JPS	*The Journal of Peasant Studies*
JSY	Janani Suraksha Yojana
KCC	Kisan Credit Card
LAMPS	Large-sized Agricultural Multi-purpose Cooperative Societies
MASR	Movement Against State Repression
MDFLP	Mother Dairy Food Procuring Limited
MGNREGA	Mahatma Gandhi National Rural Employment Guarantee Act
MIP	Minimum insured price
MLA	Member of the legislative assembly
MP	Member of Parliament
MRP	Maximum retail price
MSP	Minimum support price
NAFED	National Agricultural Cooperative Marketing Federation of India
NBTDP	North Bengal Terai Development Project
NDDB	National Dairy Development Board
NGO	Non-governmental organisation
NREGS	National Rural Employment Guarantee Scheme
NSDP	Net state domestic product
NSS	National Sample Survey
NSSO	National Sample Survey Organisation
NTR	Nandamuri Taraka Rama Rao
OB	Operation Barga
OBC	Other Backward Castes
PACS	Primary Agricultural Credit Societies
PCP	Petty commodity production
PDS	Public distribution system
PEPSU	Patiala and East Punjab States Union
PL480	Public Law 480
PPP	Public–private partnerships
SC	Scheduled Caste
SECC	Socioeconomic and Caste Census
SEZ	Special economic zone
SFDA	Small Farmers Development Agency
SHG	Self-help group
SOAS	School of Oriental and African Studies
SP	Samajwadi Party
SRMT	Sri Ramadas Motor Transport Company
ST	Scheduled Tribe

TDP	Telugu Desam Party
TOR	Terms of reference
USAID	United States Agency for International Development
UT	Union territory
WLE	Water, Land and Ecology Project
WSP	Wholesale price

Introduction

Surinder S. Jodhka

On the face of it, agriculture is simply an economic activity where individuals cultivate land and/or rear animals, the produce of which is either sold in the market or consumed at home. Like any other occupation, it is thus a source of employment and income for those engaged in the activity. Like any other enterprise, the practice of agriculture requires a certain amount of skill, investment, fixed and variable, and involves a certain degree of risk—a possibility of profit or loss. Like any other enterprise, cultivation of land and rearing of animals also requires working with others, other members of the family/kin or hired labour, the size of which would depend on the scale of the activity. As with other economic activities, the growing use of modern technology and the changing nature of demand for agricultural produce would obviously alter cropping systems or the social relations around production.

However, agriculture has been much more than simply a type or a sector of economic activity and this is so across regions and countries of the world. Its practice evokes a range of meanings and metaphors almost everywhere. Agriculture has been a civilisational epoch in the process of human evolution and it continues to matter much beyond the sphere of production, employment and markets. The question of agrarian change is not simply about economic growth or occupational mobility. It is also about social transformations and cultural shifts.

Questions of land and agriculture have also been widely written about. They have been among the most contested subjects in the modern and contemporary histories of nation states. The rise of modern-day industrial and capitalist economy in Europe in the nineteenth century, some believe, was founded on the surplus extracted from agriculture, the 'primitive accumulation of capital', as Karl Marx famously described it (see Bernstein 2001). The cultivating peasants have also been important actors in some of the major political revolutions of the twentieth century (Wolf 1969). Even when the so-called 'agrarian question' has long been resolved in the developed countries of western Europe and North America, with only a minuscule of their population directly engaged in agriculture, farming continues to be an important subject in mainstream public and political discourses and policy narratives. Discussions on food and the emerging global regimes around it can hardly escape references to agriculture. The same holds good for subjects such as folk cultures and traditions, some of the popular representations of authentic national identities or the emerging narratives on environment and sustainability. The land is not simply an economic good.

The social, cultural and economic universe of agriculture and the dynamics of its change continue to be critical questions for the Global South, even in the twenty-first century. In a country like India, even as the share of agriculture in the gross national income significantly declines, it continues to be a source of livelihood, exclusively or substantially, for a significant proportion of the population. Nearly half of the working Indians are actively engaged with agriculture for their livelihood. Patterns of its social organisation and the traditional practices of cultivation have shaped lifestyles, regional economies and political identities/processes. They continue to do so today.

Even when sections of rural populations move out of agriculture or rural settlements, they carry with them the nostalgia and the burdens of their past in a variety of different ways. For example, caste-based differences, and unequal and exclusionary structures of land ownership not only continue to be important sources of identities in rural settlements, but they also condition mobility paths out of the agrarian/rural life for individuals and communities. The patterns and outcomes of mobility for rural Dalits, for example, differ significantly from those of the traditionally land owning dominant castes (see Jodhka 2014; Jodhka and Kumar 2017). Questions of land ownership patterns, the 'land question', and the social organisation of agricultural production, the 'agrarian question', have been among the most important in shaping the nature and patterns of economic growth, human development and social change in post-Independence India.

AGRARIAN CHANGE AND THE SOCIAL SCIENCES: CONCEPTUAL FRAMES

Given the context of the emergence of the social sciences in modern and industrialising Europe, questions relating to agrarian processes and change had not been among the foundational concerns for mainstream social sciences in their theorisations of human life. Much of the mainstream social science theory, since the days of its birth in the nineteenth century, has remained preoccupied with the dynamics of urban-industrial societies. As Shanin (1987: 468) rightly points out, in its most fundamental self-image, the Western capitalist world defined itself as a 'world without peasants'. The division of societies into 'modern' and 'traditional/backward' in the evolutionist schema of early social theory also meant that conceptually the agrarian populations, or the peasants, were reduced to an unspecified part of the mixed bag of 'remainders of the past' (ibid.).

The early practitioners of social anthropology, the discipline that was supposed to study 'pre-modern' societies, in their search for 'pure' and 'primitive' cultures, invariably chose the pre-agrarian 'tribal/folk communities' for their field studies. Even when they shifted their focus to the 'village', they approached it as a closed, unchanging community of 'ascriptive groupings' organised around a normative belief system that essentialised it into the 'oppositional other' of the urban societies of the 'modern' West (Inden 1990).

Interestingly, some of the founding scholars of the early social sciences in western Europe, such as Adam Smith, David Ricardo or Marx, did make extensive references to the specific dynamics of agriculture in their writings. However, references to agrarian life soon moved to the margins and rarely found place in textbooks of economics, sociology or political science. Agriculture and rural life were almost always presented as the things that belonged to the past.

Beginnings of the Agrarian Question

It was outside the mainstream western tradition of social sciences, in peripheral eastern and central Europe, that the 'agrarian question' became an important political and intellectual agenda. The famous debate between the populist thinkers led by Russian economist A. V. Chayanov (1966) on one side, and the Marxist class-analyses of the Russian countryside by Vladimir Lenin (1908, 1960 [1899]) along with Karl Kautsky's work on the 'agrarian question' (Banaji 1976; also see Chapter 1 in this volume) on the other, laid the foundation of what later came to be known as 'the agrarian studies'.

The classical Marxist understanding of agriculture located it within the historical logic of the inevitability of capitalist penetration into all spheres of economic life. Such a process was to also transform agriculture into a capitalist enterprise through the process of differentiation and the subsequent class polarisation. With the growing sway of markets, the small and middle peasants were to disappear and dissolve into new kinds of rural classes. The social framework of agricultural production was to become like that of the industry in capitalist societies, with ownership over all the land shifting to a small agrarian bourgeoisie and large masses of peasants becoming landless proletariats. The big landowners were to transform from feudal lords to bourgeois entrepreneurs and manage their farms as factories employing rural proletariats on their fields as wage labourers.

This general Marxist formulation was expounded by Lenin for the Russian countryside in a series of texts and in his famous book, *The Development of Capitalism in Russia*, first published in 1899. However, Chayanov contested Lenin's arguments. Based on his own research on the Russian countryside and statistical evidence, he argued that the logic of peasant economy differed from presuppositions of the theory of capitalist development. G. Djurfeldt has summarised the Chayanovian position well:

> Chayanov does not deny that some differentiation takes place in the Russian peasantry. But he claims that it is to a large extent explained by the process that he terms demographic differentiation, according to which the volume of the family farm's activity expands and contracts so that the typical cycle is: a young family starts out with a little land (when ancestral property has been divided among the heirs); when the family grows, economic activity expands, to contract again when the family grows old, and when the children leave. (Djurfeldt 1982: 151).

However, this was not simply a debate between the Left-wing Marxists and the Right-wing liberals. These were, and continue to be, contentious issues in the literature on agrarian change, theoretically as well as empirically. For example, there were others such as Kautsky who, working from within the Marxist tradition, pointed to the sturdiness of middle-peasant/farmer even when penetration of capitalism had significantly advanced in a given society in twentieth-century Europe. While the agrarian economy is indeed subsumed within the logic of capitalism as cultivators come to actively participate in markets and the broader framework of commodity production, they tend to survive with no tendency toward class polarisation. As Djurfeldt argued, 'petty commodity-producing farmer has … not only survived, but has become typical of Western agriculture' (ibid.: 139).

The 'Russian debate' during the early twentieth century made substantial contributions to the field and has continued to be a source of contentions and disputes among the later-day Marxist scholars on the subject.

The *second moment* in the history of agrarian studies begins after the Second World War following decolonisation and the formation of 'new' nation states in Asia, Africa and Latin America. The most important characteristic feature of the newly emerged 'Third World' countries was the dependence of large proportions of their populations on a 'stagnant' agrarian sector. The struggle for freedom from colonial rule had also developed new aspirations among the 'masses' and the 'elites' of these societies. In some of these struggles, the peasantry had played a crucial role.

Thus, the primary agenda for the new political regimes was the transformation of their 'backward' and stagnant economies. Though the strategies and priorities differed, 'modernisation' and 'development' became common programmes in most of the Third World countries. It was in this historical context that 'development studies' emerged as one of the most important areas of interest in the global academy.

Since a large majority of the populations in these Third World countries lived in rural settlements, largely dependent on land cultivation with low productivity, understanding the prevailing structures of agrarian relations and working out ways and means of transforming them came up as important priorities within 'development studies'. Western political interest in the rural inhabitants of the Third World and the growing influence of modernisation and development theories also brought with them a good deal of funding for the study of peasant economies and societies (Silverman 1987: 11). In due course, the concept of 'peasantry' also found currency in the discipline of social anthropology. At a time when primitive tribes were either in the process of disappearing or had already disappeared, the 'discovery' of the peasantry provided a vast new field of investigation to the discipline of social anthropology (Béteille 1974: 40).

In the emerging anthropological literature of the time, 'peasant communities' came to be seen as being distinct from the isolated 'primitive communities', the tribes, but not yet evolved enough to be considered as being part of the modern social world. A well-known American anthropologist, Alfred L. Kroeber (1948), famously characterised the peasants as 'part societies with part cultures'. Another anthropologist, Robert Redfield (1965), offered a general conception of peasant communities. He argued that it was possible to identify certain core features of peasant life across regions of the world. They were all attached to their lands, and the pursuit of agriculture, for them, was a way life, not simply an occupation or an economic activity. He too distinguished peasant from tribal communities, as the former had the capacity to produce surplus that was generally transferred to a dominant group of rulers in the city (Wolf 1966: 4). Thus, unlike the primitive tribes, the peasant communities were not to be seen as simply being self-sufficient and isolated. Given that it was the surplus produced by the peasants that partially supported the activities of the rulers, they came to be part of the larger social formations and the state systems.

Drawing from these early writings, Shanin (1987: 3–5) developed an 'ideal type' of peasants with the following core features: (a) strong values attached to family life and kinship where 'peasant family' is the basic unit of production and consumption in a multi-dimensional social organisation; (b) land husbandry as typically the major source of livelihood; (c) a distinct traditional culture or a way of life linked to land-based economy; and (d) their being invariably linked to an elite, which even though invariably lives outside the community, exercises a position of domination over them and extracts a part of the surplus that the peasants produce.

Overlapping very closely in its theoretical underpinnings with the post-1950s 'peasant studies' was the American tradition of studying 'rural life' in specialised departments of rural sociology. The civil war in the late nineteenth century and the ensuing 'farm crisis' saw the emergence of farmers' organisations demanding federal aid to solve the problems of rural areas afflicted by severe depression. As an applied area of research, teaching and extension work, rural sociology came up essentially in response to this crisis (Newby 1980: 10). The primary preoccupation of 'rural sociology' during its initial decades was to understand and diagnose the social and economic problems of the American farmers, with a greater focus on questions such as the internal structure of 'community life' and the changing composition of rural populations (Schwarzweller 1984: *xi*) rather than on their relationships with land or the social aspects of agricultural production.

Theoretically, rural sociology remained caught up in binary notions of social change where the 'rural' was visualised as the opposite of the 'urban'. Even though 'rurality' was conceptualised as an autonomous sociological reality (Bonnano 1989), the framework on rural–urban binary also saw the two in an evolutionary frame where the former was to eventually dissolve and disappear with presumed inevitability of the progressive change over time. This indeed appears to have been the American story of the last century. With a steady decline of the demographically defined 'rural areas', rural sociology was confronted with a serious crisis of its disciplinary identity. The publication of W. H. Friedland's paper in 1982 with the title, 'The End of Rural Society and the Future of Rural Sociology', in *Rural Sociology*, summarised it all.

However, even when the rural declines as a demographic reality, agriculture continues to matter. Thus, scholars working in the departments of rural sociology carved out a new sub-discipline of 'sociology of agriculture' to keep themselves afloat. However, the theoretical underpinnings of the sociology of agriculture were different from those of rural sociology. The sociology of agriculture focused on studying the social framework of agricultural production, the structures of relations around land, agricultural markets and the emergent global food regimes. It raised and explored questions such as how and on what terms the agrarian sector was being integrated into the system of commodity production. It also began to focus on the questions of distribution of agricultural incomes and food across social classes and categories, nationally and globally.

Thus, the focus also shifted away from the local context of settlements and the community life of the American farmer to larger contexts of community systems and agrarian processes, which were increasingly becoming global and affecting farming practices and rural lives in countries of the developing world as well. They also explored questions such as the survival of family farms in Western capitalist societies, even while its agricultural practices actively articulated with the prevailing logic of capitalism. Thus, the sociology of agriculture distinguished itself from 'peasant studies' on the grounds that its focus was on capitalist farming, and not on the subsistence-producing peasants (Bonanno 1989; Buttel, Larson and Gillespie Jr. 1990; Friedland 1984). At the methodological level, historical inquiries became as relevant as surveys and ethnographic studies. These shifts also brought them closer to those working in the developing world with the framework of 'political economy' or 'agrarian studies'.

The study of peasant life and agrarian change became the most vibrant areas of research and discussions among those working on the Global South during the decades of the 1970s and 1980s (see Chapters 1 and 12 in this volume). A large majority of them also moved away from functionalist/evolutionary view of peasants as traditional or village communities to critical class analyses of the larger dynamics of agrarian life, which simultaneously engaged with local, regional and global processes of capitalist development and commodity production. *The Journal of Peasant Studies*, initiated by Terence J. Byres, Charles Curwen and Teodor Shanin as its founding editors in 1973, provided an important impetus to this growing interest in the field. Over the years, a large number of journals appeared with focus, entirely or partly, on agrarian issues. On the Indian scene, the *Economic and Political Weekly* (*EPW*) provided the most important and vibrant platform for discussions on agrarian issues. Beginning with 1968, the *EPW* also began to publish bi-annual special issues on 'Review of Agriculture', renamed in 2012 as 'Review of Rural Affairs'.

As 'development studies' began to lose its steam during the early 1990s with the growing shift of state policies toward greater reliance on markets during the post-Cold War period, scholarly interest in agriculture-related issues also declined. This marginalisation of agriculture soon produced a new kind of agrarian distress (see Chapters 20–21 in this volume). The increasing dependence of small marginal cultivators on the vagaries of markets raised their levels of indebtedness and vulnerability. Incidence of cultivating farmers committing suicides because of their growing debt began to be reported from all those regions, which had been at the forefront of agricultural modernisation and had shifted to the production of cash crops. However, given their demographic weight in a country like India, rural realities were hard to ignore.

At another level, the question of growing agrarian distress also hinted at the obvious fact that the economic and social dynamics of agriculture could no longer be seen within the frame of rural lives, given the context that even in the Global South agrarian lives were increasingly being integrated into the global markets, as producers and consumers of commodities. Henry Bernstein (2001: 29–32) forcefully argues that farmer sought to be seen as a category of 'petty commodity producers', almost on a par with those working in the informal and unorganised sectors of the economy (also see Lerche 2013).

This proposal does make sense, theoretically as well as empirically. Even when a substantial section of cultivating farmers in countries like India are small and marginal cultivators, working mostly with their own labour, their lives are no longer confined to the village, oriented exclusively towards their family tradition. They increasingly diversify into pluri-activities, voluntarily or out of economic compulsions. While agriculture remains a critical component of their subsistence strategy, their working lives are increasingly marked by out-migrations for work, often circular in nature (Breman 1985; Datta 2016; de Haan 2002; Deshingkar and Farrington 2009; Harriss, Jeyaranjan and Nagaraj 2010; Jodhka and Kumar 2017; also see Chapters 15, 19 and 23 in this volume). I would like to describe this convergence as the *third moment* of agrarian studies, the current moment.

Agrarian Change in India: The Colonial Context

Much before professional social scientists began to explore the dynamics of rural and agrarian lives in the region, the Indian village and its agrarian structures had been extensively documented by colonial ethnographers. Not only did the British colonisers write on the empirical details of diverse patterns or rural settlements, they also produced specific 'forms of knowledge', to use Cohn's (1987: 212) expression. Their formulations had a clear political purpose of justifying the colonial subjugation of India (ibid.). Along with the earlier writings of James Mill, Charles Metcalfe's notion of the 'Indian village community' set the tone for much of the later writings on rural India. Metcalfe, in his celebrated remark, stated:

> The village communities are little Republics, having nearly everything they want within themselves, and almost independent of foreign relations. They seem to last where nothing else lasts. Dynasty after dynasty tumbles down; revolution succeeds revolution; Hindu, Pathan, Mughal, Maratta, Sikh, English are masters in turn; but the village communities remain the same. (Quoted in Cohn 1987: 213)

This construction emphasised the homogeneity of rural settlements across the subcontinent. They also presented them as harmonious communities, relatively isolated and most importantly, they had remained unchanged for centuries. A critical assumption in this imagination of the Indian village was the absence of private ownership of land. The land presumably belonged to the village community. Since there had been no formal private rights over land, the British also believed that there would have been no significant economic differentiation in the Indian village.

Later historical research convincingly showed that this was at best a superficial understanding of the Indian village (see Chapter 11). Since land was in abundant supply, there was no sale and purchase of land in most parts of the Indian countryside. However, not everyone had equal rights of cultivation or claims over the produce. These rights were drawn from customs or from the grants made by the king (Neale 1962: 21). Some of these could even be transferred through sale and purchase (Habib 1963: 154). 'The village did not hold its land in common. Common were its officials and servants' (Neale 1962: 21).

Historians have also gathered enough evidence to show that the claims about the village being internally undifferentiated, self-sufficient and stable were wrong. Commenting on the Mughal period in the northern part of present-day India, Irfan Habib writes:

> ...economic differentiation had progressed considerably among the peasantry. There were large cultivators, using hired labour, and raising crops for the market, and there were small peasants, who could barely produce food grains for their own subsistence. Beyond this differentiation among the peasantry, there was still sharper division between the caste peasantry and the "menial" population. (Habib 1982: 247)

Writing on pre-colonial southern India, Dharma Kumar (1992) too argues that there was a sizable population of landless agricultural labourers and they invariably belonged to some specific caste groups. Villages were also not isolated. They were linked to the central authority through the revenue bureaucracy. Land revenue worked as the dominant mode of surplus appropriation during 'medieval' times. Pre-colonial agrarian relations were also not free from conflicts and tensions. Whenever the revenue demands became unbearable, the typical response of the peasantry was to flee *en masse* to other territories where conditions were more conducive to land cultivation (Habib 1963; Moore 1966: 332). There were also instances of the peasantry revolting against the local rulers. Most of these revolts, however, were unorganised, inspired by some religious ideology or a millenarian dream (Dhanagare 1983: 29).

LAND SETTLEMENTS

British rule also had far-reaching material effects on the Indian countryside. After establishing its political supremacy, the colonial regime initiated reforms in order to make their task of revenue collection easier. This process eventually resulted in the introduction of a new set of property rights on land. The first, and historically the most controversial, was Permanent Settlement introduced in Bengal Presidency in 1793. Under this, the intermediary *zamindar*s (tax-collecting officials in the earlier regime) were granted ownership rights over the lands they previously had only right to collect revenues from. Moore (1966: 345) argued that apart from simplifying things, the colonial rulers saw in the local zamindars a counterpart of the 'enterprising English landlord' who, they believed, had the capacity to 'establish prosperous cultivation' if provided with secure and permanent ownership rights over land. Some others have argued that Permanent Settlement also had politico-strategic implications, for in the landlord, the British rulers saw a possible support base in local society (Desai 1976: 39).

At least during the initial years, for the peasantry, the new system just meant an increase in revenue demands. The additional economic burden also weakened the 'traditional' structure of patron–client relations between the zamindars and local tenants, leading to a disintegration of, what Scott (1976) calls, 'the moral economy of the peasantry'. Contrary to the expectations of the colonial rulers, Permanent Settlement accelerated and intensified the trend towards 'parasitic landlordism' (Moore 1966: 346). By the middle of the nineteenth century, the entire area under Permanent Settlement was in a state of crisis.

Learning from the Bengal experience, the colonial regime tried a new arrangement in the regions of Madras, Bombay and Berar. This came to be known as the Ryotwari Settlement. Under this, the actual landholders (*ryots*) were given formal proprietary rights. The ryot in theory was a tenant of the state, responsible for paying revenue directly to the state treasury, and could not be evicted as long as he paid his revenue (Baden-Powel 1892: 126). Stokes (1978) has argued that the growing influence of utilitarian philosophy in England during the time was also a factor that produced distaste for landlordism and led to the introduction of new systems of revenue assessments.

Another variety of land settlement, known as Mahalwari or Malguzari, was introduced in the United Provinces, Punjab and the Central Provinces. Under this, the village was identified as the unit of assessment. As such the Mahalwari system was not very different from the Ryotwari system. Effective ownership of the cultivated land was vested in the cultivator here as well, but the village paid the revenue collectively. A villager of 'good social standing' was generally given the responsibility of collecting the revenue from individual cultivators and paying the assessment on behalf of the village.

Despite different settlements, the patterns of change experienced in the land relations were more or less similar in most parts of the empire. Though the new settlements changed the formal structures of authority, colonial policies also reinforced and revitalised older, 'quasi-feudal' structures, which for the peasant meant 'not less but in many cases more intensive and systematic exploitation' (Guha 1983: 7). The new land revenue systems also forced the peasants to get increasingly involved with the market, even when they did not have the capacity to produce surplus.

Commercialisation of Agriculture

The expression 'commercialisation of agriculture' is used to describe two related processes. First, a shift in the agrarian economy from production for consumption, to production for the market; and second, for a process where land starts acquiring the features of a commodity and begins to be sold and purchased in the market like other commodities.

Though it grew both quantitatively as well as qualitatively during the British rule, production for the market was not an entirely new phenomenon for Indian agriculture. As Habib (1982) points out, the big peasants during the Mughal period produced cash crops such as cotton, tobacco and sugarcane. However, these markets were generally local in nature and the demand for such things was limited. Establishment of colonial rule changed the entire scenario. The laying of the railways and the opening of the Suez Canal made the Indian village a part of the global market.

The Industrial Revolution in England around the same time generated fresh demands for some specific agricultural products required as raw materials in the new industries. The manifold increase in land revenue at the same time compelled the peasantry to shift to crops that had better market value, which effectively meant switching over from food crops to cash crops. According to one estimate, in the Rayalseema region of southern India, the area under food crops declined from 78.2 per cent in 1901–04 to 58.2 per cent in 1937–49, while on the other end, it increased from 17.0 per cent to 30.1 per cent for cash crops during the same period (Satyanarayana 1991: 57). Similarly, from the state of Punjab, a large proportion of food and non-food crops began to be exported. While there was a rapid increase in the agricultural production of the region from 1921 onwards, per capita output of food crops experienced a decline. According to Blyn's (1966) estimates for the entire country, exportable commercial crops grew more than 10 times faster at 1.31 per cent annually, compared to only 0.11 per cent increase per annum for foodgrains during 1894–1947. He also estimated that per head availability of foodgrains declined by 25 per cent during the inter-War period. This decline was the highest in Bengal, Bihar and Odisha at 38 per cent, while the relatively prosperous state of Punjab saw a decline by 18 per cent (ibid.).

One obvious consequence of this shift in cropping patterns and a growing involvement of the peasantry in the market was a significant increase in the vulnerability of the local populations to famines. Forced commercialisation of agriculture disintegrated the traditional systems of food security. India experienced a number of serious famines, particularly during the second half of the nineteenth century and the first half of the twentieth. According to an estimate, 3.5–4 million people (one-tenth to one-eighth of the total population of the region) perished during the 1876–78 famine in parts of southern India (Kumar 1982: 231).

Similarly Bengal was transformed from a prosperous region to a region with frequent famines. In one of its worst famines during 1943–44, nearly 3.5 million people died. Though the official reports and 'inquiries' by colonial rulers attributed the cause of these famines to scarcity of food due to crop failures, the per capita availability of food in Bengal in the year 1943 was not substantially different from the previous year and there were no widespread crop failures in 1942 (Greenough 1982; Sen 1976).

According to Sen (1976) it was not the scarcity of food but the changes in the 'exchange entitlements' that caused the 1943 Bengal famine. The year 1942–43 saw unprecedented inflation, mainly resulting from War expenditure, and the absolute level of prices moved rapidly upward. But the prices of different commodities did not move in the same way. While the food prices went up, wage rates, particularly of the rural unskilled labour, remained low. This was reinforced in certain regions of Bengal by a direct decline in employment arising from loss of agricultural activity due to cyclonic destruction, worsening the exchange entitlements for certain groups. While some classes ate better, benefiting from the newly created incomes of the War economy, others faced higher prices of food without a corresponding rise in the money incomes and starved (Sen 1976, 1977). Greenough (1982: 265) adds that there were also some cultural patterns specific to Bengal which explain the selective starvation and death during the famines. There was a cultural acceptance in Bengali society of 'abandoning' those dependents who were deemed inessential for the reconstitution of family and society in the post-crisis period and protection of those whose survival was held essential for the future.

Commodification of Land

While the new land settlements conferred formal and transferable/alienable rights over land, growing revenue demands and the increasing market orientation of agricultural production created conditions under which land began to acquire the features of a commodity. The new administrative and judicial system also introduced laws against defaults of legal dues that included default of rent, revenue and debts. The moneylender, who until then lent keeping the peasant's crops in mind, began to see his land as a mortgageable asset against which he could lend money. Further, an increase in population during the nineteenth century made good-quality cultivable land scarce.

As land became both scarce and transferable, and the economic environment began to change, the moneylender started advancing much more than before, provided the peasant was willing to offer his land as guarantee against a possible default. At this stage the rich landowners also entered the credit market, more with the intention of usurping the lands of smaller peasants than to earn interest. Thus began the process of 'land alienation'.

Land alienation was a pan-India development irrespective of the system, Zamindari, Ryotwari or Mahalwari (Dhanagare 1983). This impoverished the small and, often also, the middle-peasant, and strengthened the position of big landowners and moneylenders in rural society. The professional moneylender generally did not evict the peasant from his land. If the peasant could not pay back his loan, the moneylender asked for the transfer of the ownership rights over land while the peasant continued cultivating it, but as a tenant of the moneylender. Where moneylenders were also landlords, the indebted peasant could end up being a landless labourer. Thus, tenancy as well as landlessness grew significantly in most parts of the British empire. According to one estimate, out of the total population of male agricultural labourers in the state of Punjab, the proportion of those coming from peasant and land-owning castes went up from 0.8 per cent in 1911 to as much as 29.7 per cent in 1931 (Bhattacharya 1985: 136). Similarly, in the case of Odisha,

Frederick G. Bailey (1958) argues that once a market in land developed, peasants began to sell their lands whenever they were faced with a 'contingent need'.

Peasant indebtedness and land alienation acquired such gigantic proportions that even the colonial administrators began to see this as 'a problem' (Darling 1947; Thorburn 1983). Reports on growing discontent among the peasantry from different parts of the empire added to their worries. The Deccan riots of 1875 only confirmed these apprehensions. Colonial rulers responded to the growing unrest in the countryside by passing legislations such as the Deccan Relief Act of 1879 and the Punjab Alienation of Land Act of 1901. The main thrust of these legislative measures was to stop the transfers of agricultural land to members of non-agricultural castes. However, in the absence of any significant change in the revenue structure or in the overall politico-ideological framework of the colonial rule, these legislative measures hardly brought any relief to the peasantry. For the poor peasants, the only difference these measures made was that they now had to depend more on credit from the richer landowners from the cultivating castes. The discontent among the peasantry continued to grow and expressed itself in a series of revolts and protest movements, particularly during the first half of the twentieth century.

The question, 'What did the agrarian policies of the colonial rulers do to the Indian village?', has been most frequently raised by Marxist scholars. Marx himself had almost celebrated the colonial conquest of India, which he thought would break the earlier stagnant system and help private property relations, and hence contradictions, to grow in Indian society. Though guided by its own 'vilest' self-interest, Marx (1959: 18) argued that British rule was responsible for 'causing a social revolution in Hindustan'. Some later Marxists have also argued that high indebtedness of peasantry, forced commercialisation of agricultural produce, land alienation and increasing domination of rich landowners and moneylenders over the tenants and peasants was a specific form of the primitive accumulation of capital which, in the ultimate analysis, led to a formal subsumption of labour under capital (Alavi 1990; Fox 1987).

More popular has been the thesis of 'conservation-dissolution', that is, while the colonial rule destroyed some of the local pre-capitalist structures, it also preserved many. As Utsa Patnaik (1990: 41) argues, colonial rule 'broke down' the earlier structures without 'reconstituting' them, and the 'bourgeois property relations' developed without a corresponding 'development of capitalist relations of production' in Indian agriculture. In certain cases, colonial rule in fact introduced semi-feudal relations to perpetuate its rule. 'Unlike its parent mode of production in the West, distinguished historically by its continuous expansion of the productive forces, the mode of production installed in the colonies reduced the entire process of production to an immense super exploitation of the variable capital' (Banaji 1990: 126). The colonial West reinforced 'backward relations of exploitation' and transmitted to its colonies the pressures of the accumulation process in the metropolis, without unleashing any corresponding expansion in the forces of production (ibid.). Hamza Alavi (1990: 170) also argued that colonial or 'peripheral capitalism' was not the same as 'metropolitan capitalism'. While it was an integrated process of development in the West, 'peripheral capitalism brought about a disarticulated form of generalized commodity production' because the surplus generated in agriculture was reinvested not in the local economy but in the metropolitan centres.

Though with a different emphasis, Ranajit Guha (1983) too argued that the fusing of landlordism and usury by colonial rule made a possible development of capitalism difficult both in agriculture and in industry. However, unlike Alavi, Guha emphasised that 'the composite apparatus of dominance over peasantry and their subjection to the triumvirate—*sarkari* (of the state), *sahukari* (of the moneylender) and *zamindari* (of the landlord)—was primarily a political fact' (ibid.: 8).

Agrarian Changes after Independence

Independence from colonial rule in 1947, in many ways, marked the beginning of a new phase in the history of Indian agriculture. Having evolved out of a long-drawn struggle against colonial rule with the participation of the people from various social categories, the Indian state also took over the task of supervising the transformation of its stagnant and backward economy to make sure that the benefits of economic growth were not monopolised entirely by a particular section of the society. It is with this background that 'development' emerged as a strategy of economic change and an ideology of the new regime.

However, even though the political system had changed, at the micro level the structures evolved during colonial rule remained. The local interests that had emerged over a long period of time continued to matter and shaped relational structures. Speaking at the Delhi School of Economics in 1955 after his extensive trips to different parts of the country, Daniel Thorner argued that the prevailing land relations and debt dependencies, where a small section consisting of a few landlords and moneylenders (who usually belonged to the local upper castes) controlled virtually everything, perpetuated stagnation in Indian agriculture. This complex of legal, economic, and social relations uniquely typical of the Indian countryside served to produce an effect, 'a built-in depressor' (Thorner 1956: 12). Thorner's formulation was, in a sense, symptomatic of the way in which agrarian issues began to be framed at that time.

The Land Reforms

The 'land question' had become a hotly debated subject during the final years of the struggle for independence. Reforming the prevailing structure of land ownership was seen to be necessary for three different reasons. First and foremost was the need of modernising agriculture simply in order to increase productivity of land for achieving a level of food security for the entire population. This required motivating the cultivating peasant, which could be done only by developing their stakes in the production process. Second, agriculture needed to be developed to generate surplus, which was seen to be critical for India's industrial growth. Third, it was also seen as a social-justice initiative, to make rural society more egalitarian.

However, the process of agrarian reforms is inherently a political question (Ghose 1984: 6). The choices made by the Indian state and the actual implementations of land reforms were determined by the 'politics' and prevailing constellation of interests, social groups and classes that mattered. The Indian state chose to reorganise agrarian relations through redistribution of land, but not in a comprehensive and radical manner. Given that agriculture is part of the 'state-list', the central government directed the state governments to abolish intermediary tenures; regulate rent and tenancy rights; confer ownership rights on tenants; impose ceilings on holdings; distribute the surplus land among the rural poor; and facilitate consolidation of holdings. Beginning with the 1950s and through the 1970s, the state governments passed a large number of legislations.

The actual implementation of these legislations and their impact on the agrarian structures is, however, an entirely different story. Most of the legislations had intentionally provided loopholes with the help of which the dominant landowners could tamper with land records by redistributing land on paper among relatives, evict their tenants and use other means to escape the legislations. In the absence of concerted 'political will' (Joshi 1976), land reforms could succeed only in regions where the peasantry was politically mobilised and could exert pressure from below (Radhakrishanan 1989).

Despite the overall failure, land reforms succeeded in weakening the hold of absentee landlords over the rural society and assisted in the emergence of a 'class of substantial peasants and petty landlords as the dominant political and economic group' (Bell 1974: 196). The fear of losing land induced many potential losers to sell or rearrange their lands in a manner so as to escape the legislations (Byres 1974; Chakravarti 1975: 97–98; also see Chapters 4–6 in this volume). However, rarely did these reforms help the landless labourers living in the countryside, who mostly belonged to the ex-'untouchable' castes (see Chapter 16 in this volume). The beneficiaries, by and large, belonged to the middle-level caste groups who traditionally cultivated land as owner or tenant cultivators. Otherwise also the holding structure continued to be fairly iniquitous, though the proportion of smaller and medium-sized landowners had been expanding (see Chapter 7 in this volume).

Besides land reforms, the Indian state also expanded provisions of institutional credit to cultivating farmers and developed marketing networks for sale of the agricultural produce. While the land reforms were to deal with the problems of landlessness and landlordism, the hold of moneylenders over the peasantry was to be weakened by providing credit through institutional sources, initially through the cooperative credit societies and later through nationalised commercial banks.

The assessment studies on cooperative credit societies showed that much of their credit went to the relatively better-off sections of rural society, and the poor continued to depend on the more expensive informal sources (Oommen 1984; Thorner 1964). This was explained as a consequence of the prevailing structure of land tenures. The prevailing disparities in land ownership patterns shaped the rural power, which in turn also influenced distribution of the cheaper institutional credit (Herring 1977). The state response was to bureaucratise the cooperative societies.

Though in some regions this helped in releasing the credit societies from the hold of big landowners, bureaucratisation also led to a different kind of corruption. The officially appointed *babu* (accountant) began to control the process of credit disbursement and a large section of the local population began to see the cooperative society as a 'mini-bank' (Jodhka 1995a). Although banks were never controlled directly by the rural rich, the benefit of their credit has largely gone to those who had substantial holdings (Jodhka 1995b). However, despite this inherent bias of institutional credit against the rural poor, its availability played an important role in making the Green Revolution a success, and it definitely helped in marginalising the professional moneylender in the rural power structure.

The Green Revolution and After

Of all the developmental programmes introduced during the post-Independence period, the Green Revolution is considered to be the most successful. It was celebrated the world over and has been studied and debated upon quite extensively in academia. The Green Revolution led to a substantial increase in agricultural output, to the extent that it almost solved India's food problem. It also produced significant social and political changes in the Indian village and, in a sense, did bring about a kind of 'revolution' in India. In purely economic terms, the agricultural sector experienced growth at the rate of 3–5 per cent per annum (Byres 1972), which was many times higher than that during the colonial period.

However, the term 'Green Revolution' conceptualised agrarian change in purely technological terms, with a faith in the 'trickle down' theory. The term, coined in the 1960s, was a contrast to the phrase 'red revolution'. It carried the conviction that 'agriculture was being peacefully transformed through the quiet working of science and technology, reaping the economic gains of modernisation while avoiding the social costs of mass upheaval and disorder usually associated with rapid change (Frankel 1971: *v*). The United States played an active role in its conception and implementation. Many have argued that this was because of the strategic geopolitical interests that the US had at that time in the changing social and economic conditions of the countries of the Third World (Harriss 1987).

The Green Revolution was a package with high-yielding varieties of seeds as its core. But their use also required fertility-enhancing inputs, that is, chemical fertilisers, controlled irrigation conditions and plant-protecting chemicals (pesticides). The other components of the package consisted of providing cheap institutional credit, price incentives and marketing networks (see Chapters 9–10 in this volume). In order to back up the application of new technology on local farms, a large number of agricultural universities were also opened in the regions selected for the new programme. It was under the direct supervision of the Ford Foundation that the Intensive Agricultural Development Programme (IADP) was started in 1961, initially in 14 districts on an experimental basis and later extended to 114 districts (out of a total of 325) under the name of Intensive Agriculture Areas Programme (IAAP) in 1965.

Its advocates argued that the new technology was 'scale-neutral' and could be used with as much benefit by the small, as by the big landowners. However, in the actual implementation, the smaller cultivators found harder to mobilise the required resources. Thus, though theoretically the new technology was 'scale-neutral' it was certainly not 'resource-neutral' (Harriss 1987: 231). The new technology also made everyone compulsively get involved with the market. Unlike traditional agriculture, the cultivators in post-Green Revolution agriculture had to buy all farm inputs from the market for which they often had to take credit from traders or institutional sources. In order to clear the debts, they had no choice but to sell the farm yield in the market even when they needed to keep it for their own consumption, oftentimes immediately after harvesting when prices are relatively low. Later in the year, many had to buy grains for consumption when the prices were higher. Thus, though the small farmers did take to the new technology, their resources being limited, it brought in new dependencies for them as well. On the other hand, it strengthened the economic and political position of the rich farmers.

One of the manifestations of the growing market orientation of agrarian production was the emergence of a totally new kind of mobilisation by the surplus-producing farmers who demanded a better deal for the agricultural sector. Interestingly, these 'new' farmers' movements emerged almost simultaneously in virtually all the Green Revolution regions. Though initiated in the late 1970s, these movements gained momentum during the decade of the 1980s. Using the language of neo-populism (Brass 1994; Dhanagare 1991) and in some cases also invoking traditional social networks and identities of the landowning dominant castes (Gupta 1997), its leaders argued that India was experiencing a growing division between the city and the village. And the village, that is, the agrarian sector, was being exploited by the city or the industrial sector through the mechanism of 'unequal exchange'.

Those who led these movements were mostly the substantial landowners who had benefited most from the developmental programmes and belonged to the numerically large middle-level caste groups, whom Srinivas (1994) called the 'dominant castes'. This new 'social class' not only emerged as a dominant group at the village level, it also came to dominate the regional/state-level politics in most parts of India. They had an accumulated surplus that they sought to invest in ever more profitable enterprises. Some of them diversified into other economic activities or migrated to urban areas (Rutten 1991; see Chapters 17–18 in this volume) or entered agricultural trade (Harriss-White 1996). In a short piece published in the *EPW*, K. Balagopal provides a lucid account of this process:

> a typical family of this class has a landholding in its native village, cultivated by hired labour, *bataidar*, tenant or farm servants and supervised by the father or one son; business of various descriptions in town managed by other sons; and perhaps a young and bright child who is a doctor or engineer or a professor. It is this class that is most vocal about injustice done to the village. (Balagopal 1987: 1545)

The changes produced by the Green Revolution also generated an interesting debate among Marxist scholars on the question of defining the prevailing mode of production in Indian agriculture. Though the debate raised a large number of questions, the most contentious was whether capitalism had become dominant in Indian agriculture, or whether it was still characterised by the semi-feudal mode of production (see Chapter 12 in this volume).

Did the benefits of the Green Revolution 'trickle-down' to the landless labourers? How did it affect them relationally? These have been among the most debated questions in the literature on agrarian change in India. It is generally believed that the process of agricultural modernisation is accompanied by a change in the social relations of production, leading to freeing of agricultural labour from relations of patronage and institutionalised dependencies. Some scholars did report in their studies that such a process was under way in the Indian countryside, particularly in the regions where Green Revolution had been a success. Jan Breman (1974), for example, observed a process of 'depatronization' being experienced in the farmer–labourer relationship in the villages of south Gujarat. Several others confirmed that the process of formalisation of relations was indeed underway (Béteille 1971; Gough 1989; also see Chapter 13 in this volume). However, based on his work in Punjab and Haryana, two of the Green Revolution pockets, Tom Brass (1990) questioned the popular view and argued that farmers continued to use the mechanism of debt and attachment to 'discipline' labour and 'decompose/recompose' the labour market, that led to 'deproletarianization' of labour, which amounted to their being 'bonded slaves'.

This, however, was an overstatement. Even though attached labour in the post-Green Revolution agriculture involved elements of un-freedom, the system was steadily declining and their loss of freedom was increasingly becoming temporary in nature (Jodhka 1994). There were many cases where, after working for a few years, the attached labourers could come out of the relationship. The growing integration of the village with the broader market and the increasing availability of alternative sources of employment outside agriculture, along with the changing political and ideological environments, were also working to weaken the hold of the landowners over the labourers.

At another level, the increased demand for labour in the Green Revolution pockets of northwest India attracted surplus from the agriculturally depressed pockets of Bihar and eastern Uttar Pradesh, producing significant changes in the agrarian structures of those regions. Even when demands for labour declined in agriculture, migrations continued and expanded, producing long-term impact on the social organisation of rural lives everywhere. They paved the way for the loosening of dependency relationships and hierarchical ties of caste and class (see Chapter 19 in this volume).

Emergent Agrarians

In due course, Green Revolution technology spread, vertically, across agrarian classes, but also horizontally, across regions of the subcontinent. However, as mentioned earlier, even though it was not 'resource-neutral', imitating the large farmer, those with small and marginal holdings also shifted steadily to the new agrarian technology and cropping systems. However, unlike the substantial farmers, they could do so only by borrowing from institutional and informal sources. This also required them to shift the orientation of their farming, leading to their 'compulsive market participation'. Borrowings for seeds, fertilisers and pesticides required selling farm produce as soon as it was harvested. Similarly, encouraged by state agencies, traction of new technology soon moved to less-developed regions as well.

The changes in India's economic paradigm during the early 1990s shifted the state's focus away from agriculture, leaving it largely to the vagaries of market fluctuations. This has been quite challenging for the agricultural sector, particularly for those with small and marginal holdings, which make for more than 80 per cent of all landholdings in the country. The declining investments in agriculture and fluctuating markets, locally and globally, have produced a serious crisis for agriculture, manifesting itself most visibly in the growing number of farmers committing suicides across regions of the country.

The agrarian distress is not only about declining incomes of the farmers. It also has complex ecological and social/cultural dimensions. The new crops and agricultural practices were mostly adopted without giving due considerations to ecological specificities. Not only are the new practices less resilient to the vagaries of climate, they also disturb the ecological balance. The most critical in this context is that of groundwater. Similarly, the increasing commercial orientation of agriculture, coupled with other changes, has also produced a social and cultural fragmentation in the rural life, a weakening of kinship ties and a general crisis of trust and relationships (see Chapters 20–21 in this volume). Some scholars have also been working on the questions of ecology from a 'development and displacement' angle (Guha 1989; Kothari 1996) and the emergent new social movements around the question of environment (Baviskar 1995). Similarly the gender question has also become important with shifting agricultural practices and increasing out-migrations of the male members of the family (see Chapters 15 and 19 in this volume). Apart from pointing to the 'gender blindness' of much of the development theory and the empirical surveys on issues such as poverty and land rights of women in the region (Agarwal 1988, 1994; Dube 1986), students of gender and agrarian change have also shown how the new technology had a clear bias against women. It marginalised the female agricultural wage labour both in terms of work as well as earnings (Chowdhry 1994; also see Chapter 15 in this volume).

Perhaps the most important emergent trend in rural India and among those traditionally involved with agriculture is to diversify their sources of income, or pluri-activity. There has been a significant shift towards non-farm sources of employment and income generation across castes and classes in the rural areas (see Chapters 22–23 in this volume; also see Jodhka and Kumar 2017). Given the stagnant or declining rates of return from agriculture and the changing aspirations, particularly of educated young men from traditionally landed families, the trend is to move out of the village. However, not able to find 'decent jobs', some return to the village and work on their lands.

Emergent dynamics of Indian agriculture continue to be quite diverse and complex. Despite a common political history of more than a century, trajectories of agrarian change vary across regions of the country. This is not simply because of the prevailing diversities of ecological conditions. Prejudices and preferences of the developmental state have also played their role in reinforcing those diversities, some of which have led to the perpetuation of economic inequalities across regions. Dynamics of class and caste have also contributed to these processes. The success of the Green Revolution in pockets of India produced new actors in the regional political process, some of which also had their presence felt in national politics (see Frankel and Rao 1989; Rudolph and Rudolph 1987). They, in turn, played active roles in shaping the dynamics of agriculture and its relationship with the state in their regions. The churnings that accompanied economic changes in the agrarian landscapes also helped India's 'backwards', and those lower down in the social hierarchies assert and ask for citizenship (Harriss 2011; Jaffrelot 2003; Jodhka 2015).

In the aggregate economic scenario, agriculture is increasingly becoming smaller in terms of its contribution to the national income. However, given its social and demographic weight, it continues to bother policymakers. Demographics also matter politically, particularly in a democratic system. In other words, even though agriculture is no longer 'the basis of all our development', as Jawaharlal Nehru famously said soon after Independence (cited in Raina 2016: 101), it remains and will continue to remain one of the most significant sectors of the Indian economy, more significantly in the social and political life of the country for many decades, if not centuries, to come.

This volume brings together a few select and seminal readings that represent the broad contours of research on agrarian social structures and changes in India over the past century or so. We hope the book will work as a useful source for students, teachers, researchers, policy actors and lay readers who wish to understand the dynamics of the Indian agrarian scene and its contemporary history.

References

Agarwal, B. 1988. *Structures of Patriarchy: State, Community and Household in Modernising Asia*. New Delhi: Kali for Women.

———. 1994. *A Field of One's Own: Gender and Land Rights in South Asia*. New Delhi: Foundation Books.

Alavi, H. 1990. 'Structure of Colonial Formations'. In *Agrarian Relations and Accumulation: The 'Mode of Production Debate in India'*, ed. Utsa Patnaik, 165–82. Delhi: Oxford University Press.

Baden-Powell, B. H. 1892. *Land Systems of British India* (Volumes 1–3). London: Oxford University Press.

Bailey, F. G. 1958. *Caste and the Economic Frontier: A Village in Highland Orissa*. Bombay: Oxford University Press.

Balagopal, K. 1987. 'An Ideology of the Provincial Propertied Class'. *Economic and Political Weekly* 21(36–37): 2177–78.

Banaji, J. 1976. 'A Summary of Kautsky's *The Agrarian Question*'. *Economy and Society* 5(1): 2–49.

——. 1990. 'For a Theory of Colonial Modes of Production'. In *Agrarian Relations and Accumulation: The 'Mode of Production Debate in India'*, ed. Utsa Patnaik, 119–31. Delhi: Oxford University Press.

Baviskar, A. 1995. *In the Belly of the River: Tribal Conflict Over Development in the Narmada Valley.* Delhi: Oxford University Press.

Bell, C. 1974. 'Ideology and Economic Interests in Indian Land Reform'. In *Agrarian Reform and Agrarian Reformism: Studies of Peru, Chile, China, and India*, ed. D. Lehmann, 190–220. London: Faber and Faber.

Bernstein, H. 2001. '"The Peasantry" in Global Capitalism: Who, Where, and Why?'. In *Socialist Register*, eds Leo Panitch and Colin Leys, 25–51. London: Merlin Press.

Béteille, A. 1971. *Caste, Class and Power: Changing Patterns of Stratification in Tanjore Village.* Berkeley: University of California Press.

——. 1974. *Six Essays in Comparative Sociology.* Delhi: Oxford University Press.

Bhattacharya, N. 1985. 'Agricultural Labour and Production: Central and South-east Punjab'. In *Essays on the Commercialisation of Indian Agriculture*, ed. K. N. Raj, 105–62. Delhi: Oxford University Press.

Blyn, G. 1966. *Agricultural Trends in India, 1891–1947.* Philadelphia: University of Philadelphia Press.

Bonnano, A. 1989. *Sociology of Agriculture.* New Delhi: Concept Publishing House.

Brass, T. 1990. 'Class Struggle and Deproletarianisation of Agricultural Labour in Haryana (India)'. *The Journal of Peasant Studies* 18(1): 36–67.

——. 1994. 'Introduction: The New Farmers' Movements in India'. *The Journal of Peasant Studies* 3(4): 3–26.

Breman, J. 1974. *Patronage and Exploitation: Changing Agrarian Relations in South Gujarat, India.* Berkeley: University of California Press.

——. 1985. *Of Peasant, Migrants and Paupers: Rural Labour Circulation and Capitalist Production in West India.* Delhi: Oxford University Press.

Buttel, Frederick H., Olaf F. Larson and Gilbert W. Gillespie Jr. 1990. *The Sociology of Agriculture.* Westport: Greenwood Press.

Byres, T. J. 1972. 'The Dialectics of India's Green Revolution'. *South Asian Review* 5(2): 99–106.

——. 1974. 'Land Reforms, Industrialisation and Marketed Surplus in India: An Essay on the Power of Rural Bias'. In *Agrarian Reform and Agrarian Reformism: Studies of Peru, Chile, China, and India*, ed. D. Lehmann, 221–61. London: Faber and Faber.

Chakravarti, A. 1975. *Contradiction and Change: Emerging Patterns of Authority in a Rajasthan Village.* Delhi: Oxford University Press.

Chayanov, A. V. 1966. *The Theory of Peasant Economy*, eds. Daniel Thorner, Basile Kerblay and R. E. F. Smith. Homewood, IL: The American Economic Association.

Chowdhry, P. 1994. *The Veiled Women: Shifting Gender Equations in Rural Haryana, 1880–1990.* Delhi: Oxford University Press.

Cohn, B. S. 1987. *An Anthropologist among the Historians and Other Essays.* Delhi: Oxford University Press.

Darling, M. 1947. *Punjab Peasantry in Prosperity and Debt.* Bombay: Oxford University Press.

Datta, A. 2016. 'Migration, Remittances and Changing Sources of Income in Rural Bihar (1999–2011): Some Findings from a Longitudinal Study'. *Economic and Political Weekly* 51(31): 85–93.

de Haan, A. 2002. 'Migration and Livelihood in Historical Perspective: A Case Study of Bihar, India'. *Journal of Development Studies* 38(5): 115–42.

Desai, A. R. 1976. *Social Background to Indian Nationalism.* Bombay: Popular Prakashan.

Deshingkar, P., and J. Farrington. 2009. *Circular Migration and Multi-locational Livelihood Strategies in Rural India.* New Delhi: Oxford University Press.

Dhanagare, D. N. 1983. *Peasant Movements in India, 1920–1950.* Delhi: Oxford University Press.

———. 1991. 'An Apoliticist Populism: A Case Study of BKU'. In *Country–town Nexus: Study in Social Transformation in Contemporary India*, eds K. L. Sharma and Dipankar Gupta, 104–22. Jaipur: Rawat Publications.

Djurfeldt, G. 1982. 'Classical Discussions of Capital and Peasantry: A Critique'. In *Rural Development: Theories of Peasant Economy and Agrarian Change*, ed. John Harriss, 139–59. London: Hutchinson.

Dube, L. 1986. *Visibility and Power: Essays on Women in Society and Development.* Delhi: Oxford University Press.

Fox, R. 1987. *Lions of the Punjab: Culture in the Making.* New Delhi: Archives Publishers.

Friedland, W. H. 1982. 'The End of Rural Society and the Future of Rural Sociology'. *Rural Sociology* 47(4): 589–608.

———. 1984. 'Commodity Systems Analysis: An Approach to the Sociology of Agriculture'. In *Research in Rural Sociology and Development* (Volume 1), ed. H. K. Schwarzweller, 221–35. Greenwich: Jai Press.

Frankel, F. R. 1971. *India's Green Revolution: Economic Gains and Political Costs.* Bombay: Oxford University Press.

Frankel, Rancine and M. S. A. Rao (eds). 1989. *Dominance and State Power in Modern India.* New Delhi: Oxford University Press.

Ghose A. K. (ed.). 1984. *Agrarian Reforms in Contemporary Developing Countries.* New Delhi: Select Books.

Gough, K. 1989. *Rural Change in Southeast India, 1950s to 1980s.* Delhi: Oxford University Press.

Greenough, P. R. 1982. *Prosperity and Misery in Modern Bengal: The Famine of 1943–1944.* Oxford: Oxford University Press.

Guha, Ranajit. 1983. *Elementary Aspects of Peasant Insurgency in Colonial India.* Delhi: Oxford University Press.

Guha, Ramachandra. 1989. *The Unquiet Woods: Ecological Change and Peasant Resistance in the Himalaya.* Delhi: Oxford University Press.

Gupta, D. 1997. *Rivalry and Brotherhood: Politics in the Life of Farmers in Northern India.* Delhi: Oxford University Press.

Habib, I. 1963. *Agrarian Systems of Mughal India.* Bombay: Asia Publishers.

———. 1982. 'Agrarian Relations and Land Revenue: North India'. In *The Cambridge Economic History of India* (Volume 1), eds T. Raychaudhury and Irfan Habib, 235–48. Delhi: Orient Longman.

Harriss, J. 1987. 'Capitalism and Peasant Production: The Green Revolution in India'. In *Peasants and Peasant Societies*, ed. T. Shanin, 227–45. London: Blackwell.

———. 2011. 'Reflections on Agrarian Change in India since Independence: Does "Landlordism" Still Matter?'. Simons Papers in Security and Development No. 14. Available at https://www. semanticscholar. org/paper/Reflections-on-Agrarian-Change-in-India-since-Does-Harriss/3281d4734dee8271deef41318176a541fd7ea6ea (accessed 15 May 2020).

Harriss, J., J. Jeyaranjan and K. Nagaraj. 2010. 'Land, Labour and Caste Politics in Rural Tamil Nadu in 20th Century Iruvelpattu (1916–2008)'. *Economic and Political Weekly* 45(31), July: 47–61.

Harriss-White, B. 1996. *A Political Economy of Agricultural Markets in South India: Masters of the Countryside.* New Delhi: Sage.

Herring, R. J. 1977. 'Land Tenure and Credit-capital Tenure in Contemporary India'. In *Land Tenure and Peasants in South Asia*, ed. R. E. Frynkenberg, 120–58. New Delhi: Manohar.

Inden, R. 1990. *Imagining India.* Oxford: Basil Blackwell.

Jaffrelot, Christopher. 2003. *India's Silent Revolution: The Rise of the Low Castes in North Indian Politics.* Delhi: Permanent Black.

Jodhka, S. S. 1994. 'Agrarian Changes and Attached Labour: Emerging Patterns in Haryana Agriculture'. *Economic and Political Weekly* 29(39): A102–06.

———. 1995a. 'Bureacratisation, Corruption and Depoliticisation: Changing Profile of Credit Co-operatives in Rural Haryana'. *Economic and Political Weekly* 30(1): 53–56.

———. 1995b. 'Who Borrows? Who Lends?: Changing Structure of Informal Credit in Rural Haryana'. *Economic and Political Weekly* 30(39): A123–31.

———. 2014. 'Emergent Ruralities: Revisiting Village Life and Agrarian Change in Haryana'. *Economic and Political Weekly* 49(26–27): 5–17.

———. 2015. *Caste in Contemporary India.* New Delhi: Routledge.

Jodhka, S. S., and Adarsh Kumar. 2017. 'Non-farm Economy in Madhubani, Bihar: Social Dynamics and Exclusionary Rural Transformations'. *Economic and Political Weekly* 52(25–26): 14–24.

Joshi, P. C. 1976. *Land Reforms in India: Trends and Perspectives.* New Delhi: Allied Publishers.

Kothari, S. 1996. 'Whose Nation?: Displaced as Victims of Development'. *Economic and Political Weekly* 31(24): 1476–85.

Kroeber, A. L. 1948. *Anthropology.* New York: Harcourt, Brace and Co.

Kumar, D. 1982. 'South India'. In *The Cambridge Economic History of India* (Volume 2), ed. Dharma Kumar, 207–41. Delhi: Orient Longman.

———. 1992. *Land and Caste in South India.* New Delhi: Manohar.

Lenin, V. I. 1960 [1899]. *The Development of Capitalism in Russia.* In *V. I. Lenin: Collected Works* (Volume 3). Moscow: Foreign Languages Publishing House.

———. 1908 [1962]. *The Agrarian Programme of Social-democracy in the First Russian Revolution, 1905–1907.* In *V. I. Lenin: Collected Works* (Volume 13). Moscow: Foreign Languages Publishing House.

Lerche, Jens. 2013. 'The Agrarian Question in Neoliberal India: Agrarian Transition Bypassed?'. *Journal of Agrarian Change* 13(3), July: 382–40.

Marx, K. 1959. *The First India War of Independence: 1857–1859.* Moscow: Progress Publishers.

Moore, B. Jr. 1966 *Social Origins of Dictatorship and Democracy.* Middlesex: Penguin.

Neale, W. 1962. *Economic Change in Rural India: Land Tenure and Reform in Uttar Pradesh, 1800–1955.* New Haven: Yale University Press.

Newby, H. 1980. 'Trend Report: Rural Sociology'. *Current Sociology* 28(1), spring: 1–141.

Oommen, T. K. 1984. *Social Transformation in Rural India.* New Delhi: Vikas Publishing House.

Patnaik, U. (ed.). 1990. *Agrarian Relations and Accumulation: The 'Mode of Production Debate in India'.* Delhi: Oxford University Press.

Radhakrishnan, P. 1989. *Peasant Struggles, Land Reforms and Social Change: Malabar 1836–1982.* New Delhi: Sage.

Rainia, Rajeswari S. 2016. 'Agriculture and the Development Burden'. In *Routledge Handbook of Contemporary India*, ed. Knut A. Jacobsen, 99–118. London: Routledge.

Redfield, R. 1965. *Peasant Society and Culture.* Chicago: University of Chicago Press.

Rudolph, Lloyd I., and Susanne Hoeber Rudolph. 1987. *In Pursuit of Lakshmi: The Political Economy of the Indian State.* Chicago: University of Chicago Press.

Rutten, M. 1991. *Capitalist Entrepreneurs and Economic Diversification: Social Profile of Large Farmers and Rural Industrialists in Central Gujarat, India.* Rotterdam: Academisch Proefschrift.

Satyanarayana, A. 1991. 'Commercialisation, Money Capital and the Peasantry in Colonial Andhra, 1900–1940'. In *The South Indian Economy: Agrarian Change, Industrial Structure and State Policy, 1914–1947*, eds Sabyasachi Bhattacharya, Sumit Guha, Raman Mahadevan, Sakti Padhi, D. Rajasekhar and G. N. Rao, 51–77. Delhi: Oxford University Press.

Schwarzweller, H. K. (ed.). 1984. *Research in Rural Sociology and Development* (Volume 1). Greenwich: Jai Press.

Scott, J. 1976. *The Moral Economy of the Peasantry: Rebellion and Subsistence in Southeast Asia.* New Haven: Yale University Press.

Sen, A. 1976. 'Famines as Failures of Exchange Entitlements'. *Economic and Political Weekly* 11(31–33): 1273–80.

Shanin, T. (ed.). 1987. *Peasants and Peasant Societies.* London: Blackwell.

Silverman, S. 1987. 'The Concept of Peasant and the Concept of Culture'. In *Social Anthropology of Peasantry*, ed. J. Mencher, 7–31. Bombay: Somaiya Publications.

Srinivas, M. N. 1994. *The Dominant Caste and Other Essays.* Delhi: Oxford University Press.

Stokes, E. 1978. *The Peasants and the Raj.* New Delhi: Vikas Publishing House.

Thorburn, S. S. 1983. *Musalmans and Moneylenders in Punjab.* Delhi: Mittal Publications.

Thorner, D. 1956. *The Agrarian Prospects of India.* Delhi: University Press.

———. 1964. *Agricultural Co-operatives in India.* Bombay: Asia Publishers.

Wolf, E. 1966. *Peasants.* New Jersey: Prentice-Hall.

———. 1969. *Peasant Wars of the Twentieth Century.* New York and London: Harper and Row.

Section I

Conceptual Frames

1

A Post-Marxian Theory of Peasant Economy

*The School of A. V. Chayanov**

Daniel Thorner

Most of those who are today seeking to understand the economic behaviour of the peasantry seem to be unaware that they are traversing much the same ground trod from the 1860s onward by several generations of Russian economists. The problems which are today plaguing economists in countries like Brazil, Mexico, Turkey, Nigeria, India and Indonesia bear striking similarities to those which were the order of the day in Russia, from the emancipation of the serfs in 1861, right down to the collectivisation of agriculture at the end of the 1920s, to wit:

1. how to transform traditional rural society so as to overcome the misery, squalour, and illiteracy of the peasantry;
2. how to get the peasants to modernise their agriculture, especially their farming technique; and
3. how to carry out this transformation and modernisation so as to permit—indeed, to facilitate—the development of the entire national economy.

One of the first methods which young Russian idealists tried for dealing with these problems was direct action. Hundreds upon hundreds of college students, doctors, nurses, university teachers—including economists and statisticians—quit their urban life and attempted to 'go to the people'. Establishing themselves in villages, they tried to be of use to the peasantry, to get them into motion; revolutionaries among these idealists preached the virtues of socialism. The police smoked them out and rounded them up, sometimes tipped off by the peasants themselves, suspicious of outsiders from other orders of society.

* Originally published in *The Economic Weekly* 17(5–7), February 1965, annual number: 227–36.

CHASTENED INTELLECTUALS

Chastened by their experiences, many of these action-oriented intellectuals deemed it wise, before undertaking further adventures in rural philanthropy, to obtain a more precise knowledge of village realities. Scores of them offered their services when the new provincial and district assemblies, the *zemstvos*—set up to help implement the land reforms of 1861—launched in the 1870s a vast programme of economic and statistical investigations into peasant economic problems. It would be difficult to exaggerate the value of these field enquiries, which continued through four decades right down to the First World War. In sheer bulk, they add up to more than 4,000 volumes. These constitute perhaps the most ample single source of data we have on the peasant economy of any country in modern times.

More significant than the quantity is the quality of these data. From the outset, the field investigators included some of the ablest spirits of the day. Sympathetic to the peasantry and anxieties to gain insight into their problems, they were determined to carry out their enquiries with utmost thoroughness. In presenting their results, they took great pains to choose suitable categories and to design statistical tables so as to bring out clearly the basic relations among the various economic and social groups in the villages. Some of their reports were so striking that the government in 1888 passed a law forbidding any further inquiries into landlord–peasant relations, but nonetheless the work went on.

RICH ANALYTICAL LITERATURE

In the decades from 1880 onwards, Russia's leading economists, statisticians, sociologists and agricultural experts assessed, analysed and fought over the materials furnished by the successive zemstvo enquiries. Their articles and books provide the richest analytical literature we have on the peasant economy of any country in the period since the Industrial Revolution. Among the Russian scholars who participated in the debate over the zemstvo statistics, N. A. Kablukov, V. A. Kosinskii, A. N. Chelintsev, N. P. Makarov and G. A. Studenskii stand out for their attempts to formulate a theory of peasant economy. Alexander Vassilevich Chayanov, from 1919 to 1930 the leading Russian authority on the economics of agriculture, synthesised the theoretical ideas of his predecessors and contemporaries, and developed them along original lines. Translations into English of two studies by Chayanov form the core of the volume are to be published by the American Economic Association in their Foreign Translation series.

The first and, by far, the larger of these works is Chayanov's masterpiece, *Organizatsiya Krestyanskogo Khozyaistva* (Organisation of the Peasant Farm/ Economy), the title of which may be rendered in English as 'Peasant Farm Organisation'. It provides a theory of peasant behaviour at the level of the individual family farm, that is, at the 'micro' level. The second, much shorter study—*Zur Frage einer Theorie der Nichtkapitalistische Wirtschaftssysteme* (1924), which may be translated as 'On the Theory of Non-capitalistic Economic Systems'—sets forth the proposition that at the national or 'macro' level, peasant economy ought to be treated as an economic system in its own right, as a non-capitalistic system of national economy. The brief remarks which follow will be concerned chiefly with Chayanov's theory of the peasant farm, his 'micro'-theory, which Dietze (1934) has termed the most noteworthy creative synthesis so far achieved in this field, down to the present day.[1]

Chayanov's Theory of the Peasant Farm

The sure and certain way to misunderstand the peasant family farm, Chayanov held, was to view it as a business, that is to say, an enterprise of a capitalistic sort. To him the essential characteristic of business firms or capitalistic enterprises was that they operated with hired workers in order to earn profits. By contrast, peasant family farms, as Chayanov defined them, employed no hired wage labour, none whatsoever. His family farms were pure, in the sense that they depended solely upon the work of their own family members.

Chayanov's definition of the family farm may surprise us by its narrowness as compared with the much wider usage of the term in recent decades. Present-day economists familiar with model-building might assume that for his purpose Chayanov framed a special model or ideal type. In point of fact, Chayanov considered his category a real one drawn from life. He contended that 90 per cent or more of the farms in Russia in the first quarter of the twentieth century had no hired labourers, that they were family farms in the full sense of his definition. In so far as his contention was correct, his model was far from being 'ideal'; quite the contrary, it stood for the most typical farm in what was then the largest peasant country in the world.

...

Non-Euclidean Economics

Economists would have to face the fact, he held, that economies made up of family units in which the category of wages was absent belonged to a fundamentally different economic structure and required a different economic theory. Such a theoretical system, he wrote, would have the same relationship to present-day economics as N. I. Lobachevsky's geometry bore to that of Euclid. In his day Lobachevsky gave up the assumption of parallel lines; we would have to drop wages.

Chayanov's own theory—or, if the expression be permitted, his non-Euclidean economics—was not restricted to peasant agricultural production. He was concerned with the total income of the peasant family, whether from agriculture or also from crafts and trades.[2] The economic unit for which his theory was devised was the peasant *family* taken as a whole in all its works, or alternatively, the total economic activity of family labour. Thus, he saw his exposition of peasant economy as a particular form of a larger doctrine, the theory of family economy.

THE LABOUR–CONSUMER BALANCE

Chayanov's central concept for analysing family economics is what he called the labour–consumer balance between the satisfaction of family needs and the drudgery (or irksomeness) of labour. Once grasped, this concept furnishes the key to his entire position and mode of presentation. It was one of the chief weapons that he wielded in his severe critiques both of Marxian economics in Russia and of orthodox classical and neoclassical economics in the West.

In developing his concept of the labour–consumer balance, Chayanov began with the *gross* income or gross product of a peasant family household at the end of an agricultural year, assumed to be at a given level (say, 1,000 roubles). From this annual gross income certain expenses had to be deducted, so as to restore the farm to the same level of production it possessed at the beginning of that agricultural year, that is, seed, fodder, repairs, replacement of expired livestock, worn-out equipment, etc. Once these expenses had been deducted, the family was left with a *net* product or net income that constituted the return for its labour during that agricultural year. How was that net income or net product to be divided up among family budget for consumption, capital formation for raising the farm's potential level of production, and savings (insofar as there was any possibility of savings not invested in the farm)? Put simply, what should the family eat, what fresh capital should *it* invest in the farm, what should it put by?

A capitalist enterprise, Chayanov pointed out, can get objective, quantitative evidence as to how to proceed. By deducting from its gross product the outlays on materials, capital consumption and wages, a business concern can ascertain its net profits. If it wishes to increase its profits, the concern can put in more capital and obtain in due course an exact quantitative statement as to the increase, if any, in net profits. For a peasant family farm, however, there are neither wages nor net profits. The family members know roughly how many days they have worked, but Chayanov insisted, there is no *valid* way of estimating in money the value of their work. All that they can see before them is the net product of their work, and there is no way of dividing days of labour into poods of wheat.

SUBJECTIVE EVALUATIONS

The way the peasant family proceeds, according to Chayanov, is by subjective evaluation based *on* the long experience in agriculture of the living generation and its predecessors. Most peasant families, Chayanov showed, are in a position to work more hours or to work more intensively, sometimes even both. The extent to which the members of the family actually work under given conditions he called the degree of self-exploitation of family labour. The peasants would put in greater effort only if they had reason to believe it would yield an increase in output, which could be devoted to greater family consumption, to enlarged investment in the farm, *or* to both. The mechanism which Chayanov devised for explaining how the family acted is his labour–consumer balance. Each family, he wrote, seeks an annual output adequate for its basic needs, but this involves drudgery, and the family does not push its work beyond the point where the possible increase in output is outweighed by the irksomeness of the extra work. Each family strikes a rough balance or equilibrium between the degree of satisfaction of family needs and the degree of drudgery of labour.

Family 'Natural History'

In itself, Chayanov hastened to add, there was nothing novel or remarkable about this concept. It goes back, after all, to Adam Smith. What is of interest and gives value to Chayanov's book is the way he handled the concept. He showed how for different families the balance or equilibrium between consumer satisfaction and degree of drudgery is affected by the size of the family, and the ratio of working members to non-working members. He traced the 'natural history' of the family from the time of the marriage of the young couple through the growth of the children to working age and the marriage of this second generation. In relating this natural history of the family to the changing size of peasant farms from generation to generation, Chayanov developed the concept of 'demographic differentiation', which he asked his readers to contrast with the Marxian concept of class differentiation among the peasantry.

But his analysis is far from being primarily demographic. Basing himself on the zemstvo statistics, on the studies of these by his predecessors and colleagues, and on fresh-held enquiries, Chayanov examined the effects on the labour–consumer balance of a wide range of factors. He took account of size of holdings, qualities of soil, crops grown, livestock, manure, location, market prices, land prices, interest rates on capital loans, feasibility of particular crafts and trades, availability of alternative work, and relative density of population. Chayanov was not so much concerned with the individual effects of each of these factors, as with their mutual effects as they changed through time.

Marginal Utility Analysis

In weighing the influence of these *several* elements on the delicate balance between urgency of family needs and drudgery of labour, Chayanov employed some of the concepts and techniques of marginal utility analysis. His terminology included, for example, demand satisfaction and marginal expenditure of the workforce. For factors such as willingness to put in greater efforts which were not subject to any precise measurement, he constructed equilibrium graphs showing interaction under varying assumptions.

Chayanov foresaw, quite correctly, that his use of these tools of 'bourgeois' economics would shock many of his contemporaries in Soviet Russia of the mid-1920s. He countered that his work should be judged not by the genealogy of his techniques, but rather by the results which he had been able to obtain through the application of those techniques to the Russian data in the light of economic postulates firmly anchored *in* peasant behaviour.

Summing up his findings, Chayanov wrote that available income was divided according to the equilibrium of production and consumption evaluations which expressed a desire to maintain a constant level of well-being.[3] Generally speaking, an increase in family gross income led to increases in both family budget and capital formation. The precise way the gross income was divided up in each family was a question of subjective judgement by the head of the family, and hence could not be expressed in objective, quantitative terms.

According to Chayanov, the basic characteristics of the peasant family economic behaviour were fundamentally different from those of capitalistic farms in respect of the price they were prepared to pay for buying land, interest they were willing to pay in borrowing capital, rent they would pay for leasing in land, price at which they would sell their produce, etc. In conditions where capitalist farms would go bankrupt, peasant families could work longer hours, sell at lower prices, obtain no net surplus, and yet manage to carry on with their farming, year after year. For these reasons, Chayanov concluded that the competitive power of peasant family farms versus large-scale capitalist farms was much greater than had been foreseen in the writings of Marx, Kautsky, Lenin and their successors.

VIABILITY OF PEASANT FAMILY FARMS

In proclaiming the viability of peasant family farming, Chayanov set himself against the main streams of Marxist thought in Russia and western Europe. Marx had termed the peasant who hires no labour a kind of twin economic person: 'As owner of the means of production he is capitalist, as worker he is his own wage worker.' What is more, Marx added, 'the separation between the two is the normal relation in this [that is, capitalist] society.' According to the law of the increasing division of labour in society, small-scale peasant agriculture must inevitably give way to large-scale capitalist agriculture. In Marx's own words:

> [the] peasant who produces with his own means of production will either gradually be transformed into a small capitalist who also exploits the labour of others, or he will suffer the loss of his means of production ... and be transformed into a wage worker. This is the tendency in the form of society in which the capitalist mode of production predominates. (Marx 1951: 193–94)

Karl Marx and Friedrich Engels believed that the advantages of concentration and centralisation lay with the capitalist farmers who would, in the course of time, swallow up the small peasants. Two outstanding followers of Marx who adhered to this position were Kautsky, whose monograph, *Die Agrarfragc*, was published in Stuttgart in 1899, and Lenin, whose work entitled *The Development of Capitalism in Russia* appeared later in the same year in Moscow. The analyses by Kautsky for western Europe and Lenin for Tsarist Russia were each sharply challenged in a large body of literature which it is out of the question for us to discuss here.[4] What is of interest to us is that Chayanov rejected both the terms in which Marx analysed the peasant farm, and the assessment by Lenin of the importance of family farms in the Russian economy of his time.

Fictional Bifurcation

At the outset of his book on 'Peasant Economic Organisation', Chayanov assailed the characterisation of the peasant as having a twofold nature, combining in himself the attributes of both a capitalist and a wage worker. Chayanov termed this bifurcation an unhelpful fiction, what is worse, a purely 'capitalist' kind of fiction, in the sense that it was made up entirely of capitalist categories and was conceivable only within a capitalist system. For understandable reasons, Chayanov did not explicitly state that he was criticising Marx. It was all too easy, however, for anyone familiar with what Marx wrote, or with what Lenin wrote about Marx, to discern who was at least one of Chayanov's targets.[5]

Chayanov's position vis-à-vis Marx, it should be noted, was not altogether his own creation but reflected the cumulative work of the 'organisational and production school' of Russian agricultural economists from time of Kosinskii's 1905 treatise. A neat statement of the position of this group can be found in the well-known treatise on 'The Accumulation of Capital' (1921 [1913]) by Rosa Luxemburg, the most dynamic force in German socialism in the period of the First World War. Luxemburg had been born in Poland under Tsarist rule, and was thoroughly familiar with Russian literature on the peasantry:

> It is an empty abstraction to apply simultaneously all the categories of capitalistic production to the peasantry, to conceive of the peasant as his own entrepreneur, wage labourer and landlord all in one person. The economic peculiarity of the peasantry, if we want to put them ... into one undifferentiated category, lies in the very fact that they belong neither to the class of capitalist entrepreneurs nor to that of the wage proletariat, that they do not represent capitalistic production but simple commodity production. (Luxemburg 1921 [1913]: 368)[6]

Chayanov's differences with Lenin were, if anything, even sharper than his divergences from Marx. As early as 1899, Lenin had written that in Russian agriculture, the capitalist farmers, the peasant bourgeoisie, were already in the saddle. They were in a small minority, Lenin (1956: 177–78) wrote, perhaps no more than 20 per cent of the farm households. Nonetheless, in terms of the total quantity of means of production, and in terms of their share of total produce grown, 'the peasant bourgeoisie are predominant. They are the masters of the countryside'.

By what criteria did Lenin separate capitalist farmers from non-capitalist peasants? In his view, the decisive step toward capitalism came when labourers had to be hired, when '... the area cultivated by the well-to-do peasants exceed the family labour norm (i.e., the amount of land that a family can cultivate by its own labour), and compel them to *resort to the hiring of workers* ...' (ibid.: 52). For Lenin the hiring of workers had become widespread, and Russia was well on its way toward a capitalist agriculture with a peasant bourgeoisie and a rural proletariat. Chayanov's numerous references to the very small part that hired labourers played on Russian farms (for example, his assertion that 90 to 95 per cent had no hired labourers in the period 1900–25), constitute, therefore, a direct if implicit refutation of Lenin. In fact, Chayanov's whole approach, his selection of the pure family farm as the typical

Russian unit, his insistence on the survival power of such family farms, and his treatment of rural differentiation in terms of demographic cycles rather than class antagonisms was diametrically opposed to that of Lenin.

WIDER RELEVANCE OF CHAYANOV'S THEORY

Chayanov's 'micro'-theory, insofar as he was able to elaborate it before his career was cut short, is essentially a theory of one kind of individual *family farm in* Russia, the family farm that employs no hired labour whatsoever. There were other kinds of peasant farms in Russia, and there were capitalist farms as well. Once we step out of Russia, we find peasant family farms elsewhere in Europe, and in Asia, Africa and the Americas. Chayanov's theory was devised so as to take account of Russian conditions, where the kind of peasant family farm that he discussed was predominant. Does his 'micro'-theory apply to peasant family farms in other countries?

Chayanov himself conceded that his theory worked better for thinly populated countries than for densely populated ones. It also worked better in countries where the agrarian structure had been shaken up (as in Russia after the emancipation of the serfs in 1861), rather than in countries with a more rigid agrarian structure. Where the peasants could not readily buy or take in more land, his theory would have to be seriously modified.

Since Chayanov did not work out these modifications, he did not elaborate a full-blown theory of peasant family farming for any country other than Russia. Nonetheless, he indicated that he thought one single universal theory of peasant family farm at the micro level could be devised. In his view, the Russian case, which he developed so fully, was only an illustration of this larger theory.

One wonders whether he may not have been over-optimistic about the possibility of a universal 'micro'-theory of peasant family farming. We will recall that in calculating the springs of peasant decisions in Russia, Chayanov took account of the interaction of a very large number of factors, including family size and structure, land tenures, climate, access to markets and possibility of getting extra jobs in the off-seasons. He was able to construct his models the more easily since he assumed the existence of a single 'pure' type of family farm, free of hired wage labour. Extending the theory outside of Russia would at the very least involve preparation of alternative models for 'impure' peasant households, employing hired labour.

Although it encompassed a very wide range of possibilities, Chayanov's theory of peasant farming remained essentially a static one. From the 1860's through the 1920's the Russian agricultural economy underwent a rapid series of fundamental changes. There were marked sectoral and regional differences in rates of growth. Chayanov often referred to the existence of these differentials, but pitched his theory at a level of abstraction well above them.

...

Notes

1. Also, personal communication from Professor von Dietze, Summer 1964.

2. The term 'family farm' is sometimes even used for capitalistic enterprises producing essentially for export, so long as these are family-operated.

3. This is only one way, and an oversimplified one at that, of summarising Chayanov's position on a quite complex relationship. In the various chapters of his book, he spells out the nuances that are involved. For an earlier discussion of a balance between 'need' and 'labour', see Jevons (1911: Chapter 5).

4. Even before the appearance of Kautsky's book, the position and policy of the German socialists with regard to the small peasantry had given rise to sharp dispute within the party. Some of the original documents are conveniently assembled and translated into English by R. C. K. Ensor in his useful collection, *Modern Socialism* (1907: items XV, XVI and XXII). Convenient discussions of the controversy in central and western Europe are given in the works by Gerschenkron (1943) and Lichtheim (1961: Chapter 5).

5. Where Chayanov found Marx in agreement with him, he of course did not hesitate to quote him by name. Thus, he cites both in Chapters 5 and 6 the celebrated passage in which Marx states: '... with parcellated farming and small scale landed property, production to a very great extent satisfied own needs and is carried out independently of control by the general (i.e., the capitalist) rate of profit'.

It should be noted that in the 1870s, Marx learnt Russian primarily in order to read the zemstvo reports on the peasantry. He followed these closely, and as was his habit, took extensive notes. Three volumes of these notes have been translated from the German into Russian and published, and a fourth has been announced. See *Archiv Marxa i Englesa* (Volumes 11–13), 1948, 1952 and 1955, Moscow.

6. I have followed the English translation (Luxemburg 1951), but have made it more literal.

References

Chayanov, A. V. 1923. *Die Lehre von der bäuerlichen Wirtschaft: Versuch einer Theorie der Familienwirtschaft im Landbau* (The Doctrine of Peasant Economy: Test of a Theory of Family Economy in Agriculture). Berlin: P. Parey.

———. 1924. *Zur Frage einer Theorie der Nichtkapitalistische Wirtschaftssysteme. Archiv für Sozialwissenschaft und Sozialpolitik* 51(3), Heidelberg: 577–613.

Dietze, C. V. 1934. 'Peasantry'. *Encyclopedia of the Social Sciences* 12: 52.

Ensor, R. C. K. 1907. *Modern Socialism* (2nd edition). London and New York.

Gerschenkron, A. 1943. *Bread and Democracy in Germany*. Berkeley: University of California Press.

Jevons, W. Stanley. 1911. *The Theory of Political Economy* (4th edition). London: Macmillan.

Lenin, V. I. 1956. *The Development of Capitalism in Russia*. Moscow: Foreign Languages Publishing House.

Lichtheim, George. 1961. *Marxism: An Historical and Critical Study*. London: Routledge and Kegan Paul.

Luxemburg, Rosa. 1921 [1913]. *Die Akkumulaturn des Kapitals* (The Accumulation of Capital). Berlin.

———. 1951. *The Accumulation of Capital*, trans. Agnes Schwarzschild. London and New York: Routledge.

Marx, Karl. 1951. *Theorien über den Mehrvert* (Theories of Surplus Value), trans. G. A. Bonner and Emile Burns. London: Lawrence and Wishart.

2

The Agrarian Question in the Twenty-first Century*

Sam Moyo, Praveen Jha and Paris Yeros

Our intention in this chapter is to reflect on the 'classical' agrarian question and how we might look ahead to the twenty-first century.

Such a reflection continues to require a critique of Eurocentric and economistic tendencies, which have been influential in Marxian political economy, to the point of pronouncing the classical agrarian question dead, purportedly for no longer serving its primordial function, industrialisation. Absent in these approaches is acknowledgement of a series of questions, namely the national question and its land and peasant components, which are irreducible to industrialisation (Moyo, Jha and Yeros 2013). These are precisely the questions that marked the culmination of the classical agrarian question, and remain the cornerstone of contemporary agrarian questions. However, before beginning to reflect upon Archie Mafeje's views, we find it important to trace the trajectory of the 'classical myth of the agrarian question', particularly its obsession with industrialisation.

Making of the Classical Myth[1]

The notion of the 'agrarian question', which became central to Marxian political economy in the late nineteenth century, has always been a complex one, with different dimensions of a large canvas and interconnected themes getting privileged in alternative conceptual renderings. Nonetheless, soon after its inception, there was a strong tendency to shape its analytical contours in the light of Eurocentric modernisation experiences, in spite of the richly textured discourses in which it was embedded. For instance, reviewing the early literature, Terry Byres (1991) distinguishes the agrarian question in three distinct senses: (a) the Engels sense, (b) the Kautsky–Lenin sense, and (c) the Preobrazhensky sense. As he notes, each of the three senses referred to the political, social and economic dimensions of backwardness, respectively. Yet, they also converged in their underlying concern

* Originally published in *Economic and Political Weekly* 50(37), 12 September 2015: 35–41.

with obtaining, whether by capitalist or socialist means, the modern industrialised outcome that England had obtained earlier, ahead of her 'great power' rivals.

As for industrialisation, while the early European thinkers who converged around this objective had divergent views on how to obtain it, those working on the agrarian question, essentially reduced it to the question of industrialisation. It was a question which permitted a variety of perspectives on the politics and economics of industrialisation, but without managing ultimately to transcend the political and ideological limitations of turn-of-the-century Europe. In other words, the Eurocentric Marxist discourse on the agrarian question evolved largely in relation to the theme of backwardness and prescribed industrialisation as its main remedy. This binary of backwardness/industrialisation, we submit, became the basis of latter-day myth-making.

The theme of backwardness/industrialisation gained a new life after the Second World War and it got oriented either towards a radical reinterpretation, or a conservative rendition which reduced it to a technocratic exercise and accentuated Eurocentric distortions. At the crux of it were matters deeply political, namely land concentration, mass peasant populations, etc., which continued to determine the relation of forces of economies and societies, but unfortunately, these remain largely ignored. Instead, the backwardness/industrialisation binary became an axiom with strongly conservative tendencies.[2] Stating the essence of such a conception of the classical agrarian question, Byres at the close of the twentieth century remarks:

> An unresolved agrarian question is a central characteristic of economic backwardness. In its broadest meaning, the agrarian question may be defined as the continuing existence in the countryside of a poor country of substantive obstacles to an unleashing of the forces capable of generating economic development, both inside and outside agriculture. Originally formulated with respect to incomplete capitalist transition and certain political consequences of that incompleteness, the agrarian question is now part, also of the debate on possible socialist transition in poor countries. (Byres 1991: 9)

This notion of agrarian question (despite evading land reform and speaking of socialism almost stoically) is supposedly of profound relevance to all the backward countries, even though specificities in each case (of their respective agrarian questions) and the consequent trajectories of transcending economic backwardness may vary a great deal. For instance, Lenin gets drafted into this discourse through his distinction between the two broad trajectories of capitalist transition in agriculture (namely 'capitalism from above'—the Prussian path, and 'capitalism from below'—the American path), which presumably provided the necessary foundation for escaping economic backwardness (Lenin 1964: 33).[3] Subsequent Marxist scholarship on the subject has produced an impressive literature on the diversity of historical experiences. Byres distinguishes between six paths of agrarian transition, depending *inter alia* on contingent agrarian structures, the nature of state, the linkages with non-agricultural sectors and embedding of the particular country in the 'combined and uneven global capitalism'. Such explanations by then had already been established in the South, such as on the socialist transitions in Asia (Amin 1981) and the capitalist transitions in Africa, Latin America and the

Caribbean (Amin 1972; Cardoso and Faletto 1979; Mafeje 1991; Williams 1994). Yet, it is surprising that industrialisation was now being reinstated as an end in itself, even by some of the best-known and highly regarded Marxist scholars.

A FALSE RESOLUTION

Indeed, this tendency has reached new extremes, particularly in the hands of Henry Bernstein who has gone further to declare the classical agrarian question resolved on a global scale, independently of the degree or quality of industrial transitions in the South (details argued later). To understand this argument, we might recall a simpler notion of transformation, much simpler than Byres's numerous transitions above, but present in a wide spectrum of discourses in heterodox economics on structural economic transformation—or 'modern economic growth' in Simon Kuznets's expression. This notion holds that a significant spurt in agricultural growth either precedes or accompanies early to middle stages of modern economic transformation, until a stage is reached when the share of agriculture in total output, as well as labour force, starts declining: the faster this decline, the more successful and complete is supposed to be a process of agricultural transformation. Such a rendering of 'resolution' hinges on the view that agriculture plays a central role in modern economic transformation and that its success or failure may be measured with reference to the nature of overall economic transformation.

A 'minimalist' sense of resolution may specify a set of changes in economic and social relations of production within agriculture, necessarily required for significant increases in productivity and investible surplus to facilitate a process of successful transition from pre-capitalism to capitalism. Once the logic of capitalist social relations in agriculture are firmly in place (for example, agrarian capital and agrarian proletariat), resulting in technical development of enhanced surplus generation (via increased productivity of both land and labour), it may be said that the agrarian question has been addressed.

We would suggest that a substantial strand of Marxist scholarship often treated as the 'classical interpretation', appears to subscribe to this minimalist sense of the agrarian question. We have already referred to Bernstein, who is possibly one of the most prominent exponents of such a 'classical' view. In his 2004 piece in the *Journal of Agrarian Change*, Bernstein provides a 'stylised' outline highlighting what he considers to be core dimensions of the classic agrarian question, and goes on to conclude that:

> The "classic" agrarian question, I would suggest, is the agrarian question of capital. To the extent that its logic of agrarian transition succeeded (and may still succeed?) in accomplishing the social transformation and technical development of agriculture and in ways that contribute to industrialisation, then the agrarian question of capital is also that of labour as the two definitive classes of a new mode of production, representing historical progress. (Bernstein 2004: 200)

As should be evident, Bernstein's classic agrarian question hinges on what he considers to be the necessary economic and social wherewithal for the launch of capitalist development. Further, he also suggests that the logic of capitalist development in his scheme of the resolution of 'classic' agrarian question subsumes the 'agrarian question of labour' by which, presumably, he implies the absorption of dispossessed producers from agriculture (via primitive accumulation) in industrial and related non-agricultural sectors.

Bernstein goes on to argue that across the 'times and places', the changing material and social conditions underlying initiation of capitalist trajectories may imply very different expectations and demands with regards to the resolution of the agrarian question in specific contexts. He suggests that the countries of Africa, Asia and Latin America, by the time of their decolonisation and developmentalism had already been permeated by capitalist social relations of production and reproduction, and thus for them to embark on their respective (capitalist) economic transformations would have required unlocking the critical constraint of capital investments, or adequate agrarian capital. But if agrarian capital has sources beyond the local countryside, and if 'the range of non-agrarian capital' may diversify and expand over time, in accordance with expectations (Bernstein 2004: 201), then clearly the critical constraint above may be diluted both for the capitalist transformation of agriculture, as well as towards its contribution to industrialisation.

Given the nature and direction of Bernstein's argument, it leads him to suggest that:

> with contemporary "globalisation" and the massive development of the productive forces in (advanced) capitalist agriculture, the centrality of the "classic" agrarian question to industrialisation is no longer significant for international capital. In this sense, then, there *is no longer an agrarian question of capital on a world scale*, even when the agrarian question—as a basis of national accumulation and industrialisation—has not been resolved in many countries of the "South"... (Bernstein 2004: 202; emphasis in original)

To put it simply, for Bernstein, given the possibility of large capital inflows for developing countries in the era of contemporary globalisation, the classical agrarian question is dead!

Capital sans Labour?

There are a number of problems with Bernstein's arguments and it may be useful to flag the major ones. First, as stated earlier, his rendering of 'classic' agrarian question is of a minimalist variety and simply reduced to the 'question of capital'. However, even if the 'classical' agrarian question is broadly construed as social and material changes in the countryside of a poor country required for overall economic transformation, then Bernstein's reductionism is unwarranted. Second, the analytical rupture between the agrarian question of capital and the agrarian question of labour for the countries of the South, as visualised by Bernstein, seems to be misleading and is certainly a misreading of the classical perspective in which questions of capital and labour were viewed in an integrated fashion (and it was certainly not the case as Bernstein claims that in 'classic' agrarian question in capitalist transition, the question of labour was simply subsumed by the question of capital). Finally, the claim that mobility of international capital in the era of globalisation implies that the classical agrarian question no longer exists is a travesty of even the minimalist rendering of the theme, as there is no automatic/organic connection between the flow of capital and successful capitalist transitions in agriculture and elsewhere. In a nutshell, Bernstein's argument, in this sense, may be a non-starter.

Moving away from minimalist to broader renderings of the agrarian question in a classical Marxist perspective, it seems evident from the advantage of hindsight that there are significant gaps, troubling silences and even serious errors which underpin several arguments in this tradition. However, given the complex web of multi-dimensioned concerns associated with the broad sense of the agrarian question, it is hardly surprising that the meanings associated with the resolution of the agrarian question in classical Marxist discourse tend to get interpreted in conflicting ways. Sure enough, as suggested earlier, in a general sense, such a discourse organically and essentially links it to 'escape from economic backwardness' or 'successful economic transformation' (whether capitalist or socialist). But as should be evident immediately, such a general conception of resolution of the agrarian question raises more questions than answers, and in fact opens up, both analytically and empirically, slippery terrains. For instance, presumed simplistic relationship between capitalist transition in agriculture and its contribution to industrialisation (as well as overall economic transformation) has received considerable critical attention within Marxist discourses in the recent years. To take one example, by now, it seems quite clear that the transition from feudalism to capitalism in England and elsewhere in Europe was indeed characterised by a process of 'primitive accumulation', but it did not lead to 'agricultural revolution' and automatic indigenous foundations for industrialisation (Patnaik 2011).

It is not our intention in the rest of the chapter to engage in a detailed discussion of the range of problems underlying classical Marxist discourses on the agrarian question. The attempt of the arguments made in this section was to clarify how a Eurocentric and economistic version of the agrarian question has sustained a myth around industrialisation.[4] We have also suggested that this classical myth-making has not only drawn on the earlier European generation, but 'purified' it. Yet, neither did the classical agrarian question end with Preobrazhensky, nor did the original European vanguard have enough insight on, or organic experience of, the struggles and transitions in the South. The steadily escalating land-grabs in the South throughout the neo-liberal period (Moyo 2008a; Moyo, Yeros and Jha 2012), demonstrate the fact well that capital accumulation, whether linked to contemporary Western finance or Chinese industry, remains closely integrated with agriculture and this is just one of the many dimensions of the agrarian question at the current juncture. We must therefore concur with Mafeje (1997: 7) when he argues that 'the fault of socialist internationalists was to elevate the European historical experience, if that, to a universal theory'.

Looking Ahead with Mafeje

We have argued elsewhere that the classical agrarian question incorporated two sets of questions: that of industrialisation and that of national liberation (Moyo, Yeros and Jha 2012). While the earlier European vanguard, in the course of imperialist rivalries, was called upon to respond to the challenge of industrialisation, the nationalist vanguard under imperialist domination was presented most immediately with the task of liberation. As anti-imperialist nationalism spread and gained its footing in the South, the agrarian question itself evolved, reaching its most robust expression first in Maoism, then in African nationalism and the new revolutionary thought emanating from Latin America and the Caribbean. It was in these tectonic shifts of the mid-twentieth century that the political, social and economic dimensions of the agrarian question, which the European vanguard had previously articulated, were ultimately restructured and submitted to the quintessential cause of the time—national liberation. The great feat of the agrarian question of liberation was to incorporate industrialisation without surrendering to it; and thereby to create political space for the elaboration of new agrarian questions.

The key difference between the agrarian questions of industrialisation and liberation is that the latter has articulated with unprecedented clarity and conviction the requirement of sovereign industrialisation, or the safeguarding of the capacity to determine one's own external relations and internal balances. Moreover, by its very logic, it has enabled the posing of new agrarian questions in a universal way, namely gender equity and ecological sustainability—these being the dimensions that have most defined the contemporary the agrarian question—as well as the incipient debate on regional integration. Thus, the agrarian question of liberation has been the common thread between the classical and contemporary agrarian questions, consisting in the maturation of the former and cornerstone of the latter.

We submit that the agrarian question of liberation remains at the heart of the contemporary agrarian question, for its fate will continue to have a preponderant influence over the fate of gender relations, ecology or regionalism. Put differently, neither gender equity, nor ecological sustainability, nor autonomous regional integration can be expected to progress under the tutelage of monopoly capitalism. It is this which leads us to reject Bernstein's grand claim that the 'agrarian question is dead' and justifies our own exclamation—long live the agrarian question!

In looking ahead to multiple challenges of the twenty-first century, we draw inspiration on Mafeje's vision, which so distinctly embodies the continuity between the classical and contemporary agrarian questions. We draw especially on one of his last major statements, published at the turn of the century (Mafeje 2003), where one finds the wisdom acquired over a lifetime is condensed in a few pages on no less a question than 'what is to be done' in twenty-first century Africa. We highlight, in particular, three basic and interrelated issues raised: the long duration of agrarian transition, land alienation and resistance, and the role of small producers in national development.

Mafeje steadfastly argued that the specificity of agrarian transition in Africa has been obscured by concepts imported from Europe, Asia and Latin America.

He defended that Africa's long transition has differed in the persistence of a 'lineage mode of social organisation for production', which is neither a separate mode of production, nor a mere creation of the capitalist mode of production. Basic to this are social affiliation and access to land by kinship, which serve as a counterweight to individualist accumulation strategies and private use of natural resources. He further argued that the lineage system has not been restricted to subsistence production, or to the countryside, but for over a century has given structure to Africa's integration into the capitalist market and the expansion of rural–urban relations. Mafeje shared the view that the continent under colonialism embarked on three distinct transitions, identified by Amin (1972) as the peasant trade economies of the West, the concessionary economies of the central region, and the labour reserves of the South, the latter being the only region where mass land alienation occurred and a land question created. Nonetheless, the lineage system and its values continued to pervade the continent and have been remarkably resilient in structuring social relations and struggles among the exploited classes.

It is notable that Mafeje viewed the lineage system in its modern functions and as a social fact not to be taken lightly—as by modernisers of the left and right. He argued, in particular, that the 'customary' tenure relations of the lineage system are neither an obstacle to investment and accumulation, nor to technological advance. He identified the main obstacles to development as the surplus appropriated from small producers by monopoly capital and the comprador state; the domination of women, the main agricultural producers, through the same lineage system; and the degradation of the soil, possibly the main cause of productivity decline in the long run. He further argued that in the specific case of Southern Africa, where monopoly capital settled physically, peasant agriculture historically has been stifled more directly, as has accumulation by black capitalists all around, in the interest of the settler order.

From a long perspective, Mafeje's argument regarding the resilience of lineage society and its ideological force has been corroborated in the most unlikely of places, Southern Africa—indeed, the exception that proved the rule! In Zimbabwe, the alienation and privatisation of land by the white-settler minority over a whole century never obtained legitimacy, being ultimately reversed by a popular land occupation movement and a radicalised state (Moyo 1995a, 2001; Moyo and Chambati 2012; Moyo and Yeros 2007). On the other hand, the penetration of capitalism has also advanced after Independence, and especially under neo-liberalism, creating new economic facts, social classes, demographic trends, and structural tendencies. Mafeje was initially reluctant to recognise the qualitative impact of these changes, but did accept the facts when they were presented systematically (Moyo 2008a).

NEW DEBATES IN THE GLOBAL SOUTH

This new debate on transitions in Africa, in which renowned scholars such as Thandika Mkandawire, Mahmood Madmani and Samir Amin participated directly, occurred within the Council for the Development of Social Science Research in

Africa (CODESRIA) a whole decade before the onset of the major land grabs. It had the effect of placing a new land and peasant question on the research agenda in non-settler Africa, while also turning the spotlight on settler Africa, and even on South Africa where the 'proletarianisation' thesis has reigned supreme. Moreover, the debate synergised with like-minded debates among major South–South research networks, including the Dakar-based Third World Network, the Latin American Council of Social Sciences (CLASCO) and the Delhi-based International Development Economics Associates (IDEAS), to promote a peasant-friendly agenda generally across the South. Perhaps this has been the most lasting effect, galvanising a series of collaborative and autonomous research initiatives, recuperating ground on a variety of issues, inspiring young scholars and fomenting a convergent point of view on basic matters.[5] When the global land grabs escalated in 2007–08, one could indeed speak of a convergent Southern response on the nature and future of the agrarian question.[6]

This perspective has been substantially different from mainstream analyses of land alienation. Prior to the major land grabs, those who took interest in transitions construed land alienation as possibly the final blow to the 'disappearing peasantries' (Bryceson, Kay and Mooij 2000; Graziano da Silva 1999). It amounted to a narrow notion of transition, springing from an implicit (if not also explicit) desire for a post-peasant world which appeared to be on the horizon, on account of structural adjustment, out-migration and the flowering of 'multi-occupational' survival strategies. The analysis was linked to a new set of reformist and welfarist policies to be undertaken by the development industry, especially support for the 'livelihood strategies' of the dispossessed (what Bernstein called 'the agrarian question of labour') and the technical upgrading and market integration of the remaining farmers (Graziano da Silva and Tavares 2008). With the onset of major land-grabbing, such thinking could only take flight in a moralistic discourse and an empiricist vocation without a clear perspective on what is at stake. To this day, neither imperialism nor sovereignty has become relevant enough a category to the mainstream of agrarian studies to organise the discussion on the agrarian question.[7] Indeed, how can one defend the national question after having wished away the inhabitants of whole nations?

The 'multi-occupational' deepening of the last 30 years—which we have called 'semi-proletarianisation'—has been neither a new, nor a linear phenomenon. Even in non-settler Africa, as Mafeje (2003: 15) noted, 'virtually all small producers practiced more than subsistence production'. Moreover, semi-proletarianisation has never gone without a fight, which Mafeje (2003: 5) pointed out as well. So-called de-peasantisation has produced a new wave of land occupation movements, across the South, this being one of the most important political facts of our times (Moyo and Yeros 2005). The land movement in Zimbabwe may have been the most successful in reclaiming land, but the depth of the political work that has been under way on all continents has set the stage for consideration of 're-peasantisation' as a modern, sovereign project in the twenty-first century.

The forces arrayed against such a project are certainly enormous. Above all, the new scramble is set to deepen semi-proletarianisation, intensify militarisation and spread instability and conflict from one region to the next—none of which is conducive to development. But there are counter-forces at play, arising especially from small countries like Zimbabwe, Venezuela, Cuba, Bolivia, Ecuador and Nepal, which have weathered crisis and radicalisation to bring back the national question to the development agenda (Moyo and Yeros 2011). It is no coincidence that the idea of a 'return to the countryside' has been most clearly expressed in these countries, uniquely in every case. A further counter-force may also emerge from the large semi-peripheral countries, namely China, India, Brazil and South Africa. To date, these have remained contradictory in their systemic functions, but depending on the relation of forces within and around them, they do have the potential to drive a wedge in the workings of monopoly capitalism (Moyo, Yeros and Jha 2012). One indication of these contradictions, among many others, is the 'family agriculture' model for food security promoted in Brazil and now projected into the Food and Agriculture Organisation by the election of José Graziano da Silva to the top job. It amounts to a 'middle peasant' response which, by design, implies a diversion from the land question, but which is subject to capture by diverse forces, from green revolutionaries backed by Rockefeller/Gates philanthropy to radicalised states with a 'Look East' policy (Moyo and Yeros 2012).

LEARNING FROM MAFEJE

It is necessary, therefore, to start spelling out what development and modernity must mean in the twenty-first century, and there is no better mind to pick than Mafeje's. First, the peasantry is the only force which has remained untested as an agent of development in Africa (and elsewhere, with few exceptions in the South), despite the failure of all other agents. As Mafeje (2003: 28) argued: '[b]y investing in the small producers, African governments could hope to reap multiple benefits, namely, elimination of absolute poverty and acceleration of agricultural expansion by pushing into the expanded petty mode of production as many small producers as possible, and reduction/elimination of rural unemployment.'

Contrary to purist interpretations of social differentiation, broad and sustained support for small producers does not necessarily imply the unleashing of a new round of social differentiation and land alienation. Mafeje said:

> [I]f by accumulation from below is meant class differentiation, then not all forms of social exchange lead to class formation: [t]he least troublesome mode of accumulation from below that has occurred in Africa is the one that did not involve alienation of land but took advantage of customary tenure that allows perpetual use and inheritance of allotted plots of land. (Mafeje 2003: 7, 20)

Moreover, this type of accumulation from below may certainly be bolstered by collective farming and cooperatives which 'have not been given a fair chance' (Mafeje 2003: 7). Second, re-peasantisation must be accompanied by industrialisation.

This must be of the type that serves the technical upgrading of agriculture and the attainment of food sovereignty, but it does not need to originate in agriculture. Mafeje (2003: 30) defended these two conditions clearly when he stated: 'Africa will have to industrialise as a matter of urgency, not only to survive economically but also in order to meet the technical and scientific requirements for the development of agriculture.' Mafeje added:

> [t]he immediate implication is that, contrary to the usual Eurocentric assumptions, primary accumulation for industrialisation could not possibly come from the depressed African agricultural economies. The immediate task for African planners and policymakers is to make sure that agriculture can in the foreseeable future feed the rapidly growing African population. African government sought to derive great satisfaction from this for both social and financial reasons and think of other ways of financing industrialisation, which is fast becoming the sine qua non for the future of the continent. (Mafeje 2003: 30)

Finally, the new dimensions of gender equity and ecological sustainability will prove fundamental to any resolution of the agrarian and national questions. Mafeje saw the deep connections between gender and national development, mediated especially through the land question. 'The immediate solution', he argued, 'would be to grant the same usufructuary rights to men and women, whether married or not', considering that 'full usufructuary rights would enable women to expend their labour power on their own behalf and would grant them the right of disposal over the product', and given that it would be 'most unlikely that married women would neglect the subsistence needs of their households' (Mafeje 2003: 21). He concluded that 'in African agriculture it is obvious that there is a social and an economic imperative to liberate women from male domination. This is not only their democratic right but also a liberating force in the agrarian sector in general' (ibid.: 23; see also Mbilinyi 1997; Moyo 1995b; Tsikata 2003, 2009; Tsikata and Golah 2010). When combined with appropriate technology and protective measures for the soil and environment, Mafeje (2003: 30) saw a real (indeed, the only) possibility to reverse the decline in agriculture and sustain an autonomous development project.

Reclaiming the Question

Thus, unlike what is claimed by some, that 'we have been liberated from the constraints of agriculture, land and nature', the authors of this chapter believe that the agrarian question continues to evolve and is among the most fundamental questions of the twenty-first century. Indeed, this is the century in which nature, the current system of agriculture, and historical capitalism will reach their reproductive limits. The agrarian question today is a question of wresting global agriculture, land and other natural resources from the predatory logic of monopoly-finance capital and of submitting them to the logic of autonomy, equality and democracy. Under conditions of a new scramble, it still remains a question of national sovereignty.

However, what is pertinent is to understand what type of political organisation can attend to the expelled population, the semi-proletariat in town and country? And how to join the expelled with the exploited, those informal employment?

From the 1990s onwards, rural movements proliferated in Latin America (Mexico, Brazil, Bolivia, Ecuador, Colombia), Africa (most notably Zimbabwe) and Asia (Nepal, India, Philippines) have become the organising centres of the semi-proletariat and are pursuing the agenda of recuperation of land, by means of mass occupations, among many other tactics. Given that the destruction inflicted by big capital occurs most immediately at the expense of marginalised communities, the movements have often come into direct confrontation with the enduring hegemonic structures of the landed power, such as race and caste. Moreover, women, for whom land as a reproductive space is most crucial, have obtained a more pronounced role.

This explains why rural movements have converged with indigenous rights, feminist and environmental movements. Rural movements have also made few organisational inroads into urban areas. However, the journey is going to be long and arduous. The organisational unity between the rural and the urban and between the expelled and the exploited, has not materialised, or been sustained to the expectations in most cases. On the one hand, the tendency to occupational corporatism (or workerism) among conventional trade unionism continues, which lays emphasis on wages and working conditions in discrete occupational sectors; and on the other, there is an organisational segmentation among the landless, tending to single-issue platforms, such as land access and basic services.

New Alliances and Strategies

Nonetheless, there have been silver linings. A different response to the political question has been given in a handful of cases, where internal contradictions have escalated towards the radicalisation of politics, involving often the same movements. In Venezuela, Bolivia, Ecuador, Zimbabwe and Nepal, rural–urban unity has been realised by broad-based mobilisation, in the course of successive crises and political polarisation, which have fused the land and related questions with the national question as a whole. In these cases, the correlation of forces has surpassed conventional channels of political expression, to recast 'the people' and 'the nation' as belonging to the oppressed, and to clinch electoral victories. The question thus becomes—what alliances are likely to enable the resolution of the agrarian question in alternative ways? There is a need for a systematic regionalist perspective on the agrarian question (Moyo 1997, 2008b). In the interest of building broad consensus on the agrarian question, focused on a state-supported peasant path, there is an urgent need to prioritise alliances that are rural–urban and South–South, as they have the potential to confront the Eurocentric monopoly and propose an alternative global society in response to the structural imperatives of our times. Such an alternative society will most certainly be forced to take seriously 're-peasantisation' (or re-agrarianisation) as a modern project, along with new collective forms of production, labour absorption and sustainable industrialisation. Moreover, such an alternative society must be able to go beyond the nation state and propose forms of expressly regional agro-industrial integration; against the market- and rule-based integration that neo-liberalism has imposed. We take heart in the renewed interest in Mafeje's work and hope that his persistent critique of Eurocentrism, his dedication to innovative political economy and his revolutionary spirit will inspire a new generation of researchers and activists, as it has inspired us.

Notes

1. This section draws on our earlier work, Moyo, Jha and Yeros (2013).

2. We have argued elsewhere that in its most conservative rendering, backwardness was posited as a quality innate to non-European societies, and industrialisation as an end in itself, best left to trained economists and development planners. Be it in terms of 'stages of growth' of W. W. Rostow or the 'dual economies' by Arthur Lewis. The Marxian discourse of Soviet vintage running parallel to the view mentioned earlier propounded a 'stage' theory, which recognised land reform as an obstacle, but it rather chose not, for the most part, to support radical alternatives, or a peasant path, until the Chinese divergence. The 'Western Marxism' (to use Perry Anderson's term) in the meantime, drifted away from the political economy towards the political philosophy, as disenchantment and social democracy set in. There emerged a new generation of theorists, who were more organic to the peasant struggles of the Third World, but backwardness remained a dynamic process intrinsic to imperialism, and industrialisation as an aspect of a larger strategic objective national liberation even for them. Thus, the North–South dialogue remained problematic (Anderson 1976).

3. One must not forget that this speaking-of-a-new-level-of-sophistication had been raised by Lenin with special programmatic purpose, that is, to defend the American path against the Prussian, while also explicitly leaving open the possibility of a wider spectrum of transitions.

4. One of the gravest consequences of connecting the agrarian question to backwardness has been the displacement of the debate over politics and policy from North to South, absolving the North of any transformative obligation, other than providing 'aid' to the South, or removing subsidies to help the poor 'compete'. Such a line of thinking permeates both left and right, with few exceptions, arguably the Monthly Review school. Today, there is great effort in affirming one tendency—the economistic. One might again protest, pointing to the recent attempt by Henry Bernstein (2010a) to marry 'political economy' with 'political ecology' as an intellectual project. But without genuine recognition of the silences and evasions of the past, this project is likely to founder, as indeed it appears to have done in a book published simultaneously on 'the class dynamics of agrarian change' (Bernstein 2010b; Yeros 2012).

5. See Amanor and Moyo (2008); Jha (2002); Jha et al. (2007); Jha, Mahajan and Acharya (2010); Moyo (1997, 2000, 2008b,); Moyo et al. (1998); Moyo and Romadhane (2002); Moyo and Yeros (2005, 2008, 2011); Rosa (2011); Shivji (2009); Tsikata (2009); and Tsikata and Golah (2010). It is notable also that this momentum has led to the founding of a South–South journal, *Agrarian South: Journal of Political Economy*, of which Mafeje would certainly have been proud.

6. See Amin (2012); Ghosh (2012); Kamata (2012); Moyo, Yeros and Jha (2012); Patnaik (2012); and Patnaik and Moyo (2011).

7. The usual proviso applies to Monthly Review, but the challenge remains for the specialised journals, *The Journal of Peasant Studies* and *Journal of Agrarian Change*.

REFERENCES

Amanor, Kojo Sebastian and Sam Moyo (eds). 2008. *Land and Sustainable Development in Africa*. London and New York: Zed Books.

Amin, Samir. 1972. 'Underdevelopment and Dependence in Black Africa: Origins and Contemporary Forms'. *Journal of Modern African Studies* 10(4): 503–24.

____. 1981. *The Future of Maoism*, trans. N. Finkelstein. New York: Monthly Review Press.

____. 2012. 'Contemporary Imperialism and the Agrarian Question'. *Agrarian South: Journal of Political Economy* 1(1): 11–26.

Anderson, Perry. 1976. *Considerations on Western Marxism*. London: New Left Books.

Bernstein, Henry. 2004. '"Changing before Our Very Eyes": Agrarian Questions and the Politics of Land in Capitalism Today'. *Journal of Agrarian Change* 4(1–2): 190–225.

____. 2010a. 'Introduction: Some Questions Concerning the Productive Forces'. *Journal of Agrarian Change* 10(3): 300–14.

____. 2010b. *Class Dynamics of Agrarian Change*. Halifax and Sterling: Fernwood Publishing and Kumarian Press.

Bryceson, Deborah, Cristóbal Kay and Jos Mooij (eds). 2000. *Disappearing Peasantries?: Rural Labour in Africa, Asia and Latin America*. London: ITDG Publishing.

Byres, Terry. 1991. 'Agrarian Question'. In *A Dictionary of Marxist Thought*, eds Tom Bottomore, Laurence Harris, V. G. Kiernan and Ralph Miliband, second edition. Oxford: Basil Blackwell.

Cardoso, Fernando Henrique and Enzo Faletto. 1979. *Dependency and Development in Latin America*, trans. Marjory Mattingly Urquidi. Berkeley: University of California Press.

Graziano da Silva, José. 1999. *O Novo Rural Brasileiro*. Campinas: Unicamp.

Graziano da Silva, José and Lucas Tavares. 2008. 'Segurança Alimentar e a Alta dos Preços dos Alimentos: Oportunidades e Desafios'. *Segurança Alimentar e Nutricional* 15(1): 62–75.

Ghosh, Jayati. 2012. 'Accumulation Strategies and Human Development in India'. *Agrarian South: Journal of Political Economy* 1(1): 43–64.

Jha, Praveen (ed.). 2002. *Land Reforms in India: Issues of Equity in Rural Madhya Pradesh*. New Delhi: Sage Publications.

Jha, Praveen, Atul K. Singh, Namita S. Nayak and Subah Dayal. 2007. *Land Reform Experiences: Lessons from across the Globe*. New Delhi: Ekta Parishad.

Jha, Praveen, Shalini Mahajan and Nilachala Acharya. 2010. *Land Question at the Current Juncture and Some Suggestions for Reform*. New Delhi: Ekta Parishad.

Kamata, Ng'wanza. 2012. 'The Economic Diplomacy of Tanzania: Accumulation by Dispossession in a Peripheral State'. *Agrarian South: Journal of Political Economy* 1(3): 291–313.

Lenin, V. I. 1964. *Collected Works*, Vol. 22, December 1915–July 1916.

Mafeje, Archie. 1991. *The Theory and Ethnography of African Social Formations: The Case of the Inter-lacustrine Kingdoms*. Dakar: CODESRIA.

____. 1997. *The National Question in Southern African Settler Societies*. Harare: SAPES Books.

____. 2003. 'The Agrarian Question, Access to Land and Peasant Responses in Sub-Saharan Africa'. Civil Society and Social Movements Programme paper no. 6, UNRISD. Available at http://www.unrisd.org/unrisd/website/document.nsf/ab82a6805797760f80256b4f005da1ab/a2b-577c61b 19f92ec1 256d56002b5291/$FILE/mafeje2.pdf (accessed 15 October 2014).

Mbilinyi, Margaret. 1997. 'Beyond Oppression and Crisis: A Gendered Analysis of Agrarian Structure and Change in Tanzania', 317–64. In *Engendering African Social Sciences*, eds A. Imam, A. Mama and F. Sow. Dakar: CODESRIA.

Moyo, Sam. 1995a. *The Land Question in Zimbabwe*. Harare: SAPES Books.

——. 1995b. 'A Gendered Perspective on the Land Question'. *Safere* 1(1): 13–31.

——. 1997. 'Environmental Security in Southern Africa'. Research proposal, Southern African Institute for Policy Studies.

——. 2000. *Land Reform under Structural Adjustment in Zimbabwe: Land Use Change in the Mashonaland Provinces*. Uppsala: Nordiska Afrikainstitutet.

——. 2001. 'The Land Occupation Movement and Democratisation in Zimbabwe: Contradictions of Neoliberalism'. *Millennium: Journal of International Studies* 30(2): 311–30.

——. 2008a. *African Land Questions, Agrarian Transitions and the State: Contradictions of Neoliberal Land Reforms*. Dakar: CODESRIA.

——. 2008b. *The State of Food Security in Southern Africa*. Johannesburg: Southern Africa Trust.

Moyo, Sam and Ben Romadhane (eds). 2002. *Peasant Organisations and Change in Rural Africa*. Dakar: CODESRIA.

Moyo, Sam and Paris Yeros (eds). 2005. *Reclaiming the Land: The Resurgence of Rural Movements in Africa, Asia and Latin America*. London, New York and Cape Town: Zed Books and David Philip.

——. 2007. 'The Radicalised State: Zimbabwe's Interrupted Revolution'. *Review of African Political Economy* 111: 103–21.

—— (eds). 2008. *Recuperandola Tierra: El Resurgimento de Movimientos Ruralesen África, Asia y América Latina*. Buenos Aires: CLACSO.

—— (eds). 2011. *Reclaiming the Nation: The Return of the National Question in Africa, Asia and Latin America*. London: Pluto Press.

——. 2012. 'The Zimbabwe Model: Radicalisation, Reform and Resistance'. In *Land and Agrarian Reform in Zimbabwe: Beyond White-settler Capitalism*, eds Sam Moyo and Walter Chambati, 331–57. Dakar: CODESRIA.

Moyo, Sam, Paris Yeros and Praveen Jha. 2012. 'Imperialism and Primitive Accumulation: Notes on the New Scramble for Africa'. *Agrarian South: Journal of Political Economy* 1(2): 181–203.

Moyo, Sam, Praveen Jha and Paris Yeros. 2013. 'The Classical Agrarian Question: Myth, Reality and Relevance Today'. *Agrarian South: Journal of Political Economy* 2(1): 93–119.

Moyo, Sam, Prosper Matondi and Nelson Marongwe. 1998. 'Land Use Change and Communal Land Tenure under Stress'. In *Economic Policy Reforms and Meso-scale Rural Market Changes in Zimbabwe: The Case of Shamva District*, ed. Louis Masuko. Harare: Institute of Development Studies.

Moyo, Sam and Walter Chambati. 2012. *Land and Agrarian Reform in Zimbabwe: Beyond White-settler Capitalism*. Dakar: CODESRIA.

Patnaik, Prabhat. 2012. 'The Peasant Question and Contemporary Capitalism: Some Reflections with Reference to India'. *Agrarian South: Journal of Political Economy* 1(1): 27–42.

Patnaik, Utsa. 2006. 'The Free Lunch: Transfers from the Tropical Colonies and Their Role in Capital Formation in Britain during the Industrial Revolution'. In *Globalisation under Hegemony*, ed. Jomo K. S. New Delhi: Oxford University Press.

Patnaik, Utsa. 2011. 'The "Agricultural Revolution" in England: Its Cost for the English Working Class and the Colonies'. In *Capitalism, Colonialism and Globalisation*, ed. Shireen Moosvi. New Delhi: Aligarh Historian's Society and Tulika Books.

Patnaik, Utsa and Sam Moyo, with Issa G. Shivji. 2011. *The Agrarian Question in the Neoliberal Era: Primitive Accumulation and the Peasantry*. Nairobi and Oxford: Pambazuka Press and Mwalimu Nyerere Chair in Pan-African Studies, UDSM.

Rosa, Marcelo. 2011. *Engenho dos Movimentos Sociais: Reforma Agrária e Significação Social na Zona Canavieira de Pernambuco*. Rio de Janeiro: Editora Garamond.

Shivji, Issa G. 2009. *Accumulation in an African Periphery: A Theoretical Framework*. Dares Salaam: Mkuki na Nyota Publishers.

Tsikata, Dzodzi. 2003. 'Securing Women's Interests within Land Tenure Reforms: Recent Debates in Tanzania'. *Journal of Agrarian Change* 3(1–2): 149–83.

____. 2009. 'Gender, Land and Labour Relations and Livelihoods in Sub-Saharan Africa in the Era of Economic Liberalisation: Towards a Research Agenda'. *Feminist Africa* 12: 11–30.

Tsikata, Dzodzi and Pamela Golah (eds). 2010. *Land Tenure, Gender and Globalisation: Research and Analysis from Africa, Asia and Latin America*. Ottawa, Cairo, Dakar, Montevideo, Nairobi, New Delhi and Singapore: Zubaan and International Development Research Centre.

Williams, Eric. 1994. *Capitalism and Slavery, 1944*. Chapel Hill: University of North Carolina Press.

Yeros, Paris. 2012. 'Review of Henry Bernstein's Class Dynamics of Agrarian Change'. *Agrarian South: Journal of Political Economy* 1(3): 341–46.

3

GANDHI AND AGRARIAN CLASSES*

ABHA PANDYA

...

This chapter traces the development of M. K. Gandhi's views on the relationship between zamindars and *kisans* in colonial India, and discusses how his ideology on the peasant question influenced his actions as the leader of the national movement.

...

TRUSTEESHIP

Trusteeship was regarded by Gandhi as a compromise between private and state enterprise. Private enterprise, Gandhi believed, led to great and unjustified disparities of wealth. Therefore, a non-violent government and society was 'clearly an impossibility so long as the wide gulf between the hungry millions and the rich persists' (Gandhi 1944: 18). Moreover, the rich accumulate their wealth by exploiting the masses (*Young India*, 26 November 1931).

The basic idea underlying trusteeship is quite simple. The rich man will be left in possession of his wealth, of which he will use what he reasonably requires for his personal needs and will act as a trustee for the remaining to be used for society (*Harijan*, 25 August 1940). Trusteeship would eliminate all possibilities of class conflict and lead to the establishment of cooperation and harmonious relations between the conflicting classes.

Gandhi did not believe that landlords and capitalists were exploiters by any inherent necessity, or that there existed a basic and irreconcilable antagonism between the interests of the former and those of the masses. 'What is needed is not the extinction of landlords and capitalists, but a transformation of the existing relationship between them and the masses into something healthier and pure', he believed (Bose 1957: 93).

* Originally published in *Economic and Political Weekly* 13(26), 1 July 1978: 1077–79.

Fundamental to the theory of trusteeship was the principle of non-appropriation of the owners' property. Gandhi seems to make a distinction between legal and moral ownership. Legally wealth belongs to the owners, morally to the whole society—so the peasants are also owners of wealth possessed by the zamindars. Addressing the landlords, he once observed, 'I have always told mill owners that they are not the exclusive owners of mills and workers are equal sharers in ownership. In the same way, I could tell you that ownership of your land belongs as much to the ryots as to you' (Bose 1957: 91). Yet, Gandhi declared quite emphatically that in the new set-up, ownership would rest with the trustee himself (*Harijan*, 16 February 1947).

Different from Passive Resistance

This point is central to the entire idea of trusteeship, because the means proposed by Gandhi suggested that there must be voluntary conversion of the exploiting classes to the cause of socioeconomic justice. Here, his concept of trusteeship must be distinguished from that of passive resistance, though he does not always isolate one from the other. His emphasis on moral conversion includes, in addition to the moral transformation of the exploiter, the awakening of workers and peasants into a realisation of their own moral strength. Recommending non-cooperation and civil disobedience as the 'right and infallible means' of resolving social conflict, Gandhi believed that exploitation could take place only with the cooperation of the exploited classes and that non-cooperation on their part would at once deprive the exploiter of his power to exploit, leading to the establishment of equality between them (Bose 1957: 97–98). Gandhi's object was thus to eliminate not class divisions but class conflict. 'Class divisions there will be but they will be horizontal not vertical' (ibid.: 95).

In case the zamindars refuse to be converted to the new way of life, the peasants would compel his adherence through non-violent non-cooperation. If this failed, the peasants would quit the land if asked to do so, but make it clear to the landlord that all land really belonged to the tiller. Since it would be impossible to till the land, the zamindar would submit. Should he attempt to replace the non-cooperating tenants by others, agitation short of violence would then continue till he replaced the tenants (*Harijan*, 31 March 1946).

What was the actual degree of equality which Gandhi considered feasible? 'My ideal is equal distribution but as far as I can see it is not to be realised. I therefore work for equitable distribution' (*Young India*, 17 March 1927).

In answer to the question whether class war can be avoided, Gandhi said in 1931:

> we may not dispossess the zamindars and talukadars of their thousands of bighas. And among whom shall we distribute them? We need not dispossess them. They only need a change of heart. When that is done and when they learn to melt at their peasants' woes, they will hold their lands in trust for them, will give them a major part of the produce, keeping only sufficient for themselves. (*Young India*, 26 March 1931)

Gandhi in his anxiety to build harmonious relations between conflicting elements in Indian society, applied the concept of trusteeship only to their conflicts and not to those related to the alien government. During the struggle of the Champaran peasants (1916) against British indigo planters as also the Bardoli struggle (1928) against the Bombay government, the concept of trusteeship was not applied. In Champaran, the European planters asked why they alone among the landlords of Bihar became the target for a long-term, large-scale and eventually successful popular agitation (Henningham 1976: 71–72).

In another instance when the Assam Tea Garden workers went on strike against the reduction of their wages by the English planters, Gandhi justified the strike and said that 'the coolies have a substantial grievance ... and the government has failed to cope with it'. Here again any reference to trusteeship is missing (*Young India*, 8 June 1921).

Attitude to Kisan Struggles

The 1920s and 1930s saw an increasing wave of kisan struggles against the oppression of indigenous zamindars all over India, and Gandhi reacted adversely to these manifestations of kisan discontent. For instance, in 1921, Gandhi strongly condemned the social boycott and non-rent campaigns launched by rack-rented peasants in the United Provinces and called the movement an 'instrument of violence'. In Guntur, a no-tax campaign was started without the permission of the Congress. Gandhi took strong exception to it and directed that all taxes must be paid forthwith (Sitaramayya 1935: 23).

The resolutions adopted by the Congress Working Committee (CWC), presided over by Gandhi at Bardoli, in February 1922 were bitterly critical not only of the occurrence of violence in the movement, but also of any independent peasant movement inevitably developing into a kind of non-rent movement. The resolutions stated:

> *Clause 6*: CWC advises Congress workers to inform the ryots that withholding of rent payment to the zamindars is contrary to Congress resolutions.
>
> *Clause 7*: CWC assures zamindars that the Congress movement is in no way intended to attach their legal rights and that even where the ryots have grievances, the Congress desired that the redress be sought by mutual consultation and arbitration. (Dutt 1947: 270)

Gandhi himself stated that the kisan movement had received an impetus from non-cooperation but was anterior to and independent of it. He maintained that while there should be a department of the Congress to look after specific problems of the peasants, they should not be organised into an all-India organisation with a political stance. Gandhi said:

> While we will not hesitate to advise the kisans when the moment comes to suspend payment of taxes to the government, it is not contemplated at any stage of noncooperation that we would seek to deprive zamindars of their rent. The kisan movement should be confined to the improvement of the state of kisans and the betterment of relations between them and the zamindars. (*Young India*, 18 May 1921)

He advised the kisans to scrupulously abide by the terms of their agreement with the zamindars. Where custom or even a written contract was unacceptable, they should not try to uproot it by violence and an attempt should be made to arrive at a settlement (*Young India*, 1 May 1921).

In the second non-cooperation movement (1929–33), a call was given by the All-India Congress Committee (AICC) in May 1930 for non-payment of specific taxes in certain provinces to the British government. And again in the Karachi session of March 1931, the Congress called for a substantial reduction in agricultural rent paid by the peasants to the colonial government.

However, the Congress assured the zamindars that no campaign would be approved against their interests. Already after the Karachi Congress session, Gandhi had told the zamindars, 'I shall be no party to dispossessing the propertied classes ... I am working for co-operation and co-ordination of labour, capital, landlord and tenant' (Bose 1957: 91). A resolution of the Congress said:

> in as much as some misapprehensions have been created in the minds of the zamindars of UP in particular, and others in general that in discussing proposals for non-payment of rent or taxes the Congress was contemplating a class war ... [the Congress] assures the zamindars that the no-rent proposals were in no way directed at them. (Congress Working Committee 1937)

Though the Congress wanted the peasants to participate in the national movement, the emphasis throughout was on how to strengthen itself through such participation. If the peasants, through an independent movement of their own, threatened to be a divisive force in it, the Congress would have preferred doing without them (Sitaramayya 1935: 23). In fact, in December 1937, the Congress took the decision forbidding Congressmen from participating in Kisan Sabha activities. The Congress also criticised the kisan movement for being prone to violence. Gandhi believed that such a movement 'would be something like fascism'.

PROGRESSIVE RADICALISATION

By the mid-1930s, however, we notice a shift in Gandhi's stand and a progressive radicalisation of his thoughts on the peasant question. The peasant struggles, especially in Uttar Pradesh, were becoming militant in reaction to the violent resistance of the zamindars. In a message to zamindars, Gandhi warned them of the danger facing them.

> I would like the zamindars to recognise the correctness of the peasants' position and make a corresponding change in their own outlook. Let the zamindars cease to be mere rent-collectors ... thus they should become trustees of their tenants ... limit their privy purses ... forgo questionable perquisites they take from the tenants in the shape of gifts ... give them fixity of tenure ... make them feel they are their true friends ... In short, they must justify their position. (*Young India*, 28 May 1931)

By 1936, he began to realise that the concept of trusteeship was ineffective in practice. Instead of the earlier indispensibility of the zamindars, he said, 'I do not mean to destroy the zamindar but neither do I feel that zamindars are indispensible' (*Harijan*, 5 December 1936). He went on later to say that if the zamindars do not change, 'they will die a natural death' (*Harijan*, 23 April 1938).

Two years later, he had moved further from his concept of a voluntary change of heart. Replying to a socialist's question, Gandhi declared: 'the difference between your view and mine is whether the zamindar system is to be mended or ended. I say it should be mended, if it cannot be mended it should end itself' (ibid.). By 1947, Gandhi had made a radical departure from his earlier opposition to the nationalisation of the means of production. 'In the non-violent order of the future, land would belong to the state, for has it not been said "Sabhi Bhoomi Gopalki". Under such dispensation there would be no waste of talents and labour' (*Harijan*, 9 March 1947).

Gandhi had also moved from his earlier assertion that the conditions of the peasants can be improved without legislative intervention by the government. He said that the present owners of wealth would have to make their choice between class war and voluntarily converting themselves into trustees. They would be allowed to retain their possessions and use their talents to increase the wealth for the sake of society, without exploitation. The state would regulate their rate of commission and their children would inherit property only if they proved their fitness for it (*Harijan*, 9 March 1947). Voluntary conversion had thus receded further into the background.

Gandhi also did not rule out violence altogether. On being asked by Louis Fischer in 1942 what the position of peasants in a free India would be, Gandhi said that the peasant would 'seize land', that no compensation would be paid to landlords, for compensation would be 'financially impossible'. 'There might be violence in the process but the landlords might co-operate by fleeing' (Fischer 1942: 55, 91).

Here, although we notice a progressive radicalisation in Gandhi's thought, he never made it clear as to who would control the state of the future. He developed the concept of *panchayats* controlled by the kisans but did not visualise that the panchayats themselves would be dominated by vested interests.

State Intervention

Thus, his concept of trusteeship developed and changed with time. In its final form, it was substantially different from the original utopian concept. The optimistic hope that the vested interests would voluntarily transform themselves into trustees and that state intervention was similar to violence were no longer held tenable. Now he believed that if change did not come, the state would intervene and end the system of exploitation.

...

References

Bose, N. K. 1957. *Selections from Gandhi*. Ahmedabad: Navjivan Press.

Congress Working Committee. 1937. 'Congress Resolutions'. New Delhi.

Dutt, R. P. 1947. *India Today* (revised edition). New Delhi: New Age Printing Press.
Fischer, Louis. 1942. *A Week with Gandhi*. New York: Dull, Sloan and Pearce.
Gandhi, M. K. 1944. *Constructive Programme*. Ahmedabad: Navjivan Press.
Henningham, Stephen. 1976. 'The Social Setting of the Champaran Satyagraha'. *The Indian Economic and Social History Review* 13(1), March: 71–72.
Sitaramayya, B. P. 1935. *History of the Indian National Congress* (Volume 1). Allahabad: The Working Committee of the Congress.

Section II

Holding Size and Land Reforms

4

Trends in Land Relations

*A Note**

Pranab Bardhan

It is widely accepted that one result of our copious land legislation has been to reduce the importance of the parasitic intermediaries in the rural economic system and to hit at the pure rentier class, though at the expense of fairly large payments of compensation. According to the 1981 Census data, non-Ryotwari tenures constituted hardly 2.75 per cent of the total households owning or holding land from the state. This, however, does not mean that the rentier class has nearly vanished from our rural scene. It is worth noting from NSS data for the 8th and 17th Rounds that whereas in 1953–54 only 2.15 per cent of rural households owned but did not operate land, in 1960–61 the corresponding figure was 17.42 per cent. In other words, there seems to have been a rise in the percentage of rural households that act as pure rentiers so far as land interests are concerned. One explanation of this phenomenon may be that with the subdivision of land through inheritance, some of the land may become too small for cultivation and with the growth of non-agricultural employment opportunities in the rural sector, an increasing number of small landholders may be leasing out all of their land. It is also possible that the large estate of a single household has been notionally transferred to a number of households (say, of relatives) and then leased out by the latter back to the single household, giving rise to the phenomenon observed.

With the abolition of intermediary tenures, while some of the landlords who had loose connections with their land have been removed from the rural property structure, some of the erstwhile absentee landlords came back to the village, continued undisturbed possession of *khas* or *khud-bakasht* land (land kept for self-cultivation), and also enjoyed fairly liberal resumption rights on the ostensible ground of self-cultivation (in some states like Assam, Haryana, Punjab, Tamil Nadu and West Bengal, there is even a continuous right of resumption of land). The government's explicit policy of low taxation of agriculture, and the relatively liberal

* Originally published in *Economic and Political Weekly* 5(3–5), 17 January 1970: 261–66.

provision of credit and new inputs, have certainly encouraged this return of the landlords to the village. Part of the land they have leased out under various forms of open and disguised tenancy, taking extreme care that the tenants do not acquire any kind of permanent rights on the land (according to the 1961 Census data, tenants-at-will, tenants subject to the landlord's right of resumption and tenants enjoying only temporary protection constitute 82 per cent of all tenants in India); part of the land they now cultivate themselves with family and hired labour.

In the ex-Zamindari areas, where the absentee landlords have not returned and the tenants have come into direct relationship with the state, and in Ryotwari areas, in continuation of a process that started long before Independence, there has been the emergence of the well-to-do sections among the peasant castes which occupy the middle rung in the social structure in much of rural India: Marathas and Tellis, Bhumihars and Rajputs, Jats and Ahirs, Mahishyas and Sadgops, Niyars and Tilyans, Lingayats and Vokkaligas, Kammas and Reddis, Kalians and Nadars, and so on. Some of these peasant groups have acquired proprietary rights in their land, some are part-owners and part-tenants. But all of them take agriculture much more seriously than when the land was in the hands of intermediaries or as compared to those who still lease out their land. In general, one might say that in the 1950s and 1960s, a major change has been that agricultural land has passed more and more into the hands of those who take a more active interest (supervisory or cultivating) in agriculture.

This, however, does not necessarily mean that there has been a redistribution of land from the rich to the poor. Table 4.1 gives the NSS figures for the percentage distribution of land by four broad size-classes of ownership holding in 1953–54 and 1960–61. The concentration index of land ownership (including the landless households and based on a finer classification of holding sizes than given in Table 4.1) has only slightly gone down from 0.7512 to 0.7174. This insignificant decline in inequality of land ownership is thrown into lurid relief when one considers that in a country with a general absence of the law of primogeniture and continuous subdivision there should be a natural tendency towards smaller concentration. The much-publicised crop of land-ceiling legislation throughout the country, because of their defective formulation and delayed implementation, obviously had little impact on the landownership pattern.

TABLE 4.1: Percentage Distribution of Land Owned by Size-classes, 1953–54 and 1960–61

Ownership Holding Size (Acres)	*Percentage of Total Area Owned*	
	1953–54	*1960–61*
0 to below 5	16.32	19.99
5 to below 15	31.18	34.51
15 to below 30	22.05	22.59
30 and above	30.45	22.91

Source: NSS, 8th and 17th Rounds.

It is, however, worth mentioning here that according to NSS data, the proportion of landless households in the total number of rural households has appreciably gone down from 23.09 per cent in 1953–54 to 11.68 per cent in 1960–61. This might mean that the government's programme of settlement of landless people on cultivable wastelands and private forests (during the three Plan periods, 10.7 million acres of such land is reported to have been distributed by the state governments) has not been entirely fruitless. It might also be that in cases where outright eviction has been difficult, the landlords have come to private agreements with tenants that in exchange of gifts of small bits of land, the latter would voluntarily surrender all rights in any remaining land in their occupancy. In any case, while the proportion of landless households has been nearly halved, the proportion of households below 0.5 acres is not much different: it was 41.10 in 1953–54 and 37.90 in 1960–61. This only means that any settlement of landless people has been on extremely tiny plots.

On the basis of NSS and Agro-economic Research Centres' village survey data, an important observation was recently made by Dharm Narain and P. C. Joshi (1969) that there has been a significant decline in the magnitude of agricultural tenancy (as measured by, say, the proportion of operated areas leased in). In view of its importance, let us discuss this question in detail, first with respect to the genuineness of the phenomenon indicated by their observation, and second its implication for changes in land relations.

First, we might mention that the decline in tenancy in selected villages cited by Narain and Joshi (1969) from the Agro-economic Research Centre reports does not at all suggest anything conclusive. We may easily cite the cases of a fairly large number of other villages surveyed by the Agro-economic Research Centres where tenancy is reported to have *increased* over time. For example, according to the Delhi University Agro Centre, the percentage of cultivated area leased in has gone up between the original survey and resurvey points in the village of Patti Beharipur (Uttar Pradesh) from 25.2 per cent to 28 per cent, in Ghiana (Uttar Pradesh) from 12 per cent to 18.4 per cent, in Gati (Uttar Pradesh) from 9.7 per cent to 13.8 per cent, in Palanpur (Uttar Pradesh) from 9.9 per cent to 12 per cent, in Sohalpur Gara (Uttar Pradesh) from 1.9 per cent to 6.1 per cent, in Rataul Rohi (Punjab) from 44.8 per cent to 55.3 per cent, in Bahatwas (Punjab) from 30.1 per cent to 32.5 per cent, and so on. All this only means that the village survey reports are not of much help in deciding the trend in the extent of tenancy in the country as a whole.

More substantive is the NSS evidence of percentage of operated area leased in dropping from 20.34 in 1953–54 to 10.70 in 1960–61. Narain and Joshi (1969) have carefully gone into the question of any possible under-reporting bias 'based on the ground that the tenant may be afraid of speaking the truth (about his leased-in area) lest it should become known to the landlord and he may not get the land on lease again'. Of course, if this under-reporting bias has remained the same between 1933–54 and 1960–61, we may regard the declining trend in tenancy as fairly genuine. But since some of the rent-regulating and protective tenancy legislation in different parts of the country came after 1953–54, an increase in the under-reporting bias with landlords being more careful in driving tenancy underground is quite likely.

An important argument made by them in favour of the genuineness of decline in tenancy figures is as follows:

> One would expect the tenant cultivator who is reported, rather who reports himself … as an agricultural labourer to be a small operator. For obvious social reasons, a big tenant-cultivator cannot be disguised as an agricultural labourer. Therefore, the fact of tenancy having gone underground in a sizeable way would be expected to show itself in a relatively larger decline of the leased-in area of the smaller size-groups of operational holdings ... The fact, however, that the incidence of relative decline is much greater in the larger size-groups of operational holdings ... militates against this hypothesis. (Narain and Joshi 1969: A140)

The relevant evidence, as we have calculated from NSS data, is presented in Table 4.2. It shows that tenancy has declined for all size-groups of operational holdings but the smaller the size-group, the smaller is the relative decline. But this may not be conclusive proof against the hypothesis of under-reporting of tenancy by the small farm. It is an observed fact that in general, the smaller the size-group of farms the larger is the percentage of operated area leased in, and also, that with continuous subdivision of holdings through inheritance, farms over time enter smaller and smaller size-groups; other things remaining the same, these two factors may lead to a secular rise in the percentage of leased-in area for a broad class of small farms compared to a class of large farms. So a smaller relative decline in tenancy for small farms need not necessarily mean that tenancy is not being under-reported by them. Then again, it is also possible that a number of leased-in units have been put together on paper and the tenants made to look like wage-labourers, indicating a large decline in tenancy for this hypothetical large farm, whereas in reality nothing of this sort has happened. The big tenant-cultivator may not be disguised as agricultural labourer, but the small ones notionally put together may be. On the whole, we might say that there may have been some decline in tenancy in Indian agriculture, as Narain and Joshi (1969) observe, but their arguments are not sufficient to dispel the suspicion that a substantial amount of tenancy may have been driven underground. What lends partial support to this suspicion is that the number of permanent farm servants per acre of operated area, according to NSS data, has gone up by about 65 per cent between 1953–54 and 1960–61. This may indicate that an increasing number of actual tenants (particularly sharecroppers) have been reported as permanent farm servants.

TABLE 4.2: Tenancy by Size-groups of Farmers, 1953–54 and 1960–61

Size of Operational Holdings	*Percentage of Operated Area Leased in*	
	1953–54	*1960–61*
Up to 5 acres	25.76	15.32
5–15 acres	20.10	9.99
15 acres and above	18.90	6.44

Source: NSS, 8th and 17th Rounds.

While the number of permanent farm servants (or attached labour) per acre has gone up significantly, it is interesting to note that the importance of agricultural labourers as a whole (casual and attached taken together) has *declined.* According to the Second Agricultural Labour Enquiry and NSS 19th Round data, the percentage of agricultural labour households in the total number of rural households went down from 24.5 in 1956–57 to 21.8 in 1964–65. An agricultural labour household has been delined as one which derives the major share of its income from wage-paid manual labour in agriculture, and the same definition was used for both the years. In fact, what is more striking is that whereas between these two years the total number of rural households have, not unexpectedly, gone up, agricultural labour households have fallen in absolute numbers from 16.3 million in 1956–57 to 14.8 million in 1964–65. A similar relative decline is confirmed by Census data. Agricultural labourers as a proportion of total agricultural workers (cultivators as well as agricultural labourers) went down from 28.3 in the 1951 Census to 24.2 in the 1961 Census.[1]

Since dependence on wage labour is often regarded as an important aspect of capitalist agriculture, it seems on the basis of the information given earlier that assertions frequently made about the development of capitalism in Indian agriculture with increased proletarisation of agricultural workers are yet too premature. Not merely is the percentage of hired to total agricultural workers very low (according to 1961 Census data, it was only 14.64 per cent), over time there seems to have been a *decline* in the number of agricultural labourers per acre of cropped area or as percentage of total agricultural workers. Even if we are to accept Narain and Joshi's conclusion that there has been a genuine decline in tenancy, we cannot say that we are unambiguously moving towards a regime of owner-cultivation with considerably larger use of hired labour. In fact, we may have moved somewhat more towards small-scale family-farming. The average size of operational holdings, according to NSS data, has gone down from 7.6 acres in 1953–54 to 6.5 acres in 1960–61, and since it is a general characteristic of Indian agriculture (supported both by Census and Farm Management Survey data) that dependence on family labour has an inverse relationship with the size of holding, it is not entirely surprising that dependence on hired labour in Indian agriculture may have declined.

It may, of course, be argued that most of our information cited above relates to the 1950s and, at most, the early 1960s, and that since then, there has been an accelerated development towards capitalism in agriculture under explicit government sponsorship and encouragement. There is no doubt that the so-called New Agricultural Strategy followed by the government is effectively a policy of subsidising and promoting agrarian capitalism in India. In different areas throughout the country, large and middle-farmers have increasingly taken advantage of government assistance in provision of credit and now inputs, in investment in tractors, pumps and tubewells, and of the government policy of high prices for agricultural products and low taxes. We have also heard glowing accounts of the so-called 'gentleman farmers', the retired army officers and civil servants, businessmen and moneylenders, running modern capitalist farms and transforming the countryside.

But the conspicuousness of these cases often tends to obscure the general picture. After all, the IADP programme for technological breakthrough covers only about 5 per cent of cropped area under paddy, wheat and millets in the country; the High-yielding Variety Programme (HYVP), launched in 1966–67, covered, in 1967–68, only about 7 per cent of cropped area under paddy, wheat and millets. The new technology in agriculture leading to more intensive cultivation and multiple cropping is likely to increase employment of wage labour per acre. But as yet, progress in this direction has not been substantial except in a few districts. Table 4.3 shows that except in West Godavari and Ludhiana (Ludhiana is in many ways an untypical district not merely for the rest of India, but also for Punjab: for example, about 80 per cent of cultivation households in Ludhiana operate holdings of about 10 acres or more), the other IADP districts did not experience any significant expansion in labour employment per acre since the programme started. One possible explanation of slow expansion of labour employment per acre might be increased mechanisation, but mechanisation is as yet rather limited (in the country as a whole, tractors are used on only about 2 million acres), and not always labour-displacing; besides, in view of the relatively insignificant increase in real wage in most IADP districts, as shown in Table 4.3, the incentive to mechanise to substitute for labour may not have been strong.

TABLE 4.3: Index of Change in Labour Employment Per Hectare (and in Daily Real Wage Rate) in IADP Districts in 1967–68, with 1962–63 as 100

Thanjavur	*Shahabad*	*Raipur*	*Aligarh*	*Alleppey*	*Palghat*	*Mandya*
77 (116)	116 (81)	117 (71)	107 (94)	102 (139)	109 (128)	102 (86)
Surat-Bulsar	*Sambalpur*	*Burdwan*	*Cachar*	*West Godavari*	*Ludhiana*	
114 (78)	107 (120)	87 (83)	116 (84)	170 (112)	140 (116)	

Note: The bracketed numbers indicate the index of wage rate (adjusted by the estimated sales price for the principal foodgrain in the district) in 1967–68 with that in 1962–63 as base. For Burdwan and Cachar, the base year is 1963–64 for both the indices.

Source: Government of India (1969).

As for the phenomenon of gentleman farmers, one of the states most closely identified with it is Punjab, and yet we may quote from the findings of a sample survey of 261 large farms (all above 20 acres in size) in Punjab in 1968:

> Our Survey reveals that ... persons other than those who have always been peasants or landlords as yet play quite an insignificant role in the transformation that is taking place in Punjab agriculture. Large farmers of army and civil servant origin do not exceed 3 per cent of the whole lot whereas 92 per cent of the respondents claimed cultivation as the only occupation they have ever had. The mixture of farming with other occupations—trade or industry—also fails to be revealed. 96.7 per cent of the farmers denied they had any subsidiary occupation. (Rudra, Majid and Tolib 1969)

On the whole, it seems that although in the late 1960s some prosperous capitalist farms have come up in different parts of the country, sufficient in number to impress the casual visitor from the nearby city or from abroad, in general the capitalist mode of production organisation has not yet spread its roots in Indian agriculture. Consequently, the crystallisation of class interests in the form of clear-cut interest groups in mutual confrontation is still limited and localised in the Indian countryside taken as a whole. No doubt there have been in recent years sporadic cases of serious employer–employee confrontation in agriculture, as, for example, that between the Paddy Producers' Association and Agricultural Workers' Union in eastern Tanjore, occasionally erupting in violence in the classic style of class-struggle in capitalism. But such cases are still conspicuous in their isolation. There have also been several cases, particularly in West Bengal, Bihar, Orissa and Andhra Pradesh, of clashes between exploitative landlords and groups of tribal people often organised by political activists. But the exploitation in tribal areas is in the form of exorbitant usury and bonded labour, and the struggle here is more for the emancipation of serfs than for proletarian victory in a capitalist agriculture.

Although the conflicts or contradictions in Indian agriculture have not yet in general clustered in the form of class antagonism, there is no doubt whatsoever that much of the countryside today is simmering with tension; tension of various forms, social tension mostly on the basis of friction between the dominant middle castes and those below, political tension as the meagre fruits of adult franchise percolate deep down, but above all economic tension, with vast masses of as-yet-largely-unorganised small peasants getting more and more conscious of their economic interests clashing with those of the large farmers. The pattern is, of course, still in the form of a 'crazy quilt', with criss-cross lines intermingling in ample conclusion: the former group includes small farmers who are as passionate property owners as any other petty bourgeois group and landless labourers with nothing to lose; small farmers hiring themselves out as part-time agricultural labourers (according to the 1961 Census, 10.36 per cent of male and 13.06 of female cultivators had agricultural labour as a secondary occupation); and other small farmers employing wage labour from outside, particularly in peak seasons and sometimes because caste considerations necessitated hiring labour for the 'lowly' act of tilling (according to the 1961 Census data, the percentage of hired to total agricultural workers was 6.16 in holdings below 1 acre, 9.59 in holdings of between 1 to 2.49 acres, and 12.58 in holdings of between 2.5 to 4.9 acres); some tenants who have acquired occupancy rights and others without any security of tenure; some agricultural labourers who are 'attached' to landowners in a semi-feudal relationship and others who are casual labourers with no security of employment. On the other hand, the second group includes high-caste landlords depending mostly on hired labour or sharecroppers for cultivation and enterprising peasant-caste big farmers leasing in large chunks of land for own cultivation (according to the 1961 Census data, 7.57 per cent of all pure-tenancy households belonged to the size-group of 15 acres and above and 22.09 of all mixed-tenancy households belonged to this group; according to the NSS 17th Round data, of the total area leased in, 36–41 per cent was in operational holdings of 15 acres and above, and in Punjab of the total area operated under sharecropping, 43.72 per cent was in operational holdings of 15 acres and above in 1960–61); some capitalist farmers and some other large farmers still predominantly dependent on family labour (according to the 1961 Census data, the percentage of family workers in total agricultural workers was 80.07 in holdings of between 15 and 29.9 acres, 74.96 in holdings of between 30 and 49.9 acres, and 63.05 in holdings of 50 acres and above).

Such heterogeneity in each group must be exasperating for any political organiser who is interested in projecting some common code of group identification. But the palpable fact remains that one group is desperately poor and preponderantly large in number (according to NSS data, 73.76 per cent of all rural households operated holdings below 5 acres in 1960–61), whereas the numerically small other group holds a position of absurdly disproportionate importance in the rural income and property structure (according to NSS data, 45.92 per cent of total area operated was in operational holdings of 15 acres and above in 1960–61). The latter group continues to lap up the lion's share in the flow of benefits from the government's policy of modernising agriculture, while the former group smoulders with a sharp awakening of anticipations and the thwarted desire to improve their lot. Even where inequality has not increased,[2] a more politically and economically aware peasantry look upon the existing level of extreme inequality with much less patience and resignation and there are many areas, particularly the technologically more progressive areas where, on all evidence, economic disparities have increased. Even a US AID-sponsored study of five IADP districts (Ludhiana, West Godavari, Tanjore, Palghat and Burdwan) recently came to the following ominous conclusion:

> The majority of farmers—probably as many as 75 per cent to 80 per cent in the rice belt—have experienced a relative decline in their economic position; and some proportion, representing unprotected tenants cultivating under oral lease, have suffered an absolute deterioration in their living standard. The High Yielding Varieties Programme is therefore being introduced into a setting where economic disparities have already been substantially sharpened by the differential capacity of small and large farmers, and tenants and landowners, to sustain the capital outlays on land development. Given the much higher cultivation costs of the new varieties and even greater premium on timely agricultural operations—including a rigid schedule for the application of fixed amounts of water to achieve maximum potential yields—the economic disparities between the minority of cultivators who can finance land improvements and the majority who cannot is bound to widen further. (Frankel 1960)

Sooner or later the system will explode; the cracks may not be strictly on capitalist–proletarian lines, but it will be an explosion all the same. The lack of cohesion and clear-cut identification in each group may act as a damper for some time, but it has already started cracking for some districts in West Bengal and Kerala and for the rest of the country, it is only a matter of time and, above all, organisation.

NOTES

1. The 1951 data here is adjusted for comparability with the 1961 Census data. See Kalra (1962: Table 11-A for 1951 and Table 12-A for 1961).

2. It is difficult to get hold of data that accurately reflects changes in income inequality over time. As a very rough index, one might use the estimates of the share of different fractile groups in total consumer expenditure tabulated from, say, the 15th and 22nd Rounds of NSS. On the basis of them, it seems that between 1959–60 and 1967–68 the share of the bottom 60 per cent of households in rural India hardly changed (from 38.80 per cent to 39.10 per cent) and that for the bottom 90 per cent of households changed insignificantly (from 75.60 per cent to 77.39 per cent). Of course, this is a very crude index for income distribution; among other things, this does not take into account the changes in savings ratio and also the differential impact of price movements on different groups.

References

Frankel, Francine. 1960. 'Agricultural Modernisation and Social Change'. *Mainstream*, 29 November.

Government of India. 1969. 'Modernising Indian Agriculture: Report on the Intensive Agricultural District Programme, 1960–68' (Volume 1). Ministry of Food and Agriculture, New Delhi.

Kalra, B. R. 1962. 'Appendix 1: A Note on Working Force Estimates, 1901–61'. In *Census of India Paper No. 1 of 1962: Final Population Totals*, 389–413. Delhi: Government of India.

Narain, Dharm and P. C. Joshi. 1969. 'Magnitude of Agricultural Tenancy'. *Economic and Political Weekly* 4(39), 27 September: A139–42.

Rudra, A., A. Majid and B. D. Tolib. 1969. 'Big Farmers of Punjab: Some Preliminary Findings of a Sample Survey'. *Economic and Political Weekly* 4(39), 27 September: A143–51.

5

Abolition of Landlordism in Kerala

*A Redistribution of Privilege**

Ronald J. Herring

The Kerala land reforms have been widely discussed as a model for the other Indian states, the most comprehensive and far-reaching reforms of their kind in contemporary India. Most fundamentally, the reforms which came into force on 1 January 1970[1] represent what the Planning Commission termed the 'logic of development in land reforms': the conferring of ownership rights on all tenants, abolishing and rendering illegal the institutions of rentier landlordism and ground rent. But as all students of land reforms recognise, it is a long way from legislation to alteration of an agrarian system as it actually functions on the ground. The implementation of the Kerala reforms in this respect has replicated much of the experience in other parts of the subcontinent—delays, legal setbacks, irregularities, practical technical difficulties and vacillations in 'political will'. Now that the implementation of these pathbreaking reforms is virtually complete, what can we say about their impact on the agrarian structure?

. . .

The reforms under discussion have a curious political history. Legislated in 1969 by the United Front ministry led by the Communist Party of India (Marxist) (CPI-M), the reforms came into effect only on 1 January 1970 after the fall of that government, and were thus administered for a decade by coalitions led mostly by the Communist Party of India (CPI) while the CPI-M led the opposition. Second, the reforms conceptually replicate those of the first communist ministry, the Kerala Agrarian Relations Act passed in 1959 (which remained unimplemented because of the dismissal of the ministry and, later, court rulings); indeed, the two reforms were drafted under the direction of the same chief minister, E. M. S. Namboodiripad, and revenue minister, K. R. Gowry. Third, although the reforms were frequently branded as 'communist' by opponents and 'revolutionary' by supporters, in fact the legislation selfconsciously followed the recommendations of the 1949 Congress

* Originally published in *Economic and Political Weekly* 15(26), 28 June 1980: A59–69.

Agrarian Reforms Committee Report as well as Central directives on land reform. The conceptualisation was explicitly anti-feudal and pro-capitalist, not socialist.[2] The political strategy was to show that communist governments could implement progressive Congress measures which Congress governments could not.

The core of the reforms, both in 1959 and 1969, was the abolition of the landlord–tenant social organisation of production, the establishment of a relatively low ceiling on holdings to allow redistribution of land to the landless, and special measures to provide house and garden sites for a section of the largest and most disadvantaged agrarian class, the field labourers. These three measures will be analysed, in turn, with emphasis on the abolition of landlordism.

Abolition of Landlordism: How Many Tenants Were There?

The 1969 reforms, technically an amendment to the loophole-strewn and ineffectual Congress-legislated Kerala Land Reforms Act 1963, provided (in Section 72) for the vesting of all landlords' rights in the government for eventual transfer to 'cultivating tenants', with very minor exceptions. By the beginning of February 1980, there had been 3,614,834 applications filed or booked *suo moto* for transfer of landlords' rights to tenants. Disposal of these cases is now virtually complete. Applications have been allowed in 2,434,310 cases, the remainder being rejected or settled out of court. Thus, more than two-thirds (67.3 per cent) of the applications were approved, and certificates of purchase have been issued in virtually all of these cases (98.5 per cent). More than 2.4 million tenanted plots have thus become the property of their former tenants (Government of Kerala 1979b).[3]

To assess the magnitude of this structural change, one ordinarily asks the percentage of tenants who benefited through the reform. But in Kerala, in law, *all* cultivating tenants have benefited; the structural change is absolute. However, slippage in implementation is expected and it would be desirable to know what proportion of tenants was affected by the reform provisions. Unfortunately, before the land reforms, it was not known how many tenants there were. The most frequently quoted figure was 1.5 million, based on the 1966–67 Land Reforms Survey conducted by the Bureau of Economics and Statistics. That sample survey projected 1,268,425 tenants in the state; additions for population growth produced the 1.5 million figure.[4]

Government claims, however, are considerably in excess of 15 lakh tenants. The Task Force on Land Reforms, established by the State Planning Board, in its Report for the Sixth Five Year Plan in 1978, stated: 'Thus, over 23 lakh persons who were cultivating tenants have become owner operators as if by a single stroke of the pen' (Government of Kerala 1978: 4). The government of Kerala, in its Annual Plan proposals 1979–80, stated that 'the beneficiaries of land reform legislations include 23.74 lakh cultivating tenants ...' (as of March 1978) (Government of Kerala, n.d.: 25). In September 1979, the revenue minister, Baby John, stated publicly that over 25 lakh peasants became landowners through tenancy reforms, which came into effect on the first day of 1970 (Government of Kerala 1976 [1968]). The first analytical problem is to reconcile the government claim of 2.5 million tenants beneficiaries with the earlier survey estimate of 1.27 million tenants as the state total.

Obviously, if the 1966–67 survey is accurate, either the Kerala reforms were indeed remarkable, granting land to almost 200 per cent of the tenants in the state, or the official figures are exaggerated. Since official figures are notoriously unreliable with regard to implementation of land reforms, any serious analysis must establish the authenticity of the official data. To settle this question, one might turn to the 1970–71 Census. The Census does not divide cultivators into tenants and owners, but records only 1.1 million cultivators.[5] However, since holdings in Kerala are extremely small, forcing a large percentage of small landholders—tenants and owners alike—to work primarily as agricultural labourers, some percentage of the Census category, 'Agricultural Labourers', would almost certainly be tenants. The 1970–71 Census reported 1.9 million labourers. The total population of workers in agriculture thus came to about 3 million. Even if half of the agricultural population were tenants (the 1966–67 survey found that 44.9 per cent of all landholding families in Kerala were tenants), and some additions were made for population growth (though tenancies can hardly be expected to increase as fast as population), the Census figures suggest at first blush a number of tenants well below the official claim of 2.5 million beneficiaries.

Later surveys will not help solve this problem because, after 1970, tenancy statutorily ceased to exist, and the numbers of tenants reported were of dubious value. The 26th Round of the NSS, for example, in 1971–72, reported that only about 8.6 per cent of the operated area was leased in (and only 3 per cent leased out), compared to almost half in 1966–67.[6] The Third Decennial World Census of Agriculture 1970–71 reported that 8.2 per cent of the holdings, covering 13.2 per cent of the state's operated area, were wholly rented in.

The deeper one probes Kerala's agrarian structure, and the possible data sources for understanding it, the more ambiguous do the customary class categories become. Locating the tillers is conceptually problematic, and establishing their exact numbers is extremely difficult. Because the holding size in Kerala is so small (and some tree crops require so little in the way of constant attention), non-agricultural occupations among both tenants and owners are typical. The 1966–67 survey found that a majority—58 per cent—of the households with interests in land were not primarily agriculturists—that is, they did not derive the major portion of their income from agriculture (Government of Kerala 1976 [1968]: Table 7.3). By Census definition, these households would not be counted as agriculturists, despite their interests in land. Among tenants, the percentage of non-agricultural households ranged from 50 to 56 per cent. Nor will land records provide a reliable source of information on agrarian structure. A recent official study within the Revenue Department in Kerala found that the number of persons recorded as having an interest in land (*thandaper* holders, or holders of inheritance-based rights) was about half (49.8 per cent) the number of persons paying the basic tax on land. Land records were typically two decades out of date and frequently unusable (Kunhikoya 1978: Appendix A). In short, the contradiction between official claims and the exemplary 1966–67 survey cannot be settled by appeals to alternative data sources.

Scholars of land reform may have already guessed that the problem in the data is the confusion between 'cases' and 'tenants'. The Revenue Department's procedures require that a tenant file an application form for every tenanted plot; the department does not keep records of tenants, only of cases, though this distinction is ignored in official publications. Since one tenant may lease separate plots from separate landlords, there will be more cases than tenants. The 1966–67 survey projected 23.5 lakh pure tenancies (land held directly from landlords) and 2.65 lakh sub-tenancies (held from intermediaries), for a total of 26.15 lakh legitimate potential cases (Government of Kerala 1976 [1968]: Table 9.6), a figure very close to the actual implementation results of 24.34 lakh cases settled in favour of tenants. Moreover, the land area projected as tenanted in the survey (1.92 million acres) is very close to that actually turned over to tenants during the reforms. Since the survey figures are blown up from a relatively small sample, leaving margin for error, the closeness of fit of these data strongly suggests that implementation was indeed efficient, particularly when we consider the oral and informal character of many leases, the legal complications of sub-tenancies, and the magnitude of the task—about half the holdings in the state contained tenanted plots. These figures for cases then imply that the number of tenant families who received land is near the figure of 1.27 million, or about half the government's claim.

This extended detour into land data points to two important conclusions about the agrarian reforms, beyond clarification and correction of official data. First, with so few of the holdings large enough to support the proprietors as full-time agriculturalists, the alteration in distribution of property rights will have little effect on the dilemma of most tenants; most will, like the small owner-operators whose ranks they join, continue to require off-farm employment, either as agricultural labourers or in other sectors, to put together a family livelihood. More than 71 per cent of the landless tenants and 43 per cent of the owner-cum-tenants had holdings of less than 1 acre in 1966–67 (ibid.: Tables 7.7, 7.8).

Second, the fact that many, indeed a majority, of the agricultural landholders were not full-time, or even primarily agriculturalists, underlines the ambiguity in the reforms' objective of establishing 'land to the tiller'. Most tenants, like most 'owner-operators', depend heavily on hired labour to cultivate their fields. In paddy production, for example, 88.6 per cent of the total labour cost was for hired labour in 1974–75 in the state.[7] Only 28.3 per cent of the families in the state with rights in land other than *kudikidappu* (hut sites) reported having a family member 'actually engaged in agriculture',[8] and the nature of such engagement is frequently only supervisory or quite indirect.

Finally, the yawning discrepancy between land records and actual land control demonstrates concretely the vast potential for error and fraud in the implementation process, as well as the enormous technical and practical difficulties in locating surplus land and in establishing the bona fides of conflicting landlord and tenant claims; both point to the necessity of eliciting vigorous local participation in implementation, as provided in the Kerala Land Reforms Act 1963 (Section 72 EE), but never initiated below the *taluk* level.

ABOLITION OF LANDLORDISM: WINNERS AND LOSERS

The magnitude of the structural change brought about by landlord abolition in the Kerala reforms is thus indisputably significant, particularly in comparison with other Indian states and with subcontinental neighbours. The amount of land in each tenancy case was miniscule (about 0.8 acres), but the aggregate impact was dramatic—almost 2 million acres, or about 40 per cent of the operated farm area, was transferred to tenants.[9] Moreover, though the average holding distributed to a tenant family is quite small, land in Kerala is extremely productive, yielding by far the highest gross revenue output per acre in India. And the former tenants, now owners, with small-holdings are not conspicuously underprivileged in an agrarian structure in which a preponderant majority—more than 65 per cent—of the operated holdings are less than 1 acre in size. Moreover, if the average tenant had about two parcels, as seems to be the case, the average amount of land received per family would be about 1.6 acres, a size larger than the mean holding in the state.

Significantly, the combination of inflation and a low pegging of compensation have provided former tenants with a very fine land bargain. The aggregate rent that would have been paid by tenants to landlords has been officially figured at Rs 18 crores annually. The purchase price owed by tenants to the state comes to less than 5 per cent of the market value of the land in most cases, and much less in many cases.[10] In addition to the formal mechanism for transfer of land rights to tenants, the pressure of genuine land reforms in the state created over two decades an atmosphere in which many landlords sold lands to tenants, often at low prices, fearing *de facto* confiscation by the state.[11] The militancy of the agrarian movement and the real threat of official land reform combined to create a parallel unofficial land reform.

Although it can be said with assurance that virtually all tenants, including oral leasees and sharecroppers, have benefited from the land reform, in sharp contrast to the tenancy reforms typical of the subcontinent, it is certainly not obvious that the reforms benefited primarily the most oppressed agrarian classes. The 1966–67 Land Reforms Survey divided tenants (rather arbitrarily) into two numerically almost-equal groups—*kudiyirippu* tenants and 'others'. The kudiyirippu tenants were as a class the virtually landless, leasing in 99.05 per cent of the land they tilled. Very few had large operational holdings and their average income was much lower than that of 'other tenants' and owner-cultivators. Such tenants made up almost half of all tenants and constituted a class similar to the 'pure tenants' of classical theory, landless and dependent even for house sites on landlords. Their holdings were quite small: 71.2 per cent less than 1 acre, about 92 per cent less than 1 hectare. However, the 1 per cent of these tenants with holdings larger than 10 acres held almost 10 per cent of the area possessed by the stratum.

The slightly larger category of tenants, those other than kudiyirippu, exhibited more mixed class characteristics. Their average income, for example, was 63 per cent higher than that of the landless tenants and indeed 15.7 per cent higher than that of the average owner-cultivator.[12] Moreover, as a class, the 'other tenants' owned 31.72 per cent of the land they operated. Some were large owners and large operators in the Kerala context: 15.5 per cent operated more than 5 acres, and these households operated almost 60 per cent of the area operated by such tenants. A very small percentage of these tenants (0.8 per cent) operated more than 25 acres, but controlled over 12 per cent of the land operated by the stratum. This category of 'other tenants' resembles the more usual designation of owner-cum-tenant, and contained within it a large number of relatively privileged agriculturists who held a portion of the land in their control under lease arrangements. Although constituting little more than half of the tenant households, the 'other tenants' controlled more than 95 per cent of the area leased in by tenants (Government of Kerala 1976 [1968]: Tables 7.8, 9.1).[13]

Even as tenants as a category in Kerala exhibited markedly differing class characteristics, so too did landlords. Landlords in the 1966–67 survey were defined simply as households which have rental income. As a class, landlords leased in 17.83 per cent of the land they controlled. Moreover, leasing in was especially characteristic of the largest landlords; whereas only 6.81 per cent of the smallest landlords (less than 1 acre) leased in land, 45 per cent of the largest landlords (25 acres and above) did so. These largest landlord households controlled almost half (48.7 per cent) of the land possessed by all landlords (ibid.: Table 7.5). Table 5.1 presents the comparative data. The *kudikidappukars*, mostly field-labourers with hut sites on landlords' land, are included for comparison, as they both constitute the poorest class and perform the bulk of the agricultural operations on which the non-labouring agrarian classes depend.

TABLE 5.1: Some Selected Characteristics of Agrarian Classes in Kerala on the Eve of the 1969 Reforms

Class of Category	*Percentage Possessing Less than 1 Acre*	*Leased-in Area as Percentage of Possessed Area*	*Percentage with Annual Income Less than Rs 1,000*	*Agricultural Households as Percentage of Total Households**	*Average Annual Income (Rs)*
Kudiyirippu tenants	71.20	99.05	55.70	50	1,137
'Other tenants'	43.10	68.28	32.00	44	1,893
Owner-cultivators	65.10	0.00	38.10	37	1,601
Landlords	1.20	17.83	7.40	21	4,039
Kudikidappukars	100.00	—	71.40	—	869
All classes	59.70	42.60	43.90	42	1,526

Note: *'Agricultural Households' are those which have agriculture as the main source of income.
Source: *Land Reforms Survey in Kerala 1966–67*, Government of Kerala 1976 [1968], Report Tables 7.7, 7.8, 9.1, 7.5 and p. 51.

Another way to illustrate this important phenomenon is to analyse the class composition of the wealthiest stratum in rural Kerala at the time of the reforms' conception. Table 5.2 presents the characteristics of the group of landholders with incomes exceeding Rs 6,000 in 1966–67 and also indicates the percentage of each class which fell into the rich stratum. I emphasise the irony of terming such a stratum 'rich', but the relevant comparison here is to the rural poor, not to the urban rich or urban middle-class. Tenants not only constituted more than a third of the rural rich, but the 'other tenants' stand out among all agrarian classes for placing a high percentage of their members in that category (33.2 per cent). Only a tiny portion of the owner-cultivators and landless tenants, and none of the kudikidappukars, entered that stratum.

TABLE 5.2: Class Composition of the Agrarian Rich* in Kerala, 1966–67

Class	*Percentage of the Rural Rich*	*Percentage of Class Belonging to the Rich Stratum*
Landlords	16.30	18.90
Owner-cultivators	45.70	3.00
Kudiyirippu tenants	9.60	1.20
'Other tenants'	28.40	33.20
Total tenants	38.00	34.40
Kudikidappukars	0.00	0.00
	100.00	

Note: *Reporting an annual income of more than Rs 6,000.

Source: *Land Reforms Survey in Kerala 1966–67*, Government of Kerala 1976 [1968], Part III, Statistical Tables; calculations from the table.

The purpose of the preceding analysis is to demonstrate that in the concrete agrarian structure of Kerala, the abolition of tenancy relations was certain to benefit a large number of landholders whose class status was relatively high and whose position in the agrarian hierarchy was relatively privileged. The percentage of leased-in to operated area among large-holders (those possessing more than 15 acres per household) varied between 35.7 and 51.3 per cent (Government of Kerala 1976 [1968]: Table 8.6). The general point was made in a summary statistical way, in a report by the Centre for Development Studies (1975: 69–71), Trivandrum; the authors showed that in some parts of Kerala, the concentration of operational holdings was greater than the concentration of ownership holdings, meaning that in those areas, conferring ownership rights on tenanted holdings would increase the aggregate level of inequality in land control, though changing the shape of the distribution. That study concluded, however, that for the state as a whole, the abolition of tenancy would reduce rather than aggravate rural inequality in land distribution. This conclusion is sound, but more important than a summary measure of inequality is the differential impact on various classes of the abolition of landlords' property rights.

An adequate assessment of the reforms' actual impact would require a very large and elaborate field-study on the order of the 1966–67 survey cited extensively in this chapter; such a study will eventually be available. In the absence of a survey specifically aimed at measuring the impact of land reforms, it is possible to make use of other sources. One such source is an unpublished survey of 17 villages conducted in 1976 by Indian School of Social Sciences (n.d.), Trivandrum. The sample covered 1,700 households; data on landholdings are available for about half, that is, 836 households.[14]

The 1976 survey divided households into the analytical categories of capitalist landlord, rich peasant, middle-peasant, poor peasant, and an important mixed class which made up 44 per cent of the sample households.[15] 'Mixed-class' households do not cultivate their own land, and thus do not qualify as 'peasants' of any variety, but are not sufficiently wealthy to qualify as capitalist landlords. The size of this mixed class emphasises the ambiguity in the conceptualisation of land to the tiller in the Kerala reforms, as discussed previously. It is difficult to discern the source of legitimacy of the claim, either to the land or its product, of a non-cultivating 'tenant' (or owner) on land which is actually cultivated by others because the proprietor (tenant or owner) has more attractive employment opportunities or considers the land insufficient to yield a livable income.

The survey provided two categories of landlords, 'capitalist' and 'feudal', the latter defined by the dominance of rental income over income from employment of wage-labour (the mark of a 'capitalist landlord'), but none of the feudal specimen appeared in the sample. Indeed, the absence of a pure rentier class in the countryside is a marked structural change produced by the land reforms.

Although the aggregate level of change reflected by the 1976 survey gives only a partial picture of the final implementation results, and cannot be taken as unquestionably representative of Kerala as a whole, the comparisons across classes should, in general terms, delineate relative winners and losers. There are a number of ways to analyse the raw data on land gained and lost; Table 5.3 presents a variety of comparisons.

Though there are nuances in the data in Table 5.3, the clear conclusion is that the rich peasant class benefited most from the abolition of landlordism, capitalist landlords gained a great deal of land, and indeed gained a larger percentage of the land redistributed than their percentage of the population, but this class was also a significant loser. Rich peasants, on the other hand, increased their average holdings through the abolition of landlordism by a far larger percentage than other classes and by far more area in absolute terms per household, while losing land which came to only 1 per cent of the aggregate area possessed by the class. Rich peasants, like capitalist landlords, benefited disproportionately to their percentage of the population through land distribution, but for the capitalist landlords, unlike the rich peasants, this advantage was mitigated by the relatively greater loss of land (compare rows 5, 6, and 7 in Table 5.3).

Section II of Table 5.3 treats the Malabar region as a subset; that region for historical reasons was affected more than other areas of the state because of the concentration of tenancy there. Moreover, the peasant movement has its roots in Malabar, and legislative representatives from that region have historically been the most forceful advocates of radical land reform. One might thus expect different results from the reform process. The data from the seven sample villages of the Malabar region, however, indicate that essentially similar results were obtained; the loss of land by rich peasants made a slightly greater dent in their disproportionate benefit, and poor peasants received a share of the redistributed land somewhat closer to their share of the population, but the differences are slight. The analytical half-breed 'mixed class' neither gained nor lost much land, though the net gain was positive.

TABLE 5.3: Relative Winners and Losers in Kerala's Land Reforms (Abolition of Landlordism, Section 72), 1976 Survey Data

	A. By Classes					
I	*Kerala State (17 villages)*	*Capitalist Landlord*	*Rich Peasant*	*Middle-peasant*	*Poor Peasant*	*Mixed Class*
1	Area gained via land reforms as percentage of total area possessed	7.80	17.90	10.90	11.60	9.50
2	Area lost via land reforms as percentage of total area possessed	5.60	1.00	0.00	0.00	0.00
3	Net area gained per household (acres)	0.18	0.98	0.29	9.10	0.16
4	Net area gained as percentage of average holding	2.20	16.90	10.90	11.60	9.10
5	Households as percentage of sample	12.20	13.30	11.40	19.10	44.00
6	Area gained as percentage of total area redistributed	21.30	38.70	9.30	10.10	20.60
7	Net area gained as percentage of total area redistributed	6.00	36.50	9.30	10.10	19.70
II	*Malabar Region (7 villages)*					
1	Households as percentage of sample	13.4	12.1	11.4	13.7	49.5
2	Area gained as percentage of total area redistributed	20.8	41.7	8.8	10.3	18.4
3	Net area gained as percentage of total area redistributed	9.6	33.0	8.8	10.3	18.4
	B. By Size of Holding (Acres)					
	Kerala State	*2–5*	*5–10*	*10–15*	*15–20*	*>20*
1	Percentage of households*	34.20	11.50	2.50	0.60	1.20
2	Percentage of redistributed land gained	21.90	31.50	7.60	10.40	14.30
3	Net gain as percentage of total area redistributed	17.60	23.20	7.10	5.40	11.20

Note: *Excluding agricultural labourers, 65.9 per cent of whom owned some land in this sample, though averaging less than 12 acres per landholding–labourer household (0.47 acres). These are the author's calculations from original schedules. Adding the labourers to the small-holding size category would largely correct the discrepancy between the size distribution given in the table and that of the Agricultural Census.

Source: Indian School of Social Sciences (n.d.).; author's calculations from Tables 4.5, 4.4, and Appendix Tables 1.10, 2.10, 3.10, 4.10, 5.10, 6.10 and 7.10.

Part B of Table 5.3 presents a summary analysis by size of holdings.[16] The breaking point is 5 acres; households with holdings below that level, 84.2 per cent of the sample, gained a far smaller share of the land redistributed than their share of the population, a trend especially marked among the smallest holders. Households which controlled more than 5 acres, although only 15.8 per cent of the sample, received 63.8 per cent of all the land gained by sample households through the abolition of landlordism. The 84.2 per cent of the households with holdings below 5 acres received only 36.2 per cent of the redistributed area.

One curious aspect of these sample data is that every agrarian class emerged as a net beneficiary. A genuine land reform is conventionally considered a zero-sum game—some classes benefit at the expense of others. Since the survey was conducted in 1976, it reflects partial implementation results; at that time only about 40 per cent of the total tenancy eases had been processed.[17] The survey results are thus an imperfect mirror, but it must be emphasised that the analysis of the pre-reforms agrarian structure presented above demonstrated that relatively privileged groups would benefit disproportionately if tenanted lands were vested in their 'cultivators'. Most of the pure tenants had extremely small holdings; on the other hand, leasing in, often in large blocks, was characteristic of relatively large operators, many of whom owned significant amounts of land. The real losers were indeed the 'feudal landlords', the pure rentiers, who were analytically defined in the 1976 survey but were not found in the field; many were 'financially ruined'. Likewise, there were significant institutional losers, though the government has guaranteed an annuity in perpetuity to such institutions.[18] About 21 per cent of the tenanted land was owned by institutions, primarily *devaswoms* (temples) (Government of Kerala 1976 [1968]: Table 9.9).

These objective indicators of winners and losers in the reforms are congruent with the subjective perceptions of the sampled population. Table 5.4 presents the evaluation of the land reforms, and their effects on the respondents, by various agrarian classes. A majority of the capitalist landlords considered the land reforms a 'good measure', though landlord approval fell short of that of the other agrarian classes (which clustered at around three-fourths in the approval column). By a small margin, the class which expressed most frequently the opinion that it had benefited from the reforms was that of rich peasants; the lowest percentage of perceived benefits was among poor peasants. Almost half of the capitalist landlords considered themselves to have been adversely affected in some way, mostly through loss of hutment sites to kudikidappukars; over a fifth of the rich peasants expressed a similar opinion, and primarily for the same reasons.[19] In both cases, the 'adverse effects' involved tiny amounts of land, as the maximum plot size for which kudikidappukars are eligible is 10 cents (0.10 acre). The curious finding is that agricultural labourers, who objectively stood to benefit the least from the reforms, were the most consistent class in perceiving the reforms as a 'good measure'; about 87 per cent of the total agreed with that assessment.

TABLE 5.4: Perceptions of Effects of Land Reforms on Respondents by Class, 1976

Class	*N*	*Percentage Reporting*		
		Land Reforms a 'Good Measure'	*Having Benefited*	*Having Been Affected Adversely*
Capitalist landlord	102	57.8	22.5	49.0
Rich peasant	111	76.6	29.7	22.5
Middle-peasant	95	80.0	28.4	3.4
Poor peasant	160	76.9	15.6	0.6
Mixed class	368	74.7	19.3	7.9
Agricultural labourers	864	87.0	NA	NA

Source: Indian School of Social Sciences (n.d.).; calculations from Tables 5.13 and 6.18.

LAND CEILING, REDISTRIBUTION AND LABOURERS

Compared to the progress in abolition of landlordism and the conferring of rights on tenants, the progress in ceiling implementation conforms more to the all-India pattern of merely symbolic redistribution. About 92 per cent of the 70,983 returns filed under the ceiling provisions (Section 85) have been disposed of; just under 1.5 lakh acres were declared surplus, and valid orders are in force for the takeover of 116,059 acres, of which 75,831 acres has been taken, of which 47,873 acres has been redistributed. This latter figure is about 1 per cent of the operated area; the number of beneficiaries is correspondingly small: 75,483.[20]

A great deal needs to be said about the reasons for so minimal an impact, but first the ceiling must be put in context. Unlike other parts of India and the subcontinent, where the ceiling stood alone as the only measure to redistribute physical land area (after the 'abolition of intermediaries' in parts of India), in Kerala, the ceiling is part of the same legislation which abolished landlordism and tenancy. Thus, a great deal of the land in large-holdings, being tenanted, was redistributed but was not subject to the ceiling per se. The 1966–67 survey reported that in the largest holding–size group, holdings larger than 25 acres, 83.71 per cent of the households leased out land; in the aggregate, these large owners leased out 63.83 per cent of their owned area (Government of Kerala 1976 [1968]: Tables 8.13, 8.14). Thus, land redistribution in Kerala was primarily via the abolition of tenancy, rather than via a ceiling reform, and consequently favoured those with a stronger traditional claim on the land—the tenants—than that of agricultural labourers. Had there been no provisions abolishing landlordism, a much larger area would have been subject to the ceiling measures, and more labourers could have received small plots.

The impact of the ceiling was also limited by exemptions; 'plantations' were not subject to the ceiling, although plantations were defined by crops grown rather than organisation of production. Moreover, the ceiling was rather high relative to the average size of holding (20 ordinary acres for a large family compared to an average operated holding of 1.25 acres), and certain gifts and transfers were allowed. More importantly, since the abortive Agrarian Relations Bill introduced by the first communist ministry, landowners have had good reason and ample opportunity to rearrange their holdings to evade future ceilings; there is good evidence they have done so (Government of Kerala 1976 [1968]: Chapter X, 'Land Transfers'). It is also certain that large landowners engaged in fraudulent practices during the implementation of the current reforms to 'evade the ceiling, often successfully, though the aggregate effect is of course impossible to determine'.[21]

Even though the impact of the ceiling-redistributive measures in the land reforms was limited from the beginning by the level of the ceiling and the previous anticipatory manoeuvres by landlords to evade the ceiling, consideration of the disposition of the meagre surplus area is instructive. Of the 146,445 acres ordered taken over by the taluk land boards and state land board, orders covering 30,385 acres, or about 20 per cent of the area, were invalidated by high court rulings. Of the remaining 116,059 acres on which orders were in force, 75,831 acres were taken over. This leaves 40,228 acres on which orders have been passed but the land has not changed hands; more than half of this area (about 65 per cent) could not be taken because it was covered by 1,998 stay orders from the high court. Another 15,034 acres were involved in legal disputes, gift deeds or covered by separate confiscatory legislation directed at private forests. Likewise, of the land actually taken over but not yet redistributed, about 28,146 acres, all but 1,531 acres were reserved for public purposes, covered by stay orders, involved in gifts, legal disputes, vested forest conflicts, etc., and thus unavailable for redistribution.

There is an obvious lesson here: given the powers of intervention of the courts and the legal implications of land control and land legislation, effective ceiling-redistributive measures must ensure that much more land is declared surplus than is necessary to meet the redistribution goals of the reforms, and that the jurisdiction of the courts is effectively minimised. There are many slips between the cup and lip. The persistent agitations and vigilance of agrarian organisations and pressure from Left parties in the state prevented more extensive malfeasance. However, the popular committees at the village level provided for in a 1972 amendment to the Kerala Land Reforms Act 1963 (Section 72 EE), granted as a concession to popular mass agitations, were never established; such committees would almost certainly have further restricted the scope for evasion of the ceiling measures. The E. K. Nayanar government in 1980 hoped to uncover concealed surplus land, but most of the damage was done.

The distribution of surplus land from ceiling measures has thus accomplished little in aggregate terms. The 75,481 families who benefited received a total of 47,873 acres or an average of only 0.61 acres each, though again the high value of an acre of Kerala farm land and the low mean size of holding should be stressed. Most of the land redistributed was in Malabar, the area which was also most affected by the tenancy legislation. Almost a third of the land was redistributed in the Cannanore district alone (and the average plot much larger, slightly over 1 acre), another 19 per cent in the Palghat district.[22]

In addition to surplus land acquired through operation of the ceiling, the state has land resources available through other legislation. Official estimates are that a further 23,000 acres are available for redistribution from the Kannan Devan tea estate and private forest lands confiscated by the government. An additional 38,781 acres are available for redistribution under the Kerala Land Assignment Act (Government of Kerala 1979a: Table 3). But here too the aggregate impact on the agrarian structure is extremely limited because of the small area available relative to the number of the landless.

A recent amendment to the Land Reforms Act, the notorious 'gift deeds bill', which figured prominently in the resignation of the CPI-led coalition ministry on 7 October 1979, further reduced the already minimal redistributive potential of the ceiling legislation. The amendment validated gifts from owners with surplus land to their sons and daughters, or sons and daughters of deceased sons and daughters, executed between 1 January 1970 and 5 November 1974. The extent of land affected is 14,164 acres, or close to 10 per cent of the area declared surplus.[23] The number of owners affected is 1,026; given the average size of the parcel distributed up to 1980, the number of potential beneficiaries deprived by the 1979 amendment is about 23,220. The amendment thus represents a considerable negative impact on the redistributive goals of the reforms.[24]

Perhaps the most common and serious charge against the Kerala reforms is that nothing has been done for the labourers, who are not only the most depressed class in the agrarian system, but are the real tillers of the soil.[25] The most important potential benefits in the reforms for labourers were: (a) the redistribution of surplus land to the landless, and (b) the option to purchase at nominal prices, with government assistance, hut sites or kudikidappus, of up to 0.1 acres, frequently including a site for a kitchen garden and a few productive trees. The first potential was vitiated by the small amount of surplus land made available. The second applies to only those labourers who have a house site on someone else's land; these kudikidappukars traditionally occupied a status akin to that of attached labourers or agrestic slaves.

It is not known exactly how many kudikidappukars there are; the figure presented in the 1966–67 survey was 3.43 lakh (Government of Kerala 1976 [1968]: 61). Actual applications for purchase of kudikidappu came to 433,106, of which 265,829 were allowed (61.4 per cent), most of the remainder rejected or settled outside official channels. The relatively low acceptance rate should not necessarily be construed as a defeat for the hutment-dwellers; many of the cases withdrawn were settled voluntarily between landlords and kudikidappukars to the satisfaction of the latter. Moreover, about a third of all hutment-dwellers live in the Alleppey district, where successful militant struggles were waged to secure kudikidappu rights, often without formal procedures.[26]

The amount of land involved in kudikidappu cases was not large: about 21,000 acres or 0.08 acres per family. But again, the impact of the redistribution must be considered in comparison with the situation of what Aiyappan (1965) termed the 'serf-castes' historically, in comparison with the situation of landless labourers elsewhere in the subcontinent, and in the context of the tremendous rise in residential land prices in Kerala over already high prices. Moreover, some of the tiny plots are significant sources of income and food, and virtually all represent a valuable fixed asset in an inflationary market.[27]

The major thrust of the Kerala land reforms, however, was not to convert rural proletarians into poor peasants. The communist and Left Front governments of the period have attempted to alleviate the major problems of the labourers *qua* rural workers, *not* as aspiring peasant-proprietors. The most important legislation is the Kerala Agricultural Workers Act 1974, which offers some security of employment, benefits, a provident fund, etc., but has thus far remained essentially unenforced. However, it is doubtful that the traditional strategy for enhancing the wellbeing of the labourers—increasing the wage rate, already India's highest, through collective bargaining—is economically or politically viable without concomitant strategies to raise productivity and create new rural jobs. High wages threaten small and medium farmers who are caught in a serious cost-price squeeze at present. The labourers' central problem is too many days of unemployment (aggravated, but not caused, by high wages), which renders the high wage rate less significant; the going wage level matters little if one cannot find enough work.[28] Both politically and economically the problem of assuring a livable income to the labourers is obdurate, demanding far more innovative and committed programmes than those immediately apparent.

Conclusion

In summary, the agrarian structure of Kerala at the time the 1969 reforms were being formulated was such that the abolition of tenancy per se, as a legal form, would have a class-differentiated impact. Most of the area leased in was controlled by tenant-operators with holdings larger than the median holding size, a significant number of whom owned land as well. Landlords also leased in land, particularly large landlords. The relatively few tenants with large operational holdings controlled a disproportionate share of the area leased in by tenants.

These characteristics of the agrarian structure made the abolition of landlordism and the vesting of ownership in tenants a potential boon not only to poor peasants, but to rich peasants and capitalist farmers as well. Moreover, because the larger holdings contained a high percentage of leased-in land, whereas the poorest, landless tenants had very small holdings, conferring ownership rights on tenanted lands was certain to benefit relatively rich peasants more than relatively poor ones. Though households with holdings greater than 5 acres constituted only 8.1 per cent of the households with interests in land in 1968, they controlled 44.4 per cent of the leased-in area, including 61.8 per cent of the leased-in wetlands (Government of Kerala 1976 [1968]: Table 8.8).

From triangulation among official data on implementation, survey data on the pre-reforms agrarian structure, and limited survey data on the post-reforms configuration, the analysis of this chapter has demonstrated that the primary beneficiaries of the Kerala reforms, by a number of measures, were the rich peasants. The classes least benefited were those most in need of benefits—the poor peasants and agricultural labourers. The reasons for this outcome are primarily found in the strategy and conceptualisation of the reforms, not their implementation. Though implementation lapses disproportionately aided the rural privileged (superior access to legal practitioners, written records, knowledge of provisions, contacts, etc.), it must be emphasised that even perfect implementation would have produced broadly similar results. The relatively effective implementation, and relatively radical content, of these reforms are of course the product of the long, intense and costly mobilisation of the rural poor for land reforms in Kerala, and the strength of their agitations and involvement during the reform process, as well as the high level of literacy and politicisation in the state; minor lapses are inevitable, but the gross and extensive evasions and perversion of land reform measures common elsewhere in the region are virtually impossible in contemporary Kerala.

The conceptual problems in the legislation were two. First, tenancy was treated as a homogeneous type of production relations, an aspect of 'feudal' society. But, to paraphrase Lenin, there are tenants and there are tenants. For historical reasons, some tenants of Kerala were of relatively high social status and economic power, particularly the large *kanamdars*, typically employing sub-tenants or wage labourers to cultivate their holdings. Likewise, because of the lengthy, intensive commercial penetration of Kerala agriculture, tenancy became a means for rising capitalist agriculturalists of communities outside the traditional 'feudal' landholding elite (the Namboodiris and Nairs) to acquire and exploit land. The 10-acre Syrian-Christian tenant of Alleppey, employing 40–50 wage-labourers, operated a small business, paying ground rent as a small businessman would lease a firm site; such a tenant was an operative of capitalist agriculture, not an oppressed serf-like victim of feudalism. And though the reforms conferred land only on 'cultivating' tenants, 'cultivation', as in almost all Indian legislation, was defined to include supervision of hired labour, or arranging for cultivation, or simply bearing the risk of cultivation.

The majority of the tenants who received land in the reforms were indeed poor and often socially oppressed. Unfortunately, the 0.8 acres transferred in the average tenancy case left most former tenants poor, if less socially oppressed. Though most of the tenants who benefited were poor and disadvantaged, most of the *land* went to tenants who were relatively well-off and privileged. About 90 per cent of the kudiyirippu and 70.8 per cent of the 'other tenants' reported an annual income of less than Rs 2,000 in 1968. However, the very poverty of these tenants, precisely because it reflected very small holdings, ensured that they would receive very little land. Tenancy, in the concrete agarian system of Kerala, was *not* indicative of any particular social organisation of production, but rather a quasi-property form which was utilised in various configurations of production, from the feudal-like to the distinctly capitalist, with shades in between. Tenancy functionally was simply a different form of land control, and thus of labour control—control of the labour process and its surplus. The critical determinant is the size of holding of the tenants and their social and economic strength vis-à-vis the landlord. But the Kerala legislation defined tenancy in terms of formal-legal traditional relations (kanamdars, *varamdars*, etc.), essentially property relations, rather than in terms of production relations.

The connection with size of holding leads to the second conceptual problem: the ceiling level. The relatively high ceiling and the existence of several nuclear families per household in the largest households, along with the exclusion of plantations, meant that large-holders could not only retain fairly large holdings (relative to the majority), but even increase their holdings by claiming ownership of leased-in lands under the tenancy provisions in Section 72. The result was virtual exclusion of the truly landless, those whose claim on the land was more tenuous than that of the tenants.

None of the foregoing discussion is meant to constitute a condemnation of the Kerala land reforms. The reforms represented the expressed demands of the agrarian movement in the state (dominated, as elsewhere in India, historically by *pucca* tenants of higher social status rather than by sharecroppers and labourers) and were constrained in important ways by the courts and the Centre. The framers of the reforms were quite conscious of their limitations and argued explicitly that the reforms necessarily were pro-capitalist and anti-feudal in character, reflecting the primary contradiction of the period.[29]

Moreover, the reforms accomplished what most legislation in the region approaches, if at all, only in rhetoric: the abolition of rentier landlordism. Though it is common in the state to speak of 'capitalist landlords', and of the former tenants as 'new landlords', such characterisations miss an important distinction: landlords, in the true sense, lords of the land, have virtually disappeared in Kerala. Capitalist farmers enjoy only the power of capital which, strategically great though it is, is of a different character than the extra-economic subjugation, humiliation and control that characterised land relations in Kerala traditionally. These are significant changes. But the reforms do not establish land to the tiller, only land to the immediate proprietor, and much like the abolition of intermediaries elsewhere, do little for the acute problems of the numerically dominant poor peasant and agricultural labourer classes: too little land and too little work.

If the Kerala reforms are to be a model for other states, consideration must be given to a much lower ceiling, to reconsideration of the 'plantation' issue, to *de facto* absentee ownership (the majority of all landholders in Kerala who are not primarily agriculturalists), to legislation of land-use norms to prevent neglect of the land, and to more innovative attempts to avert an agro-economic *cul-de-sac* of sub-marginal peasants engaged in Chayanovian 'self-exploitation' at stagnant levels of productivity, clinging tenaciously to tiny plots while focusing their main energies on securing off-farm income. To be normatively acceptable, such reforms must simultaneously address rural–urban inequities and the anomaly of levelling the field in the countryside while ignoring the cities. Similar considerations are of course applicable in considering further land reforms in Kerala.

The cliché which closes most papers on the subject is appropriate; land reforms will not solve the central problem of too many people making a living from too little land at too low a level of productivity. But the cliché must be qualified; the necessity of seeking solutions off the farm and through greater productivity is no excuse for abandoning efforts to achieve limited social justice and economic rationality on the farm for those classes which will inevitably remain dependent on agriculture for a very long time to come. The political consequences of the Kerala model of reforms are important, intriguing and unknown. There would be a certain irony if Lenin's fears about land reforms come to pass, if redistribution of land through a process of *embourgeoisement* converted the formerly radical core of the peasant movement, which has been the heart of Left politics in Kerala, into a relatively privileged class of proprietors wedded to the *status quo* politics of defending their privileges from those less privileged. The evidence on this question is not yet in.

NOTES

1. The Kerala Land Reforms (Amendment) Act No. 35 of 1969 is the basic piece of legislation under consideration. Though technically an amendment to the Kerala Land Reforms Act 1963 (No. 1 of 1964), the 1969 legislation fundamentally altered the 1963 reforms which were filled with loopholes and never seriously implemented. For provisions, see Gangadharan (1974).

2. For a brief treatment of the progression of land reforms in Kerala, see T. K. Oommen (1975) and M. A. Oommen (1975). See Herring (1983: Chapters 6–7) for a treatment of the conceptualisation of land reforms strategically by political elites.

3. The application data reflect the situation on 1 February 1980. An additional 290,782 tenants have benefited from the abolition of intermediary tenures under acts other than the 1969 legislation. Data for progress in the implementation of 31 December 1979 are from the Land Board, Trivandrum, as yet unpublished. Also, 'Proceedings of the Land Board', dated 12 March 1980, Trivandrum.

4. Quoted in *The Indian Express*, Cochin, 26 September 1979.

5. Census of India, Series 9, Kerala, Section II-B, (i) Economic Tables, Part A.

6. National Sample Survey, 26th Round, July 1971–September 1972, Tables on Land Holdings, Table 5.1 (Report for Kerala State), Ministry of Planning, New Delhi, 1975.

7. Data from Ministry of Food and Agriculture's 'Study on Cost of Cultivation: Paddy, 1974–75', cited in Indian School of Social Sciences (n.d.). The conclusion that the 'real tillers of the soil' are the labourers, not the landholders, was affirmed in Government of Kerala (1976 [1968]). For a similar analysis, see Krishnaji (1979).

8. See Government of Kerala (1976 [1968]: Part III, Statistical Tables, Table 3).

9. Calculations from data supplied by the Land Board, Trivandrum. See also, Government of Kerala (1979a: Table 3). Acreage figures are only approximate.

10. The annual rental estimate is from Government of Kerala (1979a: 3). An aggregate rental estimate of Rs 119 crores was given in Government of Kerala (1978: 10), Sixth Five Year Plan. The estimated relationship between purchase price and land values is my own, based on local inquiries and actual compensation charges.

11. There is hard evidence of this phenomenon in the data on land transfers between 1957 and 1967 in the Land Reforms Survey, as well as in Census of India (1961: 39). My field investigations recently have confirmed this phenomenon.

12. See Government of Kerala (1976 [1968]: Table 7.7). Also, calculations from data on p. 51.

13. The 'other tenants' included tenancies such as *kanam, kuzhikanam, verumpattom, chalgeni*, etc.

14. Agricultural labourers who owned land, typically tiny amounts, were not included in the category of landholders.

15. Briefly, 'capitalist' landlords are distinguished from 'feudal' landlords by the predominance of profits rather than rents in their income from the land (that is, wage-labour over land rental as the organisation of production). Rich peasants, like capitalist landlords, hire wage-labour, but also personally work in their fields. Middle-peasants do most of their own labour and are not forced to hire out family labour. Poor peasants may hire small quantities of wage-labour but are unable to support themselves from their own holdings, and must work off the farm, typically as wage-labourers. 'Mixed-class' households are those who hire labour to work their farms because they have other occupations; they do not qualify as capitalist landlords if their income is less than Rs 12,000 per annum.

16. The size distribution of holdings is at variance with the Census and NSS results because, as explained in Table 5.3, landholders whose main income was agricultural labour were not classified as landholders. This fact does not affect the argument in the text.

17. Calculations from Indian School of Social Sciences (n.d.: Table 4.5); data on implementation from Government of Kerala (1977). The pace of implementation dramatically accelerated after the declaration of Emergency in 1975.

18. As of 31 August 1979, in only 368 cases had annuity for institutions been officially determined, of a total of 1963 cases (Government of Kerala 1979b: Statement F). Since the annuity is fixed on the basis of a decade-old 'fair rent', inflation is continuously eroding the real compensation paid through annuities.

19. Kudikidappukars, or 'hutment dwellers', were granted the right to purchase their kudikidappu (house site and garden land) up to 0.10 acres in extent in rural areas at a nominal price, assisted by the government. Most hutment dwellers are agricultural labourers and historically were frequently bound to the landowner whose land their hut occupied. About 60 per cent of the rich peasants and landlords who claimed to have been negatively affected by the land reforms mentioned loss of land to kudikidappukars (see Table 5.4).

20. See 'Proceedings of the Land Board', 15 October 1979 (Land Board, Government of Kerala, Trivandrum). Also see Government of Kerala (1979b). The latest data considered refer to the situation on 31 December 1979.

21. Besides manipulation of land transfers and gifts, *benami* transactions, and other measures familiar in ceiling reforms in the region, the tenancy provisions also created an avenue for ceiling evasion through the filing of bogus tenancy cases by landlords' co-conspirators.

22. Calculations from Government of Kerala (1979b), and later, Land Board data. In addition to the individual beneficiaries, two cooperative societies received a total of 1,817 acres.

23. Data from Land Board, Trivandrum. The 'gift deeds bill' was to replace Ordinance No. 8 of 1979: The Kerala Land Reforms (Amendment) Ordinance, Law Department, Notification No. 6110—Leg (A) 1/79/Law, 7 July 1979.

24. Other provisions in the amendment are unknown, but potentially regressive. Most important, a new Section 6C is added to the basic legislation, permitting validation of tenancies created between 1964 and 1970 (previously null and void because of the 1963 Kerala Land Reform Act) if the tenant has made significant improvements on the property. Though there may be cases of genuine tenants who benefited through this provision (that is, tenants who accepted tenancies in good faith after 1 April 1964, not realising that the transaction was legally null and void), it is likely that a number of owners who created bogus tenancies to escape the ceiling provisions will benefit as well. For examples of bona fide tenants adversely affected by the invalidation of tenancies during that period, see M. A. Oommen (1975). The E. K. Nayanar government revoked Section OC by legislation pending at the Centre.

25. See, for example, Mencher (1978); Krishnaji (1979); and M. A. Oommen (1979).

26. All accounts of the period agree that some kudikidappukars in areas of militant organisation were able to secure rights without recourse to legal channels. Of course, the obverse is also true; many in areas of minimal mobilisation were victimised by landlords and their agents. For accounts, see T. K. Oommen (1975); various articles in *Peasant and Labour* for the period; and the village interviews of Thomas Paulini (1978: 406), recorded in his thesis. Data from Indian School of Social Sciences (n.d.: Table 6.19) indicate that 3.4 per cent of the hutment dwellers in the sample who got land did so though 'forcible occupation' and another 8.5 per cent through 'other means' outside official channels.

27. I have spoken with kudikidappukars in the Trichur district who claim monthly incomes of Rs 150–200 from their plots. It is not uncommon for such plots to be sold at prices exceeding Rs 500 for each *cent* (a unit of land equal to 0.01 acre).

28. Kerala labourers have historically faced more severe problems of unemployment than those of other states.

29. For an extensive treatment of the agrarian movement in Kerala, see Paulini (1978). For the 1970s, see T. K. Oommen (1975); and Koshy (1976). Also see Hart and Herring (1977). For an extended treatment of the policy logic of the Kerala reforms, see Herring (1983: Chapter 6). Namboodiripad (1952: 61) argued that land reforms must not discourage capitalist entrepreneurs, because 'capitalism in agriculture, like capitalism in industry, is an advance on the present situation in a semi-colonial, semi-feudal country'. Also see ibid.: 27, 49.

REFERENCES

Aiyappan, A. 1965. *Social Revolution in a Kerala Village*. Bombay: Asia Publishing House.

Census of India. 1961. Volume 7, Kerala, Part VI-B, Village Survey Monographs by M. K. Devassy. New Delhi.

Centre for Development Studies. 1975. 'Poverty, Unemployment, and Development Policy: A Case Study of Selected Issues with Reference to Kerala'. United Nations, New York.

Gangadharan, A. 1974. *Law of Land Reforms in Kerala*. Cochin: K. U. Krishnan.

Government of Kerala (n.d.). 'Annual Plan Proposals, 1979–80'. State Planning Board, Trivandrum.

———. 1973. *The Third Decennial World Census of Agriculture, 1970–71: Report for Kerala State*. Bureau of Economics and Statistics, Trivandrum.

———. 1976 [1968]. 'Land Reforms Survey, 1966–67'. Bureau of Economics and Statistics, Trivandrum. [Published in 1976 as *Land Reforms Survey in Kerala 1966–67: Report 1968*; all references are to the 1976 edition.]

———. 1977. *Administration Report of the Land Board and Land Tribunals, 1975–76*. Trivandrum.

———. 1978. *Report of the Task Force on Land Reforms*. State Planning Board, Trivandrum.

———. 1979a. *Land Revolution in Kerala*. Trivandrum.

———. 1979b. *Notes on Progress of Implementation of the Land Reforms Act*. Land Board, Trivandrum.

Hart, Henry C., and Ronald J. Herring. 1977. 'Political Conditions of Land Reform: Kerala and Maharashtra'. In *Land Tenure and Peasant in South Asia*, ed. R. E. Frykenberg. Delhi: Orient Longman.

Herring, Ronald J. 1983. *Land to the Tiller: Agrarian Reform in South Asia*. New Haven: Yale University Press.

Indian School of Social Sciences (n.d.). 'Survey on Agrarian Structure and Social Change in Selected Villages in Kerala'. Typescript, under Project Director K. Mathew Kurian, Trivandrum.

Koshy, V. C. 1976. 'The Politics of Land Reforms in Kerala'. PhD thesis, Jawaharlal Nehru University, New Delhi, April.

Krishnaji, N. 1979. 'Agrarian Relations and the Left Movement in Kerala'. *Economic and Political Weekly* 14(9), 3 March: 515–21.

Kunhikoya, N. 1978. 'Work-load of Village Establishments in Kerala: A Study'. Mimeo, Board of Revenue, Trivandrum.

Mencher, Joan P. 1978. 'Agrarian Relations in Two Rice Regions of Kerala'. *Economic and Political Weekly* 13(6–7), February: 349–66.

Namboodiripad, E. M. S. 1952. *On the Agrarian Question in India*. Bombay: People's Publishing House.

Oommen, M. A. 1975. *A Study on Land Reforms in Kerala*. New Delhi: Oxford IBH.

—— (ed.). 1979. 'Land Reforms and Agrarian Change in Kerala since Independence'. In *Kerala Economy since Independence*. New Delhi: Oxford IBH.

Oommen, T. K. 1975. 'Agrarian Legislations and Movements as Sources of Change: The Case of Kerala'. *Economic and Political Weekly* 10(40), 4 October: 1571–84.

Paulini, Thomas. 1978. 'Agrarian Movements and Reforms in India: The Case of Kerala'. Thesis, Universität Stuttgart, Germany.

6

CHANGING LAND RELATIONS IN PUNJAB AND IMPLICATIONS FOR LAND REFORMS*

SUCHA SINGH GILL

...

At the time of the partition of the country, a major part of the land was under tenant cultivation. Land revenue records of Punjab indicate that land under tenant cultivation was 48.6 per cent in 1947 and 48.2 per cent in 1952 (Talib 1979). This is also confirmed by a field report of three villages in Punjab. According to this report, the area under tenant cultivation was between 37 per cent and 50 per cent in 1952 (Ladejinsky 1977). The 8th Round of NSS estimated that in 1953–54, the extent of land under tenant cultivation was 40.42 per cent in Punjab (including Delhi and Himachal Pradesh) and 37.71 per cent in the Patiala and East Punjab States Union (PEPSU) (Bardhan 1976). The Farm Management Survey data related to the Ferozepur district show that the percentage of operated area under tenancy was 37 in 1954–55 (quoted in ibid.). It is evident that at the time of enacting of land reforms legislation in Punjab and PEPSU, nearly 40 per cent of the operated area was under tenancy. Of the total leased-out area, 49.52 per cent in Punjab and 32.83 per cent in PEPSU was leased out by non-cultivating landowners. The remaining area was leased out by cultivating owners (see Table 6.1).

Tenancy was of two kinds: (a) occupancy, and (b) at will. In Punjab, occupancy tenants with inheritable rights cultivated 7–10 per cent of the cultivated area and tenants-at-will cultivated between 30 and 40 per cent of the area in 1952 (Ladejinsky 1977). According to the report of the Government of PEPSU (1953), in 1952, there were 616,799 acres under occupancy tenants and 1,046,532 acres under tenants-at-will. Thus, the major part of the tenanted area was under tenants-at-will with no security of tenure.

The tenants were further of two types: (a) purely tenants, and (b) owner-cum-tenants. Purely tenants did not own any land whereas owner-cum-tenants leased in land to increase the size of their holdings. Tables 6.1 and 6.2 show the percentage distribution of land leased out and leased in. In Punjab 19.51 per cent and in PEPSU 16.90 per cent of the households were those of purely tenants, and owners-cum-tenants

* Originally published in *Economic and Political Weekly* 24(25), 24 June 1989: A79–85.

were 35.99 and 35.85 per cent, respectively, in Punjab and the PEPSU area. They were leasing in land from both non-cultivating owners and cultivating owners. In Punjab, non-cultivating owners' contribution was the largest in leasing out land and accounted for nearly 50 per cent, followed by cultivating owners whose contribution varied between 35.64 per cent and 38.10 per cent of the total leased-out area.

TABLE 6.1: Percentage Distribution of Area Leased Out by Acerage Class, 1950–51 to 1953–54

Livelihood Class	*Percentage of Estimated Households*	*Percentage of Area Leased Out*			
		1950–51	*1951–52*	*1952–53*	*1953–54*
Punjab					
1. Cultivating owners	35.59	37.08	35.64	36.45	38.10
2. Non-owning cultivators	19.51	5.65	5.63	5.49	6.97
3. Non-cultivating owners	3.54	50.67	52.07	50.62	49.52
4. Others	40.96	6.60	6.66	7.44	5.41
Total	100.00	100.00	100.00	100.00	100.00
PEPSU					
1. Cultivating owners	35.85	52.93	53.93	53.65	50.38
2. Non-owning cultivators	16.90	2.92	2.77	2.79	3.14
3. Non-cultivating owners	7.27	30.77	30.35	30.53	32.88
4. Others	39.98	14.08	12.95	13.03	13.60
Total	100.00	100.00	100.00	100.00	100.00

Source: NSS, 8th Round.

TABLE 6.2: Percentage Distribution of Area Leased In by Acerage Class, 1950–51 to 1953–54

Livelihood Class	*Percentage of Estimated Households*	*Percentage of Area Leased In*			
		1950–51	*1951–52*	*1952–53*	*1953–54*
Punjab					
1. Cultivating owners	35.99	21.87	23.56	27.13	23.07
2. Non-owning cultivators	19.51	65.00	63.86	61.43	63.70
3. Non-cultivating owners	3.54	0.28	0.27	0.18	0.18
4. Others	40.95	12.85	12.31	11.26	8.05
Total	100.00	100.00	100.00	100.00	100.00
PEPSU					
1. Cultivating owners	35.85	57.52	60.37	61.13	54.17
2. Non-owning cultivators	16.90	36.98	32.66	31.16	39.74
3. Non-cultivating owners	7.27	—	—	0.17	0.58
4. Others	39.98	5.50	6.97	7.0	5.51
Total	100.00	100.00	100.00	100.00	100.00

Source: NSS, 8th Round.

Most of the land under tenancy was without any formal contract. Informal contracts accounted for more than 70 per cent of the land. Sharecropping was the most important method of payment of rent. Under this system, landlord and tenant shared crop on 50:50 basis. Besides, tenants were subjected to render services of various kinds to landlords. The distribution of land leased in under different types of contracts is shown in Table 6.3.

TABLE 6.3: Percentage Distribution of Area Leased In by Types of Lease, 1950–51 to 1953–54

Types of Lease	*Percentage of Area*			
	1950–51	*1951–52*	*1952–53*	*1953–54*
Punjab				
1. With formal contracts				
(a) *Cash rent*	3.60	3.28	4.85	6.95
(b) *Fixed crop rent*	0.85	0.82	1.09	1.31
(c) *Proportionate crop rent*	18.24	20.05	18.47	17.99
2. Without formal contracts:				
(a) *Cash rent*	10.81	10.82	9.95	5.6
(b) *Fixed crop rent*	2.31	3.04	2.71	3.04
(c) *Proportionate crop rent*	27.75	26.75	31.42	37.10
3. Other types	14.14	13.67	12.75	13.17
4. Unspecified	2.30	21.57	18.76	15.18
Total	100.00	100.00	100.00	100.00
PEPSU				
1. With formal contracts:				
(a) *Cash rent*	24.37	17.69	18.56	15.77
(b) *Fixed crop rent*	—	—	—	—
(c) *Proportionate crop rent*	0.91	0.93	5.43	11.16
2. Without formal contracts:				
(a) *Cash rent*	—	1.80	0.01	2.07
(b) *Fixed crop rent*	—	—	—	0.03
(c) *Proportionate crop rent*	10.64	13.20	14.55	11.82
3. Other types	15.49	15.62	18.69	16.52
4. Unspecified	48.59	50.76	42.76	42.63
Total	100.00	100.00	100.00	100.00

Source: NSS, 8th Round.

Land, which is a major source of earning and one's position in the rural area, was concentrated in a few hands. In Punjab 35.51 per cent and in PEPSU 41.52 per cent of the households were without land. The farmers owning 5 acres or less constituted 35.04 per cent in Punjab and 20.82 per cent in PEPSU of the total rural households. Their share of land was, respectively, 10.80 per cent and 5.46 per cent in Punjab and PEPSU. At the top, farmers who owned more than 30 acres of the land were 2.74 per cent in Punjab and 3.91 per cent in PEPSU. Their share of land was, respectively, 30.60 per cent and 28.03 per cent. This is evident from Table 6.4.

TABLE 6.4: Percentage of Households that Owned Land below the Specified Size of Household-ownership Holding, and Cumulative Percentage of Area Owned by Them for the Major Crop Season in Punjab and PEPSU, 1953–54

Size of Household Ownership (in Acres)	*Punjab*		*PEPSU*	
	Household	*Area Owned*	*Household*	*Area Owned*
1. 0–0.0005*	35.51	—	41.82	—
2. 1.00	50.80	0.65	50.54	0.39
3. 2.50	60.34	3.68	56.77	2.02
4. 5.00	70.50	10.80	62.64	5.60
5. 10.00	83.92	28.39	77.23	21.84
6. 20.00	93.66	53.40	90.40	50.96
7. 30.00	97.26	69.40	96.09	71.97
8. 50.00	98.99	81.23	99.11	90.30
9. 50 and above	100.00	100.00	100.00	100.00

Note: *Households either owning no land or land less than 0.005 acres.
Source: NSS, 8th Round.

The holdings of various sizes were faced with problems of fragmentation. This problem was highlighted by some studies as early as in 1920s. A study of the village Bairampur showed that 28 per cent of the holdings had over 30 fields, and in three cases, the plots were so small that they had been lost sight of by their owners and passed into the hands of others (Bhalla 1923, quoted in Darling 1925). In the village of Suner (Ferozepur), it was found that 50.3 per cent of the holdings had 1–5 fragments and 18 per cent had 6–10 fragments, and remaining had fragments between 11 and 20 (Government of Punjab 1960: 56, 1963: 41). Though in the 1930s there was some voluntary consolidation of holdings, the problem of fragmentation remained unsolved till compulsory consolidation of holdings was introduced after Independence.

The existence of intermediaries like *biswedars*, *talukdars*, etc., made the situation worse. They had no direct connections with land cultivation. But they exploited cultivators in various ways and forced *begar* (free labour) on them.

II

Land reforms adopted after Independence in the state were intended to transform the land relations to suit capitalist modernisation. They can be divided into four categories:

1. abolition of intermediaries;
2. tenancy reforms;

3. ceiling on landholdings; and
4. consolidation of holdings.

To abolish intermediaries, the Punjab Abolition of Ala Malikiyat and Talukdar Act 1951 was enacted as President's Act. This was re-enacted in 1952. In October 1952, the institution of Zaildari was abolished and in the budget session of the state legislature; in 1953, a bill was passed for the abolition of the system of Jagirdari in the state. In the PEPSU area, the PEPSU Abolition of Biswedari Ordinance was issued in 1950.

In both the areas, occupancy acts were passed, vesting proprietary rights in the occupancy tenants. The final shape to tenancy legislation was given in the Punjab Security of Land Tenures Act 1953, which was amended in 1955, and PEPSU Tenancy and Agricultural Lands Act 1955.

In both the Punjab and PEPSU acts, the maximum rent was fixed as one-third of the gross produce. With these acts, occupancy tenants got ownership rights. But landowners had the right to eject tenants-at-will and take over land up to 30 standard acres (up to 40 standard acres in case of displaced persons in PEPSU and 50 standard acres in Punjab). After ejecting tenants, landowners could either cultivate the land themselves or give it to another tenant. The laws provided that tenants were not to be ejected from an area up to 5 acres (including any other land held by them) until they had been settled on alternative land. In PEPSU laws, security given to the tenants was up to 5 acres of land whether a tenant held land from big or small owner. In the Punjab laws, a tenant on big holdings was not to be ejected at all until alternative land had been provided, while a tenant on small holdings had been given security up to 5 standard acres. PEPSU laws gave security of tenure up to 15 standard acres to a tenant with continuous possession of 12 years at the commencement of the act (3 December 1953).

Both the Punjab and PEPSU laws contained provisions enabling tenants to voluntarily acquire ownership in the non-resumable area, if they had continuous standing of six years in Punjab and 12 years in the PEPSU area. The compensation payable in the Punjab provision was one-fourth of the market value, and in PEPSU, 90 times the land revenue (including rates and cess) or Rs 200 per acre, whichever was less.

In PEPSU, the ceiling was fixed at 30 standard acres (in case of displaced persons, 40 acres). In Punjab, the state government was empowered to take over surplus land above the permissible limit of 30 standard acres (up to 50 acres in case of displaced persons).

In Punjab (both areas) exemptions were granted to land in cooperative garden colonies, land granted for gallantry to army personnel, orchards, well-run farms and tea estates.

Following the guidelines of the Central and Land Reform Committee announced on 3 August 1971, the Punjab legislature enacted the Punjab Land Reform Act 1972. A new level of ceiling was fixed in Punjab (including the PEPSU areas) at 7 hectares for double-cropping land under assured irrigation, 11 hectares for one-crop land under assured irrigation, 20.5 hectares of *barani* land (uncultivated land, completely dependent on rain for irrigation), and for other types of land at 21.8 hectares.

Ceiling had been applied to the family as a unit rather than to individual members. In Punjab Act 1972, the ceiling mentioned earlier applies to a family of five. When the number of family members exceeds five, the permissible area increases by one-fifth of the permissible area for each member in excess of five, subject to the condition that additional land shall be allowed for not more than three such members.

Exemption has been given to land belonging to any religious or charitable institutions, but not belonging to or vested in or taken in lease by the state, central government, university and educational institutions or trusts, corporations-owned or controlled by state and central governments, Bhoodan Yagna Board, agricultural cooperative societies, land mortgage banks and state or central cooperative banks.[1]

In both Punjab and PEPSU, laws were enacted for compulsory consolidation of holdings to solve the problem of fragmentation. A separate department was opened by the state for this purpose and immediately work on consolidation was started.

The land reform legislation of Punjab (and PEPSU) had many flaws in it. The passing of the land reforms legislation took a relatively longer time. A large number of landowners ejected tenants on paper as well as in practice immediately after Independence, when the land reforms became a burning question. The situation regarding ejectment as reported by the Punjab government in the state assembly is given in Table 6.5.

Table 6.5: Ejectment of Tenants by Landlords, 1950–51 to 1953–54

Year	*No. of Ejectment Notices*	*No. of Actual Ejectments*
1950–51	8,388	3,137
1951–52	7,083	3,287
1952–53	17,503	n/a
1953–54	60,358	13,700

Source: Talib (1979).

These figures only pertain to the Punjab area. The situation in the PEPSU area, though not actually known, was not different. In addition to this, powerful landowners did not allow a large number of cases of ejection to come to the notice of the state. The landlord's interest dominated the state assemblies and wielded strong influence in police and local administration. They, in collaboration with the administration, were able to suppress facts about the number of actual ejectments (Ladejinsky 1977). This resulted in the reduction of area under tenancy. This is borne out by the survey of four villages of Punjab and one of PEPSU by the committee on tenancy reforms in March 1956. As compared to nearly 40 per cent of the area under tenancy in 1953–54, the committee found that in 1956, the area under tenancy was 30 per cent in Punjab and 20 per cent in PEPSU (Planning Commission 1956).

Second, provisions like self-cultivation, 'voluntary surrenders', exemption from the provisions of ceiling of land under 'cooperative garden colonies', 'well-run farms', etc., were serious legal flaws favouring landowners, and did a lot more harm to the tenants. The rate of compensation to acquire ownership of land was too high in the Punjab region, and was beyond the capacity of the poor tenants.

A fixation of rent at one-third the produce was favourable as compared to the traditional rate of one-half. But it went against those tenants who offered to pay this rate, resulting in their eviction. The flaws in the legislation related to security of tenure of the tenants converted a benefit into loss for many tenants. In case of dispute, the tenants had to fight their case in court themselves; poor tenants could not afford this as the judicial process is a very costly affair.

The acts imposed responsibility for implementation upon the magistrates and revenue officials—collectors, revenue assistants, *tehsildars*, *naib tehsildars*, the circle *kanungo*, ending with the officer closest to villagers, the *patwari*. It is a common observation that these individuals are not in a position to insure protection of the tenants. Their normal duties are complex and time-consuming, and they are unable to devote much time. Even if they can spare time, they are biased in favour of big landowners and many of them come from such families. The implementation machinery has been successful in effectively sabotaging land reforms (Ladejinsky 1977).

Coming to implementation of land reforms, Punjab has a very poor performance in respect of tenancy reforms. A report of the Planning Commission (Bandhopadhyaya 1972) reads as follows:

> The law regarding security of tenure appears to be on the whole somewhat illusory. This is supported by the fact that the number of tenants in existence in the Punjab area at the time when the Punjab Security of Land Tenure Act was amended in 1955 has greatly decreased. From the information supplied by the state government on March 30, 1955 it appears that the total number of tenants including tenants-cum-owners was 5,83,400 ... From the information supplied by the Punjab government recently (1964) it appears that the total number of tenants who were holding land at the commencement of the act and are still holding land as tenants is 80,250. It seems difficult to account for the large difference between these two figures. Even if we treat all the post act tenants (who were admitted up to October 1960 and are going to be settled) as those in existence in 1955 the difference between the two figures still remains large. Corresponding figures of the PEPSU area are not available but the position would not be different from that obtaining in the Punjab area. (Ibid.)

Up to 1964, 19,342 tenants (in both Punjab and PEPSU) acquired proprietary rights in 127,794 acres of land (Bardhan 1976). This explains the eviction of tenants from land on a large scale. Our own study (Gill 1978) of a village in the Gurdaspur district has brought out similar results. Evidence collected by Ladejinsky (1966) on the study of tenurial conditions in Ludhiana supports these conclusions. According to the data available, there were about 28,000 tenancies in the Ludhiana district in 1953–54, and they were 40 per cent of the cultivating families (1961 Census) and cultivated 27 per cent of the total cultivated area. In 1965, the number of pure tenants was small and they were changed frequently for fear of claiming tenancy rights. In most of the cases, land had been resumed by owners for self-cultivation. NSS data show that area leased in as percentage of the total cultivated area in Punjab (including Haryana) declined from 35.39 per cent in 1960–61 to 28.01 per cent in 1970–71. But the decline in the number of landless tenants was much larger. They constituted 27 per cent of the tenants (pure tenants and owner-cum-tenants) in 1960–61, but were reduced to 13.01 per cent in 1970–71 (Bardhan 1976).

Provisions regarding the fixation of rent are not registered at all. A number of reports showed that a conventional one-half of the produce was paid by tenants to the landowners. Cases had been reported where rent exceeded even the conventional one-half of the share of produce (Gill 1978; Ladejinsky 1966, 1969, 1977).

With the implementation of the ceiling at 30 standard acres (for displaced landowners 40 acres in PEPSU and 50 acres in Punjab), about 391,837 standard acres and 106 ordinary acres were declared as surplus area. Out of this 61,177 standard acres were exempted and 264,844 standard acres were available for disposal. Up to 1964, 122,862 standard acres were utilised for resettlement of 63,520 tenants, but they had taken physical possession on 65,466 acres. At the time of the passing of the Punjab Land Reforms Act 1972, it was officially given that 5 lakh acres of land would be found surplus under the revised ceiling level. But up to June 1976, 14,832 returns had been scrutinised and 1,957 hectares had been declared surplus, and physical possession on only 394 hectares had been given. The government was expecting that a total of nearly 8,000 acres of land would be found surplus. The dismal performance of the state in this process was due to the intervention of the courts, procedural difficulties, pressure by the landlords' lobby and unwillingness of the government to risk losing political support from the influential sections (*EPW* [Commentary] 1976: 1027). On implementation of the ceiling and disposal of surplus land, the best commentary is found in the findings of the Harchand Singh Committee Report (Government of Punjab 1973). In July 1972, the governor of Punjab, with the approval of the Punjab government, appointed a committee headed by Harchand Singh to probe the setting up of sizeable agricultural farms on evacuee land by officers, their relatives and other influential public men. The surplus of evacuee land of various kinds after rehabilitation of refugees from Pakistan was inherited by Government of India which it transferred to the government of Punjab in 1960–61 at prices considerably below their market value. It was expected that the Punjab government would distribute 374,000 acres among the landless. This land was being cultivated by *abadkars*, who had brought under cultivation the wasteland in the riverbeds. The government adopted the policy of open auction to dispose of this land. Influential persons through restricted auctions and illegal deals acquired a major part of this land, causing eviction of the poor abadkars. The committee after investigation found many cases of illegal deals by influential persons, including by the agriculture minister, development minister, parliamentary secretary, assembly speaker, Congress members of Parliament (MPs), members and founder members of the Punjab state assembly, a former Akali Dal minister and also a prominent leader of CPI-M, education secretary, some senior police officials, and several provincial civil service officers. These influential persons had acquired land in the names of relatives, obliging tenants or landless Harijans. The Harchand Singh Committee observed:

> These persons, men with means as they are, had an edge over the poor tillers, who could not mobilise requisite resources to compete with them. Even otherwise, they had the goodwill and patronage of the auctioneering officers on their side. As a result, the poor and needy persons, depending upon agriculture alone, had been deprived of the opportunity of purchasing these lands and such actual landless tillers of land as were occupying the same, of course, were unauthorisedly uprooted. This was a tragic outcome of the policy of open auctions. It frustrated the cherished ideology of land for landless tillers. (Government of Punjab 1973: 71)

The most interesting part of these findings was the fact that the very elite of Punjab society, individuals in commanding political positions, lawmakers, upholders of law, or moulders of public opinion, reversed the process of land reforms. These influential persons were exonerated by the state government after the resignation of ministers and the speaker of the legislative assembly, and no follow-up action was taken.

There were two positive results of the land reforms legislation. First was the elimination of the intermediaries between the state and the cultivators. The occupancy tenants acquired ownership rights over their land. Second, the consolidation of holdings in the state was speedily achieved.

III

The decade of 1970s has brought remarkable changes in the land relations in Punjab. Pure-tenant holdings are almost completely eliminated. They constituted 13.01 per cent of total holdings in 1970–71, but were reduced to 1.56 per cent in 1980–81. The area cultivated by pure tenants declined from 7.4 per cent in 1970–71 to 0.8 per cent in 1980–81.

Punjab agriculture continues to be dominated by owner-cultivators. There is rise in the proportion of such holdings, from 80.81 per cent in 1970–71 to 82.03 per cent in 1980–81, but there is decline in the area operated on, from 82.41 per cent to 78.77 per cent. There is a 97.5 per cent increase in the owner-cum-tenant holdings during the same period. It is this category which accounted for the major part of the area under tenancy in 1980–81. Table 6.6 shows the percentage distribution in the number of holdings and area under operation of different types of holdings of various size groups. Data reveal that in 1970–71, the proportion of number and area of wholly owned holdings increased, and proportion of the number and area of wholly or partially rented holdings declined with rise in the size group of holdings.

This was reversed in 1980–81. The proportion of the number and area of wholly owned holdings declined and proportion in the number and area of wholly or partially rented holdings increased with a rise in the size group. The decline in the proportion of the number and area of wholly or partially rented holdings was concentrated sharply in the category of marginal and small holdings in 1980–81 over 1970–71.

Table 6.6: Percentage Distribution of Land Tenure in Punjab, 1970–71 and 1980–81

Size Group	*1970–71*				*1980–81*			
	No. of Holdings		*Area of Holdings*		*No. of Holdings*		*Area of Holdings*	
	Wholly Owned	*Wholly or Partly Rented*	*Wholly Owned*	*Wholly or Partly Rented*	*Wholly Owned*	*Wholly or Partly Rented*	*Wholly Owned*	*Wholly or Partly Rented*
0–1 (marginal)	79.84	20.16	79.42	20.58	92.20	7.80	92.08	7.92
1–2 (small)	79.84	20.16	79.81	20.19	83.87	16.13	83.02	16.98
2–4 (medium)	80.61	19.39	80.81	19.19	79.66	20.34	79.30	20.70
4–10 (large)	83.13	16.87	83.33	16.67	76.50	23.50	75.94	24.06
>10 (extra large)	84.26	15.74	83.80	16.20	78.60	21.40	79.86	20.14
Total	80.81	19.19	82.41	87.59	82.03	7.97	78.77	21.23

Source: Agricultural Census, 1970–71 and 1980–81.

In categories of medium, large and extra-large, there is a rise in the proportion of holdings as well as the area operated on. Marginal holdings to the tune of 20.16 per cent were wholly or partially rented, and they operated on 20.58 per cent of the area under the total marginal holdings in 1970–71. This declined to 7.80 per cent and 7.92 per cent, respectively, in 1980–81. Similarly, the proportion of holdings and proportion of area of small-holdings, respectively, declined from 20.16 per cent and 20.19 per cent in 1970–71 to 16.13 per cent and 16.98 per cent in 1980–81. There is marginal (around 1 per cent) improvement in the number and area of holdings in the medium size-group. But in case of large and extra-large groups the increase is quite high. In case of large holdings, the proportion of number and area increased, respectively, from 16.87 per cent and 16.67 per cent in 1970–71 to 23.50 per cent and 24.06 per cent in 1980–81, and in case of the extra-large group, from 15.74 per cent and 16.20 per cent, respectively, in 1970–71 to 21.40 per cent and 20.14 per cent in 1980–81. This indicates that the proportion of holdings leasing in land and the land held on lease by large and extra-large holdings is rising. This shows that tenancy is shifting from small to large operators. In fact, land is shifting from the small-holders to large-holders—a capitalist development tendency of concentration of productive resources in the hands of a few producers of large size. This is revealed by Table 6.7. There is a decline of pure-tenant holdings by 91.0 per cent during 1970–71 to 1980–81. The decline is almost even over different size-classes. In case of owner-cum-tenant holdings, there is a rise in the number by 97.5 per cent, which is fairly uneven among different size-groups.

The largest rise is experienced by medium holdings followed by large, small and extra-large and marginal holdings. Marginal holdings rose by 17.6 per cent, whereas medium holdings by 116.8 per cent and large holdings by 112.1 per cent; the small holdings rose by 90.9 per cent; extra large by 83.9 per cent. This is further confirmed by the change in the number of wholly owned holdings, which experienced a net decline by 24.7 per cent during 1970–71 to 1980–81. This is mainly experienced by marginal and small holdings which, respectively, declined by 55.8 per cent and

Table 6.7: Percentage Variation in the Number of Land Tenure in Punjab, 1980–81 over 1970–71

Size Group	*No. of Wholly Owned Holdings*		*Percentage Variation*	*No. of Owner-cum-tenant Holdings*		*Percentage Variation*	*No. of Pure-tenant Holdings*		*Percentage Variation*
	1970–71	*1980–81*		*1970–71*	*1980–81*		*1970–71*	*1980–81*	
Marginal	413,204	182,608	–55.8	8,557	10,064	17.6	95,807	5,388	–94.4
Small	207,616	167,211	–19.5	14,488	27,668	90.9	37,949	4,487	–88.2
Medium	226,585	228,965	1.0	24,907	54,013	116.8	29,611	4,445	–84.9
Large	205,948	199,835	–2.9	28,179	59,783	112.1	13,628	1,583	–88.4
Extra large	58,038	58,124	0.2	8,500	15,638	83.9	2,345	178	–92.4
Total	1,111,421	836,743	–24.7	84,631	167,166	97.5	179,340	16,081	–91.0

Source: Agricultural Census, 1970–71 and 1980–81.

19.5 per cent. The medium and extra-large holdings increased, respectively, by 1 per cent and 0.2 per cent, and large holdings declined by 2.9 per cent. This indicates that the relative position of extra-large, large and medium farmers in terms of number has improved over marginal and small holdings. This is further confirmed by changes in the land operated by different class sizes of farmers. Table 6.8 shows that there is decline in the land operated by wholly owned holdings to the extent of 6.3 per cent during this period, whereas the category of extra-large is the only one which gained land by 1.5 percent; marginal holdings experienced decline by 39.1 per cent, small holdings by 12.6 per cent, medium holdings by 2.4 per cent, and large holdings by 5.8 per cent. Owner-cum-tenant holdings experienced a considerable gain in the land operated by them. The gain in area to all such holdings was to the extent of 95.8 per cent. The gain is largest to large holdings, which experienced a rise in the land operated by 111.7 per cent, followed by medium holdings with 110.5 per cent, small holdings by 92.6 per cent and extra-large holdings by 70.8 per cent. Marginal holdings gained 17 per cent, that is, the minimum among all the categories of holdings. The pure-tenant holdings, like their number, experienced a decline in the area operated on by 89 per cent. The loss of area by different size-class followed the same pattern as that of the loss in the number of holdings. Though there was not much difference among different size-groups, the loss was more with marginal holdings and extra-large holdings compared to small, medium and large holdings. As a consequence of these changes, the total number of pure tenants and owner-cum-tenant holdings declined from 263,971 in 1970–71 to 183,247 in 1980–81, but the area operated by them increased from 699,397 hectares to 826,387 hectares. The average size of such holdings was 2.46 hectares, which was lower than 2.89 hectares; the overall average size of landholdings in the state in 1970–71 increased to 4.51 hectares in 1980–81 which became higher than 3.79 hectares, the overall average size of landholdings in the state.

The available evidence suggests a growing tendency towards capitalist agriculture in the state. There is overall decline in the total number of holdings in the state by 25.3 per cent during 1970–71 and 1980–81. There is almost negligible decline in the number of individual holdings, but there is a big decline in the number of joint holdings from 378,933 to 36,222, a decline by 90.5 per cent. This decline with some variation is experienced by all size-classes of holdings. The overall decline in the total number of holdings of all types is not evenly experienced. Whereas the marginal holdings declined by 61.9 per cent and small holdings by 23.3 per cent, the medium holdings gained by 2.3 per cent, large holdings by 8.6 per cent and extra-large by 7.3 per cent. The same pattern in change is observed in case of individual holdings as well as the area operated on. There is little evidence to suggest the large-scale sale of land by small and marginal farmers (Shergill 1986).[2]

Evidence available from various studies indicates that all class sizes of farmers participate in the land market over purchase and sale of land in the state. Small farmers buy and sell land as other classes of farmers do. In the process, land transfer takes place but there is a marginal inter-class transfer of land. A survey of the Ghanour block of the Patiala district revealed land transfer between 1973 and 1978 as given in Table 6.9.

TABLE 6.8: Percentage Variation in the Area of Land Tenure in Punjab, 1980–81 over 1970–71

Size Group	*Wholly Owned Holdings*		*Percentage Variation*	*Owner-cum-tenant Holdings*		*Percentage Variation*	*Pure-tenant Holdings*		*Percentage Variation*
	1970–71	*1980–81*		*1970–71*	*1980–81*		*1970–71*	*1980–81*	
Marginal	178,893	108,863	–39.1	5,302	6,204	17.0	41,059	3,163	–92.3
Small	266,976	233,204	–12.6	21,404	41,219	92.6	53,749	6,477	–87.9
Medium	642,576	627,171	–2.4	72,216	151,986	11.5	80,415	11,698	–85.4
Large	1,264,858	1,189,041	–5.8	173,848	368,043	111.7	78,517	8,592	–89.0
Extra Large	894,489	907,796	1.5	132,747	226,449	70.0	40,136	8,286	–94.3
Total	3,264,612	3,066,075	–6.3	405,519	791,174	95.8	293,878	32,216	–88.0

Source: Agricultural Census, 1970–71 and 1980–81.

Table 6.9: Sale and Purchase of Land in Ghanour (acres), 1973–78

Ownership Holdings	*Sale*	*Purchase*	*Net Increase*
Small up to 5	62 (12.86)	53 (11.00)	–9
Medium 5 to 15	174 (36.10)	171 (35.47)	–3
Large above 15	246 (51.04)	258 (53.35)	+12
Total	482 (100)	482 (100)	

Note: Figures in parentheses are in percentage.
Source: Singh (1982: 67–68).

Table 6.9 indicates that out of the total 482 acres of land sold during the five-year period, only 12 acres have experienced inter-class transfers. This transfer is from both the categories, that is, small and medium farmers to large farmers, and account for 2.49 per cent of the total land sold and purchased. The remaining 97.51 per cent of the land sold/purchased have remained within their respective classes. This is confirmed by our own study of the three villages each from Patiala and the Gurdaspur districts (Gill 1986).

The evidence suggests that the shift of land from small and marginal farmers to medium and large farmers is on account of leasing out of land. A study on tenancy relations revealed that in the three sampled villages of the Ludhiana district and two villages in the Faridkot districts in 1979–80, a sizeable percentage of tenants were big cultivators with a substantial land area of their own, fully endowed with modern production assets such as tractors, tubewells, etc., entrepreneurial skills and high commercial status (Singh 1985: Chapter 6, quoted in Chadha 1986: 227). This is further confirmed by another study of a Ludhiana village. It reveals that most of the leasing-out is done by small owners and leasing-in by the big operators (Grewal and Rangi 1981).

Implications for Land Reforms

The changes in land relations are the outcome of changes in modes of production of Punjab agriculture. They correspond to the capitalist mode of production. The new pattern of tenancy is capitalist in nature. This pattern of land relations has serious implications for land reforms devised to change pre-capitalist relations of production. Land reforms in India as devised in the 1950s and extended in the later period were supposed to change obsolete land relations which were obstructing the expansion of forces of production on capitalist lines. Once land relations are in tune with the new mode of production, further implementation of these reforms loses their social significance. This is evident from the emerging situation of Punjab. The implementation of the Tenancy Act providing security of tenure will lead to transfer of land from the small owners to large owners, who are leasing in land from the former to have big-sized holdings for cultivation on capitalist lines.

Originally this act was meant for the protection of small tenants cultivating land of big landlords. Now its operation will do the opposite. Second, implementation of ceiling laws and acquisition of surplus land from the big owners, and its distribution among the landless to make them small cultivators will lose purpose. This is because within the dynamics of Punjab agriculture, land is shifting towards large cultivators through a new pattern of tenancy. Whereas the operation of tenancy laws can go against the poor and small owners of land, the operation of the ceiling act as such and surplus distribution of land to the landless no longer remain capable of reducing inequality in land distribution. The situation requires necessary modifications in these acts to protect the weaker farmers.

First, operation of the Tenancy Act for the protection of tenants against eviction must be restricted to small cultivators; its use must not be allowed for large cultivators. Second, for the usefulness of ceiling laws and land redistribution among the poor, there is a need to simultaneously take steps to check the tendency of small cultivators going out of operation. Here there can be two lines of thinking: (a) small producers should be protected through various measures of the government by providing assistance and facilities serving exclusively the needs of such farmers. The experience of the past shows that in spite of such measures during the decade of 1970s, a large proportion of marginal and small farmers have gone out of cultivation. A large number of programmes meant for these farmers are, in fact, helping the medium and large farmers. (b) In absence of strong organisations of such farmers, these programmes cannot protect them. The situation immediately requires some sort of cooperative effort for the protection of poor/small cultivators. The fact that there is a large decline in joint holdings indicates that with the growth of capitalism in agriculture, the capitalist spirit of individualism and competition has been strengthened, and the community cooperative spirit has weakened. In this situation, it is difficult to visualise the success of cooperative farming by small cultivators. The widespread corruption in cooperative departments (like other areas of public life) further adds to the difficulties. The only way to check liquidation of poor/small cultivators is to introduce land reforms on Soviet and Chinese patterns (Jacoby 1980).

These days there is a lot of talk at the highest level about the strengthening of institutions of Panchayati Raj. The institution of Gram Sabha/Gram Panchayat can be assigned the historic role of reorganisation of rural life.[3] It can be made the instrument of collectivisation by entrusting ownership of the entire land of the village. It can be made responsible for the further modernisation of agriculture and organisation of non-agricultural activities in the village. In the present context, modern rural industries, particularly those engaged in processing of agricultural products can be started at the village level. This pattern of organisation of rural society has a big potential for modernisation and is capable of resolving the major problems created by the development process. It is some form of collectivisation that can protect poor cultivators from the broad dynamism of capitalist operations in agriculture. It is in this sense that land reforms are relevant and more urgently required in the state.

Notes

1. Punjab Land Reforms Act 1972, Sections 4, 14 and 27.

2. His arguments of the stabilisation effect of the Green Revolution on small and marginal farmers is valid. Calculations from his Table 1 about the average annual area sold reveal that in the pre-Green Revolution period (1952–53 to 1965–66), it was 150 acres, and in the post-Green Revolution period (1966–67 to 1978–79), it increased to 206.9 acres, leading to increased land sales due to modernisation in the sample villages of the Sangrur district of Punjab.

3. Our attention to this issue has been drawn by Suresh Ramabhai.

References

Bandhopadhyaya, D. 1972. 'Indra Lohar and the Due Process of Law'. *Report of the Task Force on Agrarian Relations*, Planning Commission, Government of India.

Bardhan, Pranab. 1976. 'Variations in Extent and Forms of Agricultural Tenancy—I: An Analysis of Indian Data across Regions and Over Time'. *Economic and Political Weekly* 11(37), 11 September: 1505–12.

Bhalla, R. L. 1923. *An Economic Survey of Bairampur*. Lahore: Government Press.

Chadha, G. K. 1986. *The State and Rural Economic Transformation: The Case of Punjab 1950–85*. New Delhi: Sage Publications.

Darling, M. L. 1925. *Punjab Peasantry in Prosperity and Debt.* London and New York: H. Milford and Oxford University Press.

EPW [Commentary]. 1976. 'Little Headway in Land Reforms'. *Economic and Political Weekly* 11(28), 10–16 July: 1027.

Gill, Sucha Singh. 1978. 'Agrarian Transformation in a Punjab Village'. *Mainstream*, 4 March.

———. 1986. 'Agrarian Structure of Punjab'. In *Agrarian Structure and Peasant Revolt in India*, ed. Amit K. Gupta. New Delhi: Criterion Publishers.

Government of Punjab. 1960. *Resurvey of Village Gijhi, District Rohtak*. Punjab: Board of Economic Inquiry.

———. 1963. *Resurvey of Village Suner, District Ferozepur*. Punjab: Board of Economic Inquiry.

———. 1973. 'Harchand Singh Committee Report'. Punjab.

Government of PEPSU. 1953. 'Land Reforms in PEPSU'. *Indian Journal of Agricultural Economics* 8(1), March.

Grewal, S. S., and P. S. Rangi. 1981. 'An Analysis of Agrarian Structure in Punjab'. *Indian Journal of Agricultural Economics* 36(4), October–December: 173–83.

Jacoby, Erich H. 1980. 'Has Land Reform Become Obsolete'. In *Peasants in History: Essays in Honour of Daniel Thorner*, eds E. J. Hobsbawm, Ignacy Sachs, Witold Kula and Ashok Mitra. New Delhi: Oxford University Press.

Ladejinsky, Wolf. 1966. *A Study of Tenurial Conditions in Package Districts*. New Delhi: Planning Commission of India.

———. 1969. 'Green Revolution in Punjab: A Field Trip'. *Economic and Political Weekly* 4(26), 28 June: A73–83.

———. 1977. 'Field Observations in the Punjab'. In *Selected Papers of Wolf Ladejinsky*, ed. L. J. Walinsky. New Delhi: Oxford University Press.

Planning Commission. 1956. *Report of the Committee on Tenancy Reforms*. Government of India.

Shergill, H. S. 1986. 'Land Sales and Land Prices in Punjab: 1952–53 to 1978–79'. *Economic and Political Weekly* 21(38–39), 20–27 September: A125–28.

Singh, Baldev. 1982. *Land Market: Theory and Practice in India*. New Delhi: Agricole Publishing.

Singh, Iqbal. 1985. 'Changing Tenancy Structure in a Developing Agricultural Region: A Case Study of Punjab'. Unpublished PhD dissertation, Centre for Study of Regional Development, Jawaharlal Nehru University, New Delhi.

Talib, B. D. 1979. *Agrarian Tensions and Peasant Movements in Punjab*. Mimeo, Centre for Study of Regional Development, Jawaharlal Nehru University, New Delhi.

7

Ownership Holdings of Land in Rural India

*Putting the Record Straight**

Vikas Rawal

Land is the fundamental means of production in an agrarian society without which no agricultural production can take place. An understanding of the pattern of ownership and operational holdings of land is, therefore, of central importance to an understanding of the agrarian class structure. Data on landholdings in India, in particular, on ownership holdings of land have been fraught with problems. Data from land and livestock surveys conducted decennially by the National Sample Survey Organisation (NSSO) are the most important source of information on distribution of landholdings in India. As part of these surveys, detailed data are collected on ownership and operational holdings, tenancy, nature of land use, status of irrigation and cropping pattern.

...

Unit-level data from the land and livestock surveys have been released for the surveys conducted as part of the 48th Round (for the reference year 1992) and 59th Round (for the reference year 2003–04). A detailed study of documents provided with these data show that published estimates of ownership holdings from these surveys pertain to all types of land owned by the households, including homestead land, and not merely to productive/agricultural land. In contrast, operational holdings refer to only agricultural land. This difference in the way ownership and operational holdings are defined is the main cause of discrepancy in the extent of landlessness by the two definitions. The proportion of households that do not own any land refers to households that do not even have homestead land of their own. In contrast, the proportion of households that do not operate any land refers to households that do not cultivate any agricultural land.

For any meaningful contribution to an understanding of the agrarian class structure, it is important to analyse the pattern of ownership of land that can be

* Originally published in *Economic and Political Weekly* 43(10), 8 March 2008: 43–47.

used in the process of production and identify landless households as households that do not own productive land.

HOMESTEAD LAND

It is, of course, true that ownership of homestead land has important implications for economic wellbeing and the social conditions of rural households, in particular, for socially disadvantaged communities. It is, therefore, important to look at the lack of ownership of homestead land separately. The problem with published reports from the NSSO has been that they have provided estimates that refer to both homestead and other lands without explicitly stating so.

As the unit-level data are available from both the 48th and 59th Rounds of the land and livestock surveys, it is possible to separate ownership of homestead and other land, and analyse the pattern of their distribution separately. Such an analysis from the 48th and 59th Rounds of the land and livestock surveys, however, has some limitations.

First, in both the 48th and 59th Round surveys, ownership holding was divided between homestead land and land other than homestead. There were, however, differences in the way the two types of land were divided and the kind of information that was collected on the two types of land.

In the 48th Round survey, only a limited amount of information was collected on productive activities carried out on homestead land. The respondents were only asked whether or not different types of productive activities including cultivation were undertaken on the homestead. Information was not collected on the extent of cultivation on homestead land. In fact, the instruction manual for the survey clearly indicated that the purpose of asking information was to cover marginal crop production in kitchen gardens. The column on whether the household produced crops on the homesteads was, by and large, used for recording marginal maintenance of kitchen gardens. In particular, the instruction manuals did not give clear instructions on how to handle cases where a household resided on a plot on which substantial crop production took place on a distinct segment. Let us consider, for example, the case of a household that owned a 10-acre plot of agricultural land. It constructed a house on part of this land and started residing there. In such a case, was all the 10 acres counted as homestead land, or only a part of it counted as homestead and the rest as agricultural? Now, let us consider a second example of a household which maintained a kitchen garden on a small part of its homestead and grew some vegetables for self-consumption on it. It is not clear how was such a case differentiated from the first example.

In the 59th Round survey, the format for collection of data on ownership holdings was changed drastically. In the schedule for the 59th Round, plot by plot data were collected for all the land owned by the household and not merely for land other than homestead. Second, the schedule for the 59th Round had provision for separately recording details of land which was a distinct part of the homestead but on which crop production took place. On the other hand, in the 59th Round schedule, respondents were not asked about whether crop production of a marginal nature was undertaken on the homestead or whether the respondents maintained a kitchen garden. The instructions did not specify explicitly how to deal with cases where the crop production happened to a small extent on an area that was not distinct from the residential part of the household.

In other words, while the 48th Round survey did not have a precisely specified method of recording information on crop production when it happened on a substantial scale on a distinct part of the same plot that was used for residence, the 59th Round survey seems to have missed out on maintenance of kitchen gardens and marginal cultivation on the homesteads.

Three Tendencies

This is important in view of three different types of tendencies that were reported from different states. First, marginal crop production on homesteads was an important source of food for the poor in many states. Second, in some states, for example in Haryana, Punjab and parts of Rajasthan, it was reported that many landowning households shifted their residence to their agricultural lands. In such cases, a small part of the agricultural land was used for residence, while crop production took place on a substantial and distinct part of the same plot. Third, in Kerala, a substantial proportion of households, including poor and households that were provided homesteads as part of land reforms, were known to cultivate commercial crops on parts of their homesteads.

All of this means that what was recorded as cultivation on homesteads was not strictly comparable between the two surveys. By the same logic, ownership of land other than homesteads was also not strictly comparable between the two surveys. As a result, it is not possible to accurately compare changes in proportion of landless households and distribution of ownership of land between 1992 and 2003–04. It may also be mentioned that the different treatment of cultivation on homestead land affects the data on operational holdings as well and, therefore, it is not possible to compare distribution of operational holdings of land between the two years. The problems of comparability of data on ownership and operational holdings of households are particularly serious in states where cultivation on a part of the homestead is widespread.

Another serious problem with the 59th Round survey was that, in that survey, information on land use and access to irrigation was not collected for ownership holdings of the households, but only for land that was operated by the household. Also, categories of land use were mixed with information on crops that were grown. For owned land, distinction was made only between homestead and all other land. Land other than homestead was not further classified into agricultural land and land under other categories of use. It is, therefore, not possible to isolate ownership of productive, agricultural, or irrigated and unirrigated lands from the 59th Round survey.

Poor Design of the 59th Round

The survey schedule for the 59th Round of the land and livestock survey conducted by NSSO was very poorly designed. This is unusual for NSSO, an organisation that is unparalleled anywhere in the less-developed world in terms of its enormous in-house expertise in organising and conducting socioeconomic surveys. The design of the 59th Round survey schedule was such that information on important aspects of landholdings was not captured. Land and livestock surveys have missed some important aspects of land relations in the earlier rounds as well. For example, these surveys do not collect information on mortgage, sale and purchase of land. The details on terms of tenancy are also inadequate. By dropping information on land use and status of irrigation on ownership holdings, the NSSO further narrowed the scope of the land and livestock survey in the 59th Round. Moreover, the data collected in the 59th Round were such that the estimates based on these are not comparable with the previous rounds.

The NSSO needs to expand the scope of these surveys and use them to collect much more detailed data on land relations and livestock. It would also be appropriate to collect these data quinquennially rather than decennially.

In this chapter, I have used unit-level data from the 59th and 48th Round surveys to provide new estimates of landlessness and inequality in ownership of land other than homestead. Given the limitation that information on land use was not available, I have tried to create variables that represent ownership of productive land as closely as possible.

Table 7.1 shows the extent of landlessness across different states by three different measures of landlessness. Column (2) of the table gives the official estimates of proportion of households that do not own any land, either homestead or otherwise. Column (3) of the table gives the proportion of households that do not have any land other than homestead (some of these may not have any homestead also). Column (4) gives the proportion of households that do not have any land other than homestead and do not cultivate any part of homestead that they may own.

It may be noted that the estimates of landlessness presented in columns (3) and (4) of the table are considerably higher than the official estimates of landlessness [column (2)]. The estimates show that in 2003–04, about 41.6 per cent of households in rural India did not own any land other than homestead (of these, about 10 per cent did not own even homestead land). About 31.1 per cent of households did not own any land other than homestead and did not do any cultivation on their homestead [column (4)].

Inter-state Variations

Table 7.1 also shows that the extent of landlessness, by whatever measure is used, varies considerably across different regions and states. The proportion of households that do not own any land other than homestead [column (3)] is highest (between 45 and 65 per cent) in agriculturally advanced states that have not had any land reforms (Punjab, Haryana, Tamil Nadu and Andhra Pradesh). All of these states also have

TABLE 7.1: Proportion of Households that Do Not Own Land (%), 2003–04

State	*Official Estimates (Households That Do Not Own Any Land Including Homestead)*	*Households That Do Not Own Any Land Other Than Homestead*	*Households That Neither Own Any Land Other Than Homestead Nor Cultivate on Owned Homestead Land*
(1)	*(2)*	*(3)*	*(4)*
Jammu and Kashmir	3.29	10.97	7.29
Himachal Pradesh	15.00	22.68	21.87
Punjab	4.57	56.89	29.51
Uttarakhand	10.64	26.40	21.15
Haryana	9.21	49.49	25.96
Uttar Pradesh	3.82	26.20	16.31
Rajasthan	5.65	19.95	12.73
Chhattisgarh	12.09	27.31	20.80
Madhya Pradesh	12.05	31.81	22.76
Gujarat	13.60	44.11	35.37
Maharashtra	17.66	44.78	38.27
Andhra Pradesh	14.33	53.19	48.75
Karnataka	14.09	40.47	30.76
Kerala	4.80	68.36	36.74
Tamil Nadu	16.55	64.52	55.43
Bihar	7.60	38.80	31.01
West Bengal	6.15	46.52	34.69
Jharkhand	4.80	39.25	18.43
Orissa	9.56	38.48	31.07
Sikkim	30.67	44.40	37.96
Arunachal Pradesh	21.59	23.50	22.59
Nagaland	8.02	15.45	10.85
Manipur	2.68	30.30	13.53
Mizoram	2.34	14.10	6.67
Tripura	8.69	59.52	33.22
Meghalaya	6.70	29.01	19.93
Assam	8.05	40.30	23.00
India	10.04	41.63	31.12

Source: Land and Livestock Survey, NSS 59th Round, 2003–04.

a substantial proportion of land in the hands of large landowners. Among these, Punjab and Haryana have a substantial proportion of households that live on their agricultural land. In these states, the proportion of landless goes down substantially when the ownership of productive land attached to homesteads is taken into account [column (4)]. On the other hand, in Tamil Nadu and Andhra Pradesh, the proportion of landless households remains very high irrespective of what measure is used. The latter is noteworthy for an extremely high degree of landlessness.

Kerala, another state where a large proportion of households do not have land other than homestead, is different in some important respects. First, about half of the households which do not have any land other than homestead cultivate a distinct part of their homestead land. Table 7.1 shows that proportion of households that do not have homestead is among the lowest in Kerala. It may be noted that a large number of households in Kerala were provided with homestead lands as part of land reforms. Research has shown that many of these households use homesteads for cultivation of commercial crops (Ramakumar 2006). Second, in Kerala, a state with very high population density, a very small proportion of land is under large landholdings.

In the eastern states, where the population density tends to be high, the proportion of landless ranges between 35 and 45 per cent. In these states, the proportion of area under large landholdings is small.

Hill states like Himachal Pradesh and Uttaranchal, most northeastern states, and Rajasthan have a relatively lower level of landlessness (between 20 and 35 per cent).

Extreme Inequality in Ownership

The distribution of ownership holding of land in India is extremely unequal. Figure 7.1 shows the Lorenz curves of ownership holdings of land other than homestead land for 2003.[1] In 2003, the Gini coefficient of ownership holdings of land (land other than homesteads) in India was about 0.76. In comparison, the official estimate of the Gini coefficient, based on ownership of all types of land, was 0.73. State-level estimates of Gini coefficient of ownership of land are provided in Table 7.2. These estimates show that the inequality in ownership holdings varies considerably across different states. Inequality in ownership of land was the highest in Tamil Nadu, Punjab, Haryana and Andhra Pradesh, the states that were earlier noted for the highest levels of landlessness. The Gini coefficient was higher than 0.8 in each of these states.

Table 7.2 also shows, for each state, the proportion of households in different size-classes of ownership holdings and the proportion of area owned by households in each size-class. Table 7.2 shows that in many states, a substantial share of land continues to be in the hands of large landowners (having more than, say, 5 hectares of land). States that are particularly noteworthy in this context are Punjab, Haryana, Gujarat, Maharashtra, Karnataka and Andhra Pradesh. Clearly, a substantial potential for land redistribution exists in these states. It may be noted that large landholding sizes in Rajasthan and in parts of some other states in central and western India are also associated with poor quality of land. In contrast, in Kerala, West Bengal and Tripura, three states where substantial land reforms have been implemented, a very small amount of land is now under large holdings. In general, the proportion of area under large landholdings tends to be relatively small in most states in eastern and northeastern India.

FIGURE 7.1: Lorenz Curves of Household Ownership Holdings of Land, 2003

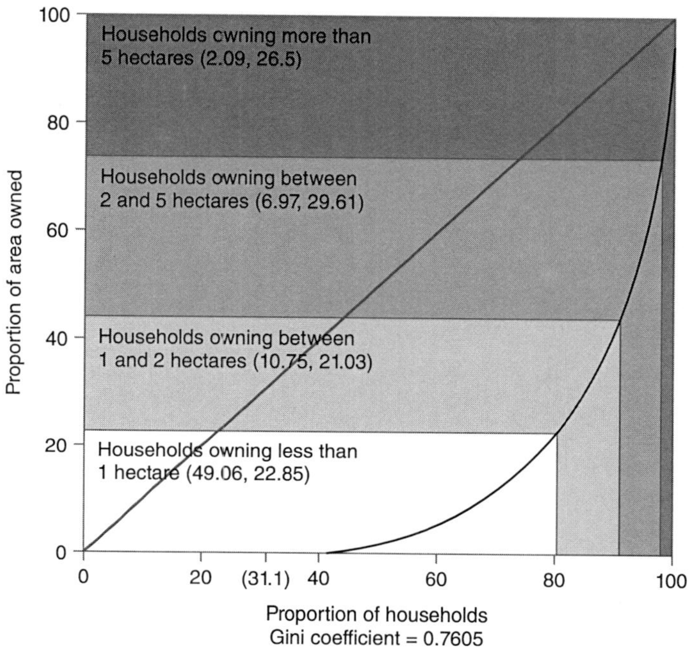

Notes: (1) The Lorenz curve has been drawn for household ownership holdings, which include all land other than the homestead land and the cultivated part of the homestead land.

(2) The shaded areas on the graph represent the proportion of households in a size-class of ownership holdings and proportion of area owned by them. The labels for shaded areas include these proportions in the parentheses.

(3) The exact point where the Lorenz curve meets the *x*-axis (31.1 per cent), representing the proportion of landless households, is marked on the *x*-axis.

Source: Based on the author's primary fieldwork.

To further explore the potential of redistribution, I estimated the extent of surplus land in different states by assuming a uniform ceiling of 20 acres. It must be remembered that official surveys are likely to underestimate the extent of large holdings and, therefore, the extent of ceiling surplus land. At the same time, limitations of using a uniform ceiling limit across states are obvious. Nevertheless, the exercise gives us ballpark estimates that are interesting and useful. Estimates based on the 59th Round land and livestock survey show that if we assume a uniform ceiling of 20 acres, there is about 15 million acres of ceiling surplus land in India. To put this in perspective, this is more than three times the total amount of land that has ever been redistributed under land reforms programmes in all states. Among the states that have a substantial amount of land above the 20 acre ceiling, particularly noteworthy are Rajasthan (5.9 million acres), Madhya Pradesh (1.8 million acres), Andhra Pradesh (1.8 million acres), Maharashtra (1.7 million acres), Karnataka (890,000 acres), Gujarat (750,000 acres), Haryana (556,000 acres) and Uttar Pradesh (471,000 acres). The availability of surplus land over the 20-acre ceiling is limited in West Bengal, Kerala and Tripura, three states which have already implemented land reforms in a substantial measure, and in all the northeastern states.

TABLE 7.2: Distribution of Ownership Holdings of Land in States (%), 2003–04

State	*Proportion of Households*								*Proportion of Area Owned*								*Gini Coefficient*
	Landless	*Less than 0.4 Hectares*	*0.4–1 Hectares*	*1–2 Hectares*	*2–3 Hectares*	*3–5 Hectares*	*5–10 Hectares*	*>10 Hectares*	*Landless*	*Less than 0.4 Hectares*	*0.4–1 Hectares*	*1–2 Hectares*	*2–3 Hectares*	*3–5 Hectares*	*5–10 Hectares*	*>10 Hectares*	
Jammu and Kashmir	7.29	40.63	29.95	14.65	4.67	1.67	0.94	0.20	0.00	9.15	20.77	21.55	13.14	7.31	6.12	21.96	0.6533
Himachal Pradesh	21.87	37.68	24.31	11.45	2.77	1.46	0.35	0.10	0.00	14.20	28.95	28.37	12.43	9.36	4.65	2.04	0.6274
Punjab	29.51	38.66	8.33	9.54	5.79	4.79	2.43	0.95	0.00	1.50	6.53	15.82	16.98	23.05	20.48	15.63	0.8225
Haryana	25.96	37.60	13.52	9.85	5.59	4.26	2.80	0.43	0.00	2.19	10.07	15.94	15.97	19.9	23.72	12.21	0.8059
Uttarakhand	21.15	48.87	22.98	5.80	0.88	0.00	0.32	0.00	0.00	26.73	40.79	21.19	6.12	0	5.17	0	0.5963
Uttar Pradesh	16.31	41.98	22.86	12.42	3.43	2.10	0.81	0.09	0.00	10.22	23.91	27.95	13.55	13.27	8.66	2.44	0.6691
Rajasthan	12.73	19.42	23.57	16.54	8.94	7.98	6.80	4.02	0.00	1.42	7.77	11.37	10.47	14.91	21.55	32.50	0.6819
Chhattisgarh	20.80	17.57	27.20	17.92	8.80	5.00	2.20	0.51	0.00	2.48	16.66	23.62	18.69	18.61	13.10	6.84	0.6283
Madhya Pradesh	22.76	16.91	22.17	17.80	7.02	8.05	4.18	1.11	0.00	0.99	10.47	18.85	12.47	23.24	21.59	12.38	0.6839
Gujarat	35.37	21.00	16.97	11.66	5.18	4.46	4.33	1.02	0.00	2.22	11.04	15.64	12.18	17.12	29.47	12.34	0.7665
Maharashtra	38.27	14.08	16.69	13.13	8.52	6.06	2.46	0.79	0.00	1.36	10.73	17.69	19.56	22.77	16.17	11.73	0.7342
Karnataka	30.76	17.97	22.49	13.90	6.69	5.12	2.34	0.72	0.00	1.66	14.41	19.28	16.20	20.95	16.13	11.37	0.7221
Kerala	36.74	49.52	9.30	3.33	0.44	0.58	0.10	0.00	0.00	20.49	27.15	26.27	6.38	14.90	4.81	0.00	0.7781
Tamil Nadu	55.43	21.20	13.65	5.64	2.16	1.30	0.60	0.02	0.00	6.62	25.12	23.53	15.66	15.01	13.44	0.63	0.8401
Andhra Pradesh	48.75	16.55	17.42	9.09	4.06	2.63	1.04	0.47	0.00	3.20	17.92	20.06	14.97	16.88	12.69	14.29	0.8072

(Contd)

Table 7.2 (Contd)

State	Proportion of Households								Proportion of Area Owned								Gini Coefficient
	Landless	Less than 0.4 Hectares	0.4–1 Hectares	1–2 Hectares	2–3 Hectares	3–5 Hectares	5–10 Hectares	>10 Hectares	Landless	Less than 0.4 Hectares	0.4–1 Hectares	1–2 Hectares	2–3 Hectares	3–5 Hectares	5–10 Hectares	>10 Hectares	
Orissa	31.07	32.33	22.96	9.17	2.60	1.26	0.56	0.04	0.00	10.82	30.82	26.79	12.90	9.91	7.54	1.21	0.6986
West Bengal	34.69	42.71	15.81	5.40	0.97	0.33	0.09	0.00	0.00	20.04	37.77	26.95	8.41	4.64	2.20	0.00	0.7361
Bihar	31.01	42.49	16.00	7.00	1.98	1.09	0.29	0.13	0.00	13.36	27.69	25.62	12.51	10.95	5.18	4.70	0.7636
Jharkhand	18.43	41.62	23.99	11.57	2.57	1.24	0.35	0.23	0.00	13.63	28.25	28.49	11.83	8.90	3.99	4.90	0.6431
Sikkim	37.96	22.70	27.64	9.35	1.32	0.60	0.43	0.00	0.00	8.33	41.31	32.25	7.15	5.12	5.82	0.00	0.6814
Assam	23.00	35.84	24.33	13.38	2.60	0.56	0.30	0.00	0.00	10.24	32.55	36.69	12.71	4.30	3.49	0.00	0.6210
Meghalaya	19.93	21.70	31.01	16.05	4.92	4.17	2.19	0.03	0.00	3.29	22.43	26.04	13.52	18.13	16.19	0.40	0.6277
Mizoram	6.67	11.64	43.39	26.08	9.19	2.04	0.53	0.45	0.00	0.36	26.05	32.60	17.70	6.17	3.72	13.39	0.5195
Manipur	13.53	41.52	31.93	10.77	2.00	0.23	0.02	0.00	0.00	12.78	46.17	28.62	9.91	2.31	0.21	0.00	0.5453
Nagaland	10.85	15.21	35.76	30.72	5.16	2.32	0.00	0.00	0.00	3.35	28.63	46.13	12.95	8.95	0.00	0.00	0.4354
Tripura	33.22	47.70	16.01	2.48	0.50	0.09	0.00	0.00	0.00	22.89	50.94	18.18	6.29	1.70	0.00	0.00	0.7136
Arunachal Pradesh	22.59	14.53	16.77	23.80	11.43	9.24	1.63	0.01	0.00	1.19	10.43	28.68	22.66	28.52	8.48	0.05	0.5866
India	31.12	29.82	18.97	10.68	4.22	3.06	1.60	0.52	0.00	5.11	16.89	20.47	13.94	16.59	15.21	11.77	0.7605

Source: Ownership holdings have been defined to include all land other than the homestead land and the cultivated part of the homestead land.

As I mentioned, because of the changes in the format of data collection, data from the 48th Round survey conducted in 1992 and the 59th Round survey conducted in 2003–04 are not strictly comparable. Comparisons become particularly problematic for states where cultivation on homesteads is important. At the all-India level, the comparisons can, at best, be seen as indicative of trends. With this caveat, if we look at the proportion of households that do not own any land other than homestead, we find that for India as a whole, the extent of landlessness went up by as much as 6 percentage points between 1992 and 2003–04. The Gini coefficient of ownership of land other than homestead increased from about 0.73 to about 0.76 over this period.

The official statistics on ownership of land are extremely problematic. Agencies involved in collection of official statistics in India need to attend to this problem. In this article, I have presented estimates of landlessness and inequality in ownership of land that correct, within the limitations posed by methodology of data collection, some problems with the official estimates. These estimates suggest that over 40 per cent households in rural India do not own land. The inequality in ownership of holdings, on a scale of zero to one, is about 0.76. The data show that, on the one hand, about 40 per cent of rural households do not own land, and on the other, a large potential for redistribution of land exists in many states.

NOTE

1. Lorenz curves are a graphical representation of inequality; the farther away a Lorenz curve from the diagonal, or the line of equality, greater is the level of inequality. The proportion of the area between the diagonal and the Lorenz curve to the total area under the Lorenz curve is a measure of inequality called the Gini coefficient. The Gini coefficient varies between 0 (perfect equality) and 1 (extreme inequality).

REFERENCES

Chaddha, G. K., Sucharita Sen and H. R. Sharma. 2004. *Land Resources: State of the Indian Farmer* (Volume 2). New Delhi: Academic Foundation.

Ramakumar, R. 2000. 'Magnitude and Terms of Agricultural Tenancy in India: A Statewise Analysis of Changes in 1980s'. *Indian Journal of Agricultural Economics* 55(3): 337.

———. 2006. 'Public Action, Agrarian Change and the Standard of Living of Agricultural Workers: A Study of a Village in Kerala'. *Journal of Agrarian Change* 6(3), July: 306–45.

Ramachandran, V. K. 1980. 'A Note on the Sources of Official Data on Landholdings in Tamil Nadu'. Data Series No. 1, Madras Institute of Development Studies, Madras.

Sharma, Naresh and Jean Drèze. 1998. 'Tenancy'. In *Economic Development in Palanpur over Five Decades*, eds Peter Lanjouw and Nicholas Stern. New Delhi: Oxford University Press.

Sharma, H. R. 1994. 'Distribution of Landholdings in Rural India, 1953–54 to 1981–82: Implications for Land Reforms'. *Economic and Political Weekly* 29(39), 24 September: A117–28.

———. 2007. 'Land Distribution and Tenancy among Different Social Groups'. *Economic and Political Weekly* 42(41), 13 October: 4183–85.

Section III

The Green Revolution and Market Edifice

8

India's Green Revolution and Beyond

*Visioning Agrarian Futures on Selective Readings of Agrarian Pasts**

Richa Kumar

Policymakers have often drawn up a vision of India's agrarian future through the lens of technological revolutions, whether an evergreen revolution (Press Trust of India 2017) or a second green revolution (Singh 2011). Drawing upon the language of productivity, they have recalled the original Green Revolution of the 1960s that is supposed to have brought forth a bounty of food, thanks to high-yielding seeds of wheat and, eventually, rice. Popular narratives suggest that India was saved from the brink of famine and destitution and that the Green Revolution averted a humanitarian disaster (Rajagopal 2016).

This productivity-centred paradigm consolidated as part of the Green Revolution has continued to be the model for all agrarian futures envisioned in the country (Raina 2015). Unfortunately, this has meant pushing for a strategy that requires extensive control over the environment. Rather than using a wide range of seed varieties across multiple crops that would fit into different agro-ecological niches, the monoculture model of the Green Revolution has promoted re-engineering of the environment to fit the needs of the single chosen seed variety—whether through plant breeding or genetic engineering.[1]

To enable a given seed variety to express its yield potential to the highest possible degree, pests, weeds, nutrients and water have to be controlled accordingly. But this pits farmers in a race against nature. They have to constantly catch up with newly evolving pests and weeds, and deal with the declining fertility of soil, which chemicals alone are unable to replace. Moreover, as the cost of cultivation increases almost every year without commensurate increases in the prices of the produce, the clamour for financial subsidies or debt relief keeps increasing. This puts farmers and the government in impossible double binds.

* Originally published in *Economic and Political Weekly* 54(34), 24 August 2019: 41–48.

Farmers, in particular, are running on a treadmill and are more prone to vulnerabilities: first, in a market where they are unable to obtain remunerative prices (even when the MSP is increased by the state); second, from the state that is finding it increasingly difficult to deliver inputs like fertiliser, electricity and fuel to them on time and at a reasonable price; third, from the scientific research on new seeds and pesticides that is playing catch-up with the ever-evolving pests and genetic vulnerability engendered by single varieties; and finally due to climatic vagaries, which irrigation and modern technology are unable to overcome.

Yet, all these consequences of the Green Revolution model have been brushed aside as collateral damage in the race to increase productivity. Much of the criticism highlighting issues of ecological toxicity, negative health impacts and rural inequality, among others (Bhalla and Chadha 1983; Byres 1983; Gupta 1998; Patel 2012; Shiva 1992) has been dismissed as unfortunate outcomes of a policy that was necessary at that time for saving lives and leading India to the path of self-sufficiency. But why are we still on the bandwagon of productivity, if India is already food-secure? Dare we ask, was India ever food-insecure, even in the 1960s, that it could not produce enough to feed itself?

This chapter argues that the productivity-oriented vision that makes these technological aspirations possible is based on a selective reading of India's agrarian past—one that labels it as backward and needing redemption through technology. It constructs India's agrarian history as beginning in the 1960s with the inception of the Green Revolution. Everything before that is lumped into one timeless static past. By re-engaging with the historical narrative that has shaped Indian agriculture, this chapter shows the ways in which the idea of a hungry, starving nation with its unproductive farmers was actively created and used to legitimise technological and institutional interventions of a specific kind.

It further argues that the Green Revolution model was never designed to solve the problem of hunger or famine, which is primarily shaped by inequity in access to food. All it gave was more wheat, which did not even form the staple diet of a majority of Indians at that time. Moreover, it did not make India self-sufficient in food, but only in wheat and rice, and that too at the cost of the rest of our plate. In the light of this, it becomes difficult to justify the enormous negative consequences arising from adopting the Green Revolution model, let alone base India's agrarian future on it. It is only through a comprehensive understanding of its agrarian past that we can begin to imagine a new vision and a new foundation for India's agrarian future.

REDEEMING INDIA'S BACKWARD AGRARIAN PAST

India's agrarian history has been characterised as one of backwardness, poor technical inputs, low productivity and a capricious environment. Economic data such as zero per cent growth rate of agriculture from 1900 to 1947 has often been presented as evidence for this. This is not surprising.

During the pre-colonial era, India's agro-industrial complex produced and exported a wide range of products, including cotton and silk textiles (fine muslin), spices, sugar, rice and others, with large domestic and international trade networks, and nearly 25 per cent of world manufacturing (Bayly 1985; Washbrook 1988). However, the backbone of Indian agriculture was broken during the eighteenth and nineteenth centuries through colonial policies that sucked the vitality out of the land and channelled the wealth to Great Britain. In collaboration with some social groups who became beneficiary intermediaries, colonial interests created pathways of unparalleled exploitation of natural resources. Cash crops like opium, jute, wheat, cotton and indigo were grown on prime agricultural land with food crops relegated to marginal areas. This was coupled with a systematic neglect of customary water harvesting and storage structures, and state takeover of the forests to harvest timber.

Colonial Misery

Under conditions of free trade, the Indian farmers growing cash crops were exposed to the price fluctuations of international markets, which caused their periodic ruin. The capstone was usurious extraction of rents from the land through a variety of land tenure systems beginning with Permanent Settlement in 1792. As the rentier economy supported by the might of the state picked up, private investment in agriculture died out (Baker 1993; Davis 2001: 311–40; Washbrook 1994). On the other hand, the common lands that were critical suppliers of food, fodder, fuel, water and building material were appropriated by the British by renaming them as wasteland. People were converted into encroachers and denied fodder and firewood from there, even during times of famine. With punitive taxes on digging wells and revenue rates for irrigated land being 10–15 times that of dryland, it paved the way for the decay of native irrigation, thus increasing the vulnerability during droughts (Satya 1997; Singh 1996).

During the last 30 years of the nineteenth century, the country saw the worst famines, with 16.6–30 million people dying (Davis 2001; Maharatna 1996). Ironically, people died while food was being exported and banquets were thrown to celebrate the monarchy's rule. It was not a crisis of production, it was a crisis of conscience (Davis 2001). But the famines took a toll on agricultural productivity. The immense loss of cattle and bullocks, and the destruction of the pastoral economy that formed the bedrock of maintaining soil fertility, had adversely affected agricultural productivity. Such eroded soils were more vulnerable to drought (Kaiwar 2000). There was nothing to fall back on—water storage systems were in tatters; the commons were inaccessible and food stores were inadequate. The extant level of yield fell by a third to a half and that of the average life expectancy by 20 per cent during this period (Davis 1951; Guha 1992).

However, this exploitative past has been quietly forgotten and replaced with a narrative of ignorant, unproductive farmers toiling away using ancient practices that had supposedly remained static over time. Overlain upon the thesis of the timeless, unchanging village (Jodhka 2002), this projected an image of India's agrarian milieu as sans experimentation, sans productivity and sans technology (Parayil 1992: 738–40; Tucker 2015: 5).[2] It is only with the coming of the Green Revolution, that things supposedly changed. It was considered to be the starting point of a transformation to a high-productivity trajectory, by providing scientific evidence of the high yields of wheat and rice.

What is missed, however, is that Indian agriculture—especially with the export of crops like wheat and jute—had recovered by the 1920s from the devastation of the late nineteenth century. By the time of the Great Depression of the 1930s, there were complaints of overproduction and a steep fall in price realisations. In 1934–35, the Crop Planning Conference decided that wheat production should be limited to 9.5 million tonnes and there should be no stimulus to increase the area under wheat (Bansil 1960: 187).[3] In 1942–43—the last year of foodgrain exports, and the same year as the Bengal Famine—undivided India produced 11.2 million tonnes of wheat and exported 3 million tonnes of foodgrains (ibid.: 190).[4]

This famine was the proverbial straw that supposedly broke the camel's back. With another 3 million people dying, India was once again condemned as a nation which could not produce enough food to feed itself. It took another 30 years for revisionist work to challenge this assertion.

Understanding Famine

Famines in the modern world have never been about an absolute shortage of food supply. In fact, globally the world has seen recurring crises of overproduction of food for the last 100 years or more. An array of scholarship over the last few decades, beginning with Amartya Sen's (1981) work on the 1943 famine, has shown that hunger and starvation are human failures rather than natural failures (Mishra 2010; Patnaik 1991; Rangasami 1985; Vasavi 1999; Vaughan 1987).[5] Famines have been driven by rising prices of food resulting from hoarding and speculation, or mismanagement of supply, making it unaffordable to the poor. Unless the prices are reduced by government action, this situation can lead to human deaths from starvation and disease. Drought and crop losses may aggravate the situation, but it is the unequal distribution of food and the inability to afford it that is culpable for the tragedy.

Even during the 1943 famine, despite halting of rice imports from Burma (due to the Japanese occupation), there was adequate food available within British India, which, if supplied to Bengal, would have reduced prices and allowed the rural households to purchase food. But the British government was diverting food to Africa and Europe for their soldiers fighting in the Second World War. Further, food available within the province was secured for the cities of Calcutta and Dacca. Though food was available, the rural poor could not purchase it. Mass starvation was created in the countryside (Mukerjee 2010).

The same analysis holds true for the series of famines at the end of the nineteenth century. The genocide of 30 million Indians between 1870 and 1901 was due to colonial policies that exacerbated droughts, destroyed agrarian communities, exported grains in the face of hunger and left millions to perish.[6] When people were dying of starvation, and disease afflicted the hungry bodies, the colonial officials were warned against displaying 'humanitarian hysterics' (Davis 2001).

The notion that famines were a natural check on undesirable population growth, especially of the wrong kind, was the dictum taught at the East India Company's famous Haileybury College. Colonial policy reflected racist prejudices against the breeding of brown Indians like rabbits. This was the perfect marriage of Malthusianism and Social Darwinism (Davis 2001). The state refused to intervene, following the diktat that the free market was supposed to take care of things. And it indeed did by letting hoarding to go unchecked, allowing grain prices to increase across the country and enabling export of grains from the famine-affected areas. Ironically, the modernising railroads and telegraph ably accelerated the process. Rather than multiplying like rabbits, Indians were dying like fleas.

Independent India has never seen such colossal famine deaths (although hunger still remains a grim reality), because the government has released food stocks to increase supply, moved grains to regions of scarcity, opened food for work-relief camps, instituted price controls and curtailed the hoarding power of traders, whenever there has been a spectre of drought. Yet, the popular understanding of famine remains trapped within the discourse that it is a natural phenomenon, which the Green Revolution's physical bounty has helped overturn.

Bringing the Green Revolution

At Independence, India was characterised as a country that could barely produce any food throughout the 1950s and 1960s, let alone enough to feed all its people. This is grossly misleading. From 1950 to 1965, Indian agriculture witnessed a surge in productivity across all crops. With the departure of the British, agriculture was freed from the shackles of punitive land revenue demands. The demolition of the Zamindari system, modest land reforms and repeal of taxes on digging wells and making improvements to the land, had given a new lease of life to farmers.

The Game of Numbers

Despite the effects of Partition, the growth rate of agriculture was 4.6 per cent for Punjab during 1950–64 (Bhalla et al. 1990: 14). Foodgrain yields rose by 45 per cent between 1950–51 and 1964–65 (Landy 2009) and foodgrain production increased at the rate of 3 per cent per annum (Srivastava 1972).[7] In fact, India's food availability per capita increased from 144.1 kg per person per annum in 1951 to 171.1 kg per person per annum in 1961 (Planning Commission 2017b).[8]

Yet, this was not recognised in the international or national discussions on food security. For instance, the World Food Budget constructed by the US government's Economic Research Service (ERS) in 1961 used only rice and wheat for its calculations, claiming that reliable data on other food crops were not available (Cullather 2010: 219). Culturally diverse, nutritious Indian diets were homogenised by mere numbers.

In 1951, India grew 19 million tonnes of millet and gram which increased to 31.1 million tonnes in 1965, almost three times the amount of wheat that had been grown.[9] Yet, wheat, which was hardly consumed locally and had been promoted as an export crop, was included in calculations. Simultaneously, lentils and oilseeds that formed a bulk of vegetarian diets almost ubiquitously across the country, let alone fish, eggs and meat, which were consumed in the highlands and coastal states, were entirely ignored. And so were the uncultivated foods sourced from common lands such as greens, berries, roots and small game, which were a significant source of nutrition in different seasons.

Further, the US ERS converted this data into calorie values and divided it by population projections. The trend showed declining availability of 'food' in Asian countries over the subsequent five years. This was then used by the US government and the Rockefeller Foundation to argue that a world food crisis was on the way unless physical production of 'food' was not increased to catch up with the predicted population increases (Cullather 2010: 219).

In the 1950s, demography had emerged as an important discipline and decolonised states facing scrutiny were evaluated using the Malthusian framework pitting food against population.[10] Rapid population growth was expected to cause high unemployment, declining incomes and economic stagnation (Perkins 1997: 121–24, 133–35; Sharpless 1997: 178). Along with pressure from international organisations, there were different threads within India that converged to provide impetus to the idea of population control at the time of Independence (Connelly 2008; Nair 2011; Unger 2015).

Even the theory of demographic transition was utilised to present a scenario of alarming population projections for Asia. Mortality rates started falling in the mid-twentieth century due to better healthcare and sanitation rather than long-term social changes. But since countries like India were still predominantly rural and 'traditional', the birth rates were not expected to fall any time soon unless drastic birth control measures were implemented (Cullather 2010: 39; Sharpless 1997: 189–90).

What this picture did not show was that the transition in Europe had taken place on the backs of exploitation of people in colonised countries. Europeans had 'begun to live longer partly *because* people in other parts of the world were suffering deprivation and dying young' (Connelly 2008: 29). Moreover, it was a throwback to the eugenic discourse of birth control in the 1930s where selective 'inferior' populations were to be controlled using new technology (ibid.: 141–42). These racialised roots of demography had been suppressed, but it begged the question—why was the 'population problem' only seen to be afflicting the newly decolonised third world?[11]

The Public Law 480 Imports

Popular proclamations that India was a Malthusian time-bomb,[12] coupled with the fact that it was importing wheat under the Public Law 480 (PL480) from the US from 1956 onwards, were used to argue that India could not produce enough food to feed itself. By the mid-1960s, the US government was successful in creating an international consensus about growing famine conditions in India and in 1966, *The New York Times* declared that India was on a 'treadmill to starvation' (cited in Cullather 2010: 223).

However, these claims had conveniently sidestepped the fact that the decision to import PL480 wheat was not because of scarcity of domestic food production. In fact, imports continued in years of high production and falling farm gate prices, reflecting the primacy of other policy considerations related to industrialisation, inflation, international trade compulsions and market imperfections (Bansil 1960). PL480 imports were a conscious choice of policymakers in the 1950s, who found them useful in dealing with multiple issues, including: (a) the need to fulfil the ration needs in the deficit areas in the country; (b) poor marketing and transportation infrastructure, and difficulty of controlling the trader lobbies[13] that were hampering foodgrain procurement; and (c) the need to save foreign exchange and extract surpluses from agriculture for pushing industrialisation.

As government policy oscillated between allowing the free movement of food and controlling supplies, while dancing to the tune of prices (Siegel 2018),[14] PL480 imports obviated the need for protracted negotiations with surplus states. Further, since it was paid for in rupees, PL480 wheat helped save foreign exchange, while providing subsidised grain to the working-class population through the ration shop system,[15] thus allowing industry to keep the wage bill low (Cullather 2010; Frankel 1978).[16]

The US gained from PL480 because first, it found markets for the surplus wheat of its domestic farmers (Friedmann 1982; Paarlberg 1985), and second, it helped pacify restive and expanding urban populations in developing countries through the provision of cheap food. The latter was critical to American security interests as this move, ostensibly, prevented countries from turning communist (Cullather 2010; Gupta 1998; Perkins 1997).

This, however, generated a domestic agrarian scenario in India that was characterised by: (a) a glut of imported PL480 wheat[17] that reduced the price of wheat for consumers, but hurt domestic wheat farmers as a consequence (Kamath 1992; Shenoy 1974);[18] (b) stagnancy in the area under wheat cultivation from 1956 to 1962 and even a decline of 7 per cent till 1966 (Shenoy 1974: 48), along with the diversion of land away from food crops, in general, to the more remunerative fibre and non-food crops; and (c) the overdependence of the PDS on the PL480 route for both provisioning and price control (Mooij 1998; Varshney 1989).[19]

In this setting, when the US threatened to stall these imports during the mid-1960s, India found itself in a vulnerable condition. In August 1965, the US decided to put PL480 wheat shipments to India on a monthly renewable contract, subject to specific conditions, including halting of India's war with Pakistan, devaluation of the rupee and opening up of the fertiliser market, to name a few. This shift of American foreign policy from being generous in doling out wheat to its conditional disbursal was partly because US grain surpluses had dwindled during this phase (Paarlberg 1985). Moreover, the US farm lobby had lost power to urban representatives in the

US Senate and Congress and the continuation of PL480 required reframing it as a response to a desperate situation of hunger, rather than as a subsidy to the American farm lobby, which it effectively was (Cullather 2010).

This 'short tether' of PL480 gave rise to the 'ship to mouth' crisis, since the US had pledged only one-fourth of the grain requested for 1965–66. Despite this, Indian government officials challenged the notion of a 1965 famine—there was rationing in some cities due to the war with Pakistan and localised crop failures, but famine sounded absurd, they argued (ibid.).[20] India failed to weather the situation using domestic wheat supplies, not only because of the PDS's overdependence on PL480, but also because the Food Corporation of India (FCI), as the coordinating agency for nationwide procurement, was unable to procure enough foodgrains due to hoarding and speculation by traders. Prices rose further when the monsoons failed in some parts of the country, resulting in localised crop failures in the kharif season (Frankel 1978).

Further, the war with China in 1962 and with Pakistan in 1965 had led to more defence spending, making foodgrain imports using foreign exchange impossible. This necessitated protracted negotiations with the Americans over several months. Finally, the Lal Bahadur Shastri government was successful in renegotiating the continuation of PL480 imports in November 1965, in return for allowing private foreign investment in fertiliser plants and the import of fertiliser, among other things (Paarlberg 1985).[21]

In 1966, India imported 8 million tonnes of wheat—the highest ever volume of import under PL480 (ibid.: 144).[22] A drought in Bihar and a monsoon failure—for the second time—in other parts of the country, had further exacerbated the already difficult situation.[23] But the very next year, 1967–68, however evidenced production recovery and bumper harvests due to favourable weather, and experts started warning of the 'problem of plenty' (Cullather 2010; Dasgupta 1977). Yet, India was compelled to agree to an additional import of 2–3 million tonnes of PL480 wheat that was dumped on her by the US as their surpluses had returned (Cullather 2010; Paarlberg 1985).

The Miracle Seeds

A series of conjunctures led M. S. Swaminathan to become a wheat breeder, brought him and others at the Indian Agricultural Research Institute (IARI) in touch with Norman Borlaug's work, and led to the planting of imported high-yielding Mexican seed varieties in C. Subramaniam's garden in Lutyen's Delhi in December 1966 (Cullather 2010: 193–98, 226). With this, the story of the seeds began with a sputtering start.

Borlaug and Swaminathan were emphasising response to nutrients like water and nitrogenous fertiliser and disease resistance, especially to rust, keeping in mind the end-goal of increasing quantitative yields.[24] Borlaug's research in Mexico had been funded by the Rockefeller Foundation, which was working squarely within the Malthusian framework. But high fertiliser prices, lack of irrigation and low wheat prices made it highly unlikely that farmers in India would adopt varieties that responded to external inputs, unless the state intervened to support them (Cullather 2010; Perkins 1997).

Subramaniam learnt of the potential of these seed varieties, and inspired, in part, by the 1964 Bell Report of the World Bank that called for betting on the strong, tried to push for a 'new agricultural strategy' in 1965. The strategy entailed providing cost and price incentives to individual farmers in the form of seeds, pesticides, power implements, chemical fertilisers and water—effectively 'guaranteeing profitability to the farmer'—in contrast to the earlier approach of the government focusing on community development programmes and land reforms. This was a massive shift away from the cheap import policy of the 1950s that had kept farm gate prices low and created disincentives for production.

But Subramaniam needed to import fertiliser for the new agricultural strategy to take off, which would have required diversion of precious foreign exchange resources meant for industrialisation (Cullather 2010; Frankel 1978). Unfortunately, he received little support. It was the impasse with the Americans and the worsening procurement situation at home that paved the way for the approval of the New Agricultural Strategy in November 1965.

The dissemination of the new seeds and fertilisers began in districts with sufficient access to water through the IADP, which had been started in 1960 with support from the Ford Foundation. High-yielding variety seeds required farmers to invest in irrigation and purchase fertilisers, failing which the seeds would not give the desired yield. Farmers who were resourceful and 'progressive', that is, typically upper caste and class, were also given extension support along with a guarantee that the government would purchase all their wheat to stock the FCI godowns and supply to the PDS, at an MSP (Cullather 2010: 201, 207; Frankel 1978).

The wheat output, which was 12.3 million tonnes in 1964–65, increased to 16.5 million tonnes in 1967–68 and further to 18.6 million tonnes in 1968–69, as more acreage was devoted to high-yielding varieties. Was this the moment of triumph? Had the Malthusian forces finally been defeated by the new technology?

In March 1968, William Gaud, director of the United States Agency for International Development (USAID), heralded the new era of plenty as a 'green revolution' in contrast to the 'red revolution' that was threatening to sweep across Asia in the face of the Vietnam crisis and the heightened tensions of the Cold War. Thanks to the seeds, the Americans claimed, restive masses across Asia would now be prevented from falling into communist hands (Fitzgerald 1986; Patel 2012). Modern seed technology was positioned as the saviour of a nation, its people, its democracy, its very existence.

Yet, the 1967–68 harvest across several countries was higher than normal in almost all crops, let alone wheat, primarily due to good weather which continued till 1970 (Dasgupta 1977; Patel 2012). Many commentators were talking of overproduction once again, but the credit for this sudden reversal from 'inevitable' famine to all-round abundance was given to the new programme.[25]

Why Wheat?

It seems strange that in a nation of rice and millet eaters, the entire discussion around food security, and its fields, was hijacked by wheat. Wheat was the food of the elite. The masses ate millet.[26] The Green Revolution changed that.

The government procurement system gave price incentives only for rice and wheat and the PDS gave poor consumers access to cheap wheat and rice. Farmers responded by switching from millet and gram to wheat (and rice). From a high of 55.6 million hectares in 1968, acreage under millet and gram fell by half to 28 million hectares in 2006 (Planning Commission 2017a). The per capita availability of wheat went up by 27.4 kg, whereas the per capita availability of millets, pulses and gram shrunk by 42 kg from 1961 to 2006.[27] This transformed staple diets across the country away from traditional millets and pulses to rice and wheat.

Since the 1990s, India has become one of the largest importers of oilseeds and pulses, primarily from Indonesia and Myanmar. Imports fulfilled nearly 35 per cent of India's domestic requirement of oilseeds and 15–18 per cent of pulses from 1992 to 2012 (Ali and Gupta 2012; *The Hindu Business Line* 2012; Sekhar 2004; Shenoi 2003). The rise in the price of pulses over the last few decades has put them beyond the reach of even middle-class households. India simply traded self-sufficiency of rice and wheat for dependence of the rest of the nutrition basket. Research by the National Institute of Nutrition has shown that the cereal-heavy diets of the poor have contributed to an epidemic of anaemia along with creating protein malnutrition and nutrient deprivation (Shatrugna 2010).[28] In quest of food security, India has compromised on nutrition security.

Self-sufficiency or Overproduction?

Most ironically, the self-sufficiency in two cereals came at the cost of another form of dependence—the import of rock phosphate for fertilisers and petroleum for irrigation pumps and tractors. Dependence on these non-renewable and fast-depleting sources of energy and minerals also made agriculture a carbon-emitting sector impacting the climate. The country did not stop being vulnerable; it became vulnerable to a different set of interests. With this, deeper ecological and existential questions have emerged.

Worse still, by the late 1970s and early 1980s, there was a crisis of overproduction and government granaries were overflowing with wheat and rice. The solution was to export the stored grain at very low prices. In effect, subsidising the poor of other countries while poor Indians continued to go hungry (Paarlberg 1985: 56–57).[29]

Further, all the input subsidies and market guarantees were going to the farmers who were already well-off—the ones who had been able to mobilise politically to successfully make demands on the government to increase the MSP—in prosperous regions in the country. Yet, farmers continued to face a crisis, with places like Punjab eventually becoming the hotbed of farmer suicides (Singh 2000). More problematically, large tracts of the country, such as the Deccan plateau drylands covering Vidarbha and Telangana, for instance, were entirely ignored—they received no support at all. Since the 1990s, as dryland farmers have increasingly adopted monoculture farming with tubewell irrigation, the same set of crises have manifested, but with a higher magnitude.

Proponents of the Green Revolution argue that the new seeds have significantly increased yields on the existing arable land, thus saving forestland from being converted into agricultural land and supporting a much higher population. Yet, Stevenson et al.'s (2013) calculations show that the amount of land 'saved' in this way was between 18 and 27 million hectares globally, about 2.6–4 per cent of the total land area under cereal cultivation (that is, 680 million hectares) as of 2004. It is amazing how much has been lost through the toxicity of our soils, our water, our health and our food, to achieve these meagre savings.

Even more surprisingly, these calculations compare yields through the lens of monoculture farming in a given season. But productivity of a single grain per unit of land in a given season is a misleading metric—it fails to account for multiple products (grains, fodder, soil fertility, carbon sequestration) that land can provide in the same season, and that in many places, multiple crops are grown on that same land across seasons. And what about the ability of the land to continue to produce into the future? Taking into account all this would drastically change the outcomes. The high yields of wheat have come at the cost of depleting/replacing soils, groundwater and the livestock economy in ways that are non-replenishable/non-renewable and carbon-emitting.

Conclusion

Despite a plethora of evidence to the contrary, India's agrarian future, whether gene-based or drone-based, continues to be driven by a productivity-focused, technology-centric vision drawing upon the Green Revolution model. Alternative visions based on different kinds of crop choices, farming systems, technologies and practices, have been dismissed as fancy thoughts of armchair intellectuals, privileged farmers, foreign-funded non-governmental organisations, or traditional obscurantists.

What would it take to bring into the envisioning process the need for healthy, nutritious food, the shepherding of our soil and water resources, the livelihoods of our farmers and farmworkers, and the situated knowledge of how to put it all together? For how long will we remain shackled to a model that focuses primarily on increasing grain productivity to the exclusion of everything else? By revisiting India's agrarian history and outlining the circumstances under which the Green Revolution model was adopted, this chapter has sought to challenge this blind adherence, and hopefully open up ways to envision futures that can begin to address the needs of the country and the countryside.

NOTES

1. Despite the availability of different varieties for a single crop, farmers are growing only a handful of very popular varieties in many crops. In soybean, for instance, the variety JS-335 was grown in approximately 90 per cent of the soybean-growing area in Madhya Pradesh throughout the 1990s and early 2000s (Kumar 2016).

2. For a contrasting view, see Howard (1943).

3. There were even a series of international conferences held by the major wheat-exporting nations, including India, to discuss how to limit the production of wheat so that its price could recover (Lindsay 1931).

4. The agricultural production data for undivided India in 1942–43 is as follows: 24.8 million tonnes of rice, 20.9 million tonnes of millet and gram, and 11.2 million tonnes of wheat (Bansil 1990: 432). Further, area under wheat cultivation in undivided India in 1942–43 was 17.1 per cent of all area under cereals (ibid.: 431).

5. Brazilian physician and public administrator Josué de Castro's book *The Geopolitics of Hunger* (1977 [1952]) was amongst the earliest to question simplistic Malthusian notions about food and population.

6. From the late 1700s, the death toll from famines and epidemics has been estimated at 55–60 million under colonial rule (Srinivasan 2017).

7. Imports of foodgrains fell from 4.7 million tonnes in 1951 to 0.8 million tonnes in 1954 (Chopra 1988: 84–106, cited in Mooij 1998). The production of major crops (except wheat) increased as much in the 15-year pre-Green Revolution period (1950–65) as it did in the 25-year post-Green Revolution period (1965–90) (Landy 2009).

8. In 2009, the food availability per capita was 162.1 kg per year, yet no one thought there was a crisis. This amounted to 444.1 grams per day. According to the National Institute of Nutrition, we need 400 grams of cereals per day along with 80 grams of pulses, 300 grams of vegetables, 30 grams of oils and 300 grams of milk, apart from a host of micronutrients (Krishnaswamy and Sesikeran 2011: 6). See also footnote 26.

9. India grew 20.6 million tonnes of rice and 6.5 million tonnes of wheat in 1951, which had increased to 39.3 million tonnes of rice and 12.3 million tonnes of wheat in 1965 (Planning Commission 2017c).

10. Thomas Malthus's famous maxim that food production grows linearly whereas population grows exponentially became the *mantra* driving this.

11. Ironically, the so-called population bombs of the 1960s (India and China) were lauded as facing a demographic dividend in the 2000s!

12. *Time* magazine even devoted a cover to such doomsday theories in January 1960 (Desrochers and Hoffbauer 2009).

13. Regulation and licensing of traders through the *mandi* system had not yet taken place—that would happen only in the early 1970s in most parts of the country.

14. Domestic procurement was never over 10 per cent of the marketed surplus of foodgrains produced in the country.

15. The rationing system had been started by the British in 1942 to control food supplies in the Second World War (Mooij 1998; Shenoy 1974).

16. PL480 imports were effectively free (aid, not trade), as the rupee payments to the US were spent in India: 15 per cent by the Americans for their expenses and 85 per cent as domestic investment (Cullather 2010: 182; Shenoy 1974: 241).

17. India imported 50 million tonnes from 1958–66, mostly through PL480 (Mooij 1998).

18. Bansil (1960) argued that farmers were not growing more wheat or rice even throughout the 1940s and 1950s despite the government offering higher procurement prices, because cheaper rice from Burma and cheaper wheat from Australia and Canada were available to urban consumers, despite import duties.

19. From 1951 to 1966, net imports averaged 72.2 per cent of total PDS off-take (Shenoy 1974: 260).

20. Foodgrain production had increased from 82 million tonnes in 1963–64 to 89 million tonnes in 1964–65, and dipped to 72 million tonnes in 1965–66. It increased marginally in 1966, clocking at 74 million tonnes (Planning Commission 2017c).

21. Research had shown that fertilisers improved the yields for several crops, and fertiliser companies were keen to access the Indian market.

22. This amount, however, 'never satisfied more than a modest 8–10% of total national food grain consumption' (Paarlberg 1985: 144). The total (net) imports in 1966 were 10.3 million tonnes, which included trade (wheat purchased using foreign exchange) and PL480 concessionary aid (Chopra 1988: 388, Table 6).

23. Even in Bihar, which saw trucks of imported PL480 wheat being sent to food camps that year, food production was 96 per cent of normal in 1966, but commercial crops like jute and sugarcane were negatively affected due to lack of water, and landless agricultural labourers found themselves unemployed. They were the ones most severely hit along with those unemployed in the cities (Cullather 2010: 227).

24. Other Indian scientists were much more concerned with features required by consumers such as colour, texture, 'chapati quality', and taste in their breeding programme, and in addressing goals of farmers such as resistance to drought and survival in low-fertility conditions (Saha 2012).

25. The quantum of improvement was as follows: increase of 8.5 million tonnes in the production of millet, pulses and gram, 7.1 million tonnes in rice and 5.1 million tonnes in wheat, totalling 21 million tonnes (Planning Commission 2017c). Only part of the latter was due to high-yielding varieties of seeds. Moreover, India continued to import wheat through PL480 till 1971 and through foreign exchange purchases until 1976 (Paarlberg 1985: 53–56; Randhawa 1986).

26. Millets are now being promoted as nutri-cereals and are slowly becoming the new food of the elite.

27. From 1961 to 2006, the per capita availability per person per year was: wheat 28.9 kg to 56.3 kg; pulses 25.2 kg to 11.8 kg; rice 73.4 kg to 72.3 kg; and millet and gram 54.6 kg to 26 kg (Planning Commission 2017b). Per person per day, this was: wheat 79 grams to 154 grams; pulses 69 grams to 32 grams; rice 201 grams to 198 grams; and millet and gram: 149 grams to 71 grams.

28. Diets also shifted away from multiple local varieties of wheat and rice to standardised varieties created by science—typically with inferior taste and less nutritive value.

29. Between 2012 and 2015, India exported 5.79 million tonnes of foodgrains to reduce excess buffer stock build-up in the FCI godowns (Kumar 2015: 5).

References

'Import of Pulses, Edible Oils May Go Up This Year: Thomas'. 2012. *The Hindu Business Line*, 27 August. Available at http://www.thehindubusinessline.com/economy/agri-business/import-of-pulses-edible-oils-may-go-up-this-year-thomas/article3827878.ece (accessed 27 January 2018).

Ali, M., and S. Gupta. 2012. 'Carrying Capacity of Indian Agriculture: Pulse Crops'. *Current Science* 102(6): 874–81.

Ambirajan, S. 1976. 'Malthusian Population Theory and Indian Famine Policy in the Nineteenth Century'. *Population Studies* 30(1): 5–14.

Baker, D. E. U. 1993. *Colonialism in an Indian Hinterland: The Central Provinces, 1820–1920.* New York: Oxford University Press.

Bansil, P. C. 1960. 'Food Resources and Population of India: A Historical Study'. *Sankhya: The Indian Journal of Statistics (1933–1960)* 22(1–2): 183–208.

———. 1990. *Agricultural Statistical Compendium (Volume 1): Foodgrains, Part 1.* New Delhi: Techno Economic Research Institute.

Bayly, C. A. 1985. 'State and Economy in India Over Seven Hundred Years'. *The Economic History Review* 38(4): 583–96.

Bhalla, G. S., and G. K. Chadha. 1983. *Green Revolution and the Small Peasant: A Study of Income Distribution among Punjab Cultivators.* New Delhi: Concept Publishing Company.

Bhalla, G. S., G. K. Chadha, S. P. Kashyap and R. K. Sharma. 1990. 'Agricultural Growth and Structural Changes in the Punjab Economy: An Input–Output Analysis'. Research Report 82, International Food Policy Research Institute and Centre for the Study of Regional Development, Jawaharlal Nehru University, August.

Byres, T. J. 1983. *The Green Revolution in India.* Milton Keynes, UK: Open University Press.

Chopra, R. N. 1988. *Food Policy in India: A Survey.* New Delhi: Intellectual Publishing House.

Connelly, M. 2008. *Fatal Misconception: The Struggle to Control World Population.* Cambridge, MA: The Belknap Press of Harvard University Press.

Cullather, N. 2010. *The Hungry World: America's Cold War Battle against Poverty in Asia.* Cambridge: Harvard University Press.

Dasgupta, B. 1977. 'India's Green Revolution'. *Economic and Political Weekly* 12(6–8): 241–60.

Davis, K. 1951. *Population of India and Pakistan.* Princeton, NJ: Princeton University Press.

Davis, M. 2001. *Late Victorian Holocausts: El Niño Famines and the Making of the Third World.* New York: Verso.

de Castro, J. 1977 [1952]. *The Geopolitics of Hunger.* New York: Monthly Review Press.

Desrochers, P., and C. Hoffbauer. 2009. 'The Post War Intellectual Roots of the Population Bomb: Fairfield Osborn's "Our Plundered Planet" and William Vogt's "Road to Survival" in Retrospect'. *The Electronic Journal of Sustainable Development* 1(3): 73–97.

Fitzgerald, D. 1986. 'Exporting American Agriculture: The Rockefeller Foundation in Mexico, 1943–53'. *Social Studies of Science* 16(3): 457–83.

Frankel, F. R. 1978. *India's Political Economy, 1947-1977: The Gradual Revolution.* Princeton: Princeton University Press.

Friedmann, H. 1982. 'The Political Economy of Food: The Rise and Fall of the Postwar International Food Order'. *The American Journal of Sociology* 88: S248–86.

Guha, S. (ed.). 1992. *Growth, Stagnation or Decline?: Agricultural Productivity in British India.* Delhi: Oxford University Press.

Gupta, A. 1998. *Postcolonial Developments: Agriculture in the Making of Modern India.* Durham: Duke University Press.

Howard, A. 1943. *An Agricultural Testament.* Oxford, UK: Oxford University Press.

Jodhka, S. 2002. 'Nation and Village: Images of Rural India in Gandhi, Nehru and Ambedkar'. *Economic and Political Weekly* 37(32): 3343–53.

Kaiwar, V. 2000. 'Nature, Property and Polity in Colonial Bombay'. *Journal of Peasant Studies* 27(2): 1–49.

Kamath, S. J. 1992. 'Foreign Aid and India: Financing the Leviathan State'. Cato Policy Analysis No. 170, 6 May. Available at https://www.cato.org/sites/cato.org/files/pubs/pdf/pa170.pdf (accessed 10 March 2018).

Krishnaswamy, K., and B. Sesikeran. 2011. *Dietary Guidelines for Indians: A Manual* (second edition). National Institute of Nutrition, Hyderabad. Available at https://www.nin.res.in/downloads/DietaryGuidelinesforNINwebsite.pdf (accessed 12 January 2018).

Kumar, R. 2016. *Rethinking Revolutions: Soyabean, Choupals and the Changing Countryside in Central India*. New Delhi: Oxford University Press.

Kumar, S. 2015. *Report of the High-level Committee on Reorienting the Role and Restructuring of Food Corporation of India*. January. Available at http://fci.gov.in/app2/webroot/upload/News/Report%20of%20the%20High%20Level%20Committee%20on%20Reorienting%20the%20Role%20and%20Restructuring%20of%20FCI_English.pdf (accessed 10 March 2018).

Landy, F. 2009. *Feeding India: The Spatial Parameters of Food Grain Policy*. New Delhi: Manohar Publishers.

Lindsay, H. A. F. 1931. 'Report on the Preparatory Conference to the World Wheat Conference of 1932'. Reference Number F-33(2)/33/Stat ICAR, 1930-31, Part I, p. 45), National Archives of India, Rome, 26 March–2 April.

Maharatna, A. 1996. *The Demography of Famines: An Indian Historical Perspective*. New Delhi: Oxford University Press.

McAlpin, M. 1983. 'Famines, Epidemics, and Population Growth: The Case of India'. *The Journal of Interdisciplinary History* 14(2): 351–66.

Mishra, A. 2010. *Hunger and Famine in Kalahandi: An Anthropological Study*. New Delhi: Pearson Education India.

Mooij, J. 1998. 'Food Policy and Politics: The Political Economy of the Public Distribution System in India'. *The Journal of Peasant Studies* 25(2): 77–101.

Mukerjee, M. 2010. *Churchill's Secret War: The British Empire and The Ravaging of India during World War II*. New York: Basic Books.

Nair, R. 2011. 'The Construction of a "Population Problem" in Colonial India 1919–1947'. *The Journal of Imperial and Commonwealth History* 39(2): 227–47.

Paarlberg, R. L. 1985. *Food Trade and Foreign Policy: India, the Soviet Union and the United States*. Ithaca: Cornell University Press.

Parayil, G. 1992. 'The Green Revolution in India: A Case Study of Technological Change'. *Technology and Culture* 33(4): 737–56.

Patel, R. 2012. 'The Long Green Revolution'. *The Journal of Peasant Studies* 40(1): 1–63.

Patnaik, U. 1991. 'Food Availability and Famine: A Longer View'. *The Journal of Peasant Studies* 19(1): 1–25.

Perkins, J. H. 1997. *Geopolitics and the Green Revolution: Wheat, Genes, and the Cold War*. New York: Oxford University Press.

Planning Commission. 2017a. 'Area Under Principal Crops: All India'. Government of India. Available at http://planningcommission.gov.in/sectors/agri_html/selagri/T%201.12.xls (accessed 27 January 2018).

———. 2017b. 'Net Availability of Food Grains (Per Annum) in India'. Data Bank on Agriculture and Allied Sectors, Government of India. Available at http://planningcommission.gov.in/sectors/agri_html/selagri/T1.25.xls (accessed 27 January 2018).

Planning Commission. 2017c. 'Production of Major Crops'. Government of India. Available at http://planningcommission.gov.in/sectors/agri_html/selagri/T%201.11.xls (accessed 27 January 2018).

Press Trust of India. 2017. 'Modi Calls for "Evergreen Revolution"'. *The Hindu*, 19 May. Available at http://www.thehindu.com/news/national/modi-calls-for-evergreen-revolution/article18510225.ece (accessed 27 January 2018).

Raina, R. 2015. 'Knowing and Administering Food: How Do We Explain Persistence?'. In *Food Security and Food Production: Institutional Challenges in Governance Domain*, ed. C. S. Reddy, 11–43. Newcastle upon Tyne: Cambridge Scholars Publishing.

Rajagopal, G. 2016. 'The Stories of Ehrlich, Borlaug and the Green Revolution'. *The Wire*, 13 October. Available at https://thewire.in/72400/paul-ehrlich-norman-borlaug-green-revolution/ (accessed 27 January 2018).

Randhawa, M. S. 1986. *A History of Agriculture in India* (Volume 4). New Delhi: Indian Council of Agricultural Research.

Rangasami, A. 1985. 'Failure of Exchange Entitlements Theory of Famine: A Response'. *Economic and Political Weekly* 20(41): 1747–52.

Saha, M. 2012. 'State Policy, Agricultural Research and Transformation of Indian Agriculture with Reference to Basic Food Crops, 1947–75'. PhD dissertation, Iowa State University. Available at http://lib.dr.iastate.edu/etd/12450 (accessed 20 January 2018).

Satya, L. 1997. *Cotton and Famine in Berar, 1850–1900*. New Delhi: Manohar Publishers.

Sekhar, C. S. C. 2004. 'Agricultural Price Volatility in International and Indian Markets'. *Economic and Political Weekly* 39(43): 4729–36.

Sen, A. 1981. *Poverty and Famines: An Essay on Entitlement and Deprivation*. New York: Oxford University Press.

Sharpless, J. 1997. 'Population Science, Private Foundations, and Development Aid: The Transformation of Demographic Knowledge in the United States, 1945–1965'. In *International Development and the Social Sciences*, eds F. Cooper and R. Packard, 176–200. Berkeley: University of California Press.

Shatrugna, V. 2010. 'The Career of Hunger: Critical Reflections on the History of Nutrition Science and Policy'. In *Towards a Critical Medical Practice: Reflections on the Dilemmas of Medical Culture Today*, eds Anand Zachariah, R. Srivatsan and Susie Tharu, 116–35. Hyderabad: Orient BlackSwan.

Shenoi, P. V. 2003. 'Oilseeds Production, Processing and Trade: A Policy Framework'. Occasional Paper 26, Department of Economic Analysis and Research, National Bank for Agriculture and Rural Development, Mumbai.

Shenoy, B. R. 1974. *PL480 Aid and India's Food Problem*. New Delhi: Affiliated East–West Press.

Shiva, V. 1992. *The Violence of Green Revolution: Third World Agriculture, Ecology and Politics*. London: Zed Books.

Siegel, B. R. 2018. *Hungry Nation: Food, Famine, and the Making of Modern India*. Cambridge: Cambridge University Press.

Singh, C. 1996. 'Forests, Pastoralists and Agrarian Society in Mughal India'. In *Nature, Culture, Imperialism: Essays on the Environmental History of South Asia*, eds David Arnold and Ramachandra Guha, 21–48. New Delhi: Oxford University Press.

Singh, M. 2011. 'PM's Address at the 83rd Foundation Day of ICAR'. 16 July. Available at http://archivepmo.nic.in/drmanmohansingh/speech-details.php?nodeid=1042 (accessed 27 January 2018).

Singh, S. 2000. 'Crisis in Punjab Agriculture'. *Economic and Political Weekly* 35(23): 1889–92.

Srinivasan, K. 2017. *Population Concerns in India: Shifting Trends, Policies, and Programs.* New Delhi: Sage Publications.

Srivastava, Uma K. 1972. 'Impact of PL480 Aid on India's Money Supply and External Debt-service Obligations: A Look Ahead'. CARD Reports, Book 48, Center for Agricultural and Economic Development, Iowa State University. Available at http://lib.dr.iastate.edu/card_reports/48 (accessed 12 January 2018).

Stevenson, James R., Nelson Villoria, Derek Byerlee, Timothy Kelley and Mywish Maredia. 2013. 'Green Revolution Research Saved an Estimated 18 to 27 Million Hectares From Being Brought Into Agricultural Production'. *Proceedings of the National Academy of Sciences* 110(21): 8363–68.

Tucker, N. 2015. 'Understanding India's Green Revolution: A Case Study for Contemporary Agrarian Reform'. Senior thesis in Economics, University of Puget Sound, Washington.

Unger, C. R. 2015. 'The Making of the Small Family Norm in Post-1947 India'. *Contemporanea* 18(3): 483–88.

Varshney, A. 1989. 'Ideas, Interest and Institutions in Policy Change: Transformation of India's Agricultural Strategy in the Mid-1960s'. *Policy Sciences* 22(3–4): 289–323.

Vasavi, A. R. 1999. *Harbingers of Rain: Land and Life in South India.* Delhi: Oxford University Press.

Vaughan, M. 1987. *The Story of an African Famine: Gender and Famine in Twentieth-century Malawi.* New York: Cambridge University Press.

Washbrook, D. A. 1988. 'Progress and Problems: South Asian Economic and Social History, c.1720–1860'. *Modern Asian Studies* 22(1): 57–96.

———. 1994. 'The Commercialisation of Agriculture in Colonial India: Production, Subsistence and Reproduction in the "Dry South", c.1870–1930'. *Modern Asian Studies* 28(1): 129–64.

9

DEVELOPMENT POLICIES AND AGRICULTURAL MARKETS*

RAMESH CHAND

In a narrow sense, the role of agricultural markets is delivering products from sources to consumers. But in a broad sense, their role extends to transmitting macroeconomic signals to producer firms, providing incentives to producers to attain the desired growth in agri-food output, improving the welfare of producers and consumers, balancing demand and supply, and promoting the efficient use of resources in the production and distribution systems. These roles require a competitive environment, strong physical and institutional infrastructure and a favourable regulatory system. These conditions cannot come up on their own, particularly in a developing country like India. Therefore, agricultural market policies are treated as an integral part of development policies and their functioning has remained an important part of public policy in India.

This chapter discusses various policies related to agricultural markets since the early 1960s, a time when major steps were taken for their transformation. It analyses how these policies have performed and their relevance, given changing production and consumption patterns, and technological and commercial developments.

POLICY INTERVENTIONS IN AGRICULTURAL MARKETS

Policy interventions in agricultural markets in India have a long history. Till the mid-1960s, it was mainly meant to facilitate the smooth functioning of markets and to keep a check on activities that were considered inimical to producers and/or consumers. Subsequently, the country opted for a package of direct and indirect interventions in agricultural markets and prices, initially targeted at procuring and distributing wheat and paddy. This gradually expanded to cover several other crops/products and aspects of domestic trade in agriculture. The present policy framework for intervention in agricultural markets and prices can be broadly grouped under

* Originally published in *Economic and Political Weekly* 47(52), 29 December 2012: 53–63.

three categories: (a) regulatory measures; (b) market infrastructure and institutions; and (c) agricultural price policy.

Regulatory Measures

The regulatory framework for agricultural markets consists of two sets of measures. One, measures for the development and regulation of wholesale markets; and two, a series of legal instruments for regulating the functioning of markets and trade activities.

Agricultural Produce Market Regulation Act

All wholesale markets for agricultural produce in states that have adopted the Agricultural Produce Market Regulation Act (APMRA) are termed 'regulated markets'. Apart from Kerala, Jammu and Kashmir, and Manipur, all other states in India have enacted marketing legislations, known as Agricultural Produce Marketing Committee (APMC) Acts. The act is implemented and enforced by APMCs established under it. It mandates that the sale/purchase of agricultural commodities notified under it are to be carried out in specified market areas, yards or sub-yards. These markets are required to have the proper infrastructure for sale of farmers' produce. Prices in them are to be determined by open auction, conducted in a transparent manner in the presence of an official of the market committee. Market charges for various agencies, such as commissions for commission agents (*arhtiyas*); statutory charges, such as market fees and taxes; and produce-handling charges, such as for cleaning of produce, and loading and unloading, are clearly defined, and no other deduction can be made from the sale proceeds of farmers. Market charges, costs and taxes vary across states and commodities.

On the whole, the APMC Acts have served some important purposes. They got rid of several malpractices and imperfections in agricultural markets, created orderly and transparent marketing conditions[1] and ensured a fairer deal to farmers selling their produce (Acharya 2004). It was a pressing need at the time and it transformed agricultural markets in most states of the country. Besides improving the way markets functioned, the acts created an environment that freed producers-sellers from exploitation by traders and mercantile capital.

In recent years, pressure has mounted to change this market regulation and remove its various restrictions. It is argued that the act was relevant when private trade was underdeveloped, exploitative, and controlled by mercantile power. The marketing monopoly provided to the state by the act is seen as preventing private investments in agricultural markets. The restrictive legal provisions of the act, such as 'all agricultural produce brought into or processed within a market area shall pass through the principal yard or sub-yard and shall not be bought or sold at any other place in the market area[2] or no such person shall carry on business and trade in agriculture produce into market area except one who holds the licence issued by the market committee', have prevented new entrants from coming in, thus reducing competition. Because of all this, the Inter-ministerial Task Force on Agricultural Marketing Reforms (2002) recommended that the APMC Acts be amended to allow for direct marketing and the establishment of agricultural markets in the private and cooperative sectors. The rationale behind direct marketing is that farmers should have the option to sell their produce directly to agribusiness firms, such as processors or bulk buyers, at a lower transaction cost and in the quality/form required by the buyers.

In response to this, the Union Ministry of Agriculture prepared a Model Act in 2003, which state governments could adopt to modify their acts (agricultural marketing is a state subject). Under the Model Act, the private sector and cooperatives can be licensed to set up markets. It also allows for contract farming and direct marketing by private traders. Barring a few, all states and Union territories (UTs) have either fully or partly adopted the Model Act. As a result, direct purchases by the private sector from farmers and contract farming have grown in some parts of the country. However, private investments in agricultural marketing have not been commensurate with the commercialisation and diversification that have taken place in the agriculture sector. The Model Act, so far, has not succeeded in persuading the private sector or cooperatives to set up agricultural marketing infrastructure as an alternative to the state-owned *mandi* (market yard) system.

Deficiencies in the Existing System and Need for Integrating the Supply Chain

As mentioned, the APMC Acts improved agricultural markets in several respects and considerably diluted mercantile power in them. However, over time, the balance of power in transactions has moved back in favour of middlemen and the trading class. It is interesting to see how these sections have entrenched themselves in mandis. When the APMRA was enacted by various states in the mid-1960s, the country was facing a serious food shortage and desperately seeking to achieve a breakthrough in food production. It was strongly felt that it would not be possible to attain and sustain food security without incentivising farmers to adopt new technology and make investments in modern inputs. Therefore, high priority was attached to enabling farmers to realise a reasonable price for their produce by eradicating malpractices from markets, protecting them from exploitation by middlemen and creating a competitive pricing environment. Simultaneously, the hold that traders and commission agents had over them by providing credit was diluted by increasing the supply of institutional credit. This, along with technology-led output growth, resulted in increased farm incomes, making farmers less dependent on the trading class for credit and cash requirements. It also gave farmers the freedom to choose markets and buyers for their produce.

The spread and success of the Green Revolution during the 1970s and 1980s led to an increase in the political power of the farming class and their clout in policymaking. This was reflected in the creation and strengthening of farmer-friendly institutions and a policy environment favourable to farmers. Marketing institutions like market committees, state-level agricultural marketing boards and many others in the public and cooperative sectors served the interests of the farming community. Over time, as the country moved close to food self-sufficiency, public policy began losing its focus. The marketing system and marketing institutions were plagued by inefficiencies, bureaucratic control and politicisation. The growth in market facilities did not keep pace with the growth in market arrivals, forcing producers to seek the help of middlemen in the market which, in turn, led to dependence on them. There was also a reversal in the credit situation after 1991, making farmers more dependent on commission agents and traders for loans.[3] The trading class quickly regained its marketing power over farmers by meeting their credit requirements with interlocked transactions, robbing producers of the freedom to decide where they would sell and whom they would sell to.

Taking advantage of the lax attitude of state governments towards marketing, the trading class consolidated their power in mandis. The so-called unorganised traders, individually small but numerically large, acquired power by organising themselves, which proved to be a potent factor in electoral politics. The ascent of the Bharatiya Janata Party (BJP) provided considerable clout and power to the trading class to influence public policy. And with populist politics, no state government wanted to undertake any market reforms that were opposed by the trading class for fear of losing its support. As a result, traders, commission agents, and other functionaries organised themselves into associations, which do not allow the entry of new players, stifling the competitive functioning of markets (Acharya 2004: 106). Middlemen successfully turned marketing policies to their benefit, dictating terms to producers, and thwarting modern capital from entering agricultural marketing. Some examples of this are: (a) increasing the commission rates of arhtiyas without any justification;[4] (b) ejecting direct payment to producers which would bypass commission agents;[5] and (c) determining prices through non-transparent methods.

These developments speak of the political clout and influence that middlemen have acquired in agricultural markets. There are also reports of collusive behaviour by wholesale buyers in markets (Banerji and Meenakshi 2001). Commission agents sometimes charge exorbitant fees for carrying out auctions. According to Gulati (2009), farmers at the Azadpur fruits and vegetable market in New Delhi have to pay commission agents a fee ranging from 6 to 10 per cent for an auction that lasts for about five minutes. Similarly, in the Vashi market in Mumbai, the commission agent's fee is 8 per cent and even goes up to 15 per cent.

The various problems facing the agricultural marketing system were summarised by the Twelfth Plan Working Group on Agricultural Marketing (Planning Commission 2011):

1. Too many intermediaries, resulting in high cost of goods and services;
2. inadequate infrastructure for storage, sorting, grading and post-harvest management;
3. private sector unwilling to invest in logistics or infrastructure under prevailing conditions;
4. price-setting mechanism not transparent;
5. ill-equipped and untrained mandi staff;
6. market information not easily accessible; and

7. Essential Commodities Act (ECA) impeding free movement, storage and transport of produce.

Thus, the APMC Act, which was enacted to protect farmers' interests and increase market efficiency and transparency, is now being used to deny them opportunities to get better prices, to prevent competition and to guard the interests of middlemen. Various researchers have reported findings on these lines.[6] A serious consequence of selling at a designated place, the yard of a mandi, is that once agricultural produce has been brought to it, it is seldom taken back in the event of any unfair deal. The costs already incurred in bringing the produce to the market and in cleaning and unloading it prevent this. This robs the producer of whatever little bargaining power she/he has in price determination. The direct sale of produce leaves this option with farmers. The system of having to go through regulated mandis also places small producers with less to sell in a disadvantageous position.

Small Traders Dominant

Agricultural markets in the country are crowded with small traders who operate on a small scale in a limited market segment. In agriculturally advanced Punjab, there are as many as 22,000 commission agents, one for every 50 farmers. Then there are a host of other middlemen such as wholesalers, transporters, labour contractors and brokers in each market. As the size of their business is small, they seek large margins on small volumes of business. Thus, the channels for marketing of agricultural produce remain long and fragmented and lack economies of scale. On an average, four to six transactions take place before the produce reaches consumers from the point of sale by producers. As each transaction involves cost and some margin for intermediaries, the price spread between consumers and producers becomes quite large, without any real value addition. Some of the middlemen are found to render no real service—they simply earn rent. Even the Model Act has failed to change the status quo. So, producers feel that they do not get value for their produce and consumers feel that they have to pay an unjustifiably higher price. The only way to address this is to integrate the supply chain, reduce the number of intermediaries and allow economies of scale in market operations. This is not possible if there are no alternative marketing options to government mandis.

A grave fallout of the present market system is declining competitiveness. This means increases in prices at the consumer level, which are the result of various factors, are not passed on to farmers. A classic example of this is the case of *arhar* (pigeon peas) in Maharashtra, where the benefit of price increases has been captured by middlemen without any benefit to farmers, as is shown in Figures 9.1 to 9.3. The price spread between the farm harvest price (FHP) of arhar (whole grain) in Maharashtra and the wholesale price (WSP) of arhar dal[7] (split and polished grain) in the Mumbai market increased from less than 25 per cent to more than 70 per cent between 2000 and 2009 (Figure 9.1). Thus, in just 10 years, the margin that middlemen earned recorded a threefold increase in the same state for the same type of product. Between 1999–2000 and 2009–10, the price that producers received for arhar increased by less than 5 per cent per year, whereas wholesale and retail prices of arhar dal increased by more than 10 per cent per year. Figure 9.2 also shows the change in minimum support price (MSP) of arhar announced by the central government relative to the change in the WSP of arhar dal. The MSP for arhar at the beginning of the 2000s was more than 50 per cent of the WSP of arhar dal in the Mumbai market. The level of support declined steadily to one-third by 2009–10. Thus, an increase in the MSP of arhar, even though notional, did not keep pace with the increase in market price in this period.[8] This illustrates a policy (price) failure in the case of pulses.

FIGURE 9.1: Ratio of Wholesale Price of Arhar Dal in Mumbai to WSP and FHP of Arhar in Maharashtra, 2000–09

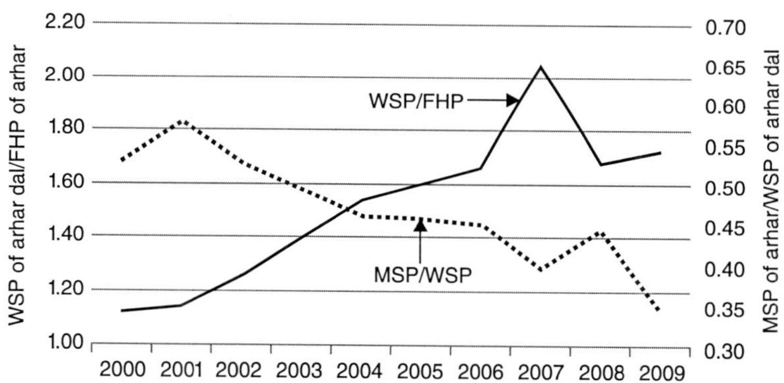

Source: *Farm Harvest Prices of Principal Crops in India*, Department of Agriculture and Cooperation, Ministry of Agriculture, New Delhi, various issues; *Agricultural Prices in India*, Department of Agriculture and Cooperation, Ministry of Agriculture, New Delhi, various issues.

FIGURE 9.2: Trend in Prices of Arhar in Maharashtra and Arhar Dal in Mumbai, 2000–09

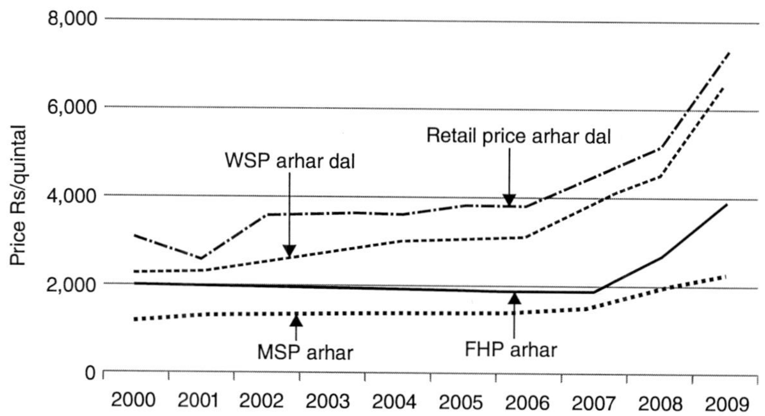

Source: *Farm Harvest Prices of Principal Crops in India*, Department of Agriculture and Cooperation, Ministry of Agriculture, New Delhi, various issues; *Agricultural Prices in India*, Department of Agriculture and Cooperation, Ministry of Agriculture, New Delhi, various issues.

FIGURE 9.3: Annual Growth Rate in Price of Arhar in Maharashtra and Arhar Dal in Mumbai, 2000–09

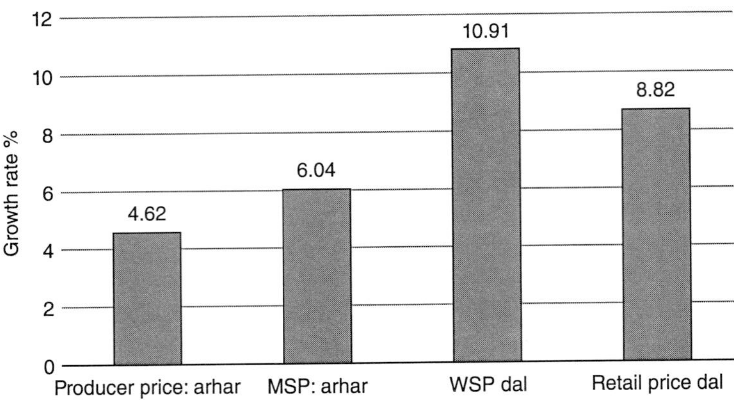

Source: *Farm Harvest Prices of Principal Crops in India*, Department of Agriculture and Cooperation, Ministry of Agriculture, New Delhi, various issues; *Agricultural Prices in India*, Department of Agriculture and Cooperation, Ministry of Agriculture, New Delhi, various issues.

The main reason for requiring that produce be sold and purchased only in a regulated market is revenue generation through collection of mandi fees and taxes. But this often stops farmers from selling produce outside the state for better price realisation. While the mandi fee is a service charge for using its services, other taxes are for state revenue. It needs to be carefully worked out whether revenue considerations are more important than increments in price realisation to producers from selling produce outside the mandi, and whether there are ways to take care of the state revenue from agriculture marketing if produce does not pass through mandis.

Legal Instruments

Apart from the APMC Acts, the activities of market functionaries are regulated by several other legal instruments promulgated and revised from time to time by the central and state governments (Acharya 1998, 2001: 131). The most important regulation is the Essential Commodities Act (ECA) 1955. Almost all agricultural commodities, such as cereals, pulses, edible oilseeds, oilcakes, edible oils, raw cotton, sugar, *gur* and jute, are included in the list of essential commodities. The act provides for instruments like licences, permits, regulations, and orders for: (a) price control, (b) storage, (c) stocking limits, (d) movement of produce, (e) distribution, (f) disposal, (g) sale, (h) compulsory purchase by the government, and (i) sale (levy) to the government. A very large number of control orders have been put into force by the central and state governments under the ECA.

To encourage quality and promote consumers' confidence in agricultural products, another act known as the Agricultural Produce Grading and Marking Act was passed in 1937. It defines standards of quality and prescribes grade specifications for a number of products. The act authorises an agricultural marketing adviser in each state to grant a certificate of authorisation to persons or corporate bodies who agree to grade agricultural produce as prescribed by it. There are Agmark grade specifications for 212 agricultural products, but the use and awareness of it have remained low despite a better understanding of quality attributes among consumers.

The main aims of the various regulations were to check the exploitation of producers and consumers by private traders through collusion and hoarding, to stabilise prices, and to raise the standards of markets and improve their performance. Many changes have taken place in the marketing and trade environment since these regulations were framed. The development of transport and communication, an expansion of marketing and increased competition make it possible for the private sector to play a larger role in agricultural marketing. It is felt that excessive control and intervention by the government have hampered the participation of private trade in agricultural marketing, which is counterproductive (Debroy and Kaushik 2002; Jha, Srinivasan and Kumar 2010). As a step towards liberalisation of agricultural trade, the Union government issued an order on 15 February 2002 which removed licencing requirements and all restrictions on buying, stocking and transporting specified commodities, including wheat, rice, oilseeds and sugar. They were further decontrolled after this. Similarly, the dairy sector was liberalised through various amendments to the Milk and Milk Product Order, beginning in 1992. The main purpose of these changes was to allow increased participation by the private sector in marketing agricultural commodities. In response, private sector investments in the dairy sector have increased and this has promoted healthy competition between cooperatives and the private sector.

However, the experience of liberalising grain trade has not been very encouraging. The 2002 change in the ECA attracted big domestic and multinational players like ITC, Cargill, Australian Wheat Board, Britannia, Agricore, Delhi Floor Mills and Adani Enterprises to the grain trade. This came after the government had accumulated excessive foodgrain during 2001–03. But soon, the domestic foodgrain demand and supply balance, particularly for wheat, turned adverse and India had to import more than 6 million tonnes of wheat in 2006–07. The imports were arranged with great difficulty and at a high price because India's wheat shortage coincided with a period of high global prices, which culminated in the global food crisis of 2007–08. Partly because of below-normal production and partly because of an increase in procurement by private trade, the official agencies could not obtain enough wheat in 2006–07.[9] The government was worried about being able to procure an adequate quantity of wheat in 2007–08 because rising global and domestic food prices were providing a strong incentive to the private sector to buy wheat coming to the market. Unrestricted trade in grains by the private sector was also found to aggravate instability in prices. These developments led the central government to reconsider and it, along with many state governments, decided to reverse the decision on the ECA.[10] This made a large section of the organised private trade (large players) withdraw from the grain market.

Some researchers have analysed the demand and supply situation of wheat and other trade issues during this period (Chand 2007a, 2007b), but in-depth information on why the government became wary of allowing freedom to market forces and the private sector in the grain trade is missing. There is a need to investigate whether it was circumstances, the conduct of private trade, or a fixed procurement price for the whole season that made it difficult for the government to manage the foodgrain economy in 2006–07 and 2007–08.

TABLE 9.1: MSP and Price Received by Farmers for Paddy and Wheat in the Highest-producing States (Rs/quintal), 1995–2010

Year	*Paddy*			*Wheat*		
	MSP	*FHP (West Bengal)*	*FHP-MSP*	*MSP*	*FHP (Uttar Pradesh)*	*FHP-MSP*
1995–96	360.0	417.00	57.00	380.0	408.00	28.00
1996–97	380.0	466.00	86.00	475.0	535.00	60.00
1997–98	415.0	580.00	165.00	510.0	484.00	–26.00
1998–99	440.0	634.00	194.00	550.0	544.00	–6.00
1999–2000	490.0	543.00	53.00	580.0	572.00	–8.00
2000–01	510.0	438.00	–72.00	610.0	529.00	–81.00
2001–02	530.0	471.00	–59.00	620.0	540.00	–80.00
2002–03	530.0	434.00	–96.00	620.0	586.00	–34.00
2003–04	550.0	469.00	–81.00	630.0	592.00	–38.00
2004–05	560.0	507.00	–53.00	640.0	615.00	–25.00
2005–06	570.0	520.00	–50.00	650.0	760.00	110.00
2006–07	580.0	562.00	–18.00	750.0	880.00	130.00
2007–08	645.0	631.00	–14.00	1,000.0	998.00	–2.00
2008–09	850.0	696.00	–154.00	1,080.0	983.00	–97.00
2009–10	950.0	772.00	–178.00	1,100.0	1,021.00	–79.00

Source: *Farm Harvest Prices of Principal Crops in India*, Department of Agriculture and Cooperation, Ministry of Agriculture, New Delhi, various issues; *Agricultural Prices in India*, Department of Agriculture and Cooperation, Ministry of Agriculture, New Delhi, various issues.

Tracking events during that period indicates that the sharp drop in procurement of wheat in two successive years, caused by the high prices offered by private players, created a panic situation of sorts and it led the ministry of food to reverse the reforms in the grain market. It is very pertinent to note that it was only in 2005–06 and 2006–07 that wheat producers in Uttar Pradesh, the largest wheat-producing state, received prices higher than the MSP after a long time. After this, the price of wheat received by them trailed far behind the MSP year after year (Table 9.1). This raises some important issues.

1. How can competitiveness in the grain market be improved while maintaining price stability?
2. How can public agencies secure supplies to meet food security obligations, like providing subsidised grain to the public distribution system (PDS), in a free market when the private sector offers more attractive prices to producers?

These issues are discussed in the section on price policy.

Agricultural marketing is a state subject and many states are either slow or reluctant to implement various reforms and legislations related to marketing, even though they are considered necessary for developing the market and trade and for improving the welfare of producers and consumers. Some experts suggest moving agricultural marketing to the concurrent list so that the required changes can be implemented quickly and smoothly.

Marketing Infrastructure

Marketing infrastructure has two broad dimensions: quantity and quality. A simple indicator of market infrastructure is the number of agriculture markets. Progress on this vis-à-vis an increase in agriculture production, as seen in the index of crop production and volume of production, is presented in Table 9.2. Between 1976 and 1991, the total number of regulated markets in the country increased from 3,528 to 6,217, a 76 per cent increase over 15 years. In the same period, agriculture production in the country increased by 74 per cent. This shows that marketing infrastructure in terms of availability of space kept pace with the growth in output. After 1991, the number of regulated markets grew only 22 per cent in 17 years, till 2008. In the same period, the volume of production increased 70 per cent. There has been no increase in the number of markets after 2006. Further, due to rising commercialisation of agriculture, market arrivals have increased at a much higher rate than the growth in production, indicating a widening gap between the increase in marketed surplus and the number of markets. As a consequence, markets are crowded, putting sellers in a disadvantageous position and providing advantages to buyers.

TABLE 9.2: Growth in Agricultural Output and Markets, 1976–2008

Year	*Crop Output (Index Number TE1981–2 = 100)*	*Quantity (Million Tonnes)**	*Regulated Markets*
1976	85.2	—	3,528
1980	102.1	—	4,446
1991	148.4	285.5	6,217
2001	179.1	373.7	7,161
2008	201.8	483.7	7,566
	Compound Growth Rate (%)		
1976 to 1991	3.769	—	3.849
1980 to 1991	3.458	—	3.095
1991 to 2001	1.898	2.729	1.424
2001 to 2008	1.719	3.755	0.789

Note: *Includes foodgrains, oilseeds, cotton, fruits and vegetables.

Source: *Agricultural Statistics in India*, Department of Agriculture and Cooperation, Ministry of Agriculture, New Delhi, various issues; *Manual on Agricultural Prices and Marketing, CSO-MAPM-2010*, Central Statistics Office, Ministry of Statistics and Programme Implementation, New Delhi, October 2010, Annexure VIII.

The experience of some states, especially in agriculturally less-developed regions, shows that mere regulation does not help in improving market performance if the required infrastructure is not there. It is reported that one-third of regulated markets in the country do not have a common auction platform. The infrastructure for marketing perishables like fruits and vegetables, which require special facilities for storage and processing, are very inadequate (Planning Commission 2007a). The Working Group on Agriculture Marketing for the Twelfth Plan highlighted the following gaps in the marketing infrastructure (Planning Commission 2011):

1. there has been virtually no progress in setting up wholesale markets, except in Kerala;
2. there are only 1,637 grading units at the primary level in the whole country;
3. of 7,246 regulated markets in India, grading units are found in less than 20 per cent of the market yards/sub-yards;
4. only around 7 per cent of the total quantity sold by farmers is graded before sale;
5. the scientific storage capacity is only 30 per cent of what is required; and
6. cold storage facilities are available for only 10 per cent of fruits and vegetables.

The appalling state of marketing infrastructure can be seen in Table 9.3, which presents data from the Directorate of Marketing and Inspection. It shows deficiencies in infrastructure that has to be provided in regulated markets according to the APMRA. These statistics reveal why producers depend on arhtiyas and traders in primary markets. A common auction platform is not available in one-third of the markets, necessitating the use of private platforms or the conduct of auctions without the proper display of produce. Producers are often not aware of acceptable moisture levels in their produce. Market yards are required to provide common areas for drying produce before it is auctioned. This facility was available in only 26 per cent of the regulated markets. Simple facilities like benches to sit on and

TABLE 9.3: Facilities/Amenities in Regulated Markets, 2010

Amenities	*No. of Markets with Facility (%)*
Common auction platform (covered)	64
Common auction platform (open)	67
Common drying yards	26
Grading equipment	30
Canteen	43
Drinking water taps	28
Seating benches	28
Public address system	34
Price display board	61

Source: *Manual on Agricultural Prices and Marketing, CSO-MAPM-2010*, Central Statistics Office, Ministry of Statistics and Programme Implementation, New Delhi, October 2010, Annexure VIII.

drinking water taps were not available in more than 70 per cent of the markets. Price information to enable producers to know the ruling price was not displayed in 39 per cent of the markets. The lack of various facilities and amenities in markets forces producers to look for them elsewhere, which means agents and traders.

The Agmark facility, which is meant to promote grades and standards, has not become popular (Table 9.4). The total quantity of produce graded at the producers' level in any year has not even reached 10 million tonnes—the highest level attained was 9 million tonnes in 2008–09. Agmark grading touched its highest total of 1.16 million tonnes in 2010–11. The highest quantity of exports under Agmark was 51,000 tonnes in 2009–10. Due to lack of awareness and extremely low brand value, the total value of Agmark-certified output did not cross even 1.5 per cent of the total value of crop produce in the country. In 2010–11, exports worth only Rs 180 crore were certified, which was 0.16 per cent of the total value of agricultural exports from India.

TABLE 9.4: Status of Grading and Agmark-certified Produce, 2010–11

		Quantity (Million Tonnes)	*Value (Rs Crore)*
1.	Grading at producers' level	8,976	—
	Share in crop output (%)	—	1.37
2.	Agmark grading		
	Total	1,060	10,844
	Share in crop output %	—	1.05
	Export	31	180
	Share in total agricultural exports (%)	—	0.16

Source: Agmark statistics, available at http://agmarketnet.nic.in/agmstat2011.pdf (accessed 8 June 2012); National Accounts Statistics 2012, Central Statistics Office.

The main reasons for poor market infrastructure are: (a) the market committees did not plough back the market fee collected into developing infrastructure, and these funds in several cases were siphoned off to the government account (Government of India 2001); and (b) the government monopoly in setting up agricultural markets has prevented the private sector from taking the initiative to develop marketing infrastructure (Acharya 2004: 107).

Institutions and Alternative Marketing Models

A large number of public sector institutions and cooperative marketing organisations were set up after Independence to improve the market structure, its conduct and performance, and to help growers realise better returns for their produce. Private trade in India at the time was underdeveloped and not equipped to meet the needs of a growing economy. Some of these institutions, such as the Food Corporation of India (FCI), Cotton Corporation of India (CCI), National Dairy Development

Board (NDDB), and National Agricultural Cooperative Marketing Federation of India (NAFED), and some commodity boards, have a strong presence in the market whereas others have become dormant or defunct. The decline has been quite serious in the case of state-level and cooperative institutions. The country needs to revive these institutions and build them on business lines as they act as a balance to the private sector and serve the purpose of attaining social objectives.

Alternative to the Mandi System

The Model Act was to add alternatives for the sale of produce and to provide competition to government mandis. The following are its salient marketing features:

1. Establishment of new markets for agricultural produce in any area by legal persons, growers and local authority;
2. contract farming with a provision for direct sale of produce from farmers' fields, without requiring it to pass through a notified committee;
3. purchase of agricultural produce through private yards or directly from agriculturists; and
4. establishment of consumer/farmers' markets to facilitate direct sale of agricultural produce to consumers.

There has been some progress in contract farming, but growth in the other aspects has been very slow, particularly the setting up of alternative mandis by cooperatives and the private sector. It is pertinent to mention two ventures that have had tremendous success: Safal Fruits and Vegetables Auction Market, a cooperative set up by Mother Dairy Food Procuring Limited (MDFPL), an NDDB subsidiary, in Bangalore, for procuring and marketing horticultural produce; and the ITC e-Choupal, a private platform for purchase of farmers' produce in Madhya Pradesh. The main reasons for the private sector not coming forward to set up an alternative market infrastructure are the reluctance of states to change the existing mandi system, a lack of enthusiasm for the Model Act, and the difficulties and cost involved in acquiring land for setting up markets.

Innovative Marketing Mechanisms

Some innovative marketing mechanisms have been developed in some states, which involve the direct sale of farm produce to consumers, the sale of produce to buyers without routing it through mandis and group marketing. Many states have attempted to promote direct contact between producers and consumers by making arrangements for sale at designated places in urban areas. Examples are Apni Mandis or Kisan Mandis in Punjab and Haryana, Rythu Bazaars in Andhra Pradesh, Shetkari Bazaars in Maharashtra, Krushak Bazaars in Odisha, and Uzhavar Sandhais in Tamil Nadu. The scale of operation of these marketing arrangements is quite small as only farmers in the vicinity of big towns can take advantage of them. But this mechanism has scope for reducing the market margin and eliminating middlemen, though it cannot cover produce separated by a geographic distance from consumers.

Another successful example of linking producers to consumers and eliminating middlemen is of Safal, a division of the NDDB. Its method of direct procurement backed with technical support has benefited farmers immensely, even without an assurance on prices. Similarly, vertical integration of poultry meat production under integrators who supply everything from inputs to technical support and pay the producer a predefined fixed price has been very successful (Birthal, Joshi and Gulati 2005).

Farm producers' organisations (FPOs) of various kinds are emerging as a new model for organised marketing and farm business. Such models include informal farmers' groups or associations, marketing cooperatives and formal organisations like producers' companies. Producers can benefit from getting together to sell their produce through economies of scale in the use of transport and other services, and raise their bargaining power in sales transactions, while marketing expenses get distributed. This results in a better share of net returns. Such models are particularly required for small farmers to overcome their constraints of both small size and modest marketable quantities.

In response to a long-pending demand from farmers' groups, the government amended the Companies Act 1956 in 2002, allowing the incorporation of producers' companies. According to the amended act, 10 or more individual producers, or two or more producer institutions, or a combination of both, and cooperatives can form a producers' company. The company can produce, harvest, procure, handle, pool, grade, market, sell and export the primary produce of members, or import goods or services for their benefit. It can also be involved in processing, including preserving, drying, distilling, brewing, canning and packaging the produce of its members. Such companies can go a long way in improving the wellbeing of producers through group action—in production, post-harvest activities, and promoting marketing and trading. Though the benefits of FPOs are obvious, they cannot be expected to come up and grow on their own. FPOs require committed and sustained help from government agencies to mobilise members, help capacity development and hand-hold them in the initial stages.

Contract farming has seen appreciable growth in most states after the legal restrictions on them were removed. This has paved the way for vertical coordination becoming a viable model for the food-processing industry as well as agri-commodity markets, and several initiatives, though on a small scale, have been taken in recent years. Yet, there are some reported dangers like the overuse of natural resources, violation of contracts, and the introduction of undesirable seeds. Keeping the pros and cons in view, the union ministry drafted a model contract farming agreement and a supportive legislation that can be inserted in the APMC Acts. The model provides for compulsory registration of contracts, a dispute settlement mechanism, the settlement of claims within three months and a ban on enmeshing farmers' land (Acharya 2006). The following are some of the suggestions to make contract farming successful:

1. Contract farming should be made legal. If contracts are violated, farmers as well as the company should be able to approach an organisation or institution, which can mediate and settle the dispute.

2. There should be an institutional arrangement to record all contractual arrangements, maybe the local market committee or panchayat or some government department. This will promote and strengthen confidence-building between the parties and also help solve disputes.
3. Contract farming should have a provision for both forward and backward linkages. Unless both input supply and market for the produce are assured, small farmers will not be able to participate in it.
4. Contracts should be managed in a more transparent and participatory manner so that there is greater social consensus in handling violations, which could avoid costly and lengthy litigation.

The direct purchase of farm produce by retailers has been steadily increasing with the growth of organised retailing in India. This is expected to accelerate with the entry of foreign direct investment (FDI) to the field. Food World (of the RPG group) is the leader among organised food-retail chains, and there are many more such as FabMall, Monday to Sunday, Family Mart, More for You, Heritage and Reliance Fresh. Most food chains are regional in nature, having one or two outlets in the main cities, but no big presence outside their states. Rapid urbanisation, urban population growth, increase in incomes and consumer spending, changing lifestyles and access to technology have been the important factors behind the expansion of food retail chains in India. Despite several factors favouring organised retail trade, it is still in a nascent stage in the country.

Integration of farmers into retail chains through contractual arrangements can fetch them higher and assured prices and allow the chains to plan the quality and quantity of supply. The other advantages of this model are reductions in transportation and handling costs, the absence of middlemen, an assured market and reduced price risk. However, this model has limited reach. Though the official view is that FDI in retail trade will be a boon to the farm sector and solve problems in the marketing system, the experience of countries where organised retail has reached a mature phase show that it can cover and benefit a maximum of 10 to 15 per cent of farm producers. Therefore, the potential of organised retail to benefit some farmers should not deflect attention from the various measures that are needed to connect retail and farm prices, and producers and consumers.

Agricultural Price Policy

The agricultural price policy is aimed at intervening in agricultural produce markets to influence the level of fluctuations in prices and the price-spread from farm gate to the retail level (Government of India 2010). The main instruments of agricultural price policy have been: (a) assured prices to producers through the system of MSPs implemented through obligatory procurement; (b) inter- and intra-year price stability through open market operations; (c) maintaining buffer stocks; and (d) distributing foodgrains at reasonable prices through the PDS. This policy has been helpful in several ways. From a situation of massive shortages, India has emerged as a net exporter of food, and food security has been attained at the national level. Prices of basic food items have remained relatively stable, and India did not face the sharp price spikes experienced by many countries during the global food crisis (Chand 2008). The policy has had a positive effect on farm income and led to economic transformation in well-endowed, mainly irrigated, regions.

Critique of Price Policy

The price policy implemented since the 1970s has mainly benefited wheat and rice among foodgrains, and sugarcane and cotton among other crops (Chand 2003). This has resulted in a shift of land and other resources away from pulses, oilseeds and coarse grains to wheat and paddy, which has created serious imbalances in the demand and supply of various agricultural commodities in the country. The country has been facing large shortages of pulses and edible oils and has to now meet about 15 per cent of its demand for pulses and 40 per cent of its demand for edible oil through imports. These imports have an adverse impact on producers in unfavourable dryland areas, while exports of wheat and rice have been pushed in some years at a huge cost to the exchequer (Chand 1999, 2001, 2005). These imbalances are against the spirit of the policy specified in the terms of reference (TOR) of the Agricultural Prices Commission (Government of India 1965), which was set up to advise the government on evolving a balanced and integrated price structure. The TOR require that a policy-induced incentive (profitability) should move in favour of crops where the domestic supply and demand balance is negative, relative to crops where it is positive and rising. The production of pulses and oilseeds in India has been growing at a slower rate than demand, whereas the demand for cereals has been growing at a lower rate than the growth in production. As a result, the country's imports of pulses and oilseeds have been rising, while exports of rice and wheat have increased, alongside a piling up of stock. The national requirement, particularly of pulses, has been bypassed by the price policy.

The per capita availability of pulses, which are the main source of protein in Indian diets, suffered a decline from 25.2 kg in 1961 to 18.7 kg in 1971, and further to 13.5 kg in 2009. This was not the result of a shift in preference but because of a decline in their availability. This is evident from that their prices have increased at a higher rate than those of cereals. The country has been importing pulses and edible oil for a long time now. On the other hand, it has been exporting a sizeable quantity of rice and occasionally also wheat. Except in 2006–07 and 2007–08, India has not had to significantly import wheat. Based on these trends in demand and supply, trade and stock, one would expect the price policy to influence a price parity in favour of pulses and oilseeds vis-à-vis rice and wheat. The actual experience on this is depicted in Figure 9.4. It shows that the ratio of MSP of wheat relative to chickpea and rapeseed-mustard declined for almost a decade beginning 1995–96, and increased sharply after that. Thus, the price of wheat relative to pulses and oilseeds remained at almost the same level where it was during the mid-1990s. The price of paddy relative to pigeon pea shows an annual decline of 1.2 per cent, but it was found to be statistically non-significant. Thus, during a period when the country moved towards surplus rice and wheat and inadequate pulses and oilseeds, no serious policy change was followed to change the price parity in accordance with the national requirement.

FIGURE 9.4: Price Parity between MSP of Cereals and Pulses, 1995–2010

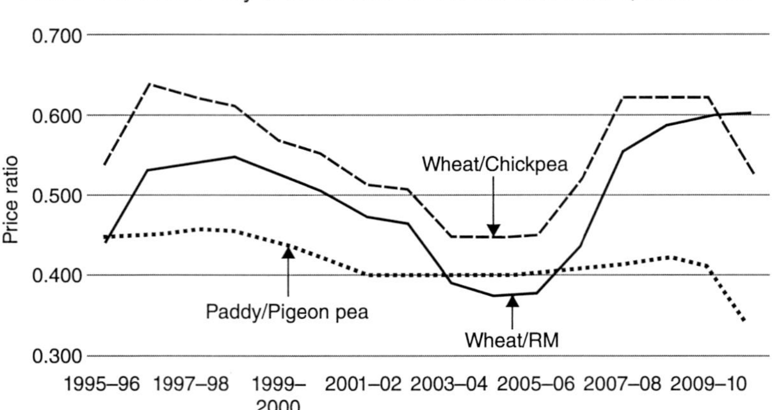

Source: *Agricultural Statistics at a Glance*, Department of Agriculture and Cooperation, New Delhi, various issues.

Policy-induced changes in production patterns towards rice and wheat have put a lot of strain on natural resources. Intensive cultivation of these two cereals, particularly rice–wheat rotation, has resulted in depletion of water, soil degradation and deterioration in water quality (Chand 2010). The price policy practised in the country since the onset of the Green Revolution ignored the TOR, which recommended developing a production pattern broadly in the light of national requirements and ensuring the rational use of land, water and other resources.

The second major criticism of the price policy is that a large number of crops and states are not covered by effective implementation of the MSP (Chand 2003). The prices received by farmers are often below the MSP in a large number of crops and in a large number of markets where it is not supported by effective procurement (Planning Commission 2007b: 67–68). This can be seen from the prices received by farmers for wheat and paddy in Uttar Pradesh and West Bengal since the late 1990s (see Table 9.1). The table shows the difference between the MSP and FHP in the two states. The average FHP in West Bengal was higher than the MSP from 1995–96 to 1999–2000. After this, the paddy price received by farmers has remained lower than the MSP in all years, with the gap widening in recent years. The story of wheat in Uttar Pradesh is similar. After 1996–97, Uttar Pradesh farmers have received a price higher than the MSP in only two years out of 13—the years the private sector was in the wheat market in a big way. In the other years, the FHP has been lower than the assured price announced by the government.

Reforming Price Policy

Till now, the price guarantee to producers has been implemented by procuring produce at the MSP/procurement price, in selected states and markets. It is not feasible for public agencies to procure the marketed surplus of each and every commodity everywhere in the country to prevent prices falling below a floor level; nor would this be desirable. Honouring price guarantee through procurement, which always involves a raise in price, also leads to serious price distortions (Chand 2009). So new mechanisms have to be devised to protect producers against the risk of the price falling below the threshold level.

One way of doing this is to provide a price guarantee for all the major crops grown in each state either through MSPs or a minimum insured price (MIP). The basis for the MIP could be the paid-out cost (A2) or average price of the past three or four seasons. The MSP should be restricted to basic staples like paddy and wheat, and it should be made effective through a procurement mechanism in all the districts that have a reasonably high surplus of the crops. All other major crops should be covered by the MIP. Under this, all farmers should be given the option of registering the quantity of surplus produce expected from their farm with the market committee at the time of sowing and insuring it against the price falling below a certain level by paying a nominal charge. If the actual market price for the produce sold in regulated markets during the specified marketing period falls below the insured price, the farmers covered by the MIP should be compensated through deficiency price payment (DPP). Another way of ensuring the MIP is through extending the market intervention scheme (which is in operation in some commodities and in some states) to all the major crops in all the states.

To sustain the food security of the country, the agricultural price policy should focus on harnessing the agricultural potential of low productivity regions like Bihar, east Uttar Pradesh, Odisha, Assam, Madhya Pradesh and Chhattisgarh. This can be done by extending foodgrain procurement operations involving remunerative and assured prices through implementation of MSPs. These states have poor marketing infrastructure and underdeveloped and exploitative private trade. Public procurement would not only help in boosting the growth of cereal output and in reaping technological gains, but also in developing a marketing system.

There is the need to maintain a distinction between the MSP and procurement price. While the MSP in its present form should continue to be announced before the sowing season, the government should separately announce a procurement price at the start of the harvest season. This price should be used as a benchmark for foodgrain procurement by the government. A cell in the ministry of food should monitor prices regularly, and if need be, change the procurement price upwards or downwards (each week or day), depending on the market situation. In this age of instant communication, there should be no problem in instructing the field staff of public agencies about the day-to-day procurement price. Under this, the government should procure all grain offered for sale at the MSP if prices fall below the threshold level. If the market price is above the MSP, the government should not distort prices to force them to the level of the MSP to achieve its procurement target. Rather, it should buy produce at the procurement price, which has been adjusted to the prevailing market reality. This requires the FCI to operate alongside private players without distorting the market, rather than seeking a space free of private trade.

CONCLUSION

Agricultural marketing suffers from inefficiency, a disconnect between the prices received by producers and the prices paid by consumers, fragmented and long marketing channels, poor infrastructure and policy distortions. Agricultural markets are not vertically integrated (Chand 2006), though they are horizontally (Jha et al. 1997). In the total value added in production and marketing, the share added in the post-harvest phase is rising and that in production is falling. In some cases, value addition in marketing is larger than value addition in production. With farm sizes getting smaller, income from agriculture produce can be improved by enabling the farmers to get a share of the value added in marketing by developing and strengthening marketing mechanisms that includes them as partners. Urgent reforms are needed in agricultural marketing to achieve such goals and address the inadequacies now prevailing in markets.

The best marketing model for producers and consumers is where producers sell directly to consumers, either as individuals or as some sort of organisation. Such models have been developed in some states and farmers are allowed to sell their produce as retail to consumers in towns on certain days without intermediaries. The scale of operation of these arrangements is quite small and only farmers near big towns can benefit from them. Such innovative marketing should be promoted on a large scale.

The demand pattern for agricultural commodities, both at the consumer and industry levels, has been changing rapidly towards processed products, quality products and specific traits. These changes favour integrated supply chains over conventional marketing channels, assured markets over open markets, and specific produce over generic produce. Such supply chains offer tremendous scope to reduce the margins paid to middlemen. A well-functioning supply chain can reduce the cost of marketing by linking farmers more closely to processing firms and consumers, and guide the production to meet changing consumer preferences for quantity, quality, variety and safety. Modern supply chains also often have strict private standards and this helps standardise product requirements over many regions or countries, enhancing efficiency and lowering transaction costs (Chand et al. 2009). The supply chain concept can be beneficial to small-holders who dominate India's agriculture. It has also been suggested that the institution of integrators who assemble small produce and sell it in the market on behalf of producers or themselves be promoted.

A few experiments such as direct procurement backed by technical support have benefited farmers immensely. These indicate that the participation of cooperatives and private sector firms in marketing agricultural produce under specific conditions can help farmers. This calls for a thorough review of existing agricultural marketing policies and implementing changes to bring producers closer to consumers.

Organised retailing in India has grown steadily since the 2000s. Despite official claims that FDI in organised retail will provide a big boost to farmers, experience elsewhere shows that it can help some pockets, but not serve the multitude of Indian farmers. Therefore, organised retail, with or without FDI, should not be seen as a panacea for addressing the problems of agricultural marketing and it should not deflect attention from other models and mechanisms for improving competitiveness and efficiency. Given the vastness and diversity of Indian agriculture, the country requires multiple approaches, including the APMC mechanism, new models and scaling up successful ventures such as cooperative milk marketing, along with organised retail. All states, in particular, need to promote producers' associations, producers' companies and cooperative marketing societies to improve the bargaining power of producers and raise their share in value addition, which is getting bigger and bigger. Most of the reforms needed in agricultural marketing are proposed in the Model Act. The states must implement the Model Act in the right spirit without diluting it to serve the interests of particular groups. This will pave the way for direct marketing and vertical coordination through contract farming. It will also provide alternative options to producers for sale of produce, and create a competitive environment for services that are now a monopoly of APMCs.

There is a pressing need to reorient our price policy to bring it in tune with the emerging demand and supply of various crops, and the sustainable use of natural resources, as laid down in the TOR for price policy. The country has to use mechanisms like deficiency price payment to avoid a bias in price support to select regions.

While increased participation of the private sector in agricultural marketing is desirable, the country also needs the strong presence and participation of the public sector and marketing models based on the participation of producers, such as cooperatives, producers' companies and producers' associations. We feel the public sector in agriculture and food marketing is as important to competitiveness as the private sector is to improving efficiency. The public sector is also essential to serve the larger social goal of maintaining price stability through market operations. The private sector has absolutely no interest in price stability; it benefits from the reverse. This is strongly borne by the global experience during 2007–12, when, in the wake of supply shocks, countries like India with a strong presence of the public sector in staple food succeeded in protecting the market from price volatility, while many developing countries with no public sector presence in food staples suffered seriously from unstable prices.

NOTES

1. Some isolated cases of price determination in a non-transparent manner still continue. This includes determining prices through negotiation and secret signals, as observed in the Azadpur market in Delhi.

2. Market area for this purpose is not restricted to a market yard or mandi; it includes the entire geographic area that comes under the purview of the market committee.

3. According to the All India Rural Debt and Investment Survey Report, the share of institutional sources in total credit received by cultivator households slipped from 66.3 to 61.1 per cent. This could have been due to a squeeze in farm incomes caused by the decline in size of holdings, the disappearance of technological gains and the mismatch between consumption expenditure and income of farm households. These changes are evident from rising farm distress in the country.

4. Agriculturally progressive Punjab increased the commission of arhtiyas from 2 to 2.5 per cent in 1999–2000 without any additional service being rendered by them. This raised the commission of arhtiyas three times, per unit of foodgrain, in 10 years.

5. The central government asked the states to directly pay farmers for cereals procured by it during 2010–11 to avoid unnecessary middlemen. The move was strongly opposed by arhtiyas, but supported by farmers. According to a survey conducted at Punjab Agricultural University, Ludhiana, 93 per cent of the farmers expressed a preference for direct payment and 84 per cent wanted the arhtiya system abolished. The state government, rather than siding with the farmers, took recourse to the APMC Act to protect the interests of arhtiyas. According to media reports, the chief minister went to Delhi a number of times to plead with the prime minister and the agriculture minister to stop direct payments to farmers (*The Tribune* 2012).

6. Krishnamurthy (2012) writes of critics who find that 'instead of protecting the interest of primary producers, mandis have thrived under a politicised and restrictive regulatory framework, strengthening mercantile control and collusion, while leaving both farmers and consumers worse off on either end of a fragmented and inefficient supply chain'.

7. The reason for choosing arhar dal instead of arhar grain for price comparison is that arhar is consumed as dal, and comparable and reliable retail and wholesale prices are available only for dal.

8. During 2010–11 and 2011–12, a substantial hike has been made to the MSP of arhar and other pulses, which will raise its ratio to the WSP.

9. Wheat procurement dropped to 9.2 million tonnes in 2006–07, which was the lowest in the last decade and around half the average procurement in the previous five years. The procurement level reached 11.1 million tonnes during 2007–08, which was again far below the procurement target of the government.

10. The Union government decided in August 2006 to keep in abeyance certain provisions of the order dated 15 February 2002 on wheat and pulses for a period of six months and subsequently extended its validity.

References

'Unwanted Middlemen: Direct Payments to Help Farmers' (editorial). 2012. *The Tribune*, Chandigarh, 11 February.

Acharya, S. S. 1998. 'Agricultural Marketing in India: Some Facts and Emerging Issues'. *Indian Journal of Agricultural Economics* 53(3): 311–32.

———. 2001. 'Domestic Agricultural Marketing Policies, Incentives and Integration'. In *Indian Agricultural Policy at the Crossroads*, eds S. S. Acharya and D. P. Chaudhri, 129–205. Jaipur and New Delhi: Rawat Publications.

———. 2004. 'State of the Indian Farmer: A Millennium Study'. Agricultural Marketing, Department of Agricultural and Cooperation, Ministry of Agriculture, and Academic Foundation, New Delhi.

———. 2006. 'Agricultural Marketing and Rural Credit for Strengthening Indian Agriculture'. INRM Policy Brief No. 3, Asian Development Bank, New Delhi.

Banerji, A., and J. V. Meenakshi. 2001. 'Competition and Collusion in Grain Markets: Basmati Auctions in North India'. Working Paper No. 91, Working Paper Series, Centre for Development Economics, Delhi School of Economics, Delhi.

Birthal, P. S., P. K. Joshi and Ashok Gulati. 2005. 'Vertical Coordination in High Value Commodities: Implications for the Smallholders'. MTID Discussion Paper No. 85, IFPRI, Washington, DC.

Chand, Ramesh. 1999. 'Liberalisation of Agricultural Trade and Net Social Welfare: A Study of Selected Crops'. *Economic and Political Weekly* 34(52): A153–59.

———. 2001. 'Wheat Export: Little Gain'. *Economic and Political Weekly* 36(25): 2226–28.

———. 2003. 'Minimum Support Prices: Changing Requirements'. *Economic and Political Weekly* 38(29): 3027–28.

———. 2005. 'Whither India's Food Policy: From Food Security to Food Deprivation'. *Economic and Political Weekly* 40(12): 1055–61.

———. 2006. 'Agricultural Markets in India: Implications for Competition'. In *Towards a Functional Competition Policy for India*, ed. Pradeep S. Mehta, 135–45. New Delhi and Jaipur: Academic Foundation and CUTS International.

———. 2007a. 'Wheat Import and Price Outlook for 2007–08: Separating the Grain from the Chaff'. *Economic and Political Weekly* 42(30): 3196–99.

———. 2007b. 'Wheat Supply, Price Prospects and Food Security'. *Economic and Political Weekly* 42(19): 1659–63.

———. 2008. 'Global Food and Financial Crisis: Experience and Perspective from India'. In *Agricultural Reforms and Trade Liberalisation in China and Selected Asian Countries: Lessons of Three Decades* (Policy Assistance Series No. 6), 151–163. Bangkok: Regional Office for Asia and the Pacific, Food and Agriculture Organisation.

———. 2009. 'Wheat Market: The Distortions Caused by Government Intervention'. *Economic and Political Weekly* 44(12): 41–46.

———. 2010. 'Understanding the Next Agricultural Transition in the Heartland of Green Revolution in India'. In *Agricultural Transition in Asia: Trajectories and Challenges*, eds Gopal B. Thapa, P. K. Viswanathan, Jayanti K. Routray and Mokbul M. Ahmad, 65–99. Bangkok: Asian Institute of Technology.

Chand, Ramesh, S. S. Acharya, P. G. Chengappa and R. S. Deshpande. 2009. 'Policies and Institutions'. In *State of Indian Agriculture*, 175–202. New Delhi: National Academy of Agricultural Sciences.

Debroy, B., and P. D. Kaushik. 2002. *Barriers to Inter-state Trade and Commerce: The Case of Road Transport*. New Delhi: Rajiv Gandhi Institute for Contemporary Studies.

Government of India. 1965. 'Government Resolution on the Terms of Reference of the Agricultural Prices', Agricultural Prices Commission, Ministry of Food and Agriculture, New Delhi.

———. 2001. *Report of the Working Group on Agricultural Marketing Infrastructure*. Ministry of Agriculture, New Delhi.

———. 2010. 'Manual on Agricultural Prices and Marketing'. Ministry of Statistics and Programme Implementation, CSO, CSO-MAPM, New Delhi.

Gulati, Ashok. 2009. 'Emerging Trends in Indian Agriculture: What Can We Learn from These?'. *Agricultural Economics Research Review* 22(2), July–December: 171–84.

Jha, Raghbendra, K. V. Bhanu Murthy, Hari K. Nagarajan and Ashok K. Seth. 1997. 'Market Integration in Indian Agriculture'. *Economic Systems* 21(3): 217–34.

Jha, Shikha, P. V. Srinivasan and A. Ganesh Kumar. 2010. 'Achieving Food Security in a Cost-effective Way: Implications of Domestic Deregulation and Liberalised Trade in India'. In *Liberalising Foodgrains Markets: Experiences, Impact and Lessons from South Asia*, eds A. Ganesh Kumar, Devesh Roy and Ashok Gulati, 47–90. New Delhi: Oxford University Press.

Krishnamurthy, Mekhla. 2012. 'All in the Name of Farmers' (opinion). *Business Line*, 2 January.

Planning Commission. 2007a. *Report of the Working Group on Agricultural Marketing Infrastructure and Policy Required For Internal and External Trade for the Eleventh Five-Year Plan 2007–12*. Agriculture Division, Planning Commission, New Delhi.

———. 2007b. *Report of the Steering Committee on Agriculture and Allied Sectors for Formulation of the Eleventh Five-Year Plan (2007–12)*. Agriculture Division, Planning Commission, New Delhi.

———. 2011. *Report of the Working Group on Agricultural Marketing Infrastructure, Secondary Agriculture and Policy Required for Internal and External Trade for the Twelfth Five-Year Plan 2012–17*. Agriculture Division, Planning Commission, New Delhi.

10

States of Wheat

The Changing Dynamics of Public Procurement in Madhya Pradesh[*]

Mekhala Krishnamurthy

Changing Landscape of Wheat Procurement

As the peak post-harvest season for wheat came to a close in July 2012, the FCI reported that a record 38 million tonnes of wheat had been procured by government agencies. This massive haul, which accounted for around 40 per cent of the total wheat production in the country for the year, consolidated a surge in state procurement that began in 2008, and represented a jump of nearly 35 per cent over the previous year's record volume.[1] In August 2012, wheat stocks held by the FCI were reported to be 76 million tonnes, which, at more than double the buffer stock requirement, generated familiar concerns about inadequate storage, price rises and the multiple challenges of foodgrain management (Das 2012b).

A much less familiar feature of this procurement picture, however, was that this year, Madhya Pradesh very nearly matched Haryana in its contribution to the central pool, having procured 8.49 million tonnes of wheat through its state agencies, just short of the 8.67 million tonnes purchased in that traditional north Indian bastion for wheat procurement (Tiwari 2012). This figure doubled Madhya Pradesh's procurement total of 3.54 million tonnes two seasons ago, and shot up by a striking 70 per cent over the previous year's high of 4.96 million tonnes. Indeed, the emergence of Madhya Pradesh as one of the leading wheat procurement states in the country over the past five years reflects remarkable and unprecedented changes in the regional distribution and dynamics of the country's grain procurement landscape.

The spatial concentration of government wheat procurement is a well-known characteristic of India's foodgrain economy. Over the preceding four decades, state procurement of wheat has been overwhelmingly concentrated in Punjab and Haryana, which have consistently accounted for between 80 and 90 per cent of

* Originally published in *Economic and Political Weekly* 47(52), 29 December 2012: 72–83.

the total volume sourced for the central pool in any given year. Since the MSP can only be ensured when the government backs it up by actually buying grain in primary markets, state price support policies for wheat have only really had an effect in these two states, and to some extent in parts of western Uttar Pradesh, regions that collectively cover only around 20 per cent of the total area under wheat cultivation across India (Chand 2003; Raghavan 2004). This serious inter-regional disparity has been an enduring element of the Green Revolution strategy—and its political legacy—of 'betting on the strong' in terms of production, price support and procurement. This has been repeatedly criticised by scholars over the years for failing poorer states and smaller farmers, further marginalising rainfed regions and dryland crops in particular (Chand 2003; Frankel 1971; Krishnaji 1990; Raghavan 2004; Shah et al. 1998).

In the case of Madhya Pradesh, which after Uttar Pradesh is the second largest state in terms of area under wheat cultivation in India, the government had traditionally played a negligible role as a buyer of wheat from farmers in the state. Moreover, the state's PDS has had a persistently poor record in providing basic food security to a very large proportion of people, and Madhya Pradesh continues to have very high levels of malnutrition.[2] While Madhya Pradesh's PDS relied on central pool allocations procured in Punjab and Haryana, in growing retail markets for wheat, the state had established a dramatically different reputation. In metropolitan cities like Mumbai and Delhi, 'MP Wheat' is carried as a brand, marked for its high quality and special taste, with the premium 'lustrous' *sharbati* varieties labelled as 'grains of gold' and marketed as the 'best wheat in India that money can buy' (Mishra 2007). In addition, the central Indian agro-ecological wheat zone is known for the production of high quality *durum* varieties of wheat, used in a range of wheat-based processed foods, such as *suji*, *sevai* and pasta.

As a result, the wheat markets of Madhya Pradesh had been largely organised around dense and diverse webs of private trade. Given its central location, the state is well situated to participate in agro-commercial networks connected to processing and retail centres in north, west and south India. Along with regional commodity traders and millers, in the 2000s, Madhya Pradesh increasingly attracted major agribusiness corporations and conglomerates—both national and multinational, among them ITC, Cargill and the Australian Wheat Board (AWB). They were all drawn by the high-quality varieties and low levels of government procurement, and by the prospect of buying not only through *mandi*-based commission agents and brokers, but also, as a result of an amendment to Madhya Pradesh's Agricultural Produce Marketing Act, directly from farmers through their own single-licence procurement centres and *choupals*.[3]

Private trade, including these major corporations, had a very profitable run in the wheat market in 2006, when a lower-than-market price MSP limited government buying, while private traders and corporations cashed in as wheat prices soared from Rs 750 per quintal in April to Rs 1,000 per quintal in September that same year (Damodaran 2007). A historic increase of Rs 200 in the MSP (inclusive of a bonus) pushed it to Rs 850 the following year, but procurement still fell short of adequately rebuilding government wheat buffer stocks. As prices rose, the government came under attack for importing large quantities of wheat at high international prices. By the 2008 marketing season, compelled to drastically step up its procurement drive, the central government hiked the MSP for wheat to Rs 1,000 per quintal, and more than doubled wheat purchases that year (Nair and Eapen 2011).

Major Shift

Given the FCI's meagre presence as a buyer in Madhya Pradesh, there was no reason to expect that the rise in the centrally declared MSP in 2008 would significantly affect the structure and dynamics of wheat marketing in the state. This time, however, the move coincided with a major shift in the state government's wheat procurement policy. In the 2008 marketing season, preceding the assembly elections held in November that year, the state government announced a bonus of Rs 100 on top of the raised MSP, taking the state-declared procurement price of wheat in Madhya Pradesh to Rs 1,100, higher than anywhere else in the country. Aware that the bonus could backfire if it was not effectively backed by actual buying, the Madhya Pradesh government prepared to rapidly expand its procurement operations in the major wheat-producing regions of the state. In the previous decade, the largest volume of wheat purchased by the FCI and state agencies in Madhya Pradesh in a year had been 0.54 million tonnes in 1999–2000. In the 2007 marketing season, it had been a mere 0.057 million tonnes. In the 2008 post-harvest period, this jumped many multiples to 2.4 million tonnes, a figure that in a single season more than matched the state's entire procurement volume from 1999 to that point. Speculation that this might only have been an election-year sweetener was dispelled when the wheat bonus became a fixture in subsequent marketing seasons, each time coming on top of a higher MSP. Five years on, the volume of wheat procured by the state had burgeoned to the record figure mentioned at the beginning (Table 10.1).

TABLE 10.1: Wheat MSP, Production and Procurement, Madhya Pradesh and India, 2006–07 to 2011–12

	Crop Year – MSP (Rs/quintal)	*Madhya Pradesh MSP + Bonus (Rs)*	*Madhya Pradesh Production (million tonnes)*	*Madhya Pradesh Procurement (million tonnes)*	*India Production (million tonnes)*	*Central Pool Procurement (million tonnes)*
2006–07	850	850	7.33	0.057	75.81	11.13
2007–08	1,000	1,100	6.03	2.41	78.57	22.67
2008–09	1,080	1,130	6.52	1.97	80.68	25.38
2009–10	1,100	1,200	7.21	3.54	80.80	22.51
2010–11	1,170	1,270	7.62	4.96	85.93	28.34
2011–12	1,285	1,385	10.58	8.49	93.90	38.15

Note: Production figures are for the crop year and procurement figures are for the corresponding rabi marketing season.

Source: *Handbook of Statistics on Indian Economy 2011–2012*, Reserve Bank of India.

...

Drawing on 18 months of ethnographic research in a primary agricultural market in Madhya Pradesh, this chapter focuses on the actors, interactions and experiences in government wheat procurement operations over consecutive marketing seasons. In doing so, it analyses some critical changes in market processes and explores their effects on different participants and on the composition and culture of the commodity market. Here, it pays close attention to the changing profiles of market agents and agencies, the particularities of market practices such as documentation and modes of payment, the importance of timing and coordination in marketing activities, and to the ways in which new systems of market management are constantly being put in place, circumvented and strengthened as part of a dynamic process. Moreover, by working at this level of detail and tracking recent and evolving developments, it is also possible to derive broad insights into the workings of agricultural markets more generally, generate productive grounds from which to raise critical questions, and to think further about how the benefits from procurement may be more effectively and equitably distributed. But first, a brief orientation to the field and market in question.

FIELD AND MARKET

The centre of action in this paper is Harda Mandi, a regulated Agricultural Produce Marketing Committee (APMC) in Harda, a small but bustling market town with a population of 65,000 (Census 2001) and the administrative headquarters of an agriculturally productive district of the same name. The Harda tehsil includes 196 villages and falls within the tail-end of the command area of the Tawa Canal. Along with Hoshangabad district, Harda is one of the best irrigated regions in predominantly rainfed Madhya Pradesh, and it has two main agricultural seasons growing rainfed kharif soybean and irrigated rabi wheat.[4]

The core material presented here is based on ethnographic fieldwork conducted between November 2008 and April 2010 and is drawn from observations, in-depth interviews and immersion in everyday activities during two consecutive marketing years (four post-harvest seasons all together) for soybean and wheat in Harda Mandi. In addition to this, I frequently visited key sites linked closely to marketing activities in and around the town—mills and processing plants, private hubs and choupals, the bazaar, banks, input dealers, cooperative societies, warehouses and the collectorate. I also spent time in a range of villages, interviewing farmers and observing agricultural, political and social activities at different points during the agricultural cycle. My fieldwork coincided with the initiation and rapid expansion of government wheat procurement operations in Harda and it provided an opportunity to closely observe as new systems and processes were put into place and tested in the market yard. The duration of fieldwork and the ethnographic approach to market life and mandi relationships provided critical context and insights into the wheat procurement process and its various dimensions that would otherwise have been difficult to access.

First, since these observations took place during a continuous engagement with agricultural activities through the marketing calendar, the action that accompanied the peak wheat season could be studied not as an isolated phenomenon, but in relation to actors and activities that took place around the year, and in continuity with, and contrast to, other commodities marketed at the same site. In particular, some of the connections and contrasts between soybean and wheat marketing in Harda are highlighted. Second, tracking processes and practices as they were implemented and experienced over the course of a procurement period and over consecutive seasons revealed how dynamic these systems were and how quickly windows of opportunity and new kinds of constraints materialised in the mandi with diverse effects and counteractions. Short follow-up visits in 2011 and 2012 and efforts to track more recent information from a distance confirmed this dynamism, and have allowed me to update, to some extent, the constantly evolving processes described in the following sections. Finally, even as one tries to keep pace with the present, it does not take long for a fieldworker in the mandi to realise that the significance of contemporary movements in agricultural commodity markets cannot be properly understood without analysing their linkages and relations to the wider political economy, and to particular agro-ecological contexts, regional histories and conjunctural changes over time. In this regard, there are four aspects to Harda Mandi that are worth mentioning, each with a critical bearing on the distinctive features of wheat procurement in Harda and in Madhya Pradesh today, and are relevant for a comparative understanding of procurement dynamics. Each is briefly described below.

Canal and Crops

Unlike soybean, which was only introduced in Harda in the 1970s and is widely considered to be a relatively new and foreign crop, wheat cultivation and trade in this region has a very long and fascinating history.[5] The current chapter in wheat production, however, springs from a much more recent point in the past, its dramatic spread vividly recalled by all those over 40 in Harda today, who have witnessed a very different mandi, dominated by cotton and filled with a range of other agricultural produce marketed in small quantities—*tuar* (red gram), *alsi* (linseed), *undi* (castorseed), *tilli* (sesame), *jowar* (sorghum) and *chana* (gram). These were variously intercropped during a single, long season of rainfed cultivation. Wheat, which today arrives in the mandi in annual volumes of more than 2 million quintals, was then grown in such small quantities that any marketed surplus was sold at a small retail wheat bazaar in the crowded market area of the town, where numerous small traders sat with their weighing scales.

All this changed with the arrival of canal irrigation, when the waters of the Tawa Canal began flowing through Harda's fields from the early to mid-1980s. At this time, across Harda, short-duration kharif soybean started replacing long-duration cotton, and irrigated winter wheat expanded as the preferred second crop. By the mid-1990s, a soybean–wheat monocropping cycle firmly dominated agricultural practice in Harda. While the canal-irrigated wheat zone of Harda and Hoshangabad is considered the most advanced in terms of productivity in Madhya Pradesh, the irrigated, heavily fertilised, high-yielding varieties grown in this area are generally rated as 'mill quality wheat'. They are not up to the high standards—and higher market prices—of wheat grown in other, largely unirrigated parts of the state. Still, in terms of wheat volumes, Harda is often heralded as the 'Punjab of MP' and both in terms of quantity and quality had attributes that made it a major site for the state government's ambitious wheat procurement programme when it took off in 2008–09 (Table 10.2).

TABLE 10.2: Government Wheat Procurement in Harda District, Rabi Marketing Season, 2008–09 to 2012–13

Procurement Year	*Procurement (tonnes)*
2008–09	2,38,665
2009–10	2,41,879
2010–11	3,14,298
2011–12	4,67,133
2012–13	5,38,627

Source: Madhya Pradesh State Civil Supplies Corporation.

Land and Caste

There is another reason that the government would have found it difficult to ignore Harda and this has to do with the relative size and strength of its farmers. In Madhya Pradesh, this small district stands out for its relatively large landholdings, which are double the size on average than the rest of the state (4.43 hectares in Harda to 2.02 hectares in Madhya Pradesh). Further, Harda is remarkable in that small and marginal farmers (below 2 hectares) comprise only 37 per cent of landowners in the district, an inversion from the rest of Madhya Pradesh, where 68 per cent of all farmers own small and marginal parcels of land. On the other end, while only 12 per cent of farmers across Madhya Pradesh own above 4 hectares and only 1.5 per cent above 10 hectares, in Harda, medium and large farmers account for 36 per cent of all landholders and those with over 10 hectares are 9 per cent of the total.

Farmers from the Scheduled Castes (SCs) and Scheduled Tribes (STs) comprise around 13 per cent and 15 per cent of all landholders, respectively, the majority of whom own small and marginal plots.[6] Landownership in Harda is mainly in the hands of the four major cultivating castes—Gujjars, Rajputs, Jats and Bishnois. Among them, the Jats and Bishnois, while numerically smaller, have been the most aggressive acquirers of land for cultivation. With the election of a Jat member of the legislative assembly (MLA) in 1993, who was re-elected for a fourth consecutive term in 2008, the Jats have grown in political power in the district and are well-known for being an agitational force in the politically charged mandi. Wheat procurement operations in Harda, then, have been implemented in the context of resourceful and vigilant farmers, and, as we shall see, have had to contend with specific acts of mobilisation and division, discipline and disregard, often with the same farmers making collective demands and manoeuvring for personal gains.

Commission Agents

Even if Harda is popularly described as 'mini Punjab' in terms of wheat production and procurement, fundamental major differences become apparent when it comes to the structure and organisation of regulated primary markets. Among the most critical contrasts is the striking absence of an old and ubiquitous intermediary found across many other agricultural markets in India—the *kacha arhatiya*.

The kacha arhatiya is a specific kind of commission agent common in primary markets who maintains long-term relationships with local farmers in a particular area, typically based on credit advances tied to the sale of produce through the arhatiya's shop in the mandi. In many mandis, farmers must sell their produce through registered arhatiyas, who conduct the auction and manage the sale and payment on their behalf, for which they deduct a commission. In the traditional procurement states of Punjab and Haryana, for instance, state agencies buy through the existing and entrenched network of mandi-based arhatiyas, who are responsible for handling the first transaction and making payments to farmers (Damodaran 2000, 2010a; Gill 2004). Arhatiyas in these states are well-organised and have forged a powerful lobby, and over the years managed to effectively resist attempts to bypass them by threatening to withhold credit and shut down mandis if payments are directly made to farmers for produce purchased by the government (Damodaran 2010a). In sharp contrast, however, in Harda and other major state-regulated mandis for foodgrains, oilseeds and pulses (but notably, not in vegetable and fruit markets) across Madhya Pradesh, kacha arhatiyas are not a feature of the current mandi system. They have not played a large part in mandi activities since the mid-1980s.

Their absence is the result of a series of reforms that was implemented by the state government led by the Congress chief minister, Arjun Singh, with Digvijay Singh as the minister for agriculture. Given the criticism the role of arhatiyas and intermediaries has attracted, their successful elimination through concerted state action across mandis in Madhya Pradesh remains curiously underappreciated by researchers and policymakers alike. But, on the ground, even today in mandis like Harda, the abolition of the *kachi arhat pratha* is still recalled by those who experienced it as having been '*krantikari*'—revolutionary—in reorganising the market. It is also important to understand that this marketing reform coincided with major improvements in agricultural production, which contributed significantly to its viability and effectiveness.

While the political calculation behind this action and the experiences associated with its implementation on the ground have been analysed in detail elsewhere (Krishnamurthy 2011), what is important to note is that, for nearly three decades now, farmers who sell their produce in Harda Mandi and other APMCs in Madhya Pradesh do so directly, in an open auction to the highest bidder without going through an intermediary, and collect their payment in cash from the buyer on the same day. The reason that this is critical to the recent expansion of wheat procurement in the state is that the state government had to rapidly work out its own mechanisms to buy grain directly from farmers across local markets. Here, on the one hand, the government did not have to contend with an entrenched and politically charged network of mandi-based intermediaries, but at the same time, it did not have the benefit of their transactional and organisational capacities in the field. The systems and processes that have been developed for this purpose will absorb our attention in the rest of this chapter.

Local Mandi Reforms

Agricultural market reforms not only require high-level political support but also local leadership and field-level capacities for implementation and regulation in market sites on the ground. Since the 2000s, Harda Mandi has had some very active mandi-level reformers, both locally elected and state-appointed, and it has a reputation as an *adarsh* or model APMC in the state, and even nationally. Among its important achievements is the installation of an electronic weighbridge—one of the first in Madhya Pradesh—after a hard-fought battle and a field trial back in 1999–2000. This is also a mandi that very consciously upgraded its infrastructure and management in response to the establishment of private-sector procurement choupals, first by ITC and then by other regional and multinational corporations. As a result, by the time the government's wheat procurement plans had to be operationalised, Harda Mandi's functionaries were well prepared to take on the challenging task of market management. The secretary at the time had managed soybean procurement in Harda in the early 1990s as part of the state's now-defunct Oil Federation, from which he was deputed to the mandi board. These capacities proved valuable in the seasons ahead, although as all the mandi functionaries admitted, none of them anticipated the scale and speed with which wheat procurement would grow in the mandi and the stress it would bring with it. It is to this complexity that we now turn our attention.

THE STATE IN THE MARKET YARD

The entry and expansion of *sarkari kharidi*, or government procurement operations, since 2008 has had a significant impact on the agricultural marketing calendar in Harda Mandi, and has dramatically altered the organisation and dynamics of its wheat season. While the volatility of soybean prices preoccupies farmers and traders in the mandi for most of the year, from mid-March to the end of June, only one rate—the annual wheat procurement price, which is the centrally sanctioned MSP plus the state-declared bonus—rules this marketplace. As the second post-harvest season of the year hits its peak, everyone in the mandi has to quickly reorient themselves to the logic and logistics of government procurement and to the dynamics of marketing defined by a fixed price and fluctuating processes.

Over a relatively short period of time, government procurement has changed the cast of characters involved in buying grain in and around the mandi and introduced new systems and practices. These have reconfigured the organisation of marketing activities, altered the duration of the season, affected the ways in which both time and space are managed and experienced in the market yard, mobilised certain kinds of social and political connections, and generated high levels of tension and new forms of assertion and exclusion. This section describes the key actors and activities in wheat procurement in Harda over the last five years, and investigates some of the critical changes in market practices and their effects on different participants, and the culture and composition of the mandi.

Agents and Agencies

With no kacha arhatiyas in the wheat mandis, the state government had to identify a new, viable, and large-scale mechanism capable of procuring grain directly from farmers in primary market sites across many districts. In 2008, the first year of major procurement, the FCI opted to use private traders with sizeable credit limits who were already well-established in the mandi. In Harda, it appointed a number of the mandi's biggest firms as commission agents for wheat purchases, dividing up a significant proportion of the volume among them and relying on their financial capacities, labour management, storage facilities and private transportation systems. The experience, however, was unfavourable, with the FCI accusing traders of huge losses in weight and of buying wheat from farmers for less than the procurement price of Rs 1,100 per quintal that year and reselling it to the government.

From the next season, the traders were dropped as commission agents and alternative arrangements for procurement were devised. As a result, full-time, licensed traders in Harda suddenly found they had little business during what would normally have been the peak trading season. Similarly, during the season, local agents for corporations were sometimes seen walking on the platforms, but were usually fretting that they had no orders to buy. Later, some of them were reassigned to look after corporate purchasing in markets in Gujarat, Uttar Pradesh and Rajasthan, where the bonus was not in play and where, in some cases, wheat prices were reportedly well below the MSP. Private hubs, including the ITC e-Choupal, registered little activity, restricting their buying to only specific high-quality varieties, of which there were limited volumes in Harda. Harda's two millers kept up some local buying throughout the season, but even they sent men to other markets in the state where procurement was less strongly enforced to meet their demands. Largely reduced to bidding on the modest quantities of soybean and chana squeezed in between the rapidly multiplying trolleys of wheat in the mandi yard, a dejected trader grumbled as he watched the action, 'It used to be the farmers who took only one crop in Harda; now thanks to the government, it is the *vyapaari* who is left to make do with only one commodity!'

In their place, the state—in the form of a range of agents and agencies—took over the market yard in the wheat procurement season. The primary responsibility for handling procurement operations in Madhya Pradesh was handed over to the Civil

Supplies Corporation (CSC). In addition to the CSC, which also manages the state PDS, the state Marketing Federation (Markfed), the nodal organisation responsible for the distribution of key agricultural inputs (seeds, fertilisers, and pesticides), was involved in a number of districts, including Harda. In village and mandi-based procurement centres, traders were replaced by Primary Agricultural Credit Societies (PACS), popularly referred to as 'societies'. Across the Harda tehsil, village-based societies were appointed to buy wheat from members, while in the mandi, four of the most fiscally healthy societies were assigned the task of buying, bagging and releasing payments to farmers. As a result, the district cooperative bank had a key role to play in managing payments and accounts across the PACS's procurement centres. The district branch of the State Warehousing Corporation was galvanised, as the target considerably exceeded the storage capacity in the district each year. And with the mandi taking on the exhausting task of market management in the yard, the district administration, led by the collector, was charged with supervising procurement operations. Clearly, government procurement of wheat now required a completely different level of coordination between multiple state agencies, set up at different levels to address different roles.

Scope for Miscommunication

As one might imagine, these arrangements afforded great scope for miscommunication, dropped linkages and non-coordination, especially in the initial phases. This was particularly visible in the relationship between the CSC and Markfed, with almost daily breakdowns in communication on different tasks. During the evening procurement meetings convened by the district collector, assembling the key functionaries of the bodies involved in the procurement process—the CSC, Markfed, the district cooperative bank, the State Warehousing Corporation and the mandi—slanging matches were routine. The CSC accused Markfed of dropping the ball on logistics and Markfed became livid at hold-ups caused by the CSC failing to arrange timely transportation, materials and finance. To be fair, the division of tasks between them left plenty of room for confusion. For instance, during an initial season, Markfed was responsible for transporting the produce from the procurement centre to the local warehouse, but the CSC for transporting it from the district to outside it. It was also the CSC's responsibility to ensure that adequate gunny bags were delivered from outside the district to Markfed's headquarters. But delivering them to village or mandi procurement centres was Markfed's duty. As a result, the two battered officials would chase each other around the collectorate table, and later around the town, as transportation failed to materialise or the delayed delivery of gunny bags held up procurement in the mandi and in village centres. The frequency of these lapses had practical implications for those dealing directly with farmers, and managing the flow of processes and produce in the market yard. But, with the state's commitment to procurement becoming more visible each year, the state agencies began responding proactively to the challenges being thrown up from the field. What was equally interesting to observe was the range of local and state identities and loyalties that were expressed at different levels of the procurement process.

FCI's Diminishing Presence

Most palpably, this sort of assertion and resistance involved the FCI. The state agencies have expanded the scale of their operations and the FCI has reduced its share of total procurement in Madhya Pradesh each year, from nearly 35 per cent in 2008–09 to 15.6 per cent in 2009–10 and to 6.7 per cent in 2010–11, all the way to zero during the subsequent two seasons. For the state agencies and their local functionaries, this was no small feat and the FCI's diminishing presence in the field was greeted rather enthusiastically. When FCI officials made an appearance in earlier seasons, its presence antagonised district officials, who were wary of the central government agency and its reputation for imposing a long list of requirements. The FCI was known to insist on running its system differently, with a high dose of attitude and scant regard for existing systems and local processes. Everyone knew that the FCI was the more powerful agency, but as a national institution, based in Delhi, it was also seen by local-level functionaries in Madhya Pradesh as a demanding and pushy outsider. As soon as the FCI entered the procurement process directly, the CSC, which until then had been the target of frustration, was embraced and defended by all district-level functionaries as one would defend one's own family.

Eyeing the FCI representative, who had just arrived in Harda and walked into the collectorate, the mandi secretary leaned over to the manager of the State Warehousing Corporation and expressed a view that resonated deeply with his fellow state functionaries, 'Our offspring (*apni aulaad*) will always remain our own, no matter how worthless (*nikamma*) he may be. In the end, the CSC is our state agency; it belongs to us. These FCI men work for the central government, and they always behave as if they are doing us some great favour by showing up.' A few days later, members of the societies and mandi staff could not contain their amusement when a row of farmers in the mandi refused to sell to the FCI, insisting that they would sell to the local societies than to this unfamiliar new agency that had suddenly entered the picture (As one agitated farmer put it, '*Yeh koi* FCI-SBI-CBI has come out of nowhere, who knows if we should sell to them!'). For his part, the FCI official, who had been specifically sent to Harda to bolster the procurement programme since the state agencies were struggling to keep up with the volume, was offended that he had to request local men to persuade farmers that the FCI was a legitimate entity and an important national institution.

If the FCI's perceived arrogance, inflexibility and status as an outsider caused problems, the local men who ran the operations of the societies brought with them a different set of issues, opening the way for a dense web of village connections to assert themselves in the mandi. The societies were manned by their appointed representatives, all of whom were farmers with landholdings that come under each society's catchment, and by salesmen and staff hired for the season, almost all of them belonged to farming families in nearby villages. During the year, the societies are responsible for disbursing agricultural credit and distributing seed and fertilisers to farmer-members. Their management and managers are important actors in the economic affairs of villages, have deep social connections there, and are thoroughly implicated in village-level politics. In sharp contrast to the traders, who are the usual buyers in the mandi, the men involved in managing wheat procurement for the societies are Jat and Gujjar farmers, not Marwari *bania*s (traders). On the platforms, the local buyers working for the societies were new faces, but for village residents, they were familiar ones. Often they would be called out to by their first names by farmers who knew them and addressed as *bhaiya* (brother) even by those less well acquainted, in contrast to the traders, who were generally referred to as *seth*s (large traders). Their appointment changed the social and political dynamics at work in the mandi where, as we shall see, the ease and speed of marketing activities now depended on what became a ubiquitous term used during the wheat season—the strength of your 'settings' with the societies' men and the mandi's functionaries.

Conflicts with Labour

Along with state agencies and village societies, government procurement brought in a whole range of local and regional *thekedar*s or contractors, who had contracts for specific elements of the process—labour, gunny bag distribution, stitching, stencilling and transportation. During this season, the societies could appoint their own labour contractors and the permanent mandi *mukkadam*s and *hamal*s (porters), attached to particular trading firms, were out of the action. They had to often seek out the labour contractors to ensure that they were included in the seasonal workforce. In addition to local labour, hundreds of hamals came to Harda to work during the second season, including those from mandis in the Malwa region that did not receive such large wheat arrivals and from as far as Bihar, who had been mobilised by local labour organisers. In the first year of large-scale procurement, in addition to dealing with the management of heavy arrivals and the multiple agents engaged in buying that year, the mandi faced a well-organised hamal *hartal*, a strike that lasted for nearly a month during the peak procurement period of April–May 2008. In the seasons that followed, therefore, mandi functionaries and procurement agencies were constantly on edge about the possibility of conflicts with labour.

While permanent labourers had to adjust to the influx of outsiders, opportunities also emerged for different types of work to be taken up by seasonal entrants to the mandi. For instance, in 2010, when the CSC had to switch to white synthetic bags due to a shortage of jute bags, a young man, whose father had been a local financier during cotton trading in the old mandi, negotiated the contract to manage the machinery and manpower required for sealing the bags. In the previous year, an enterprising young hamal assembled a team of young boys from his neighbourhood to undertake the more menial, but for him remunerative, task of manually stencilling jute bags. Bigger contracts, such as truck transportation, were given out to larger, regional operators, including Bhopal-based transporters who had taken up contracts with the CSC. But wheat not only attracted the well-connected, but also the most vulnerable and disadvantaged, who were drawn to the mandi in the hope of collecting a few grains amid the towering heaps. Every day, one could see old women and young children stooping over the cement mandi floor, sticking their fingers into fine cracks and sweeping the roads with their bare palms, trying to gather even the smallest quantities of fallen grain.

Finally, this season, the jute bags and the wheat itself seemed to have a life of their own. Even when they seemed to be just lying there, inanimate, something was happening to them that became a subject of constant debate and disagreement between the societies and the agencies. According to a widely quoted and remarkably precise estimate, a jute bag lost 165 grams of weight when it dried and the moisture evaporated from the tight bundle in which it had arrived. As with the bags, the wheat also lost moisture and therefore weight as it lay in the open. As the old and experienced manager of the State Warehousing Corporation, a man with a wry sense of humour, noted as we sat in his small office late one afternoon, 'While the wheat naturally and unnaturally loses weight, we are supposed to magically show a weight gain in each bag, and I, like Vishwakarma, the divine architect, am supposed to build brand new warehouses overnight.'

Procurement Windows and Seasonal Stresses

Unlike the licensed full-time traders and commission agents who participate in mandi-level buying as arrivals come in through the year, government wheat procurement operations take place during a specific window of time during the post-harvest season. After this, the societies quickly wrap up their buying and the high procurement price is no longer supported with active purchases. In Harda and other major procurement locations in Madhya Pradesh, this has had a significant impact on the marketing season for wheat. Since 2008–09, while the soybean season has expanded because farmers have gradually built up their holding capacities, enabling them to stagger arrivals and spread out soybean sales in anticipation of higher prices, wheat marketing has become more compressed in terms of time. When the procurement season coincides with the election, this window begins to look even shorter and more uncertain. In 2009, the Lok Sabha elections were scheduled in Madhya Pradesh in different phases from 20 April. News somehow spread among farmers that although the official procurement period was till mid-June, the state government was planning to wrap up procurement and stop paying the bonus as soon as votes were cast. As a result, everyone was in a tearing hurry to sell as much of their wheat as possible before the mandi closed for election day.

In the days immediately after procurement opened on 20 March, the arrivals began building up rapidly. And once they gathered momentum, it felt like they would never stop, as tractors bearing thousands of quintals chugged into the mandi. The auction sheds were packed, the lines to the weighbridge spilled onto the road, and every bit of space in between was filled with tractor trolleys waiting to line up. Judging from the arrivals recorded by the mandi, in the government procurements in 2009–12, even in non-election years, sales by farmers between March and June accounted for anywhere between 80 and 92 per cent of the total surplus sold in the market, with April alone accounting for around 40 per cent. During this time, everywhere you went in Harda, people were talking about the '*bhayankar aavak*' or 'terrifying arrivals' that had descended on the mandi. The wheat season built up pressure and tried one's patience in ways that were particular to this period of the year and to the specific mode of procurement that operated within this window of time.

Even before the inauguration of the current phase of large-scale government buying, the wheat season had been challenging because of the volumes of grain that came in after the second crop was harvested. Wheat, even after farmers had retained seed for the next year and set aside their annual household requirements, arrived in the mandi in annual volumes that more than doubled soybean. While farmers in Harda generally reported soybean yields in the range of 5–8 quintals per acre, their wheat yields ranged from 12–18 quintals per acre, and were increasing with the cultivation of heavily fertilised, high-yielding varieties. Therefore, very simply, there was much more wheat to be sold in the mandi.

In addition, two other factors increased farmers' urgency to market their second crop. First, as a foodgrain, wheat was harder to store than soybean and was more likely to be damaged by pests, making farmers quite reluctant to hold on to it for long periods of time. Moreover, except for the very largest cultivators, most farmers did not have adequate storage space in their homes to keep the bulk of their grain safe. Second, the period immediately after the wheat harvest in March–April, the period of Chaith-Baisakh in the Hindu calendar, is a critical period for a whole range of economic transactions, generating immense pressure on farming families. In the two-crop cycle, the first crop—soybean—is primarily 'lifted' as *laagath* or expenditure to finance critical inputs such as fertiliser and water for the winter wheat crop and to repay expenses incurred on cultivating soybean itself. Most of the formal and informal contractual and credit arrangements, however, are left to be settled after the wheat harvest comes in.

These not only include Kisan Credit Card (KCC) payments due in April, but any land deals that have been made, plots taken on *khot* or lease, settlements to be made on credit-based ration purchases, and financial agreements pertaining to new projects that households may have undertaken or are planning to undertake in the coming year. In addition, April is the wedding season with the largest number of marriage ceremonies, including all the caste *sammelans* (major social occasions hosting mass wedding ceremonies). Even before these transactions can be fulfilled, farmers have to pay Punjabi harvester operators in cash. They remain in one area only briefly and need to make their way home in time for the April harvest in Punjab. Payments to labourers which include grain but are primarily in cash also have to be settled. So, competing demands, which have all been held off till the wheat harvest, now descend on farmers all at once.

Cash, Cheques and Deposits

Farmers, with their immediate and urgent need for post-harvest cash, faced a particular problem when the government procured wheat, which had to do with the mode and timing of payments. Since all payments made by the cooperative societies in the first three seasons were by cheque, farmers invariably experienced a delay in receiving their payment after depositing their cheques, often up to a week or sometimes even longer. Those who had outstanding debts with the cooperative bank noticed that this was deducted from the final amounts credited to their account. In March 2009, even though the agencies were buying at Rs 1,130 and the market price was only around Rs 1,050–1,080, a number of farmers, especially on the first few days of procurement, did not want to sell to the societies. They preferred to sell at a lower price to traders for immediate cash payment. During this time, there was a steady flow of 'offline' transactions, where farmers brought samples of grain bundled in cloth to the side of the platform and negotiated with traders on a price to be paid in cash.

Such transactions became less visible in the following weeks as most of the immediate harvest-related cash needs had been met. The state agencies responded the following season, in 2010, by instructing societies to make payments up to Rs 20,000 by bearer cheque that could be encashed immediately. As the season progressed, government procurement took hold and news of the new system spread. Farmers also came to the mandi in the knowledge that their payments would be delayed. Many, however, informally borrowed cash on interest for short durations until the full payments were deposited in their accounts.

Cheque payments had two further effects. Once the cash constraint had been met, many farmers said they preferred cheque payments. Even more so, the direct deposit system introduced in the 2011 season, because they did not have to worry about looting, which was otherwise a common concern when carrying large sums of cash. It also meant that without cash in hand, farmers did not stop to make purchases from the bazaar and fill their trolleys with rations and other goods as they usually did after selling their produce to traders in the mandi. As a result, retailers and dealers in Harda's bazaar, who were used to estimating their business according to arrivals in the mandi, found that the new system altered their calculations during the peak season.

Documentation

To participate in the state procurement programme, farmers are required to furnish documentary proof of their landholding size in the form of their revenue record (or *rinn pustika*). Cheque payments and direct deposits are made out in the names and the account numbers listed in the formal records. Normally, sellers in the mandi do not need to prove their identity as farmers. They only have to provide a name and village that is written out on the payment slip, which also notes the price of the auctioned lot of produce, and the payments are made on the same day in cash. The additional documentation required to sell to the societies was instituted to make it difficult for local aggregators and traders who have purchased wheat at a lower price either inside or outside the mandi to sell this at the higher government procurement rate.

Unfortunately, this requirement sometimes shuts out farmers, especially small cultivators, who either do not have land titles or have cultivated land on lease (khot). This is generally not a problem for farmers, typically medium-sized landowners, who have augmented their production by taking additional plots of land on khot. They are generally able to sell under their official revenue record. The problem is for landless farmers, who often have little choice but to sell their wheat to traders. Mandi functionaries, who were aware of this issue, tried to find a way around it by allowing affidavits to be produced by such farmers with details of the land records and the lease agreement. But this is an additional process that small farmers, in any case often strapped for cash, do not easily attempt.

On the other hand, in the mandi, one encountered a number of small traders who were willing to make arrangements to sell grain to the societies, using their contacts with farmers for documentation, cashing cheques, and even direct deposits. These traders did agree, however, that these arrangements were becoming more difficult to execute with each passing season. Payments have moved to electronic transfers and there is a pre-registration system for procurement, which make it difficult to use the same documents repeatedly. As long as matching yields and total production to landholding size remains difficult, a loophole does exist, but one that has already become more complicated to pass through. Due to a large number of sellers, their greater anonymity and a larger volume of transactions, mandis are more vulnerable than village-based procurement centres where disproportionate sales easily stand out.

In the initial seasons, farmers found themselves waiting two to four days to sell their wheat to government agencies, while struggling to make sense of the system, which seemed to change daily, even hourly on certain days. For officials, the most effective method of controlling activities was to try to halt purchasing on the platform, since once farmers had their purchase slips, it was impossible to prevent them from lining up at the weighbridge. When the societies were overwhelmed as their heaps grew and labour could not keep pace, or as traffic at the weighbridge became impossible to control, purchasing would grind to a halt, sometimes for hours. Procurement agents were also frustrated by the lack of concern that farmers seemed to show after their trolleys were weighed. Throughout the season, lack of adequate transportation also meant that at intervals, the heaps and stacks built up so much that it was difficult to find room to offload more grain. On a few occasions, when clouds gathered and it looked like rain might follow, farmers sped even more urgently into the mandi, while the societies scrambled to cover the purchased stock and refused to buy until the weather cleared. Yard functionaries continuously made announcements on the loudspeaker, trying to convey the shifting situation to farmers, but there were so many different messages that their efforts were rather futile. Fights erupted at the weighbridge, trolleys collided into one another. There were soaring temperatures and frayed nerves all around the mandi yard.

No Formal Auction

It is important to note that there is no formal auction for wheat bought by the government since the societies purchase all lots at the fixed 'MSP plus bonus' rate. In a separate shed, traders carry on auctions for soybean and chana brought to the mandi, as well as for any premium varieties of wheat that are selling at market prices over the state procurement price. In the sheds filled with the vast majority of wheat trolleys for sale to the government, lots are sampled briefly by the society buyer and unless they are of very poor quality, accepted for purchase. At the beginning of the season, when the societies' buyers tried to enforce strict quality specifications, the farmers protested that not a single trolley in the mandi would meet the parameters of the sample the agents had. Furious, they stormed the collectorate, and eventually a new sample, drawn from a standing trolley in Harda, had to be agreed to by all parties before procurement could proceed.

The absence of auctions means that farmers with close ties to the society and to mandi functionaries, or with strong political connections, can use these 'settings' to push their trolleys to the front of the line. Even during the soybean season, certain farmers are known to block space in the sheds and muscle their way ahead of others already in line. However, if they want to participate in the open auction, where their produce would benefit from bidding by a range of buyers, they have no option but to wait till the traders assemble and bid on their lot. Throughout the year, there were instances of farmers selling directly to a particular trader outside the auction, but unless they were especially close to the trader, these sales were at less than the mandi price. It was generally understood that farmers opting for these direct sales required the money urgently or did not wish to remain in the mandi overnight if their trolley had not been auctioned before the end of the day.

In the wheat season, the government's rate was fixed and all the farmers lined up in sheds knew they were guaranteed the same price. They just had to wait for the society's functionary to stop by and sample their trolley, and then for the mandi staff to issue the official slip or *parchi*, after which they could move to the weighbridge. The auction was primarily used to manage arrivals and space out their movement through the weighing, downloading and payment phases. Those with connections or 'settings' in the mandi did their very best to bypass the auction sheds and go straight to the weighbridge and offload their produce there. Rather than wait like everyone else to have their slips issued, they worked the system to have the mandi 'cut parchis' (issue slips) in their names. In the 2009 season, both mandi and society officials came under enormous pressure to cut parchis for a number of large farmers, especially those with connections to various political figures. Yard functionaries, most of whom are also farmers from nearby villages, were also constantly approached by family members and close friends, asking them to make an exception. The parchi issue began to cause both personal and public tensions. For a while, it was difficult to keep track of the order in which the sheds were being organised and sold, and it was impossible to disguise that certain trolleys materialised at the weighbridge without having been in a shed. Moreover, on days that the mandi was officially closed and only bagging and transportation activities were supposed to be taking place, farmers waiting in the sheds could see selected tractors depositing their produce directly at the society's heaps. As the days progressed, the overwhelming majority of waiting farmers expressed their anger, which sometimes, when the delays were especially dire, threatened to explode.

Malpractices

The important part that parchis play in government procurement is not unique to wheat or to Madhya Pradesh. It appears to be a common feature across different commodities and regions where government support prices are backed with major purchasing by state agencies. Based on fieldwork among Jat farmers in western Uttar Pradesh, for instance, Jeffrey (2002, 2010) has documented the different ways in which rich farmers cultivate relationships with cane society officials to secure the slips they require to sell their sugarcane at competitive prices to the society in years when the government's price exceeds that at private sugar mills. Deploying a range of strategies to ingratiate themselves with officials and resorting to intimidation when these fail, the rich Jat farmers in Meerut district work hard to ensure that their supply of parchis remains constant, even if they had 'defected' the previous year by selling to private mills. The ability that some of Harda's large farmers demonstrate to access parchis shares significant similarities with Jeffrey's account of sugarcane marketing in Uttar Pradesh. In Harda, as in Meerut, the same farmers justify their micro-practice of corruption while publicly mobilising and agitating to pressure the government to keep up the high rates and high levels of procurement.

In Harda Mandi, even as these malpractices and the power of political settings were demonstrated in the blinding sunlight of summer days, tension between the different arms and agencies of the state, including conflicts between the regulated mandi and the state procurement agencies, was equally apparent. Government procurement compromised two of the important elements of mandi regulation—the fixed price led to the suspension of the open auction, while cheque payments went against the act's requirement that all buyers make full payments to farmers within 24 hours. As we have seen, the absence of both these were associated with a range of different effects on farmers selling in the mandi and for the functionaries charged with managing it. In this regard, government procurement subverted the key practices that the government itself had instituted to establish and empower regulated markets.[7]

In Harda, however, both district administrators and mandi functionaries made concerted efforts to address some of the particular problems that arose during wheat procurement. During the 2010 season, for instance, the mandi was better prepared, and put in place improvements to number and track the parchis issued, requiring countersigning by multiple functionaries and making it difficult for functionaries to cut parchis without being identified. Farmers wishing to sell to traders for direct cash payment could do so by signing the parchi, indicating that this was their own decision. In the 2011 season, under the leadership of a new district collector and new mandi secretary, a new system was developed and introduced, involving a pre-registration process and SMS messaging. Farmers were sent a text message, alerting them of the date on which they should bring their produce to the mandi. The new system has regulated the arrivals coming into the mandi on any given day and succeeded in distributing volumes more evenly across the three-month procurement period. It allows mandi officials to adjust arrivals based on the capacities of societies to buy and factor in changing transportation and storage conditions.

In the villages, in addition to a lottery system to determine the order of sales, some societies also set up 'emergency scales' for use when a farmer makes a convincing argument for the urgent sale of his produce, a request that can be easily verified by other residents in the village and by the society representatives themselves (Shrinivasan 2011). Although further work is needed to better understand the effects of these unfolding initiatives and the different ways in which they are being experienced and responded to, it is clear that wheat procurement in Harda is a dynamic and multidimensional process, dominated by a single fixed price that delivers a season defined by multiple actions and reactions, as new systems are devised, circumvented and strengthened in the mandi.

Conclusion

This chapter has drawn attention to the changing landscape of grain procurement in India, in particular to the remarkable expansion in the public procurement of wheat in Madhya Pradesh since 2008–09. This development marked a significant shift in the state government's grain procurement policy under the leadership of the chief minister, Shivraj Singh Chauhan, who made wheat procurement a high-profile initiative of his second term in power. Its defining feature has been an annual wheat bonus, announced every year since the 2008 marketing season, which, on top of a rising centrally declared MSP, has made the procurement price of wheat in Madhya Pradesh the highest in the country. This has been backed by a major decentralised procurement operation using the state's own marketing agencies and agricultural cooperative societies, dramatically altering the dynamics of wheat marketing in Madhya Pradesh, which had been structured around private trade.

Drawing on ethnographic fieldwork conducted in Harda Mandi, this chapter described the new systems and processes that have been implemented in the market yard and examined their effects on the composition of the mandi and on key market participants—farmers, traders, labourers, mandi functionaries and multiple state agencies. By focusing on the logistical life and micro-practices of procurement, it was better able to grasp the interconnections between critical, but often unnoticed or under-analysed, elements of routine market processes and their impact on market participation and outcomes. These included the timing and duration of procurement in a particular agricultural cycle and in relation to specific commodity characteristics; the different modes of payment; forms of documentation; the management of trolley traffic; and the circulation of parchis or transaction slips. Finally, this account has tried to emphasise and capture the dynamism of procurement—a period defined by a fixed price but fluctuating processes—within and across seasons, during which systems are continuously compromised and strengthened as local officials and market yard functionaries respond to, negotiate, and try to resolve new pressures, problems and loopholes.

In the initial seasons, the canal-irrigated wheat zone of the Harda and Hoshangabad districts dominated the procurement map of Madhya Pradesh, and in keeping with the popular comparisons with Punjab and Haryana, might well have led to the kind of spatial concentration in the state that is seen in the inter-regional inequality of procurement across India. The 2011–12 data on district-wise procurement is therefore particularly striking, for it shows a rapid diffusion of decentralised wheat procurement operations over much of the state, with volumes growing dramatically over the last two years (Figure 10.1). With the state government signalling every intention of rising further up the wheat procurement chart (see Tiwari 2012), these systems may further expand and dominate wheat markets in Madhya Pradesh, at least in the foreseeable future. Looking forward, there are three critical areas of tension and trade-offs that have begun to emerge and require greater attention.

FIGURE 10.1: The Changing Procurement Map of Madhya Pradesh (District-wise Distribution of Wheat Procurement in the 2008 and 2012 Marketing Seasons)

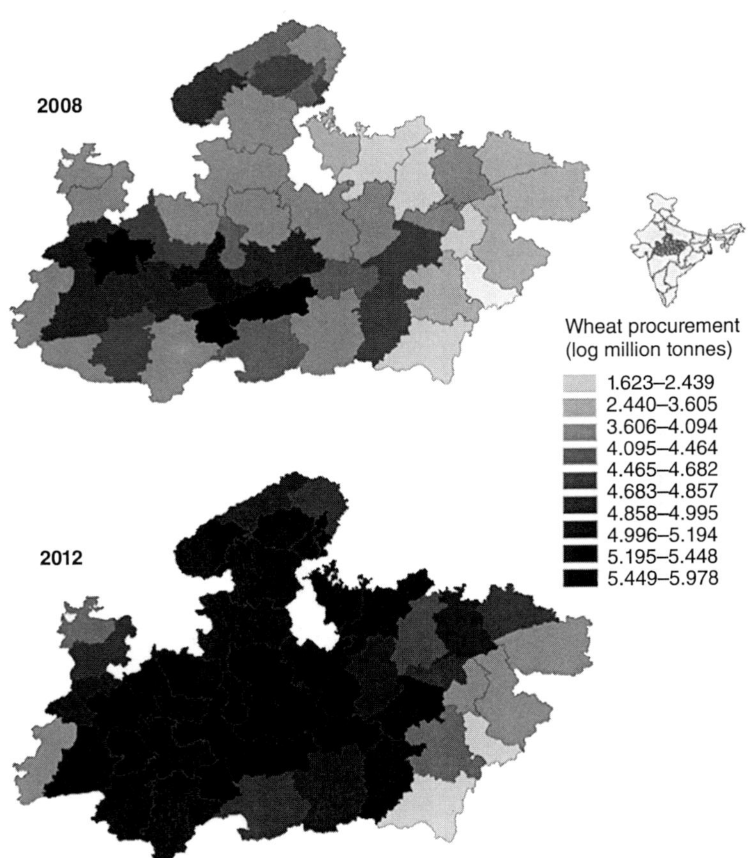

Source: Madhya Pradesh State Civil Supply Corporation.

First, given the speed with which procurement operations are being extended and the dramatic jump in the volume of wheat purchased by the state, field-level systems and capacities need to be considerably strengthened. This is especially important given the higher procurement price prevailing in Madhya Pradesh.[8] Second, with the growing volume of fixed-price procurement, it is important to understand and assess its implications on the varieties and qualities of wheat produced in the state, particularly because diversity and high quality are the great strengths of Madhya Pradesh's wheat. In Harda, which is not well-known for quality when compared to other parts of Madhya Pradesh, farmers have responded quickly to the new procurement environment by shifting to even more high-yielding varieties, but research is needed on what is happening in other districts as a result of government procurement. Finally, an urgent issue is that of distribution in a state with high malnutrition and chronic food insecurity. In Harda, as elsewhere in the state, the spread and strength of public procurement systems is far greater and more impressive than the pace of reform and change in public distribution, which was all the more palpable in the context of the wheat bonus and rising commodity prices (Tiwari 2012). If Madhya Pradesh's commitment to decentralised procurement reflects how rapidly state agencies and resources can be mobilised and how dynamically systems can be reformed and strengthened, more needs to be done if the benefits from procurement are to be more effectively and equitably distributed.

Notes

1. The national and state-wise procurement figures are from the FCI (http://fciweb.nic.in/procurements). Wheat production data and procurement as a percentage of total production has been calculated from data reported in the RBI *Handbook of Statistics on Indian Economy 2011–12* (http://www.rbi.org.in; accessed 18 November 2012). District-level data on procurement in Madhya Pradesh is from the Madhya Pradesh Civil Supplies Corporation.

2. All-India data show childhood (under-5) undernutrition levels remain exceptionally high, with 42 per cent of Indian children underweight. In Madhya Pradesh, this figure is even higher at 59.8 per cent. An 'India State of Hunger Index Report' released by International Food Policy Research Institute (IFPRI) put Madhya Pradesh in the 'extremely alarming' category (Menon, Deolaliker and Bhaskar 2009).

3. Madhya Pradesh was one of the first states to amend its APMC Act to allow private, single-licence yards to be set up outside the mandi yard. ITC began to set up its e-Choupal network here in the early 2000s.

4. The net irrigated area in Harda is recorded as 76 per cent, which makes it one of the most highly irrigated districts in Madhya Pradesh, a state which has 20 per cent of the country's drylands and where average irrigation coverage is less than 30 per cent, with most of the water coming from wells and tubewells (Vijay Shankar 2005).

5. For a rich account of wheat cultivation in this region in the mid-nineteenth century, see Charles Elliott's Hoshangabad Settlement Report (1867). Also, see Stokes (1979), Raghavan (1985), Bates (1988) and Krishnamurthy (2011), on an important chapter in regional agricultural history, known as the 'Narmada Valley wheat boom' (1880–95) in which Harda is mentioned as a key centre for the wheat trade.

6. Data on distribution of landholdings is from the Agricultural Census website: http://agcensus.nic.in/ (accessed 18 November 2012).

7. Barbara Harriss (1984) makes a similar point regarding the contradictory and conflicting roles of state intervention and regulation in foodgrain markets.

8. Here, given the direct procurement from farmers through village and mandi-based centres run by PACs, the problem is not so much that farmers will be excluded if operations open in new locations, but that it may be harder to ensure that the government does not end up buying wheat that comes in from other sites and sources, both within the state and from bordering regions. The huge jump in procurement volumes in the 2012 season, even taking into account the substantial increase in production, needs to be carefully investigated, since the data indicate that government procurement has absorbed an extraordinary 80 per cent of the total wheat production (not marketable surplus) in the state.

REFERENCES

Acharya, S. S., Ramesh Chand, P. S. Birthal, Shiv Kumar and D. S. Negi. 2012. 'Market Integration and Price Transmission in India: A Case of Rice and Wheat with Special Reference to the World Food Crisis of 2007–08'. Food and Agriculture Organisation, Rome.

Basu, Kaushik. 2011. 'India's Foodgrains Policy: An Economic Theory Perspective'. *Economic and Political Weekly* 46(5): 37–45.

Bates, Crispin. 1988. 'Class and Economic Change in Central India: The Narmada Valley 1820–1930'. In *Arrested Development in India: The Historical Perspective*, ed. Clive Dewey, 241–82. New Delhi: Manohar.

Chand, Ramesh. 2003. 'Government Intervention in Foodgrain Markets in the New Context'. Policy Paper No. 19, National Centre for Agricultural Economics and Research, New Delhi.

———. 2007. 'Wheat Supply, Price Prospects, and Food Security'. *Economic and Political Weekly* 42(19): 1659–63.

Das, Sandip. 2012a. 'Pro-farmer Policies Work Wonders as Procurement Rises'. *The Indian Express*, 25 May.

———. 2012b. 'At 76 mt, FCI Stocks More than Double of Buffer Stock'. *The Indian Express*, 11 August.

Damodaran, Harish. 2000. 'Grain Market Still under Sway of Commission Agents'. *Business Line*, 12 May.

———. 2007. 'Corporates Burn Their Fingers in Wheat as Prices Rule Flight'. *The Hindu Business Line*, 1 October. Available at http://www.thehindubusinessline.in/2007/10/01/stories/2007100151980100.htm (accessed 18 November 2012).

———. 2010a. 'Why Cash is King in Grain Market'. *Business Line*, 16 March.

———. 2010b. 'Chhattisgarh, Orissa Show the Way in Rice Procurement'. *Business Line*, 28 October.

———. 2010c. 'Grains Grow on Procurement'. *Business Line*, 2 November.

Drèze, Jean and Reetika Khera. 2010. 'Chhattisgarh Shows the Way'. *The Hindu*, 13 November.

Elliott, Charles A. 1867. *Report on the Land Revenue Settlement of the District of Hoshungabad, Central Provinces*. Allahabad: Government Press.

Frankel, Francine. 1971. *India's Green Revolution: Economic Gains and Political Costs*. New Jersey: Princeton University Press.

Gill, Anita. 2004. 'Interlinked Agrarian Credit Markets: Case Study of Punjab'. *Economic and Political Weekly* 39(33): 3741–51.

Gulati, Ashok and Pradeep K. Sharma. 1990. 'Prices, Procurement and Production: An Analysis of Wheat and Rice'. *Economic and Political Weekly* 25(13): A36–47.

Harriss, Barbara. 1984. *State and Market: State Intervention in Agricultural Exchange in a Dry Region of Tamil Nadu, South India*. New Delhi: Concept Publishing.

Jeffrey, Craig. 2002. 'Caste, Class and Clientalism: A Political Economy of Everyday Corruption in Rural North India'. *Economic Geography* 78(1): 21–41.

——. 2010. *Timepass: Youth, Class, and the Politics of Waiting in India*. Stanford: Stanford University Press.

Kingsley, John. 2011. 'Wheat Procurement Made Easy: The Harda Model, Documentation of a Successful Practice'. District Collectorate, Harda, Madhya Pradesh.

Krishnaji, N. 1976. 'Public Distribution and Procurement of Foodgrains: A Comment'. *Economic and Political Weekly* 11(8): 332–34.

——. 1990. 'Agricultural Price Policy: A Survey with Reference to the Indian Foodgrain Economy'. *Economic and Political Weekly* 25(6): A54–63.

Krishnamurthy, Mekhala. 2011. 'Harda Mandi: Experiencing Change in an Agricultural Market in Central India 1980–2010'. PhD thesis, University College, London.

Menon, Purnima, Anil Deolaliker and Anjor Bhaskar. 2009. 'The India State Hunger Index: Comparisons of Hunger across States'. International Food Policy Research Institute (IFPRI), Washington, DC.

Mishra, Ambareesh. 2007. 'Grains of Gold'. *India Today*, 15 October.

Mooij, Jos. 1999. *Food Policy and the Indian State*. New Delhi: Oxford University Press.

Nair, Sthanu R., and Leela Mary Eapen. 2011. 'Wheat Price Inflation in Recent Times: Causes, Lessons and News Perspectives'. *Economic and Political Weekly* 46(36): 58–65.

Raghavan, M. 2004. 'Politics of Procurement and Price Support'. *Economic and Political Weekly* 29(5): 506–08.

Raghavan, T. C. A. 1985. 'Malguzars and Peasants: The Narmada Valley, 1860–1920'. *Studies in History* 1(2): 169–200.

Shah, Mihir, Debasis Banerji, P. S. Vijayshankar and Pramathesh Ambasta. 1998. *India's Drylands: Tribal Societies and Development through Environmental Regeneration*. New Delhi: Oxford University Press.

Shrinivasan, Rukmini. 2011. 'Mobile Revolution in MP Wheat Market'. *The Times of India*, 19 April.

Somasekar, A. K. (ed.). 2007. *Computerisation of Paddy Procurement and PDS in Chhattisgarh 2007–08*. Chhattisgarh State Civil Supplies Corporation, Raipur.

Stokes, Eric. 1979. *The Peasant and the Raj: Studies in Agrarian Society and Peasant Rebellion in Colonial India*. Cambridge: Cambridge University Press.

Swaminathan, Madhura. 1999. 'Understanding the Costs of the Food Corporation of India'. *Economic and Political Weekly* 34(52): A121–32.

Thompson, E. P. 1971. 'The Moral Economy of the English Crowd in the Eighteenth Century'. *Past and Present* 50(1): 76–136.

Tiwari, Ravish. 2012. 'MP Set to Topple Haryana as No. 2 in Wheat Procurement'. *The Indian Express*, 5 June.

Vijay Shankar, P. S. 2005. 'Four Decades of Agricultural Development in MP'. *Economic and Political Weekly* 40(48): 5014–24.

SECTION IV

Relational Structures and Transitions

11

Relations of Production in Pre-colonial India*

Sumita Chatterjee and Ashok Rudra

It can be said about contemporary India that we have more or less a clear picture of our rural society from the point of view of production relations. Present-day landholders can be divided into a number of categories. Pure absentee landlords have largely disappeared. There are rich farmers who hold large quantities of land which they do not cultivate themselves. They get them cultivated by sharecroppers, other kinds of tenants, agricultural labourers, etc. The cultivators holding smaller areas are often self-sufficient. They work on their own and hire labour in small amounts only in the busy periods. Things may be expected to have been different in the past. We know a great deal about these matters as they were in the colonial period. But about the period immediately preceding the coming of the British, how much do we know?

This chapter represents a modest attempt to answer the question. We shall see that our body of knowledge about production relations in the period of our interest is indeed very meagre. This is no reflection cast on our economic historians. We may not be wrong in thinking that our scholars in the field have more or less exhausted all the possible sources relating to that not very ancient period. Fresh research may throw up more details about micro-regions and specific dates. It would however be surprising if one should uncover data that would drastically alter the state of the literature as presented in this chapter.

...

Communal Systems

...

Was there any collective cultivation of land or was cultivation carried out individually and separately as now?

* Originally published in *Economic and Political Weekly* 24(21), 27 May 1989: 1171–75.

One comes across indeed very little evidence about communal cultivation. The only references to such activities we find are of the nature of settlement of new areas and reclamation of new land or forest land. As to an earlier period, we have from Irfan Habib (1982b: 218) that in the Mughal period when peasants deserted old lands and settled in new ones, they did so communally.[1] As to the associated question of private ownership of land, it continues to be a matter about which different historians give answers differing from each other in shades of meaning. As is all too well known, during the sixteenth and seventeenth centuries, some European travellers originated a long-lasting myth by describing the king as the sole owner of land in India (Habib 1982a: 235). As is also well known, this idea has by now been very largely rejected. Likewise, another idea inherited from the past is that land was held in common and cultivated jointly. But this idea has also been largely rejected.

According to Walter C. Neale, however, in some areas, in the zamindari villages, 'the land-owners claimed the land jointly and their respective shares were determined by the laws of inheritance' though 'in the Bhaichara village each family owned its own lands separately. As a rule each of the original settlers or conquerors received an equal share of land' (Neale 1962: 40). About the permanent settlement regions it used to be thought for a long time that the settlement brought about ownership in land for the first time. But the idea has also been held that land was owned by zamindars more or less to the same degree and in more or less the same sense before the settlement as after it.[2]

On the question of communal ownership, the following position, once again of Neale, appears to be the most generally accepted:

> the question whether the land was owned by the raja, the talukdar, zamindar, the cultivator or the king was not a real question. Each had claim based upon custom or upon grants made by the king or a raja, or upon grants made by a talukdar or zamindar. But in addition to these claims each did or did not have the power to enforce his claims or to enlarge his claims. There was no appeal if a usurper [also] had the power to usurp. (Neale 1962: 37)

Further, 'The village did not hold its land in common. Common were its officials and servants' (ibid.: 21).

W. C. Bennet is quoted in support of this position as follows: 'The produce of the land was the common property of every class in agricultural community from Raja to the slave. No one was absolute owner more than the others but each had definite and permanent interest' (cited in Neale 1962: 24).

H. Fukazawa (1982b: 309) confirms the same when he writes about south India that 'when there were several co-sharers of a watan, they did not divide among themselves the peasant families into distinct spheres of work, but shared the total income'.[3] He further states that in the Deccan, agricultural land could be divided into: (a) ordinary owned land; (b) gifted or exempted land; (c) state land; and (d) wasteland, which incidentally confirms the existence of privately owned land (Fukazawa 1982a: 250). Similar confirmation is made by Romesh Dutt (1960: 60) who says that in Bengal during 1785–93, the *khodkhast* (self-cultivated land) ryots were given lands for cultivation for unlimited periods and that is how occupancy rights originated.

> Mirasdar peasants, mostly kunbis by caste, were permanent residents of the village and bore the regular revenue and miscellaneous cesses for the state on their miras land in which they held a fairly complete proprietary right. Though it was not a frequent practice, they could sell their own land from the late sixteenth century. (Fukazawa 1982a: 251)

This observation of Fukazawa once again confirms the existence of individual private holdings.

There are a few other points of consensus. For instance, despite the *mirasdars* (proprietary peasants) cited earlier, it is agreed by all that land mostly could not be sold and was transferred only to a limited extent by mortgage. 'The seizure and sale of land for private debt was wholly and utterly unknown—such an idea had never entered into the native imagination' (George Campbell, quoted in Neale 1962: 28). As to the origin of ownership rights, it is agreed that they depended upon: (a) who first cleared the land and made it productive, and (b) who conquered the area first.[4]

We have seen that the idea of king as the owner of land has been rejected. But that does not mean that the king did not have ownership rights over some lands. For instance the king was indeed the owner of all wastelands (see Neale 1962: 24).

We shall now see what answers we get from the existing literature to the following questions about the actual tillers of the soil.

1. Was the peasantry homogeneous or was it differentiated?
2. Were there self-sufficient peasants cultivating their land with their own labour, *without* the help of tenants or labourers?
3. If there were tenants in the present-day sense, that is, rent-paying actual cultivators, what do we know about the rent or rental share paid by them and their numerical importance?
4. If there were wage labourers, how important were they quantitatively and what do we know about the wages paid to them?
5. If there were slave labourers or bonded labourers, what do we know about their numerical importance and their conditions?
6. What do we know about moneylending by professional moneylenders or rich farmers?
7. If there were big landholders who were employers of labourers or landlords of tenants, what do we know about their role in the rural economy?

Peasant Differentiation

As is well known, there was at one time an idea that in the traditional village society there was a single class of self-sufficient peasants producing for their own consumption, Habib writes:

> To astute observers like Bernier, the Indian peasants, labourers, appeared an undifferentiated mass, all living miserably under a blind and increasing oppression.

> The picture was not an unfair one, it does not also conflict with the concept, developed later, of the Indian rural population divided up horizontally among village communities, each a self-sufficient entity, left to its own devices by the despotic regime of the court so long as the heavy land-tax was paid. (Habib 1982a: 247)

This idea, however, has now been more or less unanimously rejected. There is now a near consensus that the rural society was quite well-stratified from much before the coming of the British. We have from the authoritative pen of Habib (1982a: 247):

> economic differentiation had progressed considerably among the peasantry. There were large cultivators, using hired labour, and raising crops for the market, and there were small peasants, who could barely produce foodgrains for their own subsistence. Beyond this differentiation among the peasantry, there was the still sharper division between the caste peasantry and the "menial population".

Further,

> Depending upon their resources in seed, cattle and money, peasants might cultivate large or smaller fields. But larger land-holdings were linked to, and often resulted from, a superior position or status secured either as headmen, or as members belonging to dominant elements of the village, in contrast to the general run of the small peasantry (the reza riaya). (Ibid.: 248)

We get some similar ideas about the class composition of the village society in south India from Fukazawa. Thus, villages would consist of: (a) hereditary village officers such as headman (*patil* or *mukkadam*), accountant (*kulkarni*), and assistant headman (*chaugula*); (b) proprietary peasants, called mirasdars in Persian, or *thalkuri* or *thalvaik* in indigenous terms; (c) temporary peasants or tenants called *upari* (literally, strangers); and (d) village servants and artisans collectively called *balutedars* (Fukazawa 1982a: 250). Fukazawa further provides evidence about differentiation in the peasantry in the form of some statistical tables relating to two villages in the western Deccan.

Habib makes lots of references to what he calls dominant peasants. For instance, he writes: 'It was common in Mughal administrative literature to bemoan such exploitation of the smaller peasantry by the dominant elements within the village' (Habib 1982a: 249).

However, we do not learn from him much about the specific ways by which the so-called dominant elements carried out their exploitation. When he writes, 'The village community was thus rife with internal contradictions' (ibid.), he only means the conflicts arising from the dominant elements passing on the burden of tax revenue on the weaker elements. What we miss is any reference to the exploitative productive relations, that is, the modes of surplus extraction, as obtaining between the dominant elements and the weaker elements.

More specific references to peasant differentiation go as far as the following:

> Village society consisted broadly of three sections: first the khud-kashta, who were also called malik-i-zamin or owners of the land in the official documents ... The second section was called the pahi, or upari, outsiders. These were peasants who came from other villages to cultivate land and had their own hutments there; lastly, there were

> the muzarian or sharecroppers, who rented land from the khud-kashta peasants or the zamindars. There was also a small class of landless peasants placed at par with the village servants: the tanner, the potter, the washerman. The latter, too had little or no land, and rendered service to the peasants in return for which they received a fixed share of the produce at the time of harvest. They were sometimes given small strips of land which paid revenue at a concessional rate. They were also enrolled as casual labourers at times of harvest, sowing, etc. (Chandra 1982: 458–59)

On this point, and as far as the Bengal region is concerned, we owe a great deal to the works of Ratnalekha Ray and Rajat Ray (see Ray 1974, 1975; Ray and Ray 1973, 1975). They have forcefully argued that in the early British period there existed *from before* various types of peasants, such as self-sufficient peasant cultivators, sharecroppers, under-tenants, long-term agricultural labourers, casual labourers, bonded labourers, etc., working for superior peasant landlords.

However, what hard facts do we have about these different categories of the peasantry—their origin, their numbers, etc.? To what extent can we pin down other historians making explicit references to the existence of such peasant categories?

Self-sufficient Peasants

About self-cultivating, self-sufficient peasants, we learn about the Deccan and Maharashtra that 'many of the watandar balutedars held some plots of inam ... (rent free) land granted by the village community, such inam land also being included in the watan and obviously cultivated by themselves', and about south India that 'the small peasant households were based on personal labour' (Fukazawa 1982b: 309; Alaev 1982b: 229–30).[5] But can we be certain that *cultivated by themselves* or *personal labour* really meant that 'the raiyat or peasant produced for his household by employing on his own field his *own labour*' (Ray and Ray 1973: 104)? We cannot be certain of that even for the present day: when nowadays one refers to self-cultivation, one means no more than cultivation under one's *own supervision.* Was it different in the past? If not, who was the ultimate tiller?

Tenants

As to tenancy, one difficulty that we face is that in the literature the term 'tenant' is freely used to designate any person who enjoys a share in the surplus produced by actual tillers without being the ultimate owners. Thus, substantial farmers and even zamindars are sometimes referred to as tenants. It is difficult to locate references to such tenants who are definitely actual tillers of the soil. Sharecroppers mentioned in the extract from Satish Kumar is the kind of reference we are missing. Another such specific reference is to the 'upari' peasants, as in the following:

> Upari peasants were temporary residents of the village ... They would make an agreement with the village headman to cultivate state land or waste land therein and pay a certain amount of rent. It is also certain that many of them were tenants on inam land owned by village officers, temples, desmukhs, despandes and so on. (Fukazawa 1982a: 251)

As to terms and conditions of tenancy, we have got a huge accumulation of opinions and counter-opinions about a multitude of different kinds of tenures, occupancy rights and the various shifts in them over time. But it is very difficult to locate any information in them about the terms and conditions applying to *those particular tenants who were the actual tillers of the soil.*

As to numerical information, according to F. Buchanan, in Dinajpur, 6 per cent of the cultivating population enjoyed 36.5 per cent of the land leased in by the ryot from the zamindar, whereas 52 per cent of the agricultural workforce had no land at all and worked for rich farmers as hired labourers or sharecroppers.[6] Such fragments of information can indeed be found in profusion. However, it would be a very different task to piece them together to give estimates for any region as a whole for any particular date, and nobody seems to have attempted the task.

So far as the origin of the institution of tenancy is concerned, we know that many like Henry Thomas Colebrook argued that in Bengal an intermediary tenantry cultivating through under-tenants and sharecroppers arose after 1793 from the government's practice of raising large contributions by appointing farmers in the place of regular collectors of revenue like *amils* or zamindars. In particular, after the big famine, the area of wasteland increased. It was pointed out that in Purnea, Rajshahi and Birbhum, some rich farmers of the village drove out inferior ryots and thus secured their lands at low rates and then employed their dependents as sharecroppers, many of whom in future turned to agricultural labour. This story of the origin of tenancy in the Bengal region has, however, been strongly opposed and the view held that tenancy was an established institution from much before the coming of the British.[7]

Agricultural Labourers

As to agricultural labourers, we can infer from W. H. Moreland and F. Bernier that such labourers did exist even during the Mughal period from such references as the following: 'According to Bernier a considerable portion of good land remained untilled for want of labourers many of whom perish in consequence of the bad treatment they experience' (Raychaudhuri 1982: 175).

'W. H. Moreland doubts that there were any labourers in Mughal India free to choose their employers' (Neale 1962: 23). For a later period, L. Alaev (1982b) writes of two kinds of households: large peasant households that used to do some part of the work with family labour but mainly depended on the regular inflow of additional labour, and another type of households that got work done by labourers dependent on them and attached to the land.[8]

We can infer that the system of wage labour existed because we find plentiful references to wage rates of daily labourers for different parts of the country and for different dates. From the rates we can also infer that in some places labourers on annual contract were also prevalent. Thus, for example, Buchanan provides data like the following about the period around 1800: in south Mysore 'farm labourers got from £1 to £1.7s a year besides one meal a day and women labourers got 6s a year besides 2 meals a day' (quoted in Dutt 1960: 146). Dutt (1960: 142–43) further cites several bits of data like the following from various sources about the same period: 'In north Mysore farm servants got 29¼ bushels of gram and 13s 5d annually; the rate for day-labourers was about 3d for men and 2d for women. ... A labouring man earned 4s a month, and a woman 3s 4d.'

In Bhagalpur, 'Ploughmen ... engaged themselves by the season, received an advance of Rs 5 to Rs 20 and laboured for their masters till this was worked off' (ibid.: 165). In Behar, 'A plough servants' annual wages ranged from 16 rupees to 22 rupees a year' (ibid.: 160).

As to information about numbers of labourers, the position is no better than that for tenants. Alaev (1982b: 229) says, 'In the Madras presidency, agrestic labourers, mainly from the untouchable castes, numbered up to 10–15 per cent of the population and 17–25 per cent of the agricultural population.' But such fragments of information have not been pieced together by anybody. About the origin of agricultural labourers, we have already given some references which are common for sharecroppers and labourers.

Servile Labour

As to slave labourers and bonded labourers, one finds plentiful stray references from ancient times.[9] As to the period immediately before the coming of the British, we have fragmentary information like the following:

> Higher castes frequently had a slave-plowman who bound himself and his descendants to labour for the land-holder in exchange for a loan of Rs 100 to Rs 200. Each year the plowman received a share of the crop which he helped to cultivate. The share was normally too small to provide subsistence for himself and his family. The extra food given to him by his master was added to the debt, so that instead of releasing himself from his obligation a plowman ran more deeply into debt. It was, however, easy for him to change masters by borrowing from a new master in order to liquidate his obligation to the old! (Neale 1962: 22)

This is about south India. About Bengal, there are a lot of statements like the following: 'In Rangpur in Bengal the terms of an advance on wage was very high. Instead of this advance the labourer had to work for his master. If they could not finish the work in time the whole family became slaves and they may be sold jointly or separately' (Ray and Ray 1973: 118).

Zamindars, Big Landholders and Moneylenders

What place did zamindars have in the production conditions inside the village? The role played by them in production was very little indeed. Nowadays a landlord can and does give proposals to his tenant about details of crop production. During the pre-colonial period they seem to have had no such involvement in actual cultivation—they did not exercise any say about how individual cultivators would organise their cultivation. We do get some information about the way they controlled certain parts of the infrastructure of the rural economy. B. B. Chaudhuri (1982) provides evidence to the effect that in Bengal the zamindars used to construct as well as maintain irrigation works and embankments. Distribution of water was also part of the zamindar's responsibility, especially where a large number of villages were concerned. So was reclamation of wasteland. Chaudhuri's observations are, of course, about the colonial period, but it is safe to project the profile backwards in time. We have, of course, masses of information about the rent collecting activities of zamindars, but rent collecting relations do not constitute production relations and as such do not interest us in this article.

As to big landholders, whether strictly owners of land or not, we have recently been supplied with a lot of evidence to establish that in Bengal at least such farmers existed from long before the coming of the British.[10] As a matter of fact, these big landowners, called *jotedars* in Bengal, were themselves lease-holders or tenants. There was at one time a commonly held notion that the jotedar class emerged along with the system of tenancy after the permanent settlement. As has been mentioned earlier, it has been strongly opposed. It has been held that this class did not spring up into existence between 1760 and 1790, but had for long been a prominent element in our traditional agrarian society.[11] According to Buchanan, the rich tenant designated jotedar was under the zamindar and a large portion of cultivation of a village was carried on with money and grain advanced by them. Through this giving of credit the jotedars enjoyed command over the labour force of the village. They also brought grains from smaller cultivators at half price (Ray and Ray 1975: 84). And this held them also in their grips.

As to moneylending, there are again plentiful references though not a great deal of solid data. Moneylending in the interior was an activity of substantial villagers and grain traders who financed both agricultural and rent-collecting operations at exorbitant rates. According to some authors, in some regions cultivation was almost entirely carried on with grain advanced to the peasants by petty *mahajans* (traders/moneylenders) and jotedars. These moneylenders also acted as grain merchants. Cultivation of cash crops was mostly based on advances by sugar manufacturers, silk manufacturers, etc. (Ray 1979: 112).[12]

SERVICES AND ARTISANS

As to the way different artisans and providers of services were integrated in the village economy, we find some details in the recent writings of Fukazawa, Alaev and Neale and the earlier writings of Dutt. It is somewhat reassuring that the accounts presented by these different authors are consistent with each other. We can begin with an extensive quotation from Fukazawa about Maharashtra and Gujarat:

> Village servants and artisans called balutedars included the carpenter, blacksmith, potter, shoemaker, ropemaker, barber, washerman, astrologer, temple-keeper, mosque-keeper (being butcher as well), mahar (an untouchable caste engaged in sweeping and other menial work), and so on. Their composition was fairly uniform though their number varied according to the size of the village. They were expected to serve villagers whenever required in their respective capacities fixed by their castes, and were paid the remunerations at the two harvests of the year usually in kind, but occasionally

> in cash, such remunerations being called balute. Besides these they were entitled to certain shares of offerings dedicated to village temples, and to some other perquisites on special occasions. Moreover, many of them were given by the village a small plot of inam land, which was as a rule cultivated by themselves. (Fukazawa 1982a: 251–52)

There were three systems of payment to the balutedars:

1. All the peasants brought their respective produce to a certain place in the village and gave customary shares of it to each category of balutedars.
2. The village headman inspected the state of the harvest and then made every peasant pay a certain portion of his produce to each category of balutedars.
3. Each category of balutedar received a certain amount of cash ranging from Rs 10 to Rs 2.50 per year.

The artisans had to work for all the families of the village. Only the priests in the Deccan were employed under a certain family (ibid.: 252).

This is very similar to the account given by Neale about south India:

> The assignments of the harvest in favour of the various members of the community were of three kinds: first, on the standing crop before it was cut; second, on the whole grain heap before the main division; third, on the raja's or cultivator's separate share after the main division was made. (Neale 1962: 22)

Neale gives a very detailed description of the way different members of the rural society, for example, watchman, blacksmith, carpenter, herdsman, priest, slave-ploughman, barber, washerman, etc., were allocated shares out of the grain heap made out of all the producers according to precise rules, which also he describes in detail. 'All village artisans and menials together with the community administrative staff were known by the common appellation of ayagars ("the receivers of the ayam") and in some situations they appeared as a kind of council of representatives of all the castes living in a village. In this role the ayagars might be a collective witness to transference of land, election of the headman', and so on (ibid.: 22–23).

He says that the artisans could also sell their surplus products outside the village. They could do this only after paying the dues to the different parties (Alaev 1982a: 316–17).

Earlier, Dutt also gave detailed accounts of the payments made to different village artisans and functionaries, like astrologer, potter, accountant, *brahman*, measurer, etc., and then concluded:

> Thus a payment of 5¼ per cent of the produce of the fields secured to the villages the professional services of the barber, the potter and the blacksmith, the priest and the astrologer. Of the remainder, the deshmukh or zamindar claimed 10 per cent; and the balance was divided equally between the government and the farmer. (Dutt 1960: 141)

Revenue Collection

In pre-colonial India the revenue collecting mechanism was highly complex and elaborate, involving a number of tiers of collecting agents. In different parts of the country these agents were designated by different names but their roles were more or less the same. We indeed get a great deal of information about the revenue collecting system but that is mostly about the upper part of the ladder of revenue collectors, from the zamindars to the *diwans*. In contrast, information about the methods followed for revenue collection within the village is quite limited.

> About north India, we learn from lrfan Habib that inasmuch as it was convenient for the authorities to treat the village as a unit for collection (and even assessment), it was natural for them to rely upon the headmen or a small stratum of upper peasants. This dominant group, then, collected the tax at rates fixed by themselves from every peasant, putting the collection in a pool (fota), with its accountant, the patwari. From this pool the land revenue would be paid, so also the fees and perquisites of certain officials ...
> ... Those who controlled the pool usually evaded paying their due share of revenue. Lower rates were also levied upon some favoured elements, the khwud-kasht peasants in northern India, gharubalas in Rajasthan and mirasdars in Maharashtra. (Habib 1982a: 248–49)

The second part of the extract points at the unequal incidence of revenue but not much light is thrown on how this result is produced. That is because we are told very little by Habib about the structure of the rural society which permitted the so-called dominant groups to dominate.

The picture given above is corroborated and elaborated about the Bengal region by Ratnalekha Ray as follows:

> ... The amount due from cultivator had been left to the influential villagers. A few of the principal raiyats signed the engagement for the jama on behalf of the villagers. If there was any individual settlement, it was concluded with big huzuri jotedars (direct rayatwari holders under whom existed the actual tillers of the soil) or with revenue-farmers of villages who executed separate engagements. (Ray 1979: 65–66)

While collection of revenue was left to jotedars and another category of rich farmers called *gantidars*, Ray also refers to the role of the village headmen, called *mandais*, and officers of the zamindar like patwaris, *amins*, *shiqdar's karmacharis*, as well as *gomastas*.

CONCLUSION

The account presented here is indeed very short. Could it have been made much longer? Surely yes, if we did not want to avoid multiplying references telling the same tale. But we doubt that we would have learnt a great deal more. Relations of production is a Marxian concept defined as the relations obtaining between different human agents *around the act of production*. Most of our sources are related not to the act of production but to the act of revenue collection. As a result, we know a great deal about the complicated ramifications of the complex and ladder-like network mechanism of revenue collection. Our economic history is, therefore, very largely a history of revenue systems and not of production relations.

Notes

1. The references are all to articles in *The Cambridge Economic History of India*, Volume 1 (1982).

2. See the discussion on this point in Ray (1975).

3. The term '*watan*' is explained by Fukazawa (1982b: 308) in the following passage: 'The balutedars were divided into two classes: Watandars and Uparis. The former had a permanent right to work and receive remunerations in the village while the latter had no such right and were migratory. Such a permanent right was called Watan, which was heritable and saleable.'

4. For details, see Neale (1962: 19).

5. The expression 'granted by the village community' used in the first extract indicates some kind of communal ownership of land. This is a typical instance of the way in which the question of communal ownership and individual ownership has got clouded.

6. See details in Ray (1979: 63–64).

7. See a detailed discussion in Ray (1979: 54–56).

8. See further discussions in (Alaev 1982b: 229).

9. See, for instance, Kumar (1986).

10. See, for instance, the references to Ray and Ray (1973, 1975) mentioned before.

11. For instance, such statements as the following have been made with considerable persuasive arguments: 'Mode of production based on the relationship between the jotedar rich farmer and adhiar agricultural labour was very well established. The ruling class of the village was formed by a few influential castes or a single dominant caste employed and controlled the untouchables and tribals' (Ray and Ray 1975: 84).

And the following process is stated to have ante-dated the permanent settlement: 'Production, of commercial crops required advances, and the possibility of profits from land as a means of producing commercial crops provided an economic incentive to creditors to appropriate the lands of their debtors. There emerged a new landlord class of peasant jotedars giving credit and monopolising land, and as a corollary large sections of the peasant fraternity of the former village republics became share-croppers and agricultural labourers' (Ray 1979: 264).

12. Ray (1979: 62–62) provides lots more of information about rural moneylending, for instance: 'The rates of batta (exchange) were constantly fluctuating and were manipulated from the towns by the big sarafs (bankers and money changers). Below them were the poddars (money changers) in the villages, a very numerous class of men who possessed no shops but attended the weekly fairs from morning till evening with bags of currency.'

References

Alaev, L. 1982a. 'Non-agricultural Production: South India'. In *The Cambridge Economic History of India (Volume 1): c.1200–c.1750*, eds Tapan Raychaudhuri and Irfan Habib, 315–25. Cambridge: Cambridge University Press.

——. 1982b. 'The System of Agricultural Production: South India'. In *The Cambridge Economic History of India (Volume 1): c.1200–c.1750*, eds Tapan Raychaudhuri and Irfan Habib, 226–35. Cambridge: Cambridge University Press.

Chandra, Satish. 1982. 'Standard of Living: Mughal India'. In *The Cambridge Economic History of India (Volume 1): c.1200–c.1750*, eds Tapan Raychaudhuri and Irfan Habib, 458–71. Cambridge: Cambridge University Press.

Chaudhuri, B. B. 1982. 'Agrarian Relations: Eastern India'. In *Cambridge Economic History of India 1757-1970* (Volume 2), ed. Dharma Kumar, 91–98. Delhi: Cambridge University Press.

Dutt, Romesh. 1960. *The Economic History of India (Volume 1): Under Early British Rule.* Delhi: Publications Division, Ministry of Information and Broadcasting, Government of India.

Fukazawa, H. 1982a. 'Agrarian Relations and Land Revenue: The Medieval Deccan and Maharashtra'. In *The Cambridge Economic History of India (Volume 1): c.1200–c.1750*, eds Tapan Raychaudhuri and Irfan Habib, 249–60. Cambridge: Cambridge University Press.

———. 1982b. 'Non-Agricultural Production: Maharashtra and Deccan'. In *The Cambridge Economic History of India (Volume 1): c.1200–c.1750*, eds Tapan Raychaudhuri and Irfan Habib, 308–15. Cambridge: Cambridge University Press.

Habib, Irfan. 1982a. 'Agrarian Relations and Land Revenue: North India'. In *The Cambridge Economic History of India (Volume 1): c.1200–c.1750*, eds Tapan Raychaudhuri and Irfan Habib, 235–49. Cambridge: Cambridge University Press.

———. 1982b. 'The Systems of Agricultural Production: Mughal India'. In *The Cambridge Economic History of India (Volume 1): c.1200–c.1750*, eds Tapan Raychaudhuri and Irfan Habib, 214–26. Cambridge: Cambridge University Press.

Kumar, Dharma. 1986. 'Capitalism, Colonialism and Unfree Labour in India: A Long View'. Working Paper No. 280, Delhi School of Economics, August.

Neale, Walter C. 1962. *Economic Change in Rural India: Land Tenure and Reform in Uttar Pradesh, 1800–1955.* New Haven and London: Yale University Press.

Raychaudhuri, Tapan. 1982. 'The State and the Economy: The Mughal Empire'. In *The Cambridge Economic History of India (Volume 1): c.1200–c.1750*, eds Tapan Raychaudhuri and Irfan Habib, 172–93. Cambridge: Cambridge University Press.

Ray, Rajat and Ratnalekha Ray. 1973. 'The Dynamics of Continuity in Rural Bengal under the British Imperium'. *Indian Economic and Social History Review* 10(2), June: 103–28.

———. 1975. 'Zamindars and Jotedars in Bengal: A Study of Rural Politics in Bengal'. *Modern Asian Studies* 9(1): 81–102.

Ray, Ratnalekha. 1974. 'Land Transfer and Social Change under the Permanent Settlement: A Study of Two Localities'. *Indian Economic and Social History Review* 11(1), March: 1–45.

———. 1975. 'The Bengal Zamindars: Local Magnates and the State before the Permanent Settlement'. *Indian Economic and Social History Review* 12(3), July–September: 263–92.

———. 1979. *Change in Bengal Agrarian Society, c.1760–1850.* New Delhi: Manohar Publications.

12

SEMI-FEUDALISM OR CAPITALISM?

*Contemporary Debate on Classes and Modes of Production in India**

ALICE THORNER

For more than a dozen years Indian and foreign Marxists have been arguing with passion, subtlety and an abundance of statistics about the existing mode of production in Indian agriculture or, more broadly, in India. There have been proponents of capitalism, pre-capitalism, semi-feudalism, colonial and postcolonial modes, and recently, a dual mode. Authors of important contributions to this debate include economists: Ashok Rudra of Visvabharati University, Shantiniketan, West Bengal; Utsa Patnaik, Amit Bhaduri and Dipankar Gupta, all now of Jawaharlal Nehru University, New Delhi; Nirmal Chandra and Ranjit Sau of the Indian Institute of Management, Calcutta; Amiya Bagchi of the Centre for Studies in Social Sciences, Calcutta; Pradhan Prasad and Nirmal Sen Gupta of the A. N. Sinha Institute of Social Studies, Patna; Jairus Banaji of Bombay; Paresh Chattopadhyay and Sharat G. Lin, both teaching in Canada; and John Harriss of the University of East Anglia; social anthropologists: Kathleen Gough of Vancouver who began work in South India in 1947; and Joan F. Mencher of the University of the City of New York; and sociologists: Hamza Alavi of the University of Manchester and Gail Omvedt, an American who has adopted residence in Maharashtra. But this listing is not exhaustive.

In very large part, the successive formulations, presentations of data, critiques and rebuttals have appeared in the *Economic and Political Weekly* of Bombay. Two other journals which have published substantial contributions are *Frontier*, Calcutta, and *Social Scientist*, Trivandrum. Although a handful of relevant books have been published in India and elsewhere during the period, the cut and thrust of the argument has been carried almost exclusively in the periodicals.

* Originally published in *Economic and Political Weekly* 17(49 and 51), 4 and 18 December 1982: 1961–68 and 2061–66.

The framework and terminology of the discussion are explicitly Marxist. References to classics by Marx, Engels, Kautsky, Lenin and Mao Tse-tung (Mao Zedong) abound. Our authors are also familiar with the current international Marxist literature. They cite European and Latin American writers including Louis Althusser, Étienne Balibar, Charles Bettelheim, Samir Amin, Ciro Cardoso, Andre Gunder Frank, Michał Kalecki, Jean-Loup Herbert, Joan Martinez-Alier, Ernest Mandel, Nicos Poulantzas, Pierre-Philippe Rey, Claude Meillassoux and Rodolfo Stavenhagen, some of whose works have not been translated into English.

Gunder Frank actually intervenes briefly in the debate. But the focus remains Indian, and the concrete evidence brought forward in support of the various theses is drawn primarily from Indian experience. Thus, the different participants in the debate deal with the same body of subject matter, and they share a common theoretical commitment to Marxism. But they are very far from agreement as to how Marxist methodology should be applied to the Indian case. It is taken for granted that Marxist historical models exist; there is no consensus as to the nature of these models. In fact, questions of the Marxist legitimacy of this or that position are argued elaborately and with considerable vehemence. Despite the intrinsic interest of these strictures, we shall leave them to one side and concentrate on the substantive agreements and disagreements with regard to the nature of Indian reality.

What, then, are the main issues at stake?

1. Is there capitalism in Indian agriculture? To a significant degree? In some parts of the country only? Is it a recent phenomenon? Is it spreading? Is it the dominant tendency? Is it a guarantee of agricultural progress? By what criteria can the existence of capitalism in agriculture be proved or disproved?
2. On the contrary, is the dominant form of production relations in agriculture not capitalist but pre-capitalist or semi-feudal? What are the salient features of semi-feudal relations? Are they a brake on the productive forces? Do they resist change?
3. Can India today be characterised with one or another of Marx's well-known modes of production: slavery, feudalism, capitalism and the Asiatic mode? Is it necessary to modify one of Marx's original concepts or to bring in a new mode (or modes) to take account of Indian (or more largely, colonial) specificity? Can there be more than one mode of production in the same country at the same time? If so, are these modes necessarily in conflict, or may they be articulated in some fashion?
4. What was the mode of production or the prevailing form of production relations in India during the colonial period? At the moment of Independence in 1947?
5. What are the principal rural classes? The basis for their demarcation? Their respective shares of the rural population?
6. What are the main lines of conflict, the contradictions in rural India today? In India as a whole? What is the role of the government?
7. What implications for political action by Left parties follow from the answers given to these questions?

We shall return to this checklist when we eventually draw up the balance sheet of the debate. But we shall present the controversy in rough chronological order, as it has actually taken place. We shall see the original protagonists take up their positions, attract supporters and opponents; freebooters will enter the fray and enlarge the area of discussion; a key figure will change sides; others will regroup. In the end, to anticipate, the defenders of semi-feudalism will scatter, the champions of the colonial mode will slip away and the standard-bearers of capitalism will occupy the field, although by no means obedient to a single command.

From the beginning, the debate is carried on simultaneously at several levels: that of the individual cultivating unit, that of the agricultural sector of a particular region (for example, Punjab–Haryana or Eastern India) or of India as a whole, that of the entire economy of a region or of India as a whole; that of the colony–metropole relationship or of the imbrication of India in the world economy. A number of authors (Rudra, Patnaik, Bhaduri, Prasad, Chandra, Mencher, Harriss) bring in freshly gathered field data at the first and second levels to buttress their arguments. Others (Sulekh Chand Gupta, G. G. Kotovsky, Omvedt, Gough, as well as some of these who conducted their own rural enquiries) draw upon the vast stock of data available from official sources such as the Farm Management Studies, NSS, Rural Credit Surveys, Censuses and Agricultural Censuses and Rural Labour Surveys. Banaji and Bagchi use historical sources to document their analyses of nineteenth-century developments. Several of the economists (Patnaik, Rudra, Bhaduri, Chandra, Sau and Lin) employ mathematical models. A handful (Chattopadhyay, Sen Gupta, Dipankar Gupta and Lin) restrict themselves to purely theoretical exercises.

On the edges and over the years the discussion tends to veer off into the terrain of other familiar controversies: the Dobb–Sweezy–Takahashi debate on the transition from feudalism to capitalism in Europe and Japan: the question of the existence of the Asiatic mode of production in ancient, medieval and/or pre-colonial India; problems of agricultural efficiency such as return to scale (that is, the relation between farm size and product per acre) or differences in productivity of owner-as opposed to tenant-cultivation; assessments of the role in recent Indian politics of landlord or peasant lobbies, or of the degree to which the different parties represent different economic interest groups.

We shall try to steer clear of such temptations to digress. As far as possible we shall limit ourselves to the already very wide field embracing modes, forces and relations of production; modes of exploitation; agrarian classes; social formations, contradictions and articulations; movements and dominant tendencies; effects of imperialism and of centre–periphery links; and recommendations for praxis.

The Precursors

Sulekh Chand Gupta, G. G. Kotovsky and Daniel Thorner

As early as 1962, S. C. Gupta, then on the staff of the Agricultural Economics Research Centre of the Delhi University, offered an estimate of capitalist farming as of 1953–54. Taking as his point of departure the concentration of hired labourers on larger-acreage units shown in the Farm Management Studies, he noted that in the state of Uttar Pradesh the element of hired labour exceeded that of family labour on farms with 20 or more acres. Extrapolating in a conservative fashion to India as a whole, in parts of which the size of holdings operated mainly with year-round farm servants was as low as 7.5 acres, he proposed to take the number of households operating 20 acres or more as a rough approximation of the number of capitalist farms. Applying this procedure to the figures from the 1953–54 Census of landholding, he came up with an estimate of less than 6 or 7 per cent of all operational holdings, amounting to about one-third of the total area under cultivation.

A similarly constructed estimate was proposed by G. G. Kotovsky of the Institute of the Peoples of Asia, Moscow. In Kotovsky's (1964) judgement, the area cultivated wholly or mainly by hired labour in 1953–54 amounted to 25 or 30 per cent of the total for India. His conclusion was that the capitalist sector represented the leading tendency in Indian agriculture, but that it did not yet dominate.

Neither of these estimates appears to have provoked any wide discussion. Quite the contrary was the case with the series of four articles published in *The Statesman* (Calcutta and Delhi), on four successive days in November 1967, by Daniel Thorner. In these lively journalistic pieces, Thorner related what he had just seen in a village tour which had taken him through seven states in the northwest, north, west, south and east of India. Whereas 15 years previously his impression had been of rural stagnation (Thorner 1976 [1956]), this time he found alert, enterprising cultivators, eager to experiment with new scientific methods: quick to switch to power for traction and pumping; ready to invest in improvements; preferring to cultivate themselves with hired labour rather than, or in addition to, giving out their land on rent in small parcels; and able to obtain substantial increases in output. He wrote: 'What we are witnessing in India is the emergence of an advanced sector in agriculture that is broadly comparable to the advanced sector in modern industry. This new agriculture has been tested, has proved profitable, and is rapidly expanding' (Thorner 1980 [1967]).

Some of the new-style cultivators whom Thorner came across on his rural swing turned out to be present or former industrialists, merchants, moneylenders, civil servants, army officers, doctors, lawyers and similar persons of high economic status and caste. Thorner dubbed these agriculturists 'gentleman farmers', and pointed out that their command over funds, their education and their connections in the right places all facilitated their farming activities. He concluded that the unprecedented wave of capitalist farming foreshadowed new social and political as well as economic developments:

> Before the 1960s there used to be in the plains of India only a few pockets of genuinely capitalistic agriculture—parts of the Punjab and Western UP, Central Gujarat, Coimbatore, and Coastal Andhra. Now for the first time there has come into being in all parts of the countryside in India, a layer, thick in some regions, thinner in others, of agricultural capitalists... These capitalistic farmers seem to be the most rapidly growing group in rural India; they may already be the most powerful element. The implications

> of this are far-reaching, not only in the economic field, but for the structure of society and the future shape of politics. (Thorner 1980 [1967])

Thorner's positive, almost gleeful, description of the capitalist farmers disconcerted his Left-wing Indian colleagues. They felt they had been betrayed by someone on whom they had come to count for sharp criticisms of official policies. Neglecting to read his explicit warnings of the long-run dangers inherent in the new business-like agriculture with respect to food production, drainage, dry farming and, above all, failure to solve the underlying agrarian problem, some of them assimilated him quite unjustly to the defenders of the so-called 'Green Revolution', a term which Thorner himself never employed.

The Original Protagonists

Ashok Rudra and Utsa Patnaik

The debate proper opens with a report on a sample survey of big farmers in the Punjab by Ashok Rudra and two of his colleagues in the same Agro-economic Research Centre of the University of Delhi where S. C. Gupta had earlier worked (Rudra, Majid and Talib 1969). Rudra explained that the study was undertaken to find out what was really happening in Indian agriculture, particularly in the Punjab,

> [w]here it is being widely claimed that a veritable revolution has taken place or is taking place... One had been talking a great deal and over a long time about a certain green revolution and the emergence of a new type or even a new class of farmers... Typical of this sort of investigation are the ones reported upon by Wolf Ladejinsky and Daniel Thorner. The investigation consisted of no more than stray visits to the countryside and conversations with some farmers and other persons knowing about agricultural conditions in given areas. These reports have been extremely influential in our country... But quantitative ideas can be formed only on the basis of surveys based on random sampling. (Rudra, Majid and Talib 1969: A-143)

The sample chosen through a three-stage process included 261 farms above 20 acres in size in all 11 districts of the Punjab; and the survey was carried out in 1968–69. Why 20 acres? Rudra tells us:

> What we have been after, being more interested in the Red Revolution than the Green one, is really to get at what may be called the "capitalist farmers"... Most of the capitalist farmers, we have presumed, would have at least 20 acres of cultivated land. The rationale ... was merely to enclose in it a very large portion of what may eventually qualify as being capitalist farms. (Rudra, Majid and Talib 1969: A-145)

With regard to gentleman farmers, Rudra's initial findings were negative. Lurid pictures, he informs us, have been painted of farm households with air-conditioners and motor cars, of farmers' sons in drain-pipe trousers. True enough, says Rudra, such phenomena are blatantly present in the countryside. But their very conspicuousness blinds the observer to the surrounding, very different, reality. In his sample, 92 per cent of the large-farmer respondents claimed that cultivation was the only occupation they ever had. As many as 97 per cent denied pursuing any subsidiary calling. A bare 3 per cent were former government servants or military men. Only 1 per cent could boast of college-level education, while 69 per cent had remained illiterate.

So far as their agriculture was concerned, the land owned by these big farmers had increased by 9.5 per cent over 12 years, with those in the largest size group registering the most substantial increases. Rapid rates of capital formation were evident from the substantial rise in the value of tractors, pumping sets and tubewells, draught cattle, agricultural implements, etc.

Warmly welcoming Rudra's report, Thorner (1969) observed that if his own impressionistic account had helped to stimulate the Punjab study, it had achieved one of its principal aims. With regard to the 'intriguing but secondary question' of gentleman farmers, whose significance lies 'not in their absolute numbers but in the dynamism which they have brought to the countryside', Thorner enquired about the occupations followed by the fathers, brothers and adult sons of the respondents. As to revolutions of different hues, he wrote:

> The colour of the revolution which I have seen in one area after another of India in the 1960s is steel-grey. I call it an industrial revolution. Since Independence, hundreds of new industrial centres have sprung up. Thousands of plants using advanced technology ... have been put into operation. Millions of men have gone to work in the new factories and the auxiliary workshops ... Construction contracts and new jobs have showered purchasing power on households in city and countryside. The resulting demand for raw materials and foodstuffs has sent agricultural prices soaring ... investment in farm production has become unprecedentedly profitable. To the lure of great gain from actual farming (rather than from rural rents and usury) has responded the rise of a class of enterprising agriculturists ... their emergence as a significant group in every State is one of the facets of the industrial revolution which is today changing the face of India. (Thorner 1969)

Thorner's query about the occupations of family members is, in fact, answered in the second instalment of Rudra's (1969) survey report in the very same issue of the *Economic and Political Weekly*. It turns out that, as Thorner had suspected, in 39 per cent of the cases, one or more adult males other than the head of the household were indeed involved in work outside of agriculture. This figure gives a clear notion of the extent to which the big-farm families had, in Thorner's (1969) words, 'diversified their interests either from urban activities to agriculture or *vice versa*'.

It is also in this instalment that Rudra takes up the subject of classes among the peasantry. He does so in the context of whether or not he finds continuities in the values for each variable (for example, the ratio between land owned and land rented out, or percentage of sales to production) when distributed according to size-groups of land owned. Farm economists as well as rural sociologists, Rudra remarks, have the habit of referring to 'three categories of farmers: small peasants, middle peasants and big farmers'. But he is not at all sure this categorisation is warranted. He continues: 'Marxists in particular are wont to talk in terms of there being such subclasses among the peasantry. Now if all the important variables relating to farm economies are representable by continuous functions of size, then these concepts of big, small and middle must be quite vacuous' (Rudra 1969).

In his third and final instalment, Rudra at last sets forth his criteria for identifying capitalist, as distinguished from merely big, farmers. These are similar to Thorner's earlier descriptions. Rudra expects that the capitalist in Punjab would:

1. tend to cultivate his land himself rather than to give it out on lease;
2. tend to use hired labour in a much greater proportion than family labour;
3. tend to use farm machinery;
4. market an important share of his produce; and
5. so organize his production as to yield a high rate of return on his investments. (Rudra 1970)

As surrogates for these five characteristics, Rudra uses data thrown up by his field enquiry with respect of five variables:

1. percentage of land rented out to total land owned;
2. wage payment in cash for acre of farm size (X_2);
3. value of modern capital equipment per acre of farm size (X_3);
4. percentage of produce marketed to total produce (X_4); and
5. cash profit per acre (X_5).

He explains that X_1 is productivity defined as value of output per acre of farm size.

Rudra then argues that if indeed there existed a category of farmers who were capitalists, that is, who filled all of the listed conditions, then there should be strong positive correlations between each pair of Xs (that is, between X_2 and X_3, X_2 and X_4, etc.). His field data, however, 'fail to indicate any strong association between any of these pairs'. Hence, he concludes, there is no evidence that such a category exists.

A year later Utsa Patnaik demolished Rudra's statistical argument in a hard-hitting article which raises a great many of the points central to the subsequent discussion. She termed Rudra's method of analysis of his data 'un-historical'. His criterion of high positive association between pairs of variables, she pronounced, 'would make sense only in an unreal, idealised world in which different classes existed only in their purest form' (Patnaik 1971a: A-126); it could be satisfied 'only if the process of capitalist development has been carried to its limit so that capitalism is already the dominant mode of production' (ibid.: A-127). Historically, she contends, the capitalist is a former landlord or rich peasant. He does not suddenly appear out of the blue as a clearly defined 'pure' socioeconomic type: he develops within the pre-existing non-capitalist economic structure.

Patnaik prefers the term 'non-capitalist' to 'pre-capitalist' since it does not imply that capitalism has made no headway at all. On the contrary, Patnaik believes, 'ex-colonial countries like India are characterised precisely by a limited and distorted development of capitalism which does not revolutionise the mode of production' (ibid.: A-124). In what sense, she asks, is there today a tendency toward capitalist development which was not present earlier? The answer, she suggests, is to be found neither in the employment of hired labourers nor in production for the market. Each of these, she states, is a necessary but not a sufficient condition of capitalist organisation. Both were widely prevalent in India during the colonial period. The large force of rural wage labourers arose from the pauperisation and proletarianisation of the 'poorer majority of the peasantry' under the impact of imperialism. The choice of operating with this cheap hired labour or of leasing out to tenants represented for landowners 'a purely contingent, reversible decision taken on the basis of current circumstances' (Patnaik 1971a: A-124), that is, the comparative terms on which labourers and tenants were available in the particular locality at a particular time. Similarly, the colonial period saw a growing commercialisation of agriculture with increasing regional specialisation in cotton, sugarcane, etc. But this also was not capitalist production.

The characteristic of the genuine capitalist, Patnaik proposed, is not merely appropriation of surplus value generated by wage labour nor the sale on the market of a high proportion of produce, but also—and indispensably—accumulation and reinvestment of surplus value in order to generate more surplus value on an even-expanding scale. The capitalist in agriculture can be recognised by the 'degree of capital intensification'—that is, growth of outlay on both constant and variable capital with respect to a given land area and, over time, a tendency towards a higher than average organic composition of capital, leading to higher productivity of land and labour (Patnaik 1971a: A-126).

This process was underway in India from the mid-1950s onward, in Patnaik's view, because of the expanding domestic market created by the large governmental outlays under the Five Year Plans. In a clear break with the situation in the colonial past, it had become profitable to invest in irrigation, to turn off tenants so as to operate with hired labour, to go in for double and triple cropping rather than simply to continue with the classical pre-capitalist uses of surplus value such as trade, usury and purchase of more land to let out on tenancy.

Citing the results of her own field survey carried out in 1969 and covering 66 big farmers in five states—Orissa, Andhra, Mysore, Madras and Gujarat—Patnaik reported her conviction that a new class of capitalist farmers was indeed emerging. Whereas she started her enquiry with an extreme scepticism about the existence of any significant new trend outside of the Punjab, she was persuaded after going through her data that capitalist development was on the way, albeit in varying degrees, throughout the regions which she had studied.

Since Patnaik was not satisfied with wage labour alone as a criterion of capitalist production, she rejected S. C. Gupta's and Kotovsky's calculations. Despite Rudra's own negative conclusion, she suggested that his results showed clearly the process of capitalist development in the Punjab.

She dealt severely with Rudra's attempt to define peasant classes in terms of statistical discontinuities, as incompatible with a Marxist analysis:

> The Marxist distinction between classes within the peasantry is not derived from such a superficial statistical criterion but is a structural one based on the relations of production. The rich peasant is distinguished from the poor peasant by the fact that the former hires wage-labour to a considerable extent along with engaging himself along with family members in cultivation, while the latter is forced to hire himself out as a labourer or lease in land on onerous terms in addition to working with family labour on his own land. The middle peasant operates mainly with family labour, neither exploiting much wage labour, nor being exploited himself. (Patnaik 1971a: A-129)

In his reply, Rudra defended strongly his scepticism about the existence of peasant classes and his insistence on their being statistically separable within a Marxist framework.

> I suggest that the concept of discontinuities is the direct translation of the Marxian concept of "quantities into qualities"... If one has to undertake measurements and test hypotheses arising from Marxian analyses, one will have to undertake such translations as I have done. And for me, the Marxian concept of three classes in agriculture remains a hypothesis to be tested. (Rudra 1971)

He also stands firm on his position that the failure of his variables taken in pairs to show strong positive association indicates that there has not yet appeared a 'readily identifiable group' of capitalist farmers in the Punjab. He brings in at this point a new term: polarisation. His data, states Rudra, indicate that:

> There has not yet been among the farmers of Punjab any strong *polarisation* and I have expressed doubt whether it serves any important purpose to talk about capitalist development before polarisation has reached a sufficiently high degree... In a situation of capitalist development one should expect to find a polarisation developing such that not only would the values of the variables tend to increase among the farmers undergoing the transformation but increase *conjointly*. As long as such conjoint movement has not taken place to a considerable extent—that is, as long as there is no polarisation—we cannot say that capitalist development has taken place. (Rudra 1971; emphasis in the original.)

In a rapid riposte, Patnaik returned to her charge that Rudra had hopelessly confused two quite different propositions: (1) that there exists within the prevailing non-capitalist economy a small but growing class of capitalists, and (2) that Indian agriculture is characterised by sharp polarisation into two main classes, capitalists and wage labourers. In disproving the second one, she says, he thinks he has disproved the first, since 'he treats proposition 2 as a necessary condition for proposition 1'. This, she declares, 'is certainly not Marxist theory' (Patnaik 1971b).

With regard to indications of peasant classes, Patnaik insisted that size of holding was not a satisfactory guide. Since the available Farm Management Studies data, which are grouped by size, show that above a certain level of acres owned, hired labour predominated over family labour, with regional variations (for example, 10 acres in Bengal, 40 in Punjab), it has seemed reasonable to take the farms above these limits as roughly corresponding to rich peasant holdings. But this is a very crude procedure.

> My argument is that size of farm even as a rough indicator of rich peasant status is no longer good enough in the present situation when techniques are changing and intensive cultivation by some groups is taking place. If production techniques are intensified (more irrigation, triple cropping, mechanisation) then a farm may get smaller in terms of area, and *at the same time* get bigger as an economic unit, expand in terms of output and the extent of use of hired relative to family labour. (Patnaik 1971b; emphasis in the original.)

At this point, Chattopadhyay enters the debate in the role of a self-appointed arbiter of Marxist orthodoxy, distributing plaudits and blames to S. C. Gupta, Rudra and

Patnaik. S. C. Gupta's analysis was 'on the whole in the right direction', but he overestimated the development of capitalism in India and underestimated 'the strength of the pre-capitalist modes of production still prevalent in our agriculture' (Chattopadhyay 1972a). As for Rudra, his work 'is full of interesting empirical data', but theoretically weak. 'Most of his theoretical shortcomings have been fairly ably pointed out by Utsa Patnaik (though perhaps not in the most desirable manner) [ibid.].' Patnaik is criticised for offering 'a new notion of capitalism... not in the spirit of Marxism' (ibid.). Here, Chattopadhyay cites Lenin's definition of capitalism as 'the highest stage of commodity production where labour-power itself becomes a commodity' (ibid.). There is no need, pontificates Chattopadhyay, to specify separately accumulation and reinvestment of surplus value since they already 'fall within this definition'. Elaborating this argument, he writes, reproaching Rudra as well as Patnaik: 'The existence of a sophisticated instrument of production is not necessary for identifying a capitalist. Given the capitalist mode of production, for which capital as a relation is only required, the existence of modern equipment would only indicate a higher level of capitalism' (Chattopadhyay 1972a).

Answering Chattopadhyay, Patnaik restated her objection to taking wage labour as a sufficient condition for establishing the existence of capitalism in Indian agriculture. The bourgeoisie, which battened upon the surplus value produced by agricultural labour in India, she argued, was not Indian but British. She suggested that Chattopadhyay's proposal 'of regarding generalised commodity production as *necessarily* implying capitalist productions relations (regardless of the uniqueness of the colonial situation)' would lead, carried to its logical conclusion, to an extreme position like that of Gunder Frank's, with whom, she assumes, Chattopadhyay is not in agreement:

> Namely, all countries dominated by imperialism entered the network of world capitalist exchange relationships (and also thereby experienced generalised commodity production to a greater or lesser degree). Therefore all these countries are "capitalist." Therefore the only possible immediate programme of a revolutionary political party in each of those countries must be *socialist* revolution. I believe the fallacy in this chain of reasoning lies at the starting point, in the failure to distinguish between capital in the sphere of *exchange* and capital in the sphere of *production*... I am sure P C will not choose to draw the extreme conclusion which Gunder Frank has done; but his theoretical premise does seem to be quite close to Frank's. (Patnaik 1972: A-149; emphasis in the original.)

Banaji comes in as a professed supporter of Patnaik 'in her brilliant polemics with A. Rudra, particularly concerning the identification of capitalist development, and with P. Chattopadhyay, concerning the "specificity" of the colonial economy' (Banaji 1972). It is this second aspect, the search for a 'Marxist characterisation of the colonial economies prior to the growth of a local industrial bourgeoisie' (ibid.), which particularly interested Banaji. He rejected both the thesis that conditions in the colonial world were feudal, a thesis 'once maintained by most of the Communist parties of the colonial world who used the struggle against "feudalism" as a means of postponing the struggle for a socialist programme' (ibid.), and the more recent position arising from the work of Gunder Frank to the effect that all the colonies were capitalist because of their 'umbilical ties to a world market dominated by the capitalist mode of production' (Banaji 1972). The most striking aspect of the colonial period, according to Banaji, was precisely the 'absence of a process of capitalist expansion, for some six decades at least in manufacturing, and for about a century in agriculture' (ibid.). Banaji's own proposal was to 'accept the reality of colonial modes of production with their own coherence and laws of development' (ibid.), with, however, the proviso that they could not have come into being except within the sphere of capitalist production. Their chief historical function was to finance primary accumulation *outside* the colonial world. They served as 'the circuits through which capital was drained out of the colonies in the form of bullion, consumption goods, raw materials and so on' (ibid.). They transmitted to the colonies 'the pressures of the accumulation process in the metropolis without unleashing any corresponding expansion in the forces of production' (Banaji 1972).

Chattopadhyay returned to his disagreements with Patnaik in a substantive article published at the end of 1972. He took issue with her treatment of the role of imperialism as exclusively 'destructive' and 'negative'. In his view, 'the British preserved as well as destroyed the conditions of India's pre-capitalist economy, accelerated as well as retarded the development of capitalism in India'. On the one hand, Chattopadhyay cites evidence to the effect that the essential aspects of capitalism—*generalised* production for sale and a predominantly free class of wage labourers—were *not* present in Indian agriculture in colonial times. On the other, he holds that agricultural production 'did increasingly show its commodity character at least since the last quarter of the nineteenth century'. As proof he brings to bear statistics of the growth of non-foodgrains, the degree of differentiation among the peasantry, the percentage of cultivators engaged in money-wage relationships and the expansion of capital stock in agriculture in the years preceding Independence. 'Capitalist development' he concluded, 'was a reality in India during the British period'. But he insisted upon 'all the ups and downs, advances and retreats of this development', as well as 'the contradictions engendered by capitalism's co-existence and co-presence with the still dominating pre-capitalist relations' (Chattopadhyay 1972b). Not so far, after all, from Patnaik.

Apparently piqued by Patnaik's reference to his position as a logical extreme, Gunder Frank attacked her 'far-out definition of capitalism in agriculture'. While taking no exception to her statement that 'extended reproduction and accumulation is a criterion of capitalism', he argued that she is incorrect in defining capitalism so narrowly as to require that surplus value be invested on the very spot where it is produced, that is, in agriculture itself, or in agriculture in the same geographical area. He charged Patnaik with confusion of levels of analysis:

> UP looks for the criterion of the mode of production on the individual farm! ... No wonder if the UP method is to "extend" the criterion of extended reproduction, accumulation and reinvestment of them in each of the impoverished farms of India, that she is hard put to recognise the capitalist mode of production when she sets it. (Gunder Frank 1973)

With regard to the political implications of Patnaik's method of analysis, Gunder Frank asked how long she was prepared to put off the socialist revolution:

> Well, what conclusion will UP choose to draw from her other extreme method? That socialist revolution will not become the programmatic order of the day until capitalism by her criterion—reinvestment of surplus value produced by farm labourers on the same farm itself—has penetrated each and every one of her individual farms? (Ibid.)

Semi-feudalism, an Eastern India Syndrome

Amit Bhaduri, Pradhan Prasad, Nirmal Chandra, Ranjit Sau and, once again, Ashok Rudra

The first standard-bearer for semi-feudalism in the framework of the debate—the concept of course, being much older—is Amit Bhaduri, who published articles in 1973 in both *Frontier* and the *Economic Journal* in England. On the basis of a survey which he had conducted in 26 West Bengal villages in 1970, Bhaduri concluded that the 'dominant character of existing production relations' could best be described as semi-feudal in that they 'have more in common with classic feudalism of the master–serf type than with industrial capitalism' (Bhaduri 1973). He listed four prominent features of these semi-feudal relations: sharecropping, perpetual indebtedness of the small tenants, concentration of two modes of exploitation—usury and landownership—in the hands of the same economic class, and lack of accessibility to the market for the small tenant. Indebtedness arises from the continual need for consumption loans. In the typical situation, the creditor is the landlord, locally known as the jotedar. The tenant cannot move away without settling his debt, and he has no alternative source of credit. The rate of interest on these consumption loans is extraordinarily high: Bhaduri cites figures ranging from 25 to 200 per cent for a period of about four months. Usury is thus an important additional source of income to the semi-feudal landowner. The continuation of the double exploitation requires that the available balance of paddy with the kisan, the sharecropper, must always fall short of his family's consumption requirements. Therefore, technological improvements which might raise the productivity level of the kisan are undesirable to the landowner, since they would weaken the political and economic power of the landlord based on his being able to keep his tenant constantly indebted. In this way 'semi-feudal production relations operate as a barrier to the introduction of improved technology' (Bhaduri 1973).

Bhaduri envisages four possible developments for the future: continued stagnation, adoption of new technology together with rent increases, gradual development of capitalistic relations, or even a peasant revolt:

1. Low productivity and stagnation in agriculture will continue to maintain the existing power structure at the village level in eastern India.
2. The semi-feudal production relations themselves will be modified to accommodate profitable use of improved technology.
3. and 4. It is also possible that semi-feudal production relations will gradually give way to capitalistic production relations based on wage labour, or will be

simply overthrown by the desperate poor unless a radical land reform is carried out by the state (Bhaduri 1973).

Pradhan Prasad furnishes support for Bhaduri's thesis with data from another area of eastern India: the Purnea, Saharsa and Monghyr districts of Bihar, in which he surveyed over 2,000 households in a couple of dozen villages in 1970 and 1972. In these villages, utilisation of available irrigation facilities declines with increase in the size of holdings, larger landowners (10 acres and above) who cultivate with hired labourers, prefer 'attached' workers, indebtedness is widespread, sharecropping is a common feature, and daily wages are so low that even households with two workers employed throughout the year are forced to take consumption loans at exorbitant rates of interest. These debts run on indefinitely since the creditors 'do not expect ever to get the stipulated interest and principal from such rural poor' (Prasad 1974). Usury, Prasad continues, 'is thus practised mainly to perpetuate the indissoluble bond between the direct producer and his overlord'. Low utilisation of resources such as irrigation and low demand for labour by big landowners are essentially directed towards 'preventing the strengthening of the economic condition of the direct producer rather than maximisation of their rate of profit or rate of return' (ibid.). In the same way as Bhaduri, Prasad insists that big landowners fear that the introduction of new agricultural practices might serve eventually to free their tenants from their semi-feudal bondage.

> The essential feature of the model is thus reflected in the big landowning classes ... approaching the whole process of production and distribution with a view to strengthening their control over land and their hold on the rural masses, resulting in a set-up (which we may call semi-feudal) ... essentially characterised by the two modes of appropriation, namely sharecropping and usury. This results in semi-servile condition of living and a low level of consumption ... low productivity of land and labour (which is understood mainly in terms of disguised unemployment), under-utilisation of resources and almost negligible net investment in the agricultural sector. (Prasad 1973)

In a subsequent article Prasad argues from the evidence of various sample surveys conducted from 1951 through 1971 that his 'semi-feudal model (but for variations in details) is, by and large, valid for the most part of rural India' (Prasad 1974).

Another partisan of the semi-feudal thesis, Nirmal Chandra makes use of official data for West Bengal and explicitly links agricultural development with industrial development at the national level. He recalls the laws of motion for agriculture formulated by Kautsky and Lenin in the context of a national economy undergoing capitalist transformation: increasing returns to scale, increasing concentration of landholding, increasing proportion of agricultural labourers, decreasing extent of sharecropping, and increasing orientation of agricultural production towards the market rather than towards self-consumption by the cultivator. On the basis of data for 250 farms in five districts of West Bengal for each of the six years from 1962–1963 through 1967–1968 published by the state government, Chandra finds no unmistakable trends along these lines. He is led to suspect that 'our country has not been going through a capitalist transformation at all, and that there are important socio-economic forces impeding such a transformation' (Chandra 1974). He assigns a large share of blame for the stifling of incipient capitalism to imperialism: 'During the British Raj colonial rule undoubtedly constituted the biggest single obstacle. As a natural ally it greatly strengthened feudal or semi-feudal elements in the countryside that are primarily responsible for the indifferent progress in the postcolonial era even though the imperial yoke has been lifted (ibid.).

The basic features of semi-feudalism in the West Bengal countryside, in Chandra's view, have been most lucidly and cogently set forth by Bhaduri. But Chandra offers two emendations. First, he feels that Bhaduri has exaggerated the effect of semi-feudal relations in holding back the productive forces:

> For, technological improvements have taken place on share-tenanted land in different parts of West Bengal with working capital often provided by the landowner. If one allows for a variable share-cropping ratio, then semi-feudal relations of production can persist even after the new high-yielding varieties of crops have been introduced. By lowering the tenant's share, the landowner can keep him as poor as he always was. (Chandra 1974)

Even more important, according to Chandra, is Bhaduri's omission of the effect of 'massive underemployment in our countryside'. In several ways this critical unemployment and underemployment factor helps to explain the stability of semi-feudalism:

1. The value of labour power is pegged at the lowest possible levels so that the real income of a share-tenant is no greater than that of a hired agricultural worker.
2. From the landowner's point of view the net surplus to be extracted is the same under the one or the other system.
3. Given the weak bargaining position of labour, the landowners can arbitrarily alter the share-ratio in their own favour in case new production possibilities appear (ibid.).

Moving to the national scale, Chandra argues that large-scale rural employment 'greatly delimits the market for industrial products'. After the saturation of export markets, military demand, and the consumption requirements of an urban middle-class, stagnation becomes inevitable.

> We may then infer that labour surplus on a scale that is probably unparalleled in human history is perpetuating the semi-feudal set-up. Limited progress along the road to modernisation cannot be ruled out. Without vigorous measures to reduce considerably that surplus, we fail to see how one can get out of the vicious circle or how capitalism can strike deep root. (Chandra 1974)

Chandra does not have much faith in the ability of industrial capital in India to break out of the shackles of semi-feudalism:

> Industrial capitalism in this country, including the forces of State capitalism, is extremely weak in the relative sense. It seems to have no option but to rely on foreign capital and foreign technology, which themselves create almost insuperable barriers to industrialisation on a wide front... Since we cannot envisage how (within the confines

> of the present socio-economic formation) things might radically improve either on the industrial front or in respect of surplus labour, we cannot visualise when productive capital will dominate over usury capital in our agriculture or when the pre-capitalist crop-sharing eastern will disappear. (Chandra 1974)

Accordingly, he believes it would be more useful to characterise agrarian production relations in India as 'semi-feudal' rather than 'lumpen-bourgeois' or 'rickety capitalist'. But he takes a guarded position as to the proper designation of the mode of production: 'But one needs to explore many more facets of history, economics, politics, etc., before one can positively assert that semi-feudalism is the dominant mode of production in Indian or West Bengal agriculture' (Chandra 1974).

Ranjit Sau expresses agreement with Chandra's 'characterisation of the mode of production in Indian agriculture as semi-feudal' and also with the argument that 'the presence of enormous unemployment weakens the impulse of capitalist growth in agriculture' (Sau 1975). He adds another explanatory factor to account for the stubborn persistence of semi-feudalism: the determination of small peasants to continue cultivation, no matter how meagre the returns, because of the lack of other possibilities:

> Why does not urban industrial capital penetrate agriculture and transform the semi-feudal mode? There are certain early signs of such a shift. The celebrated 'gentleman-farmers' are indeed descending upon the countryside … This trend also would not go very far ... In the absence of alternative job opportunities in industry, the small peasants would hold on to their land by reducing consumption to an unbelievable minimum. Increasing returns to scale or no increasing returns to scale, the capitalist farmers would face insuperable barriers in ousting the small farms. (Sau 1975)

Returning to the subject in a series of three articles in *Frontier*, Chandra brings in evidence from his own study of three villages in a rice-producing tract in the Burdwan district, the most advanced area of West Bengal outside of the Calcutta conurbation, which had been chosen in the 1960s as one of the 16 districts in the country to benefit from the IADP. He found production relations in these villages had undergone some changes since Independence. An old zamindar (non-cultivating landlord, often absent) family was still on the scene and still affluent although not at the top of the economic pyramid. Otherwise the villages were dominated by jotedars (formerly occupancy-right tenants holding large blocks of land which they either leased out or got cultivated by agricultural labourers; to a varying degree involved in moneylending and trading in agricultural commodities), a class which for over a hundred years before the formal abolition of the zamindari system in Bengal in 1953 had been slowly replacing the zamindars as the leading group in the countryside.

Chandra found land ownership to be highly skewed; tenancy arrangements were predominantly of a traditional kind, with tenants taking one-half of the gross output when they bore the costs of production but only one-third to one-fourth otherwise; 'the corresponding legal ratios are three-fourths and one-half respectively'. In social terms 'most lessors come from the upper classes' (Chandra 1975). Except for one village, the vast majority of tenants came from the poorer sections, belonged to the backward castes and were personally dependent on their landlords. Individual landlords had up to eight tenants under them. One of the methods through which control is exercised is the threat of eviction: 'In the ten years prior to our survey in 1974 the number of households evicted was as high as one-fifth of the total or nearly two-thirds of the tenant households... Nearly every one of the poor tenants was evicted at one time or another over this period' (Chandra 1975).

The overall economic status of the poor peasants, Chandra calculated, was no better than that of the agricultural labourers for whom wages were the only source of livelihood. Most workers were employed on a daily basis. Only about a quarter of the total number (from both agricultural labour and poor peasant households) had annual contracts with their masters. The casual workers were employed on an average for only 126 days in the year. Landlords almost invariably charge high interest on loans given to their tenants; this exaction is not always apparent:

> Sometimes, formally speaking, the interest rate is zero. But since paddy loans are usually made in monsoon months when the price is double the post-harvest level, in effect the tenant repays a great deal more in kind. Similarly, workers for their wage advances have to repay with labour services. Taking into account both the wage cut as well as the seasonal price variations, the employer may make up to 300 per cent profit in his wage advance. (Chandra 1975)

Landlords are also able to extract various types of *begar* (unpaid or underpaid labour services), often taking the form of non-productive work in the landlord's house. Workers are typically afraid of their landlords, some of whom do not hesitate to assault them physically for slackening in their work.

In sum, Chandra argues that because of their 'activity pattern', it is the top eight to ten families in each of his villages which constitute 'the main bottlenecks to the development of productive forces', in effect, the chief obstacles to the growth of capitalism. Specifically, he charges, these families hold land in excess of legal ceilings, contribute little to paddy levies, crowd out the small farmers by obtaining an unfair proportion of institutional credit, engage in usury or usurious wage advances, and funnel their savings into the tertiary sector (Chandra 1975).

Meanwhile, in a dramatic reversal of his previous position, Ashok Rudra announces his conviction that there are increasing manifestations of characteristic features of capitalism in the agriculture of eastern India. Turning on the proponents of semi-feudalism, Rudra centres his attack on Prasad and Chandra. As against Prasad's claim of 'intimate contact with some of the rural areas of Bihar' (cited in Prasad 1974), Rudra, who had shifted from Delhi to Shantiniketan, puts forward his own 'direct first-hand knowledge of conditions prevailing in West Bengal' (Rudra 1974). In particular, he asserts, he has carried out during the past year an enquiry into agrarian relations in the different districts of the state.

Nowhere in these districts, Rudra reports, has he encountered the landowners whom Prasad and Chandra describe—a class 'that finds it more in its economic and social-power interests to resort to usury rather than to capital investments' (Rudra 1974). On the contrary, he has found in many parts of the state landowners 'who are very much engaged in capital investments in the form of irrigation, fertilisers and high-yielding variety seeds' (ibid.). This is equally true of 'landowners who give their land out on lease to sharecroppers and those who cultivate it themselves with the help of hired labour' (ibid.). The practice has become almost universal in Bengal, Rudra discovered, 'of owners paying for the irrigation costs and advancing the tenant's share of the costs of seed and fertilisers' (ibid.). These advances are repaid 'by the tenant in terms of crops at the time of the harvest. No interest is charged' (ibid.; but compare with the remarks about zero interest rates in Chandra 1975).

Similarly, although poor tenants, farm servants and casual labourers are typically bound to landlords by consumption loans, such loans 'when taken by a tenant from the landowner from whom he has leased in land or by a farm servant from the landowner for whom he works' are free of interest (Rudra 1974). They are usually repaid not in cash but in labour at the time when the landowner calls for it, the amount of labour 'being calculated at a wage rate somewhat lower than the ruling wage rate' (ibid.).

Interest at 10 per cent or more per month is charged whenever a loan is taken from a landowner or moneylender 'other than the one with whom the borrower has an attachment relation as tenant or farm servant' (Rudra 1974). Thus, usury does exist, and may serve as the 'the subsidiary source of income of the landowning class' (ibid.). But it does not appear to Rudra that 'the landowning class in West Bengal is *primarily* dependent on usury' (ibid., emphasis in the original).

Against Chandra, who questioned the development of capitalist relations in West Bengal because he found no clear trend toward concentration of landholding, Rudra uses Patnaik's argument that concentration should be measured not in acres but in the value of land held. In this sense he is sure that it has been increasing sharply 'as a result of investments on land carried out by the large land-owners' (Rudra 1974).

Criticising also Chandra's insistence on labour surplus, Rudra asserts that although there is indeed a great deal of unemployment during the lean seasons, there exists in many parts of West Bengal 'a scarcity of actual labour supply in relation to labour demand during the peak periods' (Rudra 1974). It is this high-season labour shortage, argues Rudra, which 'provides the economic incentive to the landowners to go in for arrangements that guarantee supply of labour during periods when they need it most' (ibid.).

From the labourer's or tenant's point of view, his being bound by debt and other obligations to a particular landowner means that he cannot sell his labour-power freely. If this is a characteristic of feudalism, opines Rudra, 'then such feudalistic features continue to exist in various forms both in farms cultivated by tenants and farms cultivated by hired labourers' (Rudra 1974). He announces cautiously that he prefers to postpone until after he presents his new survey findings any full-dress discussion of 'the concepts that have been used by Prasad and Chandra, e.g., capitalism, semi-feudalism' (ibid.). But in the balance it is clear that Rudra's 1974 intervention weighs heavily on the side of capitalism as against semi-feudalism. Although he had earlier failed to discern capitalism among big farmers in the Punjab, he now strongly suspects it in wide areas of West Bengal.

...

Re-entering the discussion to sharpen some of his original formulations and to comment on positions taken by Rudra, Sau and Hamza Alavi, Paresh Chattopadhyay insists notably on the 'dual role of capitalism with regard to pre-capitalism'. That it seeks both the destruction and the preservation of older forms, Chattopadhyay holds, 'is a universal Phenomenon and not confined to what is usually considered as "colonies" or "semi-colonies"' (Chattopadhyay 1980).

A two-part article by Sharat G. Lin puts forward a new term, 'a dual mode of production', for postcolonial India. Citing Banaji, Sen Gupta and Brian Davey, Lin finds overall agreement that there is a superposition of more than one mode of production. In Lin's formulation, 'the two primary modes (pre-capitalist and capitalist) interpenetrate', generating 'a single mode with dual character having, at once, both accommodating and conflicting internal dynamics' (Lin 1980). State power 'must be shared by two, historically opposed ruling classes' since it is 'based on two historically opposed primary modes'; hence, it cannot remain forever stable. Yet, Lin opines, it may last longer 'than has been the case elsewhere in the world' (ibid.). This is because the pre-capitalist mode is so well-entrenched, because of wide regional variation in the strength of capitalist forces, because of the social inertia of sheer size, and because of the role of cultural factors (ibid.).

With regard to the possibilities for revolutionary action, the oppressed classes must struggle against whichever of the two modes and elements of state power 'holds trend-dominance in the process of transition to holding status-dominance' (Lin 1980). The enemy must be carefully chosen, since a struggle against the feudal aspect which does not take into account the bourgeois aspect will lead by default to strengthening the position of the latter and 'to the type of class collaboration exercised by various left parties' (ibid.). However, it is not yet the moment for 'a stage of struggle for the socialist revolution since the Indian bourgeoisie has not completed and cannot complete the bourgeois democratic revolution' (ibid.). This democratic revolution can only 'be completed through an alliance of the proletariat and impoverished peasantry who together constitute some 90 per cent of the population' (ibid.).

Two recent articles concentrate on elements of the current rural scene which have been identified as 'feudal'. Dipankar Gupta considers the nature of sharecropping and contends that it is 'not a feudal institution but rather appears only in formations where feudal institutions have been undermined by capitalism and where capitalism has not yet appeared in all its virility' (Gupta 1980). He prefers to view the Indian economy as 'a capitalist one when capitalism has not developed uniformly' (ibid.). Although capitalism is the main enemy, a revolutionary takeover 'is not yet in the offing', so that the prospect is of a 'long period of struggle ahead' (ibid.). The Left should not rush to raise the cry of immediate socialisation of the land since slogans such as 'land to the tiller' can still motivate the majority of the peasants (ibid.).

Similarly, Aparajita Chakraborty attacks the idea that tenancy as an institution is necessarily a feature of pre-capitalist modes of production, in particular the feudal mode, and that 'capitalist development necessarily calls for its disappearance' (Chakraborty 1981). She names Patnaik, Chandra and Bhaduri as having subscribed to this erroneous and, in her opinion, un-Marxist notion. On the contrary, Chakraborty presents the view that tenancy is a flexible arrangement which 'takes different forms and embodies different mixtures of capitalist and precapitalist relations under different historical conditions' (ibid.). In India, until very recent times, tenancy has been characterised by 'very regressive features', and even today in many cases peasants are subject to 'exploitative rents' and 'exorbitant rates of interest' (ibid.). In this way, agricultural surplus is being diverted into non-productive channels, and the development of capitalism in agriculture is held back. The relations of production embodied in this process, Chakraborty concedes, 'are no doubt pre-capitalist in nature' (ibid.). But this does not mean that tenancy itself is feudal or semi-feudal: 'In India, until recently, tenancy was an institution which was very much a part of the precapitalist relations of production that characterised agriculture. But it is getting changed along with changing conditions to the point of becoming compatible with emerging capitalist relations' (Chakraborty 1981).

For his part, Rudra denies the usefulness of feudalism as a concept for analysing any period at all in Indian history. He points out that while political economists who use the term 'semi-feudal' presumably believe that the mode of production in India during some previous period was feudal, much influential opinion among historians rejects the thesis that there was ever feudalism in Indian history. After reviewing the historical debate, Rudra castigates the participants for paying insufficient attention to 'social, cultural and religious institutions' (Rudra 1981: 2143). Whereas the 'European genius' forged the features and rituals of feudalism (such as commendation, homage and fealty), the 'Indian genius' invented the caste system, the Hindu ethos (ibid.: 2146). He advances the hypothesis that whereas in the Western world the hierarchic structure of society is maintained, in the ultimate analysis, by violence, '*this particular role in Indian history was played not by violence but by ideology*' (ibid.: 2144; emphasis in the original).

This thesis, Rudra insists, 'has an extremely important implication for practice'. The political lesson that he draws is that 'the struggle against the reactionary elements of the Brahmanic ideology' should constitute an important element 'in any struggle for progress in this country' (ibid.: 2145).

This proposal of Rudra's is very close to the recommendations of a Left-wing Maharashtrian organisation, the Atyachar Virodh Samiti, at the end of a report on riots in Marathwada in which caste Hindus wreaked violence upon members of the SCs. The Samiti contends that the caste system functions as 'an extremely effective method of economic exploitation' (Atyachar Virodh Samiti 1979). Caste hierarchies reflect economic power and ownership of land. As bourgeois relations develop, the argument continues, the institution of caste starts to disintegrate, but the process is not smooth. It is at this point that caste riots, reflecting a conflict of class interests, take place. In the 'mixed capitalist economy' of today, caste persists 'as a part of feudal ideology' (ibid.). But it also serves the bourgeois system since one of its functions has been 'to prevent formalisation of consciousness and struggles on class lines' (ibid.). The Samiti calls upon all progressives and Leftists to take up issues around specific caste questions, and to support unconditionally autonomous Dalit (oppressed) movements with democratic demands against caste discrimination. 'To establish a link between fights against caste-oppression and class exploitation,' the report concludes, 'is the need of the hour' (ibid.).

In a major review of the evidence which has become available during the 1970s, Gail Omvedt gives an unequivocally affirmative answer to the question as to whether India's agriculture is now dominantly capitalist. Harking back to Thorner's 1969 formulation that the emergence of capitalist farming represented one facet of the industrial revolution which was transforming India, she stresses 'the links between agriculture and industry, city and countryside' (Omvedt 1981).

At the time of Independence, Omvedt believes, Indian agriculture was 'predominantly feudal in character, though important elements of capitalism had risen' (ibid.). This was a 'caste-structured' form of feudalism which existed before the British period. When the colonial state no longer officially enforced the caste system, 'caste' and 'class' began to represent separate social phenomena, 'but there was still a near-absolute correlation between them' (ibid.). Because of the particular caste aspect of Indian feudalism, Omvedt affirms, 'the anti-feudal movement was expressed not only through peasant revolts but also in the radical anti-caste movements of Phule, Ambedkar and Periyar' (ibid.).

For the present, Omvedt's arguments for the dominance of capitalism can be summed up as follows:

1. over half of the rural population depend upon wages;
2. all cultivators are forced to sell to some extent in the market, and their production is governed by the laws of the market;
3. the means of production in agriculture are now, to a large extent, produced industrially and acquired through the market;
4. there has been a substantial growth in the use of capital inputs such as fertilisers and oil engines;
5. there has been a genuine, if halting, growth in agricultural production;
6. generalised commodity production, including the sale of labour power, prevails;
7. the primary aspect of the relationship of the rural rich with the rural poor is as exploiters of labour power;
8. the rural semi-proletariat is, by and large, an increasingly mobile, migrant and free class, whose differences with the urban working class 'seem more those of quantity than of quality' (Omvedt 1981).

Despite the evidence that she marshals to prove the reality of capitalist development in agriculture, Omvedt emphasises her assessment that this development 'is not leading to any increased overall welfare for the rural (or urban) masses' (ibid.). She disparages the assumption of some authors that 'immiserisation, pauperisation, growing landlessness, etc., are themselves signs of "semi-feudalism" or the lack of capitalist development' (ibid.).

Omvedt's prescription for political action rests upon her faith in the revolutionary potential of the rural proletariat. She is persuaded that the agricultural labourers and poor peasants are capable 'of forming a centre around which middle peasants and other oppressed sections can be united' (ibid.). Accordingly, she deplores the tendency of the major parliamentary Left parties to call for alliances including the rich peasants, who, she contends, are in effect 'the village rulers and capitalist farmers'. The apparent weakness of the rural semi-proletariat, Omvedt tells us, is belied by 'vast numbers of diverse and unreported or under-reported clashes' involving 'agricultural labourers and other labourers as well as poor and middle peasants' (ibid.). Since 'class exploitation is compounded with caste and national oppression', many struggles assume forms which are difficult to identify as class conflicts, as for example those of the Jharkhand Mukti Morcha in the tribal area of Bihar or the Dalit Panthers in Maharashtra. Although up to now the 'rural toiling masses have not yet found their own revolutionary party', Omvedt confidently foresees for the future 'tumultous political developments' (ibid.).

Balance Sheet

What, we may now ask, has been clarified in the course of the past dozen years of debate, and what remains controversial? First of all, there would no longer appear to be any doubt that capitalism today dominates Indian agriculture, as it already was generally seen to dominate industry at the time the discussion began. Does this mean that the mode of production which prevails in contemporary India is capitalist, and subject to the Marxist laws of motion of capitalist development? Here, the answer is less evident, since India's capitalism has emerged in a particular colonial setting, markedly different from the conditions in the metropolitan countries where capitalism was born.

By what criteria has the prevalence of capitalism been established? It has been abundantly shown that the existence of widespread tenancy and/or sharecropping does not necessarily indicate the presence of feudal relations of production; nor does the concentration of landholdings together with the cultivation of small units by large numbers of peasants. By the same token, the use of wage labour cannot by itself be taken as a sure sign of capitalist relations. Yet the shift from exploitation through tenants to large-scale or intensive farming by means of hired labour is significant.

The growth of capitalist farming in India has been accompanied by—and in fact, amounts to—a transformation of the relations of production and forms of exploitation. Servile, debt-bonded, and/or traditionally tied labour has been largely supplanted by free, relatively mobile wage labour, paid (if meagrely) for the most part in cash. Investment in modern, scientific agriculture has enormously expanded, and has resulted, on the whole, in enhanced production, at least of certain crops in certain areas. Tenancy and sharecropping arrangements have, in many regions, been adapted to the new economic and technical requirements.

Yet master–servant types of behaviour, extra-economic constraints, rack-renting and usury have by no means disappeared. A particular feature of the Indian scene is the vast mass of un- or under-employed who, if they cannot emigrate and find jobs outside of agriculture, exercise upward pressure on the rental price of land, and downward pressure on wage rates. The school of thought which tried to take account of these aspects by labelling Indian agriculture semi-feudal has withdrawn from the debate after about the middle of the 1970s, but there is still talk of the persistence of feudal and semi-feudal relations of production. Similarly, the original proponents of a colonial mode have themselves dropped the term, while the term 'dual mode' has, to my knowledge, attracted no followers. But the concepts of the preservation/destruction of earlier modes of production by capitalism, and of the articulation of different modes within a single social formation continue to figure in the discussion.

Several authors who accept the leading role of capitalism nonetheless express grave doubts as to the likelihood of its further and full development. They point out obstacles to capitalist progress on a national scale, such as the relative narrowness of India's industrial base in terms of the size of the country, the dependence of this industry on foreign technology, the very limited amount of employment provided by the secondary sector, and the extreme modesty of the economic demand for consumers' goods. There is agreement that capitalism in agriculture cannot be depended upon to solve the crucial problems of access to land and to food for the entire rural population.

The set of rural classes proposed by the various authors ranges from Rudra's drastic duality to Chandra's sixfold grouping, and the even larger number of categories used by Mencher and Patnaik. This lack of accord on the array of rural classes should not surprise us. Apart from marked regional differences, it would seem that the class configuration which one sees depends primarily on one's point of view. Researchers trying variously to explain why a land reform has or has not actually been implemented; when agricultural development programmes work and when they do not; why particular candidates or parties receive the votes of specific village groups; where reform or revolutionary movements arise and spread, or where they are nipped in the bud, should obviously not be expected to come up with identical lists of classes. Under the circumstances, efforts to attach numerical values to particular classes are even less comparable. There is not even a consensus as to the identity of the typical producer; is he an independent middle peasant—or, to the contrary, is he an impoverished tenant, sharecropper or agricultural labourer?

Cut-off points in size of landholding terms are clearly inadequate for marking off agricultural classes. Combinations of landholding categories with other characteristics (such as labour relations) become unwieldy in practice. In the course of preparing this chapter, I tried to make up a table showing the relative shares of the rural population attributed to each class by the different authors who have attempted this exercise (Bhaduri, Chandra, Prasad, Mencher, Rudra, Omvedt) and to include the one-shot estimates of this or that class by other writers (for example, Alavi and Lin). But the rubrics utilised by these writers proved so disparate that I had to give up the attempt.

The various discussions of colonial India have all emphasised the detrimental effect that its involuntary integration into the world capitalist circuit had upon the older Indian economy (whether characterised as Asiatic, feudal or pre-capitalist). For some authors, British transformation of its Indian colony into a market for manufactures and a source of primary products such as wheat, cotton and jute served to establish dominant capitalist relations in late nineteenth-century India, or in certain regions of the country. For others, imperialism in its own interest shored up feudal elements in Indian economy and society. All agree that India is still a tributary to a large degree to the international market; some refer to this as a semi-colonial status. Others prefer to speak of India's peripheral capitalism in relation to metropolitan centres.

Early interventions in the debate were largely limited to economic issues. Later papers have paid increasing attention to elements of consciousness and culture, with special reference to caste. One of the weaknesses of Marxist studies on India has been precisely a failure, perhaps even an unwillingness, to deal adequately with this basic facet of Indian society. This is one of the directions which future debate can most fruitfully explore. Another is a more detailed analysis of the role of the state.

...

References

Atyachar Virodh Samiti. 1979. 'The Marathwada Riots: A Report'. *Economic and Political Weekly* 14(19): 845–52.

Banaji, Jairus. 1972. 'For a Theory of Colonial Modes of Production'. *Economic and Political Weekly* 7(52): 2498–2502.

Bhaduri, Amit. 1973. 'A Study of Agricultural Backwardness under Conditions of Semi-feudalism'. *Economic Journal* 86(329): 120–37.

Chakraborty, Aparajita. 1981. 'Tenancy and Mode of Production'. *Economic and Political Weekly* 16(13), Review of Agriculture: 5–14.

Chandra, Nirmal K. 1974. 'Farm Efficiency under Semi-feudalism: A Critique of Marginalist Theories and Some Marxist Formulations'. *Economic and Political Weekly* 9(32–34): 1309–31.

———. 1975. 'Agrarian Transition in India'. *Frontier* 7(28–30).

Chattopadhyay, Paresh. 1972a. 'On the Question of the Mode of Production in Indian Agriculture: A Preliminary Note'. *Economic and Political Weekly* 7(13), Review of Agriculture: 39–46.

———. 1972b. 'Mode of Production in Indian Agriculture: An Anti-Kritik'. *Economic and Political Weekly* 7(53), Review of Agriculture: 185–92.

———. 1980. 'Mode of Production in Indian Agriculture: An Afterword'. *Economic and Political Weekly* 15(26), Review of Agriculture: 85–88.

Gunder Frank, Andre. 1973. 'On "Feudal" Modes, Models and Methods of Escaping Capitalist Reality'. *Economic and Political Weekly* 8(1): 36–37.

Gupta, Dipankar. 1980. 'Formal and Real Subsumption of Labour under Capital: The Instance of Share-cropping'. *Economic and Political Weekly* 15(39), Review of Agriculture: 98–106.

Kotovsky, G. 1964. *Agrarian Reform in India*. Moscow: Progress Publishers.

Lin, Sharat G. 1980. 'Theory of a Dual Mode of Production in Post-colonial India'. *Economic and Political Weekly* 15(10–11): 516–29, 565–73.

Omvedt, Gail. 1981. 'Capitalist Agriculture and Rural Classes in India'. *Economic and Political Weekly* 16(52), Review of Agriculture: A140–59.

Patnaik, Utsa. 1971a. 'Capitalist Development in Agriculture: A Note'. *Economic and Political Weekly* 6(39), Review of Agriculture: 123–30.

Patnaik, Utsa. 1971b. 'Capitalist Development in Agriculture'. *Economic and Political Weekly* 6(39): 123–30.

———. 1972. 'On the Mode of Production in Indian Agriculture: A Reply'. *Economic and Political Weekly* 7(40), Review of Agriculture: 145–51.

Prasad, Pradhan. 1973. 'Production Relations: Achilles' Heel of Indian Planning'. *Economic and Political Weekly* 8(19): 869–72.

———. 1974. 'Reactionary Role of Usurers' Capital in Rural India'. *Economic and Political Weekly* 9(32–33): 1305–08.

Rudra, Ashok, A. Majid and B. Talib. 1969. 'Big Farmers of the Punjab: Some Preliminary Findings of a Sample Survey'. *Economic and Political Weekly* 4(39), Review of Agriculture: 143–46.

Rudra, Ashok. 1969. 'Big Farmers of Punjab: Second Instalment of Results'. *Economic and Political Weekly* 4(52), Review of Agriculture: 213–19.

———. 1970. 'In Search of the Capitalist Farmer'. *Economic and Political Weekly* 5(26), Review of Agriculture: 85–87.

———. 1971. 'Capitalist Development in Agriculture: Reply'. *Economic and Political Weekly* 6(45): 2291–92.

———. 1974. 'Semi-feudalism, Usury Capital, Etcetera'. *Economic and Political Weekly* 9(48), 30 November: 1996–97.

———. 1981. 'Against Feudalism'. *Economic and Political Weekly* 16(52): 2133–46.

Sau, Ranjit. 1975. 'Farm Efficiency under Semi-feudalism: A Critique of Marginalist Theories and Some Marxist Formulations: A Comment'. *Economic and Political Weekly* 10(13), 29 March: A18–21.

Thorner, Daniel. 1969. 'Capitalist Farming in India'. *Economic and Political Weekly* 4(52), 27 December: A211–12.

———. 1976 [1956]. *The Agrarian Prospect in India*. New Delhi: Allied Publishers.

———. 1980 [1967]. 'Capitalist Stirrings in Rural India'. *The Statesman*, Calcutta, 1–4 November. [Reprinted in *The Shaping of Modern India*. New Delhi: Allied Publishers.]

13

NEW RELATIONS OF PRODUCTION IN HARYANA AGRICULTURE*

SHEILA BHALLA

This chapter has three purposes: (a) to present some empirical findings about the number, composition and household origin of agricultural labourers in Haryana; (b) to give an account, in this context, of some new kinds of labour contracts and new forms of consumption indebtedness; and (c) to float some tentative ideas about the implications of these new relations of production. We begin with the agricultural labour supply and demand setting in which the new relations of production have emerged. Attention is drawn to the number of households classified by main income source at the bottom of Table 13.1. The number of landless agricultural labour households can be taken as a first rough approximation to be the 'built-in' supply of labour in each area. These figures are the product of a pre-Green Revolution adjustment between the demand and supply of agricultural labourers—*not* of post-Green Revolution migration from poor areas (such as Region C) to rich ones, such as Region A.[1] However, there has been post-Green Revolution out-migration of individuals and entire landless households from Region C, but these moved to the parts of Gurgaon adjacent to Delhi, and not to Region A.

Region A, covering the Karnal district and the adjacent highly irrigated areas, is the region to which the Green Revolution came first and consolidated itself most effectively. The impact of the new technology on agrarian relations in this part of the state is, not surprisingly, much more marked than in Region B, where the new technology has been much less widely adopted. Geographically, Region B covers most of Hissar and parts of the Rohtak district, and lies as a wide west-to-east central belt across the state. The impact of the water-seed and chemical revolution in the semi-desert Region C is negligible. The agrarian relations of this area are much as they were a decade before the field survey was conducted during 1972–73.[2]

* Originally published in *Economic and Political Weekly* 11(13), 27 March 1976: A23–30.

TABLE 13.1: Household Origin of Agricultural Labourers, by Casual/Permanent Labour Status, 1972–73

	Region A			*Region B*			*Region C*		
	Total	*Casual*	*Permanent*	*Total*	*Casual*	*Permanent*	*Total*	*Casual*	*Permanent*
I. All Agricultural Labourers									
Male	126,975 (100.0)	54,735 (43.1)	72,240 (56.9)	125,873 (100.0)	88,129 (70.0)	37,744 (30.0)	54,683 (100.0)	49,863 (91.2)	4,820 (8.8)
Female	22,599 (100.0)	21,146 (93.6)	1,453 (6.4)	23,251 (100.0)	23,251 (100.0)	—	5,084 (100.0)	5,084 (100.0)	—
(a) From landless agricultural labour households									
Male	77,396 (61.0)	22,412 (17.7)	54,984 (43.3)	65,595 (52.1)	40,232 (32.0)	25,363 (20.1)	20,204 (36.9)	15,384 (28.1)	4,820 (8.8)
Female	11,700 (51.8)	10,247 (45.3)	1,453 (6.4)	7,554 (32.5)	7,554 (32.5)	—	4,132 (81.3)	4,132 (81.3)	—
(b) From agricultural labour households with land									
Male	13,947 (11.0)	7,182 (5.7)	6,765 (5.3)	25,739 (20.4)	17,717 (14.1)	8,022 (6.4)	10,145 (19.5)	10,145 (18.5)	—
Female	2,117 (9.4)	2,117 (9.4)	—	4,311 (18.5)	4,311 (18.5)	—	—	—	—
(c) From whose main source is cultivation									
Male	29,021 (22.9)	18,530 (14.6)	10,491 (8.3)	27,602 (21.9)	23,243 (18.5)	4,359 (3.5)	13,804 (25.2)	13,801 (25.2)	—
Female	8,782 (38.9)	8,782 (38.9)	—	11,386 (49.0)	11,386 (49.0)	—	952 (18.7)	952 (18.7)	—
From other households: Male	6,611 (5.2)	6,611 (5.2)	—	6,937 (5.5)	6,937 (5.5)	—	10,530 (19.3)	10,530 (19.3)	—

(Contd)

Table 13.1 (Contd)

	Region A			Region B			Region C		
	Total	*Casual*	*Permanent*	*Total*	*Casual*	*Permanent*	*Total*	*Casual*	*Permanent*
	II. No. Classified by Main Income Source								
(a) Landless agricultural labour households	66,843	—	—	60,439	—	—	27,551	—	—
(b) Agricultural labour household with land	9,298	—	—	18,168	—	—	9,846	—	—
(c) Main income source cultivation	201,436	—	—	270,591	—	—	203,768	—	—

Note: Figures in parentheses indicate percentage of 'all agricultural labourers'.

Source: Based on the author's primary fieldwork.

The impact of the Green Revolution in enhancing the demand for labour is reflected in Region A, in the fact that labourers there enjoy the highest earnings, the highest standard of living in physical terms,[3] and the greatest continuity of employment. In fact, landless labour households in Region A earn more, on the average, than the 0–5 acre farm households in that region, and more than the 5–10 acre cultivators in Region C. In Region B, earnings and continuity of employment are much less, but the highest peak-season wage rates are recorded in Region B.

The reason for this peculiar reflection of the labour demand and supply conditions (that is, that peak-season wage rates are higher in Region B than in Region A) is intuitively obvious from Table 13.2. In Region A, there are far more landless households per household cultivating 5 acres or more than in Region B. Thus, the peak-season labour demand in Region B hits a tighter supply bottleneck than that in Region A. Wage rates hardly peak at all in Region C.

TABLE 13.2: Landless Households per 1,000 Households with 5 Acres or More, 1972–73

Region	*No. per 1,000*
A	599
B	340
C	246

Source: Based on the author's primary fieldwork.

For households with land, the relative magnitude of earnings from cultivation and earnings from agricultural labour are reflected in the number of agricultural labour households with land, recorded in Part II of Table 13.1. This is brought out explicitly in Table 13.3.

TABLE 13.3: Percentage of Households with Land whose Main Income Source is Agricultural Labour, by Acreage Class, 1972–73

Operated Acreage Class	*Region A*	*Region B*	*Region C*
0–1.25	21.6	38.4	13.2
1.25–2.50	9.3	16.2	10.0
2.50–5.00	0.0	3.3	4.6
5–10	0.0	0.0	1.8

Source: Based on the author's primary fieldwork.

Despite the widest opportunities for agricultural labour employment, and the highest earnings for those who secure it, households whose main income source is agricultural labour are found only in the very smallest acreage categories in Region A. But in Region C, the returns from cultivation are so meagre that some households from much larger acreage categories earn more from agricultural labour than from farming—and this, despite the scarcity of agricultural labour jobs, the discontinuity of this sort of employment and the consequent poor earnings from this source. The relatively high Region B figures reflect poor returns from small-farm cultivation and moderate returns from agricultural labour.

Having established the broad context, we may now refer once more to Part I of Table 13.1. These figures show only the numbers of those whose main occupation is agricultural labour, where 'main occupation' is defined by the time criterion.[4] The phenomenon of peak-season occupational shifting produces a huge additional casual agricultural labour force. For example, about 72 per cent of the women working as agricultural labourers in Region A at harvest time (above 57,000 women in all) have some other usual occupation. There are also large male occupational shifts.[5] Most shift from other gainful occupations—except in Region A, where among the women, the 'other gainfully occupied' set is exhausted first (that is, chronologically, as the seasonal graph of numbers employed begins its upward rise)—and large numbers are drawn in from the usually mainly non-gainfully occupied set subsequently. Thus, the numbers in Parts I and II are a minority subset of those who worked 'at all' as agricultural labourers during the reference year.

The more important point to note about the number of those who are by usual occupation classed as agricultural labourers is their composition. In the prime Green Revolution area, Region A, more than half the total number of male agricultural labourers are now permanent labourers. This is a post-Green Revolution inversion of the relative importance of casual and permanent labour.

Permanent agricultural labourers are defined here to mean those persons who have entered into a firm contract of employment for a specified period of one year, two years or more, to do mainly field work operations (not for care of animals).[6] Within the past 25 years, a new category of permanent labourers has arisen—the *naukar*s (employees or servants)—who only a couple of decades ago were an insignificant minority, and who account for well under 5 per cent of all permanent labourers. Today their numbers are significant even in the most backward agricultural regions, but they are much more numerous in Regions A and B.

Naukars are paid mainly in cash, but usually get fixed quantities of in-kind benefits—such as free fodder, *bidi*s, meals and tea. In recent years, they have been pressing for, and getting, a larger proportion of their wages in kind, but the combined value of their remuneration remains a predetermined payment unrelated to output in any way. Naukars, on the average, earn slightly more per year,[7] than the traditional category of permanent labourers, the *sanjhi*s (one who works on share bases of payment). Table 13.4 indicates, by region, the relative importance today of naukars and sanjhis.

Table 13.4: Percentage of Permanent Labourers Who are 'Naukars', 1972–73

Region	*A*	*B*	*C*
% of permanent labourers	44.1	43.3	28.6

Source: Based on the author's primary fieldwork.

The sanjhis,[8] who are paid a share of the crop, remain the dominant subset of the permanent labourer class. But the determination of their 'share' has altered out of all recognition. Twenty-odd years ago, the share was a standard fraction of gross output. Now that share is determined with reference to other inputs. The tubewell, bullocks, the cultivators' own unpaid family labour, fertilisers, and so on, are all imputed some share of the gross output. The result is that the share which is to go to the permanent labourer varies greatly from farm to farm,[9] depending on the range of other inputs. As the complexity of the calculations varies directly with the level of technology, the contracts in Region B are much more complex than those in Region C. And some Region A sanjhi labour agreements stand in a class by themselves, for sheer sophistication. In Region A, many sanjhis today are paid a share, not of gross output, but of net farm business income roughly estimated after deduction of a diverse set of production costs. The share thus calculated is paid in kind.

One more inter-regional contrast may be brought out, before we go on to examine the more important common features, of both naukar and sanjhi contracts, which are today found in varying degrees in all regions. Table 13.5 shows that in Regions B and C, the period of contract is usually 12 months. But in Region A, where nearly half the permanent labourers in Haryana are hired, two-year contracts are common, and three-, four- and five-year contracts are also reported. Permanent labour contracts for periods beyond one year were virtually unknown a decade ago.

TABLE 13.5: Mean Period of Permanent Labour Contracts (Months), 1972–73

Region	*A*	*B*	*C*
Mean	26.11	12.68	12.00
Standard deviation	29.30	2.77	0.00

Source: Based on the author's primary fieldwork.

Virtually all of today's permanent labour contracts have three common characteristics—all of relatively recent origin. The most outstanding general feature is the formality of these contracts. All the main details, including the mode of payment, its periodicity, the duration of contract and advances to be made, are entered in the landowner's *bahi* or account book. The agreement is finalised in the presence of three witnesses, about whom more will be said shortly. Finally, a system of advance payment of wages is built into the contracts. On the day of hiring (*namani karsi*) in the last week of June, an interest-free advance is given equivalent to the remuneration for 4–5 months' work.

The overwhelming first impression made by these new labour agreements is that the Green Revolution has served to modernise rural labour relations tremendously. Yet, despite the form of modernity, the function of these contracts in the village setting is conservative. To appreciate the role they play, an account of certain details is necessary.

Two kinds of details are discussed here: (a) the role of 'rural personages' as witnesses; and (b) the place and character of traditional and new forms of indebtedness in today's relations of production.

First, the witnesses.

Four categories of persons are identified from which the three witnesses are drawn, with care to preserve a balance between traditional and modern authority figures in the composition of the set.

1. *Rich peasant*: The criteria locally reported for identifying a suitable person from this class constitute a pragmatic list of sources of economic power in the modern Haryana village. They include distinctive ownership of agricultural machinery and equipment; ownership of land contiguous to labourers' house-sites; large unit of land; and the telling general criterion, 'that peasant who influences the village community through his economic superiority'.
2. *Traditional leader*: This set includes the following: Numberdar, ex-Safaidposh, ex-Zaildar, ex-Jagirdar, Wisbedar and Sardar. The reader will notice that many of these personages derive distinction from an office formerly held by them which today no longer exists.
3. *Modern institutional leader*: The list includes the following: Sarpanch, Panch, ex-Sarpanch, ex-Panch, Pradhan of the cooperative, member of Zila Parishad, MLA and relative of MLA. The inclusion of the cooperative director and relative of MLA among those who are called to witness permanent labour contracts brings out rather forcefully the peculiar forms taken in the evolution of authority patterns in a rural society in transition. Their position as witnesses and—by well-understood implication—as enforcers of labour contracts, brings home the 'new wine in old bottles' character of power relations in a progressive Haryana village.
4. *Others*: This miscellaneous set includes relatives of the hiring cultivator; religious teachers like the Pandit, Bhaiji and Mulla; and shopkeeper. When the shopkeeper is included, it is commonly by virtue of his function as the source of 'managed' loans, a strangely modern form of an old category of consumption indebtedness, which is discussed subsequently.

These lists are by themselves a self-sufficient commentary on the relations of power in a Haryana village. Yet it should be noted explicitly that the witnesses are all presumed by the villagers to stand on the side of the hirer, and that no case was found where a witness was included who was considered a representative for the labourer.

The second aspect of labour relations which requires detailed description is the role played by traditional and new forms of debt in tying the labourer to his employer.

Reference has already been made to the initial interest—free advance, equivalent to four or five months' emoluments, which is paid on the day of hiring. This advance payment of wages constitutes only a part of the amount which will fall due when the next payment is made, on 'Lohri' day (mid-January), which is six and a half months later. Thus, a 'gap' is built into most contracts, which tends to produce a period of financial stress for the labourer before the January 'second instalment' is received. This becomes one of the factors which makes resort to interest-bearing forms of assistance likely during the year.

In January, a labourer whom the cultivator intends to keep on after the end of the agricultural year is commonly 'overpaid'. That is, the January payment includes a substantial component of 'advance payment of wages'. Again, this is interest-free. The final accounts are settled on a day falling in the last week of June—the same day on which new contracts are formalised. If labourers have to proceed to a new employer, the accounts are 'cleared'. If not, they may receive an 'overpayment' for the previous quarter's work. In either case, the worker commonly ends the year owing in the neighbourhood of Rs 600 to the employer of the year just ending. This is 'cleared' in the cases where the labourer is hired by a different cultivator, by the repayment of the debt to the former employer by the new one. Otherwise it is cleared by an advance from the new year's first instalment of wages. In either case, for current consumption purposes, the labourer must take a loan from somewhere.[10]

This may be done via a traditional interest-bearing loan on a *tamasak* basis, that is, on the personal security of the labourer. Such loans are interest-bearing in fact, but commonly the amount of interest payable is pre-added to the principal sum, and the whole is recorded in the bahi as an interest-free advance.

More commonly today, the required money is provided through a new form described as 'managed borrowing'. 'Managed borrowing' is done on the strength of the creditworthiness of the employing cultivator, not of the labourer. In most cases, the fact that there are three parties to the loan arrangement is explicit. There is first, the shopkeeper, *arthiya*, or another landlord, who provides the money. Then there is the employer-cultivator who stands as guarantor for the loan. And finally, there is the labourer, the ultimate recipient of the borrowed money, or its kind equivalent.

But this description of the 'managed borrowing' phenomenon gives only the identifiable skeleton of this new form of consumption indebtedness. In practice, it is subject to an infinite variety of permutations and combinations. A brief account of some of them brings out the role of managed borrowing within the village labour market context.

At one extreme is the case in which the cultivator takes, in his own name, a cash loan out of which he re-lends to the labourer at a higher rate. As long as the ultimate recipient's name is recorded, this is considered a form of managed borrowing. The principal and interest are recovered via a deduction from the labourer's wages. At the other end of the spectrum is the situation in which book transactions are recorded involving the three parties—the cultivator, the labourer and the shopkeeper, arthiya, or landlord who advances money or goods on credit. In the latter case, the labourer gets supplies on credit, which is repaid from the labourer's point of view, again, via a deduction from wages. From the lender's point of view, however, the loan may be adjusted against an account already operated by the cultivator, who may even repay in kind. For example, a loan from a grain dealer may be paid via a deduction from the total sum payable to the cultivator for a grain delivery. Thus, in the system of 'managed borrowing', the labourer may never even see any cash. When the debt is repaid, it is repaid directly by the employer-cultivator to the lender.

Loans under the 'managed borrowing' system tend to be given at effective rates higher than those prevailing for direct consumption loans. This indicates that the cultivator's role as 'guarantor' is not quite what it might seem to be on the surface. Specifically, his intervention does not serve, via the security it gives to the original lender, to reduce the interest rate charged to the borrower. Finally, when the source of the loan is a shopkeeper, the labourer may be obliged to purchase from that particular shopkeeper only. Although the cultivators and village shopkeepers have never heard of the 'company stores' of North American mining towns, nor of similar earlier ventures in Industrial Revolution-era Britain, they have jointly reincarnated the institution in a form peculiarly suited to conditions in rural India.

There are two other kinds of intermediated credit, affecting tenants[11] and small farmers as well as labourers, which should be mentioned—because they constitute threads in the redesigned fabric of conservative rural power. Both have arisen because the big farmer has access to institutional credit, which is not available to labourers and marginal farm households, and in both cases he uses his position to enhance his power over the 'weaker sections' in the village.

The first can be charitably designed 're-lending'. This is the borrowing by a large cultivator from a low-interest institutional source of money, ostensibly for his own use; this is, in fact, re-lent to others at higher interest rates. This form of debt is reported commonly among end users who are tenants or small farmers, as well as among agricultural labourers. The fact that there's a third party may be supposed to be unknown to the original source of the money.

The second version takes the form of resale by big farmers of inputs acquired on credit at controlled prices. To illustrate, the large cultivator purchases fertiliser on credit from the local cooperative, again theoretically all for his own use. This fertiliser, or part of it, is then resold at a higher price, especially to tenants, but also to smaller cultivators, or the big farmers's own poorer relatives. That the higher price includes an implicit interest charge and 'commission' is understood by those who buy inputs through such arrangements. The existence of an interest component becomes perfectly obvious in those cases where the ultimate purchaser does not pay cash at the time of purchase, but months later, just after the harvest.

The repayment he makes at harvest time (which may also be in kind), includes no specific interest element, but only the 'price' which the buyer agreed to pay. Agricultural labourers from households with land, small tenants and other marginal farm operators get scarce inputs this way, which they would have no hope of getting through straightforward channels.

These re-lending and reselling operations are included here, as one of the new forms which relations of production have taken in Haryana—because, from the borrowers' point of view, they are just another strand of the web of personal indebtedness obligations which big farmers now use as part of their intuitive response to the rising bargaining power of the landless and sub-marginal farm households in the village. Taken together, the new formal labour contracts, including the witness system, advances, managed borrowing, and other forms of debt tied into the payment system under modern labour and tenancy agreements, are expressions of the adaptability of the employing cultivators and the village power structure of which they are a part, in face of other changes set in motion by the enhancement of demand for agricultural labourers.

Before going on to look at the implications of all this information, let us refer back to data related to the changes in the demand for labour.

The first point can be made by reference again to Table 13.1. From the column for Region C, it may be noted that 19 per cent of male agricultural labourers come from households designed as 'other' by main income source, but less than 6 per cent do so in the case of Regions A and B. Had the agricultural labour earnings of the men from these households been greater, many of their households would have been classified by main income source, among the landless agricultural labour households. Similarly, many individuals not counted at all as agricultural labourers in Region C work part of the year as agricultural labourers. This set have, as their main occupation (the 'other households' set have as their main income source), one out of the following three categories of employment: (a) artisans and household industry, including carpenters, masons, basket-makers or embroiders of shoes; (b) petty self-employment, including care of the households' own animal stock, collection and sale of fodder, tea shop, junk dealer and so on; and (c) unskilled PWD-type labour. It turns out that a number of the agricultural labourers in other regions also have earnings from such sources, but they are for them subsidiary, not main, occupations. That is, a number of male agricultural workers from the landless agricultural labour households of today appear to have come from the 'other households' category of 10 years ago.

Before we leave Table 13.1 finally, it may be noted also that a substantial set of men from households whose main income source is cultivation are part of the set of permanent labourers. The household origin of male permanent labourers is given by main income source of their households in Table 13.6. Item III brings out the fact that a substantial subset of these men come from households operating quite respectable acreages (by Haryana standards) in the two more prosperous regions. The majority comes from households which include more adult males than the average for their acreage class. There is no corresponding phenomenon of males from households above 2.5 acres whose main source of income is cultivation working as casual labourers. The lesser attraction of casual labour earnings does not appear to be sufficient to cause men from such households to switch from work on their own land to working for others. Thus, in Region A, a significant chunk of the enhanced demand for permanent labour is now satisfied by drawing upon the otherwise (one may infer) underemployed male labour of landed households.

What are the implications of all this?

The bare fact that the entire set of agricultural labourers has become much more numerous (it has grown by two-and-a-half times in 10 years)[12] may be considered to have altered somewhat the balance of power between classes in rural areas. One

TABLE 13.6: Household Origin of Male Permanent Agricultural Labourers by Main Income Source of Household and Acreage Class, 1972–73*

	Region A	*Region B*	*Region C*
Total permanent	72,240	37,744	4,820
I. From landless agricultural labour households	54,984	25,363	4,820
II. From agricultural labour households with land	6,765	8,022	—
(a) 0–2.5 acres	6,765	7,120	—
(b) 2.5–5.0 acres	Nil	Nil	—
(c) 5–10 acres	Nil	Nil	—
III. From households whose main income is source cultivation	10,491	4,359	—
(a) 0–2.5 acres	2,723	953	—
(b) 2.5–5.0 acres	2,723	953	—
(c) 5–10 acres	3,960	1,602	—
(d) 10–15 acres	1,676	—	—

Notes: *This is an acreage-operated classification.

A 'nil' entry indicates that for the specified household category there are no households in the specified acreage class. In Region A, for example, all households operating 2.5–5.0 acres have cultivation as the main source of income; none are agricultural labour households with land. A '—' entry is used where households exist in the specified main income source and acreage category, but no permanent labourers are reported from such households.

Source: Based on the author's primary fieldwork.

reason for this big increase in the number of agricultural labourers over the past decade has been the shift of individuals from other 'usual' occupations to agricultural labour.

About 5,000 have come from tenant households which lost their land through its resumption for self-cultivation, in each of Regions A and B. There is, in addition, a new class of agricultural labourers from households whose main income source is cultivation. Finally, there has been the 'main occupation' shift of landless persons who were formerly artisans, unskilled non-agricultural labourers or self-employed in tending animal stock.

The new class of permanent agricultural labourers from households whose main income source is cultivation appear to be least interested in collective bargaining for better terms of employment. If the competition for permanent labour jobs in time reduces opportunities for this work,[13] if the landless agricultural labourers organise themselves to present some semblance of a common front for wage bargaining with their employers, this section can be counted out of any struggle on the agricultural labourers' side.[14] The main income source of their households was, and is, petty proprietorship of land; land stands as their insurance against all forces affecting the household from outside; and the present permanent labourers from these households will stand with their households and not with the paid agricultural labour force which, as individuals, they have recently joined.

As one landless informant said, 'They do not sit with us.' He meant it literally. In the evening, when men sit around in the poorer neighbourhood of the village and talk about wages for the coming season, among many other more trifling matters, the permanent labourers from the better-off households with land are elsewhere. Thus, to the extent that the number of agricultural labourers has swelled from this source, the tilt in the relative size of the proletariat section of the rural class structure has no positive implications for support of radical programmes favouring labourers. This set will tend, instead, to support land reform and land redistribution programmes designed to help small farm operators.

This conclusion does not apply to the set of landless workers who were formerly pure tenants, artisans, unskilled non-agricultural labourers or self-employed in looking after the landless households' own cattle. In their former occupations, they were more often of the 'single workers' category, many of them obliged individually to landowners for their rented land, or for intermittent employment as carpenters and the like, or to government labour contractors. As agricultural labourers, whether permanent or casual, they now share a common experience in relation to the more substantial landowners in the village, and to the others they appear as 'personages' representing the village power structure and possible witnesses at the time permanent labour contracts are formally concluded. For the erstwhile tenants, artisans or formerly self-employed, the perspective of having been 'something else' may give a subjective vantage point from which to view their new identity as part of the ordinary agricultural labour proletariat.

But the main force making possible the emergence and consolidation of an agricultural labourers' class consciousness (as opposed to a 'Jat/non-Jat' or Scheduled Caste/non-Scheduled Caste consciousness) is the heightened demand for labour. Although this has not led to collective bargaining, it has given them individually 'a place to stand', and the beginnings of an active collective self-consciousness. Individually, the casual agricultural labourer can, and does, say on occasion to one of the cultivators who regularly hires him: 'I will not work today.' And the cultivators complain that their permanent labourers 'report sick', or go off for their sisters' marriages, more than they used to do—and that there is nothing that can be done about it.

Collectively, in action—far removed still from collective wage bargaining—labourers in a village may arrive at some sort of consensus that for the coming harvest each should stick to a demand for Rs '*y*' per day instead of the lesser sum of Rs '*x*', which was paid last year. But this is a consensus which is implemented by individuals.

The counterbalancing force is the whole process of personalised indebtedness relations being built into permanent labour contracts, very formally, on an individual labourer basis. This can best be interpreted as the landowners' response to a worrisome improvement in the bargaining position of labourers. In effect, the new contract forms and the new categories of indebtedness serve to reassert the atomistic character (from the labourer's side) of the hiring process, to institutionalise and strengthen the personal obligations of the individual labourer to the cultivators, and to back up this relationship by a combined front of powerful village personages against the labourer in a readily understood way—the very procedure of finalising permanent labour contracts.

Thus, the embryo expressions of solidarity among labourers have been nipped in the bud, and counterbalanced by the reinforcement of traditional individual relations of awe, subservience and dependency. So far, this counter-attack has been entirely successful in Haryana. Although we heard that such things were occurring, no case was found in our sample of 153 villages, of labourers forming their own harvest 'groups'. The teams of harvest workers are still put together: (a) on the basis of common membership in a family group; (b) by the cultivator who chooses members for the work team individually; or (c) by an intermediary acting as a local labour contractor. The hiring of casual labourers as members of a family team predominates much more in technologically advanced Region A than anywhere else. The success of the permanent labour policy is suggested by the fact that, at present, the casual labour set appears to be much more militant than the permanent agricultural labourers.

Conclusion

The new technology has undoubtedly improved the inherent bargaining position of agricultural labourers in the Green Revolution areas of Haryana. In practice, also, there is ample evidence that they are individually more self-assertive than they used to be. But given these facts—namely that they earn much more than they did, that their standard of living in real terms has also improved, that even the casual labourers enjoy much greater continuity of employment than before, and that large members have shifted from casual to permanent labour status—it is surprising that the Green Revolution and the post-Green Revolution periods have seen virtually no collective exercise of their apparent bargaining strength. Not only this, the newly emerged majority and 'aristocracy' of the agricultural labour force in Region A, the permanent labourers, whose formal contracts are in many respects so 'modern', seem to be even less inclined to collective action than the casual labourers.

What accounts for this?

We have argued in this chapter that it can in part be explained by the character of the new formal labour contracts. Their formality, the associated witness system, and above all the incorporation into these contracts of new forms of indebtedness, have all served to reinforce the position of the employing cultivators vis-à-vis the labourers. Whereas in Region C, where most agricultural labourers are casual workers, direct consumption loans from diverse sources still predominate; in Regions A and B, consumption indebtedness is now loosely tied in with labour agreements, and direct consumption loans from persons other than the employer have been reduced to relative insignificance—especially among the permanent labourers.

It should be noted that the factor which ties the labourer more closely to his employer is not the level of interest rates (when interest-free advances are included, the effective rates on all types of debt owed by casual and permanent labourers combined are lower in Region A than in Region C), nor is it the amount of debt. (While debt levels are certainly higher in Region A[15] than in Region C, so also are the levels of earnings. Moreover, even as the debt burden appears to be numerically comparable when debt is expressed as a proportion of income—say, one-third—one can easily be persuaded that one-third of the earnings of Rs 2,200 represent a less onerous burden than one-third of Rs 1,200.)

That is, the factor which has offset the rise in inherent bargaining strength is the direct link which has been forged in prosperous regions between employment and new forms of indebtedness. In the poor Region C, the labourer is still constrained by the scarcity of jobs, but in high-employment regions, the labourer is now kept more or less in line by a complex set of new relations of production.

A final word about the longer-term perspective. In states like Haryana, the stage is set for increased conservatism among landholders taken as a group. After at least a decade of rapid capital accumulation and heavy investment in land improvement, they are increasingly diverting their surpluses to the improvement of dwellings, ceremonial expenditures and other conspicuous consumption, and, in some areas, usury. In the mean time, there has been no proportionate shift of population out of the rural areas. In the more prosperous regions, there has been a tremendous rate of subdivision of farm holdings.

The new technology has greatly enhanced the demand for labour, especially permanent labour. But the process of the shifting down of cultivating households from higher to lower acreage operational categories over time has been much accelerated by the enhanced rate of subdivision of family land. The majority of subdivided households commonly hire no permanent labourers. They do not compensate for this by hiring an equivalent number (per acre) of casual labour days. Instead, they tend to substitute unpaid family labour for hired labour generally. Failing a fresh technological breakthrough, all this suggests that the outlook for both private farm investment and improvement of conditions of agricultural labourers is less than cheerful. What the outcome of these trends may be is yet to be decided.

NOTES

1. Two other such smaller agro-economic regions are ignored in this chapter because of the host of special features which make each difficult to compare with the rest of Haryana, without long explanations of the sources of their distinction. They are, in the north, a hill 'cho' area, and in the southeast, an area defined by a large arc to the west of Delhi.

2. Region A, the richest agricultural area of the state, grows wheat, rice, sugarcane, maize and bajra. Gross irrigated area is nearly 70 per cent of total cropped area, and 26 per cent of the total cropped area is under high-yielding variety seeds. Region B, the second most prosperous region, grows cotton, gram, wheat, bajra and jowar. Although 62 per cent of its total cropped area is irrigated, the 'quality' of the irrigation is lower than in Region A. The farmers of richer Region A use private water from their own tubewells, or that purchased from their neighbours, but Region B depends to a large extent on canal irrigation, which is not always available in the quantities and at the time it is wanted by the farmers. One consequence is that in Region B, only 14 per cent of total cropped area is under high-yielding

variety seeds. The practice of most farmers is to plant an irrigated highly remunerative crop such as cotton in one season, followed by a non-irrigated, much less remunerative, non-high yielding variety crop such as gram for the second season of the crop year. In arid Region C, bordering Rajasthan, the gross irrigated area is only 12 per cent of total cropped area, and less than 6 per cent of it is under high-yielding variety seeds. Annual crop cycles consist in some combination of bajra, gram, jowar, wheat and fallow.

3. Food consumption, housing standards and amenities.

4. Redefined on the main income source criterion, the numbers come out to be about the same, except that some men from pure-tenant households defined as cultivators on a time criterion become agricultural labourers on an earnings criterion.

5. The tables for males have not been put together yet, but it is apparent that the shifts from other gainful occupations are on a large scale.

6. A large number of boys between the ages of 9 and 15 are hired on one-year contracts for the care of animal stock. They are excluded from the agricultural labourers' set. Many permanent labourers also do odd jobs in connection with their employers' animal stock, but this is a subsidiary activity only.

7. The difference is significant in all regions, but careful checking (of debt patterns, ages and household origin) failed to produce any explanation for it.

8. The term 'sanjhi' is the one in general use to describe a permanent labourer paid by share of crop. However, the same word is also widely used to mean a sharecropper. In the vast majority of cases, there is no ambiguity whatsoever about whether an individual is a sharecropper or a permanent labourer paid on a share of crop basis. But in Region A, a significant set of borderline cases exists. To this set, we applied the locally recognised ultimate test of status. It is: 'Who owns the bullocks?' What is interesting is that the number of individuals who are in the twilight zone between labourer and sharecropper should be significant only in the highly irrigated areas.

9. Despite the variability of the fractional share, the variability of sanjhi earnings is not large, though greater than the variability of naukars' earnings.

10. The periodicity of payment descried here is typical of naukars' contracts. That of the sanjhis' may be more complex, but it produces the same effects.

11. Tenants are also often parties to 'managed borrowing' through the landlord as intermediary.

12. As a proportion of male workers, this represents an increase from 7 per cent to nearly 16 per cent in just 10 years.

13. Reasons why this may be so are discussed elsewhere (see *Secular Democracy*, annual number, January 1976).

14. They should, however, be identified as potential allies. The point is that at present, their landed status keeps them apart.

15. It may be noted that advances were never reported as debt by labourers in their responses to a separate debt questionnaire, and that they are unable to say in mid-season how much they 'now owe' in the case of managed borrowings. It is only when you come to the details of the labour contracts that the true magnitude of indebtedness begins to emerge. They tend to report direct borrowings, and managed or other intermediated borrowings, where the sum has been given to them in cash, more or less correctly.

14

Agricultural Labourers, the State and Agrarian Transition in Uttar Pradesh*

Jens Lerche

This chapter considers the development of the agricultural labourers' position within the social fabric of Uttar Pradesh during the 1990s. It addresses the question of how the situation at the local level relates to the wider economic and political development of Uttar Pradesh. The aim is to deepen our understanding of the Uttar Pradesh agricultural labourers' position, first, by relating it to the east–west differences in the general 'balance of power'[1] between the agrarian classes and, second, by contextualising this balance of power within the different agrarian transitions that are taking place in Uttar Pradesh.

It is argued that while there are clear connections between the general developments and agricultural labourers' position at the local level, this relationship does not constitute a sole dominant development trajectory. Instead, the relationship evolves around several different development paths. The argument contains three elements:

First, instead of conceptualising the east–west differences as 'capitalist agrarian development' versus 'semi-feudal stagnation', it seems more reasonable to talk about a number of different capitalist development trajectories within Uttar Pradesh agriculture.

Second, these different agrarian developments seem to give the agricultural labourers very different positions in the local class struggle. However—and this is the third point—the relationship between agrarian development and the balance of power between labourers and landowners is not simple or one-dimensional. This is, not the least because of the influence wielded by state institutions. For example, a 'development optimist' viewpoint expecting strong capitalist development to coincide with a broadening democracy, and higher wages for the labourers *can* be supported by evidence from some parts of Uttar Pradesh; but so can a more

* Originally published in *Economic and Political Weekly* 33(13), 28 March 1998: A29–35.

pessimistic viewpoint seeing capitalist development and increased non-local oppression as interlinked.

Agrarian Relations and the State

Till now, analyses touching upon these questions have had very different points of focus. Two of the most thorough writers on agrarian transition, agrarian classes and political development in north India are Utsa Patnaik and Zoya Hasan (Hasan 1989, 1994a; Patnaik 1988, 1994; Patnaik and Hasan 1995). However, their main focus is not on agricultural labourers but on dominant landowning agrarian classes. They especially investigate the extent to which, and how, these groups pursue capitalist agrarian development, their political strategies and their political importance. Patnaik is a major proponent of a dualistic understanding of India's agrarian transition. She argues that Haryana, Punjab and parts of Uttar Pradesh are characterised by a dynamic agrarian capitalism, driven by a strong middle/rich peasantry. Opposed to this, a static oppressive 'semi-feudal' capitalism, or 'Junker style agrarian capitalism of the landlords', is dominant in most of India (Patnaik 1988: 23–25, 36).

A different strand of studies from other parts of India concentrates on the influence of the state on local agrarian relations (Breman 1990; Herring 1984; Oommen 1985). In an illuminating study, Herring (1984: 201) argues that in South Asia, local agricultural labourer–landowner relations are enacted both at the local and supra-local levels. The ability to influence the state apparatus has become a crucial factor in the local class struggle. Part of the reason for this lies in the increased politicisation of the oppressed classes. In order to cope with this opposition, the rural elite makes use of the powers of the state which are easily available to them. According to Herring (1984: 240), the dominant rural classes in South Asia are often so powerful that the local power structure and the state are enmeshed to the extent where it is not possible to separate them from each other. He argues that capitalist development of agriculture might favour 'labour-repressive and extremely exploitative social organisations of production' (ibid.: 237), but to enable that, traditional oppressive means such as local patron-client relations do not suffice. Instead, 'local elites may perceive that investment in supra-local politics is more conducive to protecting their interests ...' (ibid.: 214).

Herring's argument is, however, weakened by not being well documented.[2] In fact, I will argue, a less wide-ranging conclusion along the following lines might be more appropriate: 'While state apparatuses and elected bodies are often a tool for rural elites' oppressive regimes, there are exceptions. These state institutions are contested and the outcome of these contests is no foregone conclusion.' Such a deduction certainly fits better with my own research experience.

Returning to Uttar Pradesh, to my knowledge, no study has attempted to analyse the state local-level agrarian labour struggles thoroughly. A number of studies have, however, discussed the relationship between the oppressed rural groups in Uttar Pradesh and the state in a caste rather than a class perspective. In Uttar

Pradesh, caste and class overlap to a large extent, especially among the lowest and the highest castes (Hasan 1989: 152–63, 68; Lieten 1994).[3] Agricultural labourers normally belong to the SCs,[4] and the development of these groups' relationship with the state is therefore also of interest here. Many of the caste-based studies seem to believe in the ability of the modernisation process to eradicate traditional rules and norms, and to emancipate the downtrodden. They tend to display a much more unproblematic and optimistic view than Herring's gloomy prediction of more oppressive social relations.

Of these, Oliver Mendelsohn's (1993) study deserves special mention. Mendelsohn is a development optimist. According to him, the economic and political development in India has led to the diminishing of the power of the landed elite to such an extent that it does not make sense to talk about a 'dominant caste' any longer. The village is now so integrated into India's economic, political and social life that it has lost its position as the basic unit for economic activities and, hence, also for economic, social and political domination of the lower castes. Instead, the old dominant caste elite has oriented itself towards politics at the state and national levels, and towards the modern urban sector, while the lower castes have escaped the village elite's dominance by engaging in economic activities outside the village. The causal relationship between landownership and authority/power has ceased to exist at local level, and the dominant castes have generally not been able to shift their authority to the supra-local level. This is because the overall importance of the agricultural sector and the groups involved in agriculture is on the wane, as trade, industry and state bureaucracy have gained in economic importance and political influence.

Mendelsohn's paper contains a wealth of empirical detail. Analytically, it sees 'development' as an unproblematic movement towards economic modernisation and greater political freedom and more choice for the individual. This compares unfavourably with Herring's willingness to contemplate the possibility of economic development and political oppression going hand in hand. For Mendelsohn, the greater influence of the outside world on the village is an undisputed good as the dominance of the rural elite is thereby diminished. For Herring, the rural elite will try, and will most often be successful in, using the wider arena to reinforce its position at the local level.

However, in spite of these differences, and in spite of very different theoretical points of departure, the two analyses agree in the importance of including both the local and state/supra-local levels in the analysis of local power relations.

More problematically, they also both tend to generalise their findings to cover all-India. Opposed to this, I will argue that rural social relations have developed differently in different regions. I propose that this can be linked to different agrarian transitions, that is, different development paths from pre-capitalist to capitalist agriculture. In social theory, the existence of several agrarian development paths with very different social implications is well acknowledged. For example, the 'classical' British transformation led to major upheavals in the social fabric and heralded the capitalist industrialisation of British society, whereas the German 'Junker' agrarian capitalism had the maintenance of landlord domination as a central tenet (Bernstein 1996; Byres 1986, 1991). Generally, it seems clear that the agrarian development path depends as much on existing social relations, and on the policy of the state (which again is related to the class relations), as it does on more technical issues (Byres 1986, 1991). In the following section, I will briefly present an outline of what could both be termed 'the common orthodoxy' on agrarian transition and state policy in Uttar Pradesh, and of the development of the agricultural labourers' position in rural social relations in north India. This is then discussed via two case studies.

Agrarian Transformations and Political Development in Uttar Pradesh

It is commonly accepted and well documented that during the twentieth century, west Uttar Pradesh agriculture developed more rapidly and became much more productive than agriculture in the rest of the state (Patnaik and Hasan 1995: 85; Stokes 1978). The main reason for this seems to lie in the social fabric of the area. East Uttar Pradesh has, historically, been dominated by landlords, whereas in west Uttar Pradesh, middle and large peasants are more predominant than anywhere else in the state. Importantly, the British reinforced these differences through their land tenure systems, and through the concentration of government agrarian investment in the western parts of the state (Hasan 1989: 142, 1994a: 170).

A common interpretation of the agrarian development proposed by, among others, Patnaik (1988) and Hasan (1989) is that since Independence, and land reforms abolishing zamindari, the peasant proprietors of west Uttar Pradesh, epitomised by the hardworking Jat, have developed a thriving capitalist agriculture. Opposed to this, the high-caste landlords of the east have kept this part of Uttar Pradesh in a stage of 'semi-feudal' capitalism where not even a landlord-based 'Junker' agrarian transformation has had much impact. The landlords here have by and large stuck to unproductive rent appropriation, and '... cultural and ideological domination by the high-caste landlords continues to prevail' in most of the east (Patnaik 1988: 23–24).

However, as well as cementing the peasantry structure of the west, the land reforms also created a class of small farmers in the east, mainly from middle-ranking castes such as Yadav and Kurmi, who pursue highly productive agriculture. Srivastava's (1994: 168, 170; 1995: 230) interpretation of the agrarian transition of east Uttar Pradesh pinpoints these groups as being those mainly responsible for the (modest) growth rates that actually are occurring in the east. Srivastava's contribution represents, however, more of a correction to the standard analysis than a break with it.

To put this in caste terms, landowning agricultural groups in the west consist of a mainly Jat peasantry, whereas in the east the high-caste, mainly Thakur, 'landlords' are being challenged by a numerically large group of small landowners from the medium-ranking 'Other Backward Castes' (OBCs) such as Yadav and Kurmi.

The state-level political power in Uttar Pradesh throughout the 1950s and 1960s rested with Congress Party, which encompassed both the 'Brahmin–minority groups' alliance and the dominant farming groups. Roughly speaking, the non-landlord landowners in the east and west were politically united from the late 1960s to the late 1970s on a platform supporting capitalist owner-cultivators, against, among other things, upper-caste dominance.

The politicisation of the farmers was followed by unrest among the low-caste groups. The (partial) breakdown of landlordism in the decades following Independence led to the replacement of old patron–client relations by more naked exploitation of the landless groups; but the growth of the capitalist economy and of the relatively democratic electoral system also opened up new economic and political opportunities outside the purview of the local landowners. New low-caste organisations emerged outside Congress Party's patronal network. The reaction to the untouchables' rising profile was a decade of atrocities against them. The new modern farmers and other ambitious groups used all means to strengthen their own positions. Politics, violence and organised crime became ever more enmeshed. The political parties were very much part of this development as they, more and more blatantly, appealed directly to communal interests. The elections of 1989 saw the Uttar Pradesh Congress Party crumble, while new political groups emerged.

Since then, a turbulent power struggle has unfolded. The main actors have been the high-caste and business groups' Hindu nationalist party, the BJP; the farming groups and middle castes led by Mulayam Singh's Samajwadi Party (SP); and the low castes, grouped around the Bahujan Samaj Party (BSP). All three groups have held power for a while, through a number of different coalitions and minority governments. Importantly, this has included a brief spell in power for the charismatic, female low-caste leader, Mayawati, of the BSP. Today, the BSP is the only unquestioned and politically influential crusading vehicle for the Dalits of Uttar Pradesh (Brass 1990: 208–09; Hasan 1989, 1994b; A Report from 'Mankind' 1986; Misra 1994,1996a, 1996b; R. Singh 1986; J. Singh 1992: 95, 150).

Concerning labour relations, it is commonly accepted that caste domination and other pre-capitalist oppression of agricultural labourers prevailed in the east. Opposed to this, in the west, caste relations were more egalitarian, and more 'modern' free wage labour relations, freed from pre-capitalist bonds, were emerging as part of the overall capitalist development here.

However, this picture has been modified during the 1980s and early 1990s. In west Uttar Pradesh, it has been argued that *in addition* to the relatively 'free' labour relations,[5] 'new' types of oppressive interlocking dependency relations and unfree labour relations are emerging, instigated by the capitalist farmers (Herring 1984; Lerche 1995; Srivastava 1989a, 1989b).[6] The notion of the 'semi-feudal' character of the labour relations of east Uttar Pradesh is, however, hardly challenged (though see Lerche 1995). The relationship between agrarian transformation and oppression seems more, complex than earlier expected.

CASE STUDIES

During 1992–93, two assistants and I conducted six months' fieldwork in two villages, backed up by extensive touring of the districts in which the villages were located. I returned to the two villages for a month in December/January 1995–96.[7]

The fieldwork location in east Uttar Pradesh was the village Deogaon (fictitious name) in the Jaunpur district, north of Varanasi. As is the case in most of the district, Deogaon is dominated by the Thakurs. During British rule and up to Independence they held, together with the Brahmins, all superior land rights and local political power in the area. The tenants belonged mainly to the Yadav caste, and the landless labourers were mainly from the untouchable Chamar caste.

The land reforms after Independence reduced the Thakurs to medium-scale farmers. Today, the Thakurs possess around half of the agricultural land of the village. All Thakur households own some land, and none of them work as agricultural labourers. In the main Thakur settlement, Madhya Deogaon, the average Thakur landholding is around 5 acres.[8] As in many other parts of east Uttar Pradesh, the great gainers of the land reforms have been the Yadav sharecroppers. They obtained ownership of much of the land and emerged as the most numerous group of (small) landholders. The Chamars did not gain any land rights. Today, the Thakurs have become petty commodity producers, relying on family labour and agricultural labourers. Sharecropping is negligible.

The Chamars did not only lose out in the land reforms, they have also become more delinked from agricultural production in general. The Thakur farmers have by and large taken over the courtyard work of the old Chamar farm servant; motor-driven tubewell irrigation has overtaken the earlier very widespread and extremely labour intensive mechanical tubewell irrigation;[9] tractors do half of the Thakurs' ploughing; and electrical threshers have minimised the threshing work.[10] Both Thakurs and Chamars are heavily engaged in outside activities, in the nearby towns and as migrant workers. On the other hand, the village agricultural labour market is closed; with a few exceptions no outside labourers are engaged by the Thakurs.

In western Uttar Pradesh, the fieldwork location was the village of Mirpur (fictitious name) in the Muzaffarnagar district of the old Meerut division, north-east of Delhi. Mirpur has historically been a Jat village; they hold the power and land rights in most of Meerut division (Pradhan 1966: 22; Varun 1980: 210). The Jats' cultivating practices differ from those of the Thakurs in that they themselves traditionally take part in the actual tilling of the soil, and the women may also engage in agricultural activities (Singh 1992: 12). At Independence, the Jats were the cultivators, and the Chamars were their landless agricultural workers.[11] The post-Independence land reforms gave the Jats ownership rights to practically all land in the village. Today, they still possess 95 per cent of the land, and they actively prevent outsiders and local non-Jats from buying land. The landholdings of the Mirpur Jats average around 5 acres, that is, the same size as the Deogaon Thakurs' landholdings. No Jats work as agricultural labourers. Most Jat households are also engaged in outside economic activities, but money earned through agriculture is ploughed back into production in the form of investment in machines, milch cows, etc., to a much higher extent than is done by the Thakurs of Deogaon.

As in Deogaon, the amount of work available in agriculture in Mirpur fell even before the advent of the Green Revolution, as power-driven tubewells began to take over from Persian wheels in the early 1960s. Today, there are 40 tractors in the village—whereas, in comparison, there are four in Deogaon. Power-driven wheat threshers are now common, and so are high-yielding wheat varieties. Most young male Chamars, therefore, work in brick kilns during the dry season.[12] Simultaneously with this delinking, other non-Chamar low castes have engaged themselves more in agricultural labour, but no outside workers are engaged (apart from a handful of attached labourers).[13]

Moving on to the issue of oppression and dominance, the low caste people of both villages have, along with the general development in India described earlier, experienced a lessening of this since Independence. Also, in both the case studies, it is clear that the village as an economic unit has lost some of its centrality. This means that the lower castes are not as directly economically dependent on the dominant landowning groups as they used to be, though some do depend on them for loans.

Moreover, patron–client relations and old oppressive labour relations (tied-labour relations, etc.) have lost a lot of their significance as tools of oppression in Deogaon, though they certainly still exist. In Mirpur, patron–client relations and tied-labour relations are much rarer, but here a new dependency relation connects the widespread and very lucrative cattle owning and cattle rearing among low-caste households to forced agricultural labour.[14]

However—and not so obvious from the economic outline—the case is that the class struggle position of the agricultural labourers in the east Uttar Pradesh Deogaon village was much better than that of the agricultural labourers in the west Uttar Pradesh Mirpur village. The local wages were the same in the two areas, but in Deogaon, the SC agricultural labourers were less oppressed. They could speak out openly against their high-caste employers, vote freely at elections, and organise activities ranging from religious and symbolic actions to strike actions against the landowners (approximately every third year), strikes which they generally won. A Chamar woman of the village was even the president of the women's wing of the Ambedkar Mahasabha of the Jaunpur district, and she was also in the running for a 'ticket' to stand as the Uttar Pradesh assembly candidate for the BSP.

The Mirpur Chamars' position was worse. Basically, they were not in a position to engage in open struggles, nor even in verbal rebellion against the Jats. The Jats restrained them from voting, and often cast votes on their behalf. Violence against non-Jats was not uncommon, neither were rape cases, and caste meetings for the low castes were not possible any longer. The agricultural labourers generally did not resort to strike activities, and the one time in recent memory when they did (in the late 1970s), they lost resoundingly.

Role of the State

But why are the two cases different? It is now time to return to the two earlier theories of the relationship between local dominance and the wider societal scene. As outlined earlier, Herring (1984) argues that as the state apparatus has penetrated deeper into the countryside, the rural elite has made use of it in order to cope with the increasingly politically active oppressed groups. Local oppression is not sufficient any longer, so the local elite invests in supra-local power structures instead. Mendelsohn

(1993), on the other hand, claims that local oppression has been modified as the villages have become more integrated in Indian economic, social and political life. Moreover, according to him, the dominant caste cannot easily replicate their earlier local dominance at state level because the rural sector, which they represent, has lost out in the competition for power in the modern urban sectors.

In the two villages studied here, the state has a major impact on social relations though in a slightly different way to those suggested by Herring and Mendelsohn. As described elsewhere (Lerche 1995), in Deogaon, government propaganda and agrarian legislation form part of the background to the development of a strong political group consciousness among the untouchables. Moreover, the state apparatus also interferes directly in the landowner–agricultural labourer relations. Till the early 1990s, police and courts generally acted on behalf of the high-caste landowners; but from Independence onwards limits for how blatantly this could be done have been imposed. The landowners could no longer count on the state apparatus to condone or tolerate their most atrocious actions, such as murdering the leaders of agricultural labourer strikes or burning down whole SC hamlets. The 1993 election, which brought a low-caste coalition to power in Uttar Pradesh, and the subsequent BSP government, made things even worse for the landowners. It gave an enormous confidence boost to the local agricultural labourers, and had direct practical consequences as well. For the first time, the SCs could count on a local police force and court system that would not act directly against their interests (at least if the civil servants wanted to avoid the wrath of, and sanctions from, their political superiors). This changed the balance of power in Deogaon. Hence, when the agricultural labourers went on an all-out strike for a considerable wage increase at paddy transplanting time in 1994, it was them and not the landowners that made use of the legal system. They pressed charges of assault and caste discrimination against a number of landowners, charges which they told me were *as false as* the ones the Thakurs used to press against them. The Chamars' charges were accepted by the police for investigation and, even more unusually, the strike was finally settled by the intervention of the police officer in charge who convinced the landowners to increase wages by 33 per cent, apparently impressing on them that times had changed and that they broke the law by not paying the legally stipulated minimum wage.

The Mirpur situation is quite different. Here, it is the absence of direct state influence that is important. Generally, the Jat farmers have failed to dominate Uttar Pradesh politics as they are only numerically important in west Uttar Pradesh, and as the social structure of the east only to some extent comprises farming groups with sufficiently similar interests with whom the Jat farmers can forge a strategic alliance.[15] Having so failed to take over the state apparatus (except for brief spells in the late 1960s and mid-1970s, when they managed to build an east–west farmers' alliance), the Jats have built a strong position of regional dominance in west Uttar Pradesh, especially in parts of Upper Doab. One aspect of this has been to render the Uttar Pradesh government without local influence and power. In Mirpur, the local agricultural labourers cannot rely on support from outside the state and government apparatus. The Jats have simply cut the connection between local oppressed groups and the state machinery. They have used their farmers' union, the Bharatiya Kisan Union (BKU), as well as their traditional caste organisations, to create a 'village republic' in the BKU heartland around Mirpur. In this area, police and other government officials are barred from entering the villages unless they obtain permission from the BKU leader, Mahendra Singh Tikait, or the Jat village councils. Land disputes, rape cases and even murder cases are only referred to the police and courts if the Jat village meeting and Tikait allow them to be. In Mirpur, this has strengthened the Jats' position enormously. They do not have to fear the lower castes' use of the government apparatus such as police, courts and the law any more as the local Jat village meeting together with Tikait have become the 'state' authority of the area. This means that the Jats feel safe to conduct their dominance rather openly.

The 1993 Uttar Pradesh low-caste election victory has had some influence on the Mirpur situation, though hardly a dramatic one. The low castes of the village were obstructed from voting and the BJP won most of the west Uttar Pradesh seats, supported by the Jats and BKU. Since then, BKU has officially dropped the 'village republic' policy and does again allow government officials into the villages, and has shifted its allegiance to the United Front around SP. However, up until January 1996, neither police nor courts had interfered in the agricultural labourer–landowner relations in Mirpur. At least the agricultural labourers feel strengthened by the election victory: 'We have gained self-respect/self-confidence' was a typical comment, though even that comment was only relayed to us by agricultural labourers who knew us well, and that when no Jats were around.

LOCAL SOCIAL RELATIONS, THE STATE AND AGRARIAN TRANSITION

It is clear from these two examples that the political orientation of the state and who holds influence over the state matter for the local class struggle. It is also clear that it is not only state power that is contested. Also contested is how, if at all, power at state level can be transformed into influence on local social relations. The question is: What are the decisive elements in this competition for state support? Or, to raise the question in an empirical context: Why have the Jats of Mirpur managed to neutralise the state whereas the Jaunpur SC agricultural labourers have been able to make use of it for their own ends against the Thakurs? I propose that this relates to regional differences in the balance of power between the agrarian classes, based on regional differences in the agrarian transition.

As already mentioned, it is common to analyse the agrarian transition of Uttar Pradesh within a 'semi-feudal'–capitalist dichotomy. Earlier, in the context of labour relations, this was seen as a dichotomy between the 'semi-feudal' unfree oppressive class relations and capitalist labour relations which were exploitative but which also involved the creation of a 'free' labour force. However, a number of studies seemingly point towards the conclusion that the alternative to semi-feudal oppression (as in east Uttar Pradesh) may well be unfree capitalist oppression just as severe. This would obviously leave the agricultural labourers between a rock and a hard place, with no hope of a positive development in the immediate future. The basis of such a conclusion is, however, false I would argue, as the capitalist–'semi-feudal' dichotomy does not reflect reality. Instead, there are several different capitalist agrarian development trajectories in Uttar Pradesh based on different class positions. Thus, I would argue that parts of east Uttar Pradesh are experiencing a capitalist agrarian development which has gone hand in hand with a considerable improvement in the agricultural labourers' position in the class struggle. The development is distinctively different from the west Uttar Pradesh capitalist development, and it is (obviously) also different from a static 'semi-feudal' social formation. Patnaik's 'semi-feudal' capitalism-viewpoint is based on the tenet that the landowning class of east Uttar Pradesh is dominated by landlords who tend to rely on surplus appropriation through ground rent obtained, in practice, through sharecropping. For the landlords to turn their agriculture into efficient capitalist production units would primarily require: (a) that they engaged themselves in the production process, and (b) productive investments. Patnaik argues that landlords will only undertake such investments if the returns are very high as they presently receive a return on their land without investing anything in it at all. Investments are, therefore, few and far between, and the landlord-based agrarian transformation, that is, the 'semi-feudal' capitalist path, is developing extremely slowly (Patnaik 1988).

The 'landlord capitalist' argument claims the existence of a significant number of big landlords who are to a large extent engaged in leasing out their land. But this is not the reality of the whole of east Uttar Pradesh, and certainly not of the Jaunpur district. As Cohn (1954) had concluded already in the early 1950s, land reforms and generational partitions meant that the old Thakur landlords were on their way to becoming a class of relatively small landowners who would be forced to till their land themselves. This development had actually taken place in Deogaon village when I conducted fieldwork there in 1993. Land reforms, Yadav encroachment and family partitions had reduced most of the Thakurs to petty commodity producers, tilling their land with family labour as well as agricultural labourers. Importantly, they used more machinery in the production process than the Yadavs as they could better afford to invest in threshers, tubewells and (the renting of) tractors.

Srivastava (1994: 168, 170; 1995: 230) has, as mentioned earlier, rightly pointed out that agricultural growth is actually occurring in east Uttar Pradesh. He sees the main reason for that in the class of small-scale proprietors of Yadavs, Kurmis, etc., created via the zamindari abolition reforms. However, the capitalist development of Deogaon is based as much on the Thakurs' activities as on those of the Yadavs. My trips to other parts of the Jaunpur district indicate that this is the common situation in most of the district. I would even argue that the Jaunpur situation may be similar to that in much of the south-central parts of east Uttar Pradesh, whereas parts of the north and east conform more to the 'landlord' capitalist ideal.

The Jaunpur agrarian development is less dynamic than the west Uttar Pradesh development; but a capitalist transformation of agriculture is certainly taking place, with the old Jaunpur landlords being transformed into capitalist farmers. It thus seems clear that there are several different agrarian development trajectories in Uttar Pradesh, and not just one 'semi-feudal' and one 'capitalist'.

These agrarian development paths obviously differ in how dynamic they are. Some analyses focus on this when discussing degrees of exploitation, in the sense that a dynamic capitalist class is seen as being in the best position to impose its will on others. It has thus been argued by Patnaik and Hasan (1995) that the fact that the farmers of west Uttar Pradesh (and Haryana and Punjab) produce most of India's foodgrain puts them in a very strong bargaining position. In relation to bargaining with the state, the relatively small concessions won by the farmers' union, the BKU, representing the west Uttar Pradesh farmers, leaves a question mark over this hypothesis. It is even less plausible that this is the main reason for the farmers' success in blocking the state's influence out at the local level: landlords of Bihar, who hardly compare in production efficiency with the west Uttar Pradesh peasantry, have also managed to block out the state from their oppressive actions at the local level (Kohli 1991: 205–37).

This does not mean that economic relations are unimportant, but narrow economic issues such as the rate of profit or size of production are not the essential ones. Instead, issues such as basic material interests and class are. Opposed to Mendelsohn, I would argue that in most of rural India, power and landownership are still closely interrelated.[16] The main difference with regard to class struggle positions in east and west Uttar Pradesh is, I would argue, whether or not landowners are united or not, both locally and supra-locally. In the Deogaon village, as well as in the Jaunpur district and in east Uttar Pradesh in general, the post-Independence land reforms split the land between the old landlord class (especially Thakurs) on the one hand, and OBCs (especially Yadavs) on the other. This clearly represents a division of east Uttar Pradesh landowners into two groups with different interests. Schematically, some of the differences are:

1. high caste–OBCs
2. ex-landlords–ex-tenants
3. old elite–upcoming would-be elite
4. medium-big landowners–small-medium landowners
5. the few–the many

The ex-landlords and the OBCs tend to see each other as competitors regarding landownership, access to government funds, elected office and government service posts. Opposed to this, the OBCs and the SC agricultural labourers have a common enemy: the old elite. Moreover, as the OBCs rely mainly on family labour, they do not see rising agricultural labour wages or the SC agricultural labourers' political freedom as a significant threat.[17]

It is this split within the landowning group and the subsequent alliance of the 'small castes' against the 'big castes' (Lieten 1994) that has enabled the SC agricultural labourers to develop their strong position locally. In the Jaunpur district (at least) the history of Thakur dominance has been broken both at the local level and state level, and also to some extent within the government agencies.

The west Uttar Pradesh situation is quite different. In most of Upper Doab, and particularly in the part of the Muzaffarnagar district where Mirpur is located as well as in Mirpur itself, the Jats have a near-monopoly on landownership. In short, they face no competition for land or government office locally; their dominance goes unchallenged. Moreover, opposed to the case of the Thakurs of the east, they are sufficiently numerous to physically enforce their dominance if necessary. In Mirpur, they are quite aware that their strength lies in unity, and they act accordingly. For example, all Jats meet the night before elections and decide whom to vote for; and (bar once) they have reached a common decision and enforced it on all villagers.[18] There are thus good reasons why these highly productive capitalist farmers have been capable of imposing a strict mode of oppression on their workers—but it is not because of their high productivity. Their strength and dominance have also been reinvigorated by their ability to organise a relatively efficient farmers union, the BKU; but the BKU is as much an effect of their strong position as the cause.[19]

To sum up, the west Uttar Pradesh example shows that dynamic economic development does not necessarily weaken the strong social and economic dominance of the landowners. This is the case even when the development leads to a weakening of the lower castes' direct economic dependency on the landowning groups. The east Uttar Pradesh case study, on the other hand, shows that less dynamic economic development can allow for a better position for the agricultural labourers.

These results question at least three common understandings of agrarian development in India. First, it is important to avoid a simplistic perception of agrarian transition in Uttar Pradesh (and, more generally, in India) as following either a 'semi-feudal' or a 'dynamic capitalist' trajectory. The problems with such an analysis are exacerbated if labour relations are simply 'read off' this dichotomy, thereby equating semi-feudalism with strong oppression and dynamic capitalism with less oppressive, market-led social relations. If this model is imposed on Uttar Pradesh as representing the east–west divide, a proper analysis of the position of agricultural labourers becomes impossible.

Second, the equation of economic development with an improved position for the lower castes is premature. Third, the analyses of the state's influence on rural social relations are also overly simplistic, be it: (a) in the expectation that the state machinery nowadays influences rural social relations in order to benefit the oppressed groups; or (b) in its antithesis: that the state machinery is being used by the local landed elite in order to maintain existing oppressive regimes. In these cases, once again, social and political relations are 'read off' the general theory, leaving no space for empirically grounded analyses.

The Jaunpur and Muzaffarnagar examples show that alternatives to the oppressive 'semi-feudal' and 'dynamic capitalist' agrarian transitions do exist. The forms development takes are conditioned by a complex interweaving of factors, from who holds power at a national and state level right down to the local class constellations. It is, therefore, to be expected that important regional variations in development trajectories would exist. Such an approach avoids generalisations regarding the position of the SC agricultural labourers in India, and may help us in our understanding of the number of regionally different positions held by agricultural labourers.

NOTES

1. I have argued elsewhere for the importance of what I have labelled the general 'balance of power' with regard to local agrarian relations (Lerche 1995). Such an approach follows in the theoretical footsteps of Brenner (1986) and, in an Indian context, it bears similarities to Herring's (1984) line.

2. Ironically, his main empirical evidence is from Kerala, where Left-wing governments allied with the agricultural labourers have legislated concerning minimum wages, working hours, etc. This legislation is actively enforced by the state machinery, and landowners have reacted by also engaging in supra-local activities (Heller 1995; Herring 1984: 200–01). Whereas this points to the importance of the state apparatus for local class struggle—and this is what Herring uses it for—it obviously does not support the argument of upper-class domination of rural state apparatuses. In fact, the main thrust of Herring's argument lies elsewhere: the article focuses on the extent to which oppressive social relations can go hand in hand with dynamic growth in agriculture.

3. In descriptive contexts, caste and class terms will often be used as denoting the same social group (that is, Jats/capitalist peasants of west Uttar Pradesh). This is a convenient but, admittedly, imprecise use of the terms. When used analytically, the terms are distinguished between.

4. Though, not all people from the SCs work as agricultural labourers, nor are all agricultural labourers from the SCs.

5. Brass (1990) has traced a similar development in Haryana. This has recently been disputed by Surinder S. Jodhka in a heated debate in the *EPW* [see, for example, Brass (1996) and Jodhka (1996)]. However, Jodhka's empirical material pertaining to this specific point is rather thin.

6. See Mukherji (1991) for examples of well-remunerated 'free' labour relations in west Uttar Pradesh (Meerut district), as well as for examples of modern 'unfree' labour relations in Haryana.

7. The research assistants were two sociologists: Prakash Deo Singh and Rajashree Ghosh. A third assistant, Indu Shekhar (also a sociologist), joined in during the last two months. In 1995–96, Prakash Deo Singh was my research assistant.

8. None of the Thakurs are very big landowners, nor are many of them very small. Of the 63 Madhya Deogaon Thakur households, the six biggest landowners (10 per cent) owned between 10 and 20 acres each, and seven households (11 per cent) owned 2 acres or less each.

9. The old irrigation method required at least four persons working full-time according to the Deogaon informants. The gazetteer states that three men are needed, and that up to 11 persons might have been engaged during the peak irrigation periods (Nevill 1908: 43). At the time of this fieldwork, the irrigation was mainly done by the Thakurs themselves, and labourers were largely employed for ploughing, sowing, harvesting and threshing, but some were also employed during the agricultural slack season for weeding, irrigation, hoeing, etc.

So even though the Green Revolution and tubewell irrigation allowed for new crops and a stable cropping season throughout the year, this did not lead to more man-days per year, not even before mechanisation set in.

10. This has not been a smooth process. For example, farmers did not take over the courtyard work of their own free will, but only after a dramatic sequence of strike action events when the Chamars decided not to do this polluting work. See Lerche (1995).

11. Of the 449 Mirpur households, 46 per cent were Jats and 23 per cent were Chamars.

12. A brick-kiln worker may earn between Rs 35 and Rs 65 per day, whereas the pay for a full day's agricultural work is generally Rs 25 plus food (as in Deogaon).

13. Of the 64 households engaged in agricultural labour throughout the year, 30 per cent were Chamars, while 37 per cent and 20 per cent, respectively, came from the two other low castes, the Jhimars and the Jogis.

14. Many of the low-caste households rear cattle. Some households may take a calf on lease from the Jats, who then pay them for raising it, and Chamars, who have earned money in the brick kilns, may invest in a cow of their own in order to gain an income from the sale of the milk. Altogether, around 40 per cent of the Chamars, Jogis and Jhimars have cows or buffaloes and the income from the animals may be as important for them as the income from agricultural labour. The cattle rearing involves a dependency on the Jats as the Jats have managed to institutionalise a system whereby those who collect fodder from their fields are also obliged to do the sugarcane sowing and harvesting and several other jobs. The pay for this is measly: half the sugarcane tops, which can be used for fodder. This system of unpaid work or 'begar' in relation to sugarcane growing is quite common in Uttar Pradesh, and is not always looked upon as an undesirable relation by the agricultural labourers. But in Mirpur, where sugarcane is the main crop by far, the labourers view their sugarcane begar as forced labour. Other types of dependency relations, either based on the need for fodder or on borrowing money from milkmen, are reported on from Haryana by Brass (1990: 54), and from the neighbouring Meerut district in Uttar Pradesh by Singh (1992: 68–69).

15. Mendelsohn uses the Jats of Uttar Pradesh as an example of a dominant caste which has not managed to take over the reins at state level. It is in fact his most important example, but a rather misplaced one as well. No general theory is needed to explain why they cannot be in complete control of the state apparatus; it is mainly because they only dominate in one of Uttar Pradesh's regions. This is, incidentally, also why they have chosen a different strategy vis-à-vis the state apparatus, as described subsequently. If Mendelsohn had wanted a more appropriate example, he could have chosen the Jat dominance in Haryana; but that would not have supported his overall argument: that often, the dominant castes do not succeed in reproducing their village dominance at state level.

16. There are obvious exceptions to this, as well as cases where economic activities other than agrarian production have become of more importance to the old landowning elite. See Harriss-White (1996) for a south Indian example.

17. In some parts of central and west Uttar Pradesh (and in Bihar), the OBCs are at the forefront regarding oppression of the SC people. Generally, in these areas, the class constellations are different. There, the OBCs have become the new masters and are often dependent on SC agricultural labourers. They are now trying to impose their dominance on politically aware SC people.

18. This seems to be quite common in the Muzaffarnagar district (Leiten 1996).

19. Mirpur is most probably representative of the situation in the Jat heartland, a fact reflected in the backing that the new Ajit Singh/Mahendra Singh Tikait party received in the area in the 1996 election (Ramakrishnan 1996: 22). However, the balance of power between landowners and agricultural labourers might be quite different in other parts of the highly productive west Uttar Pradesh; for example, Mukherji's (1991: 28–29) description of the strong bargaining position of agricultural labourers in some villages in the Meerut district

points towards a different balance of power here. There are thus most probably also different development trajectories within west Uttar Pradesh agriculture; but an analysis of this lies outside the scope of the present chapter.

REFERENCES

A Report from 'Mankind'. 1986. 'Countrywide Civil Disobedience Movement'. In *Agrarian Struggles in India after Independence*, ed. A. R. Desai, 83–106. Delhi: Oxford University Press.

Bernstein, Henry. 1996. 'Agrarian Questions Then and Now'. *The Journal of Peasant Studies* 24(1–2): 22–59.

Brass, Paul R. 1990. *The Politics of India since Independence: The New Cambridge History of India* (Volume 4, Part 1). Cambridge: Cambridge University Press.

Brass, Tom. 1990. 'Class Straggle and the Deproletarisation of Agricultural Labour in Haryana (India)'. *The Journal of Peasant Studies* 18(1): 36–67.

____. 1996. 'Yet More on Agrarian Change and Unfree Labour'. *Economic and Political Weekly* 31(4): 237–40.

Breman, Jan. 1990. 'From Cane Fields to Court Rooms: Legal Action For and Against Rural Labour in Gujarat, India'. In *Capitalist Development: Critical Essays*, ed. Ghanshyam Shah, 270–88. Bombay: Popular Prakashan.

Brenner, Robert. 1986. 'The Social Basis of Economic Development'. In *Analytical Marxism*, ed. John Roemer, 23–53. Cambridge: Cambridge University Press.

Byres, Terry J. 1986. 'The Agrarian Question and Differentiation of the Peasantry: Foreword'. In *Peasant and Classes: A Study in Differentiation in Bangladesh*, Atiur Rahman, *ix–xxxvii*. London: Zed Books.

____. 1991. 'The Agrarian Question and Differing Forms of Capitalist Agrarian Transition: An Essay with Reference to Asia'. In *Rural Transformations in Asia*, eds Jan Breman and Sudipto Mundle, 3–76. New Delhi: Oxford University Press.

Cohn, Bernard. 1954. 'The Chaws of Senapur: A Study of the Changing Status of a Depressed Caste'. Unpublished PhD dissertation, Cornell University.

Guha, Ranajit. 1992. 'Discipline and Mobilise'. In *Subaltern Studies VII: Writings on South Asian History and Society*, eds Partha Chatterjee and Gyanendra Pandey, 69–120. Delhi: Oxford University Press.

Harriss-White, Barbara. 1996. *A Political Economy of Agricultural Markets in South India: Masters of the Countryside*. Delhi: Sage Publications.

Hasan, Zoya. 1989. 'Power and Mobilisation: Patterns of Resilience and Change in Uttar Pradesh Polities'. In *Dominance and State Power in Modern India* (Volume 1), eds Francine R. Frankel and M. S. A. Rao, 133–203. Delhi: Oxford University Press.

____. 1994a. 'Shifting Ground: Hindutva Politics and the Farmers' Movement in Uttar Pradesh'. *The Journal of Peasant Studies* 21(3–4): 165–94.

____. 1994b. 'Party Politics and Communal Mobilisation in Uttar Pradesh'. *South Asia Bulletin* 14(1): 42–52.

Heller, Patrick.1995. 'From Class Struggle to Class Compromise: Redistribution and Growth in a South Indian State'. *Journal of Development Studies* 31(2): 645–72.

Herring, Ronald J. 1984. 'Economic Consequences of Local Power Configurations in Rural South Asia'. In *Agrarian Power and Agricultural Productivity in South Asia*, eds Meghnad Desai, Susanne Rudolph and Ashok Rudra, 198–249. Berkeley: University of California Press.

Jodhka, Surinder S. 1996. 'Interpreting Attached Labour in Contemporary Haryana'. *Economic and Political Weekly* 31(21): 1286–87.

Kohli, Atul. 1991. *Democracy and Discontent: India's Growing Crisis of Governability*. Cambridge: Cambridge University Press.

Lerche, Jens. 1995. 'Is Bonded Labour a Bound Category?: Reconceptualising Agrarian Conflict in India'. *The Journal of Peasant Studies* 22(3): 484–515.

Lieten, G. K. 1994. 'On Casteism and Communalism in Uttar Pradesh'. *Economic and Political Weekly* 29(14): 777–81.

———. 1996. 'Inclusive View of Religion: A Rural Discourse in Uttar Pradesh'. *Economic and Political Weekly* 31(23): 1411–16.

Mendelsohn, Oliver. 1993. 'The Transformation of Authority in Rural India'. *Modern Asian Studies* 27(4): 805–42.

Misra, Amaresh. 1994. 'Challenge to SP-BSP Government'. *Economic and Political Weekly* 29(8): 409.

———. 1996a. 'Revival of Old Political Alignments'. *Economic and Political Weekly* 31(32): 2127–28.

———. 1996b. 'End of a Social Revolution?'. *Economic and Political Weekly* 31(45–46): 2983–84.

Mukherji, Partha N. 1991. *Report of the Study Group on Social Constraints on Rural Labour*. Mimeo, National Commission on Rural Labour, Ministry of Labour, Government of India, New Delhi.

Nevill, H. R. 1908. *Jaunpur: A Gazetteer Being Volume XXVIII of the District Gazetteers of the United Provinces of Agra and Oudh*. Allahabad: Government Press, United Provinces.

Oommen, T. K. 1985. *From Mobilisation to Institutionalisation: The Dynamics of Agrarian Movement in Twentieth Century Kerala*. New Delhi: Sangam Books.

Patnaik, Utsa. 1988. 'Some Aspects of Development in the Agrarian Sector in Independent India'. *Social Scientist* 16(2): 17–40.

———. 1994. 'India's Agricultural Development in the Light of Historical Experience'. In *The State and Development Planning in India*, ed. Terence J. Byres, 220–64. Delhi: Oxford University Press.

Patnaik, Utsa and Zoya Hasan. 1995. 'Aspects of the Farmers' Movement in Uttar Pradesh in the Context of Uneven Capitalist Development in Indian Agriculture'. In *Industry and Agriculture in India since Independence: Social Change and Political Discourse in India, Structures of Power, Movements and Resistance* (Volume 2), ed. T. V. Sathyamurthy, 274–300. New Delhi: Oxford University Press.

Pradhan, M. C. 1966. *The Political System of the Jats of Northern India*. Bombay: Oxford University Press.

Prakash, Gyan. 1990. *Bonded Histories: Genealogies of Labour Servitude in Colonial India* (Cambridge South Asian Studies 44). Cambridge: Cambridge University Press.

Ramakrishnan, Venkitesh. 1996. 'Uttar Pradesh: A Broader Vote-base'. *Frontline*, 15 November, 21–22.

Singh, Jagpal. 1992. *Capitalism and Dependence: Agrarian Politics in Western Uttar Pradesh 1951–1991*. Delhi: Manohar.

Singh, Rajendra. 1986. 'Agrarian Social Structure and Peasant Unrest: A Study of Land-grab Movement in District Basti, East Uttar Pradesh'. In *Agrarian Struggles in India after Independence*, ed. A. R. Desai, 538–65. Delhi: Oxford University Press.

Srivastava, Ravi. 1989a. 'Tenancy Contracts During Transition: A Study Based on Fieldwork in Uttar Pradesh (India)'. *The Journal of Peasant Studies* 16(3): 339–95.

Srivastava, Ravi. 1989b. 'Interlinked Modes of Exploitation in Indian Agriculture during Transition: A Case Study'. *The Journal of Peasant Studies* 16(4): 493–522.

———. 1994. 'Planning and Regional Disparities in India'. In *The State and Development Planning in India*, ed. Terence J. Byres, 147–219. Delhi: Oxford University Press.

———. 1995. 'India's Uneven Development and Its Implication for Political Processes: An Analysis of Some Recent Trends'. In *Industry and Agriculture in India since Independence: Social Change and Political Discourse in India, Structures of Power, Movements and Resistance* (Volume 2), ed. T. V. Sathyamurthy, 219–47. New Delhi: Oxford University Press.

Stokes, Eric. 1978. *The Peasant and the Raj: Studies in Agrarian Society and Peasant Rebellion in Colonial India*. Cambridge: Cambridge University Press.

Varun, Dangli Prasad. 1980. *Uttar Pradesh District Gazetteers, Muzaffarnagar*. Rampur: Government Press, Government of Uttar Pradesh, Department of District Gazetteers.

Yadav, Yogendra. 1993. 'Political Change in North India: Interpreting Assembly Election Results'. *Economic and Political Weekly* 28(51): 2767–74.

15

De-feminisation of Agricultural Wage Labour in Jalpaiguri, West Bengal*

Loes Schenk-Sandbergen

In the conceptualisation of the Water, Land and Ecology (WLE) project, it was assumed that globalisation and climate change have triggered a negative process of 'feminisation of agriculture' in the eastern Gangetic plains, mainly because of the outmigration of men, leaving behind the women with restricted access to services, infrastructure, institutions and markets to manage productive (as well as reproductive) responsibilities. Numerous studies have pointed to the feminisation of agriculture in India and Nepal and many other parts of the world, as an effect of globalisation and the migration of men (Ganguly 2003; Gartaula, Niehof and Visser 2011; Kelkar 2006; Sugden et al. 2014).

However, Henrietta Moore had warned already in 1988 that the concept of feminisation of agriculture 'is so commonplace in "women and development" literature that it is perhaps worth considering the conceptual limitations which might underlie it' (Moore 1988: 76–79). The findings, detailed here, from the three villages—Khuttimari, Salbari and Uttar Khalpara—in the Jalpaiguri district will reveal the validity of her prediction by sketching the crises in female agricultural wage labour leading to de-feminisation. This is in line with the current discussion on statistical findings which show a substantial decline in the female labour force in India, in particular from rural areas belonging to economically poor households (Kannan and Raveendran 2012). The author seeks to contribute to this discourse by sketching in a qualitative way the root causes for the alarming decrease at the village level.[1]

The project area of Terai in North Bengal was well known to me as in the early 1990s we had conducted an in-depth study and a sample survey to evaluate the impact of the implementation of the North Bengal Terai Development Project (NBTDP)[2] on the work and status of landless and farm women and gender relations

* Originally published in *Economic and Political Weekly* 53(25), 23 June 2018: 46–53.

(Schenk-Sandbergen 1991, 2014; Schenk-Sandbergen and Choudhury 2003). In April 2015, 25 years later, I got an opportunity to have a reconnaissance with Terai to follow up my earlier research and to revisit the villages.

TWENTY-FIVE YEARS LATER: SOME IMPRESSIONS

What struck me during the first field visit to village Velkujote in 1990, was that 'feminisation of agriculture' was not an issue. It was even my impression that the large majority of the villagers were not directly engaged any more in agriculture. In Velkujote, 70 per cent of the households were landless, and women said that agricultural wage labour was scarce in all seasons (Rabi, Kharif and pre-Kharif) and had decreased considerably during the past 10 years. Nowadays, it is contract labour that is given as a piece rate; the contractor does the work with his fellow workers or wife, children or other family members. Daily wages for women are lower than those for men but that has not brought about a replacement of women doing men's wage work. Those are different circuits, and the perception is common that women simply cannot do heavy labour. Men do heavy labour and therefore earn more per day (Rs 150–200) and women earn less (Rs 100–20).

The women in Velkujote said that their husbands outmigrated as skilled (masons), or unskilled construction workers to Siliguri, Kolkata, Kerala and West Asia. They themselves stayed behind to look after the household[3] and the children, and desperately await and search for opportunities to earn money. They are not called for agricultural wage work as this is almost not available. Non-farm earning options are almost zero. They had a savings group, but the rich woman leader stole all the money and disappeared from the village. A court case is, according to them, of no use.

The women were landless, but not assetless. Under the CPI-M state government, the women got the adjudication of the land title of the homestead land in their name.[4] They could not show any document with *patta* (land title) right of this important asset, and also did not know where to go to prove that they were the owners of the land. Obviously, the adjudication of homestead land rights had not empowered the involved women as it was not embedded in other strengthening interventions.

My visit showed that there was no indication that women have to suffer increasing workloads because of 'feminisation of agriculture', suggesting that they are compelled to take over the agricultural work of their husbands. The women in Velkujote cannot dream of such a scenario of being in charge of any agricultural production, for subsistence or cash crops, as they are landless. Neither can they think of a 'feminisation of agricultural wage work' as wage labour is hardly available.

The observations during my first encounter in the field were not incidental but in line with the wider rural transformation processes in West Bengal and rural India as a whole. The Socioeconomic and Caste Census (SECC) 2011 paints a picture of rural India weighed down by landlessness and the lack of non-farm jobs. It stated that out of millions of households in India, nearly three-fourths lived in rural areas.

However, only 30 per cent of rural households depended on cultivation as their 'main' source of income. For West Bengal, this figure was even lower, at hardly 20 per cent, of which 88 per cent consisted of marginal and small farmers and farm women (NABARD Consultancy Service 2009).

Thus, rural is not agricultural anymore. Globalisation, neoliberal policies, and climate and ecosystem changes have all triggered an accelerated process of cultivating landowners spiralling to the bottom: from small to marginal farmer, from cultivator to agricultural labourer. In the Jalpaiguri district, a staggering 86 per cent of farmers experienced a decline in the rate of farm incomes since the 2000s (Shiva and Jalees 2005: 114). It is our finding that over time, the size of the landholdings for marginal farmer households came down in 25 years from 1 acre to broadly 1 bigha,[5] meaning that also male and female marginal, and even small farmers depended for their livelihood on wage labour. This created immense pressure on access to land, and on scarce, casual, sporadic and seasonal wage labour, as there were almost no alternative livelihoods.

De-agrarianisation and Landless Women

Almost No Access to Land

Wessel Kok (2016: 50) found in his study in the Uttar Khalpara village in West Bengal that access to land had become increasingly costly for the poor because of the growing population; increase in the number of landless and marginal farmers who depended on leasing agricultural land for an additional income; rising presence of outside investors who bought up land for tea gardens; equal inheritance rights of male descendants; increased land values due to unequal access to irrigation facilities; and access to good roads. This near-completely deprived the poorest community—the Rajbongshi—in the village from having access to land. On the other hand, Muslim and Santhal households had either already sold their lands to the tea-garden companies, or seasonally leased-in or mortgaged agricultural land.

In the Khuttimari village, sharecropping (*adhi*) is no option any more as it requires high investments, while the landowner gets at least half of the profit. Only 6 per cent of the people interviewed in the Salbari village were sharecroppers. Lianne Oosterbaan (2016) gives an interesting case of a farm woman and her husband who own 12 bighas of land, but they do not cultivate any of it. Instead they lease it out for a good price to poor families, and invest in mortgaging (*bandhok*) tea plantations; all the tea leaves they pick are their profit. The most common causes for mortgaging land by small and marginal farmers are weddings, funerals, medical expenses and calamities. Religion, community, or gender hardly matter when deciding whom to give land for temporary use: the deciding criterion most often is that the person should be reliable and should have a good family reputation.

In the past, poor women could forage for wild greens/vegetables, fish in the rivers, and gather forest products, cooking fuel and fodder from the grazing grounds for consumption. Now, the forest and commons have almost vanished, or are closed or privatised. Poor families are increasingly dependent on purchased food and this makes the availability of women's wage labour all the more essential.

Shrinking Female Wage Labour

In 1991, landless households derived 75 per cent of their income from agricultural wage labour (Schenk-Sandbergen and Choudhury 2003). Other sources of income were less important and concerned agricultural production (17 per cent) and self-employment in, for instance, dairy and fuel trade, brokerage or stone chipping. On an average, landless men were employed for 200 days in a year according to the findings of the sample survey and 234 days according to the in-depth study, whereas the corresponding figures for landless women were 80 and 109 days, respectively. There was a clear seasonality in the labour demand in the area, which peaked in the pre-Kharif season (during the cultivation of *boro* rice) and the Rabi season (when potato was cultivated). Thus, agricultural labourers did not get work for about six months for a male worker, and nine months for a female worker. In 2015–16, our qualitative village studies indicated that the number of working days, for landless women in particular, had declined considerably in comparison with 10 years ago; respondents often recounted a maximum of only 15 working days in Kharif season and only three to four days in Rabi. There are broadly two reasons for this disastrous de-feminisation of agricultural wage labour: agribusiness in combination with the insistent notions of the gendered division of labour.

Masculinisation of Agriculture

In Madhya Khuttimari, there is not one farmer who did not use hybrid seeds. Practically all farmers in the Uttar Khalpara village have changed their crops from traditional crops to hybrid cash crops (Kok 2016). In Salbari, majority of the farmers use high-yielding variety of seeds, whereas only 4 per cent of the informants still use traditional rice seeds, primarily due to poverty (van Andel 2016). According to an aged farmer, there is no point of return anymore. Manuring the land with cow dung is no longer possible for the fertility capacity of the land as it is too damaged by all the chemicals in modern farm inputs. With hybrid seeds, the farmers need to use chemicals, pesticides and insecticides, else the crops will fail. The original crops did not require many chemicals, but the productivity was much less, so farmers consider it worth the effort. Farmers have to spray at least once a week to protect crops from pests and insects. This is a male domain of the division of labour.

In Madhya Khuttimari, farmers who hired agricultural labourers said that they 'would not hire women to do the heavier work such as spraying chemicals, ploughing and preparing the fields, and carrying heavy bags with the harvested crops' (Oosterbaan 2016: 26). Male farmers believe that strength is a must for certain kinds of work or it would not be completed. Oosterbaan (2016) did not encounter any woman who got hired or paid to do any of these jobs. They were simply not allowed to do it. Thus, a trend of 'masculinisation of agriculture' was observed instead of feminisation.

Changes in Cultivation

The findings of our study show many other reasons for the reduction of wage labour opportunities for landless women. Rice transplanting has been replaced by the highly promoted new system of rice intensification. Cash crops such as banana and tree plantations are increasing, both requiring less female daily wage labour. More so, because of irregular rainfall due to climate change, less rice is grown in the Rabi season as investments are too high, prices too low and the risk of floods and droughts high. The 'sharecrop' cattle system has also declined due to the loss of community pasture lands, sometimes in connection with the expansion of tea gardens. The demand for making traditional puffed rice (*muri*) for selling, produced by poor women in the past, has also declined as packaged chips are selling more in the market.

On the other hand, the 'revolution' in high-yielding variety vegetables growing locally generates more wage labour for landless women. Earlier there were no beans, tomatoes and cabbage cultivation in Madhya Khuttimari. Now vegetables are grown throughout the year. We met a group of female wage labourers in the field busy plucking large green beans. It seemed that a marginal SC farmer had leased in land to grow the beans. He hired female daily wage labourers from a tribal community to pluck the beans. They were supervised by his daughter. However, some households that could grow vegetables using a (solar) dugwell for irrigation kept their land fallow in Rabi, as time and money investments are high and they have no tradition in combining non-farm work with vegetable growing.

Location-specific Opportunities

The remaining agricultural wage labour is mainly caste/community-, gender- and location-specific. Jute cultivation during the planting and harvesting phase is done by women and men of the Adivasi community. They do the hard and dirty labour of soaking and stripping jute sticks in water. An important safety net for the poorest in Salbari is stone crushing in the riverbed, which is accessible to men, women and children. The riverbed offers two work opportunities: loading of large boulders and chipping of small stones. Stone chipping is almost exclusively done by women and children, while the loading of boulders is done by both men and women. Women earn Rs 50 for each pile of small stones they make; on one day it is possible to make two or maximum three piles, and women thus earn around Rs 100–50 a day (van Andel 2016). This work is available for six days a week, barring heavy rains when the work has to be discontinued. Women from each community can be found at the riverbed; however, majority of the workers are Muslim and Rajbongshi as tribal women are preferred in tea plucking. It was remarkable that even the wife of the panchayat leader worked in the riverbed and chipped stones. Her small income and the remittances of their migrated son were the sources of survival of the household.

In Uttar Khalpara, the availability of wage labour in the tea gardens has very dramatic and historical roots. Many Adivasis, mostly Santhals, and some Muslim families were more or less forced to sell their land to the tea companies as they were desperately trying to survive, as their harvests were destroyed completely by natural disasters. Kok wrote in his village study:

> There are three major company tea gardens in the village, some exceeding village boundaries. The biggest garden is the Rajabagan company, which is owned by an Assamese company. Access to the work in this garden is reserved to those who sold three bigha or more land to the company, or by paying the company for a permanent job. Each permanent job is accompanied by a casual one, which means work for half a year. Men hold the permanent jobs more often than women, so women have to work as agricultural or private tea garden wage labourers in the other months. (Kok 2016: 27)

Government Schemes

Lastly, there are several government poverty-alleviation schemes generating wage labour for poor members of landless and marginal farmer households in the three villages. The Mahatma Gandhi National Rural Employment Guarantee Act (MGNREGA) 2005, a 100-day work-guarantee scheme, is the most important. However, in Salbari, only 28 days of employment were available in 2015, and that was not enough to uplift the socioeconomic condition of a household substantially. In Madhya Kuttimari in 2015, there were many people who wanted to participate in MGNREGA, but not everyone could be employed at once, so the work was given in shifts. Even then, there were not 100 days of work for everyone; usually it was 35 days or so.

But agribusiness, climate change, etc., are not the only reasons why landless women are faced with shrinking wage labour opportunities. Our findings showed that the revived patriarchal gender ideology that perpetuates the notion of the 'good woman' also had an impact on the allocation of access to wage labour opportunities, although gender restrictions and gender gaps were much less in poorer households (Schenk-Sandbergen 1988).

THE 'GOOD WOMAN' IDEOLOGY

The Terai region has a long historical record of peasant movements, revolts and land reforms in which women have played an important role (Dasgupta 1984; Ghose 1983; Lieten 1992; S. Roy 1992; Samanta 1984). The fearless and dynamic role of peasant and tribal women in these protest movements is fortunately well-documented (D. K. S. Roy 1992; Ghosh 1991; Sarkar 2014; Schenk-Sandbergen and Choudhury 2003; Sen 1985). Over time, zamindari relations have been whipped out by the fragmentation of land due to patrilineal inheritance, immigration of refugees and, of course, by the land reforms introduced under Operation Barga (Bakshi 2015; Mishra 2007).

Although it is true that the impact of the Bharatiya Janata Party as a political party is limited in the Jalpaiguri district, the dominant religious images of gender identity, propagated on social media outlets, is silently intruding upon the minds of people. The freedom of movement that poor farm women had in the earlier decades especially strikes us in comparison with the curbs women face nowadays (Sarkar

2014). In the three villages under study, men opined that 'women should not go outside and in particular not go to the markets' (personal interviews, 2015–16). In Madhya Khuttimari, where active, landowning Rajbongshi women grow a variety of vegetables, the men contended that, 'women are the goddesses of the house and are therefore most respected when staying inside' (Oosterbaan 2016). Even a very charismatic, active female self-help group (SHG) leader in the village relayed that after a long struggle with her husband she had to settle for the subordinated role of a housewife and mother, adhering to the 'good woman' identity and rendering her identity as a farm worker or professional woman as secondary (Oosterbaan 2016). Moreover, we witnessed on many occasions the internalised subordination of women to pay respect to men; the way women jumped up from the floor when a man was approaching; the way the grandmother of a rich family left her chair for a much younger man when he entered the veranda; the way women changed their way of talking and kept quiet when men were around. The feminist anthropologist Moore (1988: 3) wrote, 'muted groups are silenced by the structures of dominance.'

Stacey Burlet (1999) observed that in the current sociopolitical climate in India, gender problems and gender inequality are neglected and marginalised unless gender identity can be linked to religious identities. This is exactly what we observed during Surya Shashti or Chathh Puja (sun festival) in November 2015 in Jalpaiguri. The Puja was celebrated on a large scale, and promoted with big posters showing prominent political leaders depicted as spiritual saints. We went to the riverside and saw that the festival asked for extreme sacrifices from women: standing for hours in dirty water and fasting, all to ensure a good life for the husband and children. Images in social media of gender roles based on traditional Hindu culture have obviously revived the 'good woman' ideology (Banerjee 2003). This masculinisation of culture is more or less going hand in hand with the masculinisation of agriculture because of the dominance of agribusiness. This is a worldwide process, even stretching to the masculinisation of birth (Guilmoto 2015).

Our findings revealed that the intruding 'good woman' identity reinforces submissive attitudes—no need felt for (joint) land rights for women, strict gendered division of labour, wage discrimination of landless and poor women, more emphasis on endless tedious domestic duties for women, more restrictions on mobility of women, less decision-making power, shift from bride price to dowry, increasing dowries, greater domestic violence, etc.—for landowning as well as landless women. This is despite the fact that compared to other states in India, the gender ideology in West Bengal is smoothened by the absence of Brahmin dominance, a melting-pot of cultures with many tribal communities having more gender-equal ideologies, the history of revolt and peasant uprising, and more than 40 years of Left Front rule in the state. In Uttar Khalpara, the better status of tribal women is convincingly reflected in the crucial finding that dowry is still *not* demanded in Santhal and some Rajbongshi lineages (Kok 2016); only bride price is known. The 'no dowry zone' still exists in the Jalpaiguri district as also in the matrilocal Rhaba village we visited (personal interview, 2015).

But, as Oosterbaan (2016) has shown in her study, poor landless and tribal women also face restrictions of access to labour markets and wage discrimination because of the 'good woman' norms imposed on them. Unfortunately, this ideology is not only reinforced by the richer male farmers and tea-garden company owners but to a certain degree also by the class of better-off farm women, who adhere to patriarchal notions and restrictions which might protect them ('we cannot do hard labour'; 'we do not know what chemicals to spray') but simultaneously undermine and constrain the life and work of their poorest sisters. The adherence to the 'good woman' norms was also reflected in the perceptions of women on 'land rights.' As usual, women of landowning families did not own land in their own name.[6] The root causes for the exclusion of women from land rights include patrilineal kinship and inheritance rights, and patrilocal post-marriage residence pattern. Brides come from the same village, but commonly outside the block and occasionally even outside Jalpaiguri district. In general, we found that women of small and marginal farm households worked in their fields, alone, or together with the husband, mostly early morning. They expressed firmly that they did not bother about *not* having land rights. In a focus group discussion in 2015, they stated, 'So what? We work on the land, and that resource is the livelihood of the family.'[7]

We did not notice any popular disinterest among women in cultivating the land, or reluctance or less motivation to participate in agricultural work because of non-ownership of land.[8] Oosterbaan (2016: 15) mentions that women said, 'nothing would change for them if they owned land,' that is, having the land in their own name would not make any difference nor give them any personal benefits. The women agreed that the problem of 'not having land' arises when women with children are abandoned by the husband, or women become widows and sons take away the land, but that rarely happens. The opinion of many landless women was the opposite. They emphasised the need for women to own even a small piece of land. They said, 'land is status, and the right to speak. If you have no land and no assets, your opinion is not taken seriously' (personal interview, 2016). We came across only two cases of women owning 2 bighas of land. One was a gift from a father-in-law to his daughter-in-law in lieu of her care services in his old age. Even in a case of matrilocality, the inheritance rights were patrilineal. Joint patta land rights were hardly known in the research villages, and opposed by men (Brown and Chowdhury 2002). They did not see the use of co-ownership.[9]

Wage discrimination against female labourers was persistent and backed up by the 'good woman' ideology. Wages differed per task and crop, but on an average women earned around Rs 100–50 against Rs 200–50 for men. Even if men and women did exactly the same work, there was this difference in wages. Oosterbaan (2016: 13) states that 'the sermon behind the wage difference given is, that men are physically stronger and can do heavier work and women are weak.' Landless women say that they never really think about the fairness of their pay because they cannot do anything about it. They do not ask for higher wages because they fear not getting hired at all, and it is better to receive some payment than no payment at all. Landless women are, thus, forced to compete with each other, undermining solidarity as discord creeps in.

Male Migration and De-feminisation

Who Migrates?

Seasonal male migration is the most dominant survival strategy of coping with poverty and the increasing costs of living compared to 25 years ago. In the three study villages, it was found that all migrants were men, most of them very young—at times 12–14 year olds—and unmarried. These young men often quit school even before graduating Class 10 and migrated—often to Kerala or Assam—to provide an income for their parents/family, save for the construction of a house, repay a huge debt, pay for medical care or contribute to the dowry of their sisters. The study of Merel van Andel (2016) confirms this worrying process of boys leaving elementary school at a very young age to migrate and earn money for the family: 34 per cent of the sons left school before Class 10 and thus before obtaining any certificate. The main reason for discontinuing education is to contribute to the household income. Eleven per cent of the daughters too left school before reaching Class 10, mostly for marriages.[10] These drop-out rates are reasons for concern as many will remain uneducated, which of course has an impact on their overall potential for intellectual skills and development in future. Some migrants are young men in a sad position, labelled in the international literature as the 'politics of waiting' (White 2012). They are bachelors, can be missed, do not like farming, so they hang around and wait for opportunities for work.

The much higher wages in Kerala are very attractive for young men compared to the local wage rates of Rs 400–500 per day. Migrants work mainly in construction as unskilled labourers. Labour relations and conditions are often extremely hard, inhuman, traumatic for young boys and unacceptable in general. In our selected villages, women are not supposed, and allowed, to work as migrant labourers—nor do they aspire to be migrant workers. As it is hard labour, women are deemed to be unfit for the work according to our respondents. However, Neela Mukherjee (2001) came across women migrants from the Jalpaiguri district in the slums of Delhi.

Thus, our village studies did not indicate any 'feminisation of agriculture' as a consequence of the outmigration of men. Women are certainly not 'left behind' by their sons, brothers and husbands; married men only move seasonally when there is a male guardian taking over the urgent male work to be done. There was no increase in the *de facto* women-headed households and workloads *per se*. Women do not do such tasks as ploughing, land preparation, spraying pesticides and marketing of the produce, formerly done by men only. Landless women are also not hired and are paid for these 'manly' tasks at lower wages. The perception of landless and landowning women is that the division of labour in domestic and in agricultural work is 'the same' as 10 years ago. Migration is not leading to the reshaping of new gender inequalities. Nevertheless, because of migration it has become more difficult to hire men as agricultural labourers, but that does not mean that these jobs are allotted to women. Instead, landowners hire men from other villages and unemployed casual male labourers from closed tea estates.

Size of Seasonal Male Migration in the Three Villages

In Madhya Khuttimari, there was a trend of temporarily working in Kerala or Assam. Bhutan is the only foreign place some villagers have migrated to, but Bhutan is also closer to home as compared to Kerala. From the 33 interviewed households, 14 households had migrants. Among the landless households, migration is much more common. It usually takes three or more months before the first remittance is sent home by depositing the salary in a shared bank account. In Salbari, 23 per cent of the interviewed households had one or more members who migrated, mainly to Kerala or Gangtok, but also to Cooch Behar, Kolkata and Bengaluru. All migrants sent remittances home to contribute to the household income. Two-thirds of the migrants were young unmarried men whereas only one-third of the migrants were married with children.

Although men from each community migrated, among the migrants in Salbari were many Muslim boys and men. Migrants kept in touch with their families by phone. In Uttar Khalpara (Kok 2016), out of the 44 families interviewed, 18 had at least one migrant in the family. Of these, 11 were landless as may be expected and seven were landowning; five came from marginal- and small-farmer households, and two from middle-farmer households. Two families had both the husband and son migrating in alternating turns. The power of the 'good woman' norms, thus, demonstrates itself in the dominance of the 'guardianship' notions of male migrants and in the absence of female migration.

'How Far are the Left-behinds Left Behind?'

Xiang Biao (2007) raises this important question in his study of outmigration of men in China. While it seems in India that individuals have a free choice to decide who migrates and who stays back, the earlier discussion reveals that there are fundamental social, cultural and institutional determinants of such decisions. Migration of boys and young men is mainly a forced decision to cope with poverty, gender inequality and age discrimination. The point Biao makes is that the problems poor women face with outmigrated sons, husbands and brothers cannot just be attributed to being left-behind individuals; instead, the fundamental cause is that many rural communities as a whole have been left behind, economically and socially. Measures to improve regular employment and the provision of public goods in rural areas should be prioritised.

ANANDADHARA: 'FROM WHERE HAPPINESS FLOWS'

The government of West Bengal shows its concern in promoting a huge microfinance/SHG project for poor women, named Anandadhara, aiming to promote self-employment and women's entrepreneurship in order to get women into the financial flow. The implicit gender ideology of the Anandadhara project is that social empowerment will emerge from economic empowerment. SHGs are seen as new institutions of social change. In view of this discussion, our main question was: Does Anandadhara reach the poorest women, or are they 'left behind?'[11]

Why Poor Women are not Members of SHGs

In Uttar Khalpara, the two main possible productive investments are buying livestock and leasing in land for agricultural production. However, both are risky. The size of the loan does not cover the costs of leasing land and of production. Thus, the returns are minimal. Moreover, rearing livestock is difficult because there is no grassland, and goats will be poisoned when they graze around the tea gardens. The use of pesticides on tea gardens has endangered freely grazing livestock, goats in particular (Kok 2016). In Madhya Khuttimari, there were 15 active SHGs in the village. One SHG started collective activities such as leasing in a fish pond to raise fish. But the fees for leasing the pond rose, and they had to give up the project. They also tried to make a collective nursery but that project too failed. Cooking mid-day meals in Integrated Child Development Services (ICDS) and Anganwadi programmes for children is often the only collective feasible activity.

In another SHG, the leader who belonged to a rich farmer household formed a group of very poor landless tribal women out of idealism to improve the quality of their life. She was, however, disappointed as the women members did not repay the loan and spent it themselves on drinking alcohol. The Anandadhara women staff at the block level is desperately searching for modern, profitable and innovative income-generating activities. They regret that they can only provide need-based training in boring, unprofitable and traditional activities such as tailoring, embroidery, candle-, soap- and juice-making, handicrafts and cane work. As the Terai/Dooars is famous for its beautiful mountains and forests, tourism might be an option but requires huge investments. So far, the 'best practice' business activity we came across was an SHG catering to the government staff in the block government offices for coffee, tea and snacks.

In the villages, the options for profitable income-generating activities are limited. The findings revealed that farm women who managed to become members of an SHG spent their credit on non-productive investments, such as basic food and clothing, repayment of debts at the grocery store and loans from relatives, home improvements, dowries, brewing alcohol, investing in the husband's business but rarely in agriculture. This happens mostly on the demand of their husbands to buy a bag of fertiliser, to lease in a handkerchief-sized piece of land, to buy some chicken, or to sharecrop a goat or a calf. Access to money does not necessarily give women control over it. Some women said that they had bought a calf but that the animal died. For repayment, they are totally dependent on the income of their husbands and earnings of sons who have migrated.

Self-employment is, of course, more likely among those women who own land and grow vegetables. They are often leaders of SHGs and it is a positive achievement of the Anandadhara programme that the women gained knowledge on how to take loans, skills to talk to officials, increased social networks and encouraged visits to places the women had never been before, even to Kolkata. Women leaders, cashiers and secretaries of the SHGs could build an impressive network of institutional relations in numerous meetings at the village, Gram Panchayat, block as well as district levels. Increase in self-esteem, social skills, capacities and cooperation for collective action (the fight against alcoholism of men) was noticed. However, female leaders have to be cautious to shape their behaviour and preferences around the 'good woman' notions of femininity, gender roles, morality and sexual division of labour.

'Left Behind'

Our data show that there were several obvious reasons why poor women were *not* members of SHGs. Poverty is the most obvious: landless women cannot save Rs 30–40 every month for a year before they are entitled to apply for a loan. Furthermore, they are expected to repay the instalments with interest whilst continuing the monthly savings. One landless Santhal woman reasoned, 'What we earn today, we spend today.' Another woman said, 'Where is the work in the group? I only see talk about money.' That observation hits the nail on the head. 'What to sell, where, and to whom?'

Critical studies show the extent to which the discourses associated with microcredit for women and SHGs are creating new norms for 'good women' in a neoliberal framework:

> [O]ne who saves and repays regularly, puts pressure on other group members to do similarly … and is committed to the welfare of the family … it is shown that neoliberalism subsumes women into an image of the protective mother who will translate any gains from the market into the means for household survival, and will be prepared to make unlimited personal sacrifices to provide the household with a safety net against the ravages of neoliberal macroeconomic policies. Ideologically, this works to re-embed women within familial relations. (Cornwall, Gideon and Wilson 2008: 5)

It is our finding that the reality is even worse than that sketched in these critical studies. Many landless and marginal farm women in the villages could not even dream of becoming a member of an SHG, and of saving and taking a loan for investment in self-employment or self-owned small enterprises and repaying instalments in time. The Anandadhara goals of financial inclusion of poor women are promoted in a chronic patriarchal structure of society and quickly shrinking access to the means of production and resources. No wonder then that the poorest women are 'left behind' in the effort to get women into the financial flow.

CONCLUSION

The findings in the three villages of Jalpaiguri under study show that the shrinking access to (common) land, labour and money, in combination with the intrusion of the patriarchal 'good woman' ideology, causes dramatic de-feminisation of agricultural wage labour. And that rural does not mean agricultural anymore. The migration of young boys and (unmarried) men to work in insecure, casual and risky construction work in the cities of India is a coping strategy to mitigate poverty. The government of West Bengal showed its concern in promoting a huge microfinance/SHG project for poor women, named Anandadhara. The Anandadhara programme aims to achieve the financial inclusion of poor women by encouraging them to become self-employed entrepreneurs. But, the access to land, water, labour, money, forest, skills and other means of production is quickly dwindling, while reinforced patriarchal limitations of the 'good woman' gender norms keep women out of this flow. The findings showed that the landless were the real 'left-behinds' by society and government, paying the price for de-agrarianisation and 'good woman' ideologies. The measures to generate steady employment for landless women and men, and the provision of infrastructure and common goods in rural areas should have first priority.

NOTES

1. The criteria for the selection of the three villages were: variation in the composition of caste/class/community, ecosystem varieties (fringe forest, river, irrigation command area), cropping pattern combinations (rice, jute, potato, vegetables, tea), duration of existing self-help groups of the Anandadhara programme, etc.

2. An impact, in-depth study of 273 households was conducted and a sample survey, which covered 1,524 households, was carried out to put the results of the in-depth study in wider perspective. The NBTDP successfully implemented a number of practical and strategic gender-activities which contributed very much to the empowerment of the women of landless, small and marginal households (Schenk-Sandbergen and Choudhury 2003).

3. The cooking on firewood, leaves, biomass and cowdung sticks, and the type of *chulhas* (stoves), were as primitive as 25 years ago. The image of women walking along the roadside with heavy dirty sacks of leaves and firewood on their bent backs, like slaves, was degrading. Water, too, was being fetched in the same strenuous manner from the deep *guhas* or *guas* (small dug well from which water is lifted with a bamboo stick).

4. The government of West Bengal launched a 'new' homestead-allocation programme in 2009 with the primary aim of allocating land to homestead-less agricultural labourer households (Savath, Fletschner and Santos 2015). Twenty-five years ago, the CPI-M also showed much concern for gender parity by allotting homestead land to landless women selected for our hand pump programme under the NBTDP.

5. One bigha is one-third (precisely 40⁄121) of an acre. In metric units, a bigha is hence 1,333 square metre. Sometimes, landless women lease in land in which they use the smaller size name of a *katha*: there are 20 kathas in one bigha.

6. In my research 25 years ago, 7 per cent of the land pattas were in the name of women, mainly widows and families with only daughters. Now that figure is down to 6 per cent. In the matrilocal village, we visited all the women of the Rabha community-owned land, but we found that the patta rights were given to both husband and wife on the document (Schenk-Sandbergen 1998).

7. Women have, since 1967, had the legal right to inherit land, but very few will insist on it for reasons described in many studies (Agarwal 1994; Sharma 1980). For an excellent field study on women and land rights in West Bengal, see Brown and Chowdhury (2002).

8. These findings are the opposite of studies conducted in other districts where women were keen to have joint patta or land rights (Gupta 2002).

9. The state policy in West Bengal is to use public land for allocation of homestead plots to the absolute landless and homeless through legislations and government schemes giving preference to women, STs and SCs. Government schemes such as Nijo Griho Nijo Bhumi Prakalpa (My Home My Land Scheme) was introduced in October 2011 to settle 5.5 lakh landless poor and provide up to 0.05 acre to each household (World Bank 2014: 19–20).

10. For encouraging the education and all-round wellbeing of school-going girls from poor families aged 13–18 years, the West Bengal government introduced the hugely successful Kanyashree Prakalpa conditional scholarship programme in 2012, expressly so that girls are not married off before 18 owing to familial financial constraints. The Sabooj Sathi (Green Friend) launched in 2015, under which an estimated 40 lakh students of classes 9–12 were assured free bicycles, was another government scheme to inculcate self-confidence and increased mobility in adolescent girls—especially those living in remote rural areas and the hilly tea plantations, and often have to cycle 8–10 km to reach school—and encourage them to pursue higher studies. The school dropout rate for girls in rural West Bengal has fallen considerably owing to such initiatives, and promoted girls' education in the state.

11. Besides, the government of West Bengal had set up Large-sized Agricultural Multi-purpose Cooperative Societies (LAMPS), providing credit, non-credit and technical support to the tribal women in the state with the objective of empowerment and inclusive development. In Madhya Khuttimari and in Salbari, the LAMPS project was also in operation. The SHG set-up in the villages consists of at least four different types: the Swarnajayanti Gram Swarojgar Yojana, the LAMPS for tribal women, the new Anandadhara project (started in 2018), and the SHGs affiliated to local NGOs.

REFERENCES

Agarwal, Bina. 1994. *A Field of One's Own: Gender and Land Rights in South Asia*. Cambridge: Cambridge University Press.

Bakshi, Aparajita. 2015. 'Contextualising Land Reform in West Bengal: An Interview with Benoy Konar'. *Review of Agrarian Studies* 4(2): 123–36.

Banerjee, Sikata. 2003. 'Gender and Nationalism: The Masculinisation of Hinduism and Female Political Participation in India'. *Women's Studies International Forum* 26(2): 167–79.

Biao, Xiang. 2007. 'How Far are the Left-behind Left Behind?: A Preliminary Study in Rural China'. *Population, Space and Place* 13(3): 179–91.

Brown, J., and S. D. Chowdhury. 2002. 'Women's Land Rights in West Bengal: A Field Study'. *RDI Reports on Foreign Aid and Development* 116: 1–30.

Burlet, Stacey. 1999. 'Gender Relations, "Hindu" Nationalism, and NGO Responses in India'. *Gender and Development* 7(1): 40–47.

Cornwall, Andrea, Jasmine Gideon and Kalpana Wilson. 2008. 'Reclaiming Feminism: Gender and Neoliberalism'. *IDS Bulletin* 39(6): 1–9.

Dasgupta, Biplab. 1984. 'Sharecropping in West Bengal: From Independence to Operation Barga'. *Economic and Political Weekly* 19(2): A85–96.

Ganguly, A. T. S. 2003. 'Feminisation of India's Agricultural Workforce'. *Labour Education* 2–3(131–32): 29–33.

Gartaula Hom Nath, Anke Niehof and Leontine Visser. 2011. 'Feminisation of Agriculture as an Effect of Male Out-migration: Unexpected Outcomes from Jhapa District, Eastern Nepal'. *International Journal of Interdisciplinary Social Sciences* 5(2): 565–77.

Ghose, A. K. (ed.). 1983. 'Agrarian Reform in West Bengal: Objectives, Achievements and Limitations'. In *Agrarian Reform in Contemporary Developing Countries*, 91–140. London and Canberra: Croom Helm.

Ghosh, Chitra. 1991. *Women Movement Politics in Bengal*. Calcutta: Chatterjee Publisher.

Government of India. 2011. 'Socio-economic Caste Census'. Ministry of Rural Development. Available at http://secc.gov.in/welcome (accessed 23 September 2016).

Guilmoto, Christophe Z. 2015. 'The Masculinisation of Births: Overview and Current Knowledge'. *Population* 70(2): 218.

Gupta, Jayoti. 2002. 'Women Second in the Land Agenda'. *Economic and Political Weekly* 37(18): 1746–54.

Kannan, K. P., and G. Raveendran. 2012. 'Counting and Profiling the Missing Labour Force'. *Economic and Political Weekly* 47(6): 77–80.

Kelkar, Govind. 2006. 'The Feminisation of Agriculture in Asia: Implications for Women's Agency and Productivity'. UNIFEM South Asia Regional Office, New Delhi, India.

Kok, Wessel. 2016. 'Village Life in Rural West Bengal: Progress, Power and Poverty in Uttar Khalpara'. Field report for WLE Project.

Lieten, G. K. 1992. *Continuity and Change in Rural West Bengal*. New Delhi: Sage Publications.

Mishra, Surjya Kanta. 2007. 'On Agrarian Transition in West Bengal'. *Marxist* 23(2): 1–22.

Moore, Henrietta L. 1988. *Feminism and Anthropology*. Cambridge: Polity Press.

Mukherjee, Neela. 2001. 'Migrant Women from West Bengal: Ill-being and Well-being'. *Economic and Political Weekly* 36(26): 2337–39.

NABARD Consultancy Service. 2009. 'State Agricultural Plan for West Bengal 2009'. Kolkata, West Bengal.

Oosterbaan, Lianne. 2016. 'Water, Land and Ecology: Agricultural Lives, Gender Inequality and Poverty in Madhya Khuttimari'. Field report for WLE Project,

Roy, Debal K. Singha. 1992. *Women in Peasant Movements: Tebhaga, Naxalite and After*. New Delhi: Manohar.

Roy, Sankar. 1992. 'Land, Labour and Politics: A Study of Agricultural Labourers in North Bengal'. Doctoral thesis submitted to Department of Sociology and Social Anthropology, University of North Bengal, Darjeeling.

Samanta, A. K. 1984. *Left Extremist Movement in West Bengal: An Experiment in Armed Agrarian Struggle*. Calcutta: Firma LKM Private Limited.

Sarkar, Shyamal Chandra. 2014. 'The Role of Women in Tebhaga Movement in Jalpaiguri District and to Preserve Their Identity'. *African Journal of History and Culture* 6(9): 175–82.

Savath, V., D. Fletschner and F. Santos. 2015. 'Land Titling and Women's Decision-making in West Bengal'. In *Global Trends in Land Tenure Reform: Gender Impacts*, eds C. S. Archambault and A. Zoomers, 127–45. Abingdon: Routledge.

Schenk-Sandbergen, Loes. 1988. *Poverty and Survival, Kudumbi Female Servants and Their Households in Alleppey (Kerala)*. New Delhi: Manohar.

———. 1991. 'Empowerment of Women: Its Scope in a Bilateral Development Project: A Small-scale Irrigation Project in North Bengal'. *Economic and Political Weekly* 26(17): 27–35.

———. 1998. 'Gender, Culture and Land Rights in Rural Lao PDR'. Gender Studies, Monograph 7, Gender and Development Program, School of Environmental Resources and Development, Asian Institute of Technology, Bangkok.

———. 2014. 'Remembering Professor Nirendra Chandra Choudhury: Empowerment in the Terai'. *Journal of the Indian Anthropological Society* 49(2–3): 185–201.

Schenk-Sandbergen, L., and N. Choudhury. 2003. *From Heroines to Beneficiaries; From Beneficiaries to Heroines?: The Impact of a Small-scale Irrigation Project on Gender in the West Bengal Terai*. New Delhi: Manohar Publications.

Sen, Sunil. 1985. *The Working Women and Popular Movements in Bengal from the Gandhi Era to the Present Day*. Calcutta: K. P. Bagchi and Company.

Sharma, Ursala. 1980. *Women, Work and Property in North-west India*. London: Tavistock Publications.

Shiva, V., and K. Jalees. 2005. 'Impact of WTO on Women in Agriculture'. Research Foundation for Science, Technology and Ecology, National Commission for Women.

Sugden, F., S. D. Silva, F. Clement, N. Maskey-Amaa, V. Ramesh, A. Philip and L. Bharati. 2014. 'A Framework to Understand Gender and Structural Vulnerability to Climate Change in the Ganges River Basin: Lessons from Bangladesh, India and Nepal'. IWMI Working Paper No. 159, 1–42.

van Andel, Merel. 2016. 'An Insight in Salbari in Times of Change: An Anthropological Study on Livelihoods, Agriculture and Gender Inequality'. Field report for WLE Project.

White, Ben. 2012. 'Agriculture and the Generation Problem: Rural Youth, Employment and the Future of Farming'. *IDS Bulletin* 43(6): 9–19.

World Bank. 2014. 'Improving Land Governance in West Bengal: State Report'. Land Governance Assessment Framework (LANDESA), World Bank Group, Washington, DC. Available at http://documents.worldbank.org/curated/en/400881504868859280/Land-governance-assessment-framework (accessed 24 September 2016).

16

Land Distribution among Scheduled Castes and Tribes*

B. B. Mohanty

In a country like India, where agriculture is the prime source of livelihood for a vast majority of people living in rural and tribal areas, land continues to be the pivotal property in terms of both income and employment around which socio-economic privileges and deprivations revolve. Though the members of the SCs and STs mostly reside in the countryside and derive their livelihood by working on land, they are the most disadvantaged in respect to land. The incidence of landlessness is more pronounced among these groups, the bulk of whom are agricultural labourers having minuscule holdings or are sharecroppers or other types of insecure tenants (Béteille 1972; Diwakar 1999; Mungekar 1999; Murdia 1975; Sharma 1994). A majority of SCs (77 per cent) and STs (90 per cent) are landless, without any productive assets and sustainable employment opportunities.[1] Around 87 per cent of the landholders of SCs and 65 per cent of STs in the country belong to the category of small and marginal farmers (Agricultural Census 1990–91). According to the Census of India 1991, 64 per cent of main workers from the SCs and 36 per cent from the STs were agricultural labourers, as against 31 per cent of others. It also reveals that 25 per cent of SCs and 55 per cent of STs were cultivators compared to 40 per cent of others. The poorest among the poor in Indian society are largely from these groups. As per the estimates of the Planning Commission, 48 per cent of the population of SCs and 51 per cent of STs are below the poverty line.[2]

In recognition of the basic proposition that poor land ownership position of the scheduled groups accounts largely for their perpetual poverty and makes them vulnerable to social injustice and exploitation, the Government of India has made a systematic endeavour to protect and promote their rights with regard to control and use of land through land reforms and allied measures. Land reforms have been treated as one of the principal instruments for the creation of an egalitarian rural society, in tune with the socialistic spirit, as provided in the Preamble and under Part-IV of the Constitution (Directive Principles of State Policy). It has also been

* Originally published in *Economic and Political Weekly*, 36(40), 6 October 2001: 3857–68.

included in the Ninth Schedule to ensure speedy and unhindered implementation of various legislative measures. However, land reform being a state subject, the legislative as well as the administrative responsibility devolve on states, and the Union government lays down only the general guidelines. Therefore, the nature of legislative measures and their implementation and achievement are likely to vary from state to state because they are influenced by the complex interaction of historical necessities and sociopolitical and economic forces, which are largely state or region-specific. In such a context, a comprehensive and comparative analysis of the legislative measures of various states relating to the land rights of scheduled groups and their consequent effects on land distribution is imperative, as these are issues of major policy concern. Though the question of control and use of land among the SCs and STs has not been left entirely out of scientific inquiry, it has received only occasional attention.[3] The non-availability of data on landholdings of these groups was possibly one of the reasons for this gap.

II

Rural Indian society is hierarchical and inequitous, and enmeshed in feudal ethos. In such a society, to be the born into a particular social group is to be the bearer of specific rights and obligations and to be involved in a specific pattern of relationship with members of other groups. Both the privileged and the deprived believe that men are born unequal (Béteille 1974; Nair 1961). In the words of J. Parry (1979: 6), 'the "encompassing ideology" of hierarchy permeates every sphere of social life, and even the subordination of the tenant to his landlord and of the subject to his rules is expressed in the same symbolic language'. Inequality and domination are treated as the basis of social relationship. The lower castes, as per their place in social hierarchy, are supposed to serve the dominant castes and remain loyal to them. To sustain their aristocratic status the dominant castes stay aloof from the subject population and its ascribed duties (Lieten and Srivastava 1999: 39). This has been the practice as far back as the history of Indian society can be traced. The tribals, who were initially within a relatively egalitarian and homogeneous social order with a separate sociocultural and ecological milieu of their own, came under the subservience and dominance of the rich non-tribals in due course through the 'civilising' and 'modernising' effects of colonialism and planning.[4] Viewed in this perspective, SCs and STs are the historically deprived and backward sections of Indian society who languish at the lower portions of the social and economic pyramid. In a society of this kind, where inequality and domination are deeply frozen in the social structure and in the psyche of the people, it is difficult to uplift and empower the deprived groups through legislative measures because any attempt to exercise the rights created by law is often to challenge the existing order of relations (Béteille 1974). The modes of living, working and the ideology that make up this stratification constitute very real inhibitions and obstacles, and the strength of the system is evidenced by the unwillingness of the underprivileged and exploited lower strata to challenge them (Myrdal 1972: 41).

Though the SCs and STs have a combined demographic strength of one-fourth of India's population—which is greater than the population of many countries—they have not been able to emerge as a powerful combination. They continue to be ruled by the dominant elites of the upper castes[5] because of their submissiveness, tolerance and survival-mindedness. The ruling minorities, who find the existing social order beneficial, remain apathetic or lukewarm towards issues concerning the upliftment and empowerment of the people at the lower rungs as it tends to challenge their spectral dominance. Though movements have emerged time and again among scheduled population, they were mostly sporadic, unorganised and fragmented, and were suppressed or diluted by the dominant groups through various strategies (Desai 1979; Omvedt 1974; Ranadive 1979). Nevertheless, many of these movements have enlightened the members of lower castes and tribes and also produced some perceptible changes in agrarian social relations (Dhanagare 1983; Kulkarni 1983; Patankar and Omvedt 1979,). Moreover, planning in India, like in other South Asian countries, which is viewed as a 'democratic planning' in popular notion is fundamentally a political programme through which the state tries to impress the masses in order to get their support without much coercion and regimentation (Myrdal 1972: 62). Therefore, the state representing the privileged minorities formulates policies that can concede the demands of the upper strata on the one side and produce the ideological effect that it is responsive to 'popular will' on the other. To quote Myrdal (1972: 44):

> ... the south-Asian planners remain in their paradoxical position: on a general and non-committal level they freely and almost passionately proclaim the need for radical social and economic change, whereas in planning their policies they tread most warily in order to not disrupt the traditional social order. And when they do legislate radical institutional reforms ... they permit laws to contain loopholes of all sorts and even let them unenforced.

Land distribution in India closely follows social hierarchy. While the large landowners invariably belong to the upper castes, the cultivators belong to the middle castes and the agricultural workers largely to the SCs and STs (Béteille 1972; Sankaran 1996). Land being the important socially valued asset, its unequal distribution helps maintain the hierarchical structure and strengthens the basis of dominance of the privileged groups by perpetuating inequality and deprivation in various socioeconomic spheres. Seen from this point, the idea of fair distribution of land directly strikes at the roots of such social relations. Therefore, the upper castes' landed interests have opposed legislative measures with respect to land redistribution through various methods (Hiro 1976; Joshi 1975; Judge 1999; Omvedt 1993). But when the magnitude of resistance of the deprived people challenges the existing order or shows signs of potential threat, the resultant change provokes reform measures. In an insensitive democracy like India, state action is identified with people's action and people's empowerment rests on their collective resistance and agitation. The measures to promote and protect the interests of the deprived are not usually expected without persistent demands and protracted struggles. Land reforms in India have been launched in response to compelling demands expressed through agitation, struggle and movements (Dhanagare 1983; Radhakrishnan 1989). But land reform policy being fundamentally a political issue, the state passes legislation only to pacify and neutralise the agrarian tension (Suri and Raghavulu 1996). In order to monitor the implementation of such measures, the existence of strong social movements is crucial. The entrenched dominant landowning privileged groups would never like to surrender their power and privilege without exertion on them of mounting pressure from the deprived people.

Against this backdrop, this chapter attempts to examine the aspects of land distribution among SCs and STs across the major states.[6] The paper has three objectives: (a) to review the legislative measures enacted for the protection and promotion of land rights of scheduled groups and to examine their achievements; (b) to analyse the changes in land distribution among scheduled groups; and (c) to find out the causes that hinder or facilitate the improvement of the land ownership position of scheduled groups.

III

British colonialism, through its land revenue policy and elaborate exploitative bureaucratic structure, made land alienable on a large scale, especially in tribal areas. The upper caste elites who were dominating each sphere of British administration consolidated their landowning position through the state machinery, de-peasantising the tribals and lower-caste peasants. The tribals, who were cultivating land and cleaning forests within their customary norms and practices without any experience of landlessness, were compelled to work as labourers in their own land and subjected to various kinds of oppression and exploitation. Gradually it generated strong discontentment, and the simmering tensions culminated in rebellions one after another. Among them the Chotanagpur tribal revolt (1807–08), the Munda rebellion (1832, 1867–90), the Kol rebellion (1831–32), the Santal rebellion (1885–86), the Rampa rebellion (1879–90), the Madri Kalo revolt (1898) and others posed a major threat to British administration in India in general and tribal areas in particular. Though many of these movements had religious and social issues, agrarian problems were the principal mobilising force.[7] Resistance of this nature made the British Raj conscious of the rebellious potentialities of the tribals and ultimately compelled them to initiate some measures to pacify tension in the tribal areas. Possibly as a result of this, the Chotanagpur Tenancy Act 1908, the Central Provinces Land Alienation Act 1916, the Bihar Tenancy Act 1885 and the Bombay Land Revenue Code (Section 73A) were enacted. However, these measures were formally undertaken only to suppress the tribal agitation, and the British did not show any interest in their proper implementation because the provisions of these acts were affecting the interests of the upper-caste elites who were mostly landlords, moneylenders, zamindars and other intermediaries of various kinds and the main agents of British administration in India. Despite the provision for prevention of land transfers from tribals to non-tribals, land alienation through debt mechanism, tenancy and other dishonest practices continued unabated in many parts of tribal India (Haimendorf 1945; Mohanty 1997; Patnaik 1971; Rao 1987).

The tribal movements that began in the first part of the twentieth century were mostly agrarian in nature. The Srirama Raju uprising (1922–24) in West Godavari; the Gond revolt (1940) in Adilabad and the Telangana revolt (1946–51) in Nalgonda, Karimnagar and Warangal districts of Andhra Pradesh; the Warli movement (1946–48) in Thane district of Maharashtra; the Santal agitation (1937–40) in Purnea, Bihar; the Munda rising (1936–39) in Sundergarh, Orissa and the Jharkhand movement that spread over the major tribal districts in Bihar, Orissa, West Bengal and Madhya Pradesh revolved around issues relating to land alienation and exploitation by non-tribal landlords and moneylenders. Apart from this, the Halipratha movement (1920–48) in Bulsar, Surat and Bharuch districts of Gujarat against the Patidars and Kanbi landlords; the tenants' struggle (1920–21 and 1930–35) in Pratapgarh, Rai Bareli, Faizabad and Sultanpur districts of Uttar Pradesh against the Mahajans, Banias and landed aristocracies; the Tanjore revolt (1946–49) of Tamil Nadu against the higher-caste landed gentry; the Tebhaga movement (1946–47) in Jalpaiguri, Dinajpur, Malda Rangpur, Midnapur and 24-Parganas of West Bengal against the landlords, and the Kisan Sabha activities in Andhra Pradesh, Bihar, West Bengal and other states put mounting pressure on the state to protect and promote the land rights of the poor tribals and lower-caste peasants (Das 1983; Dhanagare 1983; Ekka and Danda 1983). D. N. Dhanagare's (1983) study on important peasant movements in India confirms this firmly when he says: '... each of the movements that we have examined was followed by some legislative or ameliorative measures. Some legal reforms, some modifications in the structure of land control, always followed peasant resistance.' Besides, the social reform movements with anti-Brahminical overtones led by E. V. Ramaswamy Periyar in Tamil Nadu, Narayan Guru in Kerala, Jyotiba Phule and Ambedkar in Maharashtra and Sant Ramdas in Uttar Pradesh provided the lower castes with a distinct identity and awakened the government to recognise the rights of these deprived groups and to undertake measures for the removal of social injustice and exploitation (Patankar and Omvedt 1979; Ram 1979; Ranadive 1979).

As a consequence, land reforms became a necessary part of the process of national planning for the emancipation of these deprived people. All states without exception started showing interest in land redistribution, and formulated their own legislative measures to allot land as well as protect it from being transferred to non-scheduled groups. It is rightly commented that in the post-Independence period, India was subjected to the largest body of land reform legislation ever to have been passed in so short a period in any country (Thorner 1976: 18). A statewise list of legislative measures and executive orders for the protection and promotion of land rights of SCs and STs is illustrated in Table 16.1. An analysis reveals that in many states the measures undertaken to check the alienation of land of tribal and lower-caste peasants have not been adequately framed. Though provisions have been made to prevent land transfers from scheduled groups to non-scheduled groups, in many states (for example, Orissa, Madhya Pradesh, Rajasthan, Gujarat and Kerala) such transfers can be made with the prior permission of the competent authority (collector, sub-divisional officer, among others), which ultimately left the implementation of these measures to the discretion of the bureaucrats and also made them more powerful. It has also been pointed out[8] that the rich upper castes do not find any difficulty in getting the permission of the concerned officials, and sometimes the members of scheduled groups are required to spend a certain amount for this purpose. Similarly, in Maharashtra, for example, land under new tenure could be leased out if the government is satisfied that the owner is physically incapable of tilling it. It is found that many big landowners produced medical certificates purporting to establish the incapability of tribals to cultivate their land and managed to get these lands on lease for fixed periods, after which land is seldom returned to the tribals (Murdia 1975). In Rajasthan, as per the Rajasthan Tenancy Act, land belonging to scheduled groups if transferred to non-scheduled groups can be restored provided it is brought to the notice of the government within 12 years (earlier it was only three years). As a result, the powerful landowners suppressed the facts through various means up to the restricted time period. There is rare legislative provision to check informal land transfers. Provisions are only limited to the legal ownership rights. In many cases though the land is owned by a tribal it is occupied and cultivated by non-tribals. The tribals, because of their ignorance and lack of awareness of land laws, accept the claims of the dominant non-tribals. In spite of the legislative and executive measures taken by various state governments, alienation of tribal land is reported by many studies (Haimendorf 1982; Mohanty 1997; Patel 1974; Pathy 1984; Rao 1987).

TABLE 16.1: Agrarian Legislation for Protection and Promotion of Land Rights of SCs and STs

States	*Legislative Measures*	*Description*
Andhra Pradesh	The Agency Tracts Interest and Land Transfer Act 1917.	Checks transfers of land in the agency tracts in the then composite state of Madras.
	The Andhra Pradesh Scheduled Areas and Land Transfer Regulation 1959 (amended in 1963).	Makes all transfers of ST land without the previous sanction of competent authority null and void.
	The Andhra Pradesh Scheduled Areas Land (Extension and Amendment) Regulation 1963.	Extends to scheduled areas of the Telangana region. Till then it covered the scheduled areas of the Andhra region.
Bihar	Bihar Tenancy Act 1885.	Prohibits transfer of land by certain aboriginal tenure holders, *raiyat*s or under raiyats.
	Chotanagpur Tenancy Act 1908.	Prevent transfer of land of STs, SCs and OBCs.
	Santal Parganas Act 1949.	Restores the illegally alienated land beyond 12 years but within 30 years of its alienation.
	Bihar Scheduled Areas Regulation 1969.	The government has issued instructions to allot waste or vacant lands in *khasmahal* or acquired zamindaris to SCs, STs and OBCs.

(Contd)

Table 16.1 (Contd)

States	Legislative Measures	Description
Gujarat	Bombay Land Revenue Code 1879 (Section 73A).	Prohibits transfer of land held by members of STs without the permission of the collector.
	The state government added more provisions in Bombay LR Code 1879, vide the Bombay Land Revenue Act 1980.	Restricts the transfers of occupancies of STs all over the state. The SCs and STs are given high priority in the grant of waste lands.
Karnataka	Hyderabad Tenancy and Agricultural Land Act 1950.	Provides security of land tenure to all agricultural tenants, including SCs and STs. In the Coorg area, the executive measures make provisions to transfer land permanently to SC and ST tenants, if they have been in the occupation for 12 years. The state government prohibits the alienation of lands allotted to SCs and STs for 35 years without its permission.
	Mysore Land Revenue (Amendment) Rule 1960.	Assigns land to members of SCs and STs and the land so assigned cannot be alienated for 15 years without the permission of the state government. Fifty per cent of the available land for allotment is reserved for SCs and STs.
	Scheduled Castes and Scheduled Tribes (Prohibition of Transfer of Certain Lands) Act, 1978 (Act No. 2 of 1978).	Prohibits alienation of lands granted under the Land Grant Rules, to persons belonging to SCs and STs and provides for resumption of such alienated lands and imposes penalty on the purchasers (up to six months or fine of Rs 200 or both).
Kerala	Kerala Scheduled Tribes (Restriction on Transfer of Lands and Restoration of Alienated Lands) Act 1973 (came into force from 1 January 1982).	Prohibits the alienation of land by STs to non-STs.
	Kerala Arable Forest Land Assignment Rules 1970.	States that land assigned is inheritable but not alienable for a period of five years from the date of assignment. One-third of the available land in each district should be allotted to members of SCs and STs.
	Kerala Land Assignment Rules 1964.	Provides that members of SCs can transfer their land to both SCs and STs, but STs can transfer only to STs with the prior permission of concerned authority. Twenty-five per cent of land available for assignment is allotted to SCs and STs.

(Contd)

Table 16.1 (Contd)

States	*Legislative Measures*	*Description*
Madhya Pradesh	Central Provinces Land Alienation Act 1916.	Checks the unwanted transfer of land of STs.
	Madhya Bharat Scheduled Areas (Allotment and Transfer of Land) Regulation 1954 (applicable to Madhya Bharat region only).	Restricts transfer of land of STs to non-STs without the prior permission of collector by way of sale, mortgage, lease or otherwise. The SCs and STs have been given third and fourth priority, respectively, for the allotment of government land among the landless. Freedom fighters and army personnel have been given first and second priority, respectively.
	Madhya Pradesh Land Revenue Codes 1959.	Provides protection to STs against alienation of their lands.
Maharashtra	The Maharashtra Land Revenue Code and Tenancy Laws (Amendment) Act 1974.	Restores agricultural land of the ST person involved in illegal transfer to a non-scheduled tribal effected any time before 6 July 1974.
	The Maharashtra Restoration of Land to the Scheduled Tribes Act 1974; Maharashtra Land Revenue Code 1966 (Section 36); Bombay Tenancy and Agricultural Lands Act 1948; Bombay Tenancy and Assignment Lands Act (Vidarbha Region) Act 1958; Hyderabad Tenancy and Agricultural Lands Act 1950.	Make provisions for restoration of agricultural land of STs lawfully transferred to a non-ST by way of sale mortgage, gift, etc., between 1 April 1957 and 6 July 1974. The government issued executive orders on 4 January 1961 for the disposal of land among SCs and STs as the first and second priority, respectively. But in areas other than scheduled areas they have been accorded only seventh priority. Prohibit the transfer of agricultural land of SC and ST person by sale, gift, mortgage, etc., in favour of non-scheduled groups.
Orissa	Orissa Scheduled Areas Transfer of Immovable Property (by Scheduled Tribes) Regulation 1956 (amended in 1963).	Prohibits transfer of lands from members of STs to non-STs in the scheduled areas.
	Orissa Land Reform Act 1960 (amended in 1973).	Restricts STs and SCs to sell their land to non-SCs and non-STs unless permitted by the sub-divisional officer.
	Executive Measure (there is no legislation relating to the allotment of land to SCs and STs)	The government has issued notifications for the settlement and lease of waste and encroached lands in the state in which SCs and STs have been given first and second priority, respectively. They are required to file applications before the local tehsildars for the allotment of such lands.

(Contd)

Table 16.1 (Contd)

States	*Legislative Measures*	*Description*
Punjab*	Not available	The Government of Punjab has issued orders banning transfer of land belonging to SCs. All types of surplus evacuee lands are disposed of through restricted auction to the members of SCs.
Rajasthan	Rajasthan Tenancy Act 1955.	Prohibits transfer of land from SCs and STs to non-STs without permission from competent authority. Land if transferred to others can be restored provided it is brought to the notice of the government within three years.
	Rajasthan Registration (Adoption Amendment) Ordinance 1975.	A notification has been issued under the ordinance that transfer of agricultural holdings from STs to non-STs or from a SC to a non-SC person is against public policy.
	Rajasthan Land Revenue (allotment of land for agricultural purpose) Rules 1957	Reserves 25 per cent of the available land for allotment to SCs, STs and OBCs.
	Rajasthan Bhoodan Yagna Act 1954	Makes available one-third of the land for distribution to the members of SCs/STs.
Tamil Nadu**	The Holdings (Stay of Execution Proceedings) Act 1950.	Protects STs rights in land and contains provisions for assignment of land to hill tribes. Landless poor Harijans are eligible for assignment of cultivable wasteland up to 5 acres in case of dryland and 2.5 acres in case of wetlands. STs are assigned a maximum of 10 acres of dryland and 5 acres of wetland in hilly tracts if sufficient land is available. Land assigned to the SCs cannot be alienated for 10 years and thereafter it can be transferred to SCs only.
Uttar Pradesh	Uttar Pradesh Zamindari Abolition and Land Rules Act 1950 (amended in 1969).	Restricts the transfer of lands of the members of STs to members of non-STs by way of sale, gift, mortgage or lease without the prior permission of the collector.
	Section 198 and Rule 174-A of Zamindari Abolition and Land Reforms Act 1952.	Gives priority to SCs in land allotment.
	Section 1(A) and Rule 24A(2) of UP Consolidation of Holdings Act 1953; Sections 27 and 28 of the UP Imposition of Ceilings of Land Holdings Act 1960.	Make provisions for the allotment of surplus land to the SCs.

(Contd)

Table 16.1 (Contd)

States	*Legislative Measures*	*Description*
West Bengal	The Bengal Tenancy Act 1885.	Restricts transfer of land of an aboriginal tenure holder, '*raiyat*' or under raiyat by private sale, gift, mortgage, lease or any contract or agreement unless it is transferred to another tribal included in the list. It gives priorities to SCs and STs holding not more than 2 acres of land for the distribution of government lands including *khas* land.
	West Bengal Land Reform Act 1955 (amended from time to time).	Imposes restrictions on the alienation of lands of STs and makes provision for its restoration.

Notes: * Information on legislative measures not available. The cited information is provided in Murdia (1975).
** In Tamil Nadu, there is no special legislative measure to provide protection to SCs and STs against alienation of land and to give them preferential treatment in the allotment of land.

Sources: Dubey and Murdia (1977); Patel (1974); *Report of the Commissioner for Scheduled Castes and Scheduled Tribes*, various issues.

The data on alienation and restoration of tribal lands in some states is depicted in Table 16.2. It is found that in Andhra Pradesh, Bihar, Gujarat, Karnataka, Madhya Pradesh and Maharashtra, land alienation among the tribals is remarkably higher both in terms of area and number. Excepting Gujarat, in other states a large number of registered land alienation cases have been rejected and many of them are also pending in court. While in Rajasthan 29 per cent of the registered cases have been decided in favour of tribals, in Orissa it is 31 per cent. Moreover, many of the land alienation cases are also unreported and unregistered. In states like Orissa, where the tribals and lower-caste peasants are backward on many counts, land alienation is widespread. There are a number of villages in tribal Orissa where all

TABLE 16.2: Information on Alienation and Restoration of Tribal Lands (as of November 1999)

States	*No. of Cases Filed in Court*		*Percentage of Cases Rejected*		*Percentage of Cases Decided in Favour of Tribals*		*Percentage of Cases Pending in Court*	
	No.	*Area (acres)*	*No.*	*Area (acres)*	*No.*	*Area (acres)*	*No.*	*Area (acres)*
Andhra Pradesh	65,875	287,776	48.18	52.20	40.19	36.91	11.63	10.88
Bihar	86,291	104,893	36.95	47.41	51.72	43.30	11.33	9.29
Gujarat	47,926	140,324	0.25	0.35	84.05	85.65	15.70	13.99
Karnataka	42,582	130,373	39.19	36.17	51.28	52.05	9.54	11.78
Madhya Pradesh	53,806	158,398	55.05	61.32	n/a	n/a	44.95	38.68
Maharashtra	45,634	n/a	54.08	n/a	43.70	n/a	2.21	n/a
Orissa	1,431	1,712	10.62	11.92	30.89	35.75	58.49	52.34
Rajasthan	651	2,300	8.14	8.13	28.73	25.52	63.13	66.35

Source: *Annual Report 1999–2000*, Ministry of Rural Development, Government of India.

the villagers are landless. For example, the entire land in a village in Koraput district is owned by a Keralite who operates a business farm in Thiruvananthapuram, and the management of the land is left to a non-tribal middleman (Mohanty 1997: 7).

The measures relating to allotment of land to SCs and STs are also inadequate. It is true that many states give preference to scheduled groups in the distribution of surplus land or government wasteland. But, in some states the preference is limited to scheduled areas. For example, in Maharashtra, these categories have been accorded only the seventh priority in areas other than scheduled ones. On the other hand, Madhya Pradesh gives first priority to freedom fighters and army personnel and the SCs and STs have been given third and fourth priority. In Rajasthan, only 25 per cent of the available land is reserved for scheduled groups. In Punjab, though the allotment is made exclusively to SCs, it depends upon their financial condition whether they avail such facility because land was disposed of through auction. Added to this, the procedures followed by most state governments require the eligible persons to submit their applications in the prescribed form to the concerned officers. In many places the members of SCs and STs are not aware of the procedures and formalities and being illiterate they find difficulty in filling the forms.

The availability of ceiling surplus land and its proper distribution is one of the major routes through which SCs and STs can improve their holding position. Though there is a national guideline, each state has fixed its own ceiling limits keeping in view 'local' considerations (Table 16.3). While some states have fixed the limit for various types of land uniformly for all districts, in states like Bihar,

TABLE 16.3: Ceiling Limits on Landholdings (in Hectares)

	Irrigated with Two Crops	*Irrigated with One Crop*	*Dryland*
Suggested in the National Guidelines of 1972	4.05–7.28	10.93	21.85
Actual ceilings across states			
Andhra Pradesh	4.05–7.28	6.07–10.93	16–21.85
Bihar	6.07–7.28	10.12	12.14–18.21
Gujarat	4.05–7.29	6.07–10.93	8.09–21.85
Karnataka	4.05–8.10	10.12–12.14	21.85
Kerala	4.86–6.07	4.86–6.07	4.86–6.07
Madhya Pradesh	7.28	10.93	21.85
Maharashtra	7.28	10.93	21.85
Orissa	4.05	6.07	12.14–18.21
Punjab	7.00	11.00	20.50
Rajasthan	7.28	10.93	21.85–70.82
Tamil Nadu	4.86	12.14	24.28
Uttar Pradesh	7.30	10.95	18.25
West Bengal	5.00	5.00	7.00

Source: *Agricultural Statistics at a Glance 1993*, Government of India, New Delhi.

Andhra Pradesh, Gujarat, Karnataka and Kerala it varies depending upon the 'local' agro-climatic conditions. West Bengal and Kerala have the lowest ceiling limits. On the other hand, Rajasthan has the highest limit, which is justified for its 'hilly terrain and desert area'. Moreover, except West Bengal, ceiling limits in all other states are dependent upon crop potential. This kind of fixation of ceiling limit creates enormous difficulty in the appropriate categorisation of land which gives ample scope to the dominant big landowners to avoid the ceiling laws by wrongly categorising the land in connivance with local officials (Deshpande 1998). It is also reported from several parts of the country[9] that the large landholders have avoided the ceiling laws by partitioning their families in the land record while cultivating the land jointly.

Following the implementation of ceiling laws, each state has declared surplus land and tried to distribute it to the landless (Table 16.4). The ceiling surplus land is remarkably higher in West Bengal, which is largely due to its lower limits. In many states a significant proportion of surplus land has not been taken under possession. In Karnataka, only 59 per cent of the surplus area has come under possession. In almost all the states a considerable part of the area which has been taken under possession is not distributed. While in Karnataka only 42 per cent of the area declared surplus

TABLE 16.4: Progress in Implementation of Ceiling Laws (as of March 1996)

States	*Area Declared Surplus (Acres)*	*Percentage of Area Taken Possession*	*Percentage of Area Distributed to Area Declared Surplus Possession*	*Beneficiaries (Per Cent)*					
				No.			*Area*		
				SC	*ST*	*Others*	*SC*	*ST*	*Others*
Andhra Pradesh	800,240	78.91	70.87	41.54	15.58	42.88	39.67	20.75	39.58
Bihar	488,257	81.45	62.03	61.70	11.38	26.93	59.09	12.97	27.94
Gujarat	231,172	68.76	57.65	44.38	39.75	15.87	62.13	21.85	16.03
Karnataka	280,779	59.11	42.29	60.33	3.10	36.57	60.72	3.05	36.22
Kerala	137,692	68.85	46.69	42.85	5.12	52.03	39.20	8.03	52.77
Madhya Pradesh	338,555	88.30	54.71	29.85	37.43	32.73	26.68	39.70	33.62
Maharashtra	729,644	90.93	76.05	29.84	20.78	49.38	29.14	17.65	53.20
Orissa	176,569	93.57	87.11	33.93	37.25	28.82	31.80	41.92	26.27
Punjab	132,594	79.09	77.84	39.95	–	60.05	42.53	–	57.47
Rajasthan	600,987	92.88	75.13	41.90	1.25	56.85	32.14	9.77	58.09
Tamil Nadu	191,311	89.44	83.29	44.16	0.14	55.71	38.38	0.15	61.47
Uttar Pradesh	555,350	93.84	69.13	69.33	0.23	30.43	67.56	0.38	32.06
West Bengal	1,270,965	94.57	75.66	37.22	19.51	43.27	37.24	19.37	43.39
All India	7,884,132	83.68	65.85	36.20	14.08	49.71	35.60	14.40	50.00

Source: *Rural Development Statistics 1999*, National Institute of Rural Development, Hyderabad.

has been distributed, in Kerala it comes to 47 per cent. Apart from this, though the national guideline suggests that 50 per cent of the land to be distributed through land reform measures should be made available to SC and ST beneficiaries, the distribution pattern in states like Tamil Nadu, Rajasthan, Punjab, Maharashtra and Kerala reveals a bias in favour of non-scheduled groups. Of course, in Kerala, the population of SCs and STs is much lower than in other states (10 per cent; Table 16.5). But in states like Rajasthan and Punjab where the population of scheduled groups comes to around 30 per cent, the percentage of allotted land is much lower. It is also reported that in many places 'pattas' are not issued to them even after several years of allotment of land (Murdia 1975: 1211), which invariably leads to several kinds of litigation. Even land already distributed had to be denotified in many cases, causing considerable hardship to the assignees who had invested their resources.[10]

TABLE 16.5: Distribution of SCs and STs Population (per cent)

States	*SCs*		*STs*	
	1981	*1991*	*1981*	*1991*
Andhra Pradesh	14.87	15.93	5.93	6.31
Bihar	14.51	14.56	8.31	7.66
Gujarat	7.15	7.41	14.23	14.92
Karnataka	15.07	16.38	4.91	4.26
Kerala	10.01	9.12	1.03	1.10
Madhya Pradesh	14.10	14.54	22.97	23.27
Maharashtra	7.14	11.10	9.19	9.27
Orissa	14.66	16.20	22.43	22.21
Punjab	26.87	28.31	–	–
Rajasthan	17.04	17.29	12.21	12.44
Tamil Nadu	18.35	19.18	1.07	1.03
Uttar Pradesh	21.16	21.04	0.21	0.21
West Bengal	21.99	23.62	5.62	5.60
All India*	15.81	16.73	7.83	7.95

Note: *Excludes Assam and Jammu and Kashmir.

Sources: Census of India 1991: Primary Census Abstract Scheduled Castes, Series-I, Part II-B (ii); Census of India 1991: Primary Census Abstract Scheduled Tribe Population Series I, Part II-B (iii).

Looking at the reasons why the surplus area is not available for distribution (Table 16.6), it is found that litigation withholds a major part of the land in almost all the states. Sizeable areas in Karnataka, Gujarat, Punjab, Andhra Pradesh, Tamil Nadu, Madhya Pradesh, Orissa and West Bengal have gone out of the total quantum of surplus land as a result of court decisions. It is disheartening to note that a significant portion of the area declared as ceiling surplus in many states is either unfit for cultivation or not available for distribution due to 'miscellaneous reasons'. Of the area not available for distribution, 57 per cent is unfit for cultivation in Uttar Pradesh and 41 per cent in Bihar accounts for 'miscellaneous reasons'.

TABLE 16.6: Reasonwise Area Not Available for Distribution, as of March, 1996 (Per Cent)

States	*Area Involved in Litigation*	*Area Reserved for Public Purpose*	*Area Unfit for Cultivation*	*Area Not Available for Miscellaneous Reasons*	*Total*
Andhra Pradesh	68.51	10.00	4.57	16.92	100.00
Bihar	47.94	0.98	10.22	40.86	100.00
Gujarat	85.44	12.36	2.19	–	100.00
Karnataka	92.21	6.77	1.02	–	100.00
Kerala	39.60	28.80	–	31.60	100.00
Madhya Pradesh	63.24	19.47	13.31	3.98	100.00
Maharashtra	20.00	57.59	10.29	12.12	100.00
Orissa	58.57	13.03	8.02	20.38	100.00
Punjab	85.45	–	–	14.55	100.00
Rajasthan	51.36	48.64	–	–	100.00
Tamil Nadu	67.45	32.55	–	–	100.00
Uttar Pradesh	33.10	7.66	56.57	2.67	100.00
West Bengal	56.82	25.31	17.87	–	100.00
All India	48.02	21.26	20.80	9.92	100.00

Source: *Rural Development Statistics 1999*, National Institute of Rural Development, Hyderabad.

The land obtained and distributed through the Bhoodan movement initiated by Vinoba Bhave provides some interesting information (Table 16.7). Though a sizeable amount of land was available under the scheme in some states, a large amount of this land is not distributed. In Andhra Pradesh, Bihar, Orissa and Maharashtra the proportion of land allotted was only 47.14, 25.71, 12.39 and 0.69 per cent,

TABLE 16.7: Allotment of Bhoodan Land

States	*Total Land Received (Acres)*	*Percentage of Land Allotted*	*Beneficiaries*					
			No.			*Area*		
			SC	*ST*	*Others*	*SC*	*ST*	*Others*
Andhra Pradesh (as on 31 December 1981)	195,509	47.14	35.91	8.36	55.73	28.52	14.33	57.15
Bihar (as on 21 March 1981)	2,117,756	25.71	27.83	22.91	49.26	29.28	29.60	41.12
Punjab (as on 31 March 1981)	9,801	100.00	84.70	–	15.30	95.30	–	4.70
Maharashtra (as on 31 March 1981)	88,462	0.69	56.83	18.06	21.11	57.17	15.80	27.04
Orissa (as on 31 March 1981)	1,346,966	12.39	21.77	45.63	32.60	22.56	58.01	19.44

Source: *Report of the Commissioner for Scheduled Castes and Scheduled Tribes, April 1980–March 1981.*

respectively. It is rightly commented that land amounting to only 0.27 per cent of India's 320 million acres of cultivable area were actually distributed, and some of it had been donated by poor farmers themselves.[11] The religious content[12] of the Bhoodan movement appealed to many of the religiously oriented poor rural Indians to contribute their small holdings. More than 43 per cent of land collected through this scheme (up to March 1968) from various states had been found either unsuitable for cultivation or under dispute (Murdia 1975: 1211). It was also found that in some regions many of the persons who were reported to have donated lands refused later (Francis 1996: 60; Vyasulu 1985: 65). The donated lands were by and large of inferior types requiring substantial investment to make them worthy of cultivation (Mohapatro 1987: 17; Tai 1974: 14).

It appears, as pointed out by a number of studies (Appu 1996; Deshpande 1998; Mearns 1998; Murdia 1975; Patel 1974), that the inherent loopholes and ambiguities in the legislative measures, slow proceedings at all levels of bureaucracy, lack of updated land records, the ignorance and illiteracy of the scheduled population and the escaping attitude of the large landowners are the major reasons that hinder fair distribution of land by allowing the bulk of landowners to avoid expropriation. Even a slow process of passing of the land to SCs and STs and its resultant upliftment becomes intolerable and non-acceptable to the dominant groups. They resist the allotment of land by committing atrocities on members of SCs and STs through well-organised groups, like the Ranvir Sena, Brahmarsi Sena, Bhumi Sena and Lorik Sena. In Bihar, a number of Dalits have been killed by the Ranvir Sena alone in recent years owing to issues relating to land allotment (Diwakar 1999: 75). Evidence of this type of inclement resistance abounds across the states. Because of this problem the poor SC and ST person finds it difficult to occupy the land after allotment. While describing the situation in Andhra Pradesh, S. R. Sankaran (1996: 23) writes, 'Even after the land is allotted to the poor, ensuring physical possession of it becomes a major problem, for the landlords often thwart the efforts of the poor by involving them in litigation or used threats or other coercive methods in preventing them from cultivating the land allotted to them'. Sometimes small and unorganised groups, with the tacit approbation of the powerful upper-caste landowners, forcibly grab the allotted land or throw the members of SCs and STs out of their encroached wasteland or evict them from the leased lands through atrocities ranging from setting fire to their huts to brutal murders, mostly in league with the police and the administration. Many such cases are reported from Uttar Pradesh, Bihar, Rajasthan and Madhya Pradesh.[13]

IV

The analysis of changes in the operated area among the scheduled groups would explain in more detail the achievements of land reform measures and the emerging pattern of land distribution. However, as data on operational holdings of scheduled communities is available only from 1980–81 to 1990–91, it is difficult to assess the impact of legislative measures entirely because many of these measures were undertaken in the late 1960s and early 1970s. Besides, the effects of land transfers through market mechanism also cannot be ignored.[14] Nevertheless, the trend of operational holdings (Table 16.8) will make the analysis of the aspects of land distribution more meaningful.

TABLE 16.8: Distribution of Operational Holdings among SCs and STs (Per Cent)

States	*SCs*				*STs*			
	No.		*Area*		*No.*		*Area*	
	1980–81	*1990–91*	*1980–81*	*1990–91*	*1980–81*	*1990–91*	*1980–81*	*1990–91*
Andhra Pradesh	12.62	12.70	6.87	7.50	6.42	6.90	6.29	7.20
Bihar	8.16	11.60	4.51	5.20	7.54	7.80	16.25	16.10
Gujarat	4.06	4.10	3.08	3.20	10.92	11.00	8.05	9.10
Karnataka	8.49	11.00	5.99	8.10	3.71	4.90	3.47	5.00
Kerala	8.54	9.60	2.44	2.80	0.98	1.20	1.50	1.90
Madhya Pradesh	12.85	12.60	7.93	8.10	25.11	24.70	24.84	25.20
Maharashtra	6.81	8.00	4.48	6.00	6.02	6.70	6.08	7.30
Orissa	12.17	13.70	7.86	8.60	27.58	26.60	29.90	28.70
Punjab	5.00	4.80	2.54	2.40	0.00	0.00	0.00	0.00
Rajasthan	14.26	14.70	11.31	11.70	15.36	15.40	8.35	8.40
Tamil Nadu	7.84	11.30	4.92	7.10	0.67	0.80	1.01	1.20
Uttar Pradesh	14.77	16.40	9.24	10.50	0.16	0.20	0.28	0.30
West Bengal	23.58	23.20	19.37	19.70	7.08	7.30	6.59	7.00
All India	11.31	12.50	7.03	7.90	7.71	8.10	10.20	10.80

Note: Figures are in per cent to the total number and area operated of each state.
Source: Agricultural Census Reports; figures for 1990–91 taken from *Agricultural Situation in India*.

Looking at the area operated during 1980–81 and 1990–91, it is found that the landholding position of these communities has not improved considerably even after more than five decades of planned efforts and initiatives. In many states the number of holdings and area operated by the SCs and STs is poor compared with their demographic strength (Table 16.5). However, in West Bengal, though the progress between 1980–81 and 1990–91 was negligible the landholding position of scheduled groups both in terms of area as well as number is much better than any other state. The SCs, constituting 23 per cent of the state's population, control more than 23 per cent of holdings covering 20 per cent of the operated area. Similarly, the tribals are also was well ahead of their counterparts in other states. The success is largely attributed to the Tebhaga and Naxalbari movements that spread across the districts and the consequent activities of a left-of-centre party. Though these movements were not explicitly directed against the upper castes, it could combine the landless and poor people in the rural areas through a common forum against the propertied class and the local landed power holders who were mostly from upper castes (Dasgupta 1973; Mukherji 1987). The emerging situation generated tremendous awareness among the deprived people of their own rights vis-à-vis the caste and class enemies. The level of political mobilisation as well as participation by the lower castes in this state is higher than elsewhere (Harriss 1999).

The states where the share of scheduled groups to total area operated is less compared with their population but have shown a noticeable improvement over the years are Tamil Nadu, Maharashtra and Karnataka. Tamil Nadu, with 19 per cent of SCs population has provided only 7 per cent of its operated area (1990–91) to these communities and compared with 1980–81, it has increased by more than 2 per cent. Likewise, in Karnataka, though the SCs, constituting 16 per cent of the state's population control only 8 per cent of the operated area both the number and area have increased by almost 3 per cent in the past 10 years. The position of STs has also improved considerably. Similarly, compared with their population,[15] the operated area of SCs in Maharashtra is also less but it has increased from 4 per cent in 1980–81 to 6 per cent in 1990–91. The operated area of STs also increased by more than 1 per cent during this period.

The improvement in the landholding position of scheduled groups in Tamil Nadu is primarily due to the fact that the upper-caste dominance in the state has effectively been challenged. Periyar's self-respect movement and the subsequent Dravidian movement led by the DMK, a regional party which propagated Tamil cultural rationalism, successfully mobilised the lower castes against the dominant upper castes. The achievement in Karnataka is also due to the emergence of strong Dalit movements. The districts that are included in Karnataka from Madras Presidency had exposure to a non-Brahmin movement, which was based on a wider mass mobilisation (Pani 1998: 68). The Dalit movement in Karnataka systematically started in 1968 with the emergence of the Bheem Sena under the leadership of Shyam Sunder, which went to the extent of demanding a separate land for untouchables called 'Dalitstan' (Shyam Sunder 1987: 13–15, as cited in Yadav 1998). The subsequent leadership of Basavalingappa mobilised the lower castes effectively (Yadav 1998: 115). The Dalit agitation against their oppressors in Karnataka became more active from 1973 with the emergence of the Dalit Sangharsha Samiti, a forum that educated and organised the Dalits. It became organisationally the strongest and most long-lasting Dalit movement in the country (Omvedt 1974: 337). Similarly, Maharashtra's better performance is attributed to the lower-caste and tribal movements (Kulkarni 1983; Rajasekaran 1998). Though the Satyashodhak Samaj movement was started on a social issue, it subsequently extended its coverage to the inequality in the distribution of land. The mass mobilisation by Ambedkar and the recent efforts of the Republican Party of India challenged the dominance of the upper castes and ascertained the rights of the SCs. Besides, the organised agitations of Bhil tribals in Dhule and Gadchiroli districts under the banner of Shramik Sanghatana movement during 1970–74 against tribal land alienation and the Warli movement of Koli tribals in Thane district against serf-tenure contributed towards the improvement in the proportion of operated area among the STs in the state.

Andhra Pradesh, Gujarat and Uttar Pradesh report a slow process of improvement despite their poor landholding position of SCs and STs. The SCs, with 16 per cent of the state's population, control only 7.5 per cent of the operated area in Andhra Pradesh. Compared with 1980–81, in 1990–91 the increase is less than 0.5 per cent. However, the state shows a relatively better result in the case of STs, which can be attributed to the historic Telangana movement and the contemporary Naxalite movement in the tribal pockets. The slow progress with regard to SCs is mainly due to the persistent dominance of forward castes in the state. The reason seems to be the absence of a strong and independent lower-caste movement in the state. Though there were some protests like the Adi-Andhra movement in some parts of coastal Andhra such as Rajahmundry, East Godavari and Vijayawada, they faded away after the late 1940s. The early peasant organisations like Kisan Sabha also did not project caste as a special issue in the distribution of land (Omvedt 1994: 288). Though a few backward class movements such as the Munnuru Kapu and the Padmashali movement under the leadership of Bojjam Narasimhulu and Konda Lakshman Bapuji were launched in Hyderabad state, after the formation of Andhra Pradesh they were merged into one, known as the Andhra Pradesh Backward Classes Association, and largely confined their agitation to reservation issues. The forward castes continue to dominate the society and politics of Andhra Pradesh (Harriss 1999; Reddy 1989). The same could be said for Gujarat. Here, the grip of the upper castes (Brahmins, Banias and Kshatriyas) has remained strong and their dominance extends over wide areas (Harriss 1999; Rutten 1995; Wood 1984). Ghanshyama Shah (1998: 265) rightly observed on Gujarat, 'While different classes cutting across caste boundaries are being formed, class consciousness as such is yet to develop. This situation works in favour of the upper classes of the dominant castes in perpetuating their hold over society.' He also pointed out that legislations were not rigorously implemented in Gujarat because of the implicit interference by the Patidar and Bania-Brahmin landlords who otherwise would have been adversely affected (ibid.: 233).

The rate of improvement in the landholding position of the scheduled groups in Uttar Pradesh is relatively better than these two states. With a population of 21 per cent the SCs operated 10.5 per cent of the area in 1990–91 as against 9.2 per cent in 1980–81. This comparatively better achievement was possible because the SCs are relatively organised in this state through the Dalit-based political parties like Bahujan Samaj Party (Duncan 1999; Omvedt 1998). Bihar and Uttar Pradesh are the core states of the Hindi heartland, where the upper castes are more numerous and have a strong dominance. Any measure in these states that aims for the upliftment of the lower castes is challenged by upper castes. This is one of the reasons why adoption of the recommendations of the Backward Classes Commission by the V. P. Singh government in 1990 witnessed violent protests in these states. The allotment of land to backward communities in these states leads to several atrocities on them by the powerful among the rural oligarchy.

The strong dominance and organised resistance of the upper castes primarily accounts for Bihar's poor performance in land reforms with respect to scheduled groups. Though the operated area of the SCs has increased marginally, the position of STs has gone down further. The SCs do not have an organised identity in the state. An attempt was made to build a mass movement in the 1940s through the formation of the Bihar State Backward Classes Federation under the leadership of Chandapuri, but it became weak after 1950 by the 'accommodation' strategy of the Congress Party (Frankel 1989: 84–85). Except the increasing incidences of caste-based conflict and violence, the SCs could not coordinate their efforts to organise a mass movement. Though the ruling Rashtriya Janata Dal is organising the lower castes, the major share of the benefits goes to the 'OBC group' such as the Koeris, Kurmis and Yadavs (Jaffrelot 2000; Wilkinson 2000: 788). Commenting on the performance of Bihar, P. S. Appu (1993) has stated:

> Bihar's dismal performance in the field of land reforms has been largely due to the overbearing sway of large landlords over rural society and their dominant influence over the state's politics and administration. Moreover, the legal system is heavily tilted against the disadvantaged, and there is a lack of organisation on the part of potential beneficiaries. Without a radical transformation ... there is no reason to expect any marked improvement in the implementation of land reforms ... As a result of the awakening that has taken place in some parts of rural Bihar in the wake of social mobilisation spearheaded by diverse groups of political activities, the weaker sections are becoming conscious of their rights ... Such a development may lead to better implementation of land reform laws.

Though the scheduled groups' population is around 40 per cent in Orissa and Madhya Pradesh and 30 per cent in Rajasthan, their operational holding position is extremely poor compared with many other states. While the operated area belonging to SCs has increased marginally from 7.9 to 8.6 per cent in Orissa over the past 10 years, the area of the STs has decreased noticeably. In Madhya Pradesh and Rajasthan, the area has increased only marginally both for SCs and STs. The upper-caste dominance in these states remains unchallenged and the Dalits could not mobilise themselves against the landlords and the propertied class and failed to emerge as a powerful political force. Writing about these states, John Harriss (1999) argues:

> Both Madhya Pradesh and Rajasthan constituted largely by former princely states and in both some of the former rulers have remained politically powerful ... They are states, too, in which right-wing parties have traditional base ... Neither state has offered much opportunity for left-wing political parties, or their ideologies ... The political leadership in Rajasthan is divided between brahmins, rajputs and jats and the state assemblies dominated by these groups.

While evaluating the land reforms in Rajasthan, R. S. Judge (1999: 98) says:

> ... the big landowners ... belong to rajput, brahmin, bishnoi, ahir and jat castes ... most of them belong to the ruling classes of Rajasthan, mostly they are ex-jagirdars or feudal lords ... All of them have high social status, monetary resources and connections. As a result of these resources, they acquire three abilities, viz, coercive power, manipulative power and contending power.

There are several instances in Rajasthan where the landed gentry have opposed land reform legislation through various means.[16] In both Rajasthan and Madhya Pradesh, much resistance came from the landed elites who faced little challenge from the toiling masses (Joshi 1975: 87–110).

In Orissa, on the other hand, though there were tribal movements, they were confined to only small geographical boundaries. In the post-Independence period, neither the SCs nor the STs have organised themselves against the dominant upper castes. Most of the positions in the Orissa administrative and bureaucratic structure are occupied by the forward castes and the major political parties in the state are under their control (Manor 2000: 827; Mohanty and Bahidar 1993). The Brahmins and the Karans dominate society and politics in contemporary Orissa and the failure of caste associations facilitated the continuation of upper-caste dominance in the state (Mohanty 1990: 321). The same could be established more firmly from the study of B. P. Sahu (1998: 131–32): 'Orissa does not have the advantage of the legacy of a 19th century Renaissance or sustained organised left movement as does Bengal. Nevertheless there have been no caste movements in Orissa of the kind in Maharashtra, Karnataka, etc. Although caste is socially present, it does not manifest politically'.

To analyse the Kerala situation, it is found that though the state has a long history of movements even in the post-reform period such as the Adivasi Sangham movement of 1969 in Kozhikode and Cannanore districts against tribal land alienation and the land grab agitation of 1970 in Alleppey, it has not shown any exemplary achievements like West Bengal. Of course, the ST population in the state is negligible (1 per cent, 1991 Census), and the total population of SCs and STs constitutes around 10 per cent of the state's population. The sizeable population of Christians and Muslims in the state is possibly one of the major reasons for the share of scheduled groups.

Of all the states, SCs are the most disadvantaged in Punjab. Constituting more than 28 per cent of the state's population they control only 2.4 per cent of the operated area (in 1990–91). The landholding position, instead of improving, has declined further. It is true that Punjab was also strongly affected by social reform movements with anti-Brahminical overtones in the later nineteenth/early twentieth century. The state experienced the uprising of 1890–1900 and the agrarian unrest of 1906–07 in Lahore, Amritsar, Rawalpindi. But these movements have not given adequate opportunity to the lower castes, especially the SCs, to organise themselves against the upper-caste landed interests. The early reform movements and the subsequent Ad-Dharm movement in 1926 were of a more religious and social nature and were largely under the control of upper castes. Therefore, the organisation and ideology of these movements was different from the Dalit movements of south and west India (Patankar and Omvedt 1979). In the post-Independence period, SC organisations have not developed independently like that in Uttar Pradesh and Bihar. The Dalits have so far not had a significant role in the state's politics (Jodhka 2000: 399). However, the structure of dominance around Brahmins/Kshatriyas which prevailed over most of India was not strongly developed there because of the importance of Sikhism (Harriss 1999: 3369; Jodhka 2000: 399). Moreover, the landlessness of the lower castes in Punjab was also partly caused by the migration of people from western Punjab (Pakistan) who left around 67 lakh acres of land as against the 47 lakh acres left by the people who migrated to Pakistan (Randhawa

1986, as cited in Singh 1993). The migration of many landless families, who mostly belonged to SCs, from neighbouring states to the canal-irrigated areas of this state in search of employment opportunities may also be attributed for this widespread landlessness of the SCs.

To sum up, there is a strong relationship between social movements, legislative measures and their achievements and the consequent atrocities on the scheduled population (Table 16.9). The states with a strong background of movements have relatively better legislative and executive measures for the protection, restoration and

TABLE 16.9: Movements, Legislative Measures and Atrocities on Scheduled Groups

Characteristics	*Category*			
	A	*B*	*C*	*D*
Pre-legislation movements	West Bengal, Tamil Nadu, Maharashtra	Punjab, Andhra Pradesh, Gujarat, Kerala	Orissa, Bihar, Karnataka, Uttar Pradesh	Madhya Pradesh, Rajasthan
Legislative measures	West Bengal, Karnataka, Kerala	Gujarat, Tamil Nadu, Punjab, Maharashtra, Orissa, Bihar, Uttar Pradesh	Madhya Pradesh, Rajasthan, Andhra Pradesh	–
Post-legislation movements and organisation	West Bengal, Tamil Nadu	Maharashtra, Karnataka, Kerala	Andhra Pradesh, Bihar, Uttar Pradesh	Gujarat, Orissa, Rajasthan, Madhya Pradesh, Punjab
Achievements of legislative measures	West Bengal	Maharashtra, Tamil Nadu, Karnataka	Andhra Pradesh, Gujarat, Uttar Pradesh, Bihar, Kerala	Punjab, Orissa, Rajasthan, Madhya Pradesh
Atrocities on scheduled population	West Bengal, Tamil Nadu, Karnataka	Andhra Pradesh, Kerala, Punjab	Orissa, Gujarat, Maharashtra	Madhya Pradesh, Rajasthan, Uttar Pradesh, Bihar

Notes: Category A: strong and widespread pre-legislation movements, relatively strong legislative measures, active and strong post-legislation movements and better awareness among scheduled population, significant achievement in land reforms, negligible atrocities on scheduled groups; Category B: sporadic pre-legislation movements, moderate legislative measures, post-legislation movements in many parts, noticeable achievements in land reforms, less atrocities on scheduled groups; Category C: low pre-legislation resistance, relatively inadequate legislative measures, signs of organised post-legislation protests, average achievements in land reforms, relatively more atrocities on scheduled groups; Category D: pre-legislation movements confined to a few areas, inadequate legislative measures, very low level of post-legislation awareness and resistance, miserable performance in land reforms, maximum atrocities on scheduled groups.

Pre-legislation movements are the movements that took place before the 1950s because many of the legislative measures started since then. Legislative measures, though introduced in the latter part of British rule, only the measures taken in the post-Independence period have been considered. While categorising the states in terms of legislative measures, provisions relating to fixation of ceiling limits, protection, restoration and allotment of lands have been taken into account. Post-legislation movements and organisation include movements and organised protests since the 1950s. The classification of states has been made on the basis of area (districts) covered by the movements, broad aims and objectives and achievements as reported in the available literature. Four parameters, such as, percentage of cultivable area declared as surplus, percentage of land distributed to SC and ST, present landholding position in relation to population and the extent of improvement in the holding position have been considered to classify the states in terms of achievements.

Source: Classification of states is based on the number of atrocities per one lakh population of SC and ST, as given in the *Report of the Commissioner for Schedules Castes and Scheduled Tribes, 1986–87*.

allotment of land. Of course, the legislations pertaining to protection are almost similar in many states, except for a few provisions. But with regard to the provisions for ceiling limits, restoration and allotment of land, there exist differences across the states, influenced by social movements and the awareness of scheduled groups. The achievements of these measures are relative to the nature of organisation and movements of the SCs and STs. The atrocities following land distribution are inversely related to the level of their awareness and organised action.

V

It may be summarised from the analysis in this chapter that the scheduled groups continue to be a disadvantaged section with respect to land and there has been no substantial improvement in their landholding position over the years. Rather, in some states, it has declined further. Even after more than 50 years of planned initiatives and policy measures, fair distribution of land among these backward communities appears merely hoping against hope. It is confirmed by many studies, both in India[17] and elsewhere,[18] that land reforms lead to the reduction of socio-economic inequalities and poverty, and promote agricultural growth. Moreover, as observed by A. Aiyappan (1965: 10), 'without some degree of economic freedom the underprivileged communities are seldom able to take advantage of social legislation conferring new privileges on them'. Despite this, land reforms with respect to scheduled groups evidence lugubrious performance, which raises doubts about the nature of commitment of the Indian government towards upliftment of SCs and STs. The much awaited legislative measures to protect and promote the landholdings of scheduled groups were formulated only in response to their strong and widespread resistance and movements. It is rightly remarked that 'far from being liberal gifts from enlightened governments, land reforms have been historical processes necessitated by peasant struggles' (Radhakrishnan 1989: 268). It is also revealed from the study that the achievements of legislative measures and the land distribution among scheduled communities are relatively better in those states where movements are active and people are organised. The atrocities on these groups following land allotment by the privileged landed interests are also less in these states. It seems that fair distribution of land is not possible through mere legislative measures. The law, however well framed, cannot succeed in the absence of a vigilant public opinion and active sociopolitical organisation to help the underprivileged assert their rights over land. This confirms Gandhi's remark that '... the Congress will commit suicide if its attention is solely devolved to legislative work. Swaraj will never come that way. Swaraj can only come through an all round consciousness of mass.'[19] Hence, the level of mass consciousness can be raised only through mass struggle (Prashad 1995: 210). Therefore, mass struggle seems to be the only option before the scheduled groups that could break the inertia and enable them to improve their landholding position. The submissiveness and serfdom syndrome tend to precipitate and perpetuate the subalternity and backwardness. The background of legislative measures and the magnitude of previous social movements that have provided marginal benefits provide scheduled groups adequate lessons and ample scope to choose the right option.

NOTES

1. See the Ninth Five Year Plan Draft 1997–2002, Planning Commission, Government of India, New Delhi, Vol. 2, 347.

2. Perspective Planning Division, Planning Commission, as cited in Ninth Five Year Plan Draft 1997–2002.

3. Barring Murdia (1975) and Patel (1974), studies on aspects of land distribution among SCs and STs across the states is almost non-existent. However, these early studies could not cover completely the effects of legislative measures because in many states some of the measures were introduced in the 1970s and even the 1980s, and special efforts were also made for land distribution among the scheduled groups through the Sixth and Seventh Five Year Plans. Though there are some state-level studies, they are also very limited.

4. There are a good number of studies showing how land reforms and forest policy, the associated infrastructural arrangements of British colonialism, and the planned developmental initiatives of the post-Independence period have adversely affected the socioeconomic conditions of the tribals and strengthened the basis of dominance of non-tribals in tribal areas. The pace of impoverishment, de-peasantisation, marginalisation and displacement of tribals continues to increase with the march of time. See, for example, Pathy (1984); Rao (1987); Mohanty (1997).

5. Except some of the north-eastern states where the tribal population is predominant, none of the Indian states is ruled by scheduled groups. Though the Bahujan Samaj Party was in power in Uttar Pradesh, it was only for six months and thrived on the support of the BJP, a Right-wing, upper-caste, (Brahmin)-dominated party. Similarly in Orissa, the Congress Party has made tribal leaders the chief minister of the state thrice for a very short time just before elections, to woo the tribals.

6. The analysis is limited to only 13 states. The north-eastern states, Jammu and Kashmir, Himachal Pradesh, Haryana and the Union Territories have been excluded mostly due to non-availability of data and literature. However, as most of the major states (in terms of area and SC and ST population) have been covered in the study, the exclusion of these states would not vitiate generalisation significantly.

7. It is true that many of these early movements had religious colourings. But land and forest issues had mobilised the tribals in one way or another; see Patel (1974) and Arya (1998). For more details, see Desai (1979) and Singh (1983), which provide a panoramic view of the tribal and peasant struggles in India.

8. It is revealed by various reports (see the *Reports of the Commissioner for Scheduled Castes and Scheduled Tribes*, various issues; and *Reports of the Study Team on Tribal Development Programme*, various states) that the non-tribals have purchased land from the tribals through various means. The so-called competent authority has permitted the rich non-tribals to acquire the land of the scheduled groups without much difficulty. See Mohanty (1996, 1997).

9. The studies undertaken by Rajasekar (1988) in Andhra Pradesh, Dandekar (1979) in Maharashtra, Mohanty (1996) in Orissa, and Judge (1999) in Rajasthan and Gujarat reveal that many of the large farmers have distributed their holdings among family members to avoid the ceiling laws, and also to claim to be small farmers for availing the developmental measures meant for the small and marginal holders.

10. The matter was also discussed in the conference of revenue ministers held in May 1985 and November 1986. See the *Report of the Commissioner for Scheduled Castes and Scheduled Tribes, 1986–87*.

11. See *Progress of Land Reforms*, Planning Commission, Government of India, 1963, 21.

12. The idea that to enrich their spiritual life men should share their worldly possessions, incorporated in Bhoodan philosophy, found a favourable and ready response from poor Indians of the countryside. See Tai (1974).

13. The successive reports of the Commissioner for Scheduled Castes and Scheduled Tribes have recorded some of the cases that came for legal rescue. They have provided detailed accounts of these cases with date and place of occurrence. For example, see *Report of the Commissioner for Scheduled Castes and Scheduled Tribes, 1986–87*.

14. It has been reported by some studies that the lower castes have also improved their holding position through land market. For example, see Bailey (1957); Omvedt (1993); Lieten and Srivastava (1990).

15. As per the 1991 Census, the SC population in Maharashtra is 11.10 per cent against 7.14 per cent in 1980–81. But such a substantial increase in population is mainly due to the inclusion of some communities like Neo-Buddhists in the SC groups.

16. The descriptions given in Hiro (1976) and Judge (1999) provide an interesting account of the methods and strategies adopted by the upper-caste landed interests not to implement the ceiling laws and other land reform acts.

17. The link between land reform, agricultural growth and reduction of poverty in India is well established by Besley and Burgess (1998), Haque (1995) and others.

18. It is reported that countries like China, Botswana, Egypt, South Korea and Zimbabwe have a relatively egalitarian agrarian structure due to implementation of land reforms, and these countries also maintain a good record of food production, economic growth and high level of public expenditure on health and education. See Cornia et al. (1987) and Singh (1986), as cited in Haque (1995: 67).

19. M. K. Gandhi's speech at the All-India Congress Committee. For details see the *Collected Works of Mahatma Gandhi*, Vol. 58, 11.

REFERENCES

Aiyappan, A. 1965. *Social Revolution in a Kerala Village*. Mumbai: Asia Publishing House.

Appu, P. S. 1993. 'A Modest Programme for the Nineties'. In *Land Reforms in India*, Vol. 1, ed. B. N. Yugandhar and Gopal Iyer. New Delhi: Sage Publications.

———. 1996. *Land Reforms in India: A Survey of Policy Legislation and Implementation*. New Delhi: Vikas Publishing House.

Arya, Sachi. 1998. *Tribal Activism: Voices of Protest*. New Delhi: Rawat Publications.

Bailey, F. G. 1957. *Caste and the Economic Frontier: A Village in Highland Orissa*. Manchester: Manchester University Press.

Besley, Timothy and Robin Burgess. 1998. 'Land Reform, Poverty Reduction and Growth: Evidence from India'. The Development Economics Discussion Paper Series No. 13, London School of Economics.

Béteille, André. 1972. *Inequality and Social Change*. Delhi: Oxford University Press.

———. 1974. *Studies in Agrarian Social Structure*. Delhi: Oxford University Press.

Dandekar, Hemalata. 1978. 'Rural Development: Lessons from a Village in Deccan Maharashtra'. Unpublished PhD thesis, University of California.

Das, Arvind N. 1983. *Agrarian Unrest and Socio-economic Change 1900–1980*. New Delhi: Manohar Publications.

Dasgupta, Biplab. 1973. 'Naxalite Armed Struggles and the Annihilation Campaign in Rural Areas'. *Economic and Political Weekly* 8(456): 173–88.

Desai, A. R. (ed.). 1979. *Peasant Struggles in India*. Delhi: Oxford University Press.

Deshpande, R. S. 1998. 'Land Reforms and Agrarian Structure in Maharashtra'. *Journal of Indian School of Political Economy* 10(1): 1–24.

Dhanagare, D. N. 1983. *Peasant Movements in India 1920–1950*. Delhi: Oxford University Press.

Diwakar, D. M. 1999. 'Dalit Question of Inequality, Exploitation and Mobilisation: A Micro View of Ground Realities'. *Man and Development* 21(3): 62–81.

Dubey, S. N., and Ratna Murdia. 1977. *Land Alienation and Restoration in Tribal Communities in India*. Bombay: Himalaya Publishing House.

Duncan, Ian. 1999. 'Dalits and Politics in Rural North India: The Bahujan Samaj Party in Uttar Pradesh'. *The Journal of Peasant Studies* 27(1): 35–59.

Ekka, W., and A. K. Danda. 1983. 'The Halpati Movement among the Dublas of South Gujarat'. In *Tribal Movements in India*, ed. K. S. Singh, 273–84. New Delhi: Manohar Publications.

Francis, C. 1996. 'Land Reforms: An Overview'. In *Land Reforms in India*, Vol. 3., ed. B. N. Yugandhar, 28–56. New Delhi: Sage Publications.

Frankel, F. 1989. 'Caste, Land and Dominance in Bihar'. In *Dominance and State Power in Modern India: Decline in Social Order*, Vol. 1, eds F. Frankel and M. S. Rao. Mumbai: Oxford University Press.

Haimendorf, C. V. F. 1945. *Tribal Hyderabad*. Hyderabad: Government of HEM the Nizam.

———. 1982. *Tribes in India: The Struggle for Survival*. Delhi: Oxford University Press.

Haque, T. 1995. 'Role of Land Reform in Rural Development in the Wake of Economic Liberalisation'. *Kurukshetra* 44(1): 63–69.

Hiro, D. 1976. *Inside India Today*. London: Routledge and Kegan Paul.

Harriss, John. 1999. 'Comparing Political Regimes across Indian States: A Preliminary Essay'. *Economic and Political Weekly* 34(48): 3367–77.

Jaffrelot, Christophe. 2000. 'The Rise of the Other Backward Classes in the Hindi Belt'. *The Journal of Asian Studies* 59(1): 86–108.

Jodhka, Surinder S. 2000. '"Prejudice" Without "Pollution"?: Scheduled Castes in Contemporary Punjab'. *Journal of Indian School of Political Economy* 12(3–4): 381–404.

Joshi, P C. 1975. *Land Reforms in India: Trends and Perspectives*. New Delhi: Allied Publishers.

Judge, R. S. 1999. *Social Change through Land Reforms*. New Delhi: Rawat Publications.

Kulkarni, D. S. 1983. 'The Bhil Movement in Dhulia District 1972–74'. In *Tribal Movement in India*, ed. K. S. Singh, 261–72. New Delhi: Manohar Publications.

Lieten, G. K., and Ravi Srivastava. 1999. *Unequal Partners, Power Relations: Devolution and Development in Uttar Pradesh*. New Delhi: Sage Publications.

Manor, James. 2000. 'Small-time Political Fixers in Indian States: Towel over Armpit'. *Asian Survey* 41(5): 816–35.

Mearns, R. 1998. *Access to Land in Rural India: Policy Issues and Options*. Mimeo, World Bank.

Mohanty, B. B. 1996. 'Agricultural Modernisation in Rural Orissa: Prosperity and Destitution'. *Man in India* 76(1): 81–90.

———. 1997. 'State and Tribal Relationship in Orissa'. *Indian Anthropologist* 27(1): 1–17.

Mohanty, Manoranjan. 1990. 'Class, Caste and Dominance in a Backward State: Orissa'. In *Dominance and State Power in Modern India: Decline in Social Order*, Vol. 2, eds F. Frankel and M. S. Rao. Mumbai: Oxford University Press.

Mohanty, Manoranjan and B. K. Bahidar. 1993. *Odisha Daridra Kahinki* (Oriya). Cuttack: Binod Bihari.

Mohapatro, P. C. 1987. *Economic Development of Tribal India*. New Delhi: Ashish Publishing House.

Mukherji, P. 1987. 'Study of Social Conflicts, Case of Naxalbari Peasant Movement'. *Economic and Political Weekly* 22(38): 1607–16.

Mungekar, N. 1999. 'State, Market and the Dalits: Analytics of the New Economic Policy'. In *Dalits in Modern India*, ed. S. Michael. New Delhi: Vistaar Publications.

Murdia, Ratna. 1975. 'Land Allotment and Land Alienation Policies and Programmes for Scheduled Castes and Tribes'. *Economic and Political Weekly* 10(32): 1201–14.

Myrdal, Gunnar. 1972. *Asian Drama: An Inquiry into the Poverty of Nations*, abridged in one volume by Seth S. King. Middlesex: Penguin Books.

Nair, Kusum. 1961. *Blossoms in the Dust: The Human Element in Indian Development.* London: G. Duckworth and Co.

Omvedt, Gail. 1974. 'Non-Brahmins and Nationalists in Poona'. *Economic and Political Weekly* 9(6–8), annual number: 201–16.

_____. 1993. *Dalits and the Democratic Revolution: Dr Ambedkar and the Dalit Movement in Colonial India*. New Delhi: Sage Publications.

_____. 1998. 'Kanshi Ram and the Bahujan Samaj Party'. In *Caste and Class in India*, ed. K. L. Sharma. New Delhi: Rawat Publications.

Pani, Narendar. 1998. 'Political Economy of Karnataka: 1950–1995, An Overview'. *Journal of Social and Economic Development* 1(1): 64–84.

Parry, J. 1979. *Caste and Kinship in Kangra*. London: Routledge and Kegan Paul.

Patankar, B., and Gail Omvedt. 1979. 'The Dalit Liberation Movement in Colonial Period'. *Economic and Political Weekly* 14(7–8): 409–24.

Patel, M. L. 1974. *Changing Land Problems of Tribal India*. Bhopal: Progress Publishers.

Pathy, Jagannath. 1984. *Tribal Peasantry Dynamics of Development*. New Delhi: Inter India Publications.

Patnaik, N. 1971. *Tribes and Their Development: A Study of Two Tribal Development Blocks in Orissa*. Hyderabad: National Institute of Community Development.

Prashad, P. H. 1995. 'Mass Struggle: The Only Option'. *Economic and Political Weekly* 30(4): 208–11.

Radhakrishan, P. 1989. *Peasant Struggles, Land Reforms and Social Changes, Malabar, 1836–1982*. New Delhi: Sage Publications.

Rajasekar, D. 1988. *Land Transfer and Family Partitioning: A Historical Study of an Andhra Village*. New Delhi: Oxford and IBH Publishing Company; Thiruvananthapuram: Centre for Development Studies.

Rajasekaran, N. 1998. 'Land Reforms in Maharashtra: A Regional Analysis'. *Review of Development and Change* 3(2): 238–63.

Ram, N. 1979. 'Dravida Movement in its Pre-Independence Phases'. *Economic and Political Weekly* 14(7–8): 377–402.

Ranadive, B. 1979. 'The Caste, Class and Property Relations'. *Economic and Political Weekly* 14(7–8): 337–48.

Rao, B. J. 1987. *Land Alienation in Tribal Areas of Andhra Pradesh*. Warangal: Kakatiya University.

Reddy, G. Ram. 1989. 'The Political Accommodation: Caste, Class and Dominance in Andhra Pradesh'. In *Dominance and State Power in Modern India: Decline in Social Order*, Vol. 1, ed. F. Frankel and M. S. Rao. Mumbai: Oxford University Press.

Rutten, Mario. 1995. *Farmers and Factories: Social Profile of Large Farmers and Rural Industrialists in West India.* Delhi: Oxford University Press.

Shah, G. 1998. 'Caste Sentiments, Class Formation and Dominance in Gujarat'. In *Caste and Class in India*, ed. K. L. Sharma. New Delhi: Rawat Publications.

Sahu, B. P. 1998. 'The Orissan Society: Past Trends and Present Manifestations'. In *Caste and Class in India*, ed. K. L. Sharma. New Delhi: Rawat Publications.

Sankaran, S. R. 1996. 'Introduction'. In *Land Reforms in India*, Vol. 3, ed. B. N. Yugandhar, 17–27. New Delhi: Sage Publications.

Sharma, B. D. 1994. *Dalits Betrayed.* New Delhi: Har Anand Publications.

Singh, K. S. (ed.). 1983. *Tribal Movements in India*, Vols 1 and 2. New Delhi: Manohar Publications.

Singh, Brijipal. 1993. 'Consolidation of Land Holdings in Punjab: Lessons for Bihar'. In *Land Reforms in India*, Vol. 1, eds B. N. Yugandhar and Gopal Iyer. New Delhi: Sage Publications.

Suri, K. C., and C. V. Raghavulu. 1996. 'Agrarian Movements and Land Reforms'. In *Land Reforms in India*, Vol. 3, ed. B. N. Yugandhar, 28–56. New Delhi: Sage Publications.

Tai, Hung-Chao. 1974. *Land Reform and Politics: A Comparative Analysis.* Berkeley: University of California Press.

Thorner, Daniel. 1976. *The Agrarian Prospect in India.* New Delhi: Allied Publishers.

Vyasulu, Vinod. 1985. 'Underdeveloping Koraput'. *South Asian Anthropologist* 6(1): 63–71.

Wilkinson, Steven Ian. 2000. 'India, Consociational Theory, and Ethnic Violence'. *Asian Survey* 41(5): 767–91.

Wood, J. R. 1984. 'Congress Restored?: The "KHAM" Strategy and Congress (I) Recruitment in Gujarat'. In *State and Politics in India: Crisis or Continuity*, ed. J. R. Wood. Boulder: Westview Press.

Yadav, Manohar. 1998. 'Career of Dalit Movement in Karnataka'. *Journal of Social and Economic Development* 1(1): 107–27.

17

Social Profile of Agricultural Entrepreneurs

*Economic Behaviour and Lifestyle of Middle-Large Farmers in Central Gujarat**

Mario Rutten

. . .
Based on 29 case studies, this chapter argues that besides the features usually connected with a capitalist mode of agricultural production—hiring-in of free labour to cultivate cash crops in a capital-intensive manner—the class of dominant landholders in the Charotar tract is characterised by an entrepreneurial approach to farming, a diversification of economic activities and a new lifestyle of leisure and consumption.

Introduction

Kheda district is one of the regions in Gujarat where the process of agrarian modernisation has taken place most rapidly in recent decades. On top of a relatively high level of agricultural development at the time of Independence, total production of foodgrains has almost doubled since then—from 240,100 tonnes (1949–50) to 469,900 tones (1982–83)—while the production of cash crops has increased by almost fivefold: from 75,100 tonnes in 1949–50 to 345,400 tonnes in 1982–83 (Directorate of Agriculture 1964, 1983). In comparison to the other districts of Gujarat, the percentage share in gross value of state agricultural output as well as the percentage growth rate has been considerably higher in Kheda district during this period (Sharma 1983: 236). In the last three decades production per hectare has risen for almost all the crops, especially with regard to the cultivation of tobacco, by far the most important commercial crop in this region. From an average of 683.1 kg per hectare in the 1950, the productivity of this crop went up to 1,507.4 kg per hectare

* Originally published in *Economic and Political Weekly* 21(13), 29 March 1986: A15–23.

in the last decennium. At the same time, the amount of land under double-cropping went up from a mere 1.48 per cent of the total cultivated area in 1949–50, to 9.91 per cent in 1976–77 (*District Gazetteer* 1977: 238).

An important cause of this intensification of production has been the expansion of irrigated area, particularly during the last two decades. From 7.71 per cent in 1960–61, the percentage of net-sown land under irrigation has expanded to 37.97 per cent in 1978–79. In Anand taluka, the heart of the district, it has even reached 70 per cent of the net cultivated area. Irrigation by wells is dominant in this region. In spite of a substantial increase in canal irrigation during the 1960s, as a result of completion of parts of the Mahi Right Bank Canal Project, two-thirds of the present irrigated areas is irrigated by well water (ibid. 1977: 240; District Rural Development Agency 1983: 5–6).

Partly as a result of the dominance of well irrigation, mechanisation in agriculture has made rapid strides in this district. Along with the increase in the number of tractors from 396 in 1961 to 1,760 in 1972, mechanisation has manifest itself in agriculture in the increase of electric water pumps from 870 in 1961 to 3,186 in 1971, and in the number of oil-engines which rose from 2,436 in 1961 to 8,083 in 1972 (*District Gazetteer* 1977: 269). This acceleration of agrarian modernisation has been stimulated by a large number of infrastructural provisions and institutional facilities within the region. As a result of its geographical situation, Kheda district has an extensive road and railway network which played an important role in its economic development. The Bombay–Baroda–Ahmedabad railway line as well as the Bombay–Ahmedabad National Highway No. 8 pass through the heart of the district, connecting the two towns of Anand and Nadiad which have developed into centres of considerable trade and industry in central Gujarat.

Along with these infrastructural provisions, important agricultural institutions of Gujarat are located in the centre of this district. Within the Tobacco Research Centre and the BA College of Agriculture, both located in Anand, agricultural research is being carried out on high-yielding varieties and new cultivation practices. By way of providing extension services to the farmers, these institutions have played an important role in the introduction of the 'new technology' in this region. A strong cooperative movement has been another factor in stimulating agrarian modernisation. No less than 93.6 per cent of the villages in Kheda district, the home-area of Amul Dairy, have a primary milk cooperative society. At the same time, 71.2 per cent have a primary agricultural credit society which provides inputs, credit and agricultural equipment to farmers, comparing favourably with the 42.0 per cent of Gujarat state as a whole (Gujarat State Cooperative Union 1983: 97).

The high level of agricultural development in Kheda district applies to an even greater extent to its central plains, known as the Charotar tract (pleasant land) and encompassing roughly the four southern talukas of Anand, Nadiad, Petlad and Borsad. Although not very fertile by itself, the deep sandy *goradu* soil of the Charotar tract has been made very fertile by its inhabitants over centuries, making it especially suitable for the cultivation of tobacco (Hardiman 1981: 261–62). Together with the high level of irrigation, the fertility of this soil is the main cause of the preponderating green appearance for which the Charotar tract is famous today. Intensive cultivation of the land—small, carefully tended fields on which many agricultural operations are going on the whole year around—is accompanied by an exceptional high rural density of 555 inhabitants per square kilometres (Census of India 1981).

...

It is arguable, therefore, that the majority of the present-day class of middle-large farmers consists of families from an originally middle-peasant background. The emergence of a small group from among the landlord class that underwent a transformation into capitalist farmers occurred in this region to a very limited extent and was in no way on a scale sufficient to suggest any widespread 'capitalism from above'.[1]

The focal point of my study has been the economic behaviour and lifestyle of this so-called new *kulak* class of middle-large farmers. In the winter of 1983–84, I did four months of fieldwork in six economically developed villages of the Charotar tract. All of these villages were 'Patidar-dominated',[2] but differed from each other in their cropping pattern. Altogether, I made 29 case studies of middle-large farmers with a total average operational holding of 23.4 acres, with emphasis on those households operating about 15 acres of land (Table 17.1). Out of these 29 households, 22 belonged to the Patidar community (Table 17.2).

TABLE 17.1: Operational Holding of the Selected Farming Households (in Acres)

Operational Holding	*No. of Households*	*Percentage of Households*	*Average Operational Holding*
10–15	8	27.6	11.3
15–20	9	32.1	17.2
20–25	3	10.3	21.0
25–30	4	13.8	26.8
30	5	17.2	53.4
Total	29	100.0	23.4

Source: Based on the author's fieldwork.

TABLE 17.2: Caste Composition of the Selected Farming Households

Caste	*No. of Households*
Brahmins	2
Patidars	22
Kshatriyas	'–'
Muslims	5
Total	29

Source: Based on the author's fieldwork.

Entrepreneurial Farming: Land and Capital

The major part of the areas cultivated by middle-large farmers is owned by the household itself. However, a characteristic of their economic behaviour is the fact that part of their operational holding belongs to other landowning households, including small and marginal peasants.[3] Out of the group of 29 selected farmers, the operational holding of 11 households was larger, sometimes even considerably larger than the amount of land they owned. In total, this amounted to an average of 5.4 acres of additional land per household (Table 17.3). In almost all these cases this additional part belonged to peasant households with an original operational holding of less than 5 acres.

Table 17.3: Land Owned and Operational Holding (in Acres)

Selected Households	*Land Owned*	*Operational Holding*
Average per household	18.0	23.4
Total	542.0	678.0

Source: Based on the author's fieldwork.

From the point of view of the middle-large farmer, cultivating others' property is a way of increasing land concentration at a time when there is a heavy burden on land and legal limitations on ownership. With only 2.08 acres of land available in Kheda district per head of worker in agriculture (farmers as well as agricultural labourers)—which may be even lower for Charotar proper—and a fixed ceiling of 10 acres of irrigated land of the type prevalent in the Charotar tracts, purchase of agricultural land has become increasingly difficult. Leasing-in and mortgaging are, therefore, increasingly practised by middle-large farmers to enlarge their production capacity in the most profitable way.

As far as mortgage contracts are concerned, decision-making regarding cultivation of the land passes into the hands of the larger farmer for an indefinite, often long period of time, resulting thereby in a very high rate of interest on the loan issued. With regard to leasing-in of land there is not much difference in the actual position of both parties involved. All cases of tenancy within the group of 29 middle-large farmers are on a crop-sharing basis, with half to two-thirds of the gross produce going to the middle-large farmer as a tenant. This depends, among other things, on the sharing of costs agreed on.

As a result of a lack of capital, most small peasants are not able to make the necessary investments to farm their land profitably. By leasing out part of their property and getting additional income from agricultural labour or off-farm employment, they try to make both ends meet. By doing so the ultimate sale of the land they own is being staved off or at least postponed for some time.

To the small peasant, leasing-out and mortgaging are part of a defensive strategy to counteract the downward tendency of proletarianisation. Middle-large farmers, on the other hand, enter into these contracts as part of an offensive strategy with the objective of cultivating their operational holding more profitably. These contracts of tenancy and mortgage are, therefore, in no way agreements between two equal parties—land versus capital and knowledge—as some of the middle-large farmers suggested. All the decisions regarding cultivation of the land are taken by the tenant, whereas in most cases the small peasant-owner is not able to call in the mortgage, terminate the contract and start cultivating his own land again.

Along with the quantity of land commanded, middle-large farmers are in a privileged position regarding the level of irrigation as well. The percentage of the area irrigated among these farmers is very high, even when compared to the average of the region as a whole. The total area cultivated by the 29 selected households can be irrigated throughout the year. The major part of it by well-water, pumped to the surface by way of oil-engines or electric motors. To irrigate their plots, they do not depend on others for getting the exact amount of water at precisely the right point of time. A major part of their land is irrigated by water from a well which is owned by the household itself or in partnership with other middle-large farmers. Out of the 29 farmers, 20 were part owners of a well with an oil-engine or electric water pump.

Because of the average operational holding and the type of crops predominant in this region, advanced mechanised farming is still not very remunerative, especially when compared to a wheat area as the Punjab. In the light of a labour-intensive agricultural process, the level of tractorisation within the class of middle-large farmers is relatively high. Fifteen out of the 29 selected households owned a four-wheeled tractor. As and when opportunities arose, these farmers are in a position and willing to introduce new technology on their farms. Mechanised dibbling of potatoes and the use of sprinkler-sets to irrigate the crops are two cases in point of the increasing capital-intensity within this class.

Another illustration of capital-intensive farming by these households is their specific cropping pattern. Predominant within the class of middle-large farmers is the cultivation of those crops that require single-cropping, updated agricultural knowledge, high investments as a result of material inputs needed, access to information on marketing and high risk-bearing capacity. While being highly capital-intensive, these cash crops are very lucrative at the same time, especially when sufficient financial strength enables them to postpone the ultimate sale for some months.

Out of the total area cultivated by the selected households, 70–80 per cent is occupied by this kind of capital-intensive cash crops. A few of the farmers grow grains for the market but do not differ from the others regarding their conduct of business. However, characteristic of middle-large farmers in this region is the fact that food crops such as rice, wheat and bajra are primarily grown for personal consumption and do not occupy more than a relatively small part—about 10 per cent—of their operational holding.

The main commercial crop in the present-day Charotar tract is tobacco, occupying 31.5 per cent of the net-sown area. The *bidi* type of tobacco, used for producing bidis (the Indian cigarette), is dominant in this region, and accounts for about 90 per cent of the area cultivated with tobacco (Singh and Patel 1983). Potatoes, lemon and ginger are also cash crops that require high, long-term investments and sufficient financial strength, but they are cultivated on a much smaller scale, although in some villages their concentrations can go up to more than half of the net-sown area.[4] Among the farmers with an operational holding larger than 10 acres, the percentage of the area occupied in these capital-intensive cash crops is much higher and can even go up to 80 or 90 per cent of their total operational holding.

A feature of entrepreneurial farming is not only the domination of most profitable crops requiring large amounts of capital, but also a high sensitiveness to price fluctuations in deciding which crops to grow. A number of the selected farmers stated that for a couple of years they have started to cultivate tobacco on a large scale again as a result of the recent price-rise for this crop. From an average of 41,625 hectare over the years 1975–78, the total area under tobacco in the four Charotar talukas went up to 62,484 hectare in 1979–80, an increase by no less than 50 per cent.[5]

When cultivated as a single crop, the productivity as well as the quality of the tobacco is raised. Middle-large farmers in particular are able to free their land for single-cropping and have the financial strength to be paid in instalments. This results in a high yield per acre and a better price per 20 kg as compared to the tobacco produced by small peasants. Based on economic research on tobacco growing farmers in central Gujarat and on information from farmers and local tobacco merchants, I could arrive at a calculated net profit of Rs 4,500 per acre for middle-large farmers in 1983–84. Having an operational holding of 20 acres out of which 80 per cent or 16 acres is cultivated with tobacco, this amounts to Rs 72,000 profit per household from the cultivation of tobacco for a start.[6] This profit is free of tax as a result of the fact that in India income out of agriculture is still not liable to taxation.

A growing sensitiveness to new marketing opportunities among these farmers is shown in the cultivation of potatoes. Within the last decennium, the number of cold storage buildings in the central part of the Charotar tract has increased from only two in 1974 to 13 in 1984. Before this, potatoes cultivated by the Charotar farmers had to be sent for storage to Bombay. As a result of this recent increase in storage capacity within the immediate surroundings, the area cultivated with potatoes has increased remarkably. This can be seen especially in those villages where cold storage facilities have recently become available, as, for example, in Boriavi, Chaktashi and Uttarsanda.

Renting out per square inch is the usual practice as far as the 11 private-owned cold storages are concerned. Only farmers with sufficient financial strength to postpone sale are in a position to benefit from this new opportunity. This is clearly shown in half of the 1.6-tonne storage capacity of the Gujarat Agro-industries Corporation that is being run on the same system of renting-out. More than 90 per cent of this part is rented out to farmers with an operational holding larger than 10 acres.

Ahmedabad and Bombay are the two most important market towns for selling the potatoes from central Gujarat. By telephone and post, middle-large farmers keep themselves informed as to the fluctuations in prices of this crop. What's more, they are in a position to postpone selling till some months after harvesting and are, therefore, able to earn the margin of trade (about 15 per cent) and obtain a much better price for their crop.

An important part of the working day of middle-large farmers consists of acquiring the necessary resources, including not only material inputs but also agricultural knowledge and access to new technical information. Making contacts and keeping up one's relations within semi-government organisations, banks and cooperatives forms a significant part of their day's work. In fact, they are the main beneficiaries of state-supported facilities for supplying agricultural information to the farming community.

In 1978–79 the Training and Visit System was introduced in Gujarat state under the World Bank-aided project, of which the total costs were Rs 12.65 crores, covering the period up to 1982–83. The main objective of this system of agriculture extension is to assist the farmer in raising his productivity and net income per hectare by providing appropriate technological support (Agriculture, Forests and Cooperative Department Gujarat 1982: 1–2). *Gramsevaks* (village-level workers) visit a number of farmers once in every fortnight. These so-called 'contact farmers' are selected by the village level worker and make up 10 per cent of the farming population. The role of these farmers is to transmit the latest technology conveyed by the village-level worker to the so-called 'follow farmers'. In this way, innovation is intended to spread like an oil stain to the total farming population.

Empirical research on the selected 'contact farmers' in Kheda district, however, shows that no less than 60 per cent of these farmers consists of households having a landholding of more than 10 acres. Besides, transfer of knowledge to the 'follow farmers' seems to take place on a very limited scale only (R. R. Patel 1982: 42). The same applies more or less to the agricultural exhibitions and farmers' days organised by the Agricultural College in Anand. Out of the 280 farmers who visited on the tobacco farmers' day in 1970, 64 per cent had more than 7 acres of land under tobacco cultivation for a start (Shah, Vihol and Patel, n.d.).

By introducing the Training and Visit System, the class of well-to-do farmers is given preference in the matter of technical advice, guidance and other facilities available from the state. The 'oil stain' stops at the upper stratum of rural society. This is due to the fact that the great majority of the agricultural population simply lacks the amount of land and capital needed for imitating the farming methods introduced by the governmental extension services. 'Betting on the strong' to achieve agricultural development, as it was already called at the beginning of the Green Revolution (Wertheim 1964: 259), seems to be still an important part of the policy pursued by the government today.

ENTREPRENEURIAL FARMING: LABOUR

Along with extending control over land and capital as instruments of production, the specific organisation of labour is an important part of the entrepreneurial manner in which these households manage their farms. To cultivate their land, all of the 29 selected farmers make use of wage labour only. More important, however, than the employment of hired labourers on a large scale is the fact that middle-large farmers are increasingly using a system of putting-out part of the field operations. A contract type of tenancy is practised in which the tenant is mostly a small peasant or landless labourer who is responsible for all agricultural tasks in the field and has to take care of the recruitment and supervision of labour at his own cost. In return for this, he gets 12–16 per cent of the gross produce, depending among other things on the type of crop.

Control over agricultural production is exercised by the middle-large farmer, who decides on the type and variety of crop(s) to be grown, the amount of inputs that are used and on the exact timing of the whole range of field operations. For this purpose, he provides almost all of the capital, including the advances he gives to his contract tenants, who do not have the financial strength to pay for the wages and other allowances of the hired-in agricultural labourers. This system of putting-out recruitment and supervision of labour is usually not practised on the total area cultivated by these farmers, but covers only a small part of their operational holding and does not amount to more than two to three acres per contract tenant. Out of the 29 case studies, eight households made use of this system on part of their land, mainly confined to those operations that required intensive and direct supervision on the field.

Not having sufficient relatives to supervise the execution of the work, as a result of the size of the farm, the composition of the household and activities outside farming, they increasingly make use of contract tenants on part of their operational holding. Contract tenancy is, therefore, nothing but a convenient arrangement under which a middle-large farmer who leases out in part relieves himself from the burden of labour management, while still performing the major entrepreneurial functions. Since he still does exercise control over agricultural production and since the contract is on crop-sharing basis for the duration of only one season at a time, he can be rest assured that the yield would be maximised.

Making use of an intermediate stratum of semi-permanent labourers is another manner in which these middle-large farmers have organised management of their farms. To an increasing extent, they make use of a large amount of casual labour at the peak points of the agrarian cycle alone, while employing one or two labourers on a more permanent basis. Almost all of the 29 selected households employ at least one semi-permanent labourer. These farm-hands look after irrigation, drive the tractor, take care of the farmers' livestock and perform odd jobs in and around the house. During the peak periods when more labour is required, they occupy the position of 'foreman' or 'overseer' and are responsible for recruitment and supervision of the workforce. The term of their contract is usually not more than one year, sometimes even for the length of one season only. Continuation of the relation, however, is the rule rather than the exception. Payment is done in cash along with a variety of in-kind benefits such as free fodder, clothing, bidis, occasional free meals, etc. Regular employment at a wage level of about Rs 200–50 per month—which is more than a casual labourer's wages—access to loans and the privilege to confine oneself to supervision during part of the field operations are the main advantages of being a member of this intermediate layer of semi-permanent labourers.

By way of organising the agricultural work on the field and the recruitment of labour in an entrepreneurial manner, these middle-large farmers have solved the problem of fluctuations in supply and demand of labour, while still exercising control over the process of agricultural production. This, however, is entirely at the expense of the casual labourers working in their fields, who most of the year do not earn more than Rs 6–8 per day; and that, only on the days that they are able to find work. Most of them are recruited from the overseer or contract tenant's own social milieu and are tied to him through loans advanced. Having extra-economic power over a number of labour households so that sufficient cheap labour can be supplied at any point of time is a quality required for becoming a member of this intermediate stratum and even more valued by these farmers than knowledge of agriculture as such. Thus, although not a new phenomenon, creation of an intermediate stratum has become an important aspect of the entrepreneurial way of farm management in which the responsibility for the welfare of the labourers working in the fields is abdicated to an increasing extent to a lower layer in rural society.

Underlying this type of entrepreneurial farming are not only economic reasons but also an increasing reluctance by the members of these farming households to take part in agricultural work themselves. As part of their aspiration for higher status and an ever-better position to compete with the superior Patidar landlords from the turn of this century onwards, the more wealthy among the middle Patidar peasants removed their women from engaging themselves in field labour as early as the 1930s (Pocock 1972). Until only a few decades ago, most of the present-day well-to-do Patidar farmers were still self-cultivating middle-peasants. Actually going out into the fields and doing manual work themselves, these Patidars have built up a reputation as 'good cultivators, sober, quiet, industrious and except on such special occasions as marriages also ... thrifty' (*District Gazetteer* 1977: 161). As a result of their recent economic rise, almost all of these middle-large farmers have gradually succeeded in disengaging themselves from the heavy manual labour that accompanies the life of a farmer. Out of the 22 selected Leva Patidar farmers, 21 confine themselves to supervising execution of the work without engaging themselves in any field labour whatsoever. In the 1950s, however, the head of the household of almost all of these families still did work in his own fields alongside his agricultural labourers.

This long-term process of disengaging all members of the farming household from actually working in the fields is part of the transition to a new and more respectable lifestyle in which performance of physical labour is regarded as inferior. To disengage oneself from it indicates wealth and enhances the social status of the family. Within 26 of the selected households, not a single member takes part in any of the agricultural work on the field. Besides, supervision of the agricultural work by the farmer is increasingly narrowed down to short visits. In 12 of the 26 supervising households, the members spend only a part of the working day on the fields. In the case of three households, supervision even takes place at intervals of several days (Table 17.4).

TABLE 17.4: Household Involvement in Cultivation

Type of Activity	*No. of Households*	*Percentage of Households*
Agricultural labour	3	10.3
Supervision throughout the working day	14	48.3
Supervision part of the working day	9	31.1
Supervision at intervals of several days	3	10.3
Total	29	100.0

Source: Based on the author's fieldwork.

Actual overseeing of the agricultural workforce is done by the intermediate stratum of contract tenants and semi-permanent labourers. They are the ones responsible for the entire labour job, relieving the middle-large farmer from the burden of labour management. Different systems of management are sometimes practised by one and the same farmer on different parts of his operational holding. By way of paying short visits to the fields and having regular conversations with their middlemen, these agricultural entrepreneurs acquire the information needed to take the decisions and give the instructions on the work to be done. This ongoing process of disengaging oneself from supervising execution of the agricultural work does not stand for a loss in interest in agriculture by these middle-large farmers. On the contrary, it is part of progressive agricultural management in which the farmer performs all major entrepreneurial functions and labour has become a full-fledged commodity, as is seen in the following example.

> Every afternoon from 5.00 to 7.00 pm CP visits some of his plots. He only owns half of his total operational holding of 28 acres. The other 14 acres are leased in and mortgaged from marginal and small peasants, based on loans issued by CP.
>
> Supervising execution of the agricultural work is not part of CP's day's work but is done by ten middlemen. Each of them is responsible for the entire labour job on two to three acres of land. For this they receive a fixed amount of money—about Rs 250 per month—or get a small share in the gross produce of the plots they take care of. Five of them are the original owners of parts of the land operated by CP. Knowledge of agriculture, however, was not the main reason for giving them the status of "foreman". Honesty and control, over a large group of labour households of local or migrant workers from outside, are in fact the main criteria on which CP selects his middlemen.
>
> On various occasions I accompanied him while making his round of the fields, always wearing an impeccable white *dhoti*. Within the space of two hours time and with rapid strides, he visits part of his fields on foot, while going by car to those plots situated further away.
>
> Together with the overseer/tenant he discusses the agricultural work on the field and analyses the condition of the crop. At the same time, he takes notes in a exercise-book to keep up part of his accountancy. After having finished his round, he draws up at home the programme for the following day(s). Sitting behind his desk—by looks

> indistinguishable from an urban industrial entrepreneur—he instructs his middlemen as to the timing and type of agricultural operations to be carried out (irrigation, manuring, spraying, etc.) and the amount of labour required. When necessary, he uses part of the labourers working in his tobacco factory for harvesting the crop.
>
> After instructions have been given the middlemen are allowed to go home. Before they are dismissed, however, he has them standing in front of his desk for some more minutes, visibly enjoying the feeling of power (is it because of my presence?). By this time it is 7.30 pm and satisfied with the work done, he leans back in his chair waiting for dinner to be served. (Author)

PATTERN OF INVESTMENT

Adoption by the class of middle-large farmers of the 'new technology' that became available during the Green Revolution was mainly financed by the agrarian surplus generated within the same social milieu. Early development of agriculture, especially cultivation of tobacco, has not been, however, the only source of prosperity for this class of farming households. A high level of participation of the Charotar Patidars in the process of migration abroad, which started during the period of economic deterioration around the turn of the century and accelerated during the 1920s and 1930s, has contributed to the material progress of these households as well.

> Many Patidar who had not before been further than Ahmedabad or Baroda now began to follow the trade connection which had existed for two thousand years between Gujarat and Africa ... Although few Patidar had any business experience ... within fifty years the Patidar in East Africa had turned themselves into a wealthy trading community ... Much of their new wealth was invested in land and buildings at home in Gujarat. (Pocock 1972: 63)

Those going away came '... neither from the very rich nor from the very poor. The former had resources which carried them through the bad times while many poor had nothing' (ibid.). Most of the emigrants came from the class of middle peasants whose families had been able to generate surplus to pay for the journey and could afford the costs, risks and delayed returns associated with migration. Early migration of these Patidars abroad was, therefore, not only a consequence of their economic rise, but did as much contribute to it. The fact that most of these earnings were used to acquire a superior resource endowment gave them a massive advantage in appropriating the new technology that became available by the mid-1960s.[7]

Agrarian surplus generated by middle-large farmers during the first decade of the Green Revolution was mainly reinvested in agriculture by way of increasing landholding and improving farming equipment. It is seen from Table 17.5 that nearly half of the selected households purchased land between 1960 and 1975. Most of it took place in small parts of no more than two to three acres per transaction and was originally owned by small peasants. From the mid-1970s onwards, hardly any increase in landholding took place. An important factor in this has been the further implementation of land ceiling acts, resulting for the Charotar tract in a present-day maximum of 10 acres of irrigated land. Investing in land has therefore become increasingly difficult for these owners of a substantial amount of land already in their possessions. This is in spite of the fact that with a cautious eye on imminent land reforms, they have almost always 'distributed' their lands under the names of sons, brothers and even distant relatives, while still operating it as a joint family.

TABLE 17.5: Increase/Decrease in Size of Land Owned, 1960–75

Increase/Decrease in Size of Land Owned	*No. of Households*	*Percentage of Households*
Increase by purchase of land	13	44.8
Consolidation	11	37.9
Decrease by partition	5	17.3
Decrease by sale of land	–	–
Total	29	100.0

Source: Based on the author's fieldwork.

Little by little, these middle-large farmers have begun to invest on a wider scale. In the first instance, this was mainly restricted to activities closely linked up with agriculture such as trading and processing of agricultural products. Although in central Gujarat the trade in tobacco is dominated by merchants from outside Gujarat, there are many middle-large farmers operating as agents between the merchant and the tobacco cultivator. In fact, the existence of a large number of tobacco processing factories on the countryside of Charotar from very early days on is for a major part the result of investments made by these agents/farmers.

Within the last decade in particular, concentrations of small-scale industries have emerged in the countryside of the Charotar tract, mainly restricted to the vicinity of those villages situated in between the railway and the Bombay–Ahmedabad national highway. Part of it is set up by traders, artisans and even some urban entrepreneurs. Part of the rural industrialisation in this part of Gujarat, however, is closely related to the recent economic progress of the class of middle-large farmers. Having generated a considerable amount of surplus in the last few decades, these farmers have slowly started to invest part of their capital outside the agricultural sector. Within the last 15 years, investments outside agriculture, such as in small flour mills, tiny transport companies, tile factories and private financing companies, have increased enormously among the 29 selected households (Table 17.6).

TABLE 17.6: Activities Outside the Agricultural Sector Year of Establishment

Type of Activity	*Year of Establishment*			*Total*
	Before 1970	*1970–75*	*1975–84*	
Tiny transport company	–	–	2	2
Private financing company	–	1	3	4
Manufacturing company	1	3	3	7
Other	–	1	5	6
Total	1	5	13	19

Source: Based on the author's fieldwork.

As a result of these investments outside the farm, these households are no longer solely dependent on the cultivation of crops but have at least one other source of income besides farming. In total, this amounts to a large number of different kinds of side-activities such as selling of water, hiring out the tractor, trading and processing of agricultural products, money lending and manufacturing tiles, irrigation-pipes, truck-cylinders, etc. (Table 17.7). Twenty-six of these households, however, stated that farming is still the family's major source of income. An important factor in this is the fact that in India income out of agriculture is not liable to taxation. Some of the farmers, therefore, 'suggested' that from a tax point of view it can be highly lucrative to have a farm along with industrial business and shift part of the non-agrarian income to the farming part of the household.

TABLE 17.7: Sources of Income Besides Farming

Sources of Income	*No. of Households*	*Percentage of Households*	*No. of Activities*
I. Related to the farm			
selling of water	14	48.3	14
hiring out the tractor	6	20.6	6
II. Related to agriculture			
agricultural trade	5	17.2	6
processing of agricultural products	2	6.9	2
III. Outside the agricultural sector			
transport company	2	6.9	2
private financing company	4	13.8	4
manufacturing company	4	13.8	7
other	5	17.2	6
IV. White-collar job	9	31.0	10

Source: Based on the author's fieldwork.

By way of systematically diversifying the family's interests, these farmers create employment outside farming and hope to slow down further partition of the family's landed property. It is, therefore, not uncommon to find that within one family, one member manages the family lands, while another is a trader or industrial entrepreneur. Particularly members of the younger generation are the ones to start and manage these new non-agrarian activities.

> Four sons of middle-large farmers have started an ice-cream parlour in one of the selected villages in which they sell Vadilal ice-cream from Ahmedabad. Only few villagers can afford the luxury of eating (packed) ice-cream and viability of the business is therefore not certain. At the same time they have started a video-cinema in an empty barn in which they show movies once a week, mostly to women and children. (Author)

Self-confident and with their fathers' capital—who continues to manage the family lands—they enter into new fields almost aggressively and start activities about which they have no knowledge at all in the first instance. Buying raw materials, going by or getting around government regulations, organising the process of manufacturing and marketing the finished goods are in fact operations totally different from what they are in farming. Failure in business, therefore, is not uncommon among these youngsters.

Establishing non-agrarian activities on unfamiliar ground is usually not done by one single household on its own but often takes place collectively in partnership or as a group. Out of the 19 activities that are set up outside agriculture by one of the selected households, 11 are owned in partnership. In all of these cases, the partners belong to the same caste and sometimes are even distant relatives.

Perhaps the most conclusive demonstration of the amount of money that can be involved in rural investments outside farming are the 35 pulse mills situated near one of the selected villages, out of which twelve are owned by middle-large farmers. Having a fixed capital of about Rs 4–5 lakhs and a working capital of several lakhs more, they are an illustration of the financial strength possible within this class of agricultural entrepreneurs. Diversification of risks, exchange of information and bringing in more capital are the main reasons for these households to organise along the lines of partnership. Among the owners of these pulse mills in particular, membership of the local Rotary or Lions Club is common, indicating once more their dominance in rural society.

This tendency to diversify economic activities is closely linked up with the entrepreneurial manner in which these farmers manage their farms. As a result of the fact that less supervision of the agricultural work is required by the farmer himself, members of these households have recently got more leisure time. Part of it is used to manage their non-agrarian business and to make contacts and keep up relations within government organisations, banks and cooperatives in view of official regulations, subsidies, credit facilities and matters of buying and selling. For this purpose they regularly visit Anand, Nadiad and even Ahmedabad or Gandhinagar. Their behaviour, therefore, is that of entrepreneurs whose major part of their day's work is spent outside the fields, mostly within each others' company.

Transition to a New Lifestyle

Along with economic development there has been an early spread of rural education in the Charotar countryside. The establishment of numerous secondary schools—at present one per 16.25 square kilometre (*District Gazetteer* 1977: 655)—has been partly the work of this class of middle-large farmers and in particular the result of donations given by emigrated Patidars. With the foundation in 1953 of the university town of Vidyanagar on the outskirts of Anand, university education in the Charotar tract has become easily accessible to many.

One of the main beneficiaries of this increase in educational facilities has been the rising rural middle class. From early on, these households recognised education as a valuable addition to the family property and could afford to send their children to colleges. As a result of this, families of middle-large farmers today normally have a well-educated younger generation. No less than 30 out of the 50 sons of the selected farmers—in the age-group of 20–35 years—have a Bachelor's degree. Preference is given to Science and Commerce, with Arts as a second choice (Table 17.8).

TABLE 17.8: Educational Level of the Sons in the Age-group of 20–35 Years

Level of Education	*No.*	*Percentage*
Upto primary school	10	20.0
10th, 11th or 12th standard passed	8	16.0
Diploma polytechnic	2	4.0
B-Arts	8	16.0
B-Commerce	9	18.0
B-Science	13	26.0
Total	50	100.0

Source: Based on the author's fieldwork.

Studying at university level is done with the main objective of finding a job outside farming and preferably outside the village as well. After completing their studies, these youngsters do not want to spend a large part of their working day on the farm. Being proud of the Patidars' reputation as a thrifty and industrious farming community does no longer apply to this generation to whom the occupation of farmer has a low status.

Even though they stand a relatively good chance of finding a job with the government or in a private company, most of them do prefer to manage a family-owned business instead of working under someone else. The increase in diverse investments of the family capital in activities outside farming coincides with the graduation of one of the sons. After having worked somewhere else for one or two years, some of these youngsters begin to establish tiny businesses of which they themselves become the managers.

Not being in direct contact with the labourers on their fields, as a result of the use of middlemen and of the fact that they are excused when going to college, members of this generation in particular have become increasingly insensitive to the living conditions of the socially lower classes. It is their firm conviction that the poor are themselves responsible for the position they are in today. As a result of the higher population growth within the lower classes and the recent established dominance of the Kshatriyas-Baraiyas in the elected bodies (panchayat) at village, taluka and district level (Sheth 1983: 195), according to their line of reasoning an increasing share of government budget is spent on those who do not make any contribution to economic and social development at all. In fact, they think of these classes as being a main threat to their progress and get annoyed when elder people or members of the lower castes point out their traditional responsibility of providing a minimal livelihood to those who work for them.

Only in the recent past, the Patidars of central Gujarat were famed for their thrifty and sober lifestyle (Pocock 1972: 62). But today, however, the younger generation seems to set more values on increasing consumptive expenditures and leisure time. The change in the day's work of these middle-large farmers is clearly shown in their style of dress. In contrast to the working clothes of their fellow-villagers, these farmers look spick and span all through their working-day, indistinguishable from office employees. The elder generation still prefers to wear an impeccable white *dhoti*, or bell-bottomed *pyjama* trousers, with *kurtha*. Among them, the common form of footwear is the leather *chappal*. The younger generation on the other hand favours jeans, trousers with crease, western shorts and shoes or fashionable half-boots. Wearing western clothes and sporting hairstyles, hanging around with friends in tea-stalls or *pan*-shops, and driving on scooters or even in cars, is all part of a new lifestyle pushed through particularly by the sons of these farmers. It almost seems as if they cannot wait to spend the recently acquired wealth of the family, resulting in an enormous accumulation of expensive and luxury consumer goods within these households, such as refrigerators, scooters, gas-cookers, etc. (Table 17.9).

TABLE 17.9: Luxury Consumption Goods

Consumption Goods	*No. of Households*	*Percentage of Households*	*Total Number of Goods*
Refrigerator	11	37.9	11
Gas-cooker	15	51.7	15
Television	4	13.7	4
Scooter/motor	17	58.6	21
Telephone	7	24.1	7
Car	7	24.1	9
Radio	29	100.0	60

Source: Based on the author's fieldwork.

In most of the selected cases the family lives as a joint family in one house in the centre of the village where the residential quarters of the higher castes are situated. These houses are usually spacious and well-built. Eighteen out of the 29 households live in a house built of bricks, cement and concrete. These are often three-storey buildings with light green or soft rose plaster-work on the outside, contrasting strikingly with the simple houses of bricks and mud belonging to their less prosperous caste-members living on the same street. Despite the fact that not all rooms are occupied, these farmers often own other houses in the village as well which are rented out or used as godowns for agricultural products.

In all of the 29 residential houses running water and electricity is available, and what is more, there is a large number of fluorescent lamps, fans and water taps. All of them have separate, closed bathrooms and a small number of farmers have even constructed a water tank on top of their roof to be assured of running water 24 hours of the day.

The interior of the front room normally consists of a bed, a radio, a clock, a commercial calendar with religious illustrations and a showcase with photographs of relatives abroad. A recurrent decoration of this front room and the adjoining one, in which they have also placed steel cupboards, is the display of brass, copper and stainless steel baskets, milk- and frying-pans, *thali*s and cups, hanging on the wall or put on concrete shelves. It is common among these households to have more cooking utensils and a much larger crockery than is needed for daily use, particularly within the Patidar community as a result of the still widely practised system of giving dowries. What is more, copper and brass vessels have been replaced almost completely by the much more expensive stainless steel which has become one of the new status symbols within this class. To possess a dining table and folding chairs is becoming very popular among these households as well. These pieces of furniture are not in daily use—preference is still given to sitting down on the bed, and eating food while sitting cross-legged on the floor—but are put into use only when guests are visiting the house.

The recent increase in the number of two-burner gas-cookers with gas cylinders is another illustration of rising consumptive expenditure among these households. Only one out of the 15 families that possess a gas-cooker uses it for daily preparation of food. All others do still cook by wood which they get free from their fields. In most of these households tea is the only thing being prepared on the gas-cooker. More of a status symbol than a utensil, these gas-cookers give expression to their newly acquired wealth as compared to those who at best are able to prepare tea on a paraffin-oil stove.

The main meal is taken at any time between 11 a.m. and 1 p.m. It starts with thin *rotli*s made of wheat and smeared with *ghee*, which are eaten with one or sometimes even two vegetables. This is followed by rice—sometimes *khichadi*—with *kadhi* or *dal*. The evening meal is made of thick millet, *rotla* and/or rotli with a vegetable. Daily consumption of vegetables, rice, rotli and ghee is a luxury introduced with their recent economic wealth.

The same holds true for the consumption of milk, an important factor in the nutritional value of food. Along with the consumption of large quantities of ghee, tea is prepared together with a lot of milk and granulated sugar, and a cup of milk is taken every evening at dinner. Out of the selected households, 24 have at least one buffalo or cow. The total average within the group of 29 farmers is 2.4 milk animal per household. As far as two-thirds of these households are concerned, extra income out of milk is not a motive for keeping milk animals. In contrast to small peasants who are often forced to sell almost all the milk they get from their buffaloes, these middle-large farmers are in a position to give consumption the first priority. They sell to the cooperative society only what remains after household consumption which in most cases still covers a major part of their expenses.

Today, housekeeping is the main activity of the middle-large farmers' wife. As a result of their early economic rise, for more than four to five decades already, middle-large farmers, can afford to keep their womenfolk in the house and employ labourers. Until recently, taking care of the milk animals was an important part of the day's work of the wives and daughters of these farmers. However, during the last 10–15 years, jobs such as cutting grass, milking the animals and cleaning the stable have been taken over by maid servants and permanent labourers. Nowadays, it has become customary for these women to be assisted by some of the wives and daughters of hired-in agricultural labourers who are engaged to perform the more strenuous jobs such as cleaning the house and washing dishes in the courtyard.

A large part of the women's day-work consists of preparing the food and serving the meals. Even though they work more hours per day than their male counterparts, the recent change in their day's work—which adds to the husbands' prestige—has given them more leisure time. As members of the upper stratum of rural society, they regularly pay social visits and shop in Anand and Nadiad, wearing the most beautiful silk saris.

The daughters of these middle-large farmers are well educated. A diploma course or university degree, in which preference is given to Housekeeping, Commerce and Arts, is no longer an exception. The main purpose of this is not to find employment afterwards but to stand a good chance of finding a husband from a wealthy and high-status family.

Marrying off one's daughter within the Patidar community of the Charotar tract is invariably associated with social and economic status, involving high expenses. Today, a well-to-do Patidar farmer owning more than 10 acres of irrigated land spends about Rs 1.5–2 lakhs on a daughter's wedding. Next to the costs of the wedding party, including a meal for many hundreds of guests, the dowry consists of 30–50 *tola*s of gold jewels, one steel cupboard, a large number of silk saris, stainless steel utensils, and some tens of thousands of rupees in cash.

In recent years, it has become common for Patidar daughters living in the US to bring in as a dowry their immigration visas. With the purpose of permanent settlement, there are many sons of rich Patidar farmers who hope to emigrate to the US by marrying one of these so-called 'green-card holders'.

High expenses on marriages are not only a conspicuous way of consuming surplus, but a productive investment of capital as well. The system of marriage circles extended by the richer Patidar farmers from the 1920s onwards is a valuable social network within the area. Twice a year, during the large number of recurrent wedding parties, new contacts are made and old ones reinforced. The emergence of a new lifestyle of leisure and consumption is, therefore, not only a way to enhance the social status of the family and express its newly acquired wealth, but it is also part of the entrepreneurial way in which these households manage their farms and side-businesses.

Conclusion

As an outcome of a long-term process of economic rise and upward social mobility, the class of middle-large farmers has become a vanguard of rural society in the present-day Charotar tract. Being one of the main beneficiaries of economic development from the beginning of this century onwards, the speeding-up of agrarian modernisation in the last two decades has turned them into rich farmers well provided with capital. By way of leasing in land from small peasants, they are able to enlarge their operational holding which they cultivate in a highly capital-intensive manner by using modern technology and growing the most profitable type of cash crops. Along with reinvesting their accumulated agrarian surplus in farming, these households have slowly started to diversify their economic activities and raise their consumptive expenditure in a conspicuous way. As part of a new lifestyle of leisure and consumption they have increasingly relieved themselves of the burden of labour management by shifting supervision of the agricultural work to an intermediate stratum of contract-tenants and (semi-) permanent labourers.

They have, in fact, become entrepreneurs who are increasingly extending control over land, capital and labour as instruments of production. This is, however, at the expense of those working on their fields and in their factories who, at the most, have been able to maintain their miserable, low socioeconomic position. Not recognising any obligations to those who work for them, labour has become a full-fledged commodity to these agricultural entrepreneurs.

The aim of this study was to undertake an empirically explorative investigation mainly by focusing on and confining oneself to the socioeconomic aspects of a particular class of farmers. While closely observing the economic behaviour and lifestyle of middle-large farmers, the sociopolitical milieu in which they operate and interact with other strata of community and society cannot escape one's attention. However, because of the limitations of the study, sociopolitical aspects have only been touched upon in the profile presented. Nevertheless, a serious note is taken of interesting and related questions that continued to emerge throughout the course of this exercise. They can very well be considered for future research efforts for broadening and consolidating the perspective on this theme.

The first question in this connection concerns the way in which class and caste factors operate and determine the socioeconomic and sociopolitical behaviour and interaction of these agricultural entrepreneurs. More specifically, how do these rich farmers behave and maintain social relationships with relatively poor caste members? Is there intra-class interaction and on what basis? A second question pertains to the shifts in local level dominance in Kheda district over formal elected political offices like village, taluka and district panchayats. The much suppressed Kshatriyas-Baraiyas are now capturing most of the offices of local power. The implications of this shift needs detailed investigation. Related to this is the last question to be mentioned concerning the role played by the government and governmental agencies. More specifically, the way in which the government protects and supports this class of well-to-do farmers whom it considers as the backbone of rural economy. Though of importance, these sociopolitical aspects could only be touched upon in this chapter, as the main focus of this study on agricultural entrepreneurs has been on the aspects of economic behaviour and lifestyle.

NOTES

1. From the beginning of this century onwards there has been a 'gradual disintegration of the estates of the larger landlords, illustrated by a decline in the production of proprietary holdings larger than 15 acres from 11 per cent in 1916–17 to 9 per cent in 1942–43; by 1936, in Kheda district, only 302 men held a little over 100 acres each …' (Bates 1981: 806).

2. As distinct from the 'Baraiya-dominated' villages, the 'Patidar-dominated' ones are those villages in which the Patidar community accounts for about 20–30 per cent of the population, while owning often more than 60–70 per cent of the total cultivated area.

3. Gujarat Agricultural Lands Ceiling Act 1960, as amended by the Gujarat Act 2 of 1974.

4. See, for example, A. S. Patel (1983).

5. See Singh and Patel (1983).

6. Total investment per acre for this category of farmers is about Rs 2,500: land preparation and seedbed expenses (Rs 300), manure and fertiliser (Rs 1,200), labour (Rs 800), and irrigation (Rs 200). As a result of a high yield per acre (900 kg), a good quality and the fact that they have the financial strength to be paid in instalments, middle-large farmers received in the last three years for their tobacco about Rs 150–160 per 20 kg. Figures on investment and yield are partly based on the research bulletins nos 3, 4 and 6 of the All-India Coordinated Research Project on Tobacco by S. B. Singh and G. J. Patel, 'Economics of Tobacco Production in Middle-Gujarat, 1970–80, 1980–81, 1981–82'. Figures on the current price and net profit of tobacco are based on information from farmers and local merchants.

7. Though I have not collected systematic data on this topic, from conversations with the farmers, it seems that for quite a number of the selected households, remittances from East Africa were available during this period.

References

Agriculture, Forests and Cooperative Department Gujarat. 1982. 'Training and Visit System of Agriculture: Extension in Gujarat', by M. G. Shah (Additional Chief Secretary). Gandhinagar.

Bates, C. N. 1981. 'The Nature of Social Change in Rural Gujarat, the Kheda District, 1818–1918'. *Modem Asian Studies* 15(4): 771–821.

Census of India. 1982. 'Census of India 1981, Series 5, Gujarat, Part B, General Population Tables, Primary Census Abstracts'. Ahmedabad.

Department of Agriculture Gujarat State. 1979. 'Area, Production and Yield Per Hectare of Important Food and Non-food Crops in Gujarat State, 1949–50, to 1978–79'. Ahmedabad.

Directorate of Agriculture. 1964. 'Statistics of Area, Production and Yield Per Acre of Principal Crops in Gujarat State for the Period 1949–50 to 1963–64'. Ahmedabad.

———. 1983. 'Districtwise Area, Production and Yield Per Hectare of Important Food and Non-food Crops in Gujarat State, 1980–81 to 1982–83, Based on Final Forecast Reports'. Ahmedabad.

District Gazetteer. 1977. 'Gazetteer of India, Gujarat State, Kheda District'. Ahmedabad.

District Rural Development Agency. 1983. 'The Centrally Sponsored Programme of Assistance to Small and Marginal Farmers for Increasing Agricultural Production, 1983–84, Kheda District, Gujarat'. Nadiad.

Gujarat State Cooperative Union. 1983. 'Progress of Cooperative Movement in Gujarat'. Ahmedabad.

Hardiman, D. 1981. 'Peasant Nationalists of Gujarat, Kheda District 1917–1934'. Delhi.

Patel, A. S. 1983. 'Participation of Different Groups in the Development Process: A Case Study of a Milk Producers' Cooperative in a Kheda Village'. In *Gujarat Economy: Problems and Prospects*, ed. D. T. Lakdawala, 335–50. Ahmedabad.

Patel, R. M. 1982. 'Glimpses of Change and Development in Borsad Taluka, Kheda District, Gujarat'. Agro-economic Research Centre, Indian Village Studies No. 4, Vallabh Vidyanagar.

Patel, R. R. 1982. 'Critical Study of the Role Performed by the Contact Farmers in View of the Role Expected in Training and Visit System under the World Bank Programme in the Kaira District of Gujarat State'. M.Sc. (Agriculture) thesis in Extension Education, Gujarat Agricultural University, Anand.

Pocock, D. F. 1972. 'Kanbi and Patidar: A Study of the Patidar Community of Gujarat'. Oxford.

Shah, G. n.d. 'Caste Ideology, Class Formation and Dominance in Gujarat'. Preliminary draft, Centre for Social Studies, Surat.

Shah, N., P. P. Vihol and A. U. Patel. n.d. 'Success of the Tobacco Farmers' Day'. Extension Education Institute, Anand.

Sharma, Usha S. 1983. 'Performance and Prospects of Gujarat Agriculture'. In *Gujarat Economy: Problems and Prospects*, ed. D. T. Lakdawala, 225–259. Ahmedabad.

Sheth, P. 1983. 'Caste, Class and Political Development: An Overview'. In *Gujarat Economy: Problems and Prospects*, ed. D. T. Lakdawala, 193–210. Ahmedabad.

Singh, S. B., and G. J. Patel. 1983. 'Economics of Tobacco Production in Middle Gujarat, 1981–82'. Research bulletin no. 6, All-India Coordinated Research Project on Tobacco, Anand.

Wertheim, W. F. 1964. 'East-West Parallels: Sociological Approaches to Modern Asia'. W. van Hoeve Ltd, The Hague.

18

The Farmer-capitalists of Coastal Andhra Pradesh*

Carol Boyack Upadhya

The emergence of a new kind of rural elite—a 'capitalist farmer class—is considered to be an important development of the post-Independence period in India, particularly since the Green Revolution. It has been mainly the large farmers who have benefited from the new agricultural technology, widening the economic gap between them and the mass of small farmers and landless labourers. The increased profitability of cultivation has encouraged landlords to evict tenants and begin cultivating their land directly, using hired daily labour, modern inputs and machinery. A number of studies have found the 'new farmer' to be more profit-oriented, interested only in accumulating capital, an attitude that has encouraged them to abrogate their traditional obligations towards labourers and dependents (part of the old 'feudal' agrarian system) in favour of purely functional monetary arrangements with wage workers. In short, the Green Revolution has stimulated the growth of capitalism in agriculture and the incipient 'differentiation of the peasantry into two classes: capitalist farmers and wage workers'.[1]

One characteristic of this new capitalist farmer class that has been noted by a number of observers is that its economic interests are not confined to agriculture (Sau 1988). Reviewing the available evidence, Gail Omvedt has found that:

> their property and power is not simply in agriculture. After the coming of independence, rich peasants, landlords, and the emerging capitalist farmers began to invest on a wider scale, rather than simply consuming surpluses. The establishment of tiny transport companies, tea shops, small flourmills, oil mills, brick kilns, etc., were all part of this process. Some moved into trade in direct competition with previous merchant classes/castes ... The spread of rural education with the establishment of numerous societies running schools and colleges has also been largely their work. A rural capitalist farmer family today normally has a well-educated younger generation, and systematically seeks to diversify economic activities, placing some sons in service (making them

* Originally published in *Economic and Political Weekly* 23(27), 2 July 1988: 1376–82; and *Economic and Political Weekly* 23(28), 9 July 1988: 1433–42.

doctors or lawyers if possible), setting others up with small shops or tiny businesses, and leaving only one or two to run the land and the tractor. (Omvedt 1981: A-149)

This pattern of economic diversification, particularly into small industry and other types of business means that the top households in this class 'merge into the urban and industrial bourgeoisie' (ibid.: A-150).

Diversification of interests represents the investment of accumulated agricultural surplus outside agriculture; it is also a protection against the risks of pure cultivation. While agricultural profits are invested in small businesses, often business profits are reinvested in agriculture and land, strengthening the position of the rural elite.[2] In spite of their propensity for investment outside agriculture, members of the rural elite have not entered to any great extent into the class of industrial capitalists. In most areas, they remain small businessmen engaged in trade and other non-industrial businesses, rural and urban.[3] However, with the growth of capitalist tendencies in agriculture in the last 20 years and the consequent accumulation of surpluses by big farmers, one might expect to find an increased flow of capital and entrepreneurial talent from this class into urban and rural industrial enterprises. The nature and extent of non-farm investments by cultivating households have not been studied systematically except through very general and aggregated economic statistics. Micro-level and regional studies on this topic are needed, particularly to understand the effects of social and cultural factors on investment patterns.

This chapter traces the rise of a new class of businessmen out of the class of capitalist farmers in one region of India, coastal Andhra Pradesh, and explores some of its social and economic characteristics.[4] There are many facets to this development—economic, social, cultural, political—all of which cannot be covered here. A brief sketch of the history of the region and the roots of the new capitalist class is contained in the following section. In the second section, some characteristics of the rural elite in the region are described, based on the results of village field studies. In the third section, the results of a survey of urban-based businessmen who come from the rural elite are presented. Finally, the reasons for the development of a rural-based capitalist class in this region are explored, and some of the theoretical implications are discussed.

I

Roots of Peasant Entrepreneurship: 1880–1930

The development of the new business class described below has its roots in the unique history of the coastal Andhra region.[5] The modern history of this region has been determined in large part by the construction, in the late nineteenth century, of major irrigation systems off the Krishna and Godavari rivers.[6] These canal irrigation schemes virtually obliterated subsistence agriculture and created a near-monocrop economy in the deltas, transforming them from areas of frequent famine to ones of intensive wet rice cultivation. Paddy quickly became a commercial crop, being cultivated largely for the market, and the region became an important supplier of rice for other parts of Madras Presidency. Commodity markets for agricultural products emerged, located mainly in a few fast-growing trading and transport towns such as Vijayawada, Guntur and Kakinada, and urban-based mercantile groups (particularly the Komatis and Marwaris) entered rural trade and moneylending. The growth of rice production and trade stimulated the development of local agro-processing industries, particularly rice mills, in the towns and larger villages. The expansion of trade and communications led to the integration and monetarisation of the economy of the deltas. As agriculture became increasingly commercialised, the labour force became relatively free and mobile, and payment in cash and employment on a daily basis became the norm (Rao 1985: A-63–64; Washbrook 1973: 509–11, 1976: 92–93).

Changes in land revenue policy contributed to the commercialisation of agriculture. The gradual removal of the intermediary class of zamindars, who controlled much of the land in the region, gave an impetus to agricultural growth by allowing a greater part of the profit to accrue to the cultivator (Duvvury 1986: PE-46). The introduction of the ryotwari system promoted production for the market, and by confirming ownership rights in land, it also paved the way for the development of a market in land. The enhanced productivity of delta lands after irrigation and the increase in population meant that there was growing demand for land, and land prices rose (Rao 1985: A-65–67). Agricultural production continued to increase and commerce to expand up to 1930; the continued rise in grain prices during most of this period contributed to the growth of the economy and a general increase in prosperity. Commercialisation of agriculture increased; by the end of the 1920s, more than 42 per cent of the rice produced in Guntur district was being marketed (Duvvury 1986: PE-47).

The most important outcome of these economic changes, for the purpose of this chapter, was the emergence of a relatively large class of prosperous 'peasants' or owner cultivators.[7] Because the Kammas are the most populous cultivating and landowning caste in the region, it was mainly Kammas who constituted this new 'rich peasant' class, but it included the wealthier farmers of all the major landowning castes.[8] The newly-rich peasant cultivators began to participate directly in the market, both as sellers and buyers and as traders; as a result, they came in touch with the towns (Washbrook 1973: 510–11). These 'peasant cultivators' may be termed more accurately 'commercial farmers', because they were increasingly rational and market-oriented in their agricultural practice. With higher productivity, the larger farmers were able to accumulate substantial surpluses from agriculture, and even in the early twentieth century some were looking for new and more profitable ways to invest their savings.

Purchase of additional land was the most common avenue for the investment of savings, but there was a limit beyond which land could not be cultivated profitably, and most of the fertile land had been occupied by the early twentieth century. In the Guntur villages surveyed by N. G. Ranga in the 1920s, there was no more land to be occupied, so 'all that a rich Kamma can do is to buy the already occupied land at exorbitant prices' (Ranga 1926: 36). The 'buying spree' had caused land prices sharply to increase. Some ryots speculated in land, buying unirrigated land and waiting for it to receive water, a safe gamble since the irrigation could be obtained by bribing government officials (ibid.: 37). There is some evidence that concentration of landholding increased in Krishna district between 1900 and 1930, but the increase in inequality overall was not as sharp as many have assumed. A possible reason for this is that the growing inequality of wealth manifested itself not in larger landowners buying out smaller ones, but in the former diversifying their assets by entering into trade and industry (Kumar 1975: 254–58).

Moneylending was one use to which wealthy farmers put their money. However, because of increasing indebtedness and evasion of debts in the late 1920s, moneylending was becoming less popular among rich ryots as a business, and instead, Marwari traders were becoming the major moneylenders in rural areas, and the opening of cooperative banks enabled small farmers to borrow at lower interest rates (Ranga 1926: 38).

As a result, the newly-rich delta ryots began to look for other opportunities for investment. Some entered the grain trade, buying paddy on commission and transporting it to the rice mills. About 12 ryots in each of the villages surveyed by Ranga were making profits from dealing in paddy (ibid.: 35).[9] Rich cultivators also began investing in agro-industries, and it was their capital that built many of the new rice mills that sprung up in this period (Washbrook 1973: 511).

Ranga (1926: 35) describes in detail the attempts by rich farmers in several Guntur villages to start businesses: 'In every village there are a few enterprising Kammas who have ten to twenty acres of land and who are anxious to do some sort of business or other.'

Most of those business ventures were unsuccessful, however, because of 'lack of sufficient capital, prohibitive rates of interest, lack of business bent of mind and business capacity, and the absence of commercial organisation to advise people' (ibid.).

Thus, by the early twentieth century a new stratum of rich peasants had emerged in the deltas that was rapidly developing into an entrepreneurial commercial farmer-capitalist class. In addition to agricultural growth, there were other changes in the late nineteenth and early twentieth centuries that contributed to the development of this class: rural–urban migration, the spread of education and the development of caste consciousness.

As the region prospered, the new market towns became the centres of political, cultural and social movements in which many of the rural rich participated along with more educated urban dwellers (Washbrook 1976: 92–96). Related to this increased rural–urban interaction and political ferment was the spread of literacy and higher education among the cultivating classes (Washbrook 1973: 513). The new rural elite came to value education highly (particularly in English), in part because it was the key to appointments to government office and hence to political power and influence.[10] The young men from wealthy rural families who went to towns for studies constituted the first wave of rural–urban migration, which in turn contributed to the integration of town and countryside.

An important political development of this period was the formation of the peasant castes as self-conscious, integrated political entities. The propaganda disseminated by the newly educated, politically active young men, and the organisation of caste associations, helped to cement together numerous small endogamous groups belonging to large caste categories such as Kamma and Reddi (see Elliott 1970; Washbrook 1975). The creation of Kamma caste consciousness in this period has been an important factor in the success of Kammas in business, as discussed here.[11]

Some of the rural elite began to move to towns in pursuit of their economic, political and educational goals; as a result, the dominant cultivating castes of the region contained many urban-dwellers. The rural and urban sections of these castes never split into separate sub-castes, however, because urban migrants retained close ties with their villages and there was a continuous flow of new migrants to the towns. The earlier migrants, most of whom were educated young professionals and government employees, provided role models for their rural caste-mates, and they also were leaders of caste movements.[12]

1930–1965

Christopher Baker (1976, 1978, 1984) argues that the depression was the turning point in the economic development of Madras Presidency. Up to about 1930, the rural rich had invested excess cash mainly in land, rural moneylending and trade, and the local agro-industry, but the collapse of the rural credit system and falling agricultural prices from 1929 meant that these were no longer profitable activities. The depression created a considerable 'impetus for a shift of capital, entrepreneurship, and artisan skills from country to town' (Baker 1978: 239), and there was a substantial increase in investment in joint stock companies in Madras Presidency in the late 1930s. Much of this new investment was in agro-processing industries, but in contrast to the small rice and oil mills built by rural capital earlier, now it was flowing into large enterprises, especially sugar and cotton mills (ibid.: 239–40).[13]

The early industrial entrepreneurs of coastal Andhra were mostly zamindars and large landlords, rather than ordinary rich cultivators. For example, the new film industry in Madras was heavily financed by zamindari families of the region, notably the Raja of Mirzapuram (Baker 1976: 184). Most of the new industries in the region were agro-based—most common were sugar factories—but other enterprises such as financial institutions and transport companies were also floated by wealthy landlords.

While the list of big industrialists from coastal Andhra agricultural families was still small at this time, there are many others who invested in smaller ventures in both towns and villages.

Also, many rural families sent their sons to towns for higher education, who then often entered non-agricultural occupations. Throughout the 1930s, the prices of most agricultural commodities remained depressed, and capital continued to flow out of the countryside. The Second World War caused prices to rise again and initiated a period of prosperity for the coastal Andhra farmers. Several writers have traced the influence of the Kammas in Andhra's political and economic life to this period (Harrison 1956: 381). While many of the wealthiest landowners had moved to the towns during the 1930s, some selling their lands, the war years saw the emergence of a new class of rich farmers. Those who had been able to add to their holdings while land prices were low and land was freely available were in the best position to profit from rising farm prices.

Following Independence, the government began to play an increasingly active role in the rural economy, as promoter of agricultural modernisation, procurer of produce, provider of inputs and credit, and so on. Still, the path of agricultural and economic development, and the social changes that accompanied them can be seen as continuations of what had begun earlier. Increased opportunities for education and employment and the new prosperity of cultivators following the war renewed the cycle of out-migration, in which youths of landowning families left their villages in pursuit of education or other careers in the towns. One contemporary observer attributed this trend to land reforms and thought that it spelt the end of the wealthy cultivating class: 'All Kamma youths who can afford are becoming absentee landlords to take up government service or some profession or business. Land is slowly slipping away from the hands of the middle-class and upper middle-class Kammas' (Choudary 1954: 124).

Thus, the patterns of economic diversification and urban migration were already well-established among the landowning cultivating class of coastal Andhra by 1960.

These new entrepreneurs invested primarily in small non-industrial types of business requiring low capital outlays, such as construction and public works contracting, real estate development and speculation, and transport. Trade and agro-industry continued to be the major types of business pursued by rural-based families. Some of these early ventures were successful and grew into large, diversified companies. A good example is the Sri Ramadas Motor Transport Company (SRMT), which was started by a group of local cultivators in Kakinada in 1944. Originally a small passenger transport company with a few buses running in the rural areas around the town, it later expanded into motor vehicle parts and service, acquired the Tata lorry dealership for the area and some other machinery distributorships, and started a production unit. It is now the largest firm of its type in the region, and it is still a private limited company controlled by a group of local families, mainly Kammas (Government of India 1972: 136–38).

The 1950s was a period of modest industrial growth in the region, stimulated in part by land reforms. The abolition of zamindari estates in 1949 induced the more enterprising zamindars to convert their assets into industrial capital. A large proportion of privately owned industries in East Godavari district, for example, are owned by former zamindars and estate holders, many of whom belong to the Kamma caste (Reddy 1981: 126).[14]

Post-Green Revolution Period

From 1965, the agrarian economy of coastal Andhra underwent a second major transformation in the form of the Green Revolution. The spread of modern HYV technology in paddy farming, improved irrigation and mechanisation meant that agriculture became more capital-intensive, more productive and more closely tied to the larger industrial capitalist economy. Agriculture became particularly profitable for large farmers, while technological change increased economic disparities between the landed and the landless, and led to the completion of the process of commoditisation of labour that had begun earlier. Modern large farmers displayed a business-like approach to farming, one manifestation of which was that labour became merely another input on the 'costs' side of the balance sheet. In sum, the Green Revolution strengthened capitalist tendencies in the agrarian economy, and the big and medium landowning farmers became what can best be termed 'capitalist farmers'.[15]

Yields from paddy production have increased sharply, but because the costs of cultivation have also risen, it is not clear whether net profits also have increased. Data from farm management surveys are too aggregated to be of much help in answering this question, and there is a paucity of before and after village-level studies.[16] However, it is fairly clear that large farmers have benefited from the new technology to a greater extent than small farmers, for reasons too familiar to be discussed in detail here (see Frankel 1971; Parthasarathy 1975; Parthasarathy and Prasad 1974; Thorner 1967). Furthermore, large farmers appear to get better yields and higher profits per hectare than do small farmers (Parthasarathy and Pothana 1983: A-94–96). As a result, they are able to accumulate substantial surpluses from agriculture (Parthasarathy and Pothana 1984: 582, 593). Of course, even if agricultural profits per hectare are assumed to be equal for all farm sizes, total income is directly proportional to farm size. Even before the Green Revolution, the bulk of marketed surplus (two-thirds) was being produced by the top 15 per cent of farmers (those who owned more than 4 hectares of land). Available evidence suggests that the concentration of marketed surplus in the top group has increased even though the percentage of land held in large farms has decreased (Parthasarathy and Pothana 1983: A-94–95). Furthermore, the accumulation of surplus in the agricultural sector was promoted in the 1960s by favourable domestic terms of trade (Parthasarathy 1971: 6). All these facts support the hypothesis that larger cultivators have been able to accumulate considerable capital in the last two decades.

Investment of Agricultural Surplus

Available data indicate that a very small percentage of the surplus produced in the region is reinvested in agriculture. This is attributable to the fact that there are few opportunities for productive capital investment in paddy cultivation (Parthasarathy and Pothana 1983: A-95), and to the land ceiling, which prevents large farmers from investing their profits in the purchase of additional land (Parthasarathy and Pothana 1984: 591–93). Once a big farmer has accumulated land up to or over the ceiling, purchased a tractor, other farm machinery and prize cattle, built a godown, and improved his land, there is little more he can do on his farm. He cannot buy more land nor can he increase expenditure on inputs such as fertilisers beyond a certain limit. Furthermore, large farmers may find that they are getting lower returns the more they increase their scale of operations, which some do by leasing in land (Parthasarathy and Pothana 1983: A-94–96). It is also difficult to get an adequate labour supply during the peak seasons. For these reasons, rich farmers look for other avenues for the investment of their profits.

It is commonly held that much of the agricultural surplus generated by farmers in India is spent on 'conspicuous consumption' (large, well-appointed houses, luxury goods such as automobiles, and so on) and on non-productive types of investment such as real estate and gold. It is certainly true that the wealth of the region is glaringly displayed in the houses and lifestyles of the rural rich, and that a large proportion of it is held in the form of gold and immovable property, particularly urban real estate.[17] Even so, there is significant investment in business enterprises, both rural and urban. Agro-industry and trade in agricultural commodities are the two types of business in which cultivators most commonly are engaged. Rice mills and the rice trade have been important sources of income for large farmers for a long time, as discussed earlier. The number of rice mills and other agro-processing units appears to have reached the saturation point long ago, however, and there is not much room for new investment in this field. This is why one often finds rice mills that are leased out by their owners. Trade in agricultural inputs (fertiliser, pesticides) is another field which rich farmers have entered, and many wealthy cultivators have taken up distributorships in the towns and opened retail shops in the villages. A number have become contractors for government projects in the rural areas, including irrigation, power and other construction works (Krishna Rao 1984: 48). Agricultural surplus also has flowed into the towns of the region and the state. Many landowners have set up 'chit funds' and financial corporations which give loans at high interest rates (ibid.: 30), and have constructed cinema halls, both in towns and villages. A number of former cultivators have become small industrialists, contractors and traders on a larger scale in the towns of the region.

It is argued by some that the majority of business investment by wealthy cultivators and landlords has been in non-productive (trade contracting, etc.) rather than productive types of enterprises. However, the fact that there has been a spurt in manufacturing activity in the region in the last two decades, which was also a period of agricultural growth, suggests that agricultural surplus also finds its way into that sector of the economy. Most of the growth in the small-scale industrial sector has been in agro-based units: rice and oil mills, and (in Guntur district) factories for drying and grading tobacco, and cotton gins and presses.[18] There are also a number of small engineering and manufacturing units, particularly in Krishna district, the location of the major industrial town of the region, Vijayawada (Baru 1984: 373–76). After Medak district (where many Hyderabad-based industries are located), the four delta districts had the largest number of industries in the state during 1973–76. The four districts accounted for more than one-third of all industries in the state, but for only 9 per cent of the total fixed capital, indicating that most are small industries (Government of Andhra Pradesh 1977b: 87).[19]

II

The New Rural Elite

Data collected in two village studies carried out in 1981–82 confirm the hypothesis that economic diversification is typical of wealthy cultivating households in this region.[20]

In both villages it was found that large landowners earn high profits from cultivation,[21] but that avenues for productive reinvestment of surplus in agriculture are limited, in part because of the land ceiling. Fear of confiscation prompted a few large owners to sell some of their land before the Land Ceiling Act came into effect, but most found other ways to circumvent the ceiling. Even so; it has prevented (psychologically rather than legally) owners of large holdings from acquiring more land, and it has encouraged them to invest their agricultural profits in other ways. In any case, there is a limit to how much land any one family can acquire because little land comes on the market, and because of the difficulty of managing very large farms under present technological conditions. Because farmers see the future in agriculture as uncertain (due to labour problems, possible new land reforms, and so on) and cultivation itself as relatively unprofitable, there is a strong incentive to diversify into other more lucrative activities, rather than simply to save or spend their profits.

Wealthy farmers have invested heavily in local businesses: rice mills, cinema halls, fertiliser dealerships, contracting and transport. In both villages, most of the large landowners were found to have interests in one or more such business, most located in or near the villages.

The information collected on wealthy rural families in these villages indicates that the flow of capital between agriculture and business is not one-way. In several cases, rural traders and businessmen purchased land with business profits; in others, small farmers were able to increase their landholdings only after making money in business. Even for the richest families in each village, the initial leap in prosperity came not from agriculture but from business. (The Raju family regained lost land only after prospering from its trading business; the Kamma family first became wealthy from contracting.) These cases seem to disprove the hypothesis that economic diversification is an outcome of the increased profitability of agriculture (that is, the surplus that large owners have accumulated seeks an outlet in non-agricultural business enterprises). The connection between business and agriculture is more complex and has a long history in this region. For the rural elite, they are not contradictory occupations but are complementary, because both activities can be pursued profitably by one household or individual. Furthermore, land and agriculture provide economic security but relatively low profits, while business offers an outlet for agricultural surplus and the possibility of greater accumulation, but entails financial risk.

Although this pattern is long-standing, economic development and the new technology have led to a sharp increase in the number of rural business-cum-agricultural households as well as to diversification in the type of investments made by them. With the spread of Green Revolution technology, opportunities were created for rich farmers to become dealers of fertilisers, pesticides, and agricultural machinery, a type of trade that is qualitatively different from the traditional trade in agricultural produce. Some of those who were able to get distributorships and dealerships from the manufacturing companies (mostly located in towns) prospered and expanded into other types of urban business. Contracting is another activity in which a cultivator can engage part-time; if he is successful, he may grow into a large-scale full-time contractor based in a town. New types of agro-industry and other rural-based small industries, cinema halls, and speculation in urban real estate are other 'modern' avenues of investment for the rural rich. While wealthy farmers diversify into rural-based businesses continue to be primarily cultivators, there are many others who are drawn into urban enterprises and who eventually give up agriculture. However, there are no examples in these villages of urban-based businessmen who have bought land and become cultivators; this is true only of rural trade: Thus, while capital flows in both directions, between agriculture and non-agriculture business in the rural context, between town and countryside, the flow of capital and people is more one-way. Many leave the village but few return.

Rural–urban migration is not a function only of economic diversification, but also of the high value placed on education. Although this is not a new trend, even small farmers now are able to provide educations for their children, and among wealthier families it is the norm. The switch to non-agricultural occupations and urban migration by educated children is the natural outcome of this trend. Practically every medium and large landowning family in these villages (and some with small holdings) has highly educated and/or urban-based members. As a result, there is a complex web of ties between rural and urban society, particulars within the elite, which has produced (or reinforced) an urban-oriented culture among the rural rich. This culture in turn reproduces the pattern of out-migration because town life and urban occupations are more highly valued by the rural elite than are rural life and cultivation. Wealthy families seem to have one foot already out the door, and they are awaiting an opportunity to make the move to town, an opportunity that will come to their sons and daughters if not to themselves.

These considerations suggest that a process of replacement or circulation of rural elites has been going on for a long time in coastal Andhra. Members of landed families migrate to towns, eventually selling their land, which is then purchased by upwardly mobile smaller farmers or traders who, if they accumulate enough land and capital, may enter the elite class and in turn acquire the same characteristics. Of course, not all rich families emigrate, and in some case, families have declined economically and have lost land. But, in general, there is clearly a trend of 'upward and outward' mobility in Andhra rural society.

...

Rural–Urban Connections

Urban migrant businessmen retain important social and economic ties with their rural villages. Those who have close kin (parents or siblings) in their native villages maintain social relations with them by frequent visits. Emigrant family members tend to converge on the ancestral home during summer vacations and for major lifecycle events of close relatives, such as marriages and funerals.

Most of the businessmen interviewed were not members of rural-based households, but there was a high degree of cooperation between rural and urban relatives, particularly in regard to the management of land. Urban migrants relied on their rural kin to look after their lands, even after partition of their estates. In most cases it was the father and/or brothers (present or former coparceners in the joint estate) who were the caretakers of a migrant's land, but other relatives also filled this role. The caretaker may cultivate the owner's land along with his own, sending him the profits, or it may be given to him on lease. In the case of undivided property there was usually no formal profit-sharing arrangement.

There is a close connection between continued landownership and rural–urban kin ties. The majority of informants had fathers and/or brothers living in their native villages and also owned ancestral land, and several had neither property nor kin in their villages. However, in no case did an informant have a father or brother in his native village but did *not* own land, while all of those who had no land had no father or brother in their villages. Thus, absentee landownership was contingent upon the presence of close relatives in the native village (especially a father or brother), without whom it was difficult for an urban migrant to maintain such property. However, migrants did not rely only on close agnatic kin to look after their land; most of those who had no father or brother in their villages had given it to other relatives to cultivate or leased it out. Even if the land was leased out, it was necessary to have a reliable relative present to protect the owner's interests.[22] If he did not have a close relative in his village, the absentee owner was likely to sell his land, although most did so as a last resort, when there was no other way to raise money for their businesses.

In spite of the difficulties of absentee landownership, the compulsion to keep one's land is strong, and there are important economic reasons for this. Landownership has been a crucial factor in the success of this new business class. In addition to being a source of investment capital, there are several economic advantages to the ownership of agricultural land for urban businessmen. Agricultural land provides a reliable source of income that can be used for investment in business or for household expenses when business income is uncertain. Second, because agricultural income is not taxable, a businessman may reduce his tax burden by showing business profits as agricultural profits if he owns land.[23] Third, land may be used as collateral when applying for bank loans. Fourth, land provides economic security, particularly when an entrepreneur is first starting his business and the risk of failure is great. Land is a solid piece of property as well as a source of income upon which one can fall back in case a business venture fails.

However, when asked why they have not sold their land, informants mentioned non-economic reasons as often as economic ones. Although half said that agricultural income was a source of investment capital, no one gave this as a reason for keeping his land. Rather, the most commonly mentioned economic reason was that it provides security. As one informant said, 'If you put money into a business you may lose or gain, and if you lose, you're out of your house. But if you have land and gold you have security. Nothing is sure in business.'

Others denied that there was any economic advantage to keeping one's land, citing instead 'sentimental' reasons: to 'have roots in the village', to be able 'to spend time in the village', because 'it came from our ancestors', and so on. A few who expressed the desire to return to their villages after retirement said that for this reason they would like not only to keep their land but also to increase their holdings.

Most of these businessmen, however, were permanent migrants. A few had sold all their land, and a number of others had sold some of their land to raise money for their businesses. Most were in the process of cutting off their rural connections and now regarded Visakhapatnam as their home. First-generation migrants had close relatives and land in their villages, but because rural kin become more distantly related with each generation, it is not likely that land will be retained by urban migrant families after the second generation. Many recognised that their land would have to be sold eventually, if not by them then by their children, because it will become difficult to look after it. There were several families that had retained their village roots in spite of emigration of members for more than a generation, and several of the informants were planning to return to their villages after retirement. For most, however, the relations of kinship and property that tied them to their villages were slowly being severed. Even so, the economic and social ties that the migrant entrepreneurs have with their rural villages at present are important ingredients of their success. In addition to providing financial help, rural–urban ties are important in the process of migration and in establishing new businesses. In half the cases studied, kin connections were crucial for new migrants in starting their business careers or in acquiring business partners.

Rural–Urban Flow of Resources

A key question is the extent to which economic resources flow out of rural areas into the towns as a result of urban migration and investment in urban business enterprises by cultivating families, and the extent to which urban business profits flow back into the rural economy. It is noted above that agricultural income and land were the most important sources of starting capital for these urban businessmen, including capital derived from their own land, joint family land, and investment by rural relatives. In addition to such business investments, migrants receive their shares of the profits from land that is being cultivated by their village-based brothers, and many receive agricultural produce from their land, particularly rice, for their own consumption. Their families may send some of the rice produced on jointly owned land, or they may receive rice as part of the profits which are sent to them from their own (separate) land.[24] Thus there is apparently a substantial outflow of resources from the rural areas of coastal Andhra, in cash and in kind. However, there does not seem to be much flow of capital in the other direction; there is little reinvestment of business profits in purchase of land and in agricultural production. Only three informants purchased additional land out of their business profits, and in all the cases the land was located not in their native villages but elsewhere. (Two purchased cheap drylands in Visakhapatnam district to use for eucalyptus plantations; these were really business investments.) Several informants expressed a desire to buy more land, but the majority of informants had no such intention; rather, many were intending to sell what land they had left. There was only one case, that of five brothers, in which business profits were used to build a new house in the village. (In contrast to the other informants, this family was still rural-based, having industries as well as extensive lands in or near their native village, so this investment was logical for them.) A few entrepreneurs had set up industries in rural areas, but this was in response to the government's policy of encouraging industrialisation in 'backward districts'. The only other way in which resources were transferred from towns to villages was through the economic aid that some informants gave their fathers, but such aid was found in only a few cases. Thus, there does not appear to be any significant transfer of urban business profits to rural areas, at least via this group of migrants. Instead, the net flow of resources is in the other direction; the profits and products of agriculture sent to absentee landowners have a higher total value than what returns. Out-migration of wealthy and middle-level cultivators is accompanied by outflow of resources from the rural economy.

Caste and Business

In India the term 'business community' refers to castes and religious groups whose traditional occupation is trade. The businessmen described here belong to several castes, the traditional occupation of which is cultivation. The members of this new 'business community' are united by their common class and regional origin; that is, they come from the class of landed cultivators of coastal Andhra. A central premise of this chapter is that *class*, rather than *caste*, is the important determinant of this type of entrepreneurship. Whereas most members of trading castes enter trade regardless of their economic status, among the cultivating castes, only those families with sufficient resources have the capital and the incentive to start business enterprises. The majority of Kamma, Reddi, Kapu and Raju families are not potential members of the new business community because they are small landowners or landless; it is mainly those with medium and large landholdings who go into business. For historical reasons, families of this class belong mainly to the dominant cultivating castes, but this does not mean that their entry into business is a function of their caste *per se*.

Having said this, it is necessary to consider the fact that this new business community is perceived by many to be almost a single-caste community, at least in Visakhapatnam, and that caste does play an important role in the success of new entrepreneurs. When new opportunities for business opened up, there was an influx of entrepreneurs from outside, mainly from southern coastal Andhra, who had the necessary resources and motivation to start new enterprises in the town. This 'takeover' of local business by 'outsiders' was mentioned by many, both 'outsiders' and local businessmen, and among the 'outsiders', it is mainly Kammas who are believed to have captured control of the local economy.

It is difficult to determine, in the absence of a comprehensive business survey, whether the largest number of businessmen are in fact Kammas, but it does appear that the perception has some basis in fact. What is more important is that Kammas are widely perceived to be the dominant business community. Reddis may be as important economically in the state as a whole as Kammas, if not more so, but they have not acquired the kind of reputation that have Kammas. The success of Kammas in business often is attributed to certain cultural characteristics, both positive and negative, and to their solidarity as a caste. They have a reputation for 'sticking together'—for helping one another and doing business mostly with one another—such that they have been able to monopolise business opportunities. The aggressiveness and quick success of Kammas have earned them a bad reputation, and there is resentment towards them among other businessmen. In spite of this, their success in business is attributed not only to their caste solidarity, but also to their 'enterprising', 'aggressive', 'hardworking' and 'daring' nature.

The popular perception of Kammas as the new dominant business class raises the question of whether caste is in fact a factor that influences business dealings. Most informants, particularly Kammas, insisted that caste feeling or loyalty does not affect the behaviour of businessmen, but some, particularly non-Kammas, disagreed with this view. Several Kammas admitted that there was an advantage to dealing with someone of the same caste, because 'you come with some link', or have a 'common feeling' with one's caste-mate. Although businessmen may favour others of their own caste in their business dealings, it should be noted that this is only one aspect of the general process of networking. Success in business depends largely on the ability to build extensive and useful social, networks, which may be done not only through caste connections, but also through relationships of kinship, friendship, patronage and so on. The available evidence suggests that Kamma businessmen tend to form instrumental relationships with one another, creating caste-based resource networks that exclude non-Kammas. Also, Kamma caste consciousness and solidarity have given them an edge in business because of their propensity to help one another as a means of improving the status of the caste as a whole. In a sense, then, there is an entity that can be called a 'Kamma business community', even though business is not the traditional occupation of the caste.

The functioning of caste-based networks is most apparent in the caste associations that have become active in Visakhapatnam during the past several years.[25] The Kamma. caste association in Visakhapatnam is mainly an organisation of rich Kamma businessmen (although Kammas in other occupations are also members) which promotes caste unity and the interests of Kammas. It derives its main financial support and leadership from the Kamma business community. All of the office-bearers are prominent Kamma businessmen, and all but one are contractors; these men are leaders of the local Kamma community as well as of the business community. The association provides a forum for extending social networks, and it caters to the needs of its members through projects such as the private school. It also seeks to increase Kamma power and influence by extending patronage to less wealthy caste members, for example, through providing scholarships.

IV

Conclusion

...

Economic diversification is typical of rural elites in almost every region of India, at present and in the past. In some regions this is associated with economic backwardness because of the stranglehold of a small elite over the rural economy; in others, it has led to capitalist development as agricultural and trading profits are channelled into more productive activities. In coastal Andhra and Kongunad, as in the 'dry region', wealthy farmers entered trade, but in the former the inter-penetration of agriculture and trade did not produce the vicious cycle seen in north Arcot of merchant capital reproducing agrarian stagnation reproducing merchant capital. In both coastal Andhra and Kongunad, agricultural profits tend to become trading capital, and trading profits to become industrial capital. While the outcome of this process is evident in Coimbatore, in coastal Andhra it is just beginning, and it is not yet clear to what extent this pattern will produce real industrial growth.

This comparison shows that it is necessary to look at the particular history of each region to understand the roles of various elements—landowning elites, merchant castes, cash cropping, and so on—in the development of the economy. 'Merchant capital' is not necessarily an agent of backwardness, just as the commercialisation of agriculture does not necessarily lead to a capitalist transformation (Mishra 1982). Also, the examples of the Kongunad and coastal Andhra farmers suggest that the categorisation of economic activities into 'mercantile' versus 'industrial', or 'productive' versus 'unproductive' is rather arbitrary in the context of the Indian economy (see Harriss 1981: 13–17). Agriculture, trade, industry and other economic activities are closely intertwined in these regions, in part because all may be carried out by a single social group and by a single household. Furthermore, the development of an entrepreneurial class is not a function merely of economic forces, but also of social, political and cultural processes. In the case of coastal Andhra, the social and political history of the region, and particularly of the dominant landowning castes, has played an important role in the emergence of the new business class.

...

Notes

1. There are numerous studies of the effects of the Green Revolution in India. See Byres (1972) and Omvedt (1981) for bibliographies.

2. This characteristic is not, however, simply an outcome of the Green Revolution; it was typical of rural elites even in the colonial period (see, for example, Baker 1976, 1984; Washbrook 1976). The development of capitalistic, market-oriented rural elites did not take place uniformly across regions; in some regions these tendencies are found among the rural elite in the late nineteenth or early twentieth centuries, in others more recently, and in others not at all. Furthermore, the type of diversification varies regionally. For example, where specialised merchant groups have captured the trade in agricultural commodities and dominate the rural credit market, rich farmer are less likely to become important in

these areas; consequently their capital tends to flow more into the agro-processing or service industries.

3. Historically, the Indian national and regional bourgeoisies have been composed mainly of members of the traditional merchant communities (such as Marwaris, Parsis, Gujarati Banias and Chettiars), presumably because merchants were able to accumulate sufficient capital for investment in industry and were experienced in business. Some former zamindars and large landlords were able to convert their assets into industrial capital before they were confiscated by land reforms, but ordinary 'rich peasants', small landlords and commercial farmers rarely became industrial entrepreneurs. This may be attributed to the fact that their financial resources are relatively small, to their rural location, and to their relative lack of education (Nafziger 1971). There is at least one well-documented case, however: the Coimbatore cotton mill industry was founded mainly on the capital of wealthy Gounder and Naidu cotton growers in the 1920s and 1930s (see Baker 1984: 267–76, 339–72).

4. The chapter is a summary of parts of my doctoral dissertation, 'From Kulak to Capitalist: The Emergence of a New Business Community in Coastal Andhra Pradesh, India', submitted to Yale University (New Haven, Connecticut, the US) in March 1988. The dissertation is to be published by University Microfilms (Ann Arbor, Michigan). The research on which this chapter is based was funded by a fellowship from the International Doctoral Fellowship Programme of the Joint Committee on South Asia of the Social Science Research Council and the American Council of Learned Societies for the years 1980–81; the support is gratefully acknowledged. Field research was carried out between 1981 and 1984 in two villages of coastal Andhra and in Visakhapatnam town. I would like to thank my advisor professors Harold W. Scheffler, and my readers, professor William Kelly and Helen Siu of the Department of Anthropology, Yale University, for their comments on the dissertation.

5. The focus of this study is on the canal-irrigated delta areas of the four southern coastal districts: Guntur, Krishna, West and East Godavari.

6. On the social and economic history of the region in the colonial period, see Baker (1976); Baker and Washbrook (1975); Rao (1985); Washbrook (1976).

7. According to Washbrook (1976: 68–77), the social structure that developed in this region contrasted sharply with that found in most of dryland Madras Presidency, in which rural society was dominated by a small landowning elite.

8. There are several major landowning cultivating castes in coastal Andhra, the dominant one overall in terms of land and numbers being Kammas. Kapus are probably more numerous than Kammas but they own less land. In any one village or area only one caste is dominant in regard to land ownership. The other 'peasant' castes include Reddis, Telagas, Rajus (Kshatriyas), Velamas and Naidus.

9. A contemporary report noted that 'in Bezwada [Vijayawada] there is a regular corn exchange where the price of paddy is fixed daily by the ryots with their samples, and the buyers are either merchants who buy on commission for Madras or agents of Bombay and Poona Companies ... The merchants who buy or else the *rich cultivators who are nearly all becoming traders* store their grain till prices have risen and bring it to Tenali' (Board of Revenue Report 1903, quoted in Rao 1985: A-63; emphasis mine).

10. The Madras Banking Enquiry 1933 reported that in the deltas, 'substantial sums of money were found to have been expended on the education of children' (Government of Andhra Pradesh 1977a: 158). Slater (1918: 220) remarked that every 'average villager now eagerly wants to educate his son in spite of heavy debts and great inconvenience'.

11. The concretisation of these large castes had social as well as political dimensions. Sub-caste boundaries began to break down and marriage ties to spread over wider areas, which

meant that members of a single caste for the first time were united by social relationships rather than by name alone (Elliott 1970: 141–42). The integration of the Kamma caste, for example, is demonstrated by the fact that certain social and cultural changes occurred uniformly throughout the caste, which was spread over at least six districts. Changes in social custom resulted from the new prosperity of the delta farmers and their desire to enhance the social and ritual statuses of their castes. These social changes are discussed at length in Upadhya (1988).

12. At this time there also began a trend that gathered momentum later in the century: out-migration of cultivators from the deltas to newly developed or developing areas. In the 1920s, 'energetic young Kammas' were starting to migrate to other areas of coastal Andhra, where newly converted wasteland or newly irrigated land was freely available and relatively cheap, especially in the zamindari estates (Ranga 1926: 38–39). Later a number of Kamma cultivators migrated to Karnataka and Orissa, where they converted subsistence farming drylands into areas of commercial farming. More recently, Kammas have bought up newly irrigated land in the Nagarjunasagar Project area.

13. Baker's (1976: 169–93; 1978; 1984) analysis pertains to Madras Presidency as a whole, most of which consisted of the 'dry' region or the 'plains', the rural magnates of which were different from the rich cultivators of coastal Andhra. However, it also applies to the latter, in that agriculture and agro-industry became unprofitable and rich farmers were encouraged to invest outside their rural localities. The major difference may be that the dry region magnates were more dependent on moneylending and so were harder hit by the debt crisis that followed the depression.

14. The caste factor also played a role in the success of such companies. It is said that SRMT, for example, employed mainly local Kamma youths on the recommendation of Kamma 'patriarchs', which enabled the company to pay low salaries. Other Kamma-owned industries were said to operate in the same way. Caste-based recruitment inhibits unionisation and hence benefits the owners, because the employees have patron–client ties with their employers and with their sponsors (Reddy 1981: 207).

15. These statements are based on field research in two villages, described below, results of which are presented in Chapter 3 of Upadhya (1988). They cannot be substantiated here.

16. In one West Godavari village study, only one-third of the farmers reported that their profits from rice cultivation had increased between 1965 and 1971, but few reported a decline in profits (Parthasarathy 1975: 68). In many cases, improved irrigation may have been a more significant factor determining profitability than adoption of HYV technology, because a second crop of rice could be grown; this was the case in 'Rajupalem' village studied by the author. In another study in West Godavari, large farmers estimated their incomes to have doubled between 1965 and 1970 due to the introduction of double-cropping, use of HYVs, and a partial shift to sugarcane cultivation (Frankel 1971: 70–71). There is also some statistical evidence to support the hypothesis that agricultural profits from rice cultivation are higher in the post-Green Revolution period than before (Parthasarathy and Pothana 1983: A-96).

17. There is little information on investment patterns of rich rural households. A study of rural savings and investment in Ramachandrapuram taluk found that of the total economic surplus (from agriculture) generated in the taluk of 6.6 crore in 1971–72, only one-fourth was reinvested in the taluk in the form of fixed capital for productive activity. Half of the total surplus was being exported outside the rural area of the taluk, of which one-third was being invested in residential houses and 'financial assets' (Sarveswara Rao 1978: 111–19.) Another source, the All-India Debt and Investment Survey of 1971–72,

shows that there was a sharp increase in gross expenditure and in fixed capital formation on non-farm business by cultivator households in Andhra Pradesh state between 1961–62 and 1971–72. However, fixed capital formation in residential plots and buildings was 1.5 times that on non-farm business. A disproportionate share of such expenditure was by the wealthier cultivator households. Nearly half of all the gross capital expenditure on non-farm business was by households having assets of Rs 50,000 or more (who constitute only 4 per cent of all households) (Krishna Rao 1984: 40–44).

18. This discussion focuses on the canal-irrigated deltas of coastal Andhra. However, an important section of the entrepreneurial rich farmer class comes from the 'dry' tobacco region of Guntur district. See Duvvary (1986: PE-53) for an account of how wealthy tobacco growers (mainly Kammas) have entered the tobacco processing, marketing and exporting business. One of the largest Kamma-owned export houses, Navabharat Enterprises, expanded into cigarette manufacture in the 1970s with Russian collaboration.

19. In contrast to this, Visakhapatnam district has fewer industries but a higher total fixed capital, because it is an area of large-scale industrial development.

20. The field study of a Raju-dominated village in Bapatla taluk, Guntur district, was carried out during five months in 1981. The second study of a Kamma village in East Godavari district (Ramachandrapuram taluk) was of two months' duration in 1982. The two villages are called by pseudonyms, 'Rajupalem' and 'Kammavaram', after the names of the dominant caste in each.

21. In 'Rajupalem', it was found that the average gross profit per acre in 1980–81 on a large farm for a double paddy crop was Rs 2,200, which works out to a total net profit (taking into account fixed expenses) for a 50-acre farm of about Rs 85,000, or about Rs 1,700 per acre. In 'Kammavaram' village, the gross per acre return for paddy was higher—Rs 2,500–3,000—and total incomes were higher because farmers cultivated sugarcane and other cash crops in addition to paddy. In this village, a large farmer planting 10 acres of paddy and 10 of cane can earn around Rs 38,000 per year. The average size of large farms was smaller in 'Kammavaram' than in 'Rajupalem'—20 acres and 50 acres, respectively—but the land in Kammavaram was more productive and irrigation was better.

22. Leasing out is the least preferred solution to the problem of management of rural lands belonging to absentee owners. All of those who had leased out their land had relatives in their villages who were looking after their interests had leased it to a friend or client, or were able to go frequently to their villages themselves. Several informants said that it was very difficult to maintain leased-out land unless one had a close relative in the village to look after it, because otherwise the owner would get 'cheated'. Also, it was considered risky to lease out land at all except to a 'trusted person' because of land reforms legislation that conferred ownership rights on tenants.

23. It is not clear if this tax advantage, mentioned by some informants, really exists. Some said that it does not, because although agricultural income is not taxable in itself, if one has both agricultural and other income, the former is clubbed with the latter, raising the total taxable income.

24. Even after years of living in the city, many migrants were reluctant to purchase rice, in part because of the expense, but mainly because the best quality rice is not generally available in the market. Because they take pride in eating only their own rice, many went to great trouble and expense to have their home-grown rice sent from their villages. In some cases, other provisions such as pulses, vegetable oil and vegetables were also being sent from their villages. Several informants said that they got almost all their food supplies in this way:

whatever is grown on their own land is sent to them by whomever is cultivating it and is never bought in the market.

25. Because of their lack of social respectability, the existence of these associations is not widely advertised, least of all to foreign researchers, and they are cloaked in deceptive names. The Kamma association is called the 'Kakatiya Educational and Cultural Society' and the Reddi association is called the 'Vemana Cultural Association'. Their ostensible purpose is to provide better educational facilities to poor students. The Kakatiya Society, for example, has started an industrial training institute (ITI), and it provides funds to coach and send students for the Indian Administrative Services (IAS) examinations. There were plans to build a hostel and provide scholarships for poor students attending the university, and also to build a community hall. However, the only other major accomplishment of the society has been the foundation of a private school ('public school') in Visakhapatnam, the donations for which came primarily from wealthy Kamma businessmen. The main purpose of setting up this academy is not to educate underprivileged children, but to provide better educational facilities for the rich. Because of the recent economic and population growth of the town, and the influx of wealthy business families, a demand was created for a good, expensive private school, and it is not by chance that it is being founded by a Kamma caste association.

References

Appa Rao, T. 1974. *Municipal Government in Visakhapatnam*. Visakhapatnam: Department of Politics and Public Administration, Andhra University, Waltair.

Baker, Christopher. 1976. *The Politics of South India, 1920–1937*. New Delhi: Vikas Publishing House.

———. 1978. 'Debt and the Depression in Madras, 1929–1936'. In *The Imperial Impact: Studies in the Economic History of Africa and India*, eds Clive Dewey and A. G. Hopkins, 233–42. London: Athlone Press.

———. 1984. *An Indian Rural Economy, 1880–1955: The Tamil Nadu Countryside*. Delhi: Oxford University Press.

Baker, Christopher and D. A. Washbrook. 1975. *South India: Political Institutions and Political Change, 1880–1940*. Delhi: Macmillan Company of India.

Baru, Sanjaya. 1984. 'Capitalism in Agriculture and Growth of Manufacturing: Some Issues with Reference to Andhra Pradesh'. In *Peasant Farming and Growth of Capitalism in Agriculture*, eds Y. V. Krishna Rao, et al., 365–84. Vijayawada: Visalandhra Publishing House.

Byres, T. J. 1972. 'The Dialectic of India's Green Revolution'. *South Asian Review* 5: 99–116.

Choudary, K. Bhavaiah. 1954. *A Brief History of the Kammas*. Published by the author, Sangamjagarlamudi.

Duvvury, Nata. 1986. 'Commercial Capital and Agrarian Relations: A Study of Guntur Tobacco Economy'. *Economic and Political Weekly* 21: PE-46–57.

Elliott, Carolyn. 1970. 'Caste and Faction among the Dominant Castes: The Reddis and Kammas of Andhra'. In *Caste in Indian Politics*, ed. Rajni Kothari, 129–71. New Delhi: Orient Longman.

Frankel, Francine R. 1971. *India's Green Revolution: Economic Gains and Political Costs*. Bombay: Oxford University Press.

Government of Andhra Pradesh. 1977a. *Andhra Pradesh District Gazetteers, Krishna District*. Hyderabad: Government Secretariat Press.

Government of Andhra Pradesh. 1977b. 'Report on Annual Survey of Industries, 1973–74 to 1975–76'. Bureau of Economics and Statistics.

———. 1979. *Andhra Pradesh District Gazetteers, West Godavari District.* Hyderabad: Government Central Press.

Government of India. 1964. Census of India 1961, Vol. 2, AP, Part VI, Village Survey Monographs, Monograph No. 20: Maredumaka Village, Vijayawada Taluk, Krishna District, Hyderabad. Superintendent of Census Operations.

———. 1972. Census of India 1971, Series 2, AP, Part B1, Reports on Selected Towns No. 2: Kakinada Survey, Delhi Manager of Publications. Office of the Director of Census Operations, AP.

Government of Orissa. 1966. *Koraput District Gazetteer.* Cuttack: Orissa Government Press.

Harrison, Selig. 1956. 'Caste and the Andhra Communists'. *American Political Science Review* 50: 378–404.

Harriss, Barbara. 1981. *Transitional Trade and Rural Development: The Nature and Role of Agricultural Trade in a South Indian District.* New Delhi: Vikas.

Hariss, John. 1982. *Capitalism and Peasant Farming: Agrarian Structure and Ideology in Northern Tamil Nadu.* Bombay: Oxford University Press.

Haswell, M. R. 1967. *Economics of Development in Village India.* London: Routledge and Kegan Paul.

Krishna Rao, Y. V. 1984. *Growth of Capitalism in Indian Agriculture: A Case Study of Andhra Pradesh.* Vijayawada: Visalandhra Publishing House.

Kumar, Dharma. 1975. 'Landownership and Inequality in Madras Presidency, 1853–54 to 1946–47'. *Indian Economic and Social History Review* 12: 229–62.

Mishra, Satish Chandra. 1982. 'Commercialisation, Peasant Differentiation and Merchant Capital in Late Nineteenth-century Bombay and Punjab'. *The Journal of Peasant Studies* 10(1): 3–51.

Nafziger, E. Wayne. 1971. 'Indian Entrepreneurship: A Survey'. In *Entrepreneurship and Economic Development*, ed. Peter Kilby, 287–316. New York: Free Press.

———. 1978. *Class, Caste and Entrepreneurship: A Study of Indian Industrialists.* Honolulu: University Press of Hawaii for the East-West Center.

Omvedt, Gail. 1981. 'Capitalist Agriculture and Rural Classes in India'. *Economic and Political Weekly* 16(52): A-140–59.

Parthasarathy, G. 1971. *The Green Revolution and the Weaker Sections.* Bombay: Thacker and Company.

———. 1975. 'West Godavari, Andhra Pradesh'. In *Changes in Rice Farming in Selected Areas of Asia*, 43–70. Los Banos, Philippines: International Rice Research Institute.

Parthasarathy, G., and V. Pothana. 1983. 'Capitalism in Agriculture and Peasant Farming: Case of Godavari Delta'. *Economic and Political Weekly* 18(39): A-93–97.

———. 1984. *Changing Agrarian Structure in Andhra Pradesh.* Mimeo, National Institute of Rural Development, Hyderabad.

Parthasarathy, G., and D. S. Prasad. 1974. 'The New Technology within Agriculture and Changes in Agrarian Relations: Case Study of a Delta Village in Andhra Pradesh'. In *Seminar on Changing Agrarian Relations in India.* Hyderabad: National Institute of Community Development.

Ramana, V. K. 1971. 'Caste and Society in an Andhra Town'. PhD thesis, Department of Sociology, University of Illinois, Champagne-Urbana.

Ranga, N. G. 1926. *Economic Organisation of Indian Villages (Volume 1): Deltaic Villages.* Bezwada: Vani Press.

Ranga, N. G. 1976. *Distinguished Acquaintances*. Vijayawada: Desi Book Distributors.

Rao, G. N. 1985. 'Transition from Subsistence to Commercialised Agriculture: A Study of Krishna District of Andhra, c. 1850–1900'. *Economic and Political Weekly* 20: A-60–69.

Reddy, N. V. V. S. 1981. 'Caste and Class in Andhra Politics: A Study of East Godavari District (1950–1980)'. M.Phil dissertation, Jawaharlal Nehru University, New Delhi.

Reddy, V. N. 1985. 'Pattern of Commercial Farming in Guntur District'. *Economic and Political Weekly* 20: A-137–52.

Sarveswara Rao, B. 1978. *A Study of Rural Poverty and Inequalities in a Developed District*. Madras: Sangam Publishers for Madras Institute of Development Studies.

Sarveswara Rao, B., and V. Lakshmana Rao. 1978. 'Industrial and Commercial Entrepreneurship in the Coastal Region of Andhra Pradesh'. *ICSSR Research Abstracts Quarterly* 7(4).

Sarveswara Rao, B., et al. n.d. *Commercial Entrepreneurship in Visakhapatnam City*. Mimeo, Department of Economics, Andhra University, Waltair.

Sau, Ranjit. 1984. 'Development of Capitalism in India'. *Economic and Political Weekly* 19: PE-73–80.

———. 1988. 'The Green Revolution and Industrial Growth in India'. *Economic and Political Weekly* 23: 789–96.

Slater, Gilbert. 1918. *Some South Indian Villages* (Volume 1 of Economic Studies). London: Oxford University Press.

Thorner, Daniel. 1967. 'Coastal Andhra: Towards an Affluent Society'. *Economic and Political Weekly* 1: 241–52.

Upadhya, Carol Boyack. 1988. 'From Kulak to Capitalist: The Emergence of a New Business Community in Coastal Andhra Pradesh, India'. Doctoral dissertation, Department of Anthropology, Yale University.

Washbrook, David. 1973. 'Country Politics, Madras, 1880–1930'. *Modern Asian Studies* 7(3): 475–531.

———. 1975. 'The Development of Caste Organisation in South India 1880–1925'. In *South India: Political Institutions and Political Change, 1880–1940*, eds Christopher Baker and D. A. Washbrook, 150–203. Delhi: Macmillan Company of India.

———. 1976. *The Emergence of Provincial Politics: The Madras Presidency 1870–1920*. Cambridge: Cambridge University Press.

19

INCLUSIVE DEVELOPMENT?

*Migration, Governance and Social Change in Rural Bihar**

GERRY RODGERS AND JANINE RODGERS

In a series of articles published in *Economic and Political Weekly* since 1973, we reported on economic and social change in several villages in Purnia district of Bihar (Rodgers 1973; Rodgers and Rodgers 1984, 2001). The last of these articles highlighted some striking developments in production, incomes and labour markets, as the old semi-feudal relations gave ground to market forces. In 2008 and 2009, we again visited two of these villages, in Kasba block,[1] to see whether there had been further developments: had the new economic and social relationships which emerged in the 1990s resulted in sustained growth and rising incomes? Had the acceleration of growth in the Indian economy as a whole had visible effects on the village economy? What was the impact of the political and governance changes of the last decade?

Bihar, despite recent indications of increased growth, has lagged behind as other parts of India have developed.[2] By 2004–05, output per capita amounted to only 35 per cent of the all-India average, and the incidence of poverty was high (55.7 per cent of the Bihar rural population was below the official poverty line, against 41.8 per cent of the all-India rural population; Government of India 2009a). Purnia district is, in turn, relatively backward compared with the state as a whole, with per capita output 25 per cent lower than the Bihar average.

The two villages studied are Pokharia, a small, backward caste-dominated village,[3] with 918 inhabitants in 2001; and Dubaili Biswaspur, a larger village with 4,689 inhabitants in 2001. In Dubaili Biswaspur, we concentrated mainly on one *tola*, Mazgama West, accounting for about a quarter of the households in the village, with a backward class Muslim majority and a smaller number of SC households.[4] We make no claim that these villages are representative of Bihar or even of their district. But neither is there an obvious bias in the choice of these villages.[5] The

* Originally published in *Economic and Political Weekly* 46(23), 4 June 2011: 43–50.

patterns which we observe are reproduced elsewhere in the region, and our findings can help identify the issues and impacts which merit closer attention more generally.

In the 1970s and early 1980s, these villages were backward and stagnant, and poverty was intense. Wages barely sufficed to cover basic subsistence, and real incomes were, if anything, declining. Mortality was high and production relations 'semi-feudal', in the sense that debt bondage, tenancy and attached labour were widespread, served as mechanisms of labour control and exploitation, and were resistant to change. Communications were poor, facilities limited, education levels low. The government action was extremely weak.

From the mid-1980s, things began to change, and by 1999, the picture had altered substantially. Short-term migration to northwestern India seemed to be an important trigger of change, undermining feudal relationships, creating new perspectives, generating additional income sources and pushing up local wages. Diets had improved and, to some extent, housing. Infrastructure had also improved—roads, irrigation, schools—and there had been a significant increase in agricultural productivity. At the same time, the transition was clearly incomplete, with various remnants of the semi-feudal labour and reward systems still present. Agricultural innovation was limited, gender inequality strong, and there was not much visible impact of government programmes.

This chapter explores the impact of another decade of development. After a brief introduction to the villages, it examines changes in agrarian relations, looks in more detail at migration and its impact, and considers trends in governance and in the effectiveness of state policies.

The Village Environment

Population densities are high in Bihar, and these villages are no exception: according to the Census data for 2001, there are 695 persons per square kilometre in Pokharia and 1,379 in Dubaili Biswaspur (compared with 881 for Bihar as a whole and 312 for India). Moreover, population growth is rapid. Between 1981 and 2001, the population of Pokharia almost doubled and that of Dubaili Biswaspur increased by over 75 per cent. Literacy rates have been rising, but at a very slow pace. According to the 2001 Census, even after excluding the 0–6 age group (illiterate by definition), over 50 per cent of men and over 80 per cent of women were illiterate in both villages. The last decade has, however, seen a revolution in school enrolment. New schools have opened and school attendance, especially of girls, has risen rapidly.

Within the villages, occupation remains dominated by agriculture, and the proportion of agricultural labourers has been rising—from 31 per cent of all (main) workers in 1981 to 60 per cent in 2001 in Pokharia, and from 50 per cent in 1981 to 72 per cent in 2001 in Dubaili Biswaspur, according to the Census. In 2001, 28 per cent of workers were classified as cultivators in Pokharia and 22 per cent in Dubaili Biswaspur. In Pokharia, holdings are small: no household had more than 5 acres in 2009. In Dubaili Biswaspur, some larger holdings were reported, but only 6–8 households out of the 215 in the Mazgama West *tola* were reported as having more than 8 acres. Apart from traditional occupations such as basket-making, fishing and other caste occupations, there was little non-agricultural employment in these villages.

There are few *pucca* houses, and most houses are made of traditional materials, mud and thatch (though, often now, with a corrugated iron roof), while many of the poorer households still live in simple constructions of bamboo and thatch. Access to drinking water has improved since 1999, with an increase in the number of handpumps, though some problems of water quality subsist, especially in Pokharia, where one-third of households do not have their own supply, and in the SC locality of Mazgama. Village roads and paths, and drainage show little sign of improvement, and sanitation facilities are still virtually non-existent.

The most striking and visible change concerns communications. Hard to reach in the 1980s, today, the villages are only 6 km away, along a good pucca road, from a four-lane dual carriageway.[6] This means that they are within easy reach of the local block headquarters throughout the year, and also only 40 minutes by autorickshaw from the main district market, which is in turn only a few kilometres from the district headquarters.

There were many more electricity connections in 2009 than in 1999, both legal and illegal, although electricity is available only 4–5 hours per day, and is not used for agriculture because of its unreliability. A few solar street lights have been installed, mainly outside the houses of influential villagers. There is a mobile phone in the majority of households, even among the poorest groups. There has been some growth in the number of shops, with seven in Pokharia and three in Mazgama, and several more on the road nearby, in addition to a weekly market.

CHANGES IN AGRARIAN RELATIONS

The key change observed in 1999 was the shift towards market relationships, especially in the labour market. Since earlier research had connected agricultural backwardness with semi-feudal social and economic relationships, there was reason to expect that market forces, combined with improved communications, would unleash the unfulfilled agricultural possibilities of a region with abundant groundwater and reasonable soils, and a considerable potential for triple cropping.

Agricultural Production

Between 1981 and 1999, agricultural production rose substantially as a result of both increased yields and increased cropping intensity (Rodgers and Rodgers 2001). This rise has continued over the last decade. Estimating trends in agricultural output is perilous, because of variation between cultivators and seasons, but the levels of 'normal year' agricultural output[7] in these villages, in volume terms, seemed to have increased by at least 20 per cent in the decade. Normal wheat yields were generally reported at about 2,400 kg per hectare in 2008–09, compared with an average around 2,000 kg in 1999. Aghani paddy yields were more variable, but mostly over 3,000 kg per hectare, compared with 2,000–3,000 kg in 1999.[8]

The main source of this increase seems to lie in a continued spread of tubewell irrigation, combined with the almost universal use of HYV seeds and fertiliser. Some farmers also use pesticides, and a few new composting methods. The spread of improved techniques may have been encouraged by migration. Migrants returning from Punjab are aware of the more advanced agricultural methods used there, and this may facilitate adoption locally.

By 2009, there were sufficient numbers of boring wells and pumpsets for virtually all the cropped area to be irrigated. Overall, cropping intensity has increased as a consequence, but the cropping pattern has not changed much, with the exception of a decline in jute, to some extent, replaced by maize, and some increase in the *garma* (summer) crop (maize and paddy), connected with the spread of irrigation. The growth in output has no doubt come more from higher yield than from increase in the area sown. Pulses continued their long-term decline, and there were small areas of vegetables and fruit. It is noteworthy that there was little development of new, higher-value commercial crops. Paddy, wheat and maize still accounted for 88 per cent of the entire cropped area in Dubaili Biswaspur and 68 per cent in Pokharia, according to official data; and these figures are probably underestimates, since local respondents reported even higher proportions of sown areas under cereals.

Increased yields need to be set against higher input costs (for HYV seeds, irrigation, fertiliser, pesticides and labour), which can be substantial. Labour costs, in particular, have increased, while the price of foodgrains declined relative to the price of all goods up to the beginning of 2008, compared with 1999 (although it recovered in 2009).[9] Nevertheless, detailed estimates of production costs still suggest that cereal production can be highly profitable.[10]

There have been some changes in livestock, notably a precipitous decline in the number of bullocks, because of their replacement by tractors, but on the other hand, some growth in the number of milch animals, notably among smaller cultivators and agricultural labourers. However, these are mostly local rather than cross-bred varieties and milk production is exclusively for local and domestic consumption. There also seems to have been some increase in the numbers of goats and poultry.

There is evidence here of the spread of improved techniques and growth in agricultural output. But despite improved communications, increased yields have not led to much increase in the marketing of agricultural products. This is a sign that increased output has, to a large extent, been absorbed by a growing population. Only 10 per cent of the most important crop, Aghani paddy, is marketed in Pokharia, and 20 per cent in Mazgama (but higher proportions, 40–50 per cent of the garma crop). About half of wheat produced is commercialised; jute and maize are essentially commercial crops, but they are grown on a much smaller area than paddy and wheat.

Overall, it appears that growth is not based on structural change in the production system, but rather on the intensification of an existing model. Elsewhere in Bihar, investment in the production of vegetables, fruit, flowers and medicinal plants has contributed to growing incomes, but there is no sign of such developments in these villages. And some basic disadvantages, notably vulnerability to drought and flood, have not been resolved. Improved irrigation has made agriculture more resistant to drought, but some crops, and in general, the Aghani season, remain mainly rainfed. Flood is even more problematic. While these villages were not affected by the devastating 2008 Kosi floods, in another year, it can easily be their turn; a river passes through Dubaili Biswaspur which has frequently flooded in the past. Low-lying areas often remain waterlogged. These risks still discourage high levels of investment in agriculture, and call for improved infrastructure.

Labour Relations and Wages

The market for labour has continued to tighten in these villages, and wages have risen sharply. In 1999, local wages were found to have doubled, in real terms, since 1981. Between 1999 and 2009, they rose by another 50 per cent. In 1999, casual wages (full-time, male) were mainly in the Rs 25–35 per day range. In 2009, the main range for agricultural work was Rs 67–95.[11] The Bihar consumer price index for agricultural/rural labourers rose by 76.4 per cent from April 1999 to November 2009, the relevant dates for our investigation, so in 1999 prices, the wages observed in 2009 were in the range of Rs 38–54, that is, a 50 per cent real increase at both bottom and top of the range. Almost half of this rise came in the last one year between the two visits in December 2008 and November 2009.

Women's wages had risen more than men's. Typically, Rs 20 per day in 1999, normal wages were reported as Rs 57–74 in 2009, a rise in real terms of 58–105 per cent. There was still a wage differential between men and women, but it was of the order of 15–30 per cent, rather than the 20 per cent to 50 per cent observed in 1999. However, there seemed to be more variability in women's wages, with the lowest slack season wage reported as only Rs 37.[12]

These increases in wages were accompanied by increased variability in the labour market. There was much greater diversity than in 1999 in wage rates between villages and crop operations. For instance, jute harvesting and retting was paid more because it was hard work, and there was some growth in contract work, weeding a specified area for instance, where the remuneration was negotiable depending on the area and the abundance of weeds. There was also a substantial seasonal variation.

The most likely cause of these increases in wages is the withdrawal of labour from the local labour market through large-scale temporary migration to other parts of India (which we discuss later). Increased output could, in principle, be a factor, but agricultural growth has only been of the same order as population growth, and non-agricultural output, other than construction, remains small.

The immediate consequence of the tightening labour market has been to raise the cost of cultivation, and to increase competition for labour among cultivators. It should also have increased the incentives for mechanisation. But apart from tubewells, only two types of mechanisation are widespread: tractors for ploughing and threshers. Transplanting, weeding and harvesting remain labour-intensive, and labour use for weeding and harvesting rises with yield. It is, therefore not surprising that cultivators complain of labour shortage, notably during the monsoon months of Asarh, Sawan and Bhado. The labour intensity of jute cultivation is said to be one reason for its decline; harvesting and retting of jute coincide with the paddy harvest in Punjab and Haryana, so there is a direct competition between local and distant employers.[13]

There have been differential effects across different sizes of landholding. For many small cultivators, opportunities for migration are more attractive than own cultivation. Some rent out their land, while they migrate for work, while in others women and children replace migrant male labour. Middle peasants, who were previously hiring in labour, are squeezed by the tight labour market, and may see a fall in net income. Larger cultivators, on the other hand, may have enough market power to assure a supply of casual labour at peak times, and are so better placed to take full advantage of the potential of improved seeds and cultivation practices.

Interestingly, some of the mechanisms of the semi-feudal system are still present in this new economic environment, but they function in a different way. The main exception is attached labour, which has disappeared—the labour market functions essentially on a casual, daily basis. Tenancy, on the other hand, is if anything more widespread than before, especially in Mazgama. It remains dominated by sharecropping where both inputs (fertiliser and irrigation) and outputs are shared 50:50 between landowner and tenant. Some new practices have also developed, such as fixed payment in kind for the whole year, or a smaller share for the landowner (noted in particular for the garma season). But tenancy, which is renewed annually, no longer plays a central role in economic control. Indeed, in a reversal of previous practices, it now seems that larger landowners rent in land from small landowners.

Indebtedness too appears to be as widespread as ever, much of it to traditional moneylenders at high interest rates. But the inflow of money from migration means that debts can be repaid, and indebtedness seems to be much less important as a mechanism of social control. In addition, access to institutional loans may have improved. One small cultivator-cum-agricultural labourer was able to borrow Rs 50,000 (used for his daughter's marriage) from a bank because he owned some land.

The practice of remunerating harvest labour with a share of the crop has survived the strengthening of market forces, but like daily wages, the shares have become more variable, depending on the yield and the quality of the grain, with a larger share being paid to labour where the crop is poor. The range was between one-eighth and one-twelfth for paddy and wheat, although one-eighth was the most common for paddy, as against one-ninth in 1999, suggesting some increase in the equivalent daily wage. However, given the rise in the casual daily wage for other operations, harvest shares no longer supply a bonus as they did in the past; it is likely that real wages are not very different from those in other agricultural operations.

All in all, the picture is one of increasingly atomised and diversified labour relations. There is effectively no organisation of labour within the villages, except the organisation of groups of migrants, and wage relationships appear to be individualised and short-term.

The disappearance or redefinition of the old 'semi-feudal' mechanisms has not necessarily changed the economic and social hierarchy. In some of the old 'semi-feudal' families, it seems that a new generation of cultivators has adapted to the market, and their market power may permit them to invest in more productive agriculture.

MIGRATION AND THE LABOUR MARKET

Migration has become a way of life in these two villages, as it has in many parts of Bihar. In 1999, there were already migrants to northwestern India from the majority of households, especially poorer households. Migration was almost exclusively male, short-term and seasonal, mostly between one and six months at a time. Since then migration has if anything increased further (respondents uniformly reported this), with a greater diversity of migration destinations and durations, and some move towards longer-term migration, especially to urban areas. But there is still very little permanent migration, in the sense of definitive departure of households from the village. The original reason for the growth of migration was lack of employment in the village. This reason continues to be cited by respondents, but nowadays cultivators in the village complain of labour shortage, so lack of local employment may no longer be the main factor.

The increases in local wages seen above have narrowed the gap with other parts of India. In 1999, wages for casual daily labour in northwestern India, both urban and rural, were reported as Rs 60 to Rs 65 per day, about double the wages in these Bihar villages. In 2009, migrants were reported to be getting Rs 100–150 per day in agriculture in Punjab and Haryana; compared with the wages observed in the villages of Rs 67–95 per day, the gap is down to about 50 per cent on average. In urban areas, migrants were said to be able to earn Rs 4,000–6,000 per month in a variety of casual jobs, though observations in Delhi suggest that these numbers are on the high side. All of these figures are for adult males. Very few women migrate for economic reasons.

Agricultural work (transplanting of paddy, harvesting of paddy, wheat or sugarcane) in Punjab, Haryana and nearby still seems to account for at least half of all migration. One important change has been the elimination of the middle man. Since virtually all migrants have or have access to mobile phones, it has become common for farmers in Punjab to call villagers in Bihar directly when they need labour for harvesting—this contact, of course, being carried over from year to year. Groups of villagers then migrate together, and at the place of destination they live and work together. This migration is typically for two to four months at a time, depending on the availability of seasonal work. In addition, there has been a considerable increase in migration to Delhi and other urban locations, where employment includes construction, commerce and factory work. Durations are longer; a common pattern is for the migrant to stay away for 4–6 months, return for a month or two, and then leave again. Married migrants leave their wives and children in the village. Only one case was recorded in Pokharia of a woman migrant, engaged in domestic service in Delhi, and none in Mazgama.

Migration, as noted above, is surely the primary reason for the rise in local wages. It is often argued that the National Rural Employment Guarantee Scheme (NREGS) has a similar impact, because it both creates demand for labour and (in principle, at least) pays legal daily minimum wages (Rs 89 in 2008, Rs 97 in 2009), which are higher than prevailing agricultural wages. However, in these villages, there are few NREGS projects, and the volume of employment created is at least an order of magnitude less than that obtained through migration. At most, NREGS is a supplementary factor. A similar comment can be made about the recent growth in public sector construction, notably of roads, which is also sometimes identified as a source of increased labour demand, but which is again only a secondary factor in these villages. Migration, therefore, continues to be the primary driving force for rising incomes among the poor. As noted in 1999, taking into account both the additional employment of migrants and the higher wages in the village labour market, migration probably raises the incomes of labour households by a factor of two to three.

Among the better-off households, there are frequent reports of children (mainly sons) getting secondary or vocational education outside the village. At this level, family and community networks are important. The Muslim community of Mazgama has connections with a business network both in local towns and spread across India, extending to west Asia, which provides opportunities for the second generation members of well-off families.

A form of migration that has developed recently concerns young boys aged 10–14, migrating to Moradabad, Delhi or Ferozabad to work in factories making bangles, toys, carpets or steel pots and dishes. This concerned some 25–50 households in Mazgama (out of 250). In Pokharia south tola, about 15 boys were migrating for work. The phenomenon had grown in the last two or three years. In Mazgama, it was reported that children migrate in small groups. A contractor from outside the village advances their travel expenses and gets back a percentage of the children's wages (10 per cent was mentioned). The boys concerned basically lived at the worksite, where they were given food, clothing and lodging, and a wage of Rs 600–1,000 per month for the first year, and Rs 1,000–2,000 thereafter. They would come back to the village from time to time (especially for major festivals), but would be spending 8–10 months in the year away. One respondent had a 12-year-old son who was doing this in a bangle factory near Delhi, and who was also studying—there are perhaps some elements of apprenticeship in this process. The son called home regularly—the mobile phone again!—and was reported to be 'happy'.

The overall impact of migration on the local labour market is considerable. First, there is the impact on women's work and responsibilities, which we consider below. Second, cultivators widely complain of both labour shortages and of the high cost of labour. Migrant workers do, however, tend to return for the local paddy and wheat harvests,[14] and to a lesser extent at other peak times. Third, migration also generates new skills, and there was at least one example of a person working as a tailor in Jaipur who did tailoring work in the village during spells between migrations. Skills developed in construction, in carpentry and certain other occupations may also have an outlet in the village.

The decline in wage differentials between Purnia and northwest India is striking. It suggests that migration is contributing to wage equalisation across India, and so bringing incomes in Bihar up towards the Indian mean. In fact, these labour markets are now interconnected. Unskilled wages are rising less fast than other incomes in Delhi and surrounding areas, and the inflow of migrants is surely part of the reason. The long-term dynamics of the process are unclear, but the male labour reserve in these two Bihar villages seems to be close to exhausted. That might explain the shift towards child labour. There is, of course, a female labour reserve that has hardly been tapped.

Migration generates a considerable volume of resources, both in the form of remittances and savings. Bihar has become one of the main destinations for remittances within India. If what is observed in these villages is repeated across rural Bihar, the order of magnitude of the resource flow into the state could amount to 4–7 per cent of net state domestic product.[15] From the point of view of the dynamics of development, these resources could be an important new source of investment. On the whole, however, this is not the case. Most respondents indicated that the primary use of remittances was for food, clothing, health and house repairs—that is, meeting basic needs—and education. However, in some cultivating households savings of migrants were used for current agricultural inputs—seeds, fertilisers—and one respondent had purchased a cow while others had purchased calves. Some had improved their houses, bought consumer durables (TV, radio, mobile phone) or repaid loans. Increase in dowry was also mentioned (although this may be a transfer between households rather than final consumption).

There were some isolated reports of land purchase or purchase of agricultural equipment. However, it was clear that relatively little of the resources generated by migration was going into production; perhaps this is not surprising, given that migrants came mainly from lower income groups.

IMPACT OF MALE MIGRATION ON GENDER RELATIONS

The migration of men has had some impact on the workload of women, on their responsibilities within the household and on their mobility. In 1981, women were seldom going outside the village, except to visit relatives or for severe health problems. Men went to the market and made all the household purchases. In 2009, women had more frequent contacts with the outside world. They went to the market (as a small group of women or with a male relative but also alone if need be), and in Pokharia some women mentioned going to the temple, to fairs and to bathe in the Ganga. However, mobility restrictions still affected young married women who had not borne children.

De facto head of household when men migrate, women have more responsibilities regarding the children's schooling, taking family members to the doctor and house repair. They are also more involved in the management of money. When in need they borrow from relatives or the local moneylender. However, they keep regular contact with their husband thanks to the spread of mobile phones.

While women have always played a role in agricultural production, their importance has been growing. The increase in cropping intensity, higher yields and the absence of men has increased the demand for female and child labour. In 1999, they were mainly involved in harvesting; in 2009, more women reported also doing transplanting and weeding, while women from landowning families would oversee cultivation. There has been a substantial increase in milch animals in particular among smaller cultivators and agricultural labourers. Women assume multiple roles ranging from animal care, grazing, fodder collection and cleaning of animal sheds to processing of milk and livestock products.

This increased involvement of women in agriculture includes both work on own farm and wage labour. While above a certain level in the social hierarchy women still do not work for wages, it appears that the threshold has been rising, so that, for instance, women in small peasant households who previously would not undertake wage work are increasingly reporting that they do some agricultural labour outside their own farms. The reduction in the wage differential against women also increases the incentive for women to enter the labour market.

The Role of the State and the Institutions of Governance

Since 1999, there have been important changes in the political environment of the state. The Janata Dal (United) (JDU) and Bharatiya Janata Party government (JDU-BJP), led by Nitish Kumar, which came to power in 2005, was widely seen as more effective than its predecessors. In the block office in Kasba, the block development officer reeled off an impressive list of programmes which were in operation. This was not just on paper; activities and impacts of many of these programmes could be observed in the villages. This is in sharp contrast to the situation in 1999, when state presence was weak. It may be too simplistic to attribute this only to a change of political regime, for other factors such as improved communications and awareness levels presumably also played a role. But the political change was certainly an important factor.

While we did not attempt a systematic survey of government programmes at the village level, we asked questions about awareness, impact and functioning of a variety of programmes to respondents from different social groups.

First, as noted above, there have been marked improvements in communications as a result of public investment in roads, noted by many respondents as a major dimension of progress.

There has also been a substantial increase in school enrolment and attendance.[16] This is the result of policies on both the supply and demand sides—on the supply side, through the three new schools that have opened in and around these villages and the hiring of additional teachers; and on the demand side, through scholarships for girls and a mid-day meal programme, which had started shortly before our visit, although it was far from running smoothly in Pokharia.

The improvements in public health are more modest. There are Anganwadi centres for child development in both villages, but they do not serve all segments of the community. The continued demand for medical treatment from local quacks is also indirect evidence that the public health system is not meeting local needs, and it was reported that visits by block level medical staff were infrequent. However, vaccination campaigns seem to have been effective and the Janani Suraksha Yojana (JSY) promoting institutional child delivery has scored some successes.

or

There are many beneficiaries of programmes for income transfers of various sorts. The housing scheme for backward classes and SCs [Indira Awas Yojana (IAY)] reported an increasing number of beneficiaries. In Mazgama, 20 out of 30 households in the Harijan tola had received some benefits from the programme. In Pokharia, the impact was quite visible since the IAY programme is essentially the only source of pucca (brick) houses, of which several had been built or were under construction. The scheme has been in operation for many years, so the cumulative number of beneficiaries is a significant fraction of the village population—said to be 29 households (out of 163) over 10 years.

The public food distribution system is more problematic. In 2009, villagers below the poverty line were entitled to 15 kg of rice, 10 kg of wheat and three litres of oil per month at subsidised prices. The identification of households below the poverty line raises many problems which we will not go into here. But in these villages, a voucher system was in operation which made it easy to verify the distribution. This showed that in the SC tola of Mazgama, oil was regularly available but grains were distributed only about one month in two in the five months preceding our visit. According to the manager of the shop, in the other months, there was no delivery. When grain was available, however, the full quota was distributed.

Employment under the NREGS was, as noted above, of secondary importance because of migration. While there were several projects under NREGS elsewhere in the panchayats within which Pokharia and Mazgama fell, there was little activity within these two locations—there had been only two projects in the previous two years, of which one was reported as generating 30–45 days of work for 25 men and 15 women. But no women from these two villages reported work under NREGS. Some 70–80 households had job cards in Mazgama, but in the absence of local projects they did not seem to be used.

A number of other income transfer programmes report fairly large numbers of beneficiaries, the largest being the (national) old-age pension scheme, reaching, according to official data, individuals in about 15 per cent of households below the poverty line in the panchayats concerned—and new applications which had recently been submitted would, it was stated by panchayat officials, double that number. According to official records there was also a substantial number of recipients of widow's pensions, and small (single figure) numbers receiving other benefits. Respondents made little reference to receipt of income from such programmes, but their impact can only be verified at the household level.[17]

Disappointing Development Programmes

In contrast to these 'social' programmes involving cash transfers and employment creation, state policies concerned with promoting economic development seemed to be much weaker. In principle, a variety of agricultural extension programmes exist involving loans and subsidies for investment, provision of inputs and training. But there was little impact of these programmes. A small number of loans for investment in irrigation was reported in Mazgama. Larger farmers were aware of the programmes for the distribution of new seeds and fertilisers, but complained that distribution was less than promised or of poor quality. There were demands for state borings to reduce the cost of irrigation. Many government programmes operate only on a pilot basis in a small number of blocks or panchayats, and there seem to be large opportunities which are not being exploited, for example, to support the development of milk production, or fruit and vegetables. There was little or no government support for the development of non-agricultural activities.

There was a general assumption, among village respondents, that a substantial proportion of government funds in most of these programmes was diverted into private pockets. One local official said that in the IAY housing programme, the beneficiary receives Rs 24,000 out of the Rs 35,000 allocated, with the difference taken by a middle man and public officials. Government schemes such as NREGS were diverted towards the interests of more influential sections of the village. Problems with the mid-day meal programme were reportedly, partly, because a local official was demanding a percentage. What was striking was less the examples of corruption which were cited than the lack of concern among respondents, who appeared to accept this as normal practice.

In order to ensure that these various programmes reach their intended beneficiaries, there are issues of governance at all levels—state, district, block and panchayat. Both of the villages studied are part of much larger panchayats, and respondents tended to portray their villages as relatively disadvantaged within that framework. This is perhaps not surprising in Pokharia, with a backward caste majority and no influential leaders or large landowners. There was little participation in the meetings of the Gram Sabha, the assembly of the panchayat, and little reference to its deliberations. Mazgama, on the other hand, is a significant tola of a larger village, and the location of a substantial mosque and market. Nevertheless, respondents in Mazgama believed that activities under government programmes such as NREGS were biased towards the village where the *mukhya* of the panchayat lived. However, there was much more participation in the Gram Sabha than in Pokharia [it was reported that there were 200 participants in the last meeting, although this refers to the panchayat as a whole (eight villages) and not only to Mazgama].

Conversations about the functioning of the panchayat revealed a distinct conservative bias, for instance, with respect to the effective participation of women, which did not seem to be particularly welcome. The 50 per cent reservation of seats for women in Panchayati Raj Institutions has led to the election as mukhya of a woman from a better-off household in Dubaili Biswaspur in 2005. But her role is only nominal and her husband assumes her responsibilities; it was said that real power lay with the panchayat secretary. She had not attended any meeting prior to her election and since then she attends with her husband. Her lack of experience is obviously a drawback. A learning process is, therefore, necessary but will it lead to more effective empowerment?

Beyond the political institutions, there was little effective organisation within the village. A cooperative existed on paper, but was not functioning in reality. There were no self-help groups despite the existence of a long-standing government programme to promote them. Of course, religious organisations were present and active.

CONCLUSION

Brief visits to individual villages raise questions more than they provide answers, but they do help to identify some important issues for further research concerning the pattern of development, the distribution of the benefits, the nature of social change and the role of the state.

In Pokharia and Dubaili Biswaspur there is change. The primary force is migration and other forms of communication with the outside world, but this is not the only factor. There is some shift in agricultural practices under way, universal education is likely to create new social conditions, gender relations are changing, the state is starting to look like a benefactor rather than an exploiter, the physical environment is improving, rising incomes are leading to new patterns of behaviour and expenditure, and income inequality may be falling, if only because it is among poorer groups that the gains from migration are the greatest. At the same time, local production systems are still very narrowly based, agricultural innovation is concentrated among richer farmers, pressure on land continues to rise and the sustainability of a migration-based development path has to be questioned. Social change has not greatly modified the local hierarchy, there are question marks about the functioning of local political institutions, and advances in the status of women have yet to be consolidated.

In many of these areas, knowledge of the process of change is limited. Large-scale national surveys give a very partial picture, and many issues can only be understood on the basis of in-depth, local research.[18]

Some key issues, then, emerge from this study and which need to be explored further.

1. *Sustainability and long-term impact of a development model built on migration*: In addition to the immediate effect on incomes, migration appears to have some developmental impacts, but less than one might expect—resources from migration go mainly into consumption rather than investment. Nevertheless, there are indirect impacts through the flow of knowledge and the secondary effects of changed consumption patterns, through improved communication with the outside and through changes in the structure and functioning of village labour markets. One possible negative impact concerns the implications for local agriculture of labour shortages due to migration.

2. *Changes in gender relations within the household, in the labour market and in the public sphere*: Migration is just one of a number of factors, which also include targeted policy interventions and the revolution in education, which are radically changing the role and participation of women. Women's workload has increased but their participation in the decision-making process in the domestic sphere has also increased. Women are more visible and have more frequent contacts outside the village but in the public sphere their role remains more nominal than real.
3. *Relative effectiveness of different state policies for economic and social development*: These can be broadly divided into conditional or unconditional income transfers, aimed at redistribution or at changing social behaviour; policies which create jobs through public sector action, notably NREGA; and efforts to support the improvement of the production system by providing incentives and subsidies for investment and growth. The striking feature of recent state action in these villages has been the relative success of the first group of policies, while there are questions about the effectiveness of the second and third. The central research issue is to identify the combination of state policies of different types which would most effectively promote both economic and social transformation.
4. *Distributional implications of a changing agrarian system*: In these villages, there is some reason to believe that the top and bottom of the income hierarchy are doing better than the middle, but this needs to be explored further, especially since some groups among the poor may be excluded from new opportunities. New class relations are emerging, and capitalist agriculture is likely to lead to new patterns of inequality, exclusion and adverse incorporation. Thanks to higher income and better infrastructure everyday life has become easier: food security, health, education and housing have improved, but not to the same extent for all segments of the population. A new distributional architecture may well be emerging.
5. *Weakness of non-agricultural development*: It is a striking feature of Bihar's growth as a whole that there is little industrial development; yet the potential for small-scale industry in the villages, notably in processing of primary products, is substantial. Higher income also brings increased demand for construction and services. It would be extremely valuable to identify the conditions under which a broader economic base for development can emerge within the villages, or as part of a network involving local towns.
6. *Changing pattern of governance*: Strong political pressure for developmental interventions, combined with the intelligent design of many new policies, seems to have had an impact. But there is widespread corruption, local elites control panchayat institutions, and the capacity and capability of district and block level institutions is uneven. A plethora of programmes, often short-lived, or which function mainly on paper after an initial burst of activity, does not help to generate a coherent framework. The issues of governance are complex, and embedded in local social relationships, but understanding them better is a precondition for effective state action.

7. *Undesirable side effects of the pattern of development*: One which was identified concerned the growth of new forms of migrant child labour for factory work. These phenomena may just be the tip of the iceberg; migration creates a variety of new forms of vulnerability and exploitation, and many other adverse effects may be hidden within an apparently positive development.

Forty years of visits to these villages leaves one moderately optimistic. Levels of living, health, education and infrastructure have improved to an extent which would have seemed quite implausible in the 1970s and 1980s. But development brings new issues and new aspirations. Despite progress, these villages are far from benefiting fully from the opportunities generated by rapid growth in the Indian economy as a whole. And through improved communications, villagers are well aware of the possibilities. The basic research issue remains to understand how these villages, and all sections and communities within them, can participate fully in the new Indian development path.

NOTES

1. The villages were visited in December 2008 and November 2009.

2. Recent reports of double-digit rates of growth in Bihar are probably exaggerated, but there is no doubt that growth has increased over the last decade, fuelled by a construction boom.

3. Out of 163 households recorded in 2009, 94 were Kewat, 41 Tatma and 20 Mahaldar (all OBC-I), with small numbers of other backward and SC households.

4. A total of 215 households out of 250 in this tola were Kulhaiya, a Muslim backward class, and most of the remainder Hadi, a Hindu SC.

5. They were originally chosen for their proximity to public works projects which had, in practice, little impact on the villages concerned.

6. Part of the East–West Corridor, this road appears to be a spectacular misallocation of resources, since it does not connect major centres and is built to motorway specifications when more modest improvements to a larger number of roads would certainly have been of greater benefit.

7. 'Normal' is understood to refer to years with normal rainfall, without flood or major crop infestations.

8. Farmers quoted a wide range of yields for paddy, from 8–25 md/bigha (approximately 2,000 to 5,900 kg/ha). Generally, larger farmers considered that 15–20 md/bigha (3,500–4,700 kg/ha) was attainable in a normal year in the Aghani season, and 20–25 md/bigha (4,700–5,900 kg/ha) in garma, given adequate fertiliser, pest control and irrigation; but smaller farmers reported 3,000 kg/ha or less in practice.

9. This, according to the all-India wholesale price indices, from the Office of the Economic Adviser to the Government of India, available at http://eaindustry.nic.in (accessed 18 October 2010).

10. One detailed estimate of the production costs involved in reaching a yield of 5,000 kg/ha for garma paddy gave a total of Rs 15,000–25,000 per hectare to set against the market value of the output of about Rs 40,000 (or Rs 35,000, after paying a one-eighth share to labour for harvesting).

11. Including both cash and kind components. These estimates make assumptions about the values of a breakfast (Rs 7 in 2009) and a meal (Rs 10), often included in the wage, and of other kind payments (1 kg of rice was estimated at Rs 14).

12. Some of these differences reflected different types and durations of work, so the comparisons are not always strictly accurate.

13. In addition, jute retting is an unpleasant job, shunned by workers if there are alternatives.

14. The paddy harvest falls mainly from mid-October to mid-November in Punjab, but usually peaks in the second half of November in Purnia, permitting migrants to work in both.

15. The lower estimate would amount to Rs 5,000 crore, based on one worker in every three rural households, migrating for four months and transferring Rs 2,500 per month. The higher estimate is based on an Overseas Development Institute study suggesting Rs 9,000 crore of within-country remittances (Deshingkar et al. 2006).

16. In 1999, school enrolment of girls was minimal and of boys very low among agricultural labour households. In 2009, enrolment rates in primary school were high and attendance moderately good.

17. Results from a representative survey of rural Bihar (see note 18) suggest that the old-age pension is reaching about 20 per cent of households with an eligible member.

18. A research programme to explore patterns of change in Bihar as a whole on the basis of a representative sample of villages is being carried out by the Institute for Human Development, New Delhi, titled 'Aiming at Inclusive Development in Bihar, a Research Programme' (2009).

References

Deshingkar, P., S. Kumar, H. Kumar Chobey and D. Kumar. 2006. *The Role of Migration and Remittances in Promoting Livelihoods in Bihar*. London: Overseas Development Institute.

Government of India (various years). 'Consumer Price Index for Agricultural and Rural Workers'. Labour Bureau, Government of India, Simla.

———. 1981, 1991, 2001. Census of India 1981, 1991, 2001. New Delhi.

———. 2009a. *Report of the Expert Group to Review the Methodology for Estimation of Poverty*. Planning Commission, New Delhi.

———. 2009b. 'Statewise List of Minimum Wages to Agricultural Labourers'. Press release, New Delhi, 20 July.

Rodgers, G. 1973. 'Effects of Public Works on Rural Poverty: Some Case Studies from the Kosi Area of Bihar'. *Economic and Political Weekly* 8(4–6), February: 255–68.

Rodgers, G., and J. Rodgers.1984. 'Incomes and Work among the Poor of Rural Bihar, 1971–1981'. *Economic and Political Weekly* 19(13), Review of Agriculture, March.

———. 2001. 'A Leap Across Time: When Semi-feudalism Met the Market in Rural Purnea'. *Economic and Political Weekly* 36(22), June: 1976–83.

Section V

Emergent Agrarians

20

Agrarian Distress in Bidar

*Market, State and Suicides**

A. R. Vasavi

Agrarian Distress

Between December 1997 and May 1998, 23 cases of suicides related to agricultural crop loss were reported from the north Karnataka districts of Bidar and Gulbarga. Of these, 13 suicides were by agriculturists in the district of Bidar, and a significant proportion of these was from Bhalki taluka. Though this study was initiated in response to reports of suicides in the district, the study does not focus on the actual cases/households in which distress-related suicides were reported.[1] Rather, the study considers the suicides to be symptomatic of larger and more pervasive crises in the region. The crises are ecological, economic and social, each interlinked with the other, and combining to produce distress in the region. And it is in the context of these crises that the pervasive distress in the region and the suicides by agriculturists must be understood.[2]

Ecological Crisis

The promotion of commercial agriculture, based on the utilisation of hybrid seeds, chemical fertilisers and pesticides, in a predominantly semi-arid region, has had several repercussions. There is the loss of landrace seeds as the cultivation of commercial/cash crops displaces the cultivation of local crops. Linked to the use of increased amounts of fertilisers and pesticides, there is the depletion of soil fertility and the increase in crop susceptibility to pests and diseases. As a whole, there is a lack of fit between the ecological specificity of the region and commercial agricultural practices. Climatic changes, especially changes in the rainfall pattern since the past two years (1997–98), compound the conditions of uncertainty and risk in agriculture, subjecting agriculture to an ecological crisis.

* Originally published in *Economic and Political Weekly* 34(32), 7 August 1999: 2263–68.

Economic Crisis

Though commercial agriculture is promoted on the basis of utilisation of external inputs, institutional credit facilities to purchase these inputs are available only to a limited number of agriculturists (mostly large landowners). Most agriculturists incur heavy debts in order to engage in commercial agriculture. Small and marginal cultivators for whom institutional credit is not readily or easily available resort to non-institutional debts at heavy interest rates in order to take to modern cultivation or to remain in cultivation. In times of ecological crises, such as an outbreak of pests or diseases, agriculturists incur more debts (from private creditors and from agri-business agents) to purchase pesticides. As crops are lost, due to both deficit and unseasonal rains and the outbreak of pests, several agriculturists are left with large debts, the repayment of which is beyond the immediate ability of many. As an increasingly commercial activity, agriculture increases the vulnerability of small and marginal agriculturists and provides no safety net (either locally or from the government) during periods of crises.

Social Crisis

The introduction of commercial agriculture in a predominantly dry agriculture belt has its impact on the social fabric of the region. Commercial agriculture itself forces agriculturists to submit to the prescriptions of the agricultural extension service, the market, the agribusiness agencies and credit institutions and agents. Agriculture no longer draws on the established principles of local knowledge, and on caste and kin-based ties. Instead, agriculture is a form of livelihood, to engage in which individual agriculturists depend primarily on their household and family support. As agriculture becomes an externally prescribed form of economic activity there are problems in the dissemination of knowledge, in the conduct of actual agricultural activities and in the understanding and management of situations such as crop loss.

The denouement of such conditions that can be identified as triple crises in the region necessitates that we raise several questions. What factors (economic, political, social and cultural) have combined to produce such conditions? What roles have the key agencies and agents of the government/state, the market/capital, and community played in this context? Who is responsible for the utter degradation of life conditions in this region? Who have been the victims and who have gained? Some answers to these questions may lie in understanding the general background of the region, the altered agricultural patterns and the socioeconomic trends in the region.

State Presence and Absence

In geo-physical terms, Bidar district is part of the semi-arid and drought-prone belt of northern Karnataka and has been susceptible to periodic droughts. Though some 82 per cent of the total land is cultivated, only 8 per cent of its total cultivable area is irrigated and the state's efforts to provide irrigation have been lackadaisical. The two major irrigation projects, Karanja started in 1963 and Chulkinala started in 1972, are yet to be completed. Only 2,097 hectares are irrigated by canals and tanks, while the rest, of about 30,892 hectares, are irrigated by wells and tubewells. The state of incompletion and disrepair (of the little that has been completed) of the two large irrigation projects is a telling comment on the extent of state support for the region.[3]

Compounding the lack of development of infrastructure in the region is the de-industrialisation that has set in since Independence and reorganisation of states. Though once a home to many cottage industries, such as cotton and oil-ginning mills (Government of Karnataka 1977), there are now few industries that draw on local raw materials or skills. Even the well known form of local articrafts, *bidri* ware, is in a state of decline. Increasing prices of materials, especially silver, and declining sales have meant that many of the hereditary artisans are no longer employed in the production of such ware. Literacy levels are also below the state level and currently only 45 per cent of the total population are literate (Government of Karnataka 1996–97).

A drought-prone district with little or no irrigation facilities and no alternative economic opportunities, Bidar has remained in a state of continual poverty and mass deprivation. State assessments indicate that since the 1960s there has been little or no change in its conditions of 'backwardness' measured by indices of literacy, economic development, productivity, infrastructure, etc. In 1961, the district ranked the second lowest in terms of development and by 1969 it was ranked the lowest in the state (Government of Karnataka 1977). That the conditions of 'backwardness' in economic and social criteria persist is evident in the fact that in 1971, the district was assessed to be the 'least developed district' in the state (ibid.: 305). This continues to the present where Bidar, with its average annual income of Rs 4,242 (for 1992–93 prices), ranks 19th out of 21 districts in the state in terms of per capita income (NABARD 1996).

Agricultural Interventions

Agriculture in Bidar had its own specific form. Drawing on the specificities of the local ecology, agriculture was mostly dry cultivation or rain-dependent cultivation in which a wide variety of local sorghum[4] (*jola*, the staple grain) was grown in combination with pulses, oil seeds, wheat and other cereals. Though cultivation was restricted to two periods (*rabi* or winter cultivation from August to January, and *kharif* or summer cultivation from June to September), care was taken to cultivate green manure crops of *sannhemp* and *diancha*.[5] The cultivation and use of such manure crops helped agriculturists retain the fertility of the soil, decreased the chances of external pests and diseases entering the fields, and enabled agriculturists to be self-reliant for a very significant agricultural input. Even by the 1970s, little commercial or inorganic manure or fertilisers were used (Government of Karnataka 1977).

But the agriculture of Bidar, like that of many other semi-arid regions which produced dry cereals, was considered to be 'low productive' and has been subjected to a variety of 'development programmes' that have drawn, largely, on the agenda of the Green Revolution. Drawing on programmes and policies that emphasise the need to increase agricultural productivity, the state has promoted a model of agriculture in the region that draws primarily on the model of agriculture developed for wet regions and for commercial cultivation.

In 1966–67, HYV seeds for sorghum, paddy, wheat and sugarcane were introduced (Government of Karnataka 1977: 150). Gradually, between the late 1960s and mid-1970s hybrid varieties of seeds for other crops such as cotton, pulses and sunflower were introduced. Between 1972–74, the region was subject to a prolonged drought and scarcity conditions. Government intervention in the immediate period saw to the provisioning of relief to people and cattle. But, after the end of the drought and scarcity conditions the district became part of a scheme to promote pulse cultivation.

The cultivation of *tur* or *toghri* (red gram) as a commercial crop became the primary agricultural agenda in the region. A significant proportion of land once under multi-crop and dry cultivation (especially sorghum, wheat and oilseeds) has now been dedicated to the cultivation of pulses, especially that of *kadle* (Bengal gram), and tur (Table 20.1).

TABLE 20.1: Bidar District Cropping Pattern, 1993–94 to 1995–96 (Hectares)

Year	*Paddy*	*Sorghum (Jola)*	*Millet (Sajji)*	*Wheat (Godhi)*	*Other Cereals*	*Kadle*	*Thogri (Tur)*	*Other Pulses*
1993–94	18,010	131,043	12,827	6,133	2,135	26,099	44,801	98,765
1994–95	15,656	19,953	12,811	6,757	–	31,742	48,506	103,144
1995–96	10,218	12,678	15,110	6,973	–	40,342	48,946	105,432

Source: Compiled from *District Statistical Handbook*, 1993–94, 1994–95, 1995–96.

But despite inadequate infrastructure and mass poverty, the region has been able to increase its production of tur. This is observable in the fact that yield rates of pulses were the highest in Bidar district (711 kg per hectare) compared to the state average of only 477 kg per hectare (Government of Karnataka 1995–96). As a result, since 1996, Gulburga and Bidar districts account for 75 per cent of tur cultivation in the state.

The introduction and promotion of modern agriculture resulted in the development of two key and striking contradictions in the region. Perhaps, the most significant contradiction is that while there is an alteration in the very foundation and orientation of agricultural cultivation (in the type of crops cultivated, in the new seed varieties, new inputs, etc.), there is little or no change in the social bases of the agrarian society. That is, though there is an alteration in the physical conduct of agriculture (in the types of crops grown, the cultivation patterns, etc.), it is not matched by any alteration in the ownership patterns of the agrarian society in which new agriculture is introduced. Though largely a dry cultivation belt with a predominance of small cultivators, there is a schism in the patterns of landownership. An overview of landownership patterns in the district will highlight this.

Currently, only 17 per cent of the district's agriculturists can be considered to be large landowners with holding sizes of between 4 and 10 hectares (Table 20.2).

Thirty-six per cent of agriculturists are marginal cultivators with holdings that range from 2–4 hectares. About 45 per cent are small cultivators who own lands that range from 1–2 hectares.[6] While the absence of very large holdings by a smaller proportion of persons is to be seen as an advantage (only about 2 per cent of the holdings are more than 10 hectares), it is important to note that data indicate a continual fragmentation of landholdings. In 1971, the single largest category of landholdings was that of between 5–10 hectares, and the average size of landholding was 6.2 hectares (Government of Karnataka 1995–96). But currently (1996 data), the average size of holding is only 2.8 hectares (NABARD 1996) and a majority of cultivators are those who own less than 2 hectares of land. While such units cannot be assessed to be uneconomic in terms of mere size,[7] the operators of such units face other problems.

TABLE 20.2: Land Distribution, Bidar District, 1996–97

Size Category (Hectares)	*No. of Holdings*	*Total Area (Hectares)*
<1	22,054	14,195
1–2	63,486	94,157
2–4	50,929	138,795
4–10	24,329	145,466
10+	5,229	72,948

Source: District at a Glance, 1996–97.

Given the declining size of landholdings, many small and marginal cultivators resort to renting or sharecropping. Sharecropping in the region is known as *lavani*, and there are about four different kinds of lavani arrangements that prevail in the region.[8] Insecurity of land lease, increasing production costs, inadequate returns from production, and problems in accessing and receiving credit are some of the problems that most small and marginal cultivators and lavani-holders face. Though such arrangements are not conducive to economic development, the state has not actively sought to provide security of tenure to these sharecroppers. This is evident in the fact that though tenancy is legally abolished (vide Karnataka Land Reform Act 1974), there have been no attempts to actually prevent sharecropping or to ensure transfer of titles to sharecroppers.

Of the poorer sections of the rural community, it is only the labouring class, mostly the landless and low-ranked caste groups and members of Scheduled Castes, that has, only recently, seen a slight improvement in life conditions. Linked to the fact that commercial agriculture, without high and extensive mechanisation, increases labour demands (especially for weeding, harvesting), real wages have increased (Government of Karnataka 1997–98). In addition, there has been some amount of collective political mobilisation and organisation among them as organisations such as the Dalit Sangharsh Samiti have been active in the region. Many of the labouring classes are now aware of the stipulated minimum wages, of their rights to receive ration cards and the rations with it, and of other benefits that accrue to them.

Within this context, of relatively little or no change in the economic opportunities and social structures of resource allocation, the promotion of a model of agriculture that is largely dependent on external inputs and the market has implications for the life conditions of the cultivators. Agriculturists trade low-risk, low productive agriculture (typical of agriculture in dry regions) for a high productivity but also high-risk form of agriculture. Yet, such an engagement with agriculture places cultivators in a position of vulnerability, in which neither the agency that promotes this form of agriculture (the state) nor the sources (the market forces) that drive it support them in their time of distress.

MARKET AND AGRARIAN COMMUNITY

In addition to the role of the state in initiating changes and retaining certain social features in the region, it is important to delineate and understand the role of capital and the market in influencing the conditions of the people in the region. Though modern agriculture requires inputs (seeds, fertilisers, pesticides, technology, etc.), much of the capital needed to purchase these inputs is not easily available to a majority of people. As the NABARD report for Bidar (1997–98) indicates, only large landowners are considered to be creditworthy and most institutional credit caters to their requirements. Most small and marginal cultivators, especially sharecroppers, are considered to be 'credit-unworthy' and are bypassed by institutional credit agencies (NABARD 1997–98).

Two factors are accountable for such conditions. One is the general lack of credit made available to rural and agricultural credit institutions. From 1987 to 1992, the RBI has reduced credit availability to agricultural sectors from 19.1 to 11.7 per cent (Rawal and Swaminathan 1998). As a result there is a credit crunch in the agricultural credit institutions which typically meet 67 per cent of short-term loans and 37 per cent of long-term loans in rural areas. This combines with the fact that there are sharp fluctuations in agricultural production, and loan recovery rates are poor. As the NABARD report for Bidar (1997–98) details, loan recovery rates in the district are poor, standing between only 24 per cent for cooperative banks and between 27 and 30 per cent for commercial banks. Low recovery rates further discourage the entry of additional credit into the region and lead to the marking of most small and marginal cultivators as being credit-unworthy.

A striking result of the lack of credit availability to small and marginal cultivators, when modern agricultural methods demand commercial inputs is that there is a mushrooming of non-institutional credit sources. Most of these non-institutional creditors are located in the towns of the district and in the villages. While a survey of the actual types and backgrounds of moneylenders in the region was difficult to conduct,[9] the presence and impact of two new sources of credit were evident.

The first of these are the groups of families that have either benefitted from commercial agriculture and or families with members who are employed in the urban sectors. Members of older, established landowning families, who have with the support of access to land, capital and technical advice reaped benefits from commercial agriculture, seek to utilise their surplus capital as usury. While moneylending by these households and family has always been part of the rural economy, it has now taken an impetus with the additional flow of funds that many of these households have. Urban remittances and surplus capital are ploughed into local moneylending outfits, which, with the government stipulation to be registered, call themselves 'financial corporations'. The presence and impact of these financial corporations is visible in the fact that in even small villages there are shops and houses that have boards indicating that they are 'financial corporations'. For instance, in the village of Murambi, which has only 240 households there are nine financial corporations with members drawn from different caste groups. Lending rates in these agencies are between 40 and 50 per cent per annum (as compared to the average of 17 to 23 per cent at most institutional credit agencies). Most cultivators who are unable to procure loans from cooperatives or banks depend on these agencies for agricultural and non-agricultural monetary requirements.

The second source of credit in the region is that of the agri-input agencies themselves.[10] Agents for large- and small-scale agri-input manufacturing industries not only sell fertilisers, pesticides, seeds, equipment and other agricultural requirements, but also double as creditors by linking sales of these inputs with credit. Manufacturers permit high interest rates by printing high maximum retail price (MRPs) on the items to be sold. It is left to the discretion and skill of the agent/distributor to sell the goods and retrieve the loans from the people. The availability of agri-inputs on credit acts as an incentive for most people to purchase these items.

In addition to the binding of cultivators through agri-input sales and credit, many agents also act as grain procurers. Having purchased inputs on credit, cultivators are often forced to sell their produce to these agencies, at prices that are below market rates, in order to clear their debts. While cultivators, as buyers and clients, are forced to submit to the dictates of the market, they do not have the same leverage as sellers of their produce. Sharp fluctuations in prices, as observed in the decline in prices for 'tur' in 1998, increased costs of production without assured and commensurate procurement prices are trends that mark the economic life of cultivators.

In the establishment and entrenchment of such agencies in the region there is little or no state regulation or supervision. Though pesticide dealers and agents are required to have licences and be registered, many agents and distributors in the villages are not licensed. Cultivators speak of the large-scale dilution of pesticides and the lack of guarantee of many commercial seed varieties.[11] Sales of spurious seeds and pesticides remain an allegation which the state has yet to verify.

Compounding such problems, linked to the inputs required for commercial agriculture, is also the problem of knowledge or agricultural know-how dissemination. Though the practice of commercial agriculture is promoted formally by the government through its agencies such as the department of agriculture and the agriculture extension service, and is largely backed by the promotion of commercial inputs by the agri-business agencies themselves, there are problems in the dissemination of knowledge. Though all village panchayats of the district are assigned a *gram sevaka* or agricultural assistant, contact between the agricultural assistants and the cultivators is not always assured. Most agricultural assistants maintain contacts and good rapport with only large landowners, sharing with them information about new seeds, pesticides, fertilisers and indicating ways in which to use the new inputs. In addition to this limited contact and supervision, much of the instructions for the use of agri-inputs (such as fertilisers, pesticides and seeds) are only in English and in some cases in Hindi. While a large proportion of cultivators are illiterate, even those literate in the regional and local languages, in this case, Kannada and Urdu, respectively, are unable to comprehend the instructions and directions for the use of these inputs.

This limited contact between agricultural agents and small and marginal cultivators has its effect on agricultural conditions. Agricultural practices also alter within the context of informal dissemination of knowledge and imitation. Cultivators integrate new methods and new inputs through observing others and with little or no formal instruction in the details of using the new inputs. This haphazard dissemination of agricultural knowledge and practices lends itself to problems in the context of crises situations. This was evident in the discussion relating to the use of pesticides at the time of the outbreak of the heliothesis epidemic. Members of the agricultural extension service observe that cultivators did not spray their fields at the appropriate time (when the pests were in the larvae stage) and then resorted to rampant and excessive spraying when the pests had reached the fourth stage of maturation and were not susceptible to control by pesticides. However, cultivators indicate the absence of agricultural extension personnel in the field and the lack of instruction on how to handle a situation such as the outbreak of the heliothesis pest. The resulting gap in knowledge dissemination meant that cultivators not only lost a sizeable proportion of crops, but also incurred large sums of debt. Such a situation calls attention to the problem of knowledge dissemination. While local knowledge and locally appropriate practices are being displaced, the spread of a new form of agriculture is not based on ensuring the proper dissemination and practice of new knowledge. Rather, cultivators receive and disseminate knowledge of the new practices and inputs in a rather ad hoc manner leading to confusion and even stress during periods of crises.

The result of such economic, ecological and social changes and their devastating impact on the local community was evident in the situation that developed in the agricultural seasons of 1997–98.

Season of Distress

The agricultural season of 1997–98 (between the months of June 1997 and July 1998) illustrates the conditions that prevail in the region. According to the taluk agricultural office, Bhalki, in the summer cultivation period, rainfall was 843 mm, while the average expected is 890 mm. As a result, there was a substantial decline in production. However, the winter cultivation season saw excess rains, about 153 mm when the average expected rainfall for the period is only 19 mm. The climatic conditions of long periods of cloud cover and moisture provided the right conditions for an outbreak of pests. The standing crops, predominantly that of tur, were attacked by heliothesis, also called helicoverpa. According to the assistant director, taluk agricultural office, Bhalki, heliothesis is a pest that reproduces three generations in a one-year cycle and which is difficult to control. In an attempt to bring the pests under control and to salvage the remaining crops, cultivators resorted to purchasing (mostly on credit) pesticides and rampantly and frequently spraying their fields. Yet, by the end of the season, February 1998, almost 80 per cent of the tur crops were destroyed (Table 20.3).

TABLE 20.3: Estimated Crop Loss in Some Important Crops, 1998

Crop	*Total Cropping (Ha)*	*Total Cropping Loss (Ha)*	*Loss in Production (Rs Lakh)*	*Loss in Tonnage*	*Percentage Crop Loss*
Tur	49,980	39,984	1,919	19,191	80
Jowar	35,850	24,968	747	12,472	71
Bengal gram	48,035	27,315	817	8,193	60
Sunflower	9,636	6,919	155	1,946	71

Source: Estimated from *Joint Legislative Committee Enquiry Report*, Government of Karnataka.

The loss of crops for two successive seasons has been devastating for a region that is already poor. Not only were crops meant for commercial sale lost, but the production and storage of the local staple crop, sorghum or 'jola' from the region was eroded. Having taken to the cultivation of pulses on a large scale, there was a significant decline in the cultivation of cereals, including that of sorghum. Declining area under cereal production met with two years of rainfall fluctuations and sharp decreases of crop production. The result meant that by August 1998, when we visited the area, local sorghum was not available. Many people were resorting to purchasing sorghum from stores, which did not suit their palates and which, as many people indicated, was rotten. As a result, many of the local people had stopped consuming sorghum and switched to consuming wheat rotis. While this loss of staple food, with its attendant cultural significance, is a telling comment on the food security of the region, it was the state of indebtedness of the marginal and small cultivators that triggered the sense of distress. Not only were a majority of cultivators deep in debt, but also the lack of local and external support compounded their distress. It was in this context that in some households the main earning members or heads of households, many of whom had incurred large debts, resorted to suicide. Table 20.4 gives a profile of the villages visited.

Based on a compilation of data made available by various reports, Table 20.5 provides an overview of the economic conditions of those persons who committed suicide. Even a cursory glance at the table on details of those who committed suicide will indicate that many were lavani holders with fairly substantial debts. The debts were primarily to private financial/lending agencies, which implies not only higher interest rates, but also more social and cultural pressure on these debtors. The weather fluctuations of 1996–98, and the resulting crop loss, have increased the indebtedness of cultivators. Many who borrowed did so not only for production purposes, but also to subsist. The non-availability of non-agricultural employment

TABLE 20.4: Profile of Study Villages, Bhalki Taluka

Characteristics	*Maurambi*	*Siddheshwara*	*Nittur*
Population	900	4,000	3,599
Households	275	600	715
Banks	0	0	1
Cooperatives	0	2	1
Financial corporations	9	0	3
Schools	primary, middle (government)	n/a	primary 3; high 2; pre-university 1
Pesticide and manure outlets	n/a	n/a	3

Source: Based on the author's primary fieldwork.

and institutional credit compounded the economic hardships of many. While there may be slight variations in the case history of each person who committed suicide and his/her household and family situation, their situation is representative of the larger and more pervading despair and despondency that has set in among the agriculturists in the district. A description of one of the villages, Siddheshwara, which we visited, will provide a scenario of the region and the life conditions of the people there.

TABLE 20.5: Economic Profile of Suicides

Name	*Village*	*Lavani Holder*	*Debt (Rs)*		*Own Lands (Acres)*
			Co-op Bank	*Private*	
Shivraj Mainalle	Siddeshwara	Yes	24,000	75–80,000	2.32
Prabhu	Kasarthugaon	Yes	15,000	60,000	6
Lakshmibai	Suldabka	n/a	n/a	10,000	n/a
Pandarinath	Hajnala	Yes	n/a	n/a	1
Dhanraj	Lada	n/a	n/a	n/a	n/a
Bhimrao	Bemalakeda	Yes	n/a	n/a	2.15
Vaman	Ghatbarole	Yes	65,000	30,000	3
Bijabai	Maurambi	No	60,000	na	14
Bharat	Alahalli	n/a	n/a	na	18
Basavaraj	Chondi	No	n/a	na	14
Bhojaraj Dholabba	Bhatramba	Yes	n/a	50,000	4
Basappa Balkeshwara*	Kelvadi	n/a	n/a	n/a	No
Dilip**	Kunte Sirsi	n/a	100,000	n/a	5 (shop)

Notes: * Considered to have died of snake-bite.
** Considered to have died of excessive alcohol consumption.

Source: Compiled by the author based on interviews in villages, the *Joint Legislative Committee Enquiry Report*, and newspaper reports. Newspapers sporadically reported the suicides and there are discrepancies in the numbers reported.

Siddheshwara—a temple-based village of about 600 households with a population of approximately 4,000 people—is perhaps quite typical of villages in the district. Its clutter of thatch, stone and mortar houses are linked by narrow by-lanes, which now, with the onset of the monsoon, run with water, sewage, excreta and cowdung. The temple of Siddheshwara looms large over the village and the new Basava statue, installed by the members of the local Rashtriya Basava Dal[12] marks the entry of the village and the temple. Despondency seems to be the ruling tone: poor climate, failed crops, an inefficient local government, an indifferent state apparatus. The men list their problems—the rains are unpredictable; for the past two years the winter or rabi rains have arrived at the time of harvest. Unseasonal rains have destroyed crops and the outbreak of pests has increased. The pesticides are ineffective, though vast quantities of pesticides are bought and sprayed. The pests and crop diseases have claimed the fields. Government compensation for crop loss is both inadequate and inefficient. How can a person who has lost several thousand rupees per hectare be compensated with a few hundred rupees? Worse still, the amount that is offered as compensation and the process to procure it is an insult. The government has disbursed cheques for sums so paltry that it does not even cover the cost of the bus charge required to encash the cheques at the district or taluk headquarters. Credit is hard to obtain—most people take loans from local creditors. For close to two years now there is little or no income. With increased costs of cultivation, many cultivators have incurred large debts and are unable to repay them. What are the alternatives?

Under such conditions of changing agricultural practices, minimal state and administrative support, increasing subordination to market forces, high risks in agriculture and declining community support, it is not hard to imagine the personal distress that cultivators experience. In an agrarian community, with a long history of drought-related crop loss and scarcity, it is not just the loss of crops that has created tensions. Rather, it is the experience of crop loss in a context of significantly altered form of agriculture and community relations that accounts for distress among people. As the new form of agriculture links cultivators to the larger economy and market, it compounds the schisms within the local community. Commercial agriculture with its emphasis on increased commercial inputs and capital means the conduct of agriculture on individual and household bases. Moving away from agricultural patterns that were more or less similar across households (in terms of type of crops, patterns of cultivation, knowledge base, etc.), agriculture is now primarily an independent, household or family enterprise with more links between each cultivator and the market than among cultivators themselves. Successful cultivators, primarily those with larger landholdings and with access to capital, are able to withdraw into their own enclaves. As a result, such class variations in agricultural practices also mean variations in the degree and type of crop production or crop loss, which itself is experienced on a separate household/family basis. It is this, the loss of the collective[13] and locally bound characteristic of agriculture with the increasing subordination of agriculture to market, capital, and external know-how that lends to its practice new forms of distress. Crop loss now is not uniformly experienced by all cultivators, and for those who are subject to it, in addition to the attending effects of impoverishment, there is the stigma and loss of honour that result from being indebted and penurious.

The case of Shivaraj Mainalle of Siddheshwara village illustrates this. He was a man of about 40 years with five children, the oldest of whom was in the sixth standard. He owned about 2.32 acres and was a sharecropper or *lavani* holder for another 6 acres or so. For the past two years, he had lost all crops, due to a combination of weather fluctuations and the outbreak of pests. His debts had mounted; by the end of 1997, he owed about Rs 24,000 to the local cooperative bank and some Rs 80,000 to private moneylenders. He is reported to have spent at least Rs 20,000 on pesticides alone. In this period of distress, his creditor, reportedly, asked him to return his money. Shivraj Mainalle committed suicide in December 1997.

The most popular brand of pesticide sold in the region is Endosulphan, reportedly banned in most western countries (Raithu Sahaya Committee 1998). Its advertisement jingle, 'friend of friends, enemy of enemies', can provide the epigram with which one can contextualise the impact of agri-business and commercial agriculture in the region. In the context of the devastation that has been wrought on the people, it is pertinent to ask, who have been the friends and who the enemies of cultivators in this region?

Concluding Remarks

Distress in rural India is often recognised only at the end of periods of prolonged suffering, when hunger, loss of production and destitution become either publicised or politicised events. Government machinery is largely geared towards addressing scarcity situations, linked primarily to providing relief based on indicators of distress. Food, fodder and water scarcity are considered to be reliable indicators of distress. Even conditions such as these require political will for the administration to intervene. But conditions such as in Bidar do not fall into the bureaucratic categories for assistance.

Similarly, the understanding of distress in the region has been limited. Newspaper reports have, largely, seen it as individual cases of suicide.[14] Some have questioned the claims of families to be compensated, others have assumed reports of such suicides to be opportunistic cases in which families sought to represent suicides from personal reasons as suicides from crop loss to receive government compensation. A few reports and analyses have actually linked agricultural conditions in the region to the policies of the state (Kamath 1998) and the subordination of cultivators to the market. The largely decontextualised and piecemeal approach adopted in the coverage of suicides in these regions is representative of the wide chasm between the lives of rural, agrarian residents and the urban orientation of most reporters.

The joint legislative enquiry committee, set up by the Government of Karnataka (1998), has submitted its report, which finds that most cases of suicides are linked to crop loss and indebtedness. In recognition of such crop loss, the report recommends monetary compensation to be paid to those families whose members have, as a result of experiencing crop loss and faced with high indebtedness, committed suicide. The report does not focus on the larger factors, especially those of widespread usury in the region, problems with the promotion of commercial agriculture, poor infrastructure development of the region, etc., which have combined to produce such conditions and in which suicides have been the most glaring result.

More recently, there have been calls from certain sectors of the government to send psychiatrists to the region. Resorting to psychological arguments is to deny the social and economic basis of such distress. More specifically, psychological arguments help deflect attention from the deep-rooted problems in the content, orientation, implementation and impact of economic policies. By remaining oblivious to the conditions of pervasive poverty, deprivation and collective disablement of the people, the state is laying the ground for a repeat of such distress. The state must recognise that it has been the key promoter of such an agricultural model in the region and thereby bears an onus in alleviating the risks associated with such a type of agriculture.

Distress in Bidar, of which the recent spate of suicides is only symptomatic, has resulted from a combination of crises: ecological, economic and social. Agricultural policies that overlook the ecological specificity of the region and the retention of inequitous social structures form the bedrock in producing such distress. The subordination of cultivators to market and capital forces, without any safety net to support them in times of crop loss, accounts for the devastation of rural communities. Just as the suicides are symptoms of the pervasive distress in the region, the loss of staple foodgrains in the region must also be considered to be a serious issue. As Susan George (1985) says, the loss of staple grains in any specific region without a substantial alternative economic base indicates a threat to the food security, and hence the fragility of local communities. Any intervention must seek to address these factors and not attempt to provide temporary relief such as nominal monetary compensation. It would only be fair to recognise that the victims of agrarian distress in the district are not only those who have committed suicide and their family members, but also those who continue to live there, believing, as do most cultivators, that they have an obligation to the land, to the community, to the state and to the nation to continue to cultivate the land.

Notes

1. Fieldwork for this study was conducted during 22–30 August 1998. P. K. Shetty of the NIAS was also a member of the team and has focused on the ecological dimensions of the issue (see his report, NIAS R6-99, for details). Due to the sensitivity of the issue, we did not interview many of the families in which there had been suicides. All these families had already been subject to scrutiny by the press, local and state administrators and enquiry committee members. Details of the villages visited are available in Table 20.4.

2. In writing this report I have drawn on my field and research experiences in Bijapur district, which in many ways is similar to that of Bidar. Details of my research on Bijapur are available in Vasavi (1999).

3. All data compiled from District Statistical Outline 1996–97, Karnataka Government; *District Gazetteer*, Karnataka Government; and NABARD (1996).

4. In our interviews with agriculturists in three villages, we gathered that more than 30 types of sorghum had been grown in the district. Some of the varieties that they listed were Kemp Jola, Sherkhande, Dudmangare, Sakrejola, Kanmuchike, Jingari, Haladi, Maldandi, Mussoli, Billi Jola, etc.

5. Sannhemp is called *pundi* and is a versatile green bush/shrub, the leaves of which make for a nutritious vegetable and the dried stems make good rope.

6. All data compiled from *District Statistical Handbook* (1995–96) and NABARD (1996).

7. Economic anthropology has, typically, disputed neoclassical economic arguments that consider size to be a key factor in productivity. In terms of assessing agricultural productivity in relation to size, they have argued and indicated the extent to which small parcels of landholding are utilised to maximum capacity and are thereby considered to be economically viable units.

8. The four types of lavani are: (a) a sharecropper pays a certain amount to the landowner and retains all crops and produce from the fields; (b) a sharecropper incurs all production expenses and gives half the produce to the landowner; (c) the owner and sharecropper share all the production costs and then share the produce at harvest; and (d) the sharecropper incurs all the expenses and gives one-third of the total produce to the landowner.

9. I approached the district's office of the registrar of cooperatives and moneylenders for data. However, they were reluctant and refused to share the data immediately. My request to have the necessary data (in terms of the numbers of financial corporations, moneylenders, etc., for a period of 10 years) mailed has been ignored.

10. Clive Bell (1993) documents the presence and impact of the new agricultural traders in the credit market of rural India. He however, contests government claimers that there has been a decline in the number of professional moneylenders. He links the integration of agricultural trading activities by moneylenders as camouflaging their presence.

11. Despite widespread opinions that many of the commercial seeds and pesticides are spurious, there has been no measure to either verify this or to bring to the public's notice those companies or brands which are unreliable for production.

12. The Rashtriya Basava Dal is an organisation of Lingayats that seeks to regain the religious and social heritage of Virashaivism. In the region, it is the most visible and dominant caste-based organisation and is responsible for the mobilisation of many youth into its wings, and has become the model for other castes to organise themselves. Other caste and religion-based organisations in the region are the Dalit Sangharsh Samiti, the Gondeshwara Sangha of the Kurubas or the shepherds, and the Tairik Muslim Sabha.

13. In characterising local, pre-commercial, agriculture as 'collective', I do not connote equity in terms of resource and production of all cultivators. Rather, the collective dimension of pre-commercial agriculture is to be noted in the similarity of production type, pattern, orientation, risk and productivity levels among all cultivating units.

14. For example, some newspaper reports that seem to question the authenticity of these suicides as linked to crop loss are those in the *Deccan Herald*, 6 June 1998 and *The Times of India*, 14 March 1998.

References

Bell, Clive. 1993. 'Interactions between Institutional and Informal Credit Agenciesin Rural India' in *The Economics of Rural Organisations: Theory, Practice and Politics*, eds Karla Hoff, Avisham Braverman and Joseph Stiglitz. New York: World Bank.

George, Susan. 1985. *Ill Fares the Land: Essays on Food, Hunger and Power*. London: Writers and Readers.

Government of Karnataka. 1977. *District Gazetteer*, Government Printing Press, Bangalore.

———. 1996–97. District Statistical Outline 1996–97.

———. 1995–96; 1997–98. *Report on Area, Production and Productivity and Prices of Agricultural Crops in Karnataka*.

———. 1998. *Joint Legislative Committee Report on Inquiry into Suicides by Farmers in Karnataka Due to Crop Loss*. Karnataka Vidhana Sabha Secretariat, Vidhana Soudha, Bangalore, 24 April.

Kamath, Nandan, et al. 1998. 'The Plight of Farmers in Bidar'. Student assignment for Law, Property and Development, National Law School University of India, Bangalore.

NABARD. 1996. 'Potential Linked Plan: Bidar'. Annual PLP for 1997–98, Bangalore Regional Office.

Raithu Sahaya Committee. 1998. *Farmers' Suicides in Andhra Pradesh: Report of the People's Tribunal*. Hyderabad, July.

Rawal, Vikas and Madhura Swaminathan. 1998. 'Changing Trajectories: Agricultural Growth in West Bengal, 1950 to 1996'. *Economic and Political Weekly* 33(40), 3 April: 2595–2602.

Vasavi, A. R. 1999. *Harbingers of Rain: Land and Life in South India*. Delhi: Oxford University Press.

21

Farmers' Suicides and Response of Public Policy

Evidence, Diagnosis and Alternatives from Punjab*

Anita Gill and Lakhwinder Singh

The state-led Green Revolution in Punjab increased incomes of farmers irrespective of farm size and catapulted it to the status of being called the 'grain bowl of India'. The euphoria, however, was short-lived, with the tide turning against the sector that once contributed nearly 70 per cent of wheat to the national foodgrain pool. The marginalisation of agriculture and the slowdown in industrial growth during the economic reforms period have further increased the suffering of the rural population, which has drawn the attention of policymakers, political leadership and academics alike. However, suggested policy solutions suffer from the same malaise which has already squeezed rural incomes.

This chapter attempts to examine the agrarian crisis, some of its consequences and alternative viable policy options with what we hope will be a fresh perspective. It is organised into four sections. The first section examines the emergence of the crisis of the agrarian economy of Punjab. The manifestation of the crisis in terms of the nature, extent and causes of suicides by agriculturists has been presented in the section that follows. Public policy as a remedy for this crisis, the shortcomings of public policy and possible alternative solutions have been analysed in the third section. Concluding remarks are presented in the last section of this chapter.

Growth and Structural Change in Punjab Economy

The Punjab economy has grown at a rapid rate since the ushering in of the Green Revolution. The growth rate was nearly 5 per cent per annum of the net state domestic product (NSDP) during the period 1966–67 to 1998–99. Punjab's per

* Originally published in *Economic and Political Weekly* 41(26), 30 June 2006: 2762–68.

capita income in the year 2000–01 was Rs 24,111 and was ranked number one just ahead of Maharashtra, with a difference of Rs 85 at current prices. Punjab's per capita income at constant prices was Rs 14,916 in the year 2000–01 and was ranked number two, superceded by Maharashtra with a margin of Rs 56.

Economic prosperity and the lead of Punjab in terms of per capita income are, however, now history, and other fast-growing states are quite close to surpassing this long sustained lead. This has been due to the fact that the development process in Punjab has slowed down in the post-liberalisation regime. Growth rate of NSDP declined to 4.7 per cent in the 1990s compared to that of the 1980s, which was 5.4 per cent. Major sectors of the Punjab economy showed a deceleration of the growth process in the 1990s compared with the 1980s, and the worst performance was of the agricultural sector. The rate of growth of the agricultural sector dwindled from 5.15 per cent per annum during the 1980s to 2.16 per cent in the 1990s. Growth of income generated by the agriculture sector from crops slid from a rate of 4.9 per cent per annum in the 1980s to nearly 0.4 per cent in the 1990s (Singh and Singh 2002). Previously, the agriculture sector was the engine of growth and a major contributing sector to the per capita income of the state from the mid-1960s to the early 1990s. Such a rapid deceleration of the rate of growth of the agricultural sector of Punjab has far-reaching consequences for the rest of the economy due to interdependence of the sectors, and has pushed those who are dependent for their livelihood on agriculture into an unprecedented crisis. Wide variations noticed in the growth performance of different sectors of the Punjab economy have dramatic consequences for the economic transformation of the state.

The character of the Punjab economy at the advent of the Green Revolution was fundamentally agrarian. Agriculture constituted 2.85 per cent of the gross state domestic product (GSDP) in 1966–67 and increased to 54.27 per cent in 1970–71. Thereafter, the share of agriculture sector's income in GSDP started declining continuously and dwindled to 39.22 in 2000–01. The structural transformation process has been regarded, at least in theory, as a healthy sign of economic development (Timmer 1988). However, the growth process must be underlined by technological progress and investment of capital. This implies that the structural transformation occurring under conditions of a faster rate of growth of the economy led by substantial investment and technological progress through interdependence increases the importance of dynamic sectors such as industry. It is important to mention here that the industrial sector of Punjab was not an important sector of its economy, but gained importance during the faster growth of the agriculture sector and increased its share in GSDP from 7.86 per cent in 1966–67 to 20.12 per cent in 1995–96. Thereafter, the industrial sector's share in GSDP declined and was 16.10 per cent in the year 2000–01. However, the tertiary sector has been emerging as an engine of growth during the structural transformation and generated 45 per cent of the GSDP in 2000–01 (Table 21.1). The decreasing importance of agriculture (which includes livestock) and the industrial sector, and the increasing importance of the tertiary sector is not a healthy sign of structural transformation. The rate of decline in the growth rate of the overall economy due to a sharp fall in the growth rates of the productive sectors was not neutralised by the slow acceleration of the growth of the tertiary sector of the Punjab economy.

TABLE 21.1: Sectoral Distribution of State Domestic Product, 1970–71 to 2000–01

Sectors	*1970–71*	*1980–81*	*1990–91*	*2000–01*
Agriculture and livestock	54.27	48.46	47.63	39.22
(a) Agriculture	38.51	32.22	30.69	26.76
(b) Livestock	15.76	16.24	18.94	12.46
Forestry and logging	0.76	0.99	0.59	0.14
Fishing	0.03	0.03	0.09	0.38
Mining and quarrying	0.05	0.02	0.02	0.00
Manufacturing	8.04	11.00	16.27	16.10
Electricity, gas and water supply	0.84	1.31	2.45	2.42
Construction	9.21	6.15	3.74	4.97
Trade, hotel and restaurants	10.96	14.58	11.33	12.73
Transport, storage and communication	1.73	2.05	2.32	5.67
Banking and insurance	1.80	2.55	4.67	5.48
Real estate and business services	4.79	4.26	3.20	4.22
Public administration	1.79	2.81	3.28	4.60
Other services	5.72	5.76	4.32	4.07

Source: *Statistical Abstract of Punjab*, relevant issues, Government of Punjab.

The other indicators of a structural transformation of the economy are the changes in the structure of workforce engaged across sectors and over time. In Punjab, the workforce engaged in agriculture (cultivators and labourers) was 62.67 per cent of the total in 1971, which declined to 58.02 per cent in 1981 (Census data), a reduction of 4.65 percentage points over a decade. The decline from 1981 to 1991 was only 1.95 percentage points, that is, 56.07 per cent workforce was still engaged in agriculture. From 1991 to 2001, there is some controversy regarding the figures, because according to Census data, the proportion of the workforce engaged in agriculture declined to 39.36 per cent, that is, a dramatic decline of 16.71 percentage points in a single decade. Now, this is unexplained, because if we take a look at the percentage of workforce engaged in the industrial sector, these are 11.3 per cent in 1971, 13.5 per cent in 1981, 12.28 per cent in 1991, and 8.41 per cent in 2001 (Census data). Going by Census data, this means that both agriculture and industry have shed workers, but this workforce has not found employment elsewhere also, because unemployment of both the rural and urban population increased during this period (Gill 2002). Further, the NSSO data confirm that employment has shrunk in the organised as well as unorganised tertiary sector. And if the NSSO data were to be followed, the workforce engaged in agriculture in Punjab was still 53 per cent in 2000–01 (Planning Commission 2003). Apart from the data controversy, the point that emerges is that even now a substantial percentage of the workforce

(53 per cent according to NSSO statistics or nearly 40 per cent according to Census data) is engaged in agriculture and the change (read decline) is rather slow, while the squeeze in income from agriculture has been rapid (from 40.91 per cent in 1966–67 to 26.76 per cent of SDP in 2000–01, Table 21.1). This is an obvious sign of a grave crisis.

Deceleration of economic growth of the Punjab economy in general and the agriculture sector in particular has tremendously increased the crisis of the capitalist path of economic development, especially in the liberalisation and globalisation era. A substantial proportion of the workforce still dependent on agriculture for livelihood faces a serious problem to be gainfully employed elsewhere in the backdrop of the squeezing share of agricultural income. Obviously, this is expected because of the fact that agricultural development on capitalist lines of production and a heavy dependence on market occasionally leads to this kind of situation (Timmer 1988). Therefore, a need arises to examine the process of agrarian capitalist development in Punjab in a historical perspective to provide an appropriate explanation of the emergence and rise of the agrarian crisis.

The ushering in of the Green Revolution in Punjab began with the arrival of HYV seeds for wheat and rice, along with the use of chemical fertilisers. The new technology was adopted by the Punjab farmers at a rapid rate, which had a productivity-enhancing effect mainly on two crops, wheat and rice. Not only did land and labour productivity increase many times, but it also had an income-enhancing effect across the board. Punjab peasantry was able to reap income gains proportional to their ownership of cultivable land (Bhalla and Chadha 1983). The peculiar characteristic of the early Green Revolution was that it had increased labour intensity in agricultural processes such as sowing, weeding and more so in harvesting and threshing. Farming chores were mainly done by family labour coming from the households of small, marginal and medium-sized farms, and were supplemented by hired labour during the peak seasons. However, large farmers were mainly dependent on hired labour for agricultural operations. A rise in the income of rural households increased the capacity of the farm households to employ innovations to further exploit the potential of yield increases and enhance income from agriculture. Thus, the new innovations of threshing, cultivation of land through tractors, use of pesticides and insecticides, diesel pump sets and electric tubewells increased the use of mechanical power for tilling and harvesting operations. Also biological innovations for making crops free of weeds and pest attacks started reducing the role of family labour in farm operations.[1]

The consequence of the increase in mechanisation, assured irrigation, chemical fertilisers, pesticides and insecticides and high-yielding seeds was a manifold rise in land productivity and decline in the intensity of labour. Crop yield increased at a rate of 2.43 per cent per annum during the period 1967–81, which constituted 40.91 per cent of total land productivity. The contribution of crop yield further increased at a rate of 2.71 per cent per annum during the post-Green Revolution period (1981–91) which was 52.52 per cent of the total land productivity. In the stagnation period (1991–2001), yield growth declined to 0.26 per cent and the contribution to land productivity also declined to 31.33 per cent (Singh and Sidhu 2004).

The labour-use pattern also underwent substantial changes due to the intensive use of biological and mechanical technologies. The man-days of labour use declined after the mid-1980s in the wheat crop from 52.35 to 38.9 per hectare during 1985–88 to 1998–2000, that is a 25 per cent decline. It is amazing to note that labour use in paddy crop has sharply declined from 103.60 man-days per hectare in 1981–84 to 56.32 man-days per hectare in 1998–99. Mechanical harvesting was fundamentally responsible for the sharp decline in intensity of labour use in predominant crops of Punjab agriculture (Sidhu and Singh 2004).

Mechanisation of harvesting of major crops and intensive use of biological technologies have not only reduced the household use of labour power but also substantially contributed to the rise in the cost of production. Over capitalisation of mechanical power such as tractors and tubewells has made available the use of tractors on a hire-purchase basis to the small farmers, which has reduced the use of family labour as well as completely eliminated tilling of land by bullocks even by the small and marginal farmers. The farmers have turned managers of the production processes of agriculture because the manual operations have been almost eliminated and the remaining tasks are being done by the migratory workforce available at low wages.

Rising costs along with stagnant technology and a near freeze in the minimum support price of wheat and paddy, which turned the already adverse terms of trade from bad to worse, surely reduced returns on foodgrain production. The reduction of differentials between returns and cost of production, the increasing uncertainty of weather as well as a dependence on borrowed credit at a higher rate of interest from informal lenders were the reasons responsible for increasing indebtedness among the farmers of Punjab (Anita Gill 2004; Ghuman 2001; Shergill 1998). This has compounded problems to the extent that farmers of Punjab resorted to committing suicides (Association for Democratic Rights 2000). The whole crisis is the consequence of the fact that market forces operated at much larger scale during the phase of liberalisation and globalisation, and thus reduced surpluses and increased costs leading to the distress sale of the paddy crop over a nearly five-year period during the Akali Dal rule in Punjab. The incidence of suicides in Punjab increased tremendously during this period.

FARMERS' SUICIDES: EXTENT AND DIAGNOSIS

Suicides by farmers were first highlighted by the media in Kerala, Karnataka and Andhra Pradesh. But then came reports of suicides by farmers in Punjab, which were perturbing and quite unexpected in such a prosperous region. So long as suicide remains an occasional and stray incident, it does not generate much public concern. But when the incidence shows an upward trend and affects a particular section of society, it becomes a public issue, to be viewed, studied and analysed in all its seriousness. In Punjab, suicides by the farmers became a public issue since the mid-1980s. The state government itself has admitted that 2,116 suicides had taken place since 1986, but this could just be the 'tip of an iceberg' as many more cases might have gone unreported, if not unnoticed (Dhaliwal 2005).

The gravity of the problem in Punjab has been highlighted by three main studies: by the Institute for Development and Communication (Bhalla, et al. 1998), followed by Iyer and Manick (2000), and by an NGO, the Association for Democratic Rights (2000). Table 21.2 gives the main profile of suicide victims in the survey areas of the three studies.

TABLE 21.2: Structure of Workforce in Punjab, 1971–2001

Year	*Cultivators*	*Agricultural Labourers*	*Industrial Workers*	*Other Workers*	*Total*
2001	2,099,330	1,498,976	769,047	4,774,407	9,141,760
	(22.96)	(16.40)	(8.41)	(52.23)	(100.00)
1991	1,917,210	1,502,123	749,136	1,929,905	6,098,374
	(31.44)	(24.63)	(12.28)	(31.65)	(100.00)
1981	1,767,286	1,092,225	665,442	1,402,806	4,927,759
	(35.86)	(22.16)	(13.50)	(28.47)	(100.00)
1971	1,665,153	786,705	442,070	1,018,664	3,912,592
	(42.56)	(20.11)	(11.3)	(26.03)	(100.00)

Source: *Statistical Abstract of Punjab*, relevant issues, Government of Punjab.

The studies reveal that Sangrur and Mansa are the two districts which have reported the most incidents of suicides. These are the relatively backward and poorer districts of Punjab. But, as noted earlier, this by no way is an indication that suicides in other districts have not taken place—the number could be much smaller and might have gone unnoticed and unreported. Table 21.3 also reveals that the percentage of cultivators who committed suicide is much more than agricultural labourers. And among the cultivators, it is the category of small and marginal farmers that reported the maximum number of suicides. Most of the suicide victims were illiterate. The causes of suicides, of which indebtedness figured prominently, were multiple. The other factors included economic distress, crop failure, alcoholism, marital and domestic discord, drug addiction, etc. All these causes, in one way or the other, pointed towards the poor economic status of the victims which manifested itself in various ways. Indebtedness was more towards non-institutional sources of finance, in which commission agents figured prominently. This fact has been established earlier also in the studies of Shergill (1998), Gill (2000), Gill and Kaur (2004), and NSSO (2005). Also, most of the loans (from institutional as well as non-institutional sources) taken by these victims were used for purposes that are traditionally classified as unproductive—social ceremonies, illness, house construction, etc.

The twin aspects of indebtedness (mostly to informal lenders) and the 'unproductive' use of loans need to be studied simultaneously in greater detail to analyse the true reasons behind suicides. One side of the picture is that with the

TABLE 21.3: Profile of Suicide Victims

Study by Characteristics	*Bhalla, et al. (1998)*	*Iyer and Manick (2000)*	*Association for Democratic Rights (2000)*
Districts surveyed	Gurdaspur Sangrur Mansa Ludhiana	Sangrur	Patiala Mansa Sangrur Bathinda
Villages covered	14	11	29
Households covered with confirmed cases of suicides	53	75	79
Percentage of cultivators who committed suicide	55	66.66	84.80
Percentage of agriculture labour households	45	33.33	15.20
Percentage of small and marginal farmers	25	84	65.70
Percentage of illiterates	58.50	66.25	75
Percentage of married victims	81.10	–	76
Causes of suicide (per cent)			
(i) Multiple, of which indebtedness is one	38	78.75	62
(ii) Crop failure	1.05	10	5.10
Debt exclusively from commission agents (per cent)	36.72	67.50	27.40
Debt from commission agents and other sources	–	81.25	73.60
Unproductive use of loan (per cent)	68.20	51.61	20.00*

Note: *Comprises percentage of victims who could not repay loans due to reasons like expenditure on social ceremonies, excess consumption and illness, which are conventionally regarded as unproductive expenditures.

Source: Based on the authors' primary fieldwork.

advent of the Green Revolution, the incomes of all classes of farmers increased initially, which set off the aspirations of cultivators to lead a better life in terms of living conditions and consumption. Always one to be on the ostentatious side of life, the Punjabi farmer, especially in the Malwa region (Bathinda, Faridkot, Sangrur, Mansa, Patiala and Ludhiana) now freely started spending lavishly on social ceremonies. Dowry in marriages invariably began to include a car, among other things. If there was a paucity of funds, there was always the informal lender, willing to give loans in substantial amounts. Or even a tractor loan from institutional sources could be used to give dowry. The beginning and deepening of economic crisis in agriculture shrunk the incomes of peasantry, but not their aspirations and the firmly entrenched social norms. Failure to pay back loans indebted them further, entrapping them in a debt trap. Harassment by lenders, the threat of arrest and then the public shame accompanying the impending compulsion to forsake their most prized asset—land—proved to be the last nail in their coffins.

A second but important aspect of the problem of the so-called unproductive use of loans (mostly informal loans) raises the question as to how to define the term 'unproductive'? Recalling the crisis in agriculture once again, the spending of loans for survival—essential consumption, for medical expenses, and for building a roof over one's head—is not justifiably unproductive. Spending for maintaining/enhancing one's productive capacity has now been recognised as very productive expenditures (Strauss and Thomas 1995). If an in-depth disaggregative analysis of the loan use is made, instead of just the two broad conventional categories, then a substantial proportion of the loan use classified as unproductive could possibly be deducted. The expenditure on marriages and other social ceremonies are safely classified as unproductive. But then, why is only one section of society singled out and chastised for spending on marriages when the entire set-up of the Punjab state is under the influence of this social evil. Farmers cannot be studied and analysed in isolation from what is happening in society at large because they are not autonomous from the social structure, and their actions will be influenced largely by the society in general. The problem is that farmers, unlike most other sections of society, do not have regular, assured incomes, and whatever they earn is shrinking by the day. Suicides due to drug abuse, alcohol and domestic or marital discord are just reflections of this malaise of economic crisis with grave social consequences.

Also, a less noted and thought of, albeit equally true side of the picture which is much less reported, is that not all loans, even informal loans, are misused. Yet a majority of the peasantry (and landless workers) are in a grave economic situation. It has been established by micro-empirical studies that a majority of borrowings of cultivators are used for productive short-term and long-term purposes. Gill (2000), and Gill and Kaur (2004) have established that nearly 63 and 57 per cent, respectively, of informal credit was utilised for productive purposes (Table 21.4). It was only in the case of landless workers that a greater percentage of loans were utilised for consumption or repayment of old debts. Apart from these studies, the NSSO data too confirm that in Punjab, of every Rs 1,000 of outstanding loans taken

TABLE 21.4: Utilisation of Informal Credit by Sample Households (per cent)

Size-group of Owned Holding (Acres)	*Productive Purpose*		*Consumption Purposes*	
	Patiala	*Amritsar*	*Patiala*	*Amritsar*
Landless	4.28	49.64	64.11	50.36
Up to 2.5	70.23	47.29	29.77	52.71
2.51–5.00	51.41	48.74	45.92	51.26
5.01–10.00	50.66	81.50	48.26	18.50
Above 10	68.95	71.18	29.29	28.82
Total	63.03	57.14	36.36	42.86

Note: The percentages for production and consumption in case of Patiala may not add up to 100, because it excludes the utilisation of credit for repayment of old debt of cooperative societies.

Source: Calculated by the authors based on primary survey.

by farmers, Rs 264 was for capital expenditure in farm business, Rs 360 for current expenditure in farm business, Rs 44 for non-farm business, Rs 5 for consumption, Rs 102 for marriages and ceremonies and Rs 26 for medical and other expenditure. For the country as a whole, the NSSO concluded that more than 50 per cent of indebted farmer households had taken loans for the purposes of capital or current expenditure (NSSO 2005).

The productive purposes for which informal loans are utilised is for repair, fuel, maintenance and hiring of machinery, tubewells and pump sets. The expenditure on these cannot be postponed during peak seasons, and it is only the informal loans which are immediately available. The institutional loans, on the other hand, usually have a credit limit (set on the basis of owned, not cultivated land), and are readily available only after the first loan is repaid. Hence, the cultivators have no option but to turn to the informal lenders, where red-tapism and lengthy paper work seldom exist, unlike the institutional loans. Moreover, formal credit is not able to fulfil the entire credit demands of cultivators. Table 21.5 bears ample proof of this. For most categories, the supply of formal credit is not even 50 per cent of demand for credit.

TABLE 21.5: Supply of Formal Credit as Percentage of Demand for Credit

Size-group of Owned Holding (Acres)	*Patiala*	*Amritsar*
Landless	10.77	14.58
Up to 2.5	27.12	61.93
2.51–5.00	49.51	41.43
5.01–10.00	24.96	40.07
Above 10	75.11	67.75
Total	47.85	43.67

Source: Calculated by the authors based on primary survey.

The whole situation, thus, has to be viewed in a broader macro-framework of the needs of farmers and the set-up to fulfil these needs rather than on limiting ourselves to studying just the profile of suicide victims, so that the menace can be checked before assuming gigantic proportions. In the agricultural set-up, borrowing is a necessity. It is neither objectionable nor a sign of weakness. It is the failure of the institutional set-up in supplying credit commensurate with demand that is mainly responsible for the crisis and its manifestation in the form of suicides. Commission agents are thriving as informal lenders because they have chosen crop, rather than land, as collateral, and entice farmers into interlinked contracts—pledge of sale of crop in return for a loan (Bell and Srinivasan 1989; Gill 2000). Crop is not undervalued as land is, but the rates of interest are kept exorbitantly high (Gill 2000), while keeping paper work to a minimum. Land grab is only in extreme cases, and that too in case of big landlords turned commission agents. But harassment, threats, fear of arrest and the public shame is enough to drive the borrowers to suicide, even though the loan might not have been used 'unproductively'. Hence, suicides as a manifestation of indebtedness in particular and agrarian crisis in general have to be viewed and analysed in a broad macroeconomic framework. It has to be realised that the root cause of the problem lies not just under the cursory heading of indebtedness; it has to be traced back to the entire credit set-up and then to the crisis within the agricultural sector.

Hope and Suggested Policy Measures

Despite the grave situation in which the Punjab peasantry is engulfed, there is still a ray of hope. In the previous section, an attempt was made to diagnose the problem; suitable alternatives are now suggested as remedial measures, in the light of the efforts already made at the level of the state. Since the agrarian crisis has manifested itself in suicides, the problem needs to be tackled at various levels, beginning from the immediate relief measures to the families of suicide victims, to long-term policy decisions covering the entire agricultural sector.

As a part of the immediate relief package for the families of suicide victims, there is a need to provide monetary assistance as compensation so that the aggrieved family can meet its physical survival needs. This is all the more important in the cases where the victim was the only earning member of the family. Proper identification of such families by a non-partisan organisation must precede such financial compensation. Additional financial compensation can also be provided by voluntary organisations and NGOs. Since most of the suicides are directly or indirectly related to indebtedness and economic distress (not necessarily in this order), it is proposed that a moratorium on the debt of the victim be implemented. Also the rate of interest and the loan instalments need to be substantially lowered thereafter. In case the victim was the sole earning member, waiving off the entire loan, formal or informal, would be highly recommendable.[2]

Again, taking a cue from the relief measures provided to suicide victims in Andhra, a pension scheme to the next of kin (especially if he/she is aged and/or a non-earner) should be implemented. As part of longer-term relief measures, it is suggested that provision for cost-free skill-oriented education be made for minor children. Older children could be provided suitable employment to rehabilitate the family. This would also ensure that the victim's family is made capable of paying off the debt and live a life of honour, having washed off the stigma of being a suicide victim's kin.

The growing agricultural crisis and its manifestations have not gone entirely unnoticed, with the Punjab government appointing a committee as early as in 1985 under the chairmanship of S. Johl to diagnose the problem and suggest remedial measures. The committee put forward the idea of diversification of agriculture from the existing wheat-paddy cropping pattern (Government of Punjab 1986). It was argued that this diversification from cereals to fruits, vegetables and pulses will not only increase the income of farmers, but also reduce environmental degradation for long-term sustainability of Punjab's agriculture. It may be recalled that this agriculture diversification-based rural industrialisation growth strategy met with success in the early 1980s in a number of Southeast Asian countries. The Punjab government recently tried to promote diversification of agriculture by taking the path of contract farming between farmers and the agribusiness firms (Sukhpal Singh 2004). However, the very design and implementation of contract farming left the small-sized farmers at the mercy of the private firms, which secured a monopoly situation in the market. In the absence of an enforcement agency, such profit considerations and market orientation acted against the farmers and they have been left with no choice but to continue the wheat-paddy cropping pattern (Sucha Singh Gill 2004).

Diversification of agriculture of Punjab is, no doubt, a desired goal for transformation of the economy into an industrialised one, but so long as the processing activities of agricultural production take place away from the farm gates, the agriculture sector will continue to face the threat of exploitation and a decline in rural incomes (Singh 2005; Timmer 1988). The Southeast Asian countries in general, and Taiwan in particular, have been the success stories because agricultural produce was processed on the farm gates and surpluses were ploughed back to expand rural industrial activities and also raising the level of living of the rural population. The farmers' association of Taiwan successfully bypassed the exploitative intermediary agency. The state too played its role by providing essential institutional infrastructure and investment.

The organisation of production, thus, has to be changed from individual to cooperative—not the bureaucratic state-controlled cooperative, but modern member-owned and controlled cooperatives. Amul in our own country is an example of one such cooperative. The farmers' cooperative in Junnar taluk of Maharashtra for industrialisation of grape cultivation is another success story. The Government of Punjab, too, needs to offer a strategy which is not purely private and market based, but which leads farmers to organise themselves to carry out production, processing and marketing. For this, suitable institutional and infrastructural arrangements have to be provided, and middlemen eliminated.

Specifically, addressing the problem of credit, there are no two views that it is the middleman who is exploiting the farmers the maximum and leading them into a debt trap. The remedy lies in the provision of institutional credit at cheaper rates of interest and, more important, at levels commensurate with the demand for credit. Although the recommendations of the Narasimham Committee (1991) regarding lowering of the priority sector (of which agriculture is a very important part) target of bank credit from 40 per cent to 10 per cent was not approved by the political masters in our country, the monitoring and fulfilment of targets have begun to be taken much less seriously. This is not desirable, keeping in view of the grave economic situation of agriculture. To aggravate the situation, the priority sector list is being regularly revised to the detriment of small and marginal farmers (Dasgupta 2002). For instance, in the category of direct advances to agriculture, the acquisition of jeeps, pick-up vans, etc., have been included—vehicles that are minimally made use of by small and marginal farmers. Again, the target of 18 per cent of direct advance is now being fulfilled by including a certain percentage in the form of indirect credit (*EPW* Research Foundation 2003; *The Tribune* 2003). That the supply of institutional credit is much less than the demand has already been mentioned earlier. The Punjab government's recent measure to revise the 1997 vintage land rates taken into account by cooperative banks for lending purposes has enhanced the loan availing capacity of farmers and is a step in the right direction, but the inclusion element of landownership as a basis for a loan and that too processed with considerable red tape and delays are still a problem. A lower rate of interest is of no use if the loan is not adequate, timely and without the additional costs of procuring it. These additional costs involve cost of frequent visits to the institution, payment of a fee, submission of documents (requiring payment to some *munshi* who can do the paper work for the illiterate farmers), etc. These expenses, if added to the rate of interest, make formal borrowings quite expensive.

On the other side are the informal lenders—mainly commission agents—who charge exorbitant rates of interest but provide an easy finance, commensurate with demand, while linking sale of crop to loan amounts. These practices are highly exploitative, but the farmers are forced to borrow from them out of sheer necessity. To serve rural credit needs, the experiences of Indonesian rural financial institutions, where organisations provide credit services locally, with character-based lending (Chaves and Gonzalez 1996), or like the Grameen Bank of Bangladesh can be adapted to Indian needs. And most important is the delinking of politics from credit, which turns loans into grants with every election, making the task of credit institutions difficult. The solution to indebtedness will go a long way in solving the entire agrarian crisis. Among other measures, it is suggested that formal institutions would do well to shift to crop as collateral, instead of insisting on landownership, especially for long-term loans. This would ensure that the credit is need-based. Farmers should also be provided crop insurance at par with what is available to industry, as agriculture is the sector most vulnerable to the vagaries of nature. Failure of crops almost always renders the farmers incapable of paying back the loan instalment, and if crops fail in two or more consecutive seasons, farmers invariably find themselves in a debt trap. This is exactly what is happening in some parts of Punjab, where the fury of the Ghaggar river (in the Malwa region where the maximum suicides have been reported) during monsoons wreaks havoc year after year.

Apart from this, since the farmers cannot escape certain expenditure on consumption, health and even social ceremonies, efforts can be made to set up a pool of separate funds, with matching contributions from the farmers and the government, which can then be used to give interest free loans specifically for such expenses as mentioned above. This pooling can be done at the village level, by the panchayats or some such organisations. Funds can be loaned out to member farmers on a rotational, need-based or lottery basis if the fund pool is small. The idea can be roughly similar to the chit funds or *nidhi*s operating in urban areas. However, the success of such a scheme will depend purely on the farmers and the honesty with which they operate the scheme. If such schemes can be successfully implemented, then farmers would not need to 'misuse' the borrowings from institutions or avail of informal loans for 'unproductive' purposes.

Since it has already been argued that despite using a major portion of the borrowings for 'productive' purposes, farmers are falling into a debt trap, steps have to be taken to address the entire credit needs of farmers and the very set-up of credit providing agencies, formal as well as informal.

It is also necessary that the government starts thinking in terms of setting up some sort of cooperative organisation to hire out agricultural machinery—tractors, threshers and harvest combines—on subsidised rates. This will save a lot of expenditure for the farmers. Even for irrigation, it should not be necessary that every farmer spends on installation of tubewells and pump sets individually. Government-installed tubewells, collectively operated by farmers can serve the purpose. In view of the declining water table in Punjab, submersible pump sets (deep tubewells) need to be installed. The installation cost of submersible pump sets is beyond the financial capacity of the small and marginal farmers. If such pump sets are installed by the government, water use would be more equitably distributed, in addition to saving of costs.

CONCLUSION

Remedies thus have to be found not only in terms of short-term or immediate solutions to suicides, but also long-term solutions to end the agrarian crisis itself. While immediate measures could include relief, mainly financial, to the families of suicide victims, and attempts at their rehabilitation, the long-term measures to 'nip the evil in the bud' should comprise attempts at rural industrialisation. This could be done on the lines of how and what has been undertaken in East Asian countries, especially in Taiwan. The farmers' cooperatives, sans middlemen, to produce, process and market output on the farm gates can be a way out. This would not only provide the agricultural sector with a much-needed diversification from the wheat-paddy rotation, but also prove to be remunerative in terms of incomes and employment. The farmers' organisations must engage themselves to start collectively processing and marketing enterprises rather than purely depending on agitations for more remunerative prices. Asking for rights along with engaging in industrial activities has a capacity to eliminate the middlemen who thrive on surpluses generated through processing and marketing activities. The state government, apart from supporting and extending cooperation, must become innovative to articulate policies in the fast-globalising world to prod farmers' organisations to initiate those activities which integrate the processing and marketing activities on the farm gates. This also underlines that the state and state-run financial institutions would have to alter their system of lending—loans would have to be made adequate, timely, cheap and commensurate with demand. The red tape and additional costs involved, which make institutional loans so unattractive, would also have to be reduced drastically.

Notes

1. It is important to note here that the electric tubewells installed in Punjab have been increasing continuously from 1.46 lakh in 1976 to 2.83 lakh in 1981, and were more than 8.29 lakh in 2002, which is nearly a sixfold increase. This increase in the rate of growth of number of electric tubewells could not satisfy the demand because a substantial number of applications remained continuously pending with the state electricity board (ESO 2002). The number of tractors in Punjab has increased to 3.87 lakh, which constitutes one-fourth of the total number of tractors in India, and every third farm household has a tractor keeping in view 11.17 lakh total operational holdings in Punjab (Singh 2004).

2. It needs to be pointed out at this stage that the Punjab Planning Department had announced a compensation of Rs 2.5 lakh in its Annual Plan of 2001–02, but this promise is yet to be fulfilled, unlike the case of Andhra Pradesh. In fact, highly moved by the state's apathy, a petition has been filed by the Movement Against State Repression (MASR) in the Punjab and Haryana high courts seeking instructions to the Punjab government and the Government of India to compensate and rehabilitate the families of farmers who committed suicides in the state (*Hindustan Times* 2005).

References

'Market Imperfections and Farmers Distress in Punjab'. 2003. *The Tribune*, Chandigarh, 23 December.

'Suicide by Punjab Farmers: Relief for Kin Sought'. 2005. *Hindustan Times*, Chandigarh, 22 January.

Association for Democratic Rights. 2000. 'Suicides in Rural Area of Punjab: A Report' (in Punjabi). Ludhiana.

Bell, Clive and T. N. Srinivasan. 1989. 'Interlinked Transactions in Rural Markets: An Empirical Study of Andhra Pradesh, Bihar and Punjab'. *Oxford Bulletin of Economics and Statistics* 51(1).

Bhalla, G. S., et al. 1998. *Suicides in Rural Punjab*. Chandigarh: Institute for Development and Communication.

Bhalla, G. S., and G. K. Chadha. 1983. *Green Revolution and the Small Peasant: A Study of Income Distribution among Punjab Cultivators*. New Delhi: Concept Publishing Company.

Chaves, R. A., and Gonzalez-Vega. 1996. 'The Design of Successful Rural Financial Intermediaries: Evidence from Indonesia'. *World Development* 24(1).

Dasgupta, R. 2002. 'Priority Sector Lending: Yesterday, Today and Tomorrow'. *Economic and Political Weekly* 38(41).

Dhaliwal, Sarbjit. 2005. 'Suicides by Farmers Being Underplayed: Report'. *The Tribune*, Chandigarh, 10 August.

EPW Research Foundation. 2003. 'Money, Banking and Finance: Special Statistics 33'. *Economic and Political Weekly* 38(8): 831–48.

ESO. 2002. Statistical Abstract of Punjab: Publication No. 880. Government of Punjab, Chandigarh.

Ghuman, R. S. 2001. 'WTO and Indian Agriculture: Crisis and Challenges: A Case Study of Punjab'. *Man and Development*, June.

Gill, Anita. 2000. *Rural Credit Markets: Financial Sector Reforms and the Informal Lenders*. New Delhi: Deep and Deep Publishers.

Gill, Anita. 2004. 'Interlinked Agrarian Credit Markets: Case Study of Punjab'. *Economic and Political Weekly* 39(33): 3741–51.

Gill, Anita and Gian Kaur. 2004. 'Informal Agrarian Credit Markets and Public Policy: Empirical Evidence from Punjab'. *The Global Journal of Finance and Economics* 1(2).

Gill, Sucha Singh. 2002. 'Economic Reforms, Pace of Development and Employment Situation in Punjab'. In *Reform and Employment*, ed. IAMR. New Delhi: Concept Publishing Company.

———. 2004. 'Contract Farming Hurts Farmers: Area under Wheat, Paddy Increases'. *The Tribune*, Chandigarh, 27 September.

Government of Punjab. 1986. *Report of the Expert Committee on Diversification of Agriculture in Punjab*. Chandigarh.

Iyer, K. Gopal and M. S. Manick. 2000. *Indebtedness, Impoverishment and Suicides in Rural Punjab*. Delhi: India Publishers and Distributors.

Lewis, W. A. 1954. 'Economic Development with Unlimited Supplies of Labour'. *Manchester School of Economic and Social Studies* 22(2): 139–91.

Mellor, J. W. 1976. *The New Economics of Growth: A Strategy for India and the Developing Countries*. Ithaca: Cornell University Press.

Narasimham Committee Report. 1991. *Report of the Committee on the Financial System*, New Delhi: Government of India.

Planning Commission. 2003. *Punjab Development Report*. New Delhi: Government of India.

NSSO. 2005. 'Indebtedness of Farmer Households'. NSS 59th Round, January–December 2003, Report No. 498(59/33/1), Ministry of Statistics and Programme Implementation, Government of India, May.

Shergill, H. S. 1998. *Rural Credit and Indebtedness in Punjab*. Chandigarh: Institute for Development and Communication.

Sidhu, R. S., and Sukhpal Singh. 2004. 'Agricultural Wages and Employment'. *Economic and Political Weekly* 39(37): 4132–35.

Singh, Joginder and R. S. Sidhu. 2004. 'Factors in Declining Crop Diversification'. *Economic and Political Weekly* 39(52): 5607–10.

Singh, Lakhwinder. 2005. 'Deceleration of Industrial Growth and Rural Industrialisation Strategy for Indian Punjab'. *Journal of Punjab Studies* 12(2): 271–84.

Singh, Lakhwinder and Sukhpal Singh. 2002. 'Deceleration of Economic Growth in Punjab: Evidence, Explanation and a Way-Out'. *Economic and Political Weekly* 37(6), 9 February: 579–86.

Singh, Sukhpal. 2004. 'Crisis and Diversification in Punjab Agriculture'. *Economic and Political Weekly* 39(52): 5583–90.

Strauss, J., and Duncan Thomas. 1995. 'Human Resources: Empirical Modelling of Household and Family'. In *Handbook of Development Economics* (Volume 3A), eds Jere Behrman and T. N. Srinivasan. Amsterdam: Elsevier Science Publishers.

Syrquin, Moshe. 1988. 'Patterns of Structural Change'. In *Handbook of Development Economics* (Volume 1), eds Hollis Chenery and T. N. Srinivasan, 203–73. Amsterdam: Elsevier Science Publishers.

Timmer, C. P. 1988. 'The Agriculture Transformation'. In *Handbook of Development Economics* (Volume 1), eds Hollis Chenery and T. N. Srinivasan, 275–331. Amsterdam: Elsevier Science Publishers.

22

Resurrecting Scholarship on Agrarian Transformations*

Alpa Shah and Barbara Harriss-White

How has the Indian agrarian economy transformed over the last three decades? The 1970s and 1980s saw a proliferation of scholarly research on the agrarian economy in India. The classical agrarian question set the terms of the debate: How can the rural peasant economy make the transition to capitalism and also be squeezed to provide the resources needed for industrial, urban economic development, and what are the obstacles? The questions of whether Indian agriculture is capitalist, to what degree, how unevenly it has developed, how recent it is, and the related questions of whether the dominant mode of production is not capitalist but pre-capitalist or semi-feudal were subject to extensive discussion—some of the liveliest debates on the subject internationally were found in these very pages of the *Economic and Political Weekly*. However, with the rise of the critique of village studies, the problems of categorising 'modes of production', and the push for scholarship to move to urban studies and address the urgent problems of liberalisation, in-depth research and reflection on the agrarian economy declined.

Global Capital and the Agrarian Question

Highlighting the massive changes in the global economy, Henry Bernstein (1996) argues that access to global capital may allow developing capitalist economies to generate surplus for industrial growth independently of the development of agriculture. He even asks whether under neoliberal globalisation, what he calls the 'agrarian question of capital' is relevant any longer.

Neoliberal reforms in India, at a rate second to that only of China, have indeed targeted sectors and incentivised industries catering for the urban middle classes and export markets. International finance capital has become a source for private sector investment in India. From the mid-1980s, there has been a significantly weakened

* Originally published in *Economic and Political Weekly* 46(39), 24 September 2011: 13–18.

linkage between agricultural growth and industry as a whole. Non-agricultural sectors have grown rapidly, and the agrarian economy has certainly been neglected by the policy reformers, hell-bent on ushering in a supermarket society with its highly capital-intensive supply chains.

However, paradoxically, the majority of Indians are dependent on the rural economy and in complex ways. Reflecting global patterns, 60 per cent of Indians live off agriculture as farmers and farm labourers. The *World Development Report 2008* on 'Agriculture for Development' stresses the fact that three-quarters of the world's poor live in the countryside, engaging in farming as their principal activity in conditions that do not foster a secure or sustainable livelihood (World Bank 2007). And processes of peasant differentiation may still be grinding away. Despite the claims for the 'vanishing village' (Gupta 2005) and people's aspirations to move away from farming, India does not appear to be witnessing a great civilisational shift from country to the town.

A quarter century ago, Terence Byres (1986)—after Lenin—laid out that there is no standard, unilinear or inevitable path of the transition to capitalism, and this was so even in Europe. In the last three decades, India, one of the countries with the largest agrarian population in the world, has been experiencing processes of social change that are unfolding not only in very different ways to that of the classic paths but also with vast diversity across the country. A limited number of scholars have realised the serious need to research, understand and theorise these changes. Some, such as Partha Chatterjee (2008) and Dipankar Gupta (2005), have attempted to develop their ideas into general formulations. However, only a few scholars have the research data to investigate these changes in any great depth. Some of the latter, such as Jan Breman in south Gujarat, rely on their continued long-term engagement with people from a particular set of villages. Others have restudied rural areas that they or others worked on in the past—for instance Surinder Jodhka's 2011 revisits to the Haryana villages where he pursued his doctoral research; Kalpana Wilson's 1999 visit to central Bihar villages explored earlier under the direction of Pradhan Prasad; Gerry Rodgers and Janine Rodgers' 2001 and 2011 revisits to the villages in Bihar; J. Harriss, J. Jeyaranjan and K. Nagaraj's 2010 visits to the villages studied by Gilbert Slater in Tamil Nadu; and Venugopal Rao Nellutla's visits to the villages studied by the Communist Party of India (People's War) in Andhra Pradesh—or they have combined restudies with new village studies, for instance V. K. Ramachandran, V. Rawal and M. Swaminathan's 2010 studies in Andhra Pradesh. Others are researching agrarian transformations in new areas (Anand Chakravarti in Bihar 2001; B. Harriss-White, D. Mishra and V. Upadhyay in Arunachal Pradesh 2009; or Alpa Shah in Jharkhand). A few have inspiringly tried to aggregate the lessons from some of these case studies with general trends (Basole 2010; Basu 2010; Das 2010; Lerche 2011). This growing body of work raises a number of fundamental issues which need further exploration. A recent workshop at Oxford made a start in this direction.

First, the structure of agrarian property has clearly been transformed. The land reforms of the 1950s had varied impact as did the introduction of Green Revolution technology. However, land centralisation is not the dominant trend in India. India is now an agrarian society where 63 per cent of its producers own holdings of less than 1 hectare—the structure of landholdings is pear-shaped. Moreover, NSS 2003–04 data analysis reveals that only a little over 5 per cent of the producers own more than 3 hectares and just 0.52 per cent own more than 10.

Lack of concentration of land and the persistence of small-scale cultivation have been interpreted by some as signs of semi-feudal relations but almost everywhere the logic of semi-feudalism no longer seems to be at work. In many areas mid-ranking castes, such as the Jats in Uttar Pradesh or the Yadavs, Kurmis and Koeris in Bihar, who were not the main ex-landlord group, have now become the dominant farmers. In other regions, such as parts of Tamil Nadu, while ex-landlords are still significantly powerful their role in village life has very much changed. Sharecropping arrangements in most places, even in areas such as Purnia district in Bihar, have been largely replaced by the use of wage labour in agricultural production. Thus, in many parts of India, agricultural bondage and attached labour have significantly decreased, if not disappeared, while casual wage labour has increased.

Where apparently new arrangements of attachment have appeared, settings couched in sharecropping terminology, in regions of India where sharecropping has been rare, in places in Uttar Pradesh, Haryana, Arunachal Pradesh or even Tamil Nadu, closer investigation often reveals that they are quite different from the old ones and more a piece-rate system for agriculture. Since the time of unfree labour relations pervading the semi-feudal heartlands, we seem to be watching a widespread decrease and transformation in sharecropping. These uneven changes mean that the direct confrontation that small peasants faced with exploiting classes within villages that characterised semi-feudal relations rarely exist in the same way today. These transformations have massively affected social relations in rural areas. In regions from Punjab down to the south in Tamil Nadu, Dalit landless labourers, for instance, are no longer dependent in the way they were 30 years ago on dominant landowners.

Tenancy has also declined. NSSO data in 2002–03 suggest that only 6.5 per cent of the operated area was under tenancy. Where cases of tenancy are reported, it seems important to question the classic 'feudal' model, because most landholdings now are no longer sufficient to provide for the reproduction of households. To what extent does farming income provide a major livelihood for households reported to engage in tenancy? In fact, these households are more likely to run on the salaries of teachers, government servants, shopkeepers or traders than the income from the rent of the farm or its produce. Tenancy can be part and parcel of capitalist social relations where people who have risen up the class hierarchy no longer wish to till their land themselves. And though in many of the affluent states, like Punjab and Haryana, there is a tendency towards 'reverse tenancy' in which smaller farmers lease out their land to larger, richer tenants, in other areas it is reported that people are losing their interest in village affairs and the significance of landownership as the basis of social status and political power has significantly diminished. The case for redistributive land reform certainly needs rethinking.

MULTIPLE MEANS OF LIVELIHOOD

Second, the classic push away from agricultural work at home, in which the farmer or farm labourer moves away from the village to become a factory hand in the city, is not taking place as the dominant process of labour transformation in India. Neither is the classic 'polar' differentiation of the peasant classes—the formation of a large rural proletariat and an agrarian capitalist class. The average income for farmers operating less than 4 hectares of land was shown by 2003 NSSO data to be negative. Farm incomes then are no longer sufficient to provide for the needs of most rural working people. However, growth in regular employment has been extremely slow (Bhaduri 2009) and most people are being pushed to work in the unregulated informal and unorganised sector, which has almost no labour protection but accounts for 93 per cent of the Indian workforce (Harriss-White 2004). It also seems that rather than industry *per se*, this labour is being absorbed in other sectors such as construction, workshop manufacturing, large-scale capitalist farms of other regions, or services. The vulnerability, mobility and marginality of this informal sector labour may explain the persistence of small-scale cultivation. Multiple livelihood options are necessary for the reproduction of rural households. So the rural economy has developed in very complex ways. What are the means by which rural households reproduce themselves and what kinds of differentiation might result?

To answer these questions, recent studies of labour raise the importance of the circular migration of labour for work in India's informal economy in India. In most areas, the labouring poor leave the village to work but keep coming back in a pattern of migration that is not just about becoming 'footloose labour' (Breman 1996), but remaining footloose. Some have estimated that there are 50 million Indians circulating as labour; others have suggested the figure is nearer 100 million. Casualisation is the primary feature of this labour and as J. Breman, I. Guérin and A. Prakash (2009) and others have shown, different degrees of bonded labour relations are a common condition of this capitalist work relation. While some need the advances which tie them to particular contractors in moments of crisis, others often submit to bondage simply in order to get employed. Breman points out that this neo-bondage (of varying degrees) is significantly different from the forms of agrarian bondage of the past as it comes without the guarantees of provisions of basic needs in slack seasons or when labourers were not able to work because of ill health, late pregnancy, old age, and other dependent phases of the lifecycle. He finds conditions of the rural proletariat in places like Gujarat pauperising and precarious.

There is an important regional and caste dynamic to this massive labour migration. Dalits and Adivasis predominate and central and eastern India are noted to be reservoirs of seasonal casual labour migration for the rest of the Indian economy. Adivasis and Dalits from Jharkhand, Orissa and Chhattisgarh, for instance, will commonly go to work as wage labour for six months to the brick factories of Bengal, Uttar Pradesh and Bihar, the agricultural plains of Punjab and Haryana, and more recently, to the construction companies and mills of Tamil Nadu and Kerala, but they will come back to their home villages for the rainy season where many will have small plots of land to cultivate rice that may last them a few months. It seems that these patterns of migration are increasingly prevalent and although labour from Jharkhand may go to the factories of Bihar, Bihari low-caste labour may in turn move to Delhi, Punjab or Gujarat.

Even if this migrant labour does not reinvest in agriculture back at home, migration has fostered the increased purchase of clothes, better food, healthcare and schooling, causing fundamental shifts in the agrarian economy. Rodgers and Rodgers' (2001) restudy of villages in Purnia district, areas akin to those that were seen as bastions of semi-feudalism in the 1980s, stresses the fundamental importance of temporary migration on the marketising and monetising of the rural economy and the decline in the political exactions and social mechanisms of semi-feudalism. The great transformation to industrial society does not appear to be taking place in India, but rural areas are being fundamentally transformed through migrant labour. And it is possible that this complex dynamic of rural–urban connections through circular migration is here to stay in India.

The Non-farm Economy

Moreover, while seasonal casual migration is important, there is also a significant non-farm economy which has developed within rural areas. In 2004–05, this non-farm rural economy accounted for one-fifth of total employment and for 50 million jobs more than in the rural farm economy. This includes work in construction, 'trade and hotels', manufacturing, as well as transport and storage. According to NSSO data, the largest number of new jobs is actually increasing in the category of the self-employed. The National Commission for Enterprises in the Unorganised Sector argues that 65 per cent of the agricultural sector is in fact self-employed (166.2 million people). There is a vast section of the Indian population that is involved in petty commodity production (PCP) where households control their means of production for exchange as well as exploit their own labour. Labour lawyers and economists treat it as disguised wage work. But this is often a form of more or less independent productive activity for the market, reproduced through relationships mediated by the exchange of commodities, in spheres of manufacturing, trade and services in particular, almost all of which is in the informal economy. For instance, not just food from agricultural production, but hunting, fishing, milk production, brewing, weaving, pottery, carpentry, construction, small shop keeping and producing and selling food in a restaurant or tea stall.

Most PCPs are extremely vulnerable, struggling to survive, sustaining themselves in conditions where they will not be able to grow and any surplus will be accidental. They are, as Harriss-White points out, easily susceptible to exploitation through exchange on several markets: property, raw materials, money and the finished product, other than that of the classic one of labour for wage work. Harriss-White (2010) argues that 'India's capitalist transition and ongoing transformations have created a complex social formation in which—despite rampant differentiation and the creation of advanced forms of corporate capital … together with a substantial working class—PCP *is the most common form of production.*' Moreover, she argues that 'it is not transitional'. Like seasonal labour migration, perhaps PCP too is here to stay, an element of the Indian economy as modern as the corporation. And, as in the case of labour migration, we need urgently to research and understand the widespread significance of PCP in the transformation of rural economies of India and in processes of class differentiation.

Third, the paradoxical role of the Indian state, ostensibly outside its own reach in the 'informal economy', in both propping up the poor in village India by providing infrastructure and as a potential driver of class differentiation, must not be overlooked. In remote parts of India, such as Arunachal Pradesh and Jharkhand, there is significant evidence that the state provision of commercial loans, of education and of reservations for government posts are triggering class differentiation amongst the peasantry despite the mediocre capital investment in agriculture. But more generally across the country the role of village-based anti-poverty programmes such as guaranteed employment in public work, delivery of free—or highly subsidised—food, have played significant roles in keeping the village householder alive. Chatterjee (2008), drawing on the work of Kalyan Sanyal (2007), makes this point in arguing that 'there is a growing sense now that certain basic conditions of life must be provided to people everywhere and that if the national or local governments do not provide them, someone else must, whether it is other states or international agencies or non-governmental organisations'.

NOT THE CLASSIC AGRARIAN TRANSITION

Clearly, what we are seeing in India is not the classic agrarian transition. If they ever were, poor Indians with homes in rural areas are no longer simple peasants or rural wage labourers, but people who have complex livelihoods involving both forms of work: tilling their small plots of land and now, dependent on migrant wage labour, on working in the rural non-farm economy, and on petty commodity production and trade in the capitalist economy to reproduce their household. This is a circumstance which needs new conceptual tools. We have known for a long time now that villages are not republics, but the importance of seasonal casual labour migration, the rural non-farm economy and petty commodity production stresses a new need critically to revisit the relevance of categories such as 'poor peasant', 'middle peasant' and 'rich peasant' by exploring the significance of the links that almost every single rural household seems to have for its reproduction with the wider economy beyond the village confines. Scholars of agrarian transformations in India will need to think through the relevance of Bernstein (2008) and Lerche's (2010) 'classes of labour' to the segmentation of labour in India.

Jens Lerche (2010) identifies the 'classes of labour' on the basis of different types of employment and degrees of self-employment, ordered by levels of remuneration and protection, and also by a hierarchy of powerlessness. But scholars also need to consider whether India (or at least parts of it) is witnessing a transition from peasant production to petty production in which producers embody micro capital as well as labour and do not lose entire control of the means of production but are compulsively incorporated through circuits of exchange. They also need to think through the tentative suggestion of the *Sanhati* editors that it is the Indian state (and not putative feudal lords) and its many faces which are increasingly holding back the transformations of capitalism (Das 2010). The state has an incoherent project, encouraging small-scale livelihoods, destroying them, protecting them, ignoring them, or allowing them to survive as an unintended consequence of altogether different intentions.

Changes are taking place in different ways and at dissimilar speeds across the country. Development within India means that there could be several different agrarian questions, driven by regionally disparate class constellations and development trajectories. Some agrarian regions of India have also been much better studied historically (for instance Punjab, Haryana, western Uttar Pradesh, Gujarat and Tamil Nadu) than others (for instance, the Northeast, or central and eastern India), and more theoretically informed empirical work is needed in these latter regions.

Macro-level data alone cannot unveil the nuances and implications of local transformations that are vitally important for political tactics (Ramachandran, Rawal and Swaminathan 2010). They mask significant details. They are often collected under classificatory frameworks which may no longer be the most appropriate. Case studies emanating from the village level—though in no sense does this mean treating the village as a static, bounded unit—are crucial to reveal the complexities of transformations, raise new questions and analyse continuities and changes. But they should not be used for generalisations. A dialectical treatment of case studies and new larger-scale data sets, with both being used to ask new questions of each other, must be the foundation for the way forward with this new research agenda.

References

Basu, D. 2010. 'Agrarian Change in Eastern India: The View from Bihar'. *Sanhati Journal*, 27 August.

Basole, A. 2010. 'Agrarian Change in North India: Evidence from Haryana and Uttar Pradesh'. *Sanhati Journal*, 27 September.

Bernstein, H. 1996. 'Agrarian Question Then and Now'. *The Journal of Peasant Studies* 24(1): 22–59.

———. 2008. 'Agrarian Questions from Transition to Globalisation'. In *Peasants and Globalisation: Political Economy, Rural Transformation and the Agrarian Question*, eds A. H. Akram-Lodhi and C. Kay, 239–61. London: Routledge.

Bhaduri, A. 2009. *The Face You Were Afraid to See: Essays on the Indian Economy*. New Delhi: Penguin.

Breman, J. 1996. *Footloose Labour: Working in India's Informal Economy*. Cambridge: Cambridge University Press.

Breman, J., I. Guérin and A. Prakash (eds). 2009. *India's Unfree Workforce: Of Bondage Old and New*. New Delhi: Oxford University Press.

Byres, T. 1986. 'The Agrarian Question, Forms of Capitalist Agrarian Transition and the State: An Essay with Reference to Asia'. *Social Scientist* 14(11–12): 3–67.

Chakravarti, A. 2001. *Social Power and Everyday Class Relations: Agrarian Transformation in North Bihar.* New Delhi: Sage Publications.

Chatterjee, P. 2008. 'Democracy and Economic Transformation in India'. *Economic and Political Weekly* 43(16), 19 April: 53–62.

Das, D. 2010. 'Some Aspects of Agricultural Investment in India: Part 1'. *Sanhati Journal*, 28 October.

Gupta, D. 2005. 'Whither the Indian Village: Culture and Agriculture in "Rural" India'. *Economic and Political Weekly* 40(8), 19 February: 751–58.

Harriss, J., J. Jeyaranjan and K. Nagaraj. 2010. 'Land, Labour and Caste Politics in Rural Tamil Nadu in the 20th Century: Iruvelpattu (1916–2008)'. *Economic and Political Weekly* 45(31): 47–61.

Harriss-White, B. 2004. *India Working: Essays on Society and Economy.* Cambridge: Cambridge University Press.

———. 2010. 'Capitalism and the Common Man'. Available at https://www.southasia.ox.ac.uk/sites/default/files/southasia/documents/media/oxford_university_csasp_-_work_in_progress_paper_2_capitalism_and_the_common_man_-_four_decades_of_development_in_africa_and_s.pdf (accessed 20 December 2021).

Harriss-White, B., D. Mishra and V. Upadhyay. 2009. 'Institutional Diversity and Capitalist Transition: The Political Economy of Change in Arunachal Pradesh, India'. *Journal of Agrarian Change* 9(4): 512–47.

Jodhka, S. 2011. 'What's Happening to the Rural?: Revisiting "Marginalities" and "Dominance" in Northwest India'. Paper presented at the Poverty Conference.

Lerche, J. 2010. 'From "Rural Labour" to "Classes of Labour": Class Fragmentation, Caste and Class Struggle at the Bottom of the Indian Labour Hierarchy'. In *The Comparative Political Economy of Development: Africa and South Asia*, eds B. Harriss-White and J. Heyer, 64–85. Oxon: Routledge.

———. 2011. 'Agrarian Crisis and Agrarian Questions in India'. *Journal of Agrarian Change* 11(1): 104–18.

Ramachandran, V. K., V. Rawal and M. Swaminathan. 2010. *Socio-economic Surveys of Three Villages in Andhra Pradesh: A Study of Agrarian Relations.* New Delhi: Tulika Books.

Rodgers, G., and J. Rodgers. 2001. 'A Leap across Time: When Semi-feudalism Met the Market in Rural Purnia'. *Economic and Political Weekly* 36(22), 2 June: 1976–83.

———. 2011. 'Inclusive Development? Migration, Governance and Social Change in Rural Bihar'. *Economic and Political Weekly* 46(23), 4 June: 43–50.

Sanyal, Kalyan. 2007. *Rethinking Capitalist Development: Primitive Accumulation, Governmentality and Post-colonial Capitalism.* New Delhi: Routledge.

Wilson, K. 1999. 'Patterns of Accumulation and Struggles of Rural Labour: Some Aspects of Agrarian Change in Central Bihar'. *The Journal of Peasant Studies* 26(2): 316–54.

World Bank. 2007. *World Development Report 2008: Agriculture for Development.* Oxford: Oxford University Press.

23

Agrarian Changes in the Times of (Neoliberal) 'Crises'

*Revisiting Attached Labour in Haryana**

Surinder S. Jodhka

The success of Green Revolution technology during the 1960s and 1970s, though confined only to some pockets of India, was an important turning point in the development history of India. Its implications were not confined to economic growth. It transformed rural social relations and traditional authority structures. The face of the Indian countryside in the Green Revolution pockets changed very rapidly. In terms of social groups, the most visible beneficiaries of this change were the substantial landowners from the locally dominant caste groups, who had traditionally been landowners and cultivators. The locally dominant castes consolidated their position in the regional power structure and acquired a new sense of confidence. The rise of dominant caste farmers in the 1970s also set in motion a phase of populist politics at the regional and national levels. The newly emerged agrarian elite farmer did not speak only for his own caste or class. He spoke on behalf of the entire village. His identification with the village was not just political or that of a representative of a section of the village. He saw himself to be the natural spokesperson of the village.

However, this excitement about the Green Revolution and modernisation of Indian agriculture did not last for too long. By the mid-1980s, the Indian countryside began to show a new kind of restiveness; this was particularly pronounced in the pockets that had experienced the Green Revolution. The surplus producing farmers began to mobilise themselves into unions demanding subsidies on farm inputs and higher prices for their produce. The market economy, they argued, was inherently against the farm sector and favoured the urban industry and the middle-class consumer. Given the unequal power relations between the town and countryside, they argued, the agricultural sector suffered from unequal terms of

* Originally published in *Economic and Political Weekly* 47(26–27), 30 June 2012: 5–13.

trade, the evidence of which could be seen in the growth of indebtedness among the cultivating/farming classes.

Farmers mobilised themselves in different parts of India quite successfully for over a decade. The farmers' movements of the 1980s also signalled the rise of a new mobile social category of rural people. They had prospered with the Green Revolution, which had also brought them close to the market economy. Though they spoke for agrarian interests, they aspired to go beyond the village. The agrarian economy could not satisfy their aspirations for social and cultural mobility. They were quick to move from their local seats of power to legislative assemblies in the state capitals. The surplus they generated from agriculture went into education, urban trade and other non-agricultural activities (Harriss-White 1996; Omvedt 1992; Rutten 1995; Upadhya 1988). By the early 1980s, the social profile of this class had begun to change. The following lines of Balagopal (1987) provide a lucid account of this process of growing diversification:

> … a typical family of this class has a landholding in its native village, cultivated by hired labour, *bataidar*, tenant or farm servants and supervised by the father or one son; business of various descriptions in town managed by other sons; and perhaps a young and bright child who is a doctor or engineer or a professor. It is this class that is most vocal about injustice done to the village (Balagopal 1987: 1545).

It was around this time when agrarian issues had been intensely worked on by the social scientists for nearly a decade and a half and had become politically sensitive that I initiated my doctoral research on rural indebtedness and the changing nature of debt-dependencies in rural Haryana. I selected Karnal district for my field study. Karnal had been a successful IADP district and was a typical representative of the prosperous agrarian landscape of northwest India. Keeping various sociological and methodological variables in mind, I chose three villages of Panipat tehsil for my fieldwork (Panipat later became a separate district of Haryana). I began my fieldwork in March 1988 and completed it by the middle of 1989. In terms of research questions, I looked at the different dimensions of credit and debt relations and how they institutionalised dependency relations among different social classes/categories engaged in agriculture. Given that my work was in the post-Green Revolution period in an active Green Revolution pocket, my obvious focus was on the processes of change.

Though Indian social scientists had intensely debated the emerging nature of production relations in Indian agriculture in the famous 'mode of production debate' during the 1970s and early 1980s, micro and specific dimensions of change were still being studied and debated. The question of debt-dependency and unfree labour was one such question. Since the middle of the 1970s, eradication of 'bonded labour' had also been a policy concern with the Indian state as well as global agencies like the International Labour Organisation (ILO) and the Agricultural Sustainability Institute (ASI).

The shift in India's economic orientation during the early 1990s had several implications for the agricultural sector. Apart from other things, it marginalised agriculture in the development discourse on India. Social science research on the rural and agrarian economy also declined. Agrarian questions no longer generated excitement in university seminars, or in the popular media.

By the early years of the twenty-first century a new discourse on Indian agriculture began to take shape. The preoccupation this time was with 'crisis', manifestations of which were clearly visible in the tragic rise of farmers' suicides in different pockets of India. While the Indian economy was growing at a fast pace, the agricultural sector was experiencing stagnation. The relative share of the agricultural sector in the national economy began to decline steadily. Interestingly, in this new discourse of 'crisis of agriculture', only occasionally were any references made to internal inequalities in agrarian India, even by those who swore by the political economy framework and had participated in the debate on agrarian class relations and mode of production. Unlike the 1970s and 1980s, very little empirical research was being done on the internal dynamics of the political economy of agriculture. Most formulations also seemed to be emerging from the analysis of journalistic reports, or the large data sets produced by official agencies, such as the NSSO.

Given this context, I revisited two of my three study villages during 2008–09, 20 years after my first fieldwork, with some 'old' and some 'new' questions. The new questions related to the nature of change in relation to castes and communities in the villages. The old questions were to explore the political economy of agrarian change during this period. One of these was the question of unfree and attached labour.

The Two Villages

The two villages selected for the study represent a particular type of rural setting which is becoming increasingly common in different parts of the Third World. These are villages that are actively connected to urban centres and are being changed very rapidly by technology and industrialisation. Though the two study villages are still sufficiently far from urban centres to be treated as urban peripheries, they are certainly not economically 'backward' or socially and culturally 'traditional'. The distance that the two villages have from the main towns in the region and the diverse sets of communities they are inhabited by also make them worth comparing, interestingly similar and different from each other. Of the two study villages, Village-I is located at a distance of around 9 km from the town of Panipat and the other (Village-II) around 16 km away. Both are multi-caste villages with diverse caste communities living within the villages and both experienced the Green Revolution during the 1970s.

Equally important for understanding their development has been the growing shadow of industry over the two villages. It was around the mid-1970s that the Government of Haryana decided to set up a thermal power station close to Panipat. Some of the farmers from Village-I lost a part of their agricultural land to the power project. However, it did not directly affect the agrarian economy of the village very much. The villagers whose land was acquired were considered for jobs in the thermal power station and some of them managed to get regular employment in the plant. It also generated a lot of new employment for casual labour. Over the years, the plant and the town have been expanding and new industries have also been developing in the area.

SOCIAL LIFE AND ECONOMIC RELATIONS

Until some time back, Indian rural life was almost completely identified with agriculture and activities that supported agriculture. Though there were a large number of households that never owned land, they too largely depended on agriculture for their livelihood. They either worked as casual/attached labourers with the cultivators or provided other supporting services to the cultivators. Mediated through the institution of caste, the rural society of Haryana had a system of patron–client relations within which the agrarian economy was socially organised.

This system of *jajmani* ties had begun to weaken with the introduction of commercial agriculture during the colonial period (Bhattacharya 1985) and had nearly completely disintegrated by the 1980s. However, 20 years back, the two villages still had a predominantly agrarian character. Agriculture was at the centre of rural social life. It provided employment to a majority of the working population of the village and gave them their primary identity. Cultivating farmers were at the centrestage of village life. Poor Dalits and other landless villagers looked up to them for employment, and occasionally for credit. Through credit, the richer farmers tied the labouring poor for work on land and at home, with the cattle. Those who owned big plots of land also controlled political institutions and commanded respect and authority in the village.

This has almost completely changed. The change was more visible in Village-I than it was in Village-II, but the pattern was exactly the same. Less than 30 per cent of all households identified cultivation as their primary occupation. This was even lesser in Village-I (23 per cent). As is evident from Table 23.1, the largest proportion of households is in the category of labourers. However, they are not necessarily agricultural labourers. In fact, a large majority of them earn their livelihood from working outside the agricultural sector and only occasionally work on land.

TABLE 23.1: Primary Occupation of the Respondent Households, 2008–09

Primary Occupation	*Village-I*	*Village-II*	*Total*
Cultivators	117 (23.26)	172 (35.03)	289 (29.07)
Labourers	206 (40.9)	153 (31.16)	359 (36.11)
Shopkeepers/business	39 (07.75)	45 (09.16)	84 (08.45)
Regular service/government job	108 (21.4)	63 (12.8)	171 (17.20)
No clear arrangement	33 (06.55)	58 (11.8)	91 (09.15)
Total	503 (100)	491 (100)	994 (100)

Note: Percentages are presented in parentheses.

Source: Based on the author's primary survey.

The number of people with employment outside the village in the form of regular jobs in the formal sector of the economy (17.2 per cent) is also quite significant. This becomes particularly interesting when we see it in relation to caste.

However, landownership and cultivation continue to be the prerogative of the 'dominant' and 'upper' castes in the two villages. Nearly 92 per cent of all the cultivators were from these caste communities. In contrast, more than 80 per cent of those who reported their primary occupation as labourers were either Dalits or were from Backward Castes (BCs). Occupationally, diversification had occurred among all the caste groups. As is evident from Table 23.2, a good proportion of households in each category had primary occupations outside agriculture. Interestingly, proportionately speaking, the number of Dalits with regular jobs is the highest, and it is the lowest for the BCs. Though both categories have been poor and lacking in social and cultural capital required for securing a regular job, Dalits have been able to get these jobs because of the statutory quotas in education and employment made available to them by state policies.

TABLE 23.2: Caste-wise Primary Occupation of the Respondent Households, 2008–09

Caste	*Cultivator/ Farmer*	*Labourer*	*Shopkeeper/ Business*	*Regular Service/ Government Job*	*No Regular Job*	*Total*
Dalit	7 (3.8)	106 (57.9)	0	51 (27.86)	19 (10.38)	183 (100)
BC	17 (5.5)	202 (65.37)	14 (4.5)	42 (13.5)	34 (11.0)	309 (100)
DC	201 (61.28)	25 (7.6)	23 (7.01)	55 (16.7)	24 (7.31)	328 (100)
UC	64 (36.78)	26 (14.94)	47 (27.01)	23 (13.21)	14 (8.04)	174 (100)
Total	289 (29.07)	359 (36.11)	84 (8.45)	171 (17.20)	91 (9.15)	994 (100)

Note: The category Dalit corresponds to the local ex-untouchable communities. The category BC has been in usage in the region for a long. These are, broadly speaking, 'lower' sections of the currently popular official category 'OBC'. Some of the OBC (the 'upper' layer, such as the landowning Gujjars) are the locally dominant caste (DC) and thus have been included in the category DC. Some 'upper castes' (UC), such as Brahmins, Rajput and Punjabi Aroras, have also been landowners and cultivators in the region; percentages are presented in parentheses.

Source: Based on the author's primary survey.

Apart from the economic activity, the number of working members in a household also determined the social and economic wellbeing of a household (Table 23.3). Notably, nearly half of our respondent households had more than one full-time working member and in some cases the number of working members was as high as five. Further, the pattern was almost the same across caste groups. There were also some households where there was no full-time working member.

An important aspect of this was the fact that in most cases, different members of the household were invariably employed in different occupations, reflecting a process of occupational diversification and differentiation within the household. The

TABLE 23.3: Number of Working Members in the Respondent Households, 2008–09

	1	*2*	*3*	*4*	*5*	*None*	*Total*
Dalit	82	65	24	5	4	3	183
BC	144	109	37	10	6	3	309
DC	162	99	40	13	6	8	328
UC	95	46	15	4	2	12	174
Total	483	319	116	32	18	26	994

Source: Based on the author's primary survey.

households in rural Haryana are increasingly becoming pluri-active (Jodhka 2006; Lindberg 2005). For example, apart from the reported primary occupation, more than 15 per cent (152) of the respondents also reported having a formal secondary occupation within the village or outside. In most cases, the secondary occupation was a small business, either some kind of shop within the village, or outside in the neighbouring village.

A striking change that had occurred in the two villages over the last two decades was a manifold expansion of the local market. Twenty years back the number of shops in each of the villages was around 15 to 20 and most of them were grocery shops which provided almost everything the villagers needed for their daily consumption. Most of these shops were owned and run by the local Banias or the Punjabi Aroras. This had changed significantly over the years. The number of shops in Village-I was 78 and in Village-II was 64.

AGRICULTURE

In some respects, there had not been much change over the last two decades in agrarian practices. Despite the growing shadow of industry over the two villages, not much land had been lost to 'outsiders'. On the contrary, agricultural land has grown in size as the villagers were able to work on the *banjar* (fallow) land and improve it for cultivation. In Village-I, most of the panchayat land, which was previously lying fallow, had been encroached upon by cultivators, mostly from the locally dominant communities, and was being regularly cultivated.

As was the practice two decades back, the two main crops in the region were still wheat and paddy. Some villagers also used to grow sugar cane, but over the years, they had stopped doing that. Some farmers also grew a third crop in the form of peas or lentils. The use of fertilisers and pesticides continued to grow. Farmers had almost completely stopped producing seeds for cultivation and depended entirely on the market for the supply of hybrid seeds. For their irrigational needs they depended on the canal water and tubewells. Though, unlike in some other parts of the Green Revolution areas of the north-west, the water table had not gone down much in the region, farmers installed tubewells using a new technology: submersible pumps. This was more expensive, but provided a better supply of water.

The mechanisation process that began with Green Revolution technology has continued to grow. Though a large number of farmers had tractors during the late 1980s, a good number of villagers also kept bullocks. In fact, 20 years back I came across some cases where the relatively smaller farmers, after working with a tractor for some time, had gone back to farming using bullocks, finding it more economical for their size of holdings. This was no longer the case. There were no bullocks in the two villages. The small and marginal farmers, who could not afford to buy tractors, hired tractors for ploughing. The use of combine harvesters had increased significantly, replacing the threshers for harvesting of wheat. Previously, there was some resistance to the use of combine harvesters because they only picked up the seed and left the plant on the field, a useful source for cattle fodder. Threshing machines, on the other hand, were preferred because they also processed the plant and converted it into hay (used for cattle fodder). However, the arrival of a new machine called the reaper had, to an extent, solved this problem. It plucked the plant left behind by the combine harvester and processed it into hay.

Mechanical harvesting machines were available for paddy as well, but they did not work very well for the longer plant of Basmati rice, which was popular with most of the farmers in the two villages. One of the implications, and perhaps also a reason, for this second phase of mechanisation was a steady decline in the demand for human labour in agriculture, a subject I elaborate on later.

Landholdings and Agrarian Social Structure

Despite the declining significance of agriculture in national life, agriculture continues to employ the largest number of working Indians. Though this holds good for the two villages, there is clearly a declining trend in the number of people working on land.

As mentioned above, less than 30 per cent of the households in the two villages reported agriculture or farming as their primary occupation. Also, there were significant disparities in the landownership patterns. As evident from Table 23.4, below 66 per cent of the households in Village-I and 48 per cent in Village-II reported owning no land at all. On the other hand, a small number of households owned large plots of land.

Table 23.4: Patterns of Landownership in the Two Study Villages, 2008–09

	No Land	*Less than 2 Acres*	*2–5 Acres*	*5–10 Acres*	*10–25 Acres*	*25–50 Acres*	*50+ Acres*	*No Response*	*Total*
Village-I	333 (66.2)	25 (4.97)	101 (20.1)	30 (5.96)	7 (1.39)	5 (0.99)	1 (0.19)	1 (0.19)	503 (100)
Village-II	235 (47.9)	36 (7.33)	130 (26.5)	50 (10.2)	30 (6.10)	7 (1.42)	2 (0.40)	1 (0.20)	491 (100)
Total	568 (57.1)	61 (6.13)	231 (23.2)	80 (8.04)	37 (3.72)	12 (1.20)	3 (0.30)	2 (0.20)	994 (100)

Note: The number of farming households owning and cultivating more than 10 acres of land appears to be under-reported for the obvious reasons; percentages are presented in parenthesis.

Source: Based on the author's primary survey.

When seen in relation to caste, this picture of disparity becomes even more significant. Despite many radical changes in rural social life over the last century or so, the agrarian economy of the village remains almost exclusively under the control of the dominant and upper castes, those who have traditionally been the landowning and agrarian communities. As is evident from Table 23.5 nearly 95 per cent of the Dalits and BCs were completely landless. On the contrary, only around 12 per cent of the dominant caste households were landless.

TABLE 23.5: Landownership Patterns across Caste Groups, 2008–09

	No Land	*<1 Acre*	*2–5 Acres*	*5–10 Acres*	*10–25 Acres*	*25–50 Acres*	*50+ Acres*	*No Response*	*Total*
Dalit	174 (95.08)	2 (1.09)	6 (3.28)	0	0	0	0	1 (0.55)	183 (100)
BC	293 (94.82)	4 (1.29)	9 (2.91)	3 (0.97)	0	0	0	0	309 (100)
DC	39 (11.89)	27 (8.23)	156 (47.56)	61 (18.6)	35 (10.67)	7 (2.13)	2 (0.60)	1 (0.3)	328 (100)
UC	62 (35.63)	28 (16.09)	60 (34.48)	16 (9.19)	2 (1.14)	5 (2.87)	1 (0.6)	0	174 (100)
Total	568 (57.14)	61 (6.13)	231 (23.24)	80 (8.05)	37 (3.72)	12 (1.21)	3 (0.3)	2 (0.2)	994 (100)

Note: Percentages are presented in parenthesis.
Source: Based on the author's primary survey.

However, there have been very important changes in the agrarian social structure, both in terms of relations across caste groups and class categories, as also in the attitudes of the landowners towards their occupational callings.

ATTACHED LABOUR THEN AND NOW

Most of my doctoral work was published in the *Economic and Political Weekly* (Jodhka 1994, 1995a, 1995b, 1995c, 1996). The first article I published was on the changing nature of debt dependencies in relation to the various forms of labour relations. My specific focus was on the changing patterns of attached labour. Social science literature had looked at the phenomenon of attached labour in post-Green Revolution agriculture from several different perspectives. There were many who believed that with modernisation and the development of capitalism in agriculture, all forms of traditional structures and dependency relations would disappear. Jan Breman (1974) had described this as a process of de-patronisation where labourers were not only freed from traditional ties, but they also lost the security of patronage they had earlier enjoyed.

Some others looked at it as a process of formalisation or casualisation of labour. However, empirical research showed that attached labour not only did not disappear from Green Revolution pockets, but in some cases it actually became more pronounced, albeit in different forms. Similarly, the phenomenon was also interpreted differently. T. J. Byres (1972), for example, did not find anything wrong with it and argued that this form of labour only fulfilled the changing demands of the new agrarian economy, and could work as a means of differentiating labour. Attached labour, he speculated, would be required when greater mechanisation would reduce the need for employing casual labour, and, instead, the capitalist farmer would prefer 'one attached labourer, who would be paid a regular and probably high wage and who would be trained to look after the mechanical implement' (Byres 1972: 105–09). This 'privileged class of attached labour', he expected, would also get to participate in the prosperity of the 'green revolution' (ibid.). Several years later, Rudra (1990) made a similar argument when he compared the semi-attached labour employed by the capitalist farmers of West Bengal with the regular employees of the organised sector.

Another set of scholars saw it as a form of unfreedom. Attached labour was for them a form of bondage and slavery. Amit Bhaduri (1984), for example, saw in it evidence of a continuity of pre-capitalist relations of production even in the Green Revolution pockets of India. Some others, such as Tom Brass (1990), underlined the point that their presence in post-Green Revolution agriculture was simply evidence of the fact that capitalism could be pretty comfortable with slave labour as long as it helped in wealth accumulation. He argued that the employer farmers in post-Green Revolution Haryana actively worked towards decomposing labour through the mechanism of debt using short- and long-term labour-tying arrangements, which amounted to a process of what he described as 'de-proletarianisation'.

Attached labour, indeed, existed in my study villages, though the form and content of the relationship had changed substantially and had become quite formalised, a point that had also been made earlier by Sheila Bhalla (1976). The attached labourers rarely saw themselves as being a 'privileged class', or as 'permanent employees' of the organised sector. Elements of unfreedom were also present in their relationship with the farmers. However, I did not agree fully with Brass on his conceptualisation of attached labour as a form of slavery, or that labour-tying was a growing phenomenon, a process of de-proletarianisation as he described it. In fact, the overall change in the social framework of agricultural production had opened up several choices for the labouring classes. There were many cases where, after working as attached labourers for some time the labourers had been able to move out of the relationship.

The growing integration of the village with the broader market economy and the increasing availability of alternative sources of employment outside agriculture along with the changing political and ideological environment had weakened the hold of the landowner over the labourers. They intensely disliked working in an attached relationship and chose to work only when they were in dire need of a relatively large amount of cash and had no other source of mobilising credit. They also tried to come out of the relationship as soon as they could. Dislike for the relationship by labourers often resulted in instances of violence and conflict with employers. Thanks to all these factors, and contrary to Brass's assertion, the numbers of those willing to work on annual contracts seemed to be declining in villages.

Even when they could not come out of the attached relationship, they kept changing their employers by transferring their debts after every year or two of working with one farmer. Given the shortage of those willing to work as attached labourers, it was not difficult for them to find a substitute employer who was willing to pay advance money required for clearing the outstanding debt with the previous farmer. There were some who simply ran away with the outstanding debt to the employer farmers, and the farmers could not do much to get them back or recover the advances. Recognising the significance of all these processes and their influence on relations on the ground, I conceptualised the existing forms of attached labour as a system of 'labour mortgage', an unfree relationship, but internally fragmented and frequently contested in nature (Jodhka 1994).

In several of his responses to my 1994 *EPW* article, Brass vehemently contested my claim and restated his argument that even my data showed that there was a process of de-proletarianisation underway in Haryana agriculture (Brass 1995, 1996).

Twenty Years Later

What was the nature and extent of attached labour in the two villages 20 years later? As I proceeded with my fieldwork, it was not very difficult to conclude that Brass had, indeed, overstated his argument about the process of de-proletarianisation.

As I showed through my publications based on the earlier fieldwork, by the late 1980s, agrarian relations in these villages had already changed quite radically. Farmers no longer gave their land on lease to tenants on a long-term basis. Their relationship with attached labourers had also become completely formalised (Bhalla 1976; Jodhka 1994). Most of the labour needs of the farmers were fulfilled by casual and contractual labour, mostly on a fixed cash rate. Though a good amount of peak season work was done by the migrant labour from Uttar Pradesh and Bihar, local Dalits and other landless labourers also worked on farms. Most of the middle and big farmers, who owned more than 10 or 15 acres of land, also employed attached labourers. Some of the big farmers employed up to five attached labourers. With exceptions of one or two, all attached labourers came from the same village. Only the locals could be trusted with an advance wage. Each of the villages had around 70–75 persons working as attached labourers.

Though the mechanisation process was a part and parcel of the Green Revolution technology, in its initial phase it did not lead to labour displacement. In fact, demand for labour went up considerably with the new agrarian technology making it possible to intensify cropping patterns and substantially expand land under cultivation. Thus, even when labour came from outside during the peak harvesting and sowing seasons, local labour also had enough work available on the farm.

Decline in Demand for Labour

This has changed considerably over the past 20 years. First and foremost, there has been a significant decline in the demand for labour over the years, mainly because of the second phase of mechanisation. The number of tractors in these villages has continued to grow. There are now 72 tractors in Village-I and nearly 90 in Village-II. All the ploughing work in the village is done mechanically. The wheat harvesting season, which used to go on for over a month, has come down to a mere fortnight. The combine harvesters have completely revolutionised the process of harvesting. The threshers that were earlier used had also reduced harvesting time, but they still needed a lot of labour. The combine harvesters cut down on labour significantly. Sowing of crops is becoming mechanised. Twenty years ago, paddy transplantation and its harvesting used to be the most labour-intensive work in the two villages and provided employment to a large number of people for a good number of days. This is no longer the case. Except for the transplantation of the basmati plant, everything could be done mechanically. Even weeding is increasingly done mechanically or chemically.

The decline has not only been on the demand side. The supply of labour has also shrunk. Even though they continue to be landless, Dalits no longer like working as labourers on the farms. As I have shown through my earlier work in the Punjab villages, Dalits did not wish to work on land with cultivating farmers primarily for social and political reasons (Jodhka 2002). Working with farmers implied accepting their domination and power. By refusing to work on land, Dalits expressed their dissent against the traditional structure of patron–client ties. Even if it meant cycling down to town for casual labour, and no higher wage or secure income, a Dalit would refuse to work on land. Some of them also told me that the work on the farm was much more demanding and one had to invariably work for more than eight hours in a day and put up with abuses by the farmer.

This distancing of Dalits from the agrarian economy had, of course, been made possible by the availability of alternative sources of employment in the industries and informal economy in the nearby urban centres.

Dalits have also been consolidating themselves as communities or political blocks. As mentioned above, some of them could secure regular jobs in the government sector, thanks largely to the caste-based quotas. This would have obviously decreased their dependence for short-term credit on the local cultivating farmers. In contrast, the economic position of those from landless backward castes seemed more vulnerable. They also worked as wage and attached labourers with the local farmers.

Though the two villages still have attached labourers, mostly employed by big farmers, none of them is from a local Dalit caste. The total number of attached labourers in the two villages has declined considerably. This is particularly so in Village-II, where only four or five farmers employ such labourers. The total number of attached labourers in the village would be around 10 to 15. Two decades back this figure was around 70. Their number is a little higher in Village-I, around 25 to 30. Most of them are employed by big Punjabi farmers. The Gujjar farmers no longer hire attached labourers, primarily because of the size of their holdings.

The form of contracts for their hiring has not changed much. They are generally hired in the month of June and farmers pay the annual wage in advance. In some cases when the labourer has to clear an outstanding debt with another farmer, the farmers have to pay them more than the annual wage. Though there were two cases in Village-II, where labourers are hired on a monthly basis, the contract is mostly annual.

However, there are many substantive changes. Most of the attached labourers are outsiders, though not migrants from far-off districts of Uttar Pradesh or Bihar. They are invariably from neighbouring districts of Haryana and generally have a relative living in the village. This has some implications for the contract signed between the labourer and the farmer. In place of the earlier practice of asking the local bigwig (Bhalla 1976) to be a witness, now only the local relative signed as a witness.

The employer farmers do not like to expose their attached labourers to a social science researcher from outside for the fear of them being reported as bonded labourer. Apart from the police/court case that the farmer may have to deal with, he also fears losing the advance wage paid to the worker. It was only after repeated attempts that I was able to interview 14 labourers.

As was the case 20 years ago, the attached labourers still disliked being attached and, in most cases, chose to be attached labourers out of compulsion, mostly due to a need for credit. One of them almost repeated verbatim what I was told by a respondent 20 years back: '... As an attached labourer one has to put up with the farmer like a married woman (*beer*) has to with her husband. You have to listen to his commands all the time. There is no choice!'

The annual earnings from wage work have obviously gone up, from around Rs 5,000 to around Rs 20,000. Depending on age and physical health, a labourer is normally paid anything between Rs 18,000 and Rs 22,000 for a year-long contract. In addition to the cash wage, the labourer is also given a fixed amount of wheat and, if he is an outsider, a place to stay. They work all seven days of the week but are entitled to 12 days of leave in a year. If they absent themselves beyond 12 days, they have to provide a replacement, or the farmer adds the wage of a casual labourer to the outstanding debt.

Why has the incidence of attached labour declined over the years? There are several interrelated processes that have brought this change about. First, over the last two decades, holdings have become smaller, primarily because of sub-divisions within families. Many farms that earlier required the services of a regular labourer no longer need it. Farmers could manage smaller holdings with their family labour, and by hiring casual labour as and when required. Keeping a regular farm servant also made farming unviable for such households. One of the more enterprising farmers said, 'Why should I keep an attached labourer when I can get casual labour as and when I need?'

The second related process is the growing difficulty in getting attached labourers. As the local labourers do not like working in such arrangements, attached labourers invariably have to be imported from the neighbouring districts or states. Such labourers have to be also provided with housing and other amenities for their stay in the village. Not every farmer could afford to do so. Getting an attached labourer and providing him accommodation is not easy unless you have a substantial holding.

Finally, most of the attached labourers I interviewed in 1988–89 had started their careers as *pali*s (cattle herders) at the age of 12 or 13, and graduated to becoming regular *naukars* (servants) after the age of 18 or 19. This is no longer the case. With the village commons having disappeared and the number of cattle having declined considerably, palis are no longer required.

In the changed scenario, farmers have moved to alternative modes of labour hiring, through different and innovative forms of tenurial arrangements.

Alternative Modes of Labour Attachment

One of the direct implications of land reforms legislation and Green Revolution technology was a complete decline of the old system of tenancy relations where the tenant farmer worked on land and paid one-half or one-third share of the produce to the landowner. This gave way to capitalist farming with wage labour and machines. However, over the years this too has changed. While the land market has been rather sluggish, not all landowners are cultivating farmers.

Two sets of landowners have been moving out of direct cultivation. The first are those left with small plots of land due to fragmentation of holdings and where the main working members either have a job outside or do not have the capacity to work on land. The second are the relatively bigger farmers who have diversified into other occupations but continue to live in the village and/or want to keep an active relationship with the land. Such landowners lease out their lands, invariably to smaller enterprising landowners. In such cases, land is mostly leased out on annual cash rent, which has gone up from around Rs 13,000–14,000 to around Rs 20,000–25,000. This phenomenon has been described by some economists as 'reverse tenancy' (Brar and Gill 2002), which is a misnomer. The land is leased out not only by the big landowners to small landowners, but also by small and marginalised landowners to other small landowners or enterprising farmers. Such farmers have to be not only enterprising, but also have sufficient funds to pay cash to the landowner in advance for the year. They also need to have some risk-bearing capacity. A bad crop due to poor weather or pests can mean a complete disaster. A rough estimate suggests that nearly 20–25 per cent of all the land is being cultivated under such arrangements.

Another form of tenancy arrangement, which is preferred by the relatively more active landowners, is 'labour share-cropping', which appears like the traditional system tenurial attachment. Many of the middle-size farmers and some big farmers prefer leasing their lands out on a shared basis to the labouring households. Land, in such cases, is leased out primarily to a labourer, who works on the land along with his family and gets one-fourth of the entire yield. The labourer has to also share one-fourth of the expense, which is invariably paid by the farmer and deducted from the total yield at the end of the season. Some of these labourers are also indebted to the farmers whose lands they cultivate but they are not tied to the farmer like an attached labourer. The farmer though continuing to take interest in the farm does not have to worry about everyday work.

Who then hires attached labourers and for what reasons? And how can one conceptualise this relationship? Most of the attached labourers in the two villages are currently working with big farmers who not only have large landholdings but also have occupationally diversified families. In a typical case of a family of four or five brothers, two or three work outside the village, and one or two take care of the land. They are enterprising and have invested substantially in agricultural machinery. Given their economic status and changed cultural tastes, they do not participate in any kind of physical work on land unless there is no choice. They too look towards the town for a more comfortable existence. Their children study in urban schools and aspire to an urban life. They are the ones who need attached labourers the most.

What is the nature of the attached relationship today? Interestingly, the intense tension and conflict between farmers and their attached labourers that I witnessed 20 years back did not seem to be evident any longer. This is primarily because most of the attached labourers working in these villages are outsiders, and their dependence on the employer farmers is much more than was the case 20 years back when attached labourers were mostly of local origin. These labourers have also come to work in these villages out of desperation and on recommendation of some close relative. They are also very different from the seasonal migrants who came from Uttar Pradesh and Bihar who have no kinship link with the village. As is the case with attached labourers generally, they are all indebted to their employers. Their wage rates are below the officially prescribed minimum wage. In other words, there is certainly an element of bondage and unfreedom in the relationship of attached labourers with the farmers.

GROWING DISENCHANTMENTS WITH AGRICULTURE AND ITS IMPLICATIONS

There are other, albeit indirect, factors that influence agrarian relations, such as attached labour. Globalisation and the new economic policies introduced since 1990s have had their influence on the two villages.

However, notwithstanding the intensification of the neoliberal economic policies, there is no clear indication of the classical type of capitalist development taking place where a few farmers are able to buy large plots of lands, and hire landless proletariat (Lenin 1956). Also, there has been no move towards corporate agriculture or contract farming. Only occasionally some farmers are contracted to produce seeds by seed companies. But there is no sign of this emerging as a trend in the two villages. Not much land is being sold or purchased, unless it is acquired by the industry or the state. Land sales happen only when the entire family moves out, and the next generation is unable to keep in touch with the village. As mentioned above, the first generation of landowners who have found viable urban employment prefer leasing their land out to selling it.

Interestingly, even though there is still a strong sense of attachment to land, agriculture is no longer seen as a desirable occupation. The younger generations across caste groups dislike farming. When we asked our respondents about their preferences for agriculture as a means of livelihood for their children or grandchildren (Question: Would you like your children/grandchildren to practise cultivation?), only around 8 per cent of our respondents answered in the affirmative. Surprisingly, the responses to the question were quite similar across caste and occupational categories. Dalits and upper castes (5–6 per cent) were the least interested in their families staying in farming, but even cultivating farmers of the dominant castes (9 per cent) did not want their children to practise agriculture. Only among BCs, there was some desire to continue with agriculture (11 per cent).

Interestingly, our respondents were not much opposed to living in the village. Nearly 60 per cent of them chose their homes in the village over migrating to urban centres. In fact, many of the households, or individual members of the households who had jobs outside in the neighbouring towns, continued to live in the village. Cities are invariably seen as polluted and expensive to live in.

Not only has the social and economic organisation of the village changed, but the meaning that the village had for its residents has also undergone a complete change. Choosing to live in the village did not imply any kind of commitment to, or identification with, the village and its ethos. The social order of caste hierarchy is a thing of the past and the collective identity of the village is nearly completely fragmented.

This disenchantment with village life and agrarian economy has consequences for agrarian relations. A growing distance of the traditionally rich farming classes from the agrarian economy also means their gradual withdrawal from the local context. This is also among the reasons for the growing trend toward leasing-out of their land rather than working as farm manager with attached labourers. Mode of surplus extraction is mediated through a neo-peasant type of economic arrangement where the labourers work with their families and develop personal stakes in the production process.

On the other end of the class spectrum, the growing distancing of Dalit castes from the local agrarian economy and their growing politicisation have their own implications. Moving out of the village has been one of the core elements of the Dalit political rhetoric ever since B. R. Ambedkar began to articulate a political programme for Dalit liberation. The obvious implication of such a political consolidation is a crumbling of the old framework within which social relations of production are reproduced in the local agrarian economy.

Class relations need a framework of power relations for their reproduction. As Sheila Bhalla had rightly argued, along with debt, the power of the traditional elite as 'witnesses' to contractual relations between attached labourer and the employer farmer enabled the latter to keep the labourers under control. None of this works any longer. The local framework of caste and power has changed. With the process of dissociation, distancing and autonomy in operation, the local power has become quite fluid.

REFERENCES

Balagopal, K. 1987. 'An Ideology of the Provincial Propertied Class'. *Economic and Political Weekly* 21(36–37): 2177–78.

Bhaduri, A. 1984. *The Economic Structure of Backward Agriculture*. Delhi: Macmillan.

Bhalla, S. 1976. 'New Relations of Production in Haryana Agriculture'. *Economic and Political Weekly* 11(13): 1993.

Bhattacharya, N. 1985. 'Agrarian Change in Punjab 1880–1940'. Unpublished PhD thesis, Jawaharlal Nehru University, New Delhi.

Brar, J. S., and Sucha Singh Gill. 2002. 'Tenancy Reversal and Operational Enclosures'. In *Land Reforms in India: Intervention for Agrarian Capitalist Transformation in Punjab and Haryana*, ed. Sucha Singh Gill. Delhi: Sage Publications.

Brass, T. 1990. 'Class Struggle and the Deproletarianisation of Agricultural Labour in Haryana (India)'. *The Journal of Peasant Studies* 18(1).

____. 1995. 'Unfree Labour and Agrarian Change: A Different View'. *Economic and Political Weekly* 30(13): 697–99.

____. 1996. 'Misinterpreting Unfree Labour in Contemporary Haryana'. *Economic and Political Weekly* 31(33): 2362–64.

Breman, J. 1974. *Patronage and Exploitation: Changing Agrarian Relations in South Gujarat, India*. Berkeley: University of California Press.

Byres, T. J. 1972. 'The Dialectics of India's Green Revolution'. *South Asia Review* 5(2).

Harriss-White, Barbara. 1996. *A Political Economy of Agricultural Markets in South India: Masters of the Countryside*. New Delhi: Sage Publications.

Jodhka, S. S. 1994. 'Agrarian Changes and Attached Labour: Emerging Patterns in Haryana Agriculture'. *Economic and Political Weekly* 29(39): 102–06.

____. 1995a. 'Agrarian Changes, Unfreedom and Attached Labour'. *Economic and Political Weekly* 30(31–32): 2011–13.

____. 1995b. 'Bureaucratisation, Corruption and Depoliticisation: Changing Profile of Credit Co-operatives in Rural Haryana'. *Economic and Political Weekly* 30(1): 53–56.

____. 1995c. 'Who Borrows? Who Lends?: Changing Structure of Informal Credit in Rural Haryana'. *Economic and Political Weekly* 30(39): A123–32.

____. 1996. 'Interpreting Attached Labour in Contemporary Haryana'. *Economic and Political Weekly* 31(21): 1286–87.

____. 2002. 'Caste and Untouchability in Rural Punjab'. *Economic and Political Weekly* 37(19), 11 May: 1813–23.

____. 2006. 'Beyond "Crises": Rethinking Contemporary Punjab Agriculture'. *Economic and Political Weekly* 41(16): 1530–37.

Lenin, V. I. 1956. *The Development of Capitalism in Russia: The Process of the Formation of a Home Market for Large-scale Industry*. Moscow: Foreign Languages Publishing House.

Lindberg, Steffan. 2005. 'Whom and What to Fight?: Notes and Queries on Indian Farmers Collective Action under Liberalisation and Globalisation'. Unpublished seminar paper, Punjab University, Patiala.

Omvedt, Gail. 1992. 'Capitalist Agriculture and Rural Classes in India'. In *Class, State and Development in India*, ed. B. Berberogly. New Delhi: Sage Publications.

Rudra, A. 1990. 'Class Relations in Indian Agriculture'. In *Agrarian Relations and Accumulation: Mode of Production Debate in India*, ed. U. Patnaik. Delhi: Oxford University Press.

Rutten, M. A. F. 1995. *Farms and Factories: Social Profile of Large Farmers and Rural Industrialists in West India*. New Delhi: Oxford University Press.

Upadhya, Carol B. 1988. 'The Farmer-capitalists of Coastal Andhra Pradesh'. *Economic and Political Weekly* 23(27–28): 1376–82, 1433–42.

Notes on the Authors

Pranab Bardhan is Professor Emeritus of Economics at the University of California, Berkley.

Sheila Bhalla (1933–2021) was a Professor of Economics in the School of Social Science, Jawaharlal Nehru University, New Delhi.

Ramesh Chand, an agricultural economist, is Fellow, National Academy of Agricultural Sciences and Indian Society of Agricultural Economics, and Member of NITI Aayog in the rank and status of Union Minister of State.

Sumita Chatterjee is an economist and a contributing author of the *Economic and Political Weekly*.

Anita Gill is Professor of Economics at the Punjabi University, Patiala, Punjab.

Sucha Singh Gill is a former Professor of Economics at the Punjabi University, Patiala, Punjab.

Barbara Harriss-White is Emeritus Professor and Fellow in the Wolfson College, Oxford University, Oxford.

Ronald J. Herring is Professor Emeritus in the Department of Government, Cornell University, New York.

Praveen Jha is Professor of Economics in the School of Social Science, Jawaharlal Nehru University, New Delhi.

Surinder S. Jodhka is Professor of Sociology at the Jawaharlal Nehru University, New Delhi. A recipient of the ICSSR-Amartya Sen Award for Distinguished Social Scientists, his recent publications include *India's Villages in the 21st Century* (edited with Edward Simpson, 2019); and *A Handbook of Rural India* (2018).

Mekhala Krishnamurthy is Associate Professor of Sociology and Anthropology at Ashoka University and Senior Fellow at the Centre for Policy Research, New Delhi.

Richa Kumar is Associate Professor of Sociology at the Indian Institute of Technology, New Delhi.

Jens Lerche is Reader in Labour and Agrarian Studies in the Department of Development Studies, SOAS, University of London.

B. B. Mohanty is Professor of Sociology at the Pondicherry University, Puducherry.

Sam Moyo (1954–2915) was Executive Director of the African Institute for Agrarian Studies, Harare, Zimbabwe.

ABHA PANDYA is an expert of Gandhian economics and a contributor to the *Economic and Political Weekly*.

VIKAS RAWAL is Professor of Economics in the School of Social Science, Jawaharlal Nehru University, New Delhi.

GERRY RODGERS has worked with the International Labour Organization. He is presently a Visiting Professor at the Institute for Human Development, New Delhi.

JANINE RODGERS is a Visiting Professor at the Institute for Human Development, New Delhi.

ASHOK RUDRA (1930–1992) was a Professor of Economics at the Delhi School of Economics.

MARIO RUTTEN (1958–1015) was a Professor of Comparative Sociology and Anthropology of Asia at the University of Amsterdam, Amsterdam.

LOES SCHENK-SANDBERGEN is Associate Professor of Sociology and Anthropology at the University of Amsterdam.

ALPA SHAH is Professor in Anthropology at the London School of Economics, London.

LAKHWINDER SINGH is a former Professor of Economics at the Punjabi University, Patiala, Punjab.

ALICE THORNER (1917–2005) was a Latvian-born social scientist and statistician, who worked on agrarian change in India, urban life, and gender.

DANIEL THORNER (1915–1974) was an American-born economist and economic historian. He wrote extensively on Indian agriculture and agricultural policy.

CAROL BOYACK UPADHYA is Professor in the School of Social Sciences, National Institute of Advanced Studies, Bengaluru.

A. R. VASAVI is a social anthropologist and an independent researcher based out of Bengaluru.

PARIS YEROS is Adjunct Professor of International Economics at the Federal University of ABC, São Paulo, Brazil.